VICTIMS OF THE BOOK: READING AND MASCULINITY IN FIN-DE-SIÈCLE FRANCE

FRANÇOIS PROULX

Victims of the Book

Reading and Masculinity in Fin-de-Siècle France

UNIVERSITY OF TORONTO PRESS
Toronto Buffalo London

Toronto Buffalo London
utorontopress.com

ISBN 978-1-4875-0547-9

University of Toronto Romance Series

Library and Archives Canada Cataloguing in Publication

Title: Victims of the book : reading and masculinity in fin-de-siècle France / François Proulx.
Names: Proulx, François, author.
Series: University of Toronto romance series.
Description: Series statement: University of Toronto romance series | Includes bibliographical references and index.
Identifiers: Canadiana 20190122978 | ISBN 9781487505479 (hardcover)
Subjects: LCSH: French fiction – 19th century – History and criticism. | LCSH: Books and reading – France – History – 19th century. | LCSH: Masculinity in literature.
Classification: LCC PQ653 .P76 2019 | DDC 843/.809353—dc23

This book has been published with the help of a grant from the Federation for the Humanities and Social Sciences, through the Awards to Scholarly Publications Program, using funds provided by the Social Sciences and Humanities Research Council of Canada.

University of Toronto Press acknowledges the financial assistance to its publishing program of the Canada Council for the Arts and the Ontario Arts Council, an agency of the Government of Ontario.

Canada Council for the Arts Conseil des Arts du Canada

Funded by the Government of Canada Financé par le gouvernement du Canada

Contents

Illustrations

Note on Translations and Previously Published Material

All citations of primary material are given in English translation in the body of the text, with the original French in a note.

Citations of scholarly works published in French are given in English translation only.

Translated titles of novels and essays are given in italics when a published translation exists: e.g., *Les Déracinés* (*The Uprooted*, 1897). When no published translation exists, I provide my own translation for the title, without italics: e.g., *Crise de jeunesse* (Youth in crisis, 1897).

Chapter 8 cites the translation of Proust's *Jean Santeuil* by Gerald Hopkins (New York: Simon & Schuster, 1956). Modifications to this translation are signalled in notes.

Except in a few instances, all noted, all other translations are mine.

~

Part of chapter 1 previously appeared as "*De nouveaux et étranges éducateurs*: Dangers de la lecture et remèdes littéraires, 1883–1914," *Culture & Musées* 17 (June 2011): 21–40. I thank *Culture & Musées* for permission to reuse this material.

A shorter version of chapter 5 appeared as "*À nous deux*, Balzac: Barrès's *Les Déracinés*, and the Ghosts of *La Comédie humaine*," *Nineteenth-Century French Studies* 42, nos. 3–4 (Spring-Summer 2014): 235–49. I thank *Nineteenth-Century French Studies* and University of Nebraska Press for permission to reprint.

Part of chapter 8 previously appeared as "Proust lecteur d'Emerson à l'époque de *Jean Santeuil*," *Roman 20–50: Revue d'étude du roman du XXe siècle* 67 (June 2019). I thank *Roman 20–50* and Presses universitaires du Septentrion for permission to reuse this material.

Acknowledgments

Various stages of research and writing were supported by a doctoral fellowship from the Social Sciences and Humanities Research Council of Canada, a Harvard University dissertation completion fellowship, and a research fellowship from the National Endowment for the Humanities. Any views, findings, conclusions, or recommendations expressed in this publication do not necessarily reflect those of the National Endowment for the Humanities.

In its early development, *Victims of the Book* benefited from the expert guidance of Susan Rubin Suleiman, Christie McDonald, and Judith Surkis. I am profoundly thankful to each.

Many chapters-in-progress were presented at the Nineteenth-Century French Studies Annual Colloquium, a community of scholars at once rigorous and welcoming.

I am grateful for the support of my colleagues in the Department of French and Italian as well as the Rare Book & Manuscript Library at the University of Illinois, Urbana-Champaign.

At Illinois, later phases of the project were greatly helped by the First Book Writing Group, led by Maria Gillombardo, Craig Koslofsky, and Nancy Abelmann (1959–2016), a colleague of unparalleled generosity. She is missed.

I thank the collector who kindly allowed me to reproduce the cover of *Yvon d'Or* in chapter 4.

Kirstin Ringelberg and Camille Serchuk generously offered comments on large sections of the manuscript. Two anonymous readers from the University of Toronto Press also provided numerous beneficial suggestions.

For their continued friendship I thank Daniel Bowles, Kenneth Brummel, Laura-Zoë Humphreys, Elliot Marks, Felisa Vergara Reynolds, Jessica Tanner, Michael Thaddeus, Tali Zechory, and Vivian van Blerk.

~

À mes parents.

VICTIMS OF THE BOOK

Introduction: Reading Anxieties

An impressionable reader, not yet twenty years old, seeks an escape from life's ever-growing disappointments in poetry and "daydream-filled walks." The reader's head "fills with visions" and soon becomes "a sublime muddle," where characters out of plays, poems, and novels drift past one another hazily. The reader calls out to these apparitions, but they dissipate as soon as they come into view. The scene could almost be out of *Madame Bovary* (1856–7), but this reader's name is Jean Servien, and he is the protagonist of an early novel by Anatole France, published in 1882.[1] *Les Désirs de Jean Servien* is one of dozens of French novels from the years 1880 to 1914 that stage the familiar story of Emma Bovary with a difference: the avid, easily influenced, and often ill-fated reader at the centre of the narrative is a young man. This book is about that shift: it examines how, in late nineteenth and early twentieth-century France, earlier discourses about the dangers and pernicious effects of reading were redeployed around a new object of concern, the young man. These anxieties were manifested in a profusion of novels about – as well as often explicitly addressed to – adolescent male readers.

Flaubert's *Dictionary of Received Ideas*, begun in the 1850s and posthumously published in 1911, includes a characteristically pithy entry on the novel: "Novels. – Pervert the masses."[2] That literary texts have the potential to corrupt their readers is indeed a time-worn platitude by the second half of the nineteenth century: the notion, long a literary topos, was given a prominent incarnation in Flaubert's own *Madame Bovary*. Emma Bovary reads *Paul et Virginie*, Walter Scott, and Balzac. She finds her own existence as a provincial doctor's wife "insufficient"[3] by comparison; adultery, mounting debt, and suicide ensue. Generations of readers and critics have recognized Emma as "a Don Quixote in skirts,"[4] tracing the topos of the danger of reading back to Cervantes and thus to the very origins of the novel as a genre. Taken broadly, the received idea described in Flaubert's *Dictionary* applies to both the man of La Mancha and the unhappy housewife of Yonville. Flaubert's choice of words, however, highlights three important specifics that had attached themselves to this notion by the mid-nineteenth century: the literary products most associated with danger are modern novels, not poems or chivalric romances; those most at risk are "the masses" of new, vulnerable, unsophisticated readers; and the danger incurred is "perversion," a characterization that carries a distinct whiff of the illicit or the sexual. Two further specifics could be inferred from the example of *Madame Bovary*: the victims of the dangerous practice of reading are typically female, and these dangers are represented for dramatic, not comic, effect. While the crux of the received idea – literary works pose a danger to their audience – remained the same, the details – the gender and class of the potential victims, the type of literary work incriminated, the nature of the danger, and the tone or purpose of the denunciation – had undergone a number of shifts in the two and a half centuries that separate Don Quixote from Emma Bovary.

From Cervantes to Flaubert

Don Quixote inspired a number of continuations and imitations in France,[5] among them Charles Sorel's *Le Berger extravagant* (1627), in which a young man who has read too many pastoral novels confuses the world he inhabits with the fictional realm of amorous shepherds and courtly deeds depicted, most famously, in Honoré d'Urfé's *L'Astrée* (1607–27). Sorel gave his work the subtitle *antiroman*, a term Gérard Genette adopts for his definition of this particular subgenre. For Genette, the seventeenth-century antinovel is "a complex hypertextual practice" where a narrative text represents the effects of another text or genre on a vulnerable reader, resulting in "a comical contrast, close to parody."[6] This comic effect is underlain by an anxiety regarding the potential confusions brought about by literary texts. The antinovel, by inviting its readers to have a laugh at the expense of a flawed reader, reassures them of their own ability to distinguish between reality and fiction, but also warns them of the danger of not doing so, a danger that often takes the form of imitation. Antoine Furetière's *Le Roman bourgeois* (1666), for instance, describes how a young female reader, "having taken Astrée for a model, imitated every one of her actions and words." Comparing *L'Astrée* to "a poison," this antinovel implicitly proposes itself as an antidote.[7] In the transition from comedy to morality tale, and from a male to a female reader, we observe a twofold shift towards a representation of the reader that will become predominant in French novels of the eighteenth and much of the nineteenth century: as one study succinctly puts it, "the reader is no longer extravagant but perverted ... and this perverted reader is usually female."[8]

Over the course of the eighteenth century, the effects of fiction reading (a concern that notably led to the largely unsuccessful proscription of the novel genre in 1737)[9] were the object of a number of treatises. Condillac, in his *Essai sur l'origine des connaissances humaines* (Essay on the Origin of Human Knowledge, 1749), singles out the reading of novels by adolescent girls, "whose brains are quite tender," as a common trigger to excesses of the faculty of imagination.[10] While many similar texts relayed discourses about the pitfalls of reading, some also considered the potential role of fiction in the self-construction of the reader;[11] instead of blanket condemnations, they asked what vulnerable readers should or should not read at different stages of their education. Increasingly, reading became framed as a pedagogical and familial problem, famously embodied in the relationship between student and preceptor in Rousseau's twin narratives, *Julie ou la Nouvelle Héloïse* (1761) and *Émile ou De l'éducation* (1762). The generic ambiguity of the former, where a treatise on education and family becomes a novel about love and renouncement, illustrates a persistent tension, in the representation of female readers, between the scene of pedagogy and the scene of seduction.[12] Reading, even controlled and supervised in the context of an education in taste and restraint, can lead to feverish identification and imitation: Julie and Saint-Preux read Petrarch and Tasso, and soon they are trading love letters peppered with citations.[13] The French libertine novel makes frequent use of this potential deviation: Sade, playing on an already ambiguous statement by Laclos about the relation of fiction to matters of parenting, exemplarity, and sexual morality, prefaces his *Philosophie dans le boudoir* (1795) with the indication, "mothers will prescribe this book to their daughters."[14]

Following the Revolution and the Napoleonic era, with the emergence of a national educational system, the sustained increase of literacy rates, and the rise of mass publishing,[15] the question of vulnerable readers transformed from a familial to a social concern.[16] New readers – "women, workers, peasants," in Martyn Lyons's formulation – came to be described as a potential danger, both to themselves and to the social order.[17] In the 1830s and 1840s, anxieties coalesced around the phenomenon of the serialized novel, a publishing innovation specifically targeted at these emerging reading publics. Critics expressed their distaste for this new "industrial literature"[18] and voiced apprehension over its readers, characterized as naïve[19] and in need of guidance or control lest they fall prey to "literary disorder" – "an intellectual intoxication [ivresse] a hundred times more dangerous than physical intoxication."[20] The polemic over the serialized novel largely redeployed discourses that had circulated in the seventeenth and eighteenth centuries, updating them to fit new political, social, and publishing realities.[21] The individual extravagant or perverted reader of earlier centuries became a mass of new, largely female readers, depicted as intellectually juvenile and potentially disordered, while the figuratively parental position of sophisticated reader was claimed by (adult, male, bourgeois) commentators who condemned or attempted to restrict these new readers' practices and preferences.[22] Such warnings persisted well beyond the rise of the serial novel, through the nineteenth century and into the twentieth.[23] With France's defeat in 1870 and the advent of the Third Republic, however, a different type of reader emerged as an object of concern: the young man who, by virtue of his age (and often, his class trajectory) had not yet attained the status of adult, male, bourgeois citizen. Even as reading and the study of literary texts were institutionalized as a key component of the formation of republican citizens,[24] the precocious or excessive consumption of literature made possible and fostered by education was imagined to potentially divert young men from the path to productive economic activity and its symbolic corollary, reproductive, marital heterosexuality. This new incarnation of old anxieties about the dangers of reading has hitherto not been the object of a comprehensive study; I examine it in this book.

French Masculinity at the Fin de Siècle

In the period 1880–1914, from the onset of republican reforms of education to the First World War, the figure of the adolescent was progressively constituted through scrutiny and interpellation by various texts. The period also spans, in French literary history, three decades of dominance and stagnation of the genre of the novel, from the death of Flaubert on 8 May 1880 to the publication of *Du côté de chez Swann* on 14 November 1913.[25] It has been proposed that "adolescence 'came of age' in the decades around 1900, [as] interlocking discourses about adolescence emerged in psychoanalysis, psychology, criminal justice, pedagogy, sociology, as well as in literature"[26] – a list to which we should add the nascent discipline of sexology.[27] In the French context, anxiety over the figure of the adolescent is visible in a proliferation of texts about, and often addressed to, *la jeunesse* or *les jeunes*. With titles like *Le Devoir présent de la jeunesse* (The present duty of youth, 1899)[28] or *Les Jeunes Gens d'aujourd'hui* (The youth of today, 1913),[29] these treatises, articles, and studies aim to, in the words of Ferdinand Buisson (a prominent architect of educational reforms), "speak about youth or rather speak to youth,"[30] a recurrent and significant vacillation that highlights how youth was defined as a category and described as a problem even as it was being addressed.[31]

Taking their cues from enduringly contentious debates over the 1871 Paris Commune or from journalistic accounts of sensational criminal affairs, novelists of the 1880s and 1890s exhibit a fascination with the figure of the young man as *déclassé*, murderer, or anarchist, extreme cases which they describe as symptomatic of a larger crisis affecting French youth.[32] These representative figures, as novelists depict them, all share an intense and fraught relationship to reading and literary texts, linked to class mobility. Denis Pernot observes that writers and social commentators preoccupied with the fin-de-siècle crisis of youth "perceive it ... reductively, and are mostly interested in its bourgeois, Parisian and educated component":[33] the sons of the bourgeoisie, however, share this discursive spotlight with the *déclassés*, overeducated young men of working-class background. The young man anxiously depicted in French novels of the turn of the century is the son of either an established bourgeois or a working-class father striving towards bourgeois status.[34] Both have in common a liminal, transitory position, described as precarious and fraught with the potential for veering off course. The rhetoric of crisis around adolescents stems precisely from the fact that they have not yet and may fail to attain or espouse the status of bourgeois man, because of their age, their choice of career (or failure to choose one), or their intermediate socio-economic status – all of which are linked to questions of education and reading.

Anatole France's Jean Servien offers a resonant example: he is the son of a bookbinder, who himself barely knows how to read. The narrative takes as its point of departure a generational and historical shift in working-class men's relationship to print, from artisanal production to avid and disorderly consumption, made possible by nineteenth-century developments in literacy and mechanization. For Jean's father, books are material objects, the products of a manual labour that allows him to earn a living; for Jean, raised on reading French and Latin so that he could obtain the title of *bachelier* and rise in social rank,[35] they are an object of intellectual labour, readerly passion, and ultimately, amorous, creative, and economic frustration. Jean's aspirations in matters of love and sexuality, artistic productivity, and socio-economic status are all inflected by what he reads; all are eventually disappointed. In a key scene, after he has been rebuffed by an actress (about whom he daydreams through a jumble of "Racine, Greek tragedies, Shakespeare, and Voltaire's poetry"), he watches his father's vigorous apprentice approach and seduce a working-class girl, and feels bitterly envious. He fails to compose a literary masterpiece ("his laziness, his sterility, his scruples and delicacy all stopped him after the first few lines"), and cannot find or hold on to employment, even as a meagrely paid tutor. The narrative ends with Jean's death in the upheaval of the Commune. "Why didn't you make a bookbinder out of him?"[36] a reproachful state functionary asks Jean's father, denouncing a sociohistorical trend under the guise of an individual choice. Tobias Boes proposes that, in the *Bildungsroman*, "the idealized shape of the nation comes into being through the essentially arbitrary vessel of an individual life ... in which the normative expresses itself through the contingent."[37] Jean Servien, like a vast number of similar protagonists in the French novel of formation at the turn of the century, should then be read as a negative idealization, the fictional embodiment of deep national concerns about reading, education and masculinity.

In addition to their focus on bourgeois (or liminally bourgeois), Parisian, and educated youth, turn-of-the-century discourses about *la jeunesse* systematically figure the adolescent as male. Contemporaneous representations of young women, debates about their place in the educational system, and considerations of their reading habits occupy a separate sphere of social discourse; they have been the object of a significant amount of scholarship and are not included in the scope of this study.[38] The Third Republic, born of the humiliating military defeat of 1870, is traversed with anxieties over questions of national vitality, reproductive capacity, and military adequacy; Carolyn J. Dean describes it as "a society overwhelmed by threats to the [social and individual] body's health presented by urbanization, democratization, demographic stagnation, military defeat ... and their perceived symptoms: emasculation, nervousness, weakness, enervation."[39] Anxious characterizations and appeals to male youth in the last decades of the nineteenth century redeployed and updated earlier – and often femininely coded – discourses about the uses and pitfalls of reading, in an attempt to respond to and regulate the troubling role of literature in the formation of France's future citizens. This is particularly visible in the profusion of fin-de-siècle novels about young men.

Novels of Formation

In the mid-1850s, observers could state that French literature paid little attention to youth. Hippolyte Taine, in an essay on Dickens (1856), notes that "children ... are absent from our literature";[40] George Sand, in *Histoire de ma vie* (*Story of My Life*, 1854–5), remarks that "poets and novelists have all but ignored the adolescent ... as a subject of observation and a source of poetry."[41] The same certainly no longer held true half a century later, by which time the adolescent, and the young man in particular, had become one of the most insistently scrutinized figures in the novel genre.[42] Looking back, critics of the 1920s and 1930s would ponder whether there had been a "surplus of adolescents ... in the novel" before and after the First World War, noting that the young man "occupies a central place during this period."[43] While some established novelists of the 1880s and 1890s wrote about their own childhood and adolescence in thinly fictionalized accounts,[44] numerous and often less successful others penned narratives in which the young man is a generic figure meant to embody the struggles of an entire generation, as made salient by titles like *L'Enfance d'un homme* (A man's youth, 1890), *Mémoires d'un jeune homme* (Memoirs of a young man, 1895), or *La Faillite du rêve, roman d'un jeune homme d'aujourd'hui* (The failure of dreams: A novel of today's young man, 1905).

Such novels often follow what Marc Angenot identifies as the "fin-de-siècle picaresque," a dominant template for the novelistic genre in France around 1889: a young protagonist attempts to find success in Paris, but discovers only "corruptions, lowliness, perversions." He usually ends up defeated, contemplating either suicide or a return to his native province; if he succeeds, it is only by becoming cynical and degraded.[45] These works are also often first novels, written by young writers who largely follow generic conventions; sometimes they are the only novel their author will publish, before moving on to other genres or dropping out of the literary field entirely. The career trajectory of André Lebey (1877–1938), whose novel *Les Premières Luttes* (The first struggles, 1897) I briefly examine in chapter 1, provides a typical example: born in Normandy, he had written a play and three collections of poetry by the age of twenty, when he published this first novel in Paris. A few other novels would follow, but he had a wide-ranging career as a journalist, deputy, and author of historical studies. "Neglected by history" according to his biographer,[46] Lebey is only remembered today, in the field of literary studies, as an important correspondent of Paul Valéry[47] and minor friend of Marcel Proust.[48]

Many titles of fin-de-siècle novels of formation highlight the period's concern with youth as an age of transition and uncertainty: *L'Âge incertain* (The uncertain age, 1898), *En genèse* (In genesis, 1897), *La Mue* (Moulting season, 1903). Others are explicit in their characterization of the dangers that threaten French youth – *La Vie stérile* (A barren life, 1892), *Le Vertige de l'inconnu* (The fever of the unknown, 1892), *La Mortelle Impuissance* (A deadly impotence, 1903) – at what they represent as a time of "crisis": *Crise de jeunesse* (Youth in crisis, 1897), *La Crise virile* (The crisis of virility, 1898), *Une crise* (A crisis, 1906). Prefaces and dedications[49] make clear that these novels are not only about, but also geared towards, young readers – that they engage in a double endeavour, to both represent and instruct the young man at this critical age. Karl Morgenstern, who first coined the term *Bildungsroman*,[50] defined the genre precisely in terms of this double nature in a lecture delivered in 1819: "We may call a novel a *Bildungsroman* first and foremost on account of its content, because it portrays the development of the hero in its beginning and progress to a certain stage of completion, but also, second, because this depiction promotes the development of the reader to a greater extent than any other kind of novel."[51]

Franco Moretti, who uses *Bildungsroman* to describe a broad, pan-European tradition of the coming-of-age novel (from Austen to Flaubert), proposes that it constitutes a meeting point of opposite yet "complementary" forces in the shaping of the modern subject: "The classical *Bildungsroman* [is] the synthesis that nullifies the previous opposition of *Entwicklungsroman* (novel of 'development,' of the subjective unfolding of an individuality) and *Erziehungsroman* (novel of 'education,' of an objective process, observed from the standpoint of the educator)."[52] Marianne Hirsch, however, points out that since the eighteenth-century German concept of *Bildung* is itself historically defined as "an inner-determined self-development" (i.e. what Moretti labels *Entwicklung*), *Bildungsroman* should be "limited to those novels that actually illustrate Goethe's conception of *Bildung*"; for her, *Entwicklungsroman* is the "more broadly applicable" category.[53] A definition and usage of *Bildungsroman* and its variants that would be mindful of the terms' history and etymology, yet broad enough to be applicable in non-German contexts, thus proves problematic: as Susan Rubin Suleiman has noted, György Lukács's proposed typology of the *Erziehungsroman*, drawing heavily on Goethe, tautologically ends up concluding that *Wilhelm Meister* is the only true example of the genre.[54] What, then, are we to call the abundant number of French novels written about and for young men between 1880 and 1914?

John Neubauer, following Justin O'Brien's pioneering 1937 study, proposes the label "novel of adolescence," stating that while "the *Bildungsroman* explores the transition from adolescence into adulthood," French novels from the turn of the century to the interwar period focus on somewhat younger protagonists who are often in or "just out of school."[55] Yet some of the better-known examples of the genre belie this suggestion: readers follow Jacques Vingtras, Jules Vallès's alter ego, from early childhood well into adulthood; Paul Bourget's titular *Disciple*, Robert Greslou, is twenty-nine years old. Denis Pernot, who concludes his survey of the notion of *Bildungsroman* by noting that it is "marked from the onset by a great degree of imprecision," suggests instead *roman de socialisation*, preferring this neologism to the more widely used *roman d'éducation*, which he argues is too closely associated with the concept of the didactic *roman éducatif* or pedagogical novel.[56] The label "novel of socialization," however, poses a similar problem, at least in English, since the categories invoked by Pernot, education (implicitly defined as the shaping of social subjects through institutions) and socialization (the shaping of social subjects outside of institutions), are not considered mutually exclusive by English-language sociologists.[57] Marianne Hirsch offers a more suitable compromise: noting that few or no studies rigorously "justify using the German term [*Bildungsroman*] for a non-German tradition," she goes on instead to name and define "an overarching European genre: the novel of formation."[58] The English "formation," which the *OED* defines as both a "process" and an "action," can encompass both the development of intrinsic traits (the historical meaning of *Bildung*) and the effect of external influences (institutional and not); as such, it allows for the complementarity sought by Moretti in the term *Bildungsroman*. "Novel of formation" is also something of a deliberate Gallicism, a loan translation from *roman de formation* (itself commonly used as a French translation of *Bildungsroman*) that highlights the cultural specificity of this genre to the French context.

In defining socialization as "that which, in the transmission of values, goes unseen and remains unproblematized since it is not intentionally administered by society,"[59] Pernot proposes a third term that complicates the dialectical resolution described by Moretti between the "subjective" unfolding of an innate self (*Bildung*) and the "objective" influence of intentionally directed social forces (education or *Erziehung*).[60] Pernot's "socialization" suggests that there exists another, more insidious process, through which the subject assimilates values (as well as ideas and desires) that are not transmitted through the channels of parenting, institutional education, or mentorship, but with which he or she comes in contact nonetheless, outside these channels, through acculturative practices. Chief among these practices, in the late nineteenth century, is reading. In the typology of the novel put forwards by Lukács, the novel of disillusion [*Desillusionsroman*] is defined as a subgenre where the central conflict arises from the discrepancy between the protagonist's larger-than-life "ideals" and the shortcomings of reality.[61] By holding up Balzac's *Illusions perdues* (1837–43) and Flaubert's *L'Éducation sentimentale* (1869) as its most representative examples, Lukács intimates that this is a principally French subgenre – but also that it is a subgenre about readers.[62] In both of these archetypal novels, the main characters' illusions and ideals are neither innate nor instilled through a process of education or familial upbringing; rather, they are derived from what the narrative presents as an excess of reading. Both protagonists are voracious consumers of print: before setting out into the world, Balzac's Lucien Chardon/de Rubempré was an avid reader of adventure novels and Romantic poetry, and Flaubert's Frédéric Moreau was an equally naïve, if less dedicated, reader of, as it happens, Balzac. As they make their way to Paris, both protagonists attempt to model themselves after poetic or novelistic heroes, expecting their lives to follow literary plots; the discrepancy between their "ideals" and the real world of the narrative is thus less a matter of ontology or pedagogy than a question of the problematic relationship between different versions and interpretations of "ideals" or "the real world" as mediated through books and how they are read. French novels of formation at the fin de siècle, many of them manifestly indebted to Balzac and Flaubert, can themselves be characterized as novels of disillusion in which the illusions to be lost are the product of reading. Warned against the dangers of relying on bookish knowledge to make their way in the world, the real-world young readers addressed by these novels are incited, through a negative process of *Erziehung*, to unlearn their literary education.

In Paul Flat's *L'Illusion sentimentale* (1905) – a title that neatly conflates Balzac and Flaubert – we find a description of an archetypal Parisian young man, not yet touched by the disenchantment of reality, whose desires are entirely the product of his readings:

> The young man, truth be told, was beginning to feel a need for a different kind of love, one that did not simply satisfy physical needs, but instead had some resonance in the sentimental part of his being ... Early on in his literary formation, he had formed the grand dream of a communion in the realm of intellect. His imagination had worked over the books he loved. At that age, when the harsh lessons of experience have not yet brought their disenchantment, there seems to be but one step from the dream to the realities so coveted.[63]

Time and again, from Jules Vallès to Marcel Proust, and through their numerous, less illustrious colleagues, the French novel of formation of the late nineteenth and early twentieth centuries tells the story of this young man, of his literary formation, and of his perilous encounter with the realities of experience. In doing so, the subgenre both fulfils and challenges Morgenstern's twofold definition of the *Bildungsroman*: by portraying a "hero" whose development is diverted, hindered, or even cut short by the practice of reading, it calls into question the very potential of the novelistic genre to positively further the formation of its readers.

Dynamic Reading

This book is about reading anxieties, in two distinct yet complementary ways. On one level, it examines anxieties *about* reading, as French novels of formation from the turn of the century phrase or represent them in clear ways: straightforwardly, insistently, even didactically. On another, concurrent level, it reads *for* anxieties related to reading that these same texts might suggest, hide, even deny. In doing so, it proposes a dynamic model of critical reading that integrates different approaches to literary texts sometimes conceived as opposite or difficult to reconcile. Over the past decade, critical debates about "the way we read now"[64] have highlighted how an ongoing "return to the archive"[65] in literary studies has raised challenges to modes of reading associated with literary theory. *Close reading*, the attentive, formalist study of selected (usually canonical) texts, and the related practice of *symptomatic reading*, the effort to "divulg[e] the undivulged" ideological forces[66] that, while repressed or dissimulated, nevertheless traverse and shape literary texts, are said to "not necessarily work equally well on all genres. Certain kinds of forgotten literature do not need to be decoded to be understood."[67] Alternative modes of critical reading have been proposed instead: *distant reading*,[68] the study of trends and patterns in a large corpus, often through computational processing, and more recently, *surface* or *just reading*,[69] a careful attention to what texts present on their surface in ways that can escape critical notice. While the exegetic approaches of close or symptomatic reading are associated with an overemphasis on works enshrined in the canon because of their aesthetic richness (an assumption that close reading reinforces, as ever more complexities are read into canonical texts), distant and surface reading are presented as an opposite approach that "enables us to understand ... narrative aesthetics that make no sense from the vantage point of close reading," particularly those of minor genres excluded from the canon.[70]

Victims of the Book engages in a form of distant reading in that it considers, alongside key texts endowed with various degrees of canonicity, a broad corpus of novels that have hitherto been the object of little or no critical attention. Many of these novels have never been reprinted since their original publication, and the few studies that address them touch on questions of gender or the representation of reading only fleetingly, as part of a larger project of typology of the novel of formation.[71] In doing so, this book participates in what Margaret Cohen calls "the excavation of forgotten literary forms," a project that – somewhat paradoxically – allows for a renewed approach to the canon since it makes it possible "to situate individual works in relation to their generic horizon."[72] As I mine this abundant corpus, I deploy two strategies described by Cohen: "reading for patterns," namely, the recurrence of tropes across different texts (types of scenes or characters, particular comparisons, allusions or citations), and reading for "the representative example,"[73] the isolation and analysis of a particular iteration of a trope (often due to its pronounced, highly visible character) as illustrative of a larger pattern. In my engagement with generic examples of the novel of formation, I find it useful to think of surface reading in terms of a continuum with, rather than in opposition to, close reading: as Heather Love suggests, surface reading could be defined as "a form of close reading that does not presume depth, [and] considers what texts do say, rather than what they won't or can't."[74] Yet even in reading these non-canonical texts, when coming up against moments of paradox, allusion, or silence, I choose to rely on close reading: oftentimes such texts, rather than being impervious or resistant to that approach, yield easily under its pressure. Despite their apparent lack of complexity or aesthetic sophistication, many non-canonical texts do feature contradictions, slippages, or gaps that only close critical attention can uncover and unpack. In turning to more canonical works, I rely extensively on symptomatic reading (a practice somewhat out of favour in the recent past),[75] particularly in the shape of reading for denegation.[76] Many works that partake in denunciations of the dangers of reading also insistently deny the influence of earlier literary models (including how these models represent reading) on their own narrative and stylistic constitution; a critical attention to the symptoms of this denegation reveals the unresolved paradox from which much of their complexity arises. This mobile critical approach recognizes that the distinction between canonical and non-canonical works is far from absolute or fixed: novels like *Le Disciple* or *Les Déracinés* were once acclaimed and read widely, and are much less so today; Vallès's polemical articles and *Jacques Vingtras* novels, initially met with critical hostility,[77] were republished in the prestigious Pléiade collection a century later. Overall, a dynamic combination of modes of reading can lead to a more complex understanding of the question of reading in the literary products of an era deeply preoccupied with texts and their influence on those who consumed them. Dynamic reading, a shuttling between different "ways we read now,"[78] allows me to better pose the question of the ways they read *then*, at the fin de siècle.

~

Victims of the Book comprises three parts, in turn divided into a total of eight chapters. Each part is introduced by a short case study that presents and examines (including by means of close reading) a single, non-canonical novel, framing the questions to be addressed in the chapters that follow. Part I examines a broad corpus of novels of formation from the period 1880–1914 that feature descriptions of young men's reading practices, as well as related periodical articles, polemical essays, and medical and sociological treatises. Chapter 1 shows how pedagogues and critics characterized reading as an emasculating illness afflicting French youth at the turn of the century, and how writers responded to this pathologization of reading with a profusion of novels about and geared towards adolescent male readers, paradoxically proposing these novels as potential cures. It examines pervasive metaphors of nutrition and poison in descriptions of literary consumption, as well as imaginings of antidotes to literature, from educations in self-control to the staging of dramatic, often violent renunciations. Chapter 2 turns to recurrent tropes in the depiction of readers and reading practices in the fin-de-siècle novel of formation. These patterns include the characterization of the male reader as physiologically weakened, linked to contemporary discourses about decadence and neurasthenia; depictions of libraries and other spaces of study as graveyards of the will; and frequent concurrent allusions to onanism or same-sex attachments, revealing an anxiety over the deviation of young subjects' productive and reproductive potential towards unproductive ends.

Part II investigates the three archetypal plots of the fin-de-siècle novel of formation: literary education, novelistic seduction, and writerly ambition. Each chapter examines a representative, canonical novel, with careful attention to what the novel's characters read: these intertextual links illuminate how older texts (Rousseau, Stendhal, Balzac) continued to exert a cultural pull in fin-de-siècle France, and elicited new concerns. Chapter 3 considers the work of Jules Vallès, who as early as 1861 had observed that people all around him were "victims of the book," and whose autobiographical novel *Le Bachelier* (The graduate, 1881) describes a young man struggling to survive in Paris after his literary studies fail to provide him with a useful training. Here, an important intertext is Rousseau, who warned against disorderly or excessive education as a harbinger of personal suffering and disruptive social mobility. Chapter 4 turns to the work of Paul Bourget, particularly *Le Disciple* (1889), in which a student is accused of murdering a young woman he had seduced by giving her books to read; that plot, I argue, borrows extensively from Stendhal's *Le Rouge et le Noir* (*The Red and the Black*, 1830). During the 1888 criminal trial on which Bourget's novel is based, the accused murderer had in fact been denounced for imitating Stendhal's hero; Bourget (who knew the accused) was also himself dangerously implicated in the affair. The homoerotic and homophobic implications of both the trial and Bourget's reworking of it in his novel show that the affair was a significant precursor to the Oscar Wilde trials of 1895. Chapter 5 focuses on Maurice Barrès's *Les Déracinés* (*The Uprooted*, 1897), which traces the path of seven young men from the provinces as they go to Paris to fulfil their career ambitions. This narrative arc is repeatedly linked to Balzac, even as the characters deny being influenced by the great novelist. In Barrès as in other novels from the same period, Balzac and his ambitious male protagonists have a lingering presence akin to a haunting. A sustained attention to intertexts in these three chapters demonstrates how the concept of novel reading as a seductive and disruptive practice for young men at the fin de siècle was itself produced and circulated in large part by earlier novels.

Part III shifts to consider a subsequent generation of writers who came of age reading the works discussed in Parts I and II. It highlights these new writers' strategies for overcoming the paradoxes of contagion and cure examined in earlier chapters. Chapter 6 examines Jean de Tinan's *Penses-tu réussir!* (So you think you'll succeed!, 1897) and Roger Martin du Gard's *Devenir!* (Becoming!, 1906), both of which make extensive use of irony as a strategy for confronting discursive tropes about the dangers of reading and the pitfalls of literary influence. For both novelists, irony was ultimately a flawed strategy that did not entirely allow for their stated goals of authenticity and sincerity of expression. Chapter 7 shows how André Gide, from *Les Cahiers d'André Walter* (*The Notebooks of André Walter*, 1891) to *Les Faux-Monnayeurs* (*The Counterfeiters*, 1925), increasingly embraced the antisocial dangers of reading as desirable for select individuals. Gide overcame an early failure to write a novel of formation that would solve the problem of influence by proposing a new definition of the novel *as* formation. Chapter 8 explores how reading is represented in the early work of Marcel Proust, especially the manuscript now known as *Jean Santeuil* (c. 1895–9). While Gide espoused a decidedly male-focused definition of readerly pedagogy, the Proustian model of author-reader relations is grounded in fantasies of same-sex recognition through shared reading. Rather than proposing antidotes for literary maladies or leading readers to renunciation, Gide and Proust, in different ways, put forward queer models of reading that reversed fin-de-siècle discourses about the book and its perils. An epilogue addresses how nineteenth-century denunciations of the dangers of reading evolved into warnings about cinema by the mid-twentieth century, and how today, in a remarkable reversal, male adolescents in France and elsewhere are said not to read enough.

PART I

Youth in Crisis

(Case Study: *Crise de jeunesse*, 1897)

By late 1897, France was in the throes of the Dreyfus Affair. In the weeks leading up to his famous "Lettre à M. Félix Faure" (better known as "J'accuse ...!," its headline in *L'Aurore* of 13 January 1898), Émile Zola published multiple articles in support of the wrongly convicted artillery officer Alfred Dreyfus, as well as a pamphlet titled *Lettre à la jeunesse* on 14 December.[1] While it is certainly related to questions of French masculinity at the fin de siècle,[2] the Dreyfus Affair will not be the story we follow. Instead of Zola's social purpose, I want to draw attention to his chosen rhetorical means: an address to "youth" (la jeunesse) as a distinct group, a symbol and a repository of the future of France.[3] While polemical in its support of Dreyfus, Zola's address is deeply conservative in the tropes it deploys, as it exalts the task of ensuring future national greatness through metaphors of physical toil: "O youth, youth! ... think of the great labour that awaits you. You are the builder of the future ... We ask only that you ... surpass us in your love of a life lived *normally*, in your effort wholly devoted to your work" (my emphasis).[4] "La jeunesse" is a term that only includes males, and Zola's addressees are in fact a tiny synecdoche of this group, since they are identified as "students [of the] Latin Quarter,"[5] meaning they are at least temporarily Parisian, and belong to an upper or somewhat upwardly mobile social class. In addressing a symbolic type of young male as representative of the future of the nation, Zola participates in a proliferation of discourses about young French men at the end of the nineteenth century. What is implicit in his exhortation to live life "normally" is stated rather more directly by multiple other observers: France is headed for moral and national disaster as its young men embark on lives lived *abnormally*.

Earlier in 1897, a deadly fire at a charity sale attended by wealthy upper-class Parisians prompted journalists to ask why, among the 116 victims identified, 110 were women: was chivalry dead? were men no longer men? Newspapers pointedly accused young male dandies wearing gardenias of running for the exits while ladies in distress perished in the flames.[6] In the same year of 1897, two commentators published influential tomes, each sounding a note of alarm about the current state of French male youth. The first was the novelist, journalist, and politician Maurice Barrès, whose *Les Déracinés*,[7] the first volume of his trilogy *Le Roman de l'énergie nationale* (The novel of national energy), made a narrative demonstration of the ills that awaited a group of adolescents fed an unhealthy diet of philosophy and poetry by the republican school system, and the even greater perils they faced as they left their native province for that most dangerous of milieus, Paris. The second, the sociologist Émile Durkheim, argued in his study *Le Suicide* that France's worryingly low birthrate and high suicide rate were twin symptoms of what he had earlier termed "a decline of domestic sentiments."[8] France's young men, Durkheim observed, citing statistics, married late, if at all, and were more prone to suicide because they suffered from *anomie*, which he defined as a painful discrepancy between their almost boundless socially created desires (both for economic ascension and for romantic or sexual gratification) and the very limited possibilities of satisfaction afforded to them in reality.[9] Such concerns with "the orientation of youth"[10] had been voiced regularly since the disastrous Franco-Prussian War of 1870, notably by the critic and novelist Paul Bourget in his *Essais de psychologie contemporaine* (1883–5). Yet by 1897,[11] the rhetoric of crisis around French youth, its unbound desires, and its life-threatening frustrations, seemed to reach fever pitch with the two aforementioned publications, as well as, I propose, with a third, the highly forgettable but aptly titled *Crise de jeunesse* by Albert Sueur.

This literary debut, which posterity has entirely (though perhaps not unfairly) ignored, was part of a wide contemporary production of novels of formation featuring male protagonists around the age of twenty, often geared to a readership of the same age. Many of these novels, including *Crise de jeunesse*, address young readers with a didactic purpose. They function through what Susan Rubin Suleiman has termed "negative exemplary apprenticeship"[12] – that is, they are cautionary tales, describing dangerous things that young men do and the awful consequences that ensue. These narratives implicitly urge their reader not to follow a similar path; often this is made explicit in a preface. Typically, the protagonists of these novels commit suicide or meet a similarly tragic fate; some heroes are saved through a last-minute redemption, while in other novels a parallel protagonist illustrates an alternative trajectory held up as a model (through a principle of "positive exemplary apprenticeship").[13] In much of this corpus, one of the most perilous things that young men do, strangely, is read literature.

Crise de jeunesse is no exception. It opens, symptomatically, with a reading scene:

> Fabien Després stopped reading; he lifted his gaze toward the cheerful brightness of the window, where a graceful spring morning was showing its promise, but his face showed the preoccupation of an agitated mind.
>
> The book open on the table was Stendhal's *De l'amour*. With a vivid curiosity, he had read this precise and penetrating analysis of all the sentiments of love ... And in the vague suffering of a desire, he gave himself over to the lulling charm of the images evoked in his mind.
>
> His reverie, following the suggestions of this book, evoked the skies of Spain and Italy with the poetry of faraway places ... This imaginary intoxication slowly dissipated, and as the obscure desire it shrouded became visible, the image of Jeanne Viliers appeared in the young man's thoughts. His attraction to this sweet and innocent young girl appeared feeble next to such dizzying delights, sublime emotions, fears and ecstasies. The tender sentiment he had developed toward her felt diminished by the ordinariness of their surroundings ... From his dreams, his desires, and his readings, he had formed an ideal of love and of woman ... and in his obscure torment, he felt a disproportion between his desire and its object.[14]

This incipit encapsulates all the elements of Fabien's crisis, implicitly represented as a crisis affecting a broad swath of French youth.[15] The spring morning, obviously, reflects his young age, the bright "promise" of which is darkened by looming threats. The double space of the scene – the real, natural world just outside the window, and the indoor space of reading, connoting that practice as an inner, solitary experience – mirrors the duality of the connected but conflicting worlds between which the book itself acts as a window. Fabien's immediate but ordinary surroundings contrast with the distant, "dizzying delights" evoked in his readings. Each of these worlds is inhabited by a potential object of desire: one has a name, Jeanne Viliers, and her brief introduction suffices to mark her as acceptable in gender and social terms, a proper prospect for marriage; the other is nameless, an idealized but hazy image, whose "lulling charm" shares some vague quality with "Spain and Italy," distantly Southern, dissipated realms. Fabien's tormented feeling of "disproportion" between the disappointing reality of the outside world and the boundless desires of his inner life could be labelled *anomie*, following Durkheim's contemporary theories; in an earlier decade, it might have been called *Weltschmerz*, the term coined by the poet Jean Paul to describe a similar recurring sentiment in the works of Byron.[16] A few years later, in 1902, it would perhaps be termed *bovarysme*, based on Jules de Gaultier's essay naming a sociological phenomenon after Flaubert's tragic heroine.[17] The relationship of the feeling of "disproportion" described by Albert Sueur, however we choose to label it, to the culprit he identifies, reading, has been described before: by Flaubert, of course, but also, more interestingly, by Stendhal, the very author Fabien is reading.

The book that lies open beside Fabien, *De l'amour* (*On Love*, 1822), famously gives the name "crystallization" to the process through which a desired object becomes embellished by the imagination.[18] This concept is cited by Sueur in a later work, a philosophy manual from 1920, where he defines it as a "fever of imagination that adorns the desired object with every possible seduction."[19] It is no coincidence that Fabien, whose story hinges on the seductions of imagination, reads Stendhal; by the 1890s, the very name of Stendhal had become a metonym for the imaginary seductions of novel reading. Paul Bourget, in the previous decade, had remarked on his era's infatuation and identification with Stendhal: "Henri Beyle ... happens to resemble ... many of our young contemporaries, who recognize in the writer ... a precursor of the most modern sensibility."[20] Bourget went on to describe *Le Rouge et le Noir* as "an extraordinary book, which I have seen produce on the brains of certain young people the effects of an incurable intoxication ... it casts a spell. It is a possession."[21] Maurice Barrès, likewise, would retrospectively describe the late 1880s as a time when "overall ... the sentiments ... that make up the soul of Fabrice del Dongo and Julien Sorel still ruled every heart in France. Stendhal's heroes were our brothers."[22] Both writers cite Stendhal's famous assertion in his autobiography (itself only first published in 1890, nearly fifty years after the author's death) that he would only be read and understood around 1880.[23] According to Bourget and Barrès, this prediction was proven true well beyond what Stendhal had wishfully anticipated: by the end of the nineteenth century, his readership was in no way limited to a "happy few"[24] but rather extended to young men throughout France, whom it left spellbound, intoxicated, possessed, ruled by its values as if by law, bound in a brotherhood of the book.

More than a brother, Fabien, the hero of Sueur's *Crise de jeunesse*, is a literal amalgam (Fab-ien) of Fabrice and Julien, the protagonists of Stendhal's two most widely read novels. Like them, he reads too much, a bad habit that leads to much trouble. Fabrice, the hero of *La Chartreuse de Parme* (1839), has no military training but runs off to join Napoleon's army at Waterloo, expecting to experience the "beautiful dreams of sublime and chivalrous friendship" he has read about in the epic poems of Tasso and Ariosto.[25] *Le Rouge et le Noir*, like *Crise de jeunesse*, opens with a reading scene: Julien is absorbed in his favourite book, *Le Mémorial de Sainte-Hélène*, while his brothers are diligently working in the family sawmill. As his father comes looking for him, Julien is not "in the place where he should have been"; the father, exasperated with his "odious ... mania of reading,"[26] knocks the book from his hands before striking him on the head. Linked to his reading from the start, Julien's character as out of place – echoed in Fabien's double location (not quite inside or outside, between dream and reality) in the incipit to *Crise de jeunesse* – will ensure that he escapes the path of petit-bourgeois mediocrity traced by his father and brothers. Indeed, the wonderful irony of Stendhal's novel is that while Julien, misinformed about the workings of the real world due to his excessive reading, fancies himself the protagonist of his own "novel,"[27] his failures in properly performing the role of hero are actually what lead to his successes and propel the narrative forward.[28] For instance, when he finally ascends to Mathilde de la Mole's bedroom, which in true novelistic fashion involves a hidden ladder, an unlocked window, and a dangerously bright moon, Julien is so at a loss as to what to actually say or do that he starts reciting passages from *Julie ou la Nouvelle Héloïse*, an awkward strategy for seduction that nevertheless ends in success.[29] Rousseau's novel, it should be observed, itself revolves around questions of seduction and education (and miseducation) through reading. As Julien and Mathilde mimic Rousseau's Saint-Preux and Julie, who themselves share in a reading of Abélard and Héloïse, who in turn cite Lucan, Seneca, and Ovid, a veritable continuum emerges, a chain of texts through which desire circulates not from person to person, but from book to reader, each character falling prey to the seductive model of an earlier text. Hence Stendhal writes that for Mathilde, even as she abandons herself to her lover, "passionate love was still more of a model to be imitated than a reality."[30] By the time Sueur introduces us to Fabien Després, leaving *De l'amour* open on a table in front of him, Fabien has not simply become warped by the false ideals circulated in his reading: he has in fact become a victim of the very incurable textual intoxication Stendhal both described in his own oeuvre and himself came to signify metonymically in the eyes of readers in the 1880s and 1890s.

What sets Fabien apart from Fabrice or Julien is an utter lack of success in the real world. Perhaps for want of a narrator as playful or delightfully ironic as Stendhal's, Fabien's story remains flat. Desiring to lead a life worthy of a novel, he rejects sweet, innocent Jeanne and fancies himself enamoured with a succession of unattainable women with evocative names like Madame Sallis and la comtesse de Grandlieu, all of whom reject or simply fail to notice him. To the chagrin of his father, a man of few words described as a "glorious cripple" of the Franco-Prussian War,[31] he even flirts with literary ambitions: predictably, these remain frustrated. Fabien tries to pour forth his soul in writing, but the results are worthless. To remedy this, he reads "Balzac and Flaubert ... in an effort to move beyond himself, outside the confines of his absorbing personality."[32] Fabien, instead of living fully, is confined to a barren circuit of literariness, signalled by his verbal impotence. His problem is not that he is self-absorbed, trapped in the intricacies of his own psychology, but rather that he is always already outside himself: he has no mind of his own beyond his readings. His "absorbing personality" is precisely that: a sponge, an empty vessel filled with plots and clichés culled from literary sources. Seeking a way out of his writer's block by turning to Balzac or Flaubert only furthers the problem, since these authors themselves, through characters like Lucien Chardon/de Rubempré or Frédéric Moreau, have already scripted the plot of frustrated literary ambitions. Sueur's hero can only act out a dim retread of *Illusions perdues* or *L'Éducation sentimentale*. The text spells this out squarely: when Fabien attends his first literary gathering, we are told that "he experienced a sensation of déjà vu, as scenes from Balzac and Flaubert came back to him confusedly."[33] At such moments, it is as if the narrator himself gives up, admitting his impotence in describing something other than what his readers have already read. Fabien finally abandons his writerly ambitions when he discovers that the manuscript he has been toiling on is in large part a pale copy of Goethe's *Faust*; "the comparison left him crushed."[34] In such instances, as in others when, for instance, the difficulty of getting one's first novel published is described in exhaustive detail,[35] it is almost impossible not to conflate the protagonist with Albert Sueur himself, whose first novel we are reading.

Sueur, like Fabien, appears compulsively incapable of producing a plot or scene we have not read before. Even when they are not explicitly signalled as déjà vu, many of his descriptions have a strangely familiar quality for the reader of nineteenth-century novels. His initial portrait of Fabien as "delicate" and "nervous," for instance, strongly echoes Zola's depictions of "end of race" characters and contemporary discourses on degeneration.[36] A later scene portraying Fabien as a despondent office worker leading a mechanical life echoes a similar passage from a novella by Huysmans, and even provides its title, *À vau-l'eau* (With the flow, 1882).[37] The most resonant of these citational moments comes when Fabien first declares his literary ambition: he does so by aping the poet André Chénier, as he points to his head and announces, "I, too, have got something in there."[38] There are two grave ironies here. The reference is to famous last words: Chénier is reported to have said, "and yet I had something in there!," as he was being led to the guillotine in 1794.[39] Fabien's playful exclamation, then, is ominous: he makes his entrance in the world of letters under a sign of doom. Moreover, his failure as a writer will precisely stem from the fact that he does *not* have anything "in there," except the kind of citation he is quoting. At best a sponge and at worst a void, his "absorbing personality" is composed of nothing but parroted phrases and pilfered plots, all products of his reading. His seduction by fiction is not only a product of reading books; it itself is an existing script, which he and his author merely repeat. The story of Fabien attempting to write a novel is doomed to collapse on itself, resulting in a novel of failure that is also a failed novel.

Fabien's story ends with a call to renounce the seductions of literature, by way of a religious epiphany at the church of Saint-Sulpice. Sueur's own story, about which few details have survived, appears to have followed a similar path. *Crise de jeunesse*, published in 1897, was never reprinted, nor was it followed by a second novel. In 1906 Sueur published a short essay, *Intellectualisme et catholicisme*, that aimed "against intellectualism [to] philosophically affirm [the] value of religious beliefs."[40] Inside the front cover, we find the indication, "by the same author: *Crise de jeunesse*, novel." His next publication, in 1920, was a study guide for students of the *baccalauréat* examination, *Nouveau précis de philosophie*. Inside that cover, we read, "by the same author: *Intellectualisme et catholicisme*," but see no mention of *Crise de jeunesse*, as if Sueur's youthful and unsuccessful foray into the novel genre had been erased. Among the pages of this manual, however, we find this definition:

> Imagination: ... it is the embellishment of life, the condition of progress, the master quality of inventive genius, yet it is also, when it is left unbound, a capricious faculty that fosters illusions, feeds passions, perverts the heart, and disorganises all mental life. ... But do its benefits not outweigh its dangerous seductions?[41]

~

The two chapters that follow examine how this struggle between the appeal and the peril of fiction plays out in a broad corpus of fin-de-siècle novels that both represent and address young male readers like Sueur's Fabien Després.

Chapter 1 examines how young men's reading practices in late nineteenth-century France are described as a cause for deep social concern by literary critics, sociologists, pedagogues, and philosophers. Metaphors of poison and intoxication recur throughout these denunciations, across genres and disciplines. Novelists of the period like Barrès and Bourget, writing in response to such anxieties, partake in discourses of self-control, and publish works that paradoxically hold up various forms of renunciation of literature as a cure for young readers' ills. Attempts to resolve this paradox are often made in a preface addressed to a real-life adolescent reader, or else through the representation of a violent act of disavowal – killing a character, burning a library.

Chapter 2 considers how representations of young male readers in these novels are linked to contemporary pronouncements about physiological degeneration, economic and reproductive impotence, and precarious masculinity in France's rising generations at the turn of a new century. The chapter inventories frequently used novelistic devices, such as contrasted pairs of characters (a negatively characterized reader and his positive foil), narrative sequences where reading is linked to non-reproductive sexual acts (often masturbation or same-sex dalliances), and scenes that present reading itself as disorderly (through lists of titles or authors that confuse chronology and genre). Through these devices, fin-de-siècle novels defined reading as a threat to the "normal" development of young men's productive and reproductive potential. According to their rhetoric, nothing less than the future of France was at stake.

1 Contagions and Cures

"*The Victims of the Book*, what a book that would be!" exclaims Jules Vallès in a letter printed in *Le Figaro* on 7 November 1861, when he was twenty-nine.[1] This letter, published as part of a literary game where readers were invited to select a winner among five anonymous pamphlets, is often described as a precursor to his autobiographical novel *L'Enfant* (*The Child*), published in 1879.[2] Proposing to recount "how one becomes a pamphleteer," the author, having donned a mask of anonymity, gives a lively and at times confessional account of his childhood in the hyperbolic, ironic tone that would become his novelistic signature. The exclamation is a brief aside, tossed off as Vallès remembers his "uncle" (easily identifiable as a stand-in for his father), a stern man who strove to model himself on the Roman paterfamilias described in the Latin texts that, as a lowly school instructor, he knew well.[3] As his more developed portrayal in *L'Enfant* makes clear, this man, with his delusions of classical dignity, is a victim of the book both in terms of his social standing (a promising student encouraged to set his sights on a university career, he found himself unable to move beyond the lower echelons of the teaching profession), and in terms of his own self-image, which is as far removed from his lived reality as Imperial Rome is from nineteenth-century France. If this fictional uncle is a substitute for the father, he is also, in this regard, one more mask Vallès dons to write about himself. What befalls a former student (like the father/uncle, and like Vallès) in a social and institutional structure that cannot accommodate him? How does bookish knowledge warp such a man's perception of his condition? These two interrelated questions would become central themes of Vallès's autobiographical trilogy, narrated through a further mask, the fictional character Jacques Vingtras.

Although he wrote extensively about his own victimhood in the Vingtras trilogy, Vallès never fulfilled his briefly envisioned ambition of writing a whole tome cataloguing every type of victim of the book. He did, however, develop his thoughts on the question in an article published eleven months after his letter of 1861. "Les Victimes du Livre"[4] makes a wide-reaching statement about the consequences of reading for the author's contemporaries:

> I can think of countless lives dominated, undone or redone, lost or saved by this or that passage, read by chance one morning! A maxim translated from the Chinese or Greek, taken from Seneca or St. Gregory, decided a future, weighed on a character, shaped a destiny.
>
> Often, almost always, the victims saw falsely, chose wrongly; the Book keeps dragging them further along, turning cowards into braggarts, nice young men into bad boys ... the influence is everywhere! All are subject to it, especially us, the corrupted.[5]

Vallès's claim is threefold: the influence of books affects everyone; it is so powerful that it has the potential to determine the course of entire lives; and it is overwhelmingly negative, associated with corruption, falsity, and deceit. Each of these affirmations is to some degree hyperbolic, as befits the genre of the pamphlet. By "everyone," Vallès mostly means members of his own petit-bourgeois class: his concerns do not extend to members of the rural classes, who are nowhere alluded to in "Les Victimes du Livre," nor does he give much thought to female readers, save for a late mention of three infamous criminal cases involving murderous women.[6] The unspecified countless examples of a single fragment from an obscure or distant text having irrevocably set the course of an entire existence are a rhetorical overstatement, serving to assert that books can have an effect on the lives of their readers. Vallès's third affirmation, that the influence of books is negative, appears clear from his repeated use of the word "victim." It must be noted, however, that he does not describe books themselves as being malignant; rather, he ascribes blame to the reader, since the practice of reading almost inevitably involves *mis*reading: "almost always, the victims saw falsely, chose wrongly." In Vallès's view, books are not intrinsically deceitful; it is the reader who practices self-deceit ("how many lies the book makes us tell ourselves!")[7] when he confuses their content with guidelines applicable to his own existence, or by confounding his own being with a fictional or historical character. The problem lies not with books, but with the reader who, having consumed them, goes on to misread his own life as a plot where things can and should happen as they do in novels, to misperceive himself as the hero of some great narrative. For Vallès, there are no good books or bad books: whether it be Greek texts, children's tales, illustrated adventure stories, novels by Balzac, or histories of the Revolution, all books lead to misreading. In this sense, the victims he describes are less victims of the book than victims of reading.

While he states that everyone is susceptible to the influence of books, Vallès's examples, as well as his emphasis on childhood readings, point to youth as a time of particular peril. It is individuals whose destiny is not yet traced who risk veering off the path; it is the "nice *young* man" who is most in danger of regressing into a "bad boy."[8] Paul Bourget makes this observation more pointedly, two decades later, in the foreword to the 1883 edition of his *Essais de psychologie contemporaine*:

> with the increasingly clear waning of traditional and local influences, the book becomes the great initiator. None of us, when we examine our conscience, can fail to acknowledge that we would not have quite become who we are, had we not read this or that work, be it a poem, a novel, a piece of philosophy or history. At this precise moment, as I write these lines, an adolescent – I can *see* him – is sitting at his study desk ... hunched over his book. (Bourget's emphasis)[9]

Bourget's statement echoes Vallès's in a number of ways: the influence of reading is felt by everyone (although just who his "we" includes, and excludes, is similarly problematic in terms of class and gender); it has the potential to change a person's being, to the point that one would not be the same without it; and it can stem from all texts, regardless of genre or distinctions between good and bad books. He goes on to evoke an emblematic reading scene – so readily and vividly present to his mind, he writes, that he can *see* it – in which the archetypal reader is a male adolescent, a student. Within this imagined figure of the typical adolescent, who embodies an entire generation, a tug of war of influences is taking place, and while traditional and local forces (which we may understand as shorthand for familial, religious, and provincial) are losing their grip, those of the book appear to be exerting an ever-greater pull.

Bourget presents his *Essais* as an investigation of these rising literary forces (understood to be libidinous, amoral, and Parisian). Rather than a literary critic interested in the biography or character of authors, he positions himself as a "historian of moral life." The moral life of the nation, he explains, is shaped by "elements" of which literature is "perhaps the most important."[10] The study of recent or contemporary literature, it follows, should be of interest to all concerned with the future of France, not simply because authors or their characters can be read as symptomatic cases of various social ills, but because these works actively shape the personality and destiny of rising generations.

Strange Educators

The influence of reading on the moral direction taken by young male subjects was a common concern among commentators in the first decades of the Third Republic. By the mid-1890s, a number of pre-eminent cultural critics reiterated or responded to this concern over the perceived popularity of reading in the wake of what they, like Bourget, described as the waning power of traditional and institutional forces. A polemical 1897 article by the philosopher Alfred Fouillée, linking the establishment of mandatory primary instruction in 1882 to a marked statistical rise in juvenile criminality and suicide in the years that followed, illustrates the reach of these shared anxieties.[11] Although Fouillée acknowledges that no direct causality can be proven, he asserts that the spread of education has exerted "indirect effects" on the youth of France, and laments the double-edged legacy of literacy: "the main outcome of public education has been a universal access to newspapers and novels ... by making an obligation out of knowing how to read, we have created a capacity for reading anything, and a near-inevitability of reading the very worst."[12] Responding to Fouillée by disputing his statistical inferences, the sociologist Gabriel Tarde concurs with him in suggesting that the problem lies not with school itself but with the nefarious influences that students, having learned to read, come in contact with once they leave the classroom: "it is under their father's roof that our students have suckled the poisoned milk of religious scepticism, of ambitious vanity and disrespect, of precocious greed, of vice ... if not at home, it is at work or at the café, through the suggestive power of the press."[13] A few years earlier, the educationalist Félix Pécaut expressed much the same apprehension in a report on primary school inspections:

> Yet I ask myself, with grave worry, who and what we are in fact working for, for whom and for what we train these children of the popular classes to read and to understand ... Is it to deliver these barely grown souls to new and strange educators, to cheap serialized novels, to corrupting penny press papers, adorned with the most perfid charms of illustrations?[14]

Citing Pécaut, Fouillée, and a related article by Ferdinand Buisson, the literary critic Gaston Deschamps synthesizes these concerns in a chapter of his 1899 essay *Le Malaise de la démocratie*. He describes two competing modes of learning, one inside the classroom, under the watch and guidance of state-formed instructors, and the other outside of class, beyond the reach of teachers and curricula:

> The typical Frenchman is of course capable of studying in class, but he learns even more out of class ... He has an incorrigible tendency to study what is

> not included in his curriculum of courses. He is as quick to escape the grip of pedagogues, as he is to let himself be grabbed, with great passivity, by newspapers, theatre, books, by the solicitation of things and the example of people around him.[15]

While the young man, in this picture, is always escaping the hold of the constraining if well-intentioned school system, he succumbs all too willingly to the temptations and nefarious influences of the stage and the printed word. As Pécaut points out, the particular irony of this typical and apparently inevitable shift is that access to the second, extra-institutional mode of learning is actually made possible, at least for the working classes, by the skills acquired through the first, state-sponsored mode of instruction. If it were not for the state's efforts at spreading literacy to all social ranks, the sons of the lower classes would not as easily fall prey to novels and newspapers, those strange new educators.

Fouillée, Pécaut, and Deschamps's emphasis on class in their discussion of juvenile morality stands in contrast to Bourget's stated concern for an emblematic, classless (and therefore implicitly bourgeois) adolescent. Even Ferdinand Buisson, who responds to Fouillée's 1897 article with even more scepticism than Tarde,[16] points to class contamination as the cause of the current crisis: "There is a moral crisis because the pernicious actions that, in the past, influenced the court, the nobility, and the upper bourgeoisie, are now being felt by the millions of men who are the France of today, and the millions of children who will be the France of tomorrow."[17] A stalwart republican and key architect of mandatory primary instruction, Buisson is careful to ascribe blame not to pedagogical reforms themselves, but to their unintended consequence of making citizens of all classes susceptible to some of the pleasures and temptations of the mind once available only to aristocrats. While he does not explicitly mention literacy, his explanation implicitly accepts Fouillée's claim about the "indirect actions" of education, namely, that it makes young men vulnerable to a constellation of dangerous influences (here made all the more nefarious through their association with the Ancien Régime)[18] from which they had previously been shielded.

In distinguishing between in-class and extracurricular readings, among which they specifically denounce sensational newspapers, lower-tier novels, and cheap illustrated stories, commentators from Fouillée to Buisson differ markedly from Bourget's and Vallès's suggestion that any book, any instance of the printed word, has the power to turn its reader into a victim. Nevertheless, all these observers agree that reading – broadly defined – comes to constitute a powerful alternative force in the shaping of young subjects, one that runs parallel, and often counter to, the vector of national instruction.[19] In his 1998 study of the novel of socialization,

Denis Pernot describes this conflict of forces as an opposition between "two systems of preparation to life ... the school system, and the system of literature, which is all the more popular with young people because it entices them with exciting plots."[20] While the national education system aims to foster the safe and normative development of its pupils through assigned texts, students are said to be led astray by extracurricular reading, in which they find greater or easier enjoyment.[21] This emphasis on pleasure would shape responses to the perceived crisis of the spread of reading, as pedagocially minded writers sought to harness the enjoyment of literature in the service of national education.

The captivating nature of novelistic plots is but one of the many appeals of the book; for Deschamps, as we have seen, books are part of an array of temptations whose "contagious pleasures" pose a threat to the youth and future of the nation. In his essay *Le Malaise de la démocratie*, these temptations – a popular and widespread production of novels, plays, and newspapers – are grouped under the umbrella term of "industrial literature," or, for short, "pornography."[22] Although Deschamps does not name names, his harangue appears to extend to authors of the Naturalist and Decadent schools. There is, in his judgment, no proper national literature in France in 1899, only "variegated publishing" [une librairie mêlée],[23] a statement given literal meaning when he takes his reader on a cautionary tour of a Parisian bookshop:

> you wander by the shop window at Flammarion. The covers of the latest books appear ablaze under crude lighting: blue, yellow, red, violet, green, zinzolin [reddish purple]. In large letters, the titles display their promising wares. The most recent ignominies proudly advertise their astounding sales figures [... F]rom this mound of books, a cacophony of solicitous and impertinent supplications seems to rise: "take me, monsieur, buy me, me, me ..."[24]

Here the unidentified latest books, in their luridly coloured jackets, are unmistakably depicted as prostitutes, seductively calling out to potential buyers, their titles a titillating peek at pleasures that await beneath the covers.[25] The alarming conflation of the tools of pedagogy and the commodities of prostitution is again emphasized when Deschamps observes that commercial publishers are often decorated, "not by the ministry of commerce, but by that of public instruction." Such an apparent incongruity, he explains, is in fact quite fitting, since "pornographers ... are also, in fact, educators."[26] Pornography, as Deschamps defines it, not only diverts the abilities fostered by mandatory instruction but usurps the state-sanctioned educator's role by seducing young readers into learning a different kind of knowledge, which pedagogues and essayists alike characterize as pernicious.

After the humiliating national defeat of 1870, fears about prostitution, pornography, and venereal disease gained currency alongside apprehensions regarding demographic decline, secularization, and urbanization. Rising generations of young Frenchmen were the focus of these multiple and interrelated social concerns. Carolyn J. Dean argues that, in the decades leading up to the First World War, "pornography increasingly replaced prostitution as the privileged metaphor for moral decline, commodity culture, and the loosening of spiritual bonds."[27] Each of these perceived ills could be decried as a symptom for another, almost to the point of interchangeability; all were tied to a sense of national weakness or decline, of which they were simultaneously denounced as causes and effects.[28] With pornography, as with venereal disease and its perceived corollary, prostitution,[29] young men were a particular concern, not only since they embodied the future of the Republic, but also because they were considered more easily led astray and less capable of self-control. When Deschamps writes that "now more than ever, the echo of our words, the image of our entertainments, the after-effects of our readings, the contagion of our pleasures, all affect youth,"[30] he establishes an implicit distinction between his audience of adults,[31] who are understood to be able to enjoy stage performances, books, and other indulgences without lasting consequences, and adolescents, who by nature are considered to be more easily and more profoundly susceptible to influence. Young people's vulnerability is also tied to their presumed lack of knowledge or experience; reading pornography presents a particular danger because it imparts knowledge that youths are not yet fully prepared for. Judith Surkis observes that, for turn-of-the-century syphilis specialist Alfred Fournier, "pornography ... threatened the integrity of the happy and healthy home [and, by extension, the nation] by submitting children's sexuality to a precocious publicity";[32] likewise for Buisson, pornographic materials are "the enemy" precisely because of their capacity to "prematurely stimulate appetites which are anything but noble."[33]

The argument could be extended to many types of literature beyond the already elastic category of "pornography," since reading by nature invites readers to come in contact with ideas and situations beyond the scope of their experience.[34] Books submit all readers, and perhaps particularly inexperienced ones, to a certain publicity, to information they would not otherwise have access to, whether it be by the vicarious enjoyment, through representation and plot, of realities often spatially, socially, or historically removed from them, or through the exposition of concepts or arguments they are not familiar with; these effects account in no small measure for the pleasure of reading, which, according to Deschamps, adults are able to enjoy with restraint, while youth are not – or not without consequences.

This type of statement about the particular dangers facing young readers is not only structurally similar to but, I propose, intimately bound up with contemporary discourses about prostitution and venereal disease, which, according to Surkis, are "premised on an imaginary distinction between the unknowing adolescent and the ideally knowing adult man ... capable of exercising requisite caution."[35] Fournier and other public health authorities responded to the perceived double vulnerability of youth – lack of knowledge and low self-control – with a two-tiered strategy. First, they made the case for sex education as a pre-emptive response to the danger of syphilis: by using scientific discourse, they aimed to provide adolescents with an education about matters of sexuality that counterbalanced what they might have learned from pornography or other extra-curricular sources, warning them about the dangers they faced, encouraging them to practise self-restraint, and informing them about the need to seek treatment should they, despite the best efforts of their will, one day be struck by "misfortune."[36] Second, they supported the continued regulation of prostitution as a means to diminish risk and provide young men with a safe outlet for their unbound desires.

In light of the commonplace analogy between prostitution and certain types of literature, Bourget's observation that the book has become the "great initiator" of French youth takes on particular significance. While Fournier seeks to warn adolescents against the frequentation of prostitutes, he also recognizes that such warnings are not and perhaps cannot always be heeded.[37] In doing so, he acknowledges a competing discourse – frequently represented and circulated in the nineteenth- and early twentieth-century novel – which legitimizes and even promotes the premarital sexual initiation of young men at the brothel or through other contacts with various forms of prostitution. In particular, male members of the bourgeoisie (whom Bourget specifically has in mind when he writes about adolescents) were not expected to marry with no sexual experience and instead were encouraged to sow their wild oats before taking a bride.[38] The regulation of prostitution by police and health authorities, established under the Consulate and maintained throughout the century, aimed to provide a controlled outlet for men's desires.[39] The medical surveillance of prostitutes, for Fournier, is of particular importance to the health of male youths, who, due to their "'inexperience,'" are "incapable of self-regulation," and therefore constitute, according to the statistics he compiled, the highest-risk group for syphilis.[40] The state-monitored brothel, in this sense, provided young men not only with a lower-risk outlet for satisfying their sexual curiosity, but also with an education in self-control. Rather than attempt a clampdown on all prostitution, which would have pitted them against tides of desire considered uncontrollable, state and local authorities chose to respond with a compromise that aimed to reduce the risks associated with the satisfaction of sexual drives while promoting the formation of self-regulating citizens. The response of pedagogues and novelists – Bourget among them – to the parallel dangers incurred by adolescent readers would be similar, at least in its stated intent.

Buisson explicitly recommends using the metaphorical poison of books as its own cure in an 1894 article, as he ponders the contrast between school-sanctioned readings and the cheap, sensational press enjoyed by adolescents outside the classroom. Following an indictment of "pornographic" materials, he writes:

> This poisoning of the public through a systematically demoralizing literature must be responded to with opposing readings that are just as easy and quick, attractive, low priced, multiple, and accessible to all ... *Similia similibus curantur*, goes the ancient medical adage; the same must be combatted by the same, the press by the press, the image by the image, the noxious sheet by the honest sheet.[41]

The education reformer proposes a concerted response to the fear that licentious extracurricular readings act as a powerful adverse vector in the shaping of young subjects: if such readings are luring youths away from the path traced for them by the Republic's instructors, they must be countered by other offerings that, if they are to be successful, must be just as attractive. Buisson calls on authors and publishers to make available an alternative to the products of the low-end press that would be not only as readily accessible but also equally enjoyable.[42] Since "like cures like," he reasons, the facile enjoyment of pornographic literature must be pre-empted by similarly enjoyable but morally upstanding texts; these, he argues, would shape the literary taste of young readers, making them impervious to the seductions of the tawdry press. Citing an 1893 report, he writes that students' personal reading outside the classroom should be "encouraged, guided, and controlled as much as possible" in order to "inculcate a habit of useful readings." He goes on to state his objective: "to shape taste early on, before it can be depraved or abased ... to gently inspire a taste for books, to foster a love for good and proper readings."[43] Reading, for Buisson, is not in itself a dangerous or subversive activity, but it should initially be practised in a controlled frame – one that extends beyond the classroom – in order that young readers may develop enough "taste" and self-restraint to stay away from pleasurable but morally harmful texts. Just as medical experts argue that the plague of venereal disease can be contained by the regulation of prostitution, pedagogical authorities suggest that the "poison" of dangerous literature can be countered by guiding and controlling students' reading. In both cases, state regulation is conceived not only as a palliative for youths' inherently deficient self-control, but also as an enabler of self-regulation through the formation of habits and tastes. State control is not meant to indefinitely replace self-control, but rather to teach self-control. Fourier and Buisson's strategies (allowing men supervised access to prostitutes, making available "guided" readings for young people) implicitly recognize the impossibility of eradicating prostitution or eliminating all immoral literature, and opt instead to create controlled circumstances under which future citizens can learn to enjoy texts or sex with moderation. Indeed, the development of the capacity to read and enjoy literary texts – like the development of (hetero)sexuality[44] – is an ideal, if not a condition, of full citizenship, and therefore a goal of national instruction as described by Buisson: "We want to ... create a literary atmosphere for our young men, to introduce them progressively ... into the great conversation salons of the civilized world."[45] Both strategies propose not to go against pleasure, but to harness it in the service of the education of self-regulating citizens. Controlled enjoyment is imagined to guard against excessive, disruptive enjoyment. Yet in each case there remains the unacknowledged possibility of confusion or slippage between like and like, between the proposed cure and the imagined poison: what defines and delimits textual taste and sexual habit always remains a threat to it.

Thinking of You(th), Anxiously

Fournier's double-tiered response to the menace of venereal disease is replicated in an abundant contemporary literary production addressed, at least nominally, to adolescent readers.[46] Maurice Barrès, for example, opens his second novel *Un homme libre* (A free man, 1889) with a straightforward dedication, "To a few students [collégiens] in Paris and the provinces, I offer this book," and goes on to specify, as he begins his preface, "I write for children and very young people."[47] The slippage between "young people" and the less broad "collégiens" is noteworthy, seeing as *collèges* are secondary schools, not the primary schools made mandatory in 1882. Less likely to attend a *collège*, the newly literate lower classes that so preoccupied Deschamps, Pécaut, and Fouillée are much less written about, and for, in fin-de-siècle novels than the implicitly bourgeois "adolescents" imagined by Bourget and, here, Barrès. *Un homme libre* is about, as well as for, such middle-class young men, as the narrative follows Philippe, the student protagonist of Barrès's first novel *Sous l'œil des Barbares* (Under the eye of the barbarians, 1888). Philippe first sets up a self-imposed retreat with his friend Simon, where, in a blend of decadence and asceticism that recalls Huysmans's *À rebours* (*Against Nature*,

1884), he meditates at length on the works of "spiritual intercessors" like Benjamin Constant, whose novel *Adolphe* (1816) is a classic of Romantic alienation. Later, Philippe forswears books, deciding instead to "abandon solitude," travel to Lorraine and Venice, and embrace the Church. The narrative traces a path from aimless dilettantism and "sterility" [sécheresse] to an "active life," although the latter is only imprecisely described as an ideal, a "conclusion" and a "rule of life" arrived at but not yet acted on.[48] In his original 1889 preface, Barrès presents the novel as a response to the problem of adolescent suicide:

> I have piously kept a list, for the past six or seven years, of the names of children who have killed themselves. The list is long, and I dare not publish it ... If they had read me, I believe they would not have taken so extreme a decision. It seems clear that these fragile and lazy souls had been misinformed [mal renseignées].[49]

Languid and delicate suicidal adolescents are said to be "misinformed" about the world; although the causal link between their lack of vitality and their lack of accurate knowledge is unclear, Barrès proposes that his novel can correct the former by remedying the latter with proper information. The notion of *renseignement* reappears when he revisits his first trilogy of novels (grouping *Sous l'œil des barbares*, *Un homme libre*, and the 1891 *Le Jardin de Bérénice* [The garden of Bérénice] under the overall title *Le Culte du Moi* [The cult of the self]) in "Examen des trois romans idéologiques" (1891), a short article that became the preface to the 1892 reprint of *Sous l'œil des Barbares*:

> I have attempted to write a monograph about the five or six years of development of a young intellectual Frenchman ... These monographs ... are a form of *information* [un *renseignement*] about a type of young man who is often seen, and who, I imagine, will become even more numerous among the ranks of those who are currently in secondary school [lycée]. In future years, these books ... will be consulted as documents.[50] (Barrès's emphasis)

Although terms like "monograph" and "document" suggest a detached, pseudo-scientific observation or reportage in the style of Naturalism, Barrès goes on to state that his novels are also intended to intervene in the problem they describe: "these monographs are a form of *teaching* [un *enseignement*]" (Barrès's emphasis).[51] According to his 1891 article, the novels are thus not only reporting on young people as a *renseignement* but also directed at them as an *enseignement*, in the hope of redressing what they have been taught wrong.

Barrès's early novels, *Sous l'œil des Barbares* in particular, are perhaps only retrospectively "ideological" (the qualifier he gives them in 1891); the arc they trace from dilettantism and nihilism to the cult of action is in many ways the author's own.[52] His composition of new prefaces for re-editions, in 1891 and again in 1904, attests to a desire to reframe his early trilogy in hindsight. The 1904 preface addresses a caveat formulated by Bourget in the preface to his own novel *Le Disciple* (1889), that *Un homme libre* was missing a conclusion; Barrès answers that his later work *Les Déracinés* (*The Uprooted*, 1897) picks up where the *Un homme libre* had left off:

> Indeed, *Un homme libre* told the story of a quest without giving its result, but this suspended conclusion is provided by *Les Déracinés* ... If I am not mistaken, *Un homme libre*, completed by *Les Déracinés*, is useful to young Frenchmen, in that it reconciles with the general good certain undeniable tendencies that could otherwise have easily thrown them into a fatal nihilism.[53]

Barrès justifies the apparent ideological murkiness of his first novels by claiming that it leads to the clarity of purpose of his more recent work. In a related article from 1900, he responds to a critic who claimed that he had done an opportunistic about-face, and states that his oeuvre consists "not in contradictions, but in a development [since] my errors ... remain, always fertile, at the root of each of my truths."[54] *Un homme libre*, Barrès claims, is useful because it aligns certain dispositions of adolescents with the greater social and national good. In other words, young people with a nihilistic penchant find it appealing because it appears to be in line with their sensibilities, yet they unwittingly benefit from it because the novel uses this very attractiveness to slowly guide them away from nihilism. It would be difficult, Barrès implicitly claims, to catch young readers' attention with a straightforward condemnation of their ills: instead, they must be lead along the path that he himself has traced, in a "development" from dilettantism to action. The novels use the representation of error as bait with which to veer young readers away from their own errors and towards truth.[55] *Similia similibus curantur*, as Buisson would say. In Barrès's retrospective view, his early novels function not only as documents about nihilism (like Fournier's pamphlets about syphilis), but also as a kind of education that, by permitting readers a safe, defused contact with the seductions of nihilism (like the frequentation of state-surveilled prostitutes), will ideally teach them to resist the temptation of overindulgence in it. They constitute a regulated space that allows readers to enjoy the appeals of literary nihilism while simultaneously teaching them to move beyond it. Reframed as a trilogy, and later as a series that spans two trilogies, Barrès's novels about adolescents function as an education in reading, designed to lead their readers to reject what they present as excessive bookishness.[56]

When Barrès dedicates his 1891 "Examen des romans idéologiques" to Bourget, as when he cites him in the 1904 preface to *Un homme libre*, he not only acknowledges a critic and friend who helped launch his literary career, but also cites the author of the genre-defining preface of the novel of formation under the Third Republic.[57] Bourget's preface to *Le Disciple* (1889) is a direct address to young Frenchmen, traversed by anxious questions of authorial responsibility and national morality:

> It is to you, my young countryman, that I want to dedicate this novel, you whom I understand so well, although I know ... very little about you, merely that you are between eighteen and twenty-five years old, and that you go looking, in those volumes written by us, your elders, for answers to questions that torment you. The answers you find will shape some of your moral life, some part of your soul; and that moral life of yours will in turn shape the moral life of all of France ... Knowing this, no honest man of letters, weak as he may be, can help trembling with a sense of responsibility ... you will find in *Le Disciple* a study of these responsibilities. May you also find in it some proof that the friend who writes these lines ... thinks of you, anxiously ... and has been thinking of you for a long time, since the days when you were beginning to read, at a time when we – who today are heading toward our fortieth year – were scribbling our first poems and our first page of prose, as the sound of cannons thundered over Paris.[58]

As he did in the 1883 and 1885 forewords to his *Essais de psychologie contemporaine* and in an 1888 article on *Sous l'œil des Barbares*,[59] Bourget asserts the profound importance of reading in the development of young subjects, and links this influence to the moral life of the nation itself. Yet his tone has changed slightly by 1889: as he moves from up-and-coming essayist to established novelist, he also acknowledges an important generational shift. Whereas in the *Essais* he was content to diagnose the influence of a previous generation of writers on contemporary readers, with this novel, Bourget claims for himself the position of the older generation to which a new wave of young men turn for answers. A sense of continuity between generations through reading and writing is established with a backward glance: when the author was making his first attempts at poetry and prose, his readers were just learning to read. Today, the author seems to imply, an even newer generation is learning to read, who in twenty years' time will look to the writings of today's aspiring authors for moral guidance, before in turn taking up the pen to pass down their wisdom – and their faults – to a generation as yet unborn. Looking back twenty years leads to a nod to the defeat of 1870, which later allows Bourget to link his literary enterprise to "our great duty, the restoration of the fatherland" [le grand devoir du relèvement de la Patrie].[60] For all his insistence on the writer's responsibilities, though, he does not take them up quite fully or unproblematically: as "a study of these responsibilities," his novel proposes a dramatic mise en scène of the way certain texts can have harmful effects on the actions and destiny of their reader, but offers no example as to how a text could instead have a beneficial influence. *Le Disciple* thus functions entirely as what Susan Rubin Suleiman has termed "negative exemplary apprenticeship";[61] it does not, as his later novel *L'Étape* would, offer a parallel, positive example of apprenticeship.[62] As in the *Essais*, Bourget appears exclusively preoccupied with the deleterious effects of literature on its readers, and while he ponders his tremendous responsibility as a writer, he remains silent on the possibility of a reverse, beneficial potential. The only conceivable positive role for the "honest man of letters" appears to be constituted through the paradox of a double negative: writing cautionary texts about the dangers of reading. The result for the novelist is a profound and irresolvable anxiety.

Bourget places himself in the dual role of teacher and friend: he is both a benevolent educator who warns his own disciples about the danger of following a bad master[63] and a former student who, having once been where they now stand, empathizes with his readers' predicament. This ambiguous position straddles two authorial standpoints: that of the concerned pedagogue (as embodied by the latter-day Barrès), whose greater standing and more advanced age allow him to claim moral authority, and that of the sympathetic comrade, whose claim to the adolescent reader's attention is based less on authority and more on proximity and identification. André Lebey, in the preface to his novel *Les Premières Luttes* (1897), adopts the latter standpoint through an assertion of perfectly reciprocal similarity between writer and reader: "The author of this novel is a young man, and he dedicates his novel to young people."[64] He goes on to expand this claim to include the novel's protagonist:

> But if ... you are the young man I envision, if you too are in your own way a little like Jacques Dalvèze, leaf through these pages ... and, from far away ... let us walk hand in hand. You are my brother; you are not yet twenty years old; you came into this life with a quiet smile; your illusions took flight in the blue skies of the eternal dream; you have read many books; you have lived little; you have made many attempts and you hesitate.[65]

Lebey's second-person description of his assumed reader happens to also describe his protagonist succinctly; since the reader is presumed to be somewhat like Jacques, a portrait of the latter can become a diagnosis of the former. The "you too" implies that the author is also himself like Jacques; all three, then, are "brothers," the fictional character providing the imagined link between author and reader. Holding the book that tells the story of Jacques's life is likened to holding the author's hand. Lebey uses this identification to turn his own desire for a book about his personal plight into the reader's desire to read the book he has written. Speaking of "the author of this book" in the third person, he writes:

> Alone since the day he began to look with some attention at his surroundings, he suffered from solitude and wished for a book that could help him solve his hesitations. Having never found such a book, he conceived of the ambition to write it, in the hope of sparing others, as much as he could, the suffering he had so intensely experienced.[66]

It is intimated that since the reader is like the author, he too must suffer from feeling alone; reading about the author through the fictional character Jacques, this reader is invited to both read about himself and about others like him, which should lessen his sense of isolation and thus alleviate his suffering. If the reader and the author are anything like Jacques, though, there is some unacknowledged irony here, since the novel soon tells us that, from an early age, Jacques's isolation is caused by his all-consuming passion for reading books.

The novel's first part is framed by two scenes of summer vacation, one before Jacques is seven and the other when he is sixteen and about to leave for the *collège*. Both scenes feature family members (an aunt and, in the second, Jacques's grandmother) expressing concern – "inquiétude," a recurring term – over his reading habit and his resulting propensity for isolation:

> His entire family ... saw him as strange for the first time. Less turbulent, he began to enjoy solitary walks. At Troyes, during their vacation, his aunt once caught him perched on a chair, taking volumes no one ever touched from the old bookshelves ... with time, she became concerned: he was reading too much. She confiscated the volumes from his bedroom: it was *A Thousand and One Nights*.[67]
>
> He spent [his whole vacation] hunched over books without any notion of time, barely noticing life outside, living the life of others without being a participant, so meditative and silent that his family soon began to worry ...
>
> – I've never seen such a child ... he sits for hours in front of a book or a piece of paper instead of mingling with the other youths; he's become reserved, he never speaks.
>
> – ... obviously there is something strange in his brain. No one else is like him.[68]

At the onset of Jacques's school years and the end of his childhood, reading is identified as the cause of his isolation, both literal (he takes long solitary walks) and social (even in the presence of others, he pays little attention to them). In the eyes of his family, reading makes him bizarre and not like the others. The systematic use of an exterior point of view to describe him appears to contradict the logic of identification set up in the preface: if the author is like Jacques (who is like the reader), why does he observe Jacques from an outside perspective? It may be that the reader is invited to stand with Jacques, a fellow reader, against their judgment, but in that case, he finds himself judged by association. Consistently relayed by the narrator, the aunt and the grandmother's nagging concern, halfway between worry and condemnation, has more in common with the pedagogue's stance than with the comrade's. As such, it may hint that the author-narrator is less of a brother to the reader than his preface would have us believe.

Les Premières Luttes features many characteristic elements of the fin-de-siècle novel of formation: the protagonist reads excessively from an early age; he is unhappy in school; his sexual development is shaped by a frustrated longing for inaccessible, imaginary figures drawn from literature; he indulges in dilettantism rather than engaging in productive activity; and he develops aspirations to become a writer, which are eventually disappointed. It also follows the pedagogical and ideological narrative model established by Barrès in his first trilogy, from dilettantism to action: Jacques goes from being an aimless dilettante who experiences life as a series of sad disappointments, preferring instead to read and dream ("he relived mentally every successive disillusion one by one, and felt renewed indignation at the wretchedness of life. He persuaded himself that dreams were all there really was, that they were the only true thing in life"),[69] to being a man of action disenchanted with literature and its mirages ("he now viewed literature with a smile of detached scepticism; given over entirely to life, swept up by it, he found himself unable to live it any other way than through action").[70] The very last page of the novel features a clear nod to Barrès, as the newly invigorated Jacques, sailing briskly off the coast of Italy towards an unknown but exhilarating future, is described as a "free man [homme libre] in every aspect, a double victor, who had triumphed against others but also against himself."[71] Perhaps even more than Barrès's trilogy, where the cult of action of *Un homme libre* and *Le Jardin de Bérénice* is only retrospectively made to emerge from *Sous l'œil des Barbares*'s dilettantism and nihilism, Lebey's novel appears to be constructed teleologically:[72] since *Un homme libre*, published in 1889, furnishes the novel with its final page, it is fair to say that this conclusion precedes and determines the story that leads up to it. The brotherly identification between reader, character, and author in the preface is thus revealed to be based on a rhetorical sleight of hand. The author may have once been like the presumed reader, but he is now very much unlike him, and the book he offers functions less as a consolation for the reader being who he currently is (a solitary, a voracious reader, a dilettante) than as an incitement to change and become more like what the author, through his character, now claims to be (a "free man"). A further complication also emerges: while Jacques has renounced his fruitless desire to write books in order to embrace action, the author has not; instead, he has written the book we are reading. Lebey was twenty years old when he published *Les Premières Luttes*: while his novel claims to offer a model of "action," it in fact does little more than condense and rehash Barrès's trilogy from the previous decade. It remains unclear, then, whether the adult Jacques can be unproblematically identified with his author or to what extent he should be considered a fantasmatic projection of idealized, active masculinity.

The novel of formation often employs the identification of the reader with the protagonist (and occasionally with the author) to ideological ends.[73] Authors like Barrès claim that they at first mimic the nihilistic mindset of their presumed readers in order to eventually direct them away from it; others like Bourget pose as an older and wiser version of these same readers, aiming to offer them "answers." Both seduce with sympathy ("you who I understand so well," writes Bourget) in order to better deliver pedagogy, even demagogy. Barrès, in the 1889 dedication to *Un homme libre*, makes this clear: "since my only concern is to be useful to students, whom I hold dear [aux collégiens que j'aime], I limit myself to the most childlike literary form I can think of: a diary."[74] His stated concern for students leads him to adopt an adolescent genre and style, which he knows will make the medicine he has to offer easier to swallow. The mimicked expression of adolescent nihilism is put in the service of helping adolescents grow out of it. *Similia similibus curantur*. Yet as Lebey's example shows, an unacknowledged paradox remains: if reading is the poison that causes adolescents' ills, how can a book unproblematically function as its cure?

From Consumption to Contamination

"First come children's books," Vallès declares in "Les Victimes du Livre," going on to detail how these readings, innocuous though they may seem, in fact plant the seeds of readers' future victimhood.[75] When, in *L'Enfant*, he writes about a book that his alter ego Jacques Vingtras received as a prize in school, "I devoured *Les Vacances d'Oscar*,"[76] the metaphor likewise appears innocent. Dietary metaphors about the consumption and enjoyment of books are, after all, so common in French as to usually go unnoticed. In the description of reading practices, expressions such as "se régaler" (feast on), "être nourri de" (feed on), "goûter" (savour), and most of all "dévorer" (devour) are used as a matter of habit; in linguistic terms, they are sleeping metaphors.[77] Yet within a novel as preoccupied with hunger as *L'Enfant*, and in the broader context of growing national anxiety over young subjects' consumption of books – a concern already stated by Vallès two decades earlier – the metaphor of devouring books may not be as transparent as it looks. Indeed, when considered alongside Vallès's dedication of the second volume of his autobiographical trilogy, *Le Bachelier* (The graduate) – "To those who, fed a steady diet of Greek and Latin, died of hunger"[78] – it appears to take part in a much larger reflection, which Vallès's own *L'Insurgé* (The insurgent), and, in the following decade, a sizeable production of novels of formation, would answer most alarmingly: metaphorically speaking, what are France's schoolchildren feeding on? What temperaments, what kinds of appetites are being created by this literary diet? And what happens when these appetites are left cruelly unsatisfied when confronted with reality?

The very first sentence of *L'Enfant* asks a distinctly literal, though not unrelated, question about nourishment: "Did my mother suckle me? Was it a peasant woman who gave me her milk? I have no idea." Vallès goes on: "No matter whose breast it was that I bit, I don't remember a single caress from the time I was little; I was never cuddled, petted, kissed; I was lashed a lot."[79] The next pages recount Jacques's earliest memories, all revolving around Madame Vingtras's proclivity for dispensing corporal punishment. Strikingly, this opening sequence ends on a different type of memory: the narrator, five years old and still reeling from a beating, is taught how to read. "I'm taught to read using a book where it's written, in big letters, obey your father and mother: my mother was right to beat me."[80] From the beginning, an opposition is set up that will traverse Vallès's entire trilogy. There is, on the one side, harsh reality: the real world is by and large cruel and unfair – though it may offer occasional respite from its brutality, usually in the shape of lower-class or country women such as the spinster neighbour who shelters Jacques when his mother threatens to beat him, feeding him candy instead, or the peasant woman who he imagines may have breastfed him. On the other, there are books, and these, as the narrator's bitter initiation into their world unequivocally shows, must be met with the highest suspicion. His mother is violent and unjust, yet the book tells him that he must obey her, that she is always right. His conclusion, though unspoken, appears clear: books lie.

The opposition between real life and deceitful books would be unproblematic if its terms were fully stable; however, as this early example shows, they are often not. The printed word makes claims about reality (first claim: parents must be obeyed) that, despite running counter to the narrator's experiences and emotions, are presented as authoritative ("in big letters"). The status of the corollary affirmation, "my mother was right to beat me," is profoundly ambiguous: we do not know if the narrator is still paraphrasing the book, if he is inferring a proposition from what he has read, or if he is being ironic. One might even decipher, through his possible irony, an unavowed wish: the narrator wishes the book were telling the truth, wants to believe his mother is always right, and so he transforms the book's failure to tell the truth into a failure of his own, for which he deserves to be beaten. The roundabout expression of this wish effectively blurs the line between truth and deceit – or self-deceit. From the very moment of initiation, then, the relationship of the printed word to reality is marked as complex, shot through with questions of authority and desire.

While he cannot recall whether or not he was suckled by his mother, Jacques vividly remembers, like the *Confessions*'s Jean-Jacques, his first taste of injustice.[81] Raised on a harsh diet of reprimands and beatings, trapped in a school he describes as a "prison" on a dark street, he longs for the possibility of escape, and finds it – in the practice of reading fiction.[82] The aforementioned *Les Vacances d'Oscar* provides a first glimpse into a different world, one where the sun shines and, tellingly, honest outdoor work is rewarded with a natural abundance of food. The episode Jacques remembers best is a river tableau, where two men haul in a glimmering net holding a bounty of wriggling fish. The narrator pays homage to the author of this otherwise forgotten children's book: "He'd had the skill ... to drag this large net all the way along the page, and veer that river into the corner of a chapter."[83] Here the deceit of the written word first experienced in the child's training book is presented in a new light: no longer a bitterly recognized deception, it becomes an almost Christic miracle of transposition, if not transmutation. Through this unsung author's descriptive skill, the fishermen's net moves from along the banks to along the page; from the ink of his printed words, a whole river gushes forth. The evocative power of reading ruptures the barrier between what is on the page and what is experienced.

Jacques's escapist consumption of children's novels finds its most intense and memorable occurrence when he encounters a better-known book, albeit one that shares the aquatic theme of *Les Vacances d'Oscar*: Defoe's *Robinson Crusoe*, discovered by chance, dug up like buried treasure from a gap between desks in an unheated empty classroom to which he was confined as punishment. Enthralled by his discovery, "devoured by curiosity, glued to Robinson's side,"[84] he spends hours absorbed in his reading, well past nightfall, until hunger strikes him suddenly, and he wonders whether he, like Robinson, will have to survive on grilled rat. A teacher finally remembers him and, embarrassed for having apparently left him locked in punishment so long in the cold, offers him whatever modest sustenance he can put together. Jacques does not go to bed but continues to read: "I throw myself into the book I'd hidden between my shirt and my skin, and I devour it – with a bit of tuna, and a few drops of cognac – in front of the chimney fire. I feel like I'm in a ship's cabin or an island shack."[85] Here the nutritional metaphor returns, along with a manifold confusion of lived experience with written tableaux. Hunger for the narrative initially obscured real hunger (indeed it was the reader, in a reversal of the usual metaphor, who was "devoured"); when the latter resurfaces, the fleetingly envisioned solution of grilled rat conflates the reader's predicament with Robinson's; later, both hungers are satisfied simultaneously – using the same verb, *dévorer* – while the reader's real setting fades into a fictional one.

Defoe's adventure narrative holds sway over young Jacques's imagination and existence for a long time, up to his last year at the *lycée*, when he concocts a Crusoe-inspired scheme of escaping his schoolboy's existence and finding work aboard a ship at the seaport of Toulon. This fantasy leads him to masochistically seek out punishment, as he imagines he needs to toughen up in anticipation of a harsh life at sea:

> It's going to be hard on the ship. I have to *break myself in* for the job, or rather have myself *broken in* ahead of time; so here I am for weeks on end saying I broke some dishes, lost some ink bottles, ate all the paper! – I have to say I'm always eating paper and drinking ink, I can't help myself. My father has no idea ...! (Vallès's emphasis)[86]

Whereas his initial encounter with reading involved punishment unjustly received for an offence not committed, a violence ironically sanctioned by the written word's untrue declaration that parents are always right, Jacques's prolonged contact with *Robinson Crusoe* has led to a full reversal: he now actively seeks out corporal punishment for acts he did not commit, hoping that the beatings will toughen him up in preparation for a harsh life at sea. In order to do so, he uses a most literary stratagem: he tells stories, he lies. What's more, the strange tale he makes up involves a form of bibliophagia: eating paper, drinking ink. Here, as in his earlier expression of disbelief at the book's affirmation of parents' infallibility, the narrator's statement is irresolvably ambiguous: it is impossible to know if the sentence that begins with "I have to say" (Il faut dire) is meant as an admission of guilt (I now confess I actually was eating paper and drinking ink) or as an admission of the stratagem (I had to falsely declare I was eating paper and drinking ink in order to get beaten). The narrator may be ironically justifying his false claim of having consumed vast quantities of paper and ink by facetiously emphasizing the compulsive nature of this fictional mania ("I can't help myself"); or he may be admitting that this claim actually was true, which would then contradict his earlier suggestion of having told tales.[87] In either case, the child/narrator lies, relishing his father's – and perhaps his reader's – cluelessness ("my father has no idea") and delighting in his own status as "such a hypocrite!"[88] Jacques has consumed enough paper and ink, whether metaphorically or literally, to be able to produce, in his turn, the commixture of truth and deceit that is the defining characteristic of the written word.

In 1885 Anatole France described *Robinson Crusoe* as "the great classic of childhood literature for the past hundred years,"[89] and indeed it is cited with great frequency in French novels of formation, among them Daudet's *Le Petit Chose* (1868), Zola's *La Joie de vivre* (1884), and Bourget's *André Cornélis* (1887).[90] In 1910, an example of the genre even appears under the title *Robinson*.[91] Defoe's novel is emblematic of childhood reading, not simply because it is widely read, but because, as Vallès shows, its tale of shipwreck and island life offers a strong metaphor for the escapist quality of the practice of reading (as does *Paul et Virginie*, the other title most frequently mentioned in childhood novels of the period). It also, conversely, provides a potent symbol for the alienation experienced by readers upon their return to the real world. In *Le Bachelier*, Vallès's narrator thus describes his first night spent on the streets of Paris: "I'm as scared as a Crusoe shipwrecked on an abandoned shore, but in a land with no green trees or red berries."[92] Barrès uses a similar comparison to illustrate the worsening predicament of two of the seven protagonists of *Les Déracinés*: "Racadot and Mouchefrin are struggling mightily ... Lost in the Parisian desert, like Crusoe on his island, they know they have to hustle."[93] In both cases, the citation has a double function: it identifies the characters as modern-day adventurers who, driven at least in part by what they have read, left their homes and set out for the dangerous terrain of Paris; simultaneously, it performs a cruel inversion of the logic of escapism by using the very emblem of their readerly fantasy to describe the harshness of their subsequent encounter with reality.

Like his citation of *Robinson Crusoe*, Vallès's use of dietary metaphors is a recurring trope of novels of formation in the following decades,[94] including those of Barrès. *Les Déracinés* opens with the narrator comparing a classroom where a new teacher (Bouteiller, the iconic *mauvais maître*) is giving his first lesson, to a stable thrown into commotion because oats are being distributed instead of hay. The image is striking in its implications: schoolchildren are institutionally raised, like horses or cattle,[95] and the texts and ideas they are presented with ("the various rudiments they were chewing on") are like the feed used to foster animals' growth.[96] Unlike Vallès's descriptions of a hearty appetite for books, however, Barrès's metaphors often carry a clear connotation of danger. The diet of Kantianism and Romantic poetry fed to his group of impressionable schoolboys is "nearly undigestible"; susceptible as they are to "moral epidemics" and "fevers of imagination," the boys risk being irrevocably pushed to nihilism by an "overdose."[97] With these last examples, the nutritional metaphor leaves the realm of delectable foods suggested by Vallès and his lexicon of hunger and devoration, and veers instead towards the vocabulary of medicine, of disease. In his use of this related trope, Barrès is clearly indebted, once again, to Bourget – to whom *Les Déracinés* is dedicated. In the foreword to the second volume of his *Essais de psychologie contemporaine* (1885), Bourget explains how his work has sought to investigate the causes of what he describes as the predominance of a "melancholy" and "profoundly, continually pessimistic" state of mind among his young contemporaries. "A whole swath of our contemporary youth is in crisis," he writes; "it displays the symptoms ... of a disease of moral life having reached its most acute stage."[98] The agent of contamination he singles out is literature – specifically, the works bequeathed to the youth of the 1880s by their elders of the previous generation, among them Baudelaire, Flaubert, and the Goncourt brothers. "Works of literature and art are the most potent means of transmission of this psychological heritage," he claims.[99] Bourget employs the medical analogy throughout his foreword, pondering how far this "contagion" will spread and explaining how he sought to isolate "the germ of melancholy."[100] In *Le Disciple*, published four years later, he makes further use of this analogy as he details the treacherous workings of what he names "the general law of literary intoxication."[101] The metaphor of reading as toxic runs through the narrative ("my fantasies had drunk in the most dangerous poisons in life"),[102] and comes to be literalized when the protagonist is accused of having poisoned a young noblewoman to whom he had lent books.

In *Les Déracinés*, likewise, the trope of poison is deployed in a manner that combines metaphors of consumption and contamination. Barrès details how François Sturel, one of the young men his novel follows from their native Lorraine to the dangerous playing field of Paris, has been exposed to a variety of dangerous intellectual influences, all represented through images of noxious vapours or particles: in philosophy classes he breathed in "faraway oriental perfumes of death, filtered through a network of German thinkers"; later there comes an "exaltation when, at the age of seventeen, the star of poetry had risen from his books ... all these elements and many others floated inside the young man."[103] These "melancholy vapours," Barrès explains, coalesce through a phenomenon of "general condensation" when François is seduced by Astiné Aravian, an alluring and mysterious Armenian heiress who enthrals him with tales of her exotic travels.[104] Astiné's story is itself described through an agglomerate of metaphors that combine orientalist clichés with military, medical, and chemical terms: it is at once an "unnerving invasion from Asia," a cloud of "toxic dust," a "poison cup," and a "precipitate of death."[105] The scene's final sentence further condenses all these images of danger into a striking double metaphor: "Astiné is an admirable book he leafs through [qu'il feuillette]; he poisons himself avidly with every sentence."[106] Here the book, long a tenor for metaphor (book as food, book as poison), has become a vehicle (woman as book), through a play on the orthographic similarity between *feuilleter* (leaf through) and *effeuiller* (literally, "remove the leaves" – a metaphor for the action of undressing). The success of the sentence's first metaphor relies on what is reiterated in the second; because books are established to be poisonous, they become an apt vehicle through which to describe Astiné. The double figure suggests reciprocity: if Astiné is like a book in her toxicity, she is also the intoxicating danger of reading personified. As such, her eventual murder at the hands of the two most destitute *déracinés* – the same two who had earlier been compared to Crusoe lost on his island – is more than a simple plot point: it stages a symbolic vengeance for the victims of the book.

Literary Remedies

In their sustained use of metaphors of poison and intoxication to describe the pernicious effects of literary representations, Vallès and Barrès show themselves to indeed have been "fed a steady diet of Greek and Latin":[107] such metaphors have been a mainstay of antimimetic discourses since Plato. In *The Republic*, we find a passage where, as in *Les Déracinés*, the future guardians of the city are compared to a herd of grazing animals unwittingly exposed to a poisonous substance: "We would not have our guardians grow up amid images of mortal deformity, as in some noxious pasture, and there browse and feed upon many a baneful herb and flower day by day, little by little, until they silently gather a festering mass of corruption in their own soul."[108] Taken up again in the writings of church fathers like Tertullian (in *De Spectaculis*) and Augustine (in the *Confessions*) against stage performances, these metaphors recur in seventeenth-century condemnations of theatre in France, which rely in large part on the authority of the ancients.[109] The Jansenist Pierre Nicole, in his *Lettre sur l'hérésie imaginaire* (1665), denounces the "novel-maker" and the "playwriting poet" alike as "a poisoner of the public."[110] Bossuet, in his *Maximes et réflexions sur la comédie* (1694), compares stage actresses to "those sirens described by Isaiah" and denounces "the poison they spread through their song."[111] As numerous nineteenth-century commentators would later do, Plato points to youth as a time of particular susceptibility to the dangerous habit of imitation that stems from contact with noxious mimetic art: "imitations, beginning in early youth and continuing far into life, at length grow into habits and become a second nature, affecting body, voice, and mind."[112] In such characterizations, we recognize Plato's concern with the worrisome potential of mimesis to supplement and potentially supplant, as a second nature, the natural, the good, and the true.[113] Sylviane Léoni notes that this Platonic model of mimesis as corruptive and condemnable exists alongside, in the Western heritage of ancient texts, a competing Aristotelian model according to which the mimetic representation of various dangers can lead to a desirable *catharsis*, that is, the experience of certain painful emotions made safe or sanitized for the audience of a poetic or stage work. Aristotle's concept of catharsis through representation, Léoni observes, implies "the idea of a betterment rather than a degradation."[114] The curative strategies deployed by French novels of formation under the Third Republic reflect the lasting influence of both models, as well as their enduring, if uneasy and often paradoxical, coexistence. By denouncing the literary intoxication of French youth, novelists like Bourget and Barrès, as well as commentators like Fouillée, adopt what could be described as a moderately Platonic stance.[115] None of them, of course, argue for the exclusion of writers from the Republic; yet by proposing that the works of certain poets, novelists, and philosophers are harmful to many of its future citizens, they implicitly invite the critical banishment of these texts from the channels of republican education, both in and outside the classroom. Conversely, in choosing to write novels themselves, these same novelists display a faith in the Aristotelian model of catharsis, or, more broadly defined, in the potential of controlled representations of danger or negative examples to participate in the education and betterment of their stated audience, young men. Whether explicitly, like Joseph Hudault, who, in the preface to *La Formation de Jean Turoit* (1911), compares himself to "a doctor advertising his remedy" and promises his reader that, if he accepts his novel's lesson, "you will once more be a man";[116] or with more circumspection, like Bourget, who claims that *Le Disciple* primarily aims to "show" his reader the ravages of intellectualism, and can only hope to be "beneficial" to him in doing so,[117] these writers propose that their novels can act as a cathartic cure for young men's literary ills.

Like Barrès, who sought to reframe his early trilogy *Le Culte du Moi* through prefaces to new editions in 1892 and 1904, effecting a shift from observational *renseignement* to salutary *enseignement*, Bourget prefaced his *Essais de psychologie contemporaine* three times, moving from the purported near-neutrality of a diagnostic to outright didacticism. The 1883 foreword, built around the description of an emblematic reading "adolescent," states that the *Essais* only aim to "define a few of the types of sentiment that certain writers of our era propose to very young people as examples for imitation."[118] The foreword to the second volume of *Essais* in 1885, as we have seen, makes sustained use of a medical lexicon ("symptoms," "disease," "contagion"); it also goes on to express a certain unresolved uneasiness stemming from the critical reception to the 1883 *Essais*. "Do you propose a remedy," Bourget asks, paraphrasing his critics, "to the ills you describe so complacently?" For the time being, "I humbly admit that I have no possible conclusion to give to this study" is his only response.[119] *Le Disciple*, published four years later, constitutes a more elaborate answer, as well as a shift from observation to intervention, with its stated hope of being "beneficial," if not quite yet the awaited potent remedy. A later preface to the *Essais*, written in 1899, is in contrast explicitly prescriptive: "for the moral maladies of contemporary France ... the Christian faith is now the sole and necessary hope for a cure."[120] In the intervening decade, Bourget married in 1890,[121] renewed ties to Catholicism (which he had renounced at fifteen), and was elected to the Académie française in 1894 (at the young age of forty-two). The 1899 edition of the *Essais*, which coincided with his public enlistment in an anti-Dreyfusard organization, includes a number of appendices, among them Bourget's *Discours de réception à l'Académie française*, here given a significant new title, "The Disease of the Will: A Recovery." An introductory note states in no uncertain terms that the addition is meant to provide an answer to the question left hanging in earlier editions: "I present it today after these *Essais*, to which it can serve as a conclusion."[122] Here, then, is the deferred conclusion of the previous decade's *Essais*, Bourget's long-awaited description of a cure to his era's literary maladies.

As is customary, Bourget's *Discours* is an oration in praise of the previous occupant of his assigned seat at the Académie: in this case, the writer Maxime Du Camp (1822–94), today mostly remembered as Flaubert's friend and travel companion in the Middle East. Bourget's narration of Du Camp's youthful years is remarkable in that it deploys nearly every single one of the characteristic tropes – one might even say clichés – about the excessively literary formation of nineteenth-century bourgeois young men that Bourget's own essays and novels had earlier defined. In other words, the young Du Camp, through Bourget's lens, becomes yet another specimen of adolescent literary malady; his biography is written as a short novel of formation about the intoxication of reading, one that ends in a cure. The narrative Bourget traces opens immediately with a depiction of the young

Du Camp in school, where "he hid himself in a corner to read ... the most recent volumes by contemporary poets"; it then goes on to describe how, by reading Lamartine, Sand, and Gautier, "he imbued himself, saturated himself with the complex and dangerous Ideal held up by the Romantics."[123] The adolescent Du Camp and his friend Flaubert, in this familiar picture, both end up "victims of the same imbalance [and of] all the contradictions [and] the worst anxieties of their era."[124] Later, as an adult, Du Camp publishes some volumes of poetry followed by a number of novels, among which Bourget chooses to cite two heavily symptomatic titles: *Mémoires d'un suicidé* (Memoirs of a suicide, 1855) and *Les Forces perdues* (The lost strengths, 1867). Du Camp, according to Bourget's biographical sketch, is a sufferer among others, "a melancholy type ... a tormented soul" – a specimen of the widespread and debilitating "Romanticism of education" that turns French youths into morally weak men unable to lead productive lives because "they dream of nothing but literature."[125] What singles him out as an object of praise, however, is his miraculous "recovery"; such recoveries are "rare in our day," the newly minted academician acknowledges, but he emphatically insists they "are possible."[126]

Bourget's account of this cure follows Du Camp's narration of a life-changing episode in his *Souvenirs littéraires* (1882–3). Until the age of forty, Du Camp writes, "I had been able to read indefatigably."[127] In May of 1862, however, recurring eye pain leads him to consult an optician, who prescribes glasses. "Age was taking its toll. I did not welcome it gladly. *But I submitted to it.* I ordered spectacles" (Bourget's emphasis).[128] Bourget attaches tremendous weight to this formulation:

> You will notice, Messieurs, this phrase, *I submitted* [*je me soumis*], and the tone in which it is uttered. The phrase will elucidate the remainder of this rather simple yet quite significant anecdote. The writer does not merely address this phrase to age, you see. He addresses it to all of life, to reality, to the social community, of which, from that moment on, he will strive to make himself a useful member, a beneficial artisan. (Bourget's emphasis)[129]

The anecdote continues: the optician needs half an hour to prepare the lenses, so Du Camp steps out of his shop and wanders around Paris. As he crosses the Pont Neuf and sees the statue of Henri IV, that "relic of dear old France," he experiences a revelation.[130] What if he were to write a monumental tome about the capital – not a novel or a poem, but a painstakingly detailed, factual account, a document for the ages? The optical symbolism of the episode is fairly transparent: the young Du Camp had used his vision to read indefatigably, even excessively, and in doing so failed to really see the world and the city around him. By contrast, the mature Du Camp, struck with far-sightedness that makes it difficult for him to read, is able to look around him and truly see for the first time. The project conceived at that moment would become a six-volume study titled *Paris, ses organes, ses fonctions, sa vie* (Paris: Its organs, its functions, and its life, 1869–75), the work of Du Camp's mature years. Bourget characterizes this change of genre, from fanciful poetry and fiction to the rigidly documentary monograph, as a radical transformation of Du Camp from sickly dilettante to virile worker: "The child of the century, grown weary of empty passions, useless melancoly, and romantic adventures, transforms himself into a vigorous and valiant worker of the pen, who will henceforth have in front of him a single work, but a work that is large, masculine, and civic-minded."[131] Under Bourget's own pen, the shift in genre becomes a shift in gender. The writer figure who emerges from this epiphanic transformation is a fantasy of authorial virility, a projection of idealized worker-like masculinity all the more striking in that the stated condition for his metamorphosis is the renunciation of the novel (he forswears anything "novelistic"), one if not the very genre for which Bourget is being named to the Académie and hence asked to give this speech.[132] Bourget emphatically reiterates this point by citing Du Camp's own characterization of poetry and the novel as nebulous, insubstantial genres that he chose to give up in favour of the solidity and reliability of the monograph – "I grasped something solid, on which I could lean."[133] The genre of the monograph, Bourget concludes, is a social good because it reconciles the power of the word with the truth of the world. Citing Fénelon – himself an academician under Louis XIV – he ascribes the genre a motto: "To use the word only for thought, and thought only for truth."[134] The result of this rhetorical manoeuvre is nothing less than the fantasmatic collapse of the word onto truth. In this anti-Platonic fantasy, the writer achieves a fullness of presence and social purpose – systematically coded as masculine – by closing the gap between reality and literary mimesis. Such full presence, Bourget insists, can be achieved only at a price, the writer's repudiation of youthful imaginings and subjective sensitivities, and his surrender to objectivity: "Had he attempted to translate his vast investigation into novelistic settings and characters ... he would have revived within himself the powers of imagination and sensitivity that he had to keep dormant; he would not have practised an absolute submission to the object, the submission that cured him."[135] This, for Bourget, is the cure to literary intoxications: renunciation, submission. Again he cites Du Camp: "*I have been disciplined by truth*" (Bourget's emphasis).[136]

I proposed earlier that Third Republic educationalists sought to counter the effects of what they themselves described as the poison of dangerous readings by guiding and controlling young people's tastes and habits as they formed. This regulatory drive, I argued, was intimately bound up with related efforts to curtail the spread of venereal disease among young French men through both education and controlled access to medically surveilled prostitution. In both cases, state regulation was conceived as a measure that would not simply palliate young men's intrinsically (though temporarily) deficient self-control, but ultimately teach them self-regulation. Providing adolescents with what was imagined as safe, controlled access to the objects of their presumed desires (texts; sexually available women) was meant to assist the formation of their own individual habit of self-control. These measures, in other words, aimed to facilitate adolescents' eventual repudiation of tendencies or desires considered excessive (voracious and undiscerning reading, masturbation, indiscriminately directed sexual drives) and impart a deference to an accepted moral, economic, and social re/productive order. Renunciation and submission, in this regard, emerge not only as the cure to youthful maladies of the mind and body, but as the very conditions of adult male subjectivity in the Republic.[137]

In *Dialectic of Enlightenment* (1947), Theodor Adorno and Max Horkheimer famously offer a definition of modern bourgeois subjectivity based on the Homeric myth of Odysseus and the Sirens. While these Sirens are not the biblical (and apocryphal) sirens evoked by Bossuet, the significant recurrence of the term "submission" under Bourget's pen, along with the enduring trope of the book as an enticing but perilous poison – in another metaphorical figuration, a siren – leads me to consider their proposition. "The history of civilization," they write, "[is] the history of renunciation." Odysseus, they assert, is the "prototype of the bourgeois individual" because he is able to "train himself in lordly self-mastery." His bondage to the ship's mast, which he willingly chooses and in fact orders, becomes an allegory for mastery through submission and restraint. The song of the Sirens has "power as art" because it contains "irresistible promise of pleasure" but also "knowledge."[138] Odysseus is able, through his power of restrictive self-mastery given literal form in the ropes of his bondage, to both enjoy and resist its seductive call. A perilous promise of knowledge and pleasure in which one risks losing oneself, and from which the adult bourgeois subject learns to keep a restrained distance in order to experience enjoyment without danger – what if, following Bossuet and Bourget, we were to reframe the mythical story of the Sirens' song as a scene of reading:

> [T]he lure of the Sirens remains overpowering. No one who hears their song can escape. Humanity had to inflict terrible injuries on itself before the self – the identical, purpose-directed, masculine character of human beings – was created, and something of this process is repeated in every childhood ... The

> fear of losing the self, and suspending with it the boundary between oneself and other life ... is twinned with a promise of joy which has threatened civilization at every moment ... Odysseus's idea, equally inimical to his death and to his happiness, shows awareness of this ... The bonds by which he has irrevocably fettered himself to praxis at the same time keep the Sirens at a distance from praxis: their lure is neutralized as a mere object of contemplation, as art.[139]

Odysseus's wilful self-bondage, then, could be an allegory for the bourgeois male subject's relation to the siren song of literature: the mimetic remains accessible and even sanctioned as an object of his enjoyment, on the condition of his maintaining a restrained distance from its lure, of his continued and "absolute submission to the object," his self-fettering to the solidity of the real – in Du Camp's words, "something solid, on which I could lean." The condition of the reader's accession to adult male subjectivity is that he remain "disciplined by truth."[140]

Adorno and Horkheimer's reading of Homerian myth also brings into stark relief the questions of class. Odysseus is able to train himself in self-mastery only because of his status as a "landowner," "free of practical cares." He can have himself tied to the mast and safely enjoy the perilous song only because he "has others to work for him." The allegory, in their reading, is built around a rigid and impervious demarcation between classes: above deck, the prototype of the bourgeois subject can enjoy art through his self-restraint, while below deck, the workers toil away, their "urge toward distraction" suppressed through the blocking of their ears.[141] In the context of the Third Republic, however, this demarcation is anything but solid: the development of a meritocratic national educational system and the related, continued rise of a petit-bourgeois class of bureaucrats and office clerks[142] continuously threaten the traditional division between landowners and workers. The instatement of mandatory primary education in 1882 further erodes the distinction between a bourgeois class whose formation in self-restraint allows its members to enjoy the pleasures of mimesis as art, and the ever-increasingly literate masses for which it becomes incumbent on the Republic to provide an equivalent training, lest they throw themselves to the Sirens. "We want to ... create a literary atmosphere for our young men, to introduce them progressively ... into the great conversation salons of the civilized world,"[143] writes Buisson: this gradual formation aims to bring, in allegorical terms, a whole generation above deck – hence the insistently stated and staged anxiety of the appointed pedagogical and literary masters of the nation's youth. The almost systematic absence of the working class in the literary production that represents and targets young men in this period is symptomatic not only of its authors' own affiliations and aspirations, but of this very problem: the contemporary crisis of French youth is a crisis of class upheaval imputable to education, and its embodiment is the socially ascendant *étudiant* imagined and interpellated by Bourget.

Where does this leave the novel of formation? I proposed earlier that many novels addressing and representing young readers are the locus of an uneasy coexistence between a Platonic condemnation of mimesis and an Aristotelian model of catharsis that allows controlled representation as means of betterment. In some of the more patently didactic of these novels, these competing paradigms converge in the dramatic mise en scène of a renunciation of literature. Two novels by Joseph Hudault illustrate possible iterations of this convergence. In *La Formation de Jean Turoit* – prefaced, as we have seen, with an appeal to the reader as a "my young countryman" that echoes Bourget – the titular protagonist, a twenty-three-year-old law student, initially spends his days in the Sorbonne library and dreams of becoming a writer. The narrator characterizes his existence as aimless and in need of more solid fettering: "Sense of family, sense of place, sense of traditions and common religion: those are strong ties ... Jean feels that, if he wanders aimlessly, and wastes his energy in the most disparate directions, it is because he has not made good use of these ties."[144] When the young woman Jean loves marries another man, he realizes that what he desired was an overly literary version of her: "impossible dream! ... in the manner of *Ruy Blas*. I had mostly loved Simone with my brain."[145] He declares his renewed faith in Catholicism and leaves Paris to settle instead in his native Beauce, where the towers of Chartres cathedral stand out in the plain like an immense marker, "the centre of this landscape."[146] Finally anchored, his days occupied with physical labour, he is able to forget his literary education. Doing Odysseus one better, Jean renounces the Sirens' song altogether and fetters himself below deck, ears blocked: "The vast Beauce plain spreads out around him ... And while he toils, having forgotten his complications, he is happy. He is tired. He thinks of his next rest, of the joy of loving and being loved. Everything else, he forgets. He no longer suffers over insignificant and imaginary things."[147] Hudault's next novel, *Le Pavillon aux livres* (1914), reprises the theme of renunciation through a plot of multiple seductions and eventual atonement revolving around the personal library that the protagonist, Robert, inherits from his freethinking grandfather. The library's morally dangerous content (Stendhal, Renan, Voltaire) is unrelentingly incriminated as the cause of every ill that befalls the young household: Robert becomes a hapless, devirilized, apathetic "dilettante";[148] his wife and his former fiancée are both seduced by the same lecherous friend; one of their sons is born abnormally feeble and dies. The novel ends on a note of vengeful repudiation, as Robert vows to restore the library to its pre-revolutionary function as a chapel, and condemns its contents to the flames:

> His gaze lost in the blaze, he looked on as the fictions that had once allured him now dissipated. It seemed to him that, in the flutter of the flames, they were drifting to sow elsewhere, in innocent and desirous hearts, their seeds of godlessness and disenchantment ... He saw them as in a procession, those warlocks and magicians who had misused their art: the Romantics with their pride and their sick passion for themselves, the Naturalists who had forgotten to give their heroes a soul, the sceptics who had been his favourite, destructors of ideals, professors of impotence and uncertainty.[149]

In *Le Pavillon aux livres*, the paradox of the fiery denunciation of literature through literary means is laid so bare as to be almost untenable: how can a novel that relies so centrally and repeatedly on the plot of adulterous seduction (one of the subplots even involves the discovery of the unfaithfulness of Robert's mother-in-law, through a letter she left hidden in a volume of Montaigne's *Essais*) denounce *Le Rouge et le Noir* (among others) with utter seriousness? The answer may lie in the violence of the required repudiation: like the figure of Astiné Aravian in Barrès's *Déracinés*, the all-alluring library in *Le Pavillon aux livres* can be indulged in and loved only on the condition of its destruction – the woman-book is brutally murdered, the library is set ablaze. Like Bourget's version of Maxime Du Camp, Hudault's characters are allowed their youthful literary passions on the condition that they eventually cure themselves through sharp renunciation. The price of their accession or return to idealized, productive masculinity is their surrender and subjection to what Bourget calls "traditional" and "local" forces.[150] Hudault himself would put into practice this glorification of action over intellectualism advocated by his master Barrès: he died fighting at Les Éparges in Lorraine, in 1915.[151]

2 Representing the Fin-de-Siècle Reader: Exhaustion, Deviation, Impotence

In his autobiographical *Confession d'un enfant d'hier* (1903), Abel Hermant writes:

> You know what men of my generation are called: children of the conquest. It is well known that the facts of war, which we witnessed but barely understood, left on us an indelible trace: they humiliated our energy and weakened our temperament ... They made us brittle, egotistical, pessimistic.[1]

By the turn of the century, it was indeed an admitted, received idea that the military defeat of 1870 and the chaos of the Paris Commune of 1871 had left an imprint on the generation that came of age in the 1890s, leaving it weak-willed and temperamentally fragile. The defeat itself, early on, had been explicated in terms of decadence and national decline;[2] in the decades that followed, it was continually returned to as both a consequence of decadence and a cause of further decline. Zola's *Rougon-Macquart* cycle, published between 1871 and 1893, famously develops this interpretation, as it depicts the moral excesses of the Second Empire culminating in the "debacle" of 1870. In the early decades of the Third Republic, writers like Zola and Taine proposed to investigate the defeat's causes, while others like Barrès expounded on its consequences, all as part of a more or less explicitly stated project of national regeneration. Daniel Pick proposes that Durkheim, though "very different" from any of these writers in his methods and affiliations, nevertheless himself "perceived 1870, year of defeat, as the moment of inception of a sociology in which certain pathologies of 'hypercivilization' were opened up to investigation."[3] The lexicon of pathology was inextricably wed to these observations and analyses of national decline and has been the focus of much historical scholarship.[4] Anxieties over the perceived ill health of the social body traversed and inflected a number of interrelated discourses, notably around questions of education and literature.

By 1897, diagnoses of national degeneracy and decadence had become enough of a commonplace that Michel Provins[5] could list, in the preface to his play *Dégénérés!*, a string of ubiquitous terms related to and, he argued, subsumed under his title:

> Over the last few years, expressions like fin de siècle, end of race, decadence, corruption, Symbolism, Naturalism, self-interested amorality, reign of money, multiplied like the facets of a gem, and the truth seemed to sparkle on the surface of each for an instant. All were attempts at labeling a generalized disease for which the diagnostic had not yet been made ... We needed, in order to name it correctly, the all-compassing word that a German doctor was to whisper in our ear: degeneration![6]

The German doctor in question (actually Hungarian) is Max Nordau, whose 1892 essay *Entartung*, translated into French in 1894 as *Dégénérescence*, went through no less than seven editions before the end of that year.[7] Nordau had lived in Paris, and studied under the eminent Jean-Martin Charcot, a specialist of hysteria and other neuroses. *Entartung* opens with descriptions of the "various manifestations" of degeneracy Nordau observed among Parisians, not in the Salpêtrière Hospital where Charcot worked, but on the street, in salons and concert halls; in subsequent chapters he goes on to lambast a succession of "degenerate" French writers, including Baudelaire and Huysmans but also Zola and Barrès, citing racy or lurid morsels of their oeuvre for effect. Nordau emphatically partakes in the medical discourse on national decline. To explain why the "pathological phenomena" he ascribes to "the effect of contemporary civilization" have taken a particular hold in France, he cites the disaster of the Franco-Prussian War: "upon this nation, nervously strained and predestined to morbid derangement, there broke the awful catastrophe of 1870."[8] Pick notes that Nordau's opus was "sometimes celebrated, but also frequently denounced as charlatanism"; he goes on to explain that "by the 1890s, [as] the critique of *dégénérescence* was gathering pace ... the word was slowly losing its specificity and its mystique, its point of difference from heredity in general, in serious medicine and psychiatry."[9] Yet despite being an increasingly imprecise, contestable concept, degeneration gained in scope as a discursive trope through that decade; as Robert Nye explains, "by the 1890s degeneracy was no longer simply a clinical theory of abnormal clinical pathologies, but a social theory of persuasive force and power ... widely employed as an explanation for the whole range of pathologies from which the nation suffered: alcoholism, prostitution and pornography, suicide, and the incapacity (or unwillingness) to procreate."[10] A nexus of national anxieties, social concerns, scientific or pseudoscientific diagnostics, and literary trends, the discourse of degeneration echoed through the turn of the century (at which point it in many ways shaped responses to the Dreyfus Affair):[11] certainly, by 1897, it had become a topos.

Carolyn J. Dean observes that Nordau, like other "mainstream critics," diagnosed degeneracy and its literary manifestations in gendered terms: "Nordau argued quite conventionally that behind great literature was a virile male body whose virility provided the necessary energy needed to transcend ... man's creaturely status ... 'Degenerate' writers were instead eunuchs ... weak, nervous men with deteriorating bodies, evidence of a sterile, agonized manliness symptomatic of cultural decline."[12] For him, she argues, "literature reflected the 'masculinity crisis'" that characterized the end of the century in France.[13] Dean borrows the phrase "masculinity crisis" from Michelle Perrot, who in an influential article from 1987 described this crisis as rooted in "fear of women's sexual and economic liberation," embodied in the threat of the New Woman;[14] more recent scholarship problematizes the "crisis model" according to which a "formerly stable" masculinity found itself threatened by social changes at the fin de siècle (including the increasing emancipation of women), and instead proposes to examine the category of masculinity as "a contingent norm, constituted by ever-present possibilities of abnormal deviation."[15] In the literary field, perceived deviations from an ideal of authorly masculinity, as Perrot notes, were denounced across the political spectrum, and writers as ideologically disparate as Zola, Barrès, and Octave Mirbeau all railed against what they saw as a deficiency of French literary virility.[16] Indeed, for male authors of all political affiliations as for Nordau, literary products not only "reflected" but inflected the health and virility (or fecundity) of the social body; they were seen not only as "evidence" or symptoms, but as potential agents of destabilization and devirilization. Nordau underscores this point in his dedication of *Entartung* to Cesare Lombroso, the father of criminal anthropology and himself a theorist of social degeneration:

> Degenerates in literature, music and painting have in recent years come into extraordinary prominence ... This phenomenon is not to be disregarded. Books and works of art exercise a powerful suggestion on the masses. It is from these productions that an age derives its ideals of morality and beauty. If they are absurd and anti-social, they exert a disturbing and corrupting influence on the views of a whole generation. Hence the latter, especially the impressionable youth ... must be warned and enlightened.[17]

Nordau's expression of concern for "the masses" and "impressionable youth" mirrors many of his contemporaries' pronouncements about reading practices and the dangers they pose to segments of society perceived as vulnerable; yet like most of them, he remains unable to resolve (or perhaps is simply oblivious to) the paradox of his "warning and enlightening" project, parts of which read like a catalogue of literary salacities.[18]

Provins's 1897 preface goes on to inadvertently suggest a complex relationship between literature and degeneration:

> Many men who have worn themselves thin [qui se sont usés] in the whirling and factitious life of great cities have become degenerates, to varying degrees ... from superior degenerates whose flaw [fêlure] is above all an excess of intellectualism, down to simple mattoids [i.e., eccentrics], without forgetting graphomaniacs.[19]

The passage presents intellectual activity, including writing and, presumably, reading, as both a cause ("excess of intellectualism") and a symptom ("graphomaniacs") of degeneracy, in accordance with Nordau's diagnostic. Yet it is perhaps most revealing as a web of citations: aside from Nordau, who is transparently alluded to earlier in the preface, the passage is woven through with terms borrowed, directly or not, from various theoreticians and critics of decadence. "Graphomaniacs" (individuals afflicted with a pathological compulsion to write) and "mattoids" (eccentrics bordering on, but not fully given over to, insanity) are two of the categories of degenerates described by Lombroso and adopted by Nordau; *fêlure* is one of the most heavily significant terms in Zola's oeuvre, where it designates the hereditary "crack" or flaw that perpetuates itself among the Rougon-Macquart.[20] The notion of *usure* (wear and tear, structural weakening) appears in Bourget's 1882 essay on Flaubert, reprinted in *Essais de psychologie contemporaine* the following year, where the critic describes three interrelated types of "weakening."[21] Provins's preface thus shows how literature, aside from being both one of its symptoms and one of its causes, is also a vehicle for degeneration as a concept; increasingly, the terms this concept relies on (*fêlure*, *usure*, "intellectualism," even "degenerate" itself), as they gain discursive currency, lose their precision and become literary commonplaces.

Bourget's description of three types of *usure* among his contemporaries juxtaposes physiological symptoms with mental and behavioural ones:

> Physiological weakening [L'usure physiologique] ... can be observed in the deformations of the human type visible at every street corner in large cities. Modern man, as we see him coming and going along the boulevards of Paris, bears in his frail limbs, in the overly expressive physiognomy of his face, in the excessively sharp look in his eyes, the obvious trace of a thinned blood, a diminished muscular energy, an exaggerated nervosity ...

> The weakening of feeling [L'usure du sentiment] through thought is likewise effected in diverse ways. At times, the creation of an over-refined ideal feeds passion [and] pushes men to strange and dangerous excesses ... Other times, obsessive habits of mental analysis are to blame ...
>
> The weakening of the will [L'usure de la volonté] completes this destruction, and here a number of diseases yet to be classified pullulate in the most fearsome way. The multiplicity of points of view, which can be the mark of a rich intelligence, ends up ruining the will, since it produces dilettantism, and the enervated impotence of men who spread themselves too thin.[22]

Bourget bases his diagnostic on Flaubert's characters (first among them the protagonists of his three contemporary novels: Frédéric Moreau, Emma Bovary, Bouvard and Pécuchet – all avid readers), but states that the physiological signs of illness he describes can be seen everywhere on the streets of Paris, significantly conflating literary representations and field observations. The symptoms he lists (frailty, oversensitivity, weakened blood, "nervosism") echo recurring contemporary descriptions of weakened male bodies, exemplified in fiction by the devirilized, "end of race" members of Zola's Rougon-Macquart clan (the slender and effeminate Maxime of *La Curée*; frail and "bloodless" Charles in *Le Docteur Pascal*)[23] and linked, in medical discourse, to a newly defined condition: neurasthenia.

Usure physiologique: Readerly Bodies

Durkheim, as we have seen, identified "hypercivilization" as the source of the anomic and egotistical tendencies he observed in his contemporaries; in his treatise *Le Suicide*, he notes that "one of the effects of hypercivilization ... is the over-refinement of nervous systems, which become exceedingly delicate."[24] This phenomenon, attributed to the ever-increasing mental demands of bourgeois modern life and the disappearance of physical labour, was given the name "neurasthenia" by American neurologist George Miller Beard in an influential medical article from 1869. The concept was rapidly integrated in French psychiatric discourse, and by the 1880s it was notably present in pedagogical debates over the perceived prevalence of intellectual exhaustion ["surmenage intellectuel"] among students in the republican school system.[25] Two French treatises on, and titled, *La Neurasthénie* appeared in 1891,[26] followed in 1897 – the same year as Durkheim's *Le Suicide* – by *L'Hygiène du neurasthénique*, by Drs Adrien Proust (Marcel's father) and Gilbert Ballet. Part of a collection of medical textbooks, this publication confirmed neurasthenia's place among diseases of the age described in other volumes of the series, including tuberculosis, asthma, and syphilis.

Proust and Ballet define neurasthenia as a nervous illness ["névrose"] resulting from the exhaustion of the superior nervous system, and although they argue (refuting Beard) that it has most likely always existed and is thus not intrinsically a modern affliction, they acknowledge that it has become more common in the 1890s than earlier in the century. Among its potential causes, they list heredity, "defective education," class mobility, cerebral exhaustion, and excessive intellectual work or schoolwork.[27] Robert Nye notes that, while they and Durkheim are largely in agreement "on the social origins of this illness ... to a greater extent than Durkheim, Proust and Ballet and many of the other commentators on the syndrome emphasized the great range of physical infirmities to which these 'weakened' neurasthenics were susceptible."[28] The physical and mental symptoms they describe include excessive thinness; pallor; muscular weakness; depression; lack of willpower; and excessive suggestibility.[29] Neurasthenia, according to Proust and Ballet, is much more common among men than women, especially in adolescents; teenage neurasthenics, they write, "are almost always of the masculine sex."[30] Christopher E. Forth points out that, while concern over the health of men with intellectual occupations had been the subject of medical literature since at least the eighteenth century,[31] by the end of the nineteenth century, with the rise of a class of petit-bourgeois bureaucrats (a phenomenon propelled by the new republican system of "educational meritocracy"), such discourse found new social resonance. Forth goes on to argue that

> distrust of the effects of excessive mental labor ... was one of the most crucial catalysts of the period's gender anxieties ... Like the stereotypical bureaucrat and Jew, the man whose work was *intellectuel* (as opposed to *manuel*) was not really a "man" in the full sense of the word, at least not when compared to traditional images of the man of action ... The men who seemed to thrive during the 1890s – functionaries, *intellectuels*, and dandies – were all combined in a single category of decadent and weak men.[32]

The neurasthenic thus embodied the "gender anxieties" of the fin de siècle as an increasingly visible (indeed "ever-present") medicalized possibility of deviation from standards of masculine somatic and mental health. In many ways tied to the discourse of degeneration,[33] he constituted a symptomatic figure, an incarnation of national concerns over social transformations resulting from the increased intellectualization of rising generations. As such, neurasthenia, whether explicitly named or implicitly described, became a privileged trope in literary representations of the young male reader.

Nineteen-year-old Paul, the bookish and eventually suicidal protagonist of Marc Elder's *Une crise* (1906), is a "young man whose nervous and unhealthy sensitivity" is defined by a "neurasthenic temperament, always wavering."[34] Valentin, the aimless and despondent anti-hero of Édouard Rod's *L'Indocile* (1905), is simultaneously presented as an avid reader and as a physically degenerate specimen of manhood:

> he went down almost directly to the river banks [quais], where the booksellers knew him well. He was a young man of short stature, with frail limbs, a rounded forehead under his flimsy, flat brown hair, and a thin, pinched mouth only faintly framed by the lightest hint of a reddish mustache. Given his myopia, which had spared him from military service, he had to wear a pince-nez that magnified his grey eyes. His hands were pale, scrawny, always hot, and extremely clumsy. His sallow, highly mobile facial traits ... seemed to reflect an inner storm where complicated thoughts roiled ... sparked by an overactive imagination.[35]

Unfit for military service, hypercerebral, and vulnerable to excessive suggestibility, Valentin is the very picture of the turn-of-the-century degenerate: a cross between the neurasthenic and the mattoid, fittingly at home among the wares of Parisian booksellers. In André Mellerio's *La Vie stérile* (1892) – a novel that bears the dedication "TO YOUNG MEN" – excessive reading is presented as having had a direct, debilitating effect on the physical development of Philippe, one of the two main characters:

> He had in no way made a gradual acquaintance with reality, in proportion with the normal growth of a mind. All at once, he had touched the highest spheres through books, losing himself, absorbing himself in them, without living life. His ideas had developed with the strange glow, the hurried and sickly exuberant growth of plants raised in the artificial atmosphere of hothouses. His body reflected this ... his overly developed forehead, his scrawny waist, his long frail limbs ... all displayed a contradiction, a defect of being, a lack of balance and healthy proportion, as there was in his mind.[36]

The comparison to strange, "sickly exuberant" hothouse plants is a commonplace of literary depictions of decadence: in Zola's *La Curée*, a luxuriant hothouse is the symbolic breeding ground of a doubly perverse (because incestuous and gender inverted) affair between Renée Saccard and her stepson Maxime.[37] Here, the trope is used to make explicit a parallel between precocious intellectual development under abnormal stimulation (the implied "hothouse" of readerly excess) and its imprint on the body, the physiognomic symptoms of adolescent neurasthenia.

In Mellerio's novel, the botanical metaphor is taken up again after Philippe's internment and death at the insane asylum of Charenton, when the other main character, André (who shares the author's first name), reflects upon learning of the death of his friend: "a precocious bloom doomed to rot on a feeble branch – putrefaction, disintegration before maturity. That had killed Philippe!"[38] At that point André has not seen Philippe for over a year; while Philippe lived the aimless existence of a dilettante, punctuated by "solitary wanderings and long bouts of daydreaming," as well as hapless attempts at writing, André has gotten married and will soon have a child.[39] The contrast between "sterile" Philippe and fruitful André (whose very name derives from the Greek *andros*, "manly") is a recurring device in the fin-de-siècle novel of formation, which often depicts neurasthenic young men against a more masculine foil. This point of comparison is sometimes the father, as in Albert Sueur's *Crise de Jeunesse* (1897), where the bookish dilettante Fabien is depicted as fundamentally dissimilar from his stern and quietly disapproving begetter, a "glorious cripple" of the Franco-Prussian War:

> With a single glance, one could see in him a life of honour, discipline, and personal disinterest; his infirmity made him seem to tower even higher, evoking the last glorious charge, out there on the battlefield, from which so few had returned. When he talked about Fabien, he sometimes said: "He takes after his mother."[40]

Identified with his mother, Fabien represents a rupture in the male lineage of military valour. The generational contrast between fathers who fought (and sometimes died) in the war of 1870 and their devirilized offspring is exploited in a number of novels, perhaps nowhere as melodramatically as in Ferri-Pisani's *Les Pervertis: roman d'un potache* (1905), which stages a confrontation between the protagonist Alberti and his father:

> – I've always thought that a military career was an absurdity! ... I want to be a writer ...
>
> – And you think I'll allow you to stay under my roof, doing nothing? ... Who ever heard of such a thing? Who could have put such ideas in your head? ...
>
> His son! That was his son! And in the furor of his thoughts, he remembered the religion he had instilled in him, the homeland he had taught him to cherish as a child ... His son! That was his son, this anarchist!
>
> A single tear welled in his eye, rolled down his white beard, and fell on his poor mutilated leg.[41]

While the trope of the father's mutilated body emphasizes the older generation's courage and patriotic sacrifice in contrast to the rising generation's aimlessness, it also complicates the dichotomy. Rather than a mirror opposition between generations – virile elders, weak offspring – it suggests a genealogy of decadence: the son's deviation from an implied ancestral masculinity appears as an extension of the father's mutilation, the amplification and incarnation of a loss of potency. The maiming of the father's leg embodies a fantasmatic national castration, perpetuated and aggravated in the son. The generational problem is then not only a matter of deficient parenting, as the father's ideals are rejected by the son, but also one of all too effective filiation, as the parent's debilitating wound is reinscribed in the adolescent's weakened temperament and body.[42] Fabien and Alberti, in this way, are truly "children of the conquest."

Social and occupational change between generations can be depicted as a "natural" progression, as in Paul Flat's *L'Illusion sentimentale* (1905):

> It was quite normally, over the course of two generations, without any rush or commotion, that he had become a *cérébral*, one of those strange beings for whom intellectual play offers greater pleasure than any other form of activity. The grandfather had been a peasant; the father ran a business: no sudden burst of change along those steps that, as naturally as can be, had led to the birth of an intellectual. (Flat's emphasis)[43]

Yet even here, the description carries a hint of worry, as the multiplication of adverbs insisting on normalcy suggests the ironic denial of a threat of abnormality. Indeed, this intellectual grandson of a peasant, the young Charles Hérial, who nevertheless displays "an unspoiled vigour and the most robust build, still untouched by any flaw," will soon form an intense, possibly amorous friendship with his classmate Lucien d'Entraygues, himself portrayed as "svelte, highly elegant, with small features, a frail build and very little heft ... in him, all is cerebral [tout est cérébralité]."[44] This peculiar bond, forged over a shared love of Baudelaire and Musset, will by the end of the novel lead Charles to demand legal separation from his new wife, incurring social opprobrium; in the last scene, he and Lucien travel to Italy arm in arm.[45] The implicitly patriarchal and traditional values of his father and grandfather, whom the novel never mentions after his initial description, are destabilized and eventually upturned as Charles sheds the role of husband and paterfamilias; the promise of reproductive vigour implied in his physical description ends up thwarted by his shared "cerebrality" with a frail and unmanly companion who also shares his passion for reading.

Alcanter de Brahm's *L'Arriviste* (1893) similarly presents generational relations in terms of a gradual progression from rustic grandparents to an overeducated son. Here again the description is traversed with concern over the son's potential "fruitfulness":

> the young dreamer's aspirations were made possible by the father's character: a model of rectitude, devotion, and care, working assiduously in that legal office where, over the last twenty years, his seniority had earned him respect ...

> this father, the son of good peasants among whom he had received only a rudimentary education ... now and then asked himself worriedly whether the fine education he was providing for his own son, costing him enormous sacrifices, would some day bear any fruit.
>
> He was willing to make these sacrifices because he felt that Claudius's heart bore the same qualities and flaws as his own: the same aspiration to learning and to the healthy reading of books that provide intellectual education better than the best teachers. If, he told himself, I give my son in his twentieth year the same baggage it took me half a century to assemble, surely he will, soon enough, make a life for himself.[46]

The father's fears are confirmed when his son Claudius (described as a "vaporous personality") founds a student magazine devoted to literature and Parisian gossip; shortly after, upon the father's death, Claudius abandons mathematics for the study of letters, and professes his desire to become a writer.[47] As in *L'Illusion sentimentale*, the father appears as an intermediary stage between traditional rural values and occupations, represented by the grandparents, and modern fickleness and dislocation, embodied in the son. While the father has adopted a modern profession (significantly, a low-level bureaucratic post in the ministry of justice), he has devoted his existence to regular, diligent work, and has accepted his station in life; he has, in other words, preserved ancestral values even as he adapted to a world different from that of his parents. The father's "aspiration" to "intellectual education" through schooling and books is benign, but something goes awry when they are passed on to the son; without the anchoring of traditional values, Claudius ends up valuing books in a different way – as an object of enjoyment and desire rather than as a means to a modest end – and rejects the professional path traced for him. Between generations, the "healthy reading" advocated by the father has given way to something different – the likely fruitless pursuit of reading and writing for their own sake.

In Henry Bérenger's *L'Effort* (likewise published in 1893), the protagonist is also presented in contrast to his father: while Georges Lauzerte's illustrious begetter is a fully accomplished "great doctor, member of the Academy, officer of the *Légion d'honneur* and millionaire," he himself is described as a "nervous being," characterized by a "frail elegance" and an "eternal dilettantism."[48] Georges is a voracious reader; his hunger for books, his world-weariness, and his debilitating propensity for overanalysis are described as traits passed down by his mother:

> Madame Lauzerte was above all an intellectual ... Lamartine and George Sand had given her young self aspirations that were soon shattered ... At twenty, she had already read every book and judged most men ... She had no gift for love: ideas were her only interest. In that world, she was extraordinary; she

> was immensely well read. She delighted in the latest works of Taine, Flaubert, Stuart Mill, Spencer. More than anything, she enjoyed the strange and precise labors of Max Muller and Huxley, or else the cruel analyses of Baudelaire and the wry irony of Renan.[49]

The heritage of this intellectual woman, uninterested in love but enamoured with the world of ideas, shapes Georges (perhaps named after Sand) to the point that his physical resemblance to his father is diminished: "father and son resembled each other ... but the strong build of the father had dwindled in the son. Every trait of the face had become slighter, more spiritual."[50] Physically, as in terms of temperamental vigour, Georges is a shadow of his father. Faced with this wan double of himself, Doctor Lauzerte comes to question the success of his parental guidance, and even rhetorically doubt his paternity: "could that really be his son, this tall and over-refined youth ... Had his efforts to shape him and launch him into the world only turned the lad into a kind of intellectual Hamlet?"[51] Feminized through his intellectual identification with his mother, devirilized through his physical description, bookish, mentally gifted but weak willed, Georges is, as Bérenger puts it in his preface, "the very type of the intellectual ... in our generation."[52] In addition to his father, the novel paints him in clear contrast to a second, more fully developed foil: Jean Darnay, his sister's eventual love interest.

L'Effort explicitly sets up Georges and Jean as opposite figures: "The contrast between the two young men was striking: Georges was frailer ... his face thinner ... Jean was more vigorous and manlier, with his great height."[53] While contrasting pictures of fathers and sons highlight the advance of decadence across generations, suggesting a bleak prognosis for the nation, depictions of physiologically and temperamentally opposed types within the same generation serve a different ideological purpose. Jean, for instance, is presented as having overcome the afflictions that have shaped Georges: "struck, like his friend, by the same intellectual diseases between the age of seventeen and twenty, [he] had bravely overcome them, and achieved by now a rather admirable type of moral harmony."[54] After Georges commits suicide, it is suggested that Jean will go on to marry his sister Marthe, thus taking Georges's place as his father's heir, the new link in filiation that his friend failed to become. By presenting a contrasting fate to that of the degenerate or neurasthenic "intellectual type," novels like *L'Effort* aim to propose an alternative narrative that leads to a fantasmatic possibility of regeneration.[55] Bérenger states his intention clearly in his preface:

> I would not have dared to describe the invasion of intellectualism in a soul destined to suicide, if I had not also conceived of a way to escape from this

> disease, if I had not been able to oppose Jean Darnay to Georges Lauzerte ... To the passive male [Au passif], as immense as he is, I needed to oppose an active male [un actif].[56]

The juxtaposition of an "active" and a "passive"[57] character from the same generation rearranges the chronologically twofold structure that illustrated a progressive shift, within a single protagonist, from nihilism to action in novels like *Un Homme libre* and *Les Premières Luttes*,[58] into parallel narratives that trace two inverse trajectories, one coded positively (often ending in marriage and successful social integration) and the other negatively (often ending in death through illness or suicide). This type of contrasting characterization[59] relies on overdetermination, or what Susan Rubin Suleiman has analysed as "redundancy"[60] between the culturally coded qualities of a character and his or her role in a narrative. The "passive" character, a composite of implicitly or explicitly negative traits (overly intellectual, dilettantish, frail, temperamentally weak, neurasthenic, degenerate, sexually ambiguous), is destined to perish, while the "active" character (physically robust, temperamentally strong, morally upstanding, resolutely heterosexual) comes to live up to his productive and reproductive potential. The narratives of *L'Effort* and *La Vie stérile* are less about apprenticeship or development than about inevitability: in both novels, the overlying plot arc is the gradual dissolution of the two protagonists' initially close friendship, as each follows his (over)determined trajectory.

If single-protagonist narratives of development from nihilism to action rely on the reader's initial identification with a dilettante main character, in order to lead him to a straighter path, it is worth asking how double narratives of juxtaposed passivity and activity lay claim to the reader's attention. Indeed, while the didactic purpose of these double narratives is evident (they implicitly – or in the case of Bérenger's preface, explicitly – propose that the reader model himself after the positive rather than the negative example), it is less clear how the reader, precisely *as* a reader, is meant to situate himself in a binary structure that systematically places reading on the side of negatively coded activities and qualities. The place of the author is similarly problematic, since the desire to write is inevitably attributed to the negatively described, "passive" protagonists, as part of their characterization as overly intellectual and incapable of a productive effort (Mellerio's Philippe, for instance, spends his days writing "vague notes without order or style, haphazardly scribbled from fleeting impressions, almost instantly forgotten").[61] *L'Effort* and *La Vie stérile* address this paradox by presenting the "active" characters as having overcome the literarily inflected passivity that has taken hold of their friend.

Jean, addressing his parents and later Georges's sister, describes such a transformation:

> Think back to five years ago. Wasn't I ensnared in the worst illusions [chimères]? ... I couldn't find my place. Paris and books had gone to my head. I had read too much Balzac and Baudelaire. I wanted right away to become a great man or a very rich man ... I was simply out of kilter [détraqué] ...
>
> I found two infallible remedies: I sprung to action and I loved. When, after romanticism and pessimism, I felt dilettantism starting to take over, I threw myself wholly into action.[62]

Yet this triumph over passivity is introduced retrospectively, outside the time frame of the narrative; from the time they appear, Jean and André are already destined to survive and thrive, as suggested by their insistent characterization as physically vigorous. The "passives," although they lead their existence concurrently with their foil until their death, are eventually described as embodying an earlier stage in the development of the "actives," as made explicit by André's reflection after Philippe's burial: "This friend buried with such sorrow that very morning, didn't he represent a line in André's own existence? His whole carefree youth, inexperienced, unthinking, had ended there."[63] André symbolically buries his own youth in the person of Philippe, and the reader is implicitly invited to follow his example. But the question of identification lingers unresolved: if the reader initially identifies with the "passive" character (including by virtue of being a reader), it remains unclear just how he should make the jump to modelling himself on the "active" one, aside from possibly putting down the book he is reading.

These novels' descriptive fascination with "passives" raises the related question of readerly and authorial interest: since the positive example of activity is so clearly favoured, and retrospectively integrates (as having vanquished) the characteristics of passivity, why lavish such sustained narrative attention on protagonists like Georges and Philippe? One answer is that they provide pathos: a novel solely devoted to the likes of Jean or André, whose story consists of accepting their class station and choosing a socially suitable bride, would be much less compelling than the tragic tale of a doomed intellectual degenerate. Another, not unrelated answer could have to do with what readers (and writers) like to read (and write) about: the "passive" characters present them with a negative narcissistic image of themselves as readers, distorted and exaggerated through contemporary tropes of degeneration, while "active" characters are the projection of a fantasmatic positive image of a virile, productive man who has left behind the world of books. Lastly, the symmetrical contrast between passives and actives, often figured in implicitly gendered terms, is rife with dramatic potential for a complex depiction of opposition and complementarity (a situation taken to one possible extreme with the homoerotic couple of *L'Illusion sentimentale*); some authors represent the relationship between these pairs of characters not simply as one of friendship, but rather as a thorny mix of mutual fascination and disgust, competition and envy. In Gustave Toudouze's *Le Vertige de l'inconnu* (1892), for example, the "passive" protagonist Alain (described as "constantly buried in books and the study of literature"), becomes so fixatedly preoccupied with Fernand (presented as someone who "at first sight ... seduced all admirers of physical vigour and masculine beauty"), the antagonist who will eventually marry his sister and lay claim to the position of paterfamilias, that he loses sleep obsessing over him:

> he studied Fernand down to the bottom of his soul, reading him like the pages of an open book ... with but one look at him, he had understood his positive, wholly material nature, and guessed his hungers and needs. That young man was to be his antithesis in every way, morally as well as physically, and he immediately felt toward him, not exactly repulsion, but an instinctive suspicion, as in the presence of some hidden danger.[64]

Alain's sleepless night, throughout which he returns to the remembered image of Fernand chatting with his sister, arouses a sense of shame:

> at the same time, he scolded himself bitterly over the bizarre trouble that tore through him. Was it simply a blind and fanatical devotion to family that made him instantly look upon this newcomer as an enemy of his kin's happiness, and of his own ... Or was it some other, more redoubtable feeling, more dangerous to ponder? ... A bit of shame rose from the bottom of his being, and blood flushed to his face.[65]

The cause of this trouble is never made clear: it might be that Alain is so deeply jealous of his sister that he is hostile to any suitor, suggesting a potentially incestuous desire; it might be that he is jealous of his sister in a different way (who exactly are these "admirers of physical vigour and masculine beauty"?).[66] By the end of the novel, Alain manages to wrest ownership of the familial domain back from Fernand, but the effort of the confrontation costs him his sanity, and he joins Philippe and Georges among the ranks of doomed readers.

Usure du sentiment: Woman and Her Shadow

The binary opposition between over-readers (implicitly or explicitly neurasthenic, "passive") and non-readers or cured readers (virile, "active") among young male characters is often replicated when fin-de-siècle novels of formation represent the practice of reading itself. In such depictions, the contrast is recast as a series of interrelated dichotomies – between the reader's inner experience and the outside world, the imaginary and the real, the artificial and the natural. These multiplied oppositions do not always overlap seamlessly: in the same breath, reading can be described as both an experience of interiority, of shutting out the outside world, and as an invasion of outside influences. We have seen how Bourget, in the 1883 preface to his *Essais de psychologie contemporaine*, imagines the archetypal reader as *un adolescent*;[67] that preface goes on to describe, in attentive detail, both the outside setting this young man neglects in favour of his book, and the inner process that takes hold of him as he immerses himself in the printed word. The result is an emblematic reading scene:

> At this precise moment, as I write these lines, an adolescent – I can *see* him – is sitting at his study desk on this beautiful evening of a June day. Flowers blossom amorously below the window. The tender gold of the sun, now set, spreads along the horizon with a lovely subtlety. Young women chat in the nearby garden. The adolescent is hunched over his book, perhaps one of the very ones mentioned in these *Essais*. It's *Les Fleurs du Mal* by Baudelaire, it's *La Vie de Jésus* by Renan, *Salammbô* by Flaubert, *Thomas Graindorge* by Taine, *Le Rouge et le Noir* by Beyle ... "Oh, but he should live instead!" the wise will say ... Alas! How he does live at this very moment, and a life more intense than if he picked the scented flowers, than if he gazed at the melancholy West, than if he held the delicate fingers of one of the girls. His entire being glides into his favourite writer's sentences. He converses with him, heart to heart, man to man. He listens to his pronouncements on how to enjoy love and practise debauchery [...] every word is a revelation. These words introduce him to a world of sensations [sentiments] only barely glimpsed before now. From this initial revelation to the imitation of those sensations, the distance is short, and the adolescent has soon crossed it. A great observer once said that many men would never have been in love if they had never heard of love. To be sure, they would have loved in a different way [d'une autre façon].[68]

The "adolescent," further categorized as a "student," is pictured as occupying an undefined interior space, set against an exterior garden scene where flowers and young girls are metonymically juxtaposed (the flowers are blooming "amorously"). The window, a topos of the scene of reading,[69] serves as a point of contact and division between these two spaces, but also as a point of contrast, for the reader is not looking through it but at (and, in a sense, through) another, metaphorical window, that of the book. If, in the highly similar scene we examined in *Crise de jeunesse*, the spring morning symbolized the reader's youth,[70] here the June evening evokes a more complexly characterized time of life: June, the moment of transition from spring to summer, seems to imply both the impending passage from adolescence to adulthood and the possible lateness or delay of that passage (shouldn't the reader, the passage asks, be outside courting the girls?). The moment of sunset, specified almost oxymoronically as the "evening of a ... day," likewise suggests both transition and delay: June evenings, building up to the summer solstice, are the latest evenings of the year. Poetic commonplaces around sunset, which Bourget does not shy from ("the tender gold of the sun"), include rest and contemplation but also languor, even decline; indeed, according to the *Essais*, the books this reader is most likely immersed in are the products and reflections of a decadent nation, a civilization at sunset. The scene is thus organized around a series of thresholds: the contrasting thresholds of the window, opening an indoor space to the outside world, and of the book, linking an individual consciousness to outside influences; the threshold of adulthood, potentially delayed; and the threshold of individual and national decline, possibly already crossed – the sun, after all, has "now set." The golden light of the scene is but the remaining glint of a shining moment that has already faded, just as the listed books are the products of a bygone literary generation, still lighting the way but belonging to the past. This sense of the passing of time is complicated by the description of a multiple simultaneity: Bourget states that the scene he describes is taking place "at this precise moment, as I write these lines," a claim empathically emphasized by the italicized "I can *see* him" and the sustained use of the present tense. The passage in fact sets up a quadruple simultaneity through four imbricated levels of specularity: 1) Bourget "sees" and writes about 2) a scene in which an adolescent is reading 3) an unspecified scene taking place in a book; all of which 4) Bourget's readers can "see" in their own present, when they read the passage. The written word is thus implicitly described as that which is always potentially of the present, even when it belongs to the past; that which, scandalously, takes the place of the present and replaces it with the past, the absent, that which *is* not, or is not *here*, and yet is seen ("I can *see* him") as though it were. The adolescent *should* be living in the present ("he should live instead!" the wise exclaim, in the conditional), he *should* be crossing the threshold into adulthood – entering the symbolic garden, holding hands with the girls – but he is instead held back by his reading, his intermediary state prolonged (June, between seasons; sunset, between day and night), his transition into manhood delayed. This, for Bourget, is the crux of the "crisis" he diagnoses in the contemporary youth of the 1880s: the literary productions of previous generations "continue to weigh on youth"; they propagate, in the present and ever more widely, "what was called, around 1830, the malady of the century [le mal du siècle]."[71]

The 1883 preface describes reading as a conversation "man to man": like the characterization of the reader as an "adolescent" and "*étudiant*" (a student of the secondary level or higher), this leaves much of the French reading public of the 1880s outside the scope of Bourget's consideration. Beyond this limitation, the phrase is revealing in that it depicts reading and writing as a male-to-male network[72] of apprenticeship and initiation from which women, although they may be a favoured topic of discussion, are nevertheless excluded as participants: "young women," in Bourget's vision, are relegated to the periphery of the scene. The discussion of desire and sexuality between writer and reader revolves around a series of abstract terms: "love," "debauchery," "sensations." More concrete terms, including "women," are avoided. The extent of this exclusion of women may be appreciated in the passage's paraphrase of a maxim by La Rochefoucauld, obliquely referred to as a "great observer" (a matter of rhetorical discretion rather than vague attribution – it is assumed that the citation will be recognized by the reader): the maxim is cited almost without modification, except that Bourget substitutes "many men" [beaucoup d'hommes] for La Rochefoucauld's gender-neutral "some people" [il y a des gens].[73] The passage further suggests an intimate proximity that goes beyond mere dialogue, as the (explicitly male) reader's "entire being glides into" the sentences of the (presumed male) writer. The image operates a confusion of sender and receiver: where we might expect the sentences to pass into the reader, it is the reader who glides wholly into them, indicating a depth of communion that goes well beyond the presented alternative, holding hands with one of the young women. For the adolescent reader to prefer *Les Fleurs du Mal* to "the scented flowers" that bloom by his window, both literal and figurative, is indeed to love "in a different way."

In observing his exclusion of women from the imagined conversation of literature, I do not mean to suggest that Bourget, however implicitly, posits a causal link between reading and male homosexuality. Rather, I want to propose that the anxiety (tinged with fascination) he expresses over reading as a privileged means of apprenticeship and initiation – "introduction," "revelation," "imitation" are the terms he uses – into matters of love (and implicitly, sexuality) is closely bound up with contemporary discourses denouncing the perceived threat of same-sex activity among adolescents, particularly in secondary school dormitories.[74] In those discourses, reading and homosexuality are often presented in parallel as causing deviation from what is implied to be the natural evolution of the young man's sentimental attachment and sexual desire, a diversion from what should be its eventual target and destination: the young woman. Both are described – and decried – as particular dangers to the adolescent because they threaten to permanently stall his development or irrevocably steer it away from its heterosexual, reproductive goal. For instance, many of the "passive," readerly protagonists of contemporary novels of formation have mistresses who, unlike the love interests of their "active" foils, do not offer a path to marriage and procreation. In *L'Effort*, Georges frequents Léa, an "educated and domineering" New Woman who has read Barrès;[75] in *La Vie stérile*, Philippe falls under the spell of a married woman with the resonant name of Madame Bartès, who is likewise well read and not inclined towards reproductive sexuality: "she had read the most extreme illicit books, and would question Philippe ... about putrid vices and unspeakable passions."[76] These domineering, gender-transgressive women, as thoroughly versed in contemporary literature as their neurasthenic male counterparts, embody an object of attachment that, while heterosexual, deviates perilously from the path of familial reproductivity. They also present an inverted, perversely complementary image of weakened male readers: whereas reading has made Georges and Philippe into failed men, it has conversely virilized their female equivalents to what the narrative presents as an equally threatening degree.[77]

Bourget's emblematic reading scene implies that the natural course of evolution for the adolescent would be to step outside to the garden, to pick the flowers, to touch the girls, while instead he remains inside, pulled ever deeper into "a world of sensations" that were once unknown to him. Depictions of the natural, contrasted with the artificially sentimental productions of art and literature, are another recurring trope in the fin-de-siècle novel of formation. In a scene from Frantz Jourdain's *L'Atelier Chantorel: mœurs d'artistes* (The Chantorel atelier: Artists' mores, 1893), we follow Gaston, a student at the École des Beaux-Arts, as he wanders through that most typical strolling ground of late-nineteenth century Parisian students, the Jardin du Luxembourg. Gaston was raised by a spinster aunt who, "spurred by her own passion for literature, had put in the hands of her young nephew a great many books, the kind that were usually off-limits to readers before they had a mustache"; as an adolescent, like the reader of Bourget's preface, he read *Les Fleurs du Mal*.[78] Walking through the gardens, he reflects:

> All those poets had more than spoiled nature for him, and its inner meaning eluded him. Behind every branch, every blade of grass, every flower, every

> stream, every pebble, a hemistich lay in wait, an epithet slid into view. With ... its phony exclamation marks, its vibrations in imitation bronze ... its mummified idyllic embraces, academic lyricism had deflowered his first outpourings. He felt nauseous at the thought of raising to his lips the same cup where the insufferable pedantry of the entire world had gargled itself for centuries. Gaston remembered the torrents of ink poured to glorify birdsong, the reams of paper covered with lithographs and etchings representing the celestial joys bestowed by the tweeting of the nightingale. In all honesty, was the chirping of even the most melodious bird worth a sonata by Beethoven or a melody by Schumann?[79]

The scene hinges on the lexical ambiguity of the past participial "deflowered" [défloré], which designates both the spoiling of an experience through prior description and the defloration of a virgin. Nature is described as "spoiled" – *gâtée*, Jourdain writes, bringing to mind Bourget's *usure* – by the ardour of countless poets, and later compared to a vessel that priggish writers have figuratively used for gargling over centuries. What should have been a scene of the young man's ardent communion with nature is instead a tableau of impossibility and revulsion: behind or around every feature of the natural world, a ready-made literary description lurks, obstructing the possibility of direct contact or impression. Virgin, unmediated perception is foreclosed: every element of the scenery has been experienced in literature before it has been discovered in life. The result is a feeling of disgust with both nature (implicitly figured as a "spoiled" woman) and its representation (the residue of her "deflorations" by older artists, understood to be other men). Gaston had wandered into the park by following an attractive woman enjoying a promenade, but his musings there have thrown him off course, and he does not pursue her further. He concludes by expressing a preference for melodies by Schumann over birdsong – modern human productions over animal phenomena, the artificial over the natural.[80]

The disgust with nature voiced by Jourdain's protagonist finds a mirror image in an inclination for the "unnatural." Few fin-de-siècle novels of male formation depict protagonists who explicitly manifest same-sex inclinations, but in many the menace of homosexuality lurks in the background, particularly in school settings. Stéphane, the protagonist of Amédée Rouquès's *Le Jeune Rouvre* (1909) – described as "enfeebled, enervated, in moral despair" – suffers insomnia in his dormitory, and attempts to write verse:

> He tried to write lyrics that had rhythm: they lacked any sense, but their rhythm delighted him. His memory was overcrowded with thousands of

> lines of French and Latin verse, but he was ignorant of the most elementary rules of prosody, so he scribbled awkward poems.

Meanwhile, he hears suspicious noises:

> At times, there were other noises, much closer, and then there could be no mistake. Beads of sweat trickled on his torso. Hushed murmurs, bare feet scurrying away, muffled kisses.[81]

Here, the student's surcharge of cultural baggage is depicted against a background of "unnatural" acts, literalizing the threat obliquely suggested in Bourget and Jourdain. The same juxtaposition occurs in *Les Pervertis*, where a same-sex pair openly flaunts their scandalous affair in boarding school while the Corsican protagonist, Alberti, struggles with his desire to write. His own vice, during his days as a student, is not homosexuality but masturbation:

> Alberti closed the novel and drifted into a dream of love ...
>
> Little by little, his nerves became dulled, and no longer transmitted exterior impressions to his brain: the student no longer heard his neighbours' whispers, or the sound of school desks being opened ... The harsh gaslight, veiled by his lowered eyelids, filled his sight with a soft and warm pinkness ... [...] His mind, entirely free, searched through images he vaguely remembered: silhouettes glimpsed, one after the other, passed in his memory ... [...]
>
> An unreal being of impalpable shape, that Alberti nevertheless thought he could seize, if he wanted to ... Around Her [Elle], the scene shimmered in a dizzying whirl [...]
>
> Suddenly he was alone with Her in a bedroom ... How had he gotten there?
>
> One thing was real: he saw Her in front of him, he fell to his knees, he held her waist, but did not feel the resistance of the corset or the flesh under his fingers; [...]
>
> Alberti had a mad desire to touch that ankle, and then to caress softly, with his hand, a little higher, but he touched only the void ... [...]
>
> Slowly, his sensitive nerves were awakened by an outside noise ... From very far away, as if out of an abyss, a voice, the woman's voice perhaps, yelled:
>
> – Someone's ripped off my Lorrain novel! Have you seen it?[82]

The sensual after-effects of sentimental or titillating reading are a trope of love narratives: upon closing the book, the confusion of fiction and reality lingers, leading to daydreams or illicit acts. In Canto V of Dante's *Inferno*, Francesca and Paolo famously recount how, having read together the tale of Lancelot and Guinevere's adulterous love, they gave in to an analogical passion: "That day we read no farther."[83] No Francesca is present in the dormitory, so Alberti conjures one out of thin air: shapeless, nameless, *Elle* is but an amalgam of metonymic and synechdochal female parts – the corset, the waist, the ankle, the leg. Her ghostly, visual presence arouses a desire to touch, the satisfaction of which is always denied by the fact of her absence. Her apparition relies on shutting out the stimuli of the present, outside world: the noises of the school, the harsh gaslight. When these come crashing back into the scene, the sensual spell is broken, to comic effect. That the pilfered novel is by the decadent Jean Lorrain (1855–1906), who was somewhat notoriously queer, only adds to the collapse of heterosexual fantasy in the scene.

The passage elliptically suggests that Alberti engages in masturbation; other fin-de-siècle novels are more explicit.[84] In *Une crise*, a similar scene links reminiscences of poetry to the practice it names "solitary pleasures," with quotation marks:

> All these reminiscences rushed up to his overheated brain: poems of debauchery and poems of love rang in his ears, and beautiful, naked flesh laid in front of him. – Oh, to remember the most ardent ecstasy! oh! to embrace another body! to hold it in a wild spasm! – He dug his fingers in the sheets. – [...] oh! come! I beg you, I love you! ... – He was speaking out loud in the silence. Then he felt soothed and indulged in "solitary pleasures."[85]

These scenes all depict how protagonists piece together disparate and fragmentary elements – scenes or images remembered from books, glimpses of silhouettes furtively caught – into a vague but titillating imaginary scene of erotic passion. Condillac, in his *Essai sur l'origine des connaissances humaines* (1749), defined the imagination precisely as the capacity to both conjure up and recombine various situations in their absence: "our ability to wake our perceptions in the absence of objects gives us the ability to combine and bring together the most disparate ideas."[86] As a particular peril associated with this capacity, he singled out the reading of novels by adolescent girls. Historians including Jan Goldstein have considered Condillac's essay alongside Samuel-Auguste Tissot's oft-cited treatise *L'Onanisme* (1760), observing that both voice concern over parallel "eighteenth-century figures whose solitary practices were also widely decried and attributed to overactive imagination – namely, the masturbator and the (usually female) reader of novels." Goldstein, citing the analyses of Thomas Laqueur and Vernon A. Rosario, notes that

> the brunt of [Tissot's] attack was not so much that masturbation depleted vital spermatic fluid or that it sexualized the young precociously but rather that ...

> it was a transaction occurring entirely in the realm of the imagination ... its fundamental danger as a practice – its true scandal – lay in the fact that, by dint of its largely imaginary nature, it eluded all natural, interpersonal, and social limitation. In its ceding of ultimate authority to the imagination, masturbation effectively established an order of disorder.[87]

In the late nineteenth-century novel of formation, masturbation (often spurred by reading or the memory of reading) is depicted as a temporary outlet that allows male adolescents to redirect their erotic desire away from its socially sanctioned (but absent) object, and towards imaginary, immaterial combinations of vague literary tropes. Its "true scandal," as explicitly represented in a number of novels, is that this temporary redirection constantly threatens to become a permanent deviation. "What arduous or dangerous conquest of a flesh-and-bone woman," asks the first-person protagonist of Paul Margueritte's *Les Jours s'allongent* (The days grow longer, 1905), "could be worth, to my eyes, the woman I could possess freely and without effort, like a magician conjuring up the most seductive and beautiful ghosts?"[88] The solitary, imaginary practices of the adolescent – reading, masturbation – pose the risk of taking the place of the "real" and proper object whose absence they are meant to supplement.[89] Novels of formation allude to this anxiety by representing the masturbator's return to reality, and particularly the reality of heterosexual sex, as a rude comedown, marked by disappointment and disgust. In *Les Pervertis*, Alberti, shortly after his masturbation scene, meets a prostitute in the street and expectantly takes her up on her offer; yet after this encounter, he is disconcerted and dissatisfied: "Once the student found himself back on the street, he felt overcome by an immense disgust. So this was all there was to the love that haunted his boyhood dreams!"[90] By the novel's conclusion, this protagonist, who has lusted after imaginary and unattainable women since his schooldays, will end up joining the ranks of the "perverted." In a final scene of erotic hallucination, the ideal female forms he has long yearned for, only to be met with disillusion in reality, dramatically meld into young male torsos, and the faces of the effeminate, sexually transgressive boys who used to haunt the boarding school come back to claim him:

> The reverberation of the sun on the asphalt forced the Corsican to shut his eyes: soon, he had unknown visions ... At first, there were only vague nude shapes, and then little by little, the lines sharpened to give shape to women whose breasts then blurred into youths' torsos ... He who had loved Marguerite and dreamed of Camille had thought himself strong; but the law was inexorable and the seed of unnatural sexual instincts [instincts insexuels],

> caught at boarding school, would soon germinate under the breath of female disappointments and grow imperiously in his soul.[91]

In *Les Jours s'allongent*, the protagonist's imaginary longings are similarly depicted against the background menace of adolescent same-sex practices in the dormitory:

> The dainty boys [peaufins] are the ephebes, the pretty adolescents. They can easily find a protector ... males will fight over them. No surprise that a languidly graceful blond or a provocative brunet should naturally adopt a feminine gait: sidelong glances, swaying hips. They have women's nicknames: the English Girl, Baby ... One hears rumours, in hushed tones, of what goes on in the older boys' dormitory: prostitution without women, and yet with women. It's inevitable: the natural instinct, unsatisfied, deviates.[92]

The juxtaposition does not, as in *Les Pervertis*, lead to the protagonist inexorably joining the ranks of deviants, yet it similarly highlights the threat of deviation brought on by the non-satisfaction of "natural" instincts aroused to a frenzy in the suffocating space of the all-boys school, where Hugo and Musset are read with "unknown emotion ... shot through with warm languor and feverish spasms."[93] The story retrospectively follows the progress of an unnamed narrator, born in Algeria but raised near Paris; the trajectory it traces (as outlined in the chapter titles: Children's prison, The crisis, Woman and her shadow, The two chimeras, The choice of a career) is in many ways typical of the fin-de-siècle novel of formation. The protagonist suffers through his secondary education, where he nevertheless finds passionate enjoyment in the discovery of literature; schooled through novels and poetry in matters of sentiment and sexuality, he experiences a series of amorous disappointments in reality; he entertains the ambition of becoming a writer, but eventually settles for an existence as a government bureaucrat. The threat of "deviation" alluded to in the description of same-sex practices at boarding school is presented not specifically as a dangerous potential contagion, but as a resonant synecdoche for a larger pattern of dissatisfaction that eventually overtakes every aspect of the protagonist's life, a pattern ascribed entirely to his reading habits:

> The exclusively bookish conceptions that overwhelmed my casuistry (?) and my experience (!) of love, the total invasion of my soul by illusion, all led to an absolute paralysis ... my soul had false conceptions of the possible and of the taste for truth. A disgust of action, a fear of trying were my only rewards for the delicious ecstasies of waking sleep ...

> I do not believe that this strange malady was mine alone: in my case it lasted for years ... It inflected not only my heart and my senses, but it deviated the very operation of my mind, the way I conceived of more and more things. Measuring my actions to a purely sentimental criterion, judging life based on books, – and what books? Novelistic novels [les romans romanesques], the least apt to teach me about it, – I belonged to illusion. It was its toy.[94]

The recurrence of the term "deviate" highlights the structural similarity between the deviation of some students' libidinal drive towards each other and the deviation of the protagonist's own drives (to learn, to love, to produce) towards insensible, ultimately unattainable and unproductive goals. "Bookish conceptions" of love and of the world, he claims, caused him to lose sight of what is possible or true, and sapped his potential for "action." They irreversibly inflected the course of his life – in his choice of an educational path (he obtains a degree in literature), in his choices in love, and in his choice of career. As he points out, this "strange malady" was not at all exclusive to him, but indeed endemic among the novelistic embodiments of his generation.

Usure de la volonté: From Disorder to Impotence

Scenes of reading in the fin-de-siècle novel of formation depict intricate conflicts between interiority and outside influence, the real and the illusory, "innate" desires and "unnatural" deviations. Implicitly or explicitly, novels repeatedly describe the long-term effects of these struggles on readers' bodies and drives – as degeneracy, neurasthenia, and other strange ills or "diseases yet to be classified."[95] The immediate effects of reading are likewise depicted through a medical lexicon, in recurrent characterizations of the practice as a fever. In Mellerio's *Jacques Mérane* (1891), the eponymous protagonist's favoured activity as a child is represented as an agitated transport, both emotional and illusorily geographical:

> He preferred to read, that was his favorite occupation, as soon as he was finished with his homework. Then he would devour books about adventure and travel. A whole world opened up before him. His chest heaved, his temples throbbed, his mind became feverish. Faraway journeys took him over immense seas, into strange countries.[96]

The passage is notable for its use, in close proximity, of a number of tropes associated with reading: hunger and consumption, feverishness, displacement, strangeness. Jacques, like *La Vie stérile*'s Philippe, develops a readerly "lassitude with everything" as he approaches adulthood, but in order to win the affection of his cousin Marthe – whose status as a non-reader is presented as a guarantor of her earnestness ("she did not read novels, and never analysed. That was precisely why she remained deep and sincere") – he eventually renounces his literary ambitions and becomes more like Philippe's active foil André. The novel ends with Jacques's marriage to Marthe: "through her, he started a family anew, one that would grow."[97]

The depiction of reading as a fever[98] appears again in Amédée Rouquès's *Le Jeune Rouvre* (1909), in an extended passage that describes a group of adolescent friends' shared, progressive discovery of many of the salient names of nineteenth-century French literature:

> It was the time for great literary discoveries: Stéphane, for the new year, had received the complete works of Musset; Varenne, Hugo's poetic works; Margelin, while exploring the library inherited from his grandfather, had discovered a first edition of Lamartine ... It was a fever of passionate readings, without pause, without choice. Every single poem moved them in the very depths their soul and revealed to them a piece of that soul. It was their sorrow, their desire, their hope they found expressed in "Le Lac," "Olympia," "Souvenir." It was truly, after the revelation of life and love, the revelation of poetic beauty that began.
>
> Soon, it was no longer enough.
>
> Hugo, Musset, Lamartine, Chénier, Vigny, read and reread haphazardly, Baudelaire admired mostly by reputation, they went on to the prose writers. Balzac stupefied them. Zola, for them, had all the attractions of a particularly forbidden fruit. The Goncourt brothers and Daudet, finally, overwhelmed them with a strange trouble through their modernism, with their analyses of impressions and sensations that they imagined to be so close to their own.[99]

Here, "fever" denotes less a bodily disorder than a lack of logical order: reading is done "without choice," "haphazardly." Yet the narration seems to undercut these assertions of readerly disorder by listing writers in more or less chronological order (Baudelaire comes after the Romantics; Zola and the Goncourts, after Balzac), as well as drawing a clear line between poets and novelists – soon to be followed by contemporary critics ("Sainte-Beuve, Taine ... Renan, France, Lemaitre") and philosophers of various periods and nationalities ("The Stoics and the Epicureans, Descartes and Gassendi, Locke and Kant").[100] The portrayal of the group of friends' literary education is thus a meeting point of two opposite tendencies: the commonplace representation of inexperienced readers' consumption of books as haphazard and disorderly,[101] and the increasing categorization and chronologizing of literary works associated with the rise of literary history as an academic discipline. The influence of the latter on Amédée Rouquès is made clear in the dedication of his novel, "To my dear master Gustave Lanson."[102]

Lanson, the author of a seminal *Histoire de la littérature française* (twelve editions between 1894 and 1912), famously aimed to dissociate the practice of literary history from what he characterized as the subjective or "impressionistic" excesses of literary criticism as practised by Taine or Brunetière. In addition, he established textual explication as a mainstay of the teaching of literature in the French educational system.[103] While Lanson sought to situate literary works as expressions of historical, social, and biographical phenomena linked to the time of their composition (a practice much questioned by his later detractors, most famously Roland Barthes), he also, conversely, argued that the study of literary works from all periods had an important social function in the present. Textual explication by students, he stated, should always include "the search for current uses and applications of the work studied": through it, "young people will always be prepared to face the great problems that arise in every conscience and every society."[104] In this preoccupation with the role of literature in the formation of young subjects, as well as his advocacy of the study of nineteenth-century works (the French canon having hitherto been dominated by the seventeenth and eighteenth centuries),[105] Lanson displays an affinity with Bourget's *Essais* from the previous decade. However, unlike Bourget's social critique, which was grounded in subjective appreciations and made broad pronouncements about the state of contemporary French society, Lanson's literary history lays claim to a "pedagogical neutrality": in his view, students' supervised contact with literary texts leads not to imitation, but to the development of analytical faculties, including those that deal with moral and social problems.[106] In their recurring enumerations of young characters' favoured readings, novels of formation from the turn of the century show the pull of Bourget's and Lanson's differing yet related views.

In Bérenger's *L'Effort*, for example, Georges's literary self-education is described in medical terms – very much in Bourget's style – as a succession of afflictions; yet the chronology of this progression, as the protagonist "successively" suffers from the influence of various literary schools or masters in the order in which they appeared over the course of the century, bears the imprint of literary history:

> Born sensitive, but devoid of moral resistance, he had successively been a victim of all the psychological maladies that so strangely tormented Europe in the nineteenth century and that might very well, if they are to continue,

> indicate the weakening [usure] of a race. Romantic at seventeen, Baudelairian at eighteen, Pessimistic at nineteen, he had become Renanian and Barresian between the age of twenty and twenty-three.[107]

Bourget's model of imitative influence is exemplified by Rouquès's observation that Romantic poems "reveal ... a piece of their soul" to his characters, or that they find, in the novels of Daudet and the Goncourt brothers, "impressions and sensations that they imagine to be so close to their own." Tinged with hyperbolic irony ("Every single poem moved them in the very depths of their soul"),[108] these observations suggest a dynamic of wilful identification rather than simple self-recognition. Poems and novels do not merely reflect, mirror-like, the pre-existing feelings and impressions of the young friends: instead, the adolescents imagine themselves ("s'imaginent") reflected by them, that is, they project themselves into them, make themselves believe the texts reflect them, and therefore (re) make themselves in the texts' image.

Rouquès follows his description of this imitative fever with a significant qualification: the adolescents having reached, with Daudet and the Goncourts, the end point of their formative journey along the chronology of nineteenth-century literature, they come to identify themselves not merely with the impressions and moods represented in their works, but with the writers themselves, as students and future competitors of these latest literary masters: "But this time, their enjoyment is no longer blindly avid: their trouble is inflected by a new curiosity; they admire the tricks of the trade [le métier] as much as the story and their obscure kinship with the hero; they see, in front of them, models to be imitated, masters only a generation older, whose secrets they want to capture."[109] Again introduced with unmistakable irony[110] ("it was the revelation, the supreme illumination [...] that determines vocations [...] To write! ... Suddenly they had no more doubts, the clarity was dazzling; it was their destiny: they would write!"),[111] the adolescents' choice of a vocation as writers is presented as the ineluctable conclusion of a process of ever-increasing identification with and self-fashioning after literary texts. From naïve and overly eager consumers of print, it seems inevitable, according to this narrative, that the group of friends would become equally naïve and overeager would-be producers. The novel ends ambiguously, with the friends' disheartened realization that "life has been hidden from them" after one of them dies of diphtheria, an affliction that literalizes their literary fevers – described by the doomed member of the group as "the malady of our time."[112]

A similar trajectory from agitated discovery to frustrated authorial ambitions can be observed in Paul Margueritte's *Tous Quatre* (All four of us, 1885), where Tercinet, the protagonist, emerges from a long succession of literary discoveries, from Hugo and Balzac to Mallarmé, with a desire to write. His first collection of poems, *Les Reflets* (a title that clearly signals their derivative nature), sells only seven copies (a metaphor for inadequate reproductivity). Later, as he finishes his debut novel, his young son dies – also, incidentally, of diphtheria – and his wife takes a female lover, again emphasizing his deficient virility. Tercinet's discovery of contemporary novelists, like that of Rouquès's band of friends, is described as a confused jumble of the Goncourts, Zola, Daudet, and Flaubert: "he could not form a general impression of this formidable reading that amalgamated *Charles Demailly*, *La Curée*, *Manette Salomon*, *Le Ventre de Paris*, *Fromont jeune*, *Salammbô*, *L'Éducation sentimentale*, etc., etc., etc."[113] Flaubert himself, in *Madame Bovary*, famously made use of the trope of the naïve, disorderly reader: Emma, as a bored housewife, reads Balzac, Sue, and Sand alongside gossipy newspapers and fashion catalogues.[114] Whereas the mid-century discourses cited (and to some extent parodied) by Flaubert typically characterized this dangerously impressionable reader as female, working class, or very young,[115] the late nineteenth-century novel of formation, taking its cues from contemporary concerns about education and persistently circulated diagnostics of fin-de-siècle malaise among France's male youth, recasts this vulnerable and overly malleable reader as a young man – one who not only vainly attempts, like Emma Bovary, to model his existence after literary plots, but also entertains largely ill-fated fantasies of becoming a writer himself. Such writerly fantasies are presented as equally dangerous and destabilizing to the social and gender order as Emma's own behaviour.

The topos of the list of formative readings, like the received idea that books have the potential to corrupt certain readers, predates the nineteenth century entirely. In the eighteenth-century libertine novel, aristocrats' literary erudition is cited as a foundation and indicator of their worldly, cynical ways. The Marquise de Merteuil, the master manipulator of *Les Liaisons dangereuses* (1782), peruses her book collection ("a chapter from the *Sopha*, a letter from Héloïse and two *Tales* by La Fontaine")[116] in order to review the various tones and attitudes she intends to adopt in her latest campaign of seduction. Like the late nineteenth-century student, the Marquise reads broadly and assiduously: unlike her latter-day counterpart, though, she builds and wields her literary knowledge as a means to an end. She reads not with "passion" but for the purpose of observation, and in order to gain control over herself and those around her.[117] The libertine's personal library, a corollary of the topos of the reading list, provides an illustration for this shift from strong-willed aristocrats to languid adolescents when contrasted with the late fin-de-siècle novel of formation's own representation of book collections. Whereas the libertine library is a space of seduction, in which books serve as initiators or even tokens of exchange for salacious interactions,[118] the novel of formation repeatedly depicts personal libraries as mortuary spaces, full of gloom and deathly emanations. Lebey's *L'Âge où l'on s'ennuie: chronique contemporaine* (The age of apathy: a contemporary story, 1902) opens with the protagonist, twenty-three year-old Paul, contemplating the book-lined walls of his study:

> Their ranks tightly closed, books appear to form a single volume; they meld into a kind of peaceful army, though they are destructive, invincible et haughty ... A precipitate of nothingness [Un néant condensé] emanates from all this. Despite the wonders it contains and the life that animates it, each flat block pressed against the wall is nothing but paper; the spine of every book fluctuates, contracts, undulates, expands, suggesting now an urn, then a coffin, and the library seems a sublime necropolis.[119]

The "wonders" that seems to spring from each individual book reveal themselves to be illusory, as the accumulation of volumes in immediate proximity instead turns out to exude the essence of morbidity. The initially innocuous and positive characteristics of books (peacefulness, "life") quickly give way to their reverse (destructiveness, death). A military metaphor frames the reader's visual confrontation with the tightly packed ranks of his books as a relationship of enmity. Many of these same descriptive devices – enmity, "nothingness," the book as tombstone – appear in Henry Bérenger's "Portrait d'un jeune homme" (1897):

> Charner turned around, crept along the walls, shot a disgusted glance at the worktable that had become a table of torture, and came face to face with his library. Here they were, all piled up, his dearest confidents, and also his most feared enemies: masterpieces. Now they exalted him to heroism, now they dejected him to the point of suicide. When he aspired to match them, they seemed like precious relics; when they drove him to despair, they were miserable tombs. They contained the whole essence of beauty, and all of its nothingness [néant] as well. And the disgust of heaping more corpses onto these corpses repulsed him more often than he felt intoxicated by an enthusiasm to add one more immortality to their immortalities.[120]

Bérenger sets up pairs of antonymic descriptions – confidents and enemies, agents of exhilaration and despondency, reliquaries of immortality and tombs for cadavers – but ultimately states that the negative elements outweigh the positive. The desire to work and write, born of the reader's feverish and formative contact with the masterpieces of literature, gives way to the "torture" of creative impotence and despair. To write another book would not extend life through artistic filiation but rather produce a revolting, stillborn "corpse." In a similar line, Tercinet, in Margueritte's *Tous Quatre*, does not father any more children after the death of his young son; instead, he writes five further novels (in addition to a volume titled *Poèmes névrosés*), all of which gather dust in his study, unpublished. As he rereads and revises his oeuvre, he is struck by self-doubt, and ends up destroying the manuscripts: "everything died, in his books."[121]

Jean Morgan's *En genèse* (1897) features a scene similar to Lebey's and Bérenger's depictions of the young man's study as a space at once of familiar comfort and oppressive enmity: Jacques, the protagonist, "looking all around him, in the room where books were the only furniture," thinks to himself: "Oh, books ... the best friends, the worst enemies!"[122] By the end of the novel, he contemplates suicide. The narrative had opened with a priest's remonstrance to Jacques as an archetype of his exhausted generation: "You suffer from the disease that afflicts the current generation ... we have dilettantes and wonderfully corrupted men ... but we have no men of will; that is a trait that tends to disappear among intellectuals. Sensitive types, analysts, subtle thinkers ... it is a brilliant degeneration, but a degeneration nonetheless ... As for you, my son, what you lack is energy."[123] The opposition between impotent dilettantism and wilful energy, as we have seen, is a mainstay of discourses on the perceived crisis of contemporary youth exemplified by Barrès and Bourget (from the latter's *Essais*: "The multiplicity of points of view, which can be the mark of a rich intelligence, ends up ruining the will, since it produces dilettantism").[124] In deploying lists of names and titles, and staging crucial scenes in the emblematic space of the library, many novels of formation inculpate reading as the root cause of this imagined shift between active (re)productivity and passive impotence. It is in his personal study, for instance, that Georges's body is found after he commits suicide in *L'Effort* – sitting at a worktable "covered with books and papers strewn about [en désordre]."[125] The young man's library, the collection of his formative readings, is cast as a place and agent of disorder, the symbolic and, at times, literal graveyard of his life-will. His body marked by degeneration, his drives deviated from productive goals, his will to create spurred only to be fatally sapped, the readerly protagonist of the fin-de-siècle novel of formation is depicted over and again as a victim of the book.

PART II

The Three Dangers of Literature

(Case Study: *Les Trois Legrand*, 1903)

In 1903, André Beaunier published his second novel, *Les Trois Legrand, ou le danger de la littérature*.[1] In a lightly comic mode, the narrative follows the three members of the Legrand family as their lives are ruined by reading. The trio initially moves to Paris so that the adolescent son, Pierre Legrand, can obtain a *baccalauréat* and launch his literary career. When he fails to qualify, he abandons his studies on the advice of a mediocre but fashionable poet (who exclaims, "I had no need for such a diploma ... neither did Coppée!")[2] in order to devote himself entirely to writing. That poet goes on to seduce Pierre's mother, Virginie Legrand: in what is depicted as a cynically routine ploy of conquest, he lends her a few novels by George Sand. The father, Ange Legrand, has hitched his social and monetary ambitions to his son, and pushes him to move from poetry to lowbrow pornographic prose and journalism, in a futile pursuit of commercial success. The whole family is ironically named, as the Legrands turn out to have no great qualities: Ange is no angel, Virginie no blushing virgin, and Pierre no bedrock for future posterity. By the end of the narrative, the parents have exhausted their last savings with the desperate purchase of a shabby brasserie on the outskirts of Paris, while Pierre, ostensibly researching a novel on the criminal underbelly of this seedy neighbourhood, ends up instead drawn into it:

> This is where [Ange] ends up, fallen from his lofty ambitions, his pride exhausted, reduced to the indignity of having to serve drinks to city guards. His prodigious dreams of art and literature, his son's glory expected too quickly, fortune, luxury and their disappointing illusions! ... The man of letters [Pierre] is out wandering, who knows where. He has not been seen all day. At his family's watering hole, on the ramparts, by the gates, he is making contacts. He will never write [his novel]; he will live it instead.[3]

As a novel, *Les Trois Legrand* occupies a slippery and indefinite position between social satire and literary parody.[4] Some evidence suggests that

Beaunier did not conceive of his work as entirely facetious: the dedication of his 1911 novel *L'Homme qui a perdu son moi* – to Paul Bourget – states that "the meeting of ideas and souls ... is the subject of all my books."[5] Yet he would also, over the following decades, develop a clearly stated position rebutting those who would hold literature accountable for social ills. A 1923 essay, "Sur les dangers de la littérature," strongly disputes Jean Carrère's polemical treatise *Les Mauvais Maîtres* from the previous year, which had argued that Rousseau, Stendhal, Balzac, and other major figures of eighteenth and nineteenth-century literature continued to exert, in spite of – or rather because of – their greatness and their charm, a demoralizing influence on French youth, teaching them excessive melancholy, cynicism, and ambition.[6] Regardless of whether it was intended as social critique, *Les Trois Legrand* works effectively as a parody of the fin-de-siècle novel of formation because it relies on a number of narrative tropes that are easily recognizable as such by 1903. For this reason, it provides a useful template for defining the three archetypal plots of this genre: literary education, novelistic seduction, and writerly ambition.[7]

Literary Education

Pierre Legrand's disappointment with the promises of republican higher education provide the impetus for the novel, which opens with a dramatic scene of the failure of his examination for the *baccalauréat*, staged "in the middle of the Sorbonne."[8] His humble provincial origins and his struggles with the heavily classical and literary program of the nation's secondary schools make him akin to Jules Vallès's iconic *Bachelier*, the somewhat autobiographical character Jacques Vingtras (who succeeds in obtaining the *baccalauréat*, but goes on to become no less of a failure). Although Vallès's trilogy of novels is set before the advent of the Third Republic, the arc it traces from unhappy childhood to desperate and socially volatile destitution – neatly summarized in the titles *L'Enfant*, *Le Bachelier*, and *L'Insurgé* (The child, The graduate, The insurgent) – crucially places the failure of state education, and specifically education in classical letters, at the centre of its impassioned indictment. The timeliness of this denunciation was far from lost on readers and critics of the 1880s. Like Beaunier's Pierre, Vallès's young Jacques is made to believe that his intellectual and literary aptitudes, channelled through the centralized institutions of republican higher education, give him a rightful claim to upward social and economic mobility – in other words, that education constitutes what another novel ironically and insistently calls *La Clé des carrières*, the key to all careers.[9] The frustration of these aspirations, coupled with the often one-way geographical trajectory of similar young men from the provinces to Paris, created what came to be described as a population of successive and increasingly large generations of overeducated, displaced malcontents in the capital – in Barrès's phrase, "a proletariat of diploma-holders."[10] The socially threatening figure of these disappointed students would loom large in the many contentious educational debates and reforms of the years 1881 to 1905 (from the institution of free primary education to the controversial law separating church and state),[11] as it would in novels of formation throughout the period.

Novelistic Seduction

The seduction of Pierre Legrand's mother Virginie at the hands of the (no less ironically named) poet Hyacinthe Perdrix is a minor narrative turn in Beaunier's novel. Its expedited treatment is a testament to the familiarity and legibility of the plot of novelistic seduction. A hitherto blameless married mother is introduced to sentimental readings, and her virtue falters:

> He lent her some books ... She asked for novels, perversely, since she had been raised to consider these kinds of works as frivolous and full of danger ... George Sand caused her the greatest shock: she was at first indignant, then seduced. It had never occurred to her that love might have intractable rights.[12]

The "perverse" appeal of such readings is precisely their known danger: their reputation is both a warning and an incitement. Virginie Legrand is familiar with the long-standing discourse linking the reading of novels with women's moral strayings, as are the presumed readers of this briefly sketched scene. From Rousseau's Julie to Flaubert's Emma and their multitude of counterparts, the seduced female reader is omnipresent in eighteenth- and nineteenth-century fiction,[13] as well as in contemporaneous social discourse concerned with the habits of new and presumed naïve consumers of literature. By 1903, the trope is so worn as to have become a stock figure, a comedic subplot. A variant of this character had already emerged in the preceding decades: the young man morally compromised, and in many ways seduced, by his own reading habits. Critically imagined in Bourget's *Essais*, this young man would become a fully fledged object of fictional and social concern in his novel *Le Disciple* (1889),[14] and in the sustained debates that surrounded its publication.

Writerly Ambition

Ange Legrand is the driving force behind his son Pierre's literary ambitions, which he sees as the family's ticket to wealth and social recognition. Early on, he rationalizes the trio's move to Paris by explaining to his sceptical wife that "every time [Edmond] Rostand writes a play, he earns a million francs";[15] once there, he convinces her to give their son money so that he can go find inspiration in the company of disreputable women, since "it's a known fact that great poets necessarily indulge in fairly bad behaviour."[16] When Pierre's mediocre poetry fails to find a publisher, Ange takes him to the booksellers' quarter in order to discover exactly what kinds of books are being published and sold. The titles they see displayed provide an unmistakable answer: "*A Woman's Body*, *Flesh Gone Wild*, *Killer Love*, *The Passionate Ones*, *Courtesans of the Salons*, *The Demon Women* ..."[17] The father questions a store clerk:

> – Seems that poetry's less in demand, Mr. Legrand said hesitantly [...]
>
> – For sure, poetry! ... If we didn't have pornography to make ends meet, it'd be impossible to run a bookshop [...] People write more and more, and read less and less. It's what they call the crisis of the book! Anyone who would've been a reader, in the old days, is now a writer ...[18]

Ever pragmatic, Ange concludes that his son should abandon poetry and write pornographic novels instead. He conceives of literature less as an artistic pursuit than as a career, a potentially lucrative gamble, a means to social advancement – and he is far from alone in thinking this, since nearly everyone, according to the bookseller, is now an aspiring writer facing an overcrowded market. In the contemporary publishing climate, Ange reckons, "Dante would write *Flesh Gone Wild*. Homer too, Virgil as well. Or else they'd be losers."[19] As the father pushes his son from lyric poetry to salacious novels, and later to sensational journalism, literary value matters less than the pursuit of success. In this preoccupation with financial and social ascension, even at the price of lofty literary ideals, Ange proves himself a descendant of a literary archetype: the ambitious Balzacian hero.[20] Jean Carrère, against whom Beaunier would write his 1923 article, thunders against Balzac as an enduring fount of ill-conceived ambitions even in the twentieth century:

> We can thank the author of the *Comédie humaine* for the ever-growing onslaught of the most vulgar ambitions ... It is he who ... goes around all our provinces and rings, in the all-too-receptive ear of every plebeian still dirty with the earth of his native soil, a call to the conquest of Paris! It is he who ... through the glimmer of his examples ... has led to the rise, from the troubled dregs of our race, of a nefarious and innumerable type, the swarm whose buzzing is a curse on our country ... the social climber![21]

As Beaunier's rebuttal argues, such a denunciation is itself a literary cliché by 1922, and a dated one at that; by 1903, it was already on its way to being one, as the comic tone of *Les Trois Legrand* suggests. In fact, the condemnation appears as early as 1887, in an article penned by Barrès;[22] ten years later, in *Les Déracinés*, Barrès would examine the effects of this "contagion" of Balzacian ambition on a group of seven young provincials who, like the Legrands, abandon their native soil to seek success in Paris.

~

In the chapters that follow, I examine a representative novel for each of the three archetypal plots encapsulated in *Les Trois Legrand*, with particular attention to each novel's complex relation to one or more influential older texts. In chapter 3, I consider Vallès's *Le Bachelier* (1879–81), the sequel to *L'Enfant*, in the context of nineteenth-century debates about the importance of Greek and Latin in the national education curriculum. I show how Vallès engages with eighteenth-century texts including Rousseau's hybrid educational novel-treatise *Émile* (1762) and Sébastien Mercier's *Tableau de Paris* (1781–8) on the question of the uneasy encounter between classical ideals and modern realities.

Chapter 4 turns to the work of Paul Bourget, particularly *Le Disciple* (1889), in which a student is accused of murdering a young woman he had seduced through their shared reading of novels; that plot, I argue, is heavily indebted to Stendhal's *Le Rouge et le Noir* (1830). During the 1888 murder trial on which Bourget's novel is based, the accused murderer Henri Chambige had in fact been denounced for emulating Stendhal's hero. Retracing how the trial unfolded in transcripts and newspapers, I reveal how Bourget (who knew the accused student) was dangerously implicated in the queer networks underlying what became known as the Chambige affair.

In chapter 5, I focus on the work of Maurice Barrès, especially *Les Déracinés* (1897), a novel I briefly examined in chapter 1 during a larger discussion of the common metaphor of reading as poison. That novel's narrative arc, as it follows seven young men from the provinces who go to Paris to fulfil their career ambitions, is repeatedly linked to Balzac's cycle *La Comédie humaine* (1830–50), even as the characters deny being swayed by the great novelist. I show how, in Barrès as in a number of novels from the same period, Balzac has an effaced but lingering presence best described as a haunting. Barrès's characters are marked by a ghostly masculinity, manifested in either melancholy and impotence, or cynical and violent overcompensation.

Vallès may seem like an unlikely juxtaposition to the more conventional pairing of Bourget and Barrès.[23] Born ten years apart, Bourget (1852–1935) and Barrès (1862–1923) followed similar trajectories from pessimistic and notorious "princes of youth" (a moniker bestowed on both at different times)[24] to conservative members of the literary and political establishment. Both became anti-Dreyfusards and academicians;[25] in the early twentieth century, Bourget declared himself a Catholic and royalist, and Barrès held a seat as a right-wing member of the Assemblée nationale for seventeen years. Much of their later output has long been regarded as "romans à thèse" of limited literary value, save as examples of an ideologically inflected genre.[26] Their reciprocal exchange of favourable articles, reviews, and dedications attests the public visibility of their association in the 1880s and 1890s.[27] Barrès's manuscripts reveal that Bourget provided suggestions and even rewrote some of the concordances for the 1892 re-edition of *Sous l'œil des Barbares*, most notably those that emphasize the influence of formative readings on the protagonist. Bourget therefore not only found an illustration of his theories about reading in Barrès's early works, he made sure the connection was emphasized more strongly.[28]

Vallès (1832–85), by contrast, belonged to an earlier generation. He was an advocate of the political left as a journalist in the 1860s, and held an elected post in the Paris Commune of 1871. After a decade in exile following the repression of the Commune, he returned to France in 1880 and died in 1885. Yet Bourget suggests a link between Vallès and his and Barrès's own diagnostics about the ills affecting French society – as well as those made earlier by Stendhal, Balzac, and Flaubert – when he writes, in 1912, that "Julien Sorel, Lucien de Rubempré, ... Flaubert's Emma Bovary, Vallès's Jacques Vingtras ... are all subjectivities undergoing a change of class"; each of these well-known characters, he explains, illustrate "the danger represented by [what] Barrès has very aptly termed uprootedness."[29] The protagonists of famous novels by Stendhal, Balzac, and Flaubert, in Bourget's view, wander astray from "a strong local, professional, and familial environment";[30] the perils of such a path are shown anew, he proposes, in novels by Vallès and Barrès, as well as in his own work. As the emblematic mid-century figures of Julien, Lucien, and Emma are led to their doom by what they read, so will the late-century work of Vallès, Bourget, and Barrès revolve around characters who fall prey to the siren song of the book in matters of education, seduction, and ambition. Therein, as Beaunier's potentially parodic novel shows, lies yet another danger of literature: its denunciation as an intoxicating and socially disruptive practice may reveal itself to be a literarily produced and circulated notion, a received idea, a cliché – the result of a tendency, on the part of critics and novelists, to see their contemporary reality through an overly literary lens.

3 Vallès, the *Déclassé*, and the Pitfalls of Education

Year after year, an outdated university system churns out throngs of overeducated candidates who, having spent of much of their youth toiling towards an all-important degree, find themselves competing for a disproportionally small number of teaching and administrative positions. Does this describe the early twenty-first century PhD, or the late nineteenth-century *bachelier*?[1] A 2007 essay by François Moureau, decrying how "the enormous standardizing machine of the university creates a product [that is] too often ill-suited to the needs of the market,"[2] connects the two periods through its title, *Le Nouveau Prolétariat intellectuel*, an echo of a 1901 tract by Henry Bérenger, *Les Prolétaires intellectuels en France*.[3] Yet aside from this implicit citation, Moureau – an eminent scholar of eighteenth-century French literature – does not look back earlier than 1955. If he had, he might have pointed out a number of striking continuities between the contemporary problem he examines, common to France and the United States, and descriptions of the bleak economic outlook faced by would-be upwardly mobile graduates drifting around Paris in centuries past. Louis-Sébastien Mercier's *Tableau de Paris* (1781–8), as we will see, already portrayed the degree-holding dwellers of the capital's Latin Quarter as socially dangerous malcontents with too many grand aspirations and too few marketable skills. A century later in the 1880s and 1890s, French essayists and pedagogues employed similar characterizations to critique the increasingly anachronistic institutional pre-eminence of the Latin-based *baccalauréat* degree, a holdover from pre-revolutionary times, in the new political and economic reality of the Third Republic. During those decades, polemical tracts as well as novels depicted a swelling, unproductive, and restless mass of overeducated and underemployed male graduates, an intellectual proletariat (in Bérenger's phrase) whose discontent and economic desperation threatened the social order of the young Republic. The most emblematic of these novels may well be Jules

Vallès's *Le Bachelier* (1879–81). In his constant preoccupation with nourishment – encapsulated in the epigraph to that novel, "To those who, fed a steady diet of Greek and Latin, died of hunger"[4] – Vallès's fictional double Jacques Vingtras is not far removed from current-day depictions of doctoral degree holders, whether in light-hearted comics (Mike Slackenerny, the long-suffering postdoc of the popular online series *Piled Higher and Deeper*, is amusingly single-minded in his pursuit of the free food served at academic functions)[5] or in anything-but-comical journalism: as a 2012 article informs us, "The Ph.D. Now Comes with Food Stamps."[6]

Lives of Not-so-Illustrious Men

In Paul Brulat's *Le Nouveau Candide* (1902), a first-person narrator takes a foreign prince on a comprehensive tour of turn-of-the-century Paris. Clearly indebted to Voltaire but also to Montesquieu's *Lettres persanes* (1721) and the tradition of reverse travel literature, in which an imagined foreign visitor provides a falsely naïve, critical perspective on national mores and institutions, this narrative setup allows for a series of satirical tableaus, as the narrator guides the wide-eyed prince through what he ironically calls "the wonders of our civilization."[7] Among these modern wonders is a character simply called "the poet," whom the travelling pair meet at a sordid *café-concert*. The poet welcomes a chance to perorate, and explains how his extensive education has led to his wretched condition:

> two master's degrees and a doctorate, that's more than enough to die of hunger, in the times we live in. Instead of helping me earn a living, all this erudition made a fool of me. In pursuing it, I used up all the vitality and energy of my youth: and now here I stand, powerless in the gruelling struggle for life. Perhaps I could have amounted to something, had my father, an honest peasant, not bled himself from every vein in order to make someone out of me [...] My teachers all promised me a brilliant future, since I was a good student. [...] I learned *De viris illustribus* by heart – a harmful book if there ever was one. By the seventh grade, it had already given me dreams of glory; later, it turned me into an oddball, a crank, a *déclassé*, an idiot, totally deprived of common sense, a dreamer and a mooch, so useless in business that I had never heard, although I had a law degree, of a letter of credit or a promissory note ... Would you have some coins to lend me?[8]

The overeducated *déclassé* (a somewhat untranslatable term denoting social out-of-placeness), doomed to a lowly and embittered existence not despite but precisely because of his education, was a familiar figure in the discursive landscape of the fin de siècle. That the poet singles out *De viris illustribus*, an eighteenth-century school manual by the Abbé Lhomond, as the single book most responsible for his unhappy fate is no accident. Lhomond's *De viris*, itself based on a long tradition of exemplary literature in Latin,[9] is a collection of stories about a hundred or so illustrious Romans, from Rhea Silvia (mother of Romulus and Remus) to Augustus, designed for first-year *collège* (that is, secondary school) students. It enjoyed enduring, nearly continual use in French schools from its first publication in the 1770s to the middle of the twentieth century. The poet's doomed trajectory towards the status of *déclassé* thus began in the classroom, as he learned – memorized, to be exact, and the distinction will prove important – a Latin text. Just as significantly, this most fateful book was not composed in the ancient world, but rather recomposed, from disparate classical sources, by a French clergyman living under the Ancien Régime. Both these features, the primacy of rote memorization and the problematic filtering of a distant classical age through the more recent eighteenth century, will feature prominently in Vallès's critique of the centrality of Latin in state education.

In 1902, the year Brulat's novel appeared, a ministerial decree established an official equivalency between the newer *baccalauréat moderne* (without Greek or Latin) and the *baccalauréat classique*, ending, in theory if not quite in practice,[10] the centuries-old privilege of classical studies, and particularly the study of Latin, as the sole means of entry to French university programs in the liberal professions as well as in letters and sciences. The decree was based on the recommendations of the Ribot Commission,[11] itself one of the culminating points of a series of widely debated reforms of the French education system undertaken in the 1880s. Calls to transform and modernize all levels of the nation's schools had appeared soon after the disastrous Franco-Prussian War of 1870 and the suppression of the Commune of 1871.[12] It had been a journalistic commonplace to explain France's defeat as the victory of a more modern Germanic model of education: the enemy armies, the story went, were better organized, better disciplined, more physically fit, and had superior technical knowledge; many Prussian officers spoke French whereas few of their counterparts knew any German, and the invaders had better geographic knowledge of the battlefields than the French themselves.[13] French primary education, by contrast, stood accused of forming easily swayed, semi-literate malcontents (the typical depiction of Communards in the conservative press), while secondary education was said to produce voluble aesthetes ill-fitted to the service of the nation: "our institutions of higher learning tend to produce nothing but a population of dilettantes and delicate minds, pompous lawyers, salon thinkers and pleasant writers ... This is the source of the practical carelessness and recklessness that have precipitated us into such terrible disasters."[14] Republican policymakers, led by Jules Ferry, responded by making primary education free, mandatory, and secular, through a succession of laws passed between 1881 and 1886; a first set of secondary school reforms was enacted in 1890, paving the way for the transformations of 1902.[15]

Nineteenth-century commentators and more recent scholars alike note that French secondary education remained largely unchanged from the Ancien Régime to the 1880s. In the midst of a century of dramatic regime overthrows, scientific discoveries, and cultural effervescence, the *collège* (briefly renamed *lycée* under the Empire, and again under the Republic) had remained a remarkably stable, even ossified institution.[16] This continuity is visible in at least three constants: secondary education remained the exclusive province of boys (a provision not challenged until the 1860s) from families who could afford its expense; its goal was to prepare them for the all-important *baccalauréat* examination; and the means of this preparation was the extensive study of Latin texts through recitation, translation, and imitation, exercises that occupied more class time than any other.[17] The debates that preceded and accompanied the reforms of 1890 and 1902 took on many of these entrenched traditions: was the expense justified, both in terms of financial costs to middle-class or petit-bourgeois families and of years of young men's lives, given what secondary education did or did not provide in return? Was a single and classically oriented examination really the most adequate entrance requirement for university studies and training in the liberal professions – and if obtained, did it effectively guarantee access to these careers? Could the study of Latin, a holdover from pre-revolutionary times, still be considered an effective program for the mental, moral, and social formation of the future citizens of the modern Republic? Dramatically negative answers to these questions coalesced in the recurring figure of the *déclassé*.

The Novel of *Déclassement*

In sociological terms, *déclassés* are defined by status incongruence, a discordance between individuals' education or background and their current economic status. *Déclassement* should not be understood as a decrease in social status, but instead as the loss of a clear place in the class system: the male student turned *déclassé* fails to fit in an established socio-economic category. Rather than a figure of downward mobility,[18] he is the victim of an unsuccessful attempt at upward mobility that leaves him unable or unwilling to reintegrate the lower class from which he came. While his economic status fails to improve, the *déclassé* no longer fits in his original social class. Here again, the garrulous poet of Brulat's novel summarizes the phenomenon when he refers to "my father, an honest peasant" – the intimation being that the poet would have been better off if he had remained in the provinces and become a man like his father, making a modest but honest living instead of haunting Parisian drinking holes and ranting about dreams of success that never materialized. The failed scholar muses that he should have been content with "amounting to something" instead of going along with his father's ill-advised ambition of turning him into a "someone."[19] The problem of the *déclassé* comes down to a conflict between the revolutionary ideal of equality – or rather, the more moderate republican principle of the equality of opportunity, as embodied in a national education system that grants access to prestigious careers through standardized examinations – and the enduring fact of familially inherited social and economic privilege. Education is the nexus of this conflict, since it holds out the possibility of social mobility for students, but also because teaching posts are themselves envisioned as intermediate positions, as steps on the ladder from the rural or working classes to the urban bourgeoisie[20] – a promise often not borne out, as frequently depicted in turn-of-the-century novels about the difficult working conditions and frustrated aspirations of teachers.[21]

Two novels of formation by Alphonse Daudet illustrate the failure of class mobility through education and teaching. These novels, written thirty years apart, bookend both Daudet's career and the concurrent period of deep social concern with questions of education and *déclassement*. In the first, *Le Petit Chose* (*Little What's-His-Name*, published as a serial in 1866–7, and as a volume in 1868), the son of a small fabric mill owner is sent to a *collège* in Lyon while his brother remains in the family business. The titular *petit Chose* goes on to a miserable existence first as a *pion* (a classroom supervisor, the lowliest teaching grade), and later as a struggling would-be poet in Paris. When his lyrical magnum opus ("The Pastoral Comedy," comprising such sections as "The Adventures of a Blue Butterfly")[22] fails to find a publisher, his brother arranges to have it privately printed, but even then, the book does not sell. After his brother dies, *le petit Chose* arranges for the remaining copies of his book to be used as wrapping paper for egg cups shipped to Madagascar. He has humiliatingly and ironically come full circle: the poetic product of his education proves to have no value, and its material traces end up recycled in the kind of commerce his father used to live from – except that his family no longer owns the means of production. The second novel, the posthumous *Soutien de famille* (The support of the family, published as a serial in 1897, and as a volume in 1898), likewise contrasts the destinies of two brothers. Raymond, the eldest, studies German philosophy and aspires to be a writer, while Antonin, the youngest, moves to England to work as a factory supervisor. The novel opens dramatically with the suicide of their father, the owner of a furniture-making business who has bankrupted himself to send his sons to the prestigious Lycée Charlemagne in Paris; it ends with Raymond's realization that the younger Antonin, with his steady work and more pragmatic aspirations, has all along been "the real support of the family." When the failed writer Raymond learns that his fiancée is pregnant, he leaves her to Antonin and his wife's care while he, desperate to earn a living for his new family, enrols in a military expedition to Indochina: "After so many incarnations, so many sterile efforts in literature, medicine, and politics," he writes them in a letter, "I thought I should at least be good for something."[23] Here again, the father's blind faith in the potential of secondary education to lift his progeny to greater social heights – "my boys will know Latin," he had declared resolutely[24] – and the son's resulting literary ambition lead to a form of *déclassement.* Raymond never would have had to face poverty, and later risk his life as a colonial footman, had he simply been groomed to take over his father's manufacturing business. In the novel's very last lines, the former student pleads with his brother and sister-in-law to spare his own child from the curse of classical education: "I beg you, do not make my child learn Latin or study the classics. In asking these things of his own son, my father brought me nothing but misfortune."[25]

In his sustained discussion of the figure of the *déclassé* in the first decades of the Third Republic, Fritz Ringer does not bring up Daudet's novels (which, although representative, were not epoch making), opting instead to focus on two highly influential works: Paul Bourget's *Le Disciple* and Maurice Barrès's *Les Déracinés.*[26] Judith Surkis, similarly, examines the question through the writings of Barrès and Henry Bérenger.[27] Each of these works is indeed deeply preoccupied with the problem of *déclassement*, yet none of them pays much heed to an issue that, as the final exclamation of Daudet's 1897 novel reminds us (and as Ringer and Surkis both acknowledge),[28] was the central symbol of republican debates on secondary education and its relation to class mobility: the notorious "Latin question."[29] That question, by contrast, is at the very heart of a series of three novels that both Bourget (as we have seen, in a 1912 article) and Barrès (in an early article from 1886, "The lesson of an insurgent")[30] acknowledged as an antecedent: Jules Vallès's *Jacques Vingtras* trilogy.

Jules Vallès and *Jacques Vingtras*

Vallès had long been a vocal critic of France's educational practices and institutions, starting with his journalism of the 1860s. During the Commune, he was a member of the revolutionary government's committee on education (Commission de l'enseignement); *L'Insurgé* represents this in a number of scenes, taking potshots at Jules Ferry and Jules Simon, who first rose to prominence in the fledgling republican government of 1870 and would go on to lead the education reforms of the 1880s.[31] His *Jacques Vingtras* trilogy – *L'Enfant*, *Le Bachelier*, and *L'Insurgé*, a succession of titles that neatly encapsulates the menacing failure of secondary education – functions along two parallel chronologies. On a first level, as a somewhat autobiographical enterprise, the narrative follows Vallès's double Jacques Vingtras from his childhood under the July Monarchy and the short-lived Second Republic, through the coup d'état of 2 December 1851 (described in a chapter of *Le Bachelier*) and Jacques's subsequent years as a down-and-out journalist under the Second Empire, before culminating in his active involvement in the Commune of 1871 and his flight from France following its brutal repression. Yet save for the events of 1851 and 1871, the novels avoid alluding to dates altogether; the long sequences of chapters that describe Jacques's misery in school, or his struggles as an unemployed *bachelier* in Paris, are not set in specific years. Given this historical indeterminacy, Vallès's readers were free to relate his damning portrayal of the French education system to the polemics that swirled around that very topic at the time the novels appeared.[32] Indeed, a second chronology, that of the trilogy's publication and reception, closely coincides with the major educational debates and reforms of the 1880s. The first two tomes were written in exile in London. *L'Enfant* appeared as a serial in 1878 and as a volume in 1879, and *Le Bachelier* in 1879 and 1881; Ferry's reforms of primary education, first undertaken in 1879 and hotly debated through 1881, were mostly in place by 1882.[33] A first version of *L'Insurgé*, composed after Vallès's return to Paris when amnesty was granted to Communards in 1880, appeared as a serial in 1882–3, but the revised text was left unfinished at the time of Vallès's death in February 1885; it was published in book form, thanks to the editorial efforts of Vallès's collaborator Séverine, in May 1886,[34] just as educationalists and critics were busily debating Raoul Frary's polemical *La Question du latin* of 1885.[35]

The question of Latin traverses Vallès's novels in four interrelated ways: as the root cause of a familial drama of failed ambitions; as an educational practice that foments social unrest; as a body of knowledge that makes possible a problematic imitation of historical models; and as a set of references and rhetorical devices that comes to undermine the authenticity of personal expression.

1) The Latinist Father: A Familial Drama

The familial consequences of the teaching of Latin are most salient in the figure of Jacques's father, whose personal history is succinctly recounted in the first chapter of *L'Enfant*:

> We're from the country.
>
> My grandfather was a peasant who, out of pride, wanted his son to study and become a priest. My father was sent to live with an uncle who was a vicar so he could learn Latin, then he was shipped off to a seminary.

> My father ... didn't stay there: he thought he could be a *bachelier* instead, and land a prestigious post ... in the evenings, he came home and wooed a farm-girl who became my mother ...
>
> I'm the first child of this blessed union. I was born in an old wooden bed riddled with bedbugs from the village and fleas from the seminary.[36]

Jacques thus introduces himself as the spawn of an unholy coupling of village life and Latinate education. What should have been an uncomplicated story of farmer's son meets farm girl is troubled by the father's half-successful education – characterized as the result of the grandfather's prideful desire for upward social mobility. Instead of raising a new generation of peasants, the father (who has become a lowly teacher) will strive to make his own son into the *bachelier* he himself never managed to become, even as this resolution goes against the son's inclinations. At every turn of *L'Enfant*, Jacques protests that he would rather do manual labour than pore over his schoolbooks ("I'd rather be making haystacks than read my [Latin] grammar"),[37] but his pleas go unheard. His father's unflinching resolve is itself presented as the product of his education; as an early article by Vallès makes explicit, the father wilfully models himself on what he imagines to be the classical ideal of the paterfamilias, strong, impassible, and cold.[38] Only at the very end of *L'Enfant* does the father acknowledge – in a conversation overheard by Jacques from another room – that this play-acting got the better of him, supplanting what should have been his more gentle parental disposition: "I can't help it! Being a teacher has turned me into a mean old man: I needed to look like a killjoy, and I ended up becoming one ... *I wanted to act like a Roman*, I was cruel."[39] Father and son both, as well as the relationship between them, are thus depicted as victims of classical education.

The recurrence of the figure of the overly ambitious father in Daudet's as well as Vallès's novels suggests that the Vingtras trilogy partakes in a wider topos about education and class. *L'Enfant*, most notably in its depiction of school as a space of misery, has much in common with Daudet's earlier novel, a debt it acknowledges on its very first page when a neighbour comments, upon hearing Jacques being beaten, "there's *le petit Chose* getting the strap again."[40] It also reworks, in its depiction of a father blindly driving his son to pursue classical studies, a much older text, Mercier's *Tableau de Paris* (1781–8), which Vallès knew: in 1882, he undertook a series of articles under the same title for the newspaper *Gil Blas*. The first article opens with a direct nod to Mercier.[41] In Mercier's 1781 *Tableau*, a chapter entitled "Latinists" paints a comical yet alarming picture of petit-bourgeois fathers who, in their drive for social ascension, push their sons to learn Latin:

> These days the petit bourgeois (who is illiterate) absolutely wants to make his son a Latinist. He tells all his neighbours ... as he explains his silly project: Oh! Latin leads to everything; my son will know Latin. This is a great ill. The son goes to the *collège*, where he learns nothing: upon leaving, he has become a layabout who turns up his nose at manual labour ... and has nothing but disdain for his father's profession ... And yet he must earn a living: what profession will he enter? What is he good for? Since his father has no fortune, he is thrown into the dusty office of some lawyer or notary. Now our young man applies for some position as a clerk, an assistant, or an agent: most often he fails. Oh! Latin leads to everything.
>
> Isn't it ridiculous and deplorable to see shopkeepers, artisans, domestics even, want to raise their children as the higher classes do, and delight themselves with an imaginary profession for their progeny, as they repeat idiotically, parroting the middle school teacher: Oh! Latin leads to everything.[42]

Mercier's harangue could almost serve as a plot summary for *L'Enfant* and *Le Bachelier*: Jacques, upon exiting the *collège*, will indeed find himself unsuited for manual labour. In a highly symbolic scene, the freshly minted *bachelier* is turned away from a printer's shop where he wants to enrol as an apprentice:

> The printer answered: "You should have come when you were twelve.
>
> – When I was twelve, I was a prisoner at the *collège*! I had my shoulder to the wheel of Latin.
>
> – Even more reason not to take you! In these revolutionary times, we don't like *déclassés* who jump from the classroom to the workshop. They spoil the others."[43]

Jacques's figurative toiling at the wheel of Latin precludes him from working on a literal machine. Instead of happily operating the press, he will struggle to earn a living as a writer or journalist, someone who produces written content for the press. As in Anatole France's *Les Désirs de Jean Servien*, where the father is an illiterate bookbinder,[44] the young man's relationship to print is illustrated by his exclusion from a material relationship to productivity. This dematerialization is connoted as a devirilization, drawing on a long tradition representing intellectual pursuits as physically debilitating and unmanly.[45] At the end of *Le Bachelier*, Jacques will, as a last resort, resign himself to work as a teacher like his father, and earn a meagre wage by propagating knowledge he knows to be useless, a "peddler of dead tongues."[46] Unlike his father, he will not sire children: over the span of three generations, from peasant to *bachelier*, the dead tongue of Latin brings about the death of a bloodline, foreclosing not only economic productivity but biological reproductivity.

Many turn-of-the-century novels of formation stage similar conflicts between the possibilities supposedly opened by the classical *baccalauréat* and the reality of limited career prospects faced by those who hold it.[47] Mercier's ironic repetition of the mantra "Latin leads to everything" is updated, in Abel Faure's *La Clé des carrières* (1904), in the recurring and equally ironic assertion that the *baccalauréat* is "the key that opens all doors."[48] An echo of Mercier's "my son will know Latin," as we have seen, opens Daudet's novel *Soutien de famille* (1897). And the protagonist of Frantz Jourdain's *L'Atelier Chantorel* (1893), another *bachelier*, finds himself the butt of a Vallèsian joke when a prospective employer asks him what foreign languages he knows:

> – What about German?
> – No, sir.
> – Spanish?
> – Neither! You know, at the *lycée* ...
> – Right, Greek and Latin. Sadly, we have no business relations with Themistocles or Brutus.[49]

Such conflicts find their most pared-down expression in a scene from *Le Bachelier*, where Jacques is asked a straightforward question by a wealthy man to whom he has come looking for a job, and finds himself unable to answer.

> – What are your skills? [...]
> – I am a *bachelier*.
> Monsieur Bonardel repeats his question louder; he must think I'm deaf.
> – WHAT ARE YOUR SKILLS?
> I fondle my hat, I search for an answer ... Monsieur Bonardel waits for a moment, gives me two minutes. After two minutes, he reaches for a bell pull.
> – Show this young man out. [...]
> WHAT ARE MY SKILLS????
> I racked my brain all night, I couldn't think of any.[50]

Foreseen by Mercier ("Now our young man applies for some position as a clerk, an assistant, or an agent: most often he fails"), the scene encapsulates the tragic fate of the *bachelier*: his hard-earned classical education has no practical use, no technical or economic value.[51] The cultural prestige it carries is worthless without existing familial capital, which Jacques most definitely does not have, as his tragicomic struggle to get to his interview without muddying his clothes reminds us – it is raining, and he has no money to hire a ride. Whereas he could have lived a contented existence of manual labour (at least, so he insistently tells the reader), Jacques's education instead leads him to a life of economic struggle and, ultimately, revolt.

2) The Latinist Student: A Social Threat

As early as Mercier's *Tableau* of 1781, the phenomenon of petit-bourgeois Latinists was described less as a Molièresque comic oddity than as a pressing social problem:

> Our *collèges* ... indiscriminately open to all, do nothing but pour out to the streets of Paris a stream of useless subjects who, with their hollow education, go on to corrupt any position where they manage to land. This plague keeps growing, and it threatens society with a flood of layabouts and do-nothings. ... it would be time to close these *collèges*, if the government does not want the next generation of Parisians to be made up of nothing but blabbers, libertines, and half-doctors, of that whole race who spend the last of their father's money loitering at concerts, cafés, and houses of ill repute ... The petit bourgeois should be required to give their sons a trade, instead of sending them to sit on school benches ... This gangrene is spreading among the petite bourgeoisie: the disease is worsening, and the time has come to apply a serious remedy.[52]

Mercier's screed is strikingly similar to the alarmed descriptions of a swelling, unproductive, and restless mass of "intellectual proletariat" that would repeatedly be made a century later, including in front of the Ribot commission on secondary school reform.[53] In his 1885 *La Question du latin*, Raoul Frary makes explicit the link between classical education, economic unproductivity, and what he calls "the increasingly menacing invasion of these *bacheliers*":

> Classical education fails to prepare young Frenchmen for any productive career ... it turns them into *déclassés* ... by launching them into the world to earn a living with a degree in their pocket, a head full of Latin and nothing else. The government ... causes society a great harm by pushing an ever-growing number of Frenchmen toward unproductive careers. These young men could have made themselves useful ... if they had been given a less literary education.[54]

Here again, the polemist might as well be writing about Jacques Vingtras; Vallès's *Bachelier*, whose misfortunes appeared in print a mere four years before Frary's tract, wholly embodies this warning about the social pitfalls of classical education.

The threat of the *déclassé* to the economic and political order is not only linked to his unproductivity, but also to the revolutionary values circulated in his wide readings. In *L'Enfant*, Vallès contrasts Jacques's oppressive schoolbooks – above all his Latin grammar – with other types of reading presented as enjoyable and liberating.[55] First come a series of seafaring and adventure novels, chief among them *Robinson Crusoe*;[56] later, Jacques breathlessly discovers the history of the French Revolution:

> This time, it was no longer Latin. They were saying: we're starving! We want to be free! ... I leapt from a dead world into a world of the living. – The history I now devour is no longer a story of gods, kings or saints ... it's the story of Pierre and Jean, of Mathurine and Florimond, the story of my country, of my village ... I hear about the people, about citizens, saying *Liberté* instead of *Libertas*.[57]

The antithesis can appear clear-cut: one set of books represents a world that is dead, distant, irreducibly foreign, while the other is alive, close, and strikingly familiar. Yet two observations trouble the dichotomy. First, the opposition is uncannily symmetrical, pitting book against book.[58] Though they may appear closer or more relatable, the people and events described in the modern books are no more actually present than those represented in the Latin ones. Jacques imagines he has found an escape from the deadening reach of the printed word, yet his choice of more books suggests that there can be, for him, no true escape. Second, *Liberté* and *Libertas* are anything but unambiguously dissimilar: their clear etymological filiation short-circuits the opposition.

In *Le Bachelier*, Jacques comes to terms with the strange historical link between the Latin books he detests and the revolutionary books he loves. The shock of this realization is cloaked in his characteristic irony,[59] as he parodies the bombastic discourse that circulates among the group of political agitators he has recently joined: "1793, THE APEX OF HISTORY; THE NATIONAL CONVENTION, AN ILIAD; OUR FATHERS, SUCH GIANTS."[60] When he is asked to contribute an article for a newspaper they plan to launch, he suggests a panegyric to the fallen heroes of the Revolution – collapsing a morbid classical form onto what should have been, according to the binary set up in *L'Enfant*, its opposite, a vividly modern subject. His proposed title, "Revolutionary Tombs,"[61] neatly conflates the two elements of the dichotomy, the distant world of dead forms and the still-close real life of 1789 and 1793. Confounded by the contradiction, Jacques realizes that he is unable to write about the topic that most stirs his heart without drawing on his loathed classical training:

> I was always repeating the same thing, every time I invoked the dead ... And I quoted Latin phrases ... Sparta, Rome, Athens ... I used to joke about it at school, I thought it was useless and stupid, the ancient republics, Greek and Roman! ... Now I see what it's good for. You can't write for republican newspapers without knowing your Plutarch through and through.[62]

Even more startlingly, he comes to see that the men who shaped the Revolution were themselves aping, in their discursive postures, models from the ancient world:

> Is there a single page by ... our Jacobin writers that doesn't mention Hannibal, Fabricius, Aristogeiton? ... We can't do without. It would be rude not to tell the men of 1793 that they resemble the great men of our schoolbooks.[63]

What was once imagined as a black-and-white opposition between deadening Latin manuals and vivid histories of the Revolution is thus revealed to be a continuum, a hall of mirrors. Jacques finds himself utterly unable to write his article.

3) Problematic Historical Models

The study of Latin had specific political implications in the emergent Third Republic: advocates of classical education held up the Roman model as historically essential to the formation of proper republican citizens. What seemed self-evident under a republic had been flagged as a hazardous contradiction a century earlier, under a monarchy, by critics like Mercier. Just as he had described the rising tide of restless, unproductive Latinists already flooding the streets of Paris in 1781, Mercier noted the perplexing fact that the *collèges* of the Ancien Régime dispensed a classical education that glorified republican, even regicidal, values: "Studying the Latin language results in a certain taste for republics: students find themselves wanting to revive the one whose vast and glorious history they read ... they hear about the senate, about the freedom and dignity of the Roman people, its victories, the righteous murder of Caesar ... yet it is under a monarchy that that these young men are perpetually exposed to such foreign ideas."[64] In the wake of the Revolution, commentators would make similar observations. Chateaubriand, in his 1797 *Essai sur les révolutions*, stated that "our Revolution was produced in part by men of letters who, being citizens of Rome and Athens more than of their own country, sought to bring Europe back to the values of Antiquity."[65] Half a century later, the link between revolutionary beliefs and the heavily Latin curriculum of French secondary education was brought up again: in a tract provocatively titled *Baccalauréat et socialisme* (published in 1850, under the short-lived Second Republic), Frédéric Bastiat lambasts the enduring institution of the classical curriculum as the ideological breeding ground of the bloody events of 1848: "The subversive doctrines called socialism and communism are the result of classical education, whether dispensed by the church or the university ... Is there any doubt that these teachings have spread [in the public opinion] a slew of false ideas, brutal sentiments, subversive utopias, and fatal experiments?"[66] Some critiques were more nuanced, and suggested that the revolutionary legacy of classical education has more to do with potent rhetoric than with clearly defined political ideas.[67] Volney, in his *Leçons d'histoire* (1795), asserted that Latin texts had contributed to recent revolutionary events as subversive conveyors of mere imitative enthusiasm: "Those classical books, the works of these famed poets, orators, and historians, indiscriminately placed in the hands of young people ... offer them certain men, certain actions as models, and ignite in them a natural desire for imitation ... yet, being beyond their capacity to understand, these books only manage to sway them with the blind sentiment known as enthusiasm."[68] The distinction between actual comprehension and blind sentiment is important, and would be taken up again by opponents of classical education in the second half of the nineteenth century.

Nineteenth-century proponents of Latin recognized that its study did not provide much in the way of "concrete knowledge" but defended it as a useful form of mental "gymnastics" that prepared boys attending secondary school for the future challenges of advanced learning.[69] Critics like Frary responded that Latin deadened students' natural intellectual curiosity, fostering mindless imitation instead.[70] Opponents also linked Latin to the violent excesses of revolutionary movements, a sensitive subject in the wake of the 1871 Commune. Frary argued that classical education as it was practised in French *lycées* – the superficial study and imitation of fragmented or apocryphal texts, emphasizing the flowers of rhetoric over any substantial engagement with ideas – did not provide adequate democratic models, but instead fostered intellectually deleterious habits of piecemeal mimicry and discursive hyperbole.[71] Michel Bréal, cited by Frary as an important forerunner, warned of this as a social danger in his 1872 treatise: "Sixteen-year-olds are taught to consider the subject as an ancillary matter, and to place literary merit above the substance of ideas ... [W]hen the whole youth of a country is raised with this exclusive preoccupation with style, the soul and the moral direction of the nation are in danger."[72] In *Le Bachelier* and *L'Insurgé*, Jacques consistently uses classical tropes in his polemical journalism and his incendiary political speeches, confirming the potency of this menace.[73] Yet Vallès also shows how Jacques struggles deeply with his paradoxical reliance on classical references and models.

In a review from 1864, Vallès decries this very flaw in the recently republished *Memoirs* of Manon Roland, an important figure of the revolutionary Girondin party who was guillotined in 1793. Madame Roland, for Vallès, was a "beautiful and sad victim of Antiquity," an eighteenth-century "Emma Bovary" who modelled her marital life and her political convictions on classical models: she could only have chosen her much older husband, for instance, because she saw him as "a rough Spartan or an old Roman."[74] This imitative delusion, he goes on to observe, was endemic among revolutionaries. Echoing Mercier, Chateaubriand, and Bastiat, he writes:

> The republican eighteenth century only wanted to mimic Antiquity. It sacrificed ideas and men to this fixation! The orators and proconsuls of that dark, tormented period drew inspiration from Plutarch and cited Tacitus, without knowing that what Tacitus and Plutarch called liberty was merely the fierce selfishness of the homeland.[75]

Further damning her, Vallès accuses Madame Roland of having written her memoirs under the spell of Rousseau. Rather than as a token of autobiographical honesty or literary daring, he reads her mention of a mild sexual incident as a slavish imitation of the *Confessions*.

> You think her spontaneous and free, that woman writing her confessions? Not so: she is but an overzealous student, who seeks to ape Rousseau with these immature audacities ... Her obsession surfaces in many places, and betrays itself visibly and surely ... Enough about her writings: *o imitatores, servus pecus*! She was an imitator, nothing more. You will see that her politics were no different.[76]

Remarkably, Vallès's reproof of Madame Roland's imitative mania is shot through with classical references, starting with "O imitators, you slavish herd," a quotation of Horace's *Epistles*.[77] He refers uncomfortably to other childhood scenes from her *Memoirs* involving a chamber pot or a spanking at the hands of her father, using a classically flavoured periphrasis ("non-sacred vase") and a learned reference to the Spartan commander

Eurybiades.[78] His emphasis on the influence of Rousseau is equally striking: a decade later, Vallès would go on to write *L'Enfant*, which opens with the scene of Jacques being unjustly beaten, a clear echo of the famous scene in Book I of the *Confessions*.[79] Even his faint praise of the moments where Madame Roland forgets her models – "when she forgets history and becomes herself again, which is to say simple and natural, we are moved to feel attachment and almost admiration"[80] – is positively Rousseauian in its privileging of nature and simplicity over learned affectation. What Vallès singles out and castigates in Madame Roland, then, seems to be his own persistent struggle with influence.

4) The Struggle for Authenticity

Recent scholarship and nineteenth-century readers both note a paradox: Vallès constantly uses classical tropes and allusions to attack the institution of classical education. A striking and concise example appears in an 1882 article on the dangers of the university: "I said it yesterday, I say it today, I will say it tomorrow. *Delenda Carthago*. The Carthage of today is that city of prigs whose fortress is the Sorbonne."[81] In his review of *L'Insurgé* in 1886, the young Maurice Barrès put it succinctly: "[Vallès], whose genius is made of the best of Antiquity, enjoys ridiculing it like no other."[82] Readers can hardly fail to note, for instance, the self-conscious allusion to mythology in very first lines of *Le Bachelier*:

> I have an education. "You are now armed for the struggle," my teacher tells me as he bids me farewell. "He who triumphs at the *collège* enters his career as a conqueror." What career? ... Entering a career means: to march forward in the path of life; to place yourself, like Hercules, at the crossroads. *Like Hercules at the crossroads!* I haven't forgotten my mythology. Come on! That's at least something.[83]

Multiple ironies are at work here: the new *bachelier* enters life "armed" with nothing but a multifarious knowledge of classical references and rhetoric, including the one he deploys to describe his situation; this knowledge is about as useful in the modern struggle for life as he himself resembles Hercules, which is clearly not much at all. The self-mocking repetition of the comparison reveals an awareness of its comical inadequacy. Passages in this vein show that Vallès, in composing and revising the trilogy, was quite mindful of the paradoxical presence of classical tropes in his prose. In a detailed study of his "contradictory attitude" towards antiquity, Corrine Saminadayar-Perrin demonstrates,[84] by comparing the versions of the three novels revised as volumes with their earlier incarnations as newspaper articles or serials, that Vallès actively sought to remove classical references from the trilogy as he reworked it for publication in book form.[85] "This enormous task of eradication," she writes, "shows the extent to which the facile effects of conventional rhetoric characterize Vallès's spontaneous writing."[86] For the author of *Le Bachelier*, spontaneity means the opposite of authenticity, since what inevitably first bursts onto the page is the product of secondary education – ancient allusions, memorized fragments, hollow rhetoric. The desire for a textual voice that would be true to his deeper self, "which is to say simple and natural" (as Vallès characterized the few passages he admired in Madame Roland), becomes a treacherous process of extirpation from formative influences though self-editing and negation.

Two complementary scenes from the trilogy illustrate the troubling facility with which Vallès's autobiographical double uses disparate and decontextualized elements of classical culture to compose his own texts – troubling because these resulting texts, as he is the first to admit, can hardly be called his "own." Required to write a composition in Latin verse, the young Jacques cobbles together fragments from his various schoolbooks, with little regard for accuracy or originality:

> I steal left and right, I pick up stray words [rejets][87] in the corners of books. Sometimes I'm even dishonest. I need an epithet: so what if that means sacrificing the truth! I open the dictionary and choose a word that fits, even if it means the opposite of what I wanted to say.[88]

Expecting to be punished for this transgression, Jacques confesses to his teacher, who instead laughs it off. The teacher's answer gives the dietary metaphor that runs through *L'Enfant*[89] a rather nauseating twist: "that's the only reason you're in school, to chew and chew again on what has already been chewed by others!"[90] Even more disconcertingly, Jacques discovers that his father, the would-be paterfamilias, proceeds no differently as he prepares for the *agrégation*, the competitive examination for secondary school teaching positions.[91] The young narrator thus realizes that Latinists of every stripe, from student to father to teacher, partake in a chain of near-mindless copying, from which any trace of true meaning has disappeared. Opponents of classical education had long deplored that the practice of Latin compositions led students to approach ancient texts only superficially, as repositories of material to be copied and reassembled.[92] Jules Simon, in his 1874 essay *La Réforme de l'enseignement secondaire*, pondered the implications of this practice on young people's capacity for authentic expression:

> Are we truly developing young men's imagination, when we ask them to compose Latin verses? Are we not merely developing their memory instead? Are their verses anything but mere pastiche? What they call finding an

> idea – is it not instead finding a half-line, and indeed finding it ready-made in their Latin dictionary? And what is this type of imagination, if it has nothing to do with taste or with common sense, and consists instead in assembling the most verses on a given topic, utterly dispassionately, without including any idea or emotion?[93]

In this description of a perverted and ill-named faculty of imagination, the images of language, pieced together from anthologized fragments, exist in a strange state of living death, detached from ideas and emotions. In some ways the opposite of the potential for excessive and irrational sentiment (the "blind enthusiasm" decried by Volney), the cynical detachment described by Jules Simon is the flip side of a same threat: both imply a loss of the supposedly natural, sensible, authentic self, in the face of a takeover of the text.

In *Le Bachelier*, as we have seen, the adult Jacques struggles with a near inability to write without regurgitating the dead images and rhetoric he absorbed in school. Vallès's manuscript depicts a moment of despair as he tries to find comfort in the possibility of writing a book:

> I pushed my suffering back inside me, I tried to drown it in the idea of writing a book ... But I stumbled against the stupidities of the studies [*bachellerie*] that had filled my head with Greek ... Before writing a book like you would load a cannon, you have to clear the baggage that's in the way ... My book is in my heart, not on the page. What's the use! There's no field of reeds where I could scream my rage![94]

Jacques's fantasy is to write a book that would be pure self-expression, liberated from all past books, an explosive book where, freed from the baggage of his literary education, he would have a direct conduit from his heart to the page. "One must be true to one's self, and throw away all books," Vallès had written about Madame Roland in 1864.[95] But the obstacle remains: the *bachelier* cannot undo his *bachellerie*. There is no thicket of reeds, he writes, to which he could entrust his despair – symptomatically slipping into an erudite reference to the story of Midas, as recounted in Ovid's *Metamorphoses*.[96] King Midas, freed from his famous curse, goes on to anger Apollo, who gives him donkey ears in retribution. Midas attempts to hide his animal ears under a turban, but his barber discovers his secret and is unable to keep it. The barber digs a hole in a field, whispers the secret into the ground, and covers it up; later, a patch of reeds grows where the hole was, and the secret is heard whenever the wind blows through it. Like Midas and his golden touch, everything Jacques touches turns to Greek and Latin – even this attempt to express his rage at the deadening effect of his classical education. For him, unlike the mythical king, there can be no cure. As he did with other similar slip-ups, Vallès cut the scene from the serialized and book versions of *Le Bachelier*.

The Statue of Jean-Jacques Rousseau

In 1878 (the year *L'Enfant* appeared as a serial) a proposal for a statue of Rousseau was presented at the Paris municipal council. The project stalled under opposition from the political right – resistant to any glorification of the Revolution, and, by association, the recent Commune – but in 1885 (the year of Vallès's death) a commission was formed that led to a statue being erected on the Place du Panthéon and unveiled on 3 February 1889.[97] The inscription reads, on the left side of the base: "to the author of *Émile* and *The Social Contract.*"[98] It would be an exaggeration to state, as John Grand-Carteret did in his collection of homages to Rousseau published the following year, that "All our programs of education and teaching are laid out in *Émile.*"[99] Rousseau's treatise recounting the idealized mentoring, at an almost complete remove from the world, of a single boy who happens to be both orphaned and wealthy, is in no way a straightforward program for the education of the masses across the nation.[100] Yet its influence on the school reforms undertaken under the Revolution and throughout the nineteenth century has been well documented.[101] Following the defeat of 1870, critics of the French school system noted that it had been in Germany, rather than in France, that Rousseau's ideas on education had taken root, while France still clung to older teaching methods inherited from the Ancien Régime and the clergy.[102] Vallès – who, as many have noted, was much more at ease as an unrelenting critic of the French education system across its transformations than as champion of proposals for reform[103] – was not indifferent to these ideas.

One of the few times Vallès ventured to make educational proposals, in a fiery article from 1882, the pedagogical revolution he envisioned turned out to be singularly Rousseauian:

> If our educational system were renewed and made modern, students could learn the sciences without effort, at the pace of their journey through life ... We would only have to set loose, in the countryside, in gardens, in forges, in hospitals, all those young people we keep imprisoned, chained to books that speak only of the dead, under the roofs of sad and noxious institutions.[104]

Vallès's fantasy of an education that would wrest young people away from books and send them instead into nature and traditional workplaces takes a page from *Émile*, where we read that "reading is the plague of childhood."

"Therefore, I closed all books. There is but one left open in front of me: the book of nature," Rousseau goes on to write. He prescribes that Émile should learn a manual trade, since constant sedentary study debilitates the body.[105] He also takes a stand against teaching Greek and Latin to children before they are twelve or even fifteen, arguing – as Mercier, Jules Simon, Vallès, and Raoul Frary would after him – that young students are not actually taught to read and appreciate classical languages, but instead to memorize denatured fragments that they then reassemble in perfunctory imitations:

> Since the everyday use of these languages has long been lost, we limit ourselves to imitating what we find written in books, and we call it speaking Greek or Latin. That is the level of teachers – imagine their students! No sooner have they memorized the most basic elements, while understanding absolutely nothing, than they are taught ... to stitch together as prose a few sentences from Cicero, and as verse some fragments of Virgil.[106]

Yet Rousseau's relationship to classical texts in *Émile*, no less than Vallès's in the trilogy, is fraught with paradox. Once Émile becomes an adolescent in Book IV, his mentor decrees that he should learn to read the likes of Demosthenes and Cicero.[107] More importantly, all of Book V is structured around an imitative relationship to a classical text, or rather, to a seventeenth-century adaptation of a classical text, Fénelon's *Les Aventures de Télémaque* (1699), which draws on Homer's *Odyssey* to stage the pedagogical journey of Odysseus's son Telemachus and his tutor, Mentor. When Émile meets Sophie, the young woman his preceptor Jean-Jacques has selected as his future mate, references to Fénelon's novel abound. Sophie, who has read *Télémaque*, is enamoured with the fictional character, and progressively comes to see Émile as that character's real-life double; Émile himself compliments her family's hospitality with a reference to Homer; Sophie's father compares Jean-Jacques to the character Mentor; and the preceptor compares Sophie to Eucharis, one of Calypso's nymphs who tempts Telemachus as her mistress had tempted Odysseus.[108] Once introduced, the classical paradigm and its compelling story of two competing passionate attachments (Mentor and Telemachus, Telemachus and Eucharis) comes to dominate the chapter, to the point that the narrative voice makes the peculiar admission, "I have led myself astray."[109]

As he had accused Madame Roland of aping the author of the *Confessions*, Vallès criticizes Rousseau, in *Le Bachelier*, for imitating classical authors: "He never laughs, that Rousseau, he's stuck-up, teary-eyed; his writing is overblown instead of coming from the heart; he perorates for the Romans, as we used to have to do in our homework ... He reeks of the *collège*."[110] In doing so, he echoes essayists from Volney to Bastiat,[111] who earlier observed, as we have seen, that the discourse of the forerunners and actors of the Revolution – the ideas and values it put forward, but in particular the rhetoric it deployed – was heavily indebted to classical education. As was the case with his reproof of Madame Roland, Vallès's disparagement of Rousseau singles out the very struggle that traverses and defines his own writing. The author of *Le Bachelier*, in his rush to denigrate his eighteenth-century predecessors as mindless or inauthentic imitators of the ancients (and, in the case of Madame Roland, of each other), reveals the depth of his anxiety over this question in his own work.

A novel published twelve years after *L'Insurgé*, L. Achille's *Âme neuve* (New soul, 1898), stages a Rousseauian education in the late nineteenth century. Rousseau is never mentioned, but his educational prescriptions permeate the narrative, albeit in simplified form. Like Émile, Yves, the young protagonist, is both orphaned and rich; he is raised on a secluded provincial estate by a watchful tutor, his grandfather. In a crucial early scene, the grandfather decrees that Yves will not be taught how to read:

> I heard the brave manservant tell grandpapa:
>
> – If he knew how to read, he could pass the time, he would find distractions, discover interests ...
>
> Before he could even finish, grandpapa struck him silent with a commanding look.
>
> – Quiet, he said gravely, quiet, do you hear? Reading! ... I do not want him to learn to read ... It would bring him sorrow, as it has brought me, as it has brought other men ... [...]
>
> I naïvely asked my grandfather whether reading was a game.
>
> – No, my child, grandpapa answered dolefully. It is something men invented, and it is largely because they know how to read that they are vicious and cruel.
>
> – In that case, I said, I do not want to learn it.[112]

Sheltered from the deleterious influence of reading, Yves leads an idyllic childhood, free to roam in the woods of the family domain and practise every outdoor activity from horseback riding to ice skating. When he reaches the age of seventeen, disaster strikes after his athletic physique catches the eye of an impressionable teenage girl ("Yves? The most handsome adolescent a woman could dream of! That warrior's countenance, that height, those muscles ...").[113] The girl kills herself when he innocently rejects her advances; around the same time, his grandfather passes away. Yves soon leaves for Paris where he is watched over by the grandfather's faithful manservant, who proves to be no match for the task. A series of misadventures ensue, from Yves causing a commotion when he goes for a nude swim in the Seine, to an imbroglio with a prostitute that leads him to hire the services of a lawyer. The lawyer takes him on a civilizing tour of Paris (not unlike the tour offered to the foreign prince in Paul Brulat's *Nouveau Candide* of 1902), teaches him to read, and shows him the ways of the world – but ends up betraying him by marrying the woman Yves loves. The blow is fatal, and Yves dies in a sanatorium. The latter-day Émile's ignorance of cultural codes proves to be just as lethal[114] as the *bachelier*'s excess of culture; if books smother the child's, and later the adult's, authenticity under the deadening burden of influence ("the baggage that's in the way," according to Vallès),[115] authenticity alone appears no more viable. Readers and writers are left to negotiate some middle measure between unfettered nature and mindless imitation.

4 Bourget, the Chambige Affair, and the Queer Seductions of the Novel

That sigh you heard is but a citation,
– the woman you held against your heart, a volume.

Bourget, *Physiologie de l'amour moderne*[1]

On 25 January 1888, in Sidi-Mabrouk, near the Algerian city of Constantine, Henri Chambige, a twenty-two-year-old aspiring writer who had studied in Paris, shot and killed Magdeleine Grille, the wife of a railroad engineer and a mother of two, before firing into his own mouth – and failing to kill himself. Two bullets were found in Madame Grille's skull, and two others pierced his cheek, leaving but a minor wound. Because of Chambige's connection to Parisian letters, what could have remained a negligible incident in a distant colonial town became one of the year's most widely commented stories in France. By early November, in the days leading up to the murder trial, newspapers were breathlessly reporting on what had become "a famous case."[2] In the courtroom as in the press, the events at Sidi-Mabrouk gave rise not only to conflicting, sensational interpretations – was the incident a tragic, half-missed double suicide, or a calculated rape and murder cynically masquerading as a lovers' death pact? – but to a broader debate about a rising generation of disaffected, amoral young men and the potential responsibility of "so-called decadent" contemporary literature.[3] After the trial concluded, *l'affaire Chambige* raged on. While critics like Anatole France and Ferdinand Brunetière sparred over its weighty moral and social implications, the affair inspired no fewer than four novels,[4] among them Paul Bourget's *Le Disciple* (1889), which transformed its author's literary standing and remains his most famous work.[5]

Even before the Chambige trial began in Constantine, details of the case were recounted for the Parisian reading public through a frame laden with literary references. A three-part article in *Le Figaro* opens with two comparisons, to an 1838 case in which a young doctor and his mistress attempted suicide after reading George Sand's *Indiana* (1832), and to a poem by Alfred de Vigny, "Les Amants de Montmorency" (1830), about a couple who elope to the woods and kill themselves after three days. What took place in Sidi-Mabrouk, the article promises, is "even more novelistic [romanesque] and more poignant."[6] During the trial and its aftermath, Chambige was made to embody *le romanesque*, a highly charged and peculiarly recurrent term in discussions of the case both in and outside the courtroom. Through Chambige, the novelistic was put on trial – by prosecutors claiming to protect the familial and social order, and by critics eager to rescue French letters from what they described as a slide into decadent excess and imitative delusion. In its conflation of the fictional (decried as inauthentic, artificial, false) and of perilous seductions (including the implied possibility of same-sex attachments), the Chambige affair prefigured the Wilde trials of 1895, where *The Picture of Dorian Gray* was cited as evidence of the promotion of "sodomitical and unnatural habits, tastes and practices."[7] The affair's most celebrated commentator, Bourget, knew Wilde; the two had met in Paris in 1883, and they saw each other "frequently" that year, according to one source.[8] Their starkly differing fates in the years that followed call attention to all that Bourget publically and symbolically renounced at the time of the affair, including his infatuation with the *romanesque*.

Novelistic Cases

Romanesque is a qualifying adjective (for instance, a *romanesque* turn of events), but unlike "novelistic" or "novelesque" in English, it is sometimes used as an adjectival noun. One can use it with a definite article – *le romanesque* – to name the quality that a real-life situation shares with events usually found in novels: unlikely coincidences, surprising reversals, heart-tugging denouements. Significantly for our purposes, the term can also be used with an indefinite article – *un romanesque* – to name a real-life character type, someone whose words or actions suggest they expect their own life to unfold as a series of novelistic occurrences. *Le romanesque*, the novelistic quality of an event, is not quite the opposite of the verisimilar or the true, since such an event is an occurrence that seems unlikely, but actually happened, like the incident at Sidi-Mabrouk. Rather, *le romanesque* exists in tension with verisimilitude: that which is *romanesque* is neither fully impossible nor entirely likely. Because the word denotes a grey area between reality and fiction, it can name moments of slippage or confusion between the two – or people who are prone to such confusions. As with much discourse about reading and the consumption of fiction, the term is linked to a question of dosage: a little *romanesque* in real life (an unexpected twist of fate, a tragic scene) can be touching, but too much of it (expecting such occurrences to happen, or actively setting them up, the hallmarks of *un romanesque*) is culturally coded as dangerous.

Examples listed in Littré's *Dictionnaire de la langue française* of the 1870s highlight the long-standing implicit association of the *romanesque* with falseness, sentimentality, and femininity. The entry cites Rousseau's *Dialogues* (1777), "he dreamt up *romanesque* and false ideas about men and society, of which no number of disastrous experiences were able to cure him," and Madame de Staël's *Corinne* (1807), "women enjoy sadness, as long as it is properly *romanesque*."[9] The dissociation of the novel as a genre from the conventionally negative, feminine connotations of the *romanesque* was a key preoccupation for many male novelists over the course of the nineteenth century.[10] In an 1875 essay, for instance, Zola lauded Flaubert as a precursor to a new genre of scientific, non-*romanesque* novel: "the first characteristic of the Naturalist novel, of which *Madame Bovary* is the originator, is the precise depiction of life, the absence of any *romanesque*."[11] Claiming to excise the novelistic from the novel was a way of laying claim to a writerly authority coded as rational, detached, and masculine, based on observation rather than imagination;[12] the "experimental" novel described by Zola was purportedly free of the fanciful situations and excessive sentimentality culturally associated with older or lower-brow novels, especially novels written by or perceived as written for women. Although Bourget was a rival of the Naturalist school, he employed a similar strategy. As we have seen, he gave a career-defining speech lauding precisely this renunciation of the trappings of the novel in the non-fictional works of Flaubert's friend Maxime Du Camp, his predecessor in seat 33 at the Académie française, when he was elected in 1894.[13] This induction, at the young age of forty-one, capped a remarkable transformation in Bourget's literary persona.

Over the course of the 1880s, Bourget had emerged as an influential critic, and published four relatively well-received novels. A practitioner of what would be dubbed the "psychological novel" or "novel of analysis" (in opposition to the Naturalist novel, which in the eyes of its detractors was exceedingly concerned with scabrous descriptions of plebeians and degenerates), his output consisted mostly of intricately detailed stories of adultery and similar temptations of the Parisian upper bourgeoisie. He frequented literary circles and aristocratic salons; his essays earned him something of a following among students, while his risqué yet tasteful fiction made him a fashionable novelist among taste-making *salonnières* like the Princesse Mathilde (Napoleon's niece) and Geneviève Straus (who would go on to become an important correspondent for Proust).[14] Bourget was also a notable proponent of the critical and popular resurgence of Stendhal in the 1880s, decades after the novelist's death in 1842: his essay on Stendhal, first published in 1883 and included in the first series his *Essais de psychologie contemporaine*, was reprinted as a preface for *Le Rouge et le Noir* in 1886.[15] Bourget's reputation as a refined analyst of the tortured minds of *romanesque*, Stendhalesque protagonists – such as bookish students and adulterous bourgeois women – made him a prime target for those who would seek to incriminate contemporary writers in the Chambige affair.

Henri Chambige, born in colonial Algeria on 13 May 1865, had attended school in Bordeaux before he gravitated to the student and literary milieus of the Parisian Left Bank.[16] He first met Magdeleine Grille (née Jackson), eight years his senior, on a visit to his family in 1886; in the following months, he was a frequent guest in her home. While according to him they came to share a desperate, all-consuming passion, her husband met this assertion with stern disbelief, and testified he was certain that Chambige's affections were never returned. In defending his late wife's honour, Monsieur Grille emphatically described her as "the most pure, naïve, and honest woman ... she was *anti-romanesque*, ignorant of evil ... a model mother and wife." How could such a woman, he argued, have given in to the novelistic fancy of a doomed affair? By contrast, Chambige according to him was "*romanesque*, with a gloomy disposition."[17] The moral polarity between what is *romanesque* (seduction, adultery, suicide) and the opposite (purity, honesty, simplicity) is overlaid, in the journalistic commentary that frames various accounts of the trial, with a marked physical contrast: while Chambige is "thin ... pale, and seems profoundly sad," Monsieur Grille is described as "tall, strong [and] serious."[18] These analogous moral and physical characterizations are combined, in Monsieur Grille's testimony, through a further contrast between Chambige's rarefied life of the mind and the shared pursuits of "honest folk" such as the Grilles: "physical exercise," "working together," "loving their children." For this upstanding and unsuspecting husband, Chambige was an "interesting" guest to have at dinner, but his "weak and sickly" constitution inspired pity rather than masculine rivalry.[19] Chambige's version of events (related in a declaration he composed for his defence, from which *Le Figaro* published long excerpts) also emphasized the polarity between him and the manly Monsieur Grille. Claiming to paraphrase his beloved Magdeleine, he explained that his own lack of virility had actually been key to his romantic success: "instead of Grille, that Hercules, she loved me, because I was *a very sweet weakling*" (original emphasis).[20] They initially bonded over a shared experience of loss, as he was grieving the sudden death of his sister, and she had just lost a young son. A bereaved weakling's love for his dead sister, a mother's love for a lost child: it was in this highly feminized "community of sorrow," over the course of many tear-filled scenes, that their transgressive passion would come to grow.[21] Entrance to the family home and access to the married Madame Grille were granted to Chambige because of his effete physicality and sentimental temperament. Neither a strong male nor physically female, he never seemed a menace to familial and marital unity. Monsieur Grille's blindness to the sexual threat posed by the young student corresponded precisely with his lack of appreciation for literature – indeed Chambige faulted him for having indulged in "that innocuous habit of men of science, which is to scoff at poets."[22]

A bookish young man is introduced into a bourgeois family, seduces the slightly older married woman, and eventually stands accused of her murder: the outline of the Chambige case likely appeared familiar to readers of *Le Figaro*, as it bears close resemblance to the plot of Stendhal's *Le Rouge et le Noir* (1830). Many journalists drew links between the case and the famous novel, for instance dubbing Chambige "the Julien Sorel of the *brasserie*."[23] The sensational appeal and lasting resonance of the case for Parisian readers and writers – in other words, its very readability – owed much to this connection. The basic narrative canvas of Stendhal's novel was itself taken from a real-life criminal case, the Berthet trial of 1827, which the novelist likely followed in the newly founded *Gazette des tribunaux*,[24] the same periodical that published daily accounts of the Chambige case six decades later. In July 1827, Antoine Berthet, age twenty-five, fired two shots on Madame Michoud, a forty-one-year-old bourgeois wife and mother, in the middle of a crowded small-town church near Grenoble, before turning his weapon on himself. Both perpetrator and victim survived their wounds, and Berthet was tried for attempted murder. The son of a blacksmith, Berthet had been a seminary student from 1818 to 1822, when ill health forced him to withdraw. Later that year, the Michouds hired him as a live-in preceptor for their children, but in 1823 he was let go due to suspicions that he had become Madame Michoud's lover. The *Gazette*'s unsigned articles described him as "slender, with a delicate complexion," and went on to state that "a frail constitution, little disposed to physical labour, an intelligence higher than his position, a taste for advanced study displayed early on" had set him apart from his working-class peers.[25] Thus characterized, Berthet constituted a double threat: his potential for overstepping his social position, coupled with his apparent powers of seduction, disrupted both the class order and the bourgeois family as embodied by Madame Michoud, who according to the *Gazette* had enjoyed an "intact reputation" prior to meeting him. The prosecution latched on to these fears by depicting him as a gifted young man whose unusual intelligence made him a "perverse soul," unable to control his own passions yet capable of provoking and manipulating them in others.[26] Berthet was found guilty, and executed on 23 February 1828.

Le Rouge et le Noir's Julien Sorel inherits, among other traits, Berthet's delicate complexion, and it is the very first thing the married Madame de Rênal notices about him. The pair's initial meeting also happens to be marked by the first appearance of the word *romanesque* in the novel:[27] "The young peasant's complexion was so pale, his eyes were so sweet, that Madame de Rênal's slightly *romanesque* mind first imagined he might be a young girl in disguise."[28] A few pages later, the narrator states that "Julien's extreme beauty" and "the feminine shape of his features" ensure that Madame de Rênal does not see him as a menace to her honour, and therefore paradoxically allows herself to develop a fondness for him: "the masculine character usually thought to be essential to a man's beauty would have scared her."[29] Such descriptions of Madame de Rênal's lack of fear of Julien echo the gender ambiguity that traverses courtroom retellings of Chambige's meeting with Madame Grille; Stendhal's narrator, however, provides a number of indications (such as the ironic understatement "slightly *romanesque*") that Madame de Rênal's initial impression of Julien is suffused with denegation[30] regarding both the possibility of female same-sex attraction and her own taste for the novelistic. We read, for instance, that she does not conceive of her growing attachment to Julien as a nascent love since "she regarded as an exception, something completely against nature, love as she had found it described in the very small number of novels upon which chance had made her lay her eyes." As the narrator ironically protests her "ignorance" and that she remains "perfectly happy" in her marriage (even as she becomes "constantly occupied with Julien"),[31] we understand that she has succumbed to the very thing she denies knowing or being attracted to: novelistic love.

As would be the case for Chambige, Julien's amorous success is due to stealth. Because Julien appears unthreateningly feminine, and because Madame de Rênal views her existence as unquestionably unnovelistic, he is allowed into it, and eventually, into her bed. Stendhal's narrator plays further with the question of the normal and the literary when he contrasts the "natural" development of their affair to how it might have played out in Paris:

> In Paris, Julien's position with Madame de Rênal would have soon been simplified; but in Paris, love is the child of novels. The young preceptor and his shy mistress would have found in three or four novels ... an explanation for their position. Novels would have outlined the roles they should play and given them a model to imitate ... [whereas] in a small town ... our poor young man ... sees each day a sincerely virtuous thirty-year-old woman, fully occupied with her children; never would she find in novels examples to follow. Everything unfolds more slowly, more gradually in the provinces, things are more natural.[32]

One of the many ironies at play as their adultery progresses is its dual characterization as both natural and against nature. Their love is purportedly free of novelistic influence, yet it echoes the gender-bending tropes of popular romances;[33] it is both the "natural" attraction of a young man to a slightly older mother figure (the affair is not without an Oedipal component) and the disruptive incursion, in a bourgeois marriage bed, of an unsuspected lower-class interloper. Like his real-life model Berthet – and like his later avatar Chambige – Julien is given access to a well-to-do family because of his unusual intellectual gifts; like them, his androgynous charm hides a threat to heterosexual marriage. But Julien is no run-of-the-mill seducer of married women. He has other, greater interests besides Madame de Rênal, among them his passionate love of books.

In Stendhal's novel, the intrusion of Julien's menacing difference – class discrepancy, gender ambiguity – under the guise of sameness is mirrored in the Rênal household's relationship to books. Early in his tenure as preceptor, Julien manages to persuade Monsieur de Rênal that his children would benefit from reading books on the history of the local gentry, that is, books about families like the Rênals. Such books are assumed to be safe and proper reading because they simply reflect the household. Julien adds that, since neither himself (a theology student) nor his employer (a reputable mayor) could be seen patronizing the local bookseller (whose politics are known to be subversive), they should have one of the servants take a subscription. His suggestion is entirely self-interested: the sight of the bookseller's wares has made his heart "palpitate," and he devises this stratagem to get his hands on them without arousing suspicion. In one of his first successful acts of hypocrisy (a major theme in the novel), Julien thunders against the dangers of novels, "the most odious of books," in order to overcome the mayor's hesitations. He proposes a strict guideline: "It should be specified that the servant should borrow no novels. Were they to enter the house, such dangerous books could corrupt Madame's housemaids, and the manservant as well."[34] Having set up this arrangement, he goes on to order books largely for his own consumption rather than the children's; later, he also has a friend send him novels he does not dare procure through the servant.

We are told that Julien prefers this illicit reading to Madame de Rênal's nightly company: "only at night did he dare open them ... often he would have preferred not to be interrupted by a visit."[35] Dangerous volumes thus serve as a metonym for the equally dangerous preceptor, whose perversity is such that he prefers reading to sleeping with his married mistress. Both Julien and his books make their way into the familial home under a false pretence of class similarity and moral harmlessness. Julien's overly zealous tirade condemning novels, when in fact he desires them intensely, echoes and casts further doubt on Madame de Rênal's earlier denial that what she feels for the preceptor has anything to do with such books. Was it truly unwittingly that this irreproachable wife managed to read a few novels "upon which chance had made her lay her eyes"? Can one truly say, given her eventual course of action with Julien, that she "in no way found in novels examples to follow"? The intrusion of the preceptor who loves books – and with him of everything *romanesque* – into her life and household brings about a confusion between the honest woman and the adulterous wife, between sincerity and deception, including self-deception. The odious danger represented by Julien and his books is not merely the danger of adultery (which simply amounts to a form of sameness: a married woman sleeps with another man), but instead the danger and seduction of deceit, of the confusion between truth and fiction. Madame de Rênal pretends not to have read books even as she models her amorous conduct after them; Julien pretends to condemn novels, and perhaps even pretends to love Madame de Rênal, all so that he can read more books. Like books, Julien circulates dangerously, surreptitiously, in disguise, between naïve virtuousness and hypocritical duplicity, across classes and professions (in an early scene, he changes clothes to take part in a military parade and a religious procession in quick succession), even across genders. Like novels, he blurs the line between truthful representation and unlikely imaginings. Armed with little cunning of his own but with a prodigious memory, he makes his way in the world by reciting the texts he has learned by heart. Although he has few heroic qualities, he ardently desires for his life to unfold as if he were the hero of a *roman* – which, in the central irony of Stendhal's novel, he is, and it will. The fictional double of a criminal, he is, as he shifts between social and ontological categories, a patron figure of the *romanesque*. He would go on to spawn his own imitators, even decades after Stendhal's death.

From Chambige to Bourget

While the Berthet trial of 1827 was only retrospectively read through a literary text,[36] almost every actor in the 1888 Chambige affair, at every stage of its unfolding – from the accused, to various witnesses and lawyers in the courtroom, to reporters and critics of different affiliations writing about the case, to Bourget, who would reframe the debate in *Le Disciple* the following year – read and commented on the case through a novelistic lens. Ludovic Trarieux, the lawyer representing Madame Grille's family, devised his closing argument around a portrayal of Chambige as a thoroughly literary entity. "This man is Werther, he is Antony, he is Julien Sorel, he is ... Raskolnikov," he thundered; "the man who murdered Magdeleine Grille belongs to this redoubtable lineage."[37] Trarieux dismissed the narrative presented by the defence – that Chambige and Madame Grille, modern-day star-crossed lovers, planned a double suicide as a desperate apotheosis to their doomed affair – as "*romanesque* fabrications and pure lies,"[38] and laid out a different version of their story. Chambige, according to Trarieux, was not a true Werther: he had no real intention of killing himself. Instead, he was a would-be Julien Sorel, who shot a married woman because she would not give in to his novelistic fantasies of adulterous passion.

Trarieux depicted the accused as a monstrous conflation of three literary roles – writer, actor, and character. Chambige was first "a perverse novelist [who] dreamt up a whole calumnious tale about the motives for his actions": he concocted a novelistic love story to hide the true events leading up to the murder.[39] As evidence, the lawyer paraphrased Chambige's unpublished manuscript for a novel, *La Dispersion infinitésimale du cœur* (The infinitesimal dispersion of the heart), in which the narrator professes all-encompassing scepticism, cynically observing that "all our emotions, even the sentiment of love, are but our imagination chasing illusions."[40] Seeing as his world-weary narrator does not believe in love, why would the jury, Trarieux asked, believe the author's version of the events at Sidi-Mabrouk as a love-mad suicide pact? Second, he was "a redoubtable actor," who managed to ingratiate himself with the innocent Madame Grille without arousing suspicion. Like Julien Sorel, he had trained himself to become a consummate "hypocrite."[41] Everything about him was tied to falsity: Trarieux argued that Chambige most likely forged the letters his lawyer presented as evidence of the couple's shared love ("not surprising, coming from a man who has mastered the art of writing novels"), and that he may have used hypnotic "suggestion" or a narcotic poison on his victim in the hours leading to her death.[42] Third, Chambige was a "sinister hero from some novel," a "wayward imagination"[43] who fancied himself the protagonist of a fin-de-siècle narrative, and ended up murderously blurring the line between Decadent literary aesthetics and reality. As the most damning evidence supporting this portrayal, the lawyer read at length from *Yvon d'Or*, a novel published earlier that year by Léopold Martin-Laya, who was a friend of the accused – "an intimate acquaintance," as Trarieux put it.[44] The novel was dedicated to Chambige, and he allegedly even appeared on its cover, in an illustration depicting a dissolute group of three men and one woman (see figure 1). "Look here," Trarieux told the jury, "in the middle of a group of artists, there stands, in an affected and pretentious pose ... the character named Yvon d'Or. Those are the traits, that is the countenance of Chambige."[45] The image, signed by Ernest Biéler (1863–1948),[46] indeed represents a standing male figure striking a theatrical pose, sinuously leaning on one hip, his head thrown back in either song or laughter; the figure's traits resemble depictions of Chambige that accompanied press coverage of the trial (see figure 2).

Figure 1. Ernest Biéler, cover for Léopold Martin-Laya, *Yvon d'Or* (Paris: Dentu, 1888). Private collection.

Figure 2. Henri Thiriat, "H. Chambige. D'après la photographie de M. J. Cougot, à Constantine." *L'Illustration*, 8 December 1888, 424. © *L'Illustration*. Used by permission.

Yvon d'Or, the fictional character, is a young man who, in the bohemian student milieus of Paris, practices "a superior scepticism." He breaks the hearts of the women he seduces by revealing, after he has bedded them, that his own "heart is empty" and that he is "incapable of love." In a melodramatic scene, Yvon's mother begs him to renounce his fiendish ways, but he rebuts her. Ever lucid, he calmly envisions his fate as that of a new Julien Sorel: "I'll be sent to the scaffold, won't I?"[47] This, the lawyer asserted, was the true character of Chambige – "it is Chambige himself."[48] In other words, a character in a novel ostensibly based on Chambige (Yvon d'Or), which itself mirrors a character from a much more famous novel (Julien Sorel), provided the key to Chambige's true character – though the notion of truth finds itself troubled in the proposition, since the very nature of this character is duplicity, affectation, pose. Accordingly, the narrative of shared, tragic love described by Chambige could only be a "hideous novel, a monstrous aberration."[49] For Trarieux, Chambige's monstrosity lay precisely in this bleeding of fiction into life. Literary character became true nature, and the novelistic crossed over into the real: "[The attempted seduction of Madame Grille] was his own novel, the novel in which his vanity revelled, where his ferocious egotism sought its hour of joy. Tragically that novel became history, and he emerged from it covered in blood that any tears he might shed can never erase."[50] The underlying queerness of the menace of the *romanesque* was signalled when Trarieux read aloud from the dedication of *Yvon d'Or* to Chambige, where Martin-Laya refers to the protagonist as "our Yvon."[51] As the prosecutor homed in, describing the character as "this Yvon, their Yvon ... who belongs to both of them,"[52] he seemed to suggest that the character's nihilistic amorality, his dangerous potential slippage into tragic reality, and his improbable literary paternity by two men, were somehow connected.

Le Rouge et le Noir itself plays constantly with the confusion between the novelistic and the real. It is at its core the story of a young man who falls prey to seductive "romanesque ideas,"[53] no small thanks to his covert arrangement with the subversive bookseller at Verchères. The narrator often comments on Julien's unfolding story as "his novel," and the character himself, shortly before his schemes crumble and he is sent to the guillotine, self-satisfiedly reflects that "my novel has come to an end."[54] In an irony that Stendhal might have appreciated, then, a novel where the protagonist models his own story on literary examples was used as a template for a court case, over sixty years after the trial on which the novel was itself based. Defence and prosecution presented equally novelistic versions of the events leading to Madame Grille's death, and a wide readership followed the case in the press as if it were a gripping serial. Yet whereas *Le Rouge et le Noir* is told in a lightly comic, ironic mode, the tone of the 1888 affair was markedly graver. Julien Sorel, while he embodied the allure of the *romanesque* in his shifts across degrees of class, gender, and truth, still bore resemblance to the endearingly bumbling heroes of the seventeenth-century picaresque; but Chambige, as depicted by the prosecution, was the personification of a menacing and furtively queer literary perversion. Trarieux was perhaps not without literary talents or aspirations of his own, and his eloquent arguments in the infamous case were published as part of a stand-alone tome in 1903.

Henri Chambige's own account of events – his "novel," as it were – unfolded in the pages of *Le Figaro* in the days leading up to the trial. In his articles presenting the case, Albert Bataille did not explicitly favour either of the competing versions presented in court, but he devoted considerable space to what he called Chambige's "confession,"[55] a type of deposition composed by the accused after his arrest.[56] Chambige's narrative of his childhood and education deploys almost every trope of the late nineteenth-century novel of formation. As a boy, he writes, "I threw myself into fantastic tales with great fervour"; in adolescence, "I spent night after night reading Hugo ... I read prodigiously, especially poetry."[57] His first experiences of love left him bitterly disappointed, and he came to see himself as a specimen of fin-de-siècle degeneration – "I was a failed being, impotent, the end of a bloodline! ... a pathological case, a cerebral."[58] He turned to books for consolation, or at least for some answers – Montaigne, Sainte-Beuve, Renan, Taine – but found only more pessimism, more doubt, more questions: "My thoughts sped up to a mad pace. Books echoed back to me every question that, on my own, I had ever pondered ... in my jumbled and overheated brain."[59] The story of his meeting with Magdeleine Grille is equally shot through with literary references. Shortly before meeting her, he read Balzac's *La Femme de trente ans* (*A Woman of Thirty*, 1842); when they did meet, they formed a bond over their recent losses, she of an infant son, he of his sister, whom he compares to the writer Eugénie de Guérin;[60] in subsequent letters and conversations with his Parisian friends, he quoted Goethe's *Werther* to describe the unfolding affair. On the afternoon of 25 January 1888, as they were driven to Sidi-Mabrouk, he remembers singing a line from Gounod's *Faust*.[61] Chambige thus portrays himself as twice over a victim of the book: as a sufferer of the contemporary reading illness documented in Bourget's *Essais* of the mid-1880s (which include chapters on Sainte-Beuve, Renan, and Taine, as well as Stendhal), and as a doomed, melancholy lover belonging to an illustrious literary lineage.

In his rebuttal to Chambige's account, Jules Maillet, the prosecutor for the case, implicitly referenced Vallès's 1862 essay "Les Victimes du Livre." Refusing to put French literature on trial, Maillet preferred, as was common following the defeat of 1870, to direct the blame at German philosophy:

> Chambige is not a victim of the book ... He is merely his own victim ... The admirable psychological studies of the descendants of the great Balzac should not be held responsible for his neurosis. This grave illness is the neurosis of failures like Henri Chambige: men who have a lust for life, yet become consumed and embittered by their impotence. If certain books are to be blamed for the state of mind of the accused, we must look beyond France, where today's youth still chants the motto of Montaigne and Molière: "High and clear!" We must instead direct our gaze at those emanations from across the Rhine.[62]

Other commentators were not as quick to let French letters off the hook. Many pointed fingers: Ludovic Trarieux, leading the charge, stated that the case "should give pause to the leaders of a certain literary movement."[63] Albert Bataille made a point of characterizing Chambige as a "mind that had fed on Herbert Spencer[64] and the young masters of the contemporary novel,"[65] but he refrained from naming novelists' names. Trarieux pointedly mentioned one: Paul Bourget.

Bourget had been publishing a serial in *La Vie parisienne* under the title *Physiologie de l'amour moderne* (Physiology of modern love) since August 1888. The poet and playwright Émile Bergerat, in an acerbic column published in *Le Figaro* (like Bataille's articles) on the day the trial opened, 8 November 1888, stated that Chambige "is a descendent of Julien Sorel, who is much admired, among devotees of modern love and crystallization."[66] Not content with this already clear allusion, Bergerat went on to call out Bourget by name. He reproached him for having lavished endless attention, in his narrative studies of adultery, on the whims and sorrows of unfaithful women as a fascinating "psychological problem," while glossing over the silent plight of their cuckolded husbands – just as, he observed, the suffering of the stoic Monsieur Grille was barely mentioned in newspaper accounts of his wife's death.[67] Weeks later, in its satirical "prophetic almanac" for the coming year, the periodical *L'Illustration* made a sarcastic prediction for January 1889: "Paul Bourget publishes *Physiology of Modern Murder*, with a letter-preface by Henri Chambige."[68] Bourget was being implicated from all sides.

He had a personal connection to the case, since he knew Chambige, who was one of his student admirers, and had received him several times at his Paris home to discuss his literary projects.[69] A letter from Chambige to Bourget was reproduced in a special supplement of *L'Indépendance belge* on 1 January 1889: the missive, signed "your friend (?), Henri Chambige," with a question mark, expresses "stupefied" admiration for Bourget's 1887 novel *André Cornélis*.[70] A rumour circulated that Bourget would take the stand to defend him in Constantine – but he never did.[71] His response came in the form of a novel, *Le Disciple*, which began to appear as a serial in *La Nouvelle Revue* in February 1889, a mere three months after the trial. He also wrote a preface for Bataille's *Causes criminelles et mondaines de 1888*, a volume containing the journalist's reports on cases covered for *Le Figaro*. This preface, dated 13 March 1889, includes a recollection of Chambige that faintly echoes Bourget's vision of a young reader in the 1883 preface to his *Essais* ("an adolescent – I can *see* him" ["un adolescent, que je *vois*"]): "I can still see him, that bright-eyed young man whose physiognomy seemed so expressive, so intelligent, walking into my study less than two years ago. He brought me some pieces of literary criticism, a few fragments of short stories that showed glimpses of a fine talent."[72] Bourget goes on to plead his own defence as a writer using, as he had in his preface to the 1885 edition of the *Essais*, an extended medical analogy:

> It is easy to make literature responsible for the moral malady that took hold of [Chambige's] mind ... Those who inveigh against writers who were particularly beloved by the man condemned in Constantine, should instead ask themselves whether, in the past fifty years, anything at all has been done in France to create anew for young men a moral life, an atmosphere of healthy willpower. Such critics find it convenient to disparage writers who have devoted their life to revealing the intellectual and emotional ills of contemporary youth, while doing their best to search for a cure.[73]

He may not yet have found a suitable a cure, Bourget intimates, but he is actively looking for one – *Le Disciple*, its publication already underway, would constitute a first attempt. Just as he had done to answer detractors of his *Essais*, he asserts that his endeavours are those of an observer and diagnostician, not an agent of contamination. In support of this claim to observational neutrality, Bourget invokes a famous passage from ... *Le Rouge et le Noir*, comparing the genre of the novel to a mirror carried along a road.[74]

Schools on Trial

Less directly implicated than Bourget, but nevertheless concerned that literature was being put on trial along with Chambige, several other writers responded to the unfolding affair by shifting the blame away from fiction, and back onto the accused as a flawed and constitutionally weak reader. Anatole France, in his column for *Le Temps* on 11 November

1888, asserted that while Chambige was most closely linked to "so-called decadent literature," no literary school should be held responsible for his crime. "Anything can trouble the unhinged," he remarked, and Chambige was clearly deranged. His father had committed suicide, and the young Henri had inherited "an incurable neurosis." To hold fiction accountable for his crime would be "an odious affront to the dignity of literature."[75] In the courtroom, Ludovic Trarieux and Jules Maillet had portrayed Chambige's alleged crime as a despicable affront to the sanctity of the family: by murdering a married woman and then claiming that she had died willingly in the name of their adulterous love, he had cynically sought to depict a grave social transgression by using false novelistic colours. In a remarkable rhetorical sleight of hand, France made literature the true victim of Chambige's actions – it was no longer Magdeleine Grille, but rather "the Muses he betrayed and compromised."[76]

The same day, in *Le Figaro*, Maurice Barrès penned his own commentary on the affair. *Sous l'œil des Barbares* had appeared earlier that year, and Barrès, who was then writing *Un homme libre*, saw many parallels to his work in Chambige's story. The protagonist of what would become the trilogy *Le Culte du Moi*, we are told in the first tome, had grown up "surrounded by his books" (the title of that novel's opening chapter); "at eighteen, he had gorged himself with the most outrageous paradoxes of human thought."[77] Barrès recognized that the accused student displayed "the main features of the contemporary soul," and acknowledged that some recent fiction "described, and even created some of the ways of feeling found in Chambige." Yet he disputed those who would put what he called "the elevated literature of our time" on trial. Instead, like France, he faulted Chambige as a flawed reader. The accused, he wrote, lacked "strength." The model reader Barrès envisioned, by contrast, would never let his troubling analyses get the better of his self-control: "The Chambige I imagine would not have allowed love to dominate him. That is crucial. The best analysts do not let themselves get carried away. They keep a firm grasp on themselves."[78] Contemporary writers, Barrès insisted, did not merely depict and foster the listless, self-absorbed behaviour displayed by Chambige: they accompanied this description with "crucial guidelines" that helped their readers grow out of such tendencies. That endeavour would become increasingly clearer in Barrès's own work, starting with *Un homme libre*.[79]

On the same day that France and Barrès's articles appeared, 11 November 1888, the trial drew to a close in Constantine. Henri Chambige was found guilty of premeditated murder with attenuating circumstances, and sentenced to seven years of hard labour in the penal colony of Cayenne, in French Guyana. His lawyer quickly sought and obtained an intervention from the President of the Republic, Sadi Carnot, who commuted the sentence to seven years in prison. Chambige would be granted an early release in October 1893.[80]

Both France and Barrès cited Chambige's novelistic prison confession, relayed through Bataille's articles for *Le Figaro*. France chose a damning sentence to illustrate his characterization of the accused as a young man who, by nature, was morbidly drawn to deception: "even more than women, I loved deceit."[81] Barrès quoted a similar excerpt in support of his portrayal of Chambige as a refined analyst of his own mental processes: "The woman I love is not as beautiful as I imagine her to be. When I think that I love a woman, I love only the error of my own mind."[82] Both passages are similar in their unspoken intimations. Chambige, by his own admission, did not love women as much as he relished the strange workings of his own mind. He did not love women in a straightforward or usual way; his desires had, over the course of his overheated and excessively literary self-education, acquired a strange bent. Gabriel Tarde, in an article written for *Archives de l'anthropologie criminelle* the following month, would take these insinuations further, citing testimony from two of Chambige's former classmates at a religious boarding school:[83]

> Here is another [event] that, in the history of his heart, may have had just as great an influence, if my sources are correct. But I will need a few circumlocutions in order to be properly understood. I am told that, in his first year of high school, which is to say, around the time of early puberty, "one of those *liaisons* that occur between schoolmates" appeared to have a profound impact on his character.[84] "He daydreamed frequently, he exchanged letters with his friend every day, often in verse. He seemed to take the whole thing very seriously and maintained this intimate relationship [cette intimité] the whole time he was at school." (Tarde's emphasis)[85]

As he indicates, Tarde's circumlocutions are not meant to obscure his meaning, but instead to direct the informed readers of this specialized journal towards a phenomenon they are assumed to know. Tarde takes pains to preface his affirmation with a double hypothetical ("may have," "if") and to follow it with a string of distancing terms ("repugnant," "aberrations," "corruptions," "monstrous degenerations," and so on),[86] yet these rhetorical gestures in no way banish the spectre of male same-sex attachment that has been conjured. They are required performances in its invocation, and serve to define and mark it as unspeakable yet explicable, an object of both moral condemnation and scientific knowledge. He goes on to justify his hypothesis with a personal reminiscence of boarding school that attests the existence of strange liaisons between adolescent boys, while at the same time exonerating the participants, placing the blame squarely on their all-male environment: "I remember having seen, with stupefaction, such attachments ... I hold the institution of the boarding school responsible, since to a certain point it makes these confusions of the heart almost inevitable." While the prosecutor's narrative and Chambige's own confession depicted the accused as a victim of literature, Tarde states that he was also "one of the most pitiable victims of the boarding school."[87]

Crucially, Tarde weaves these two strands together when he compares the young man's apprenticeship in matters of intimacy to an artistic education based on faulty models:

> Nothing is more excusable, yet nothing is more regrettable than to set out in this way. To learn music on an out-of-tune piano [un piano faux], to use, as a first model for drawing, lithographs full of anatomical mistakes [fautes], to be introduced to poetry through ill-metered and falsified verses, each of these could distort [fausser] one's ear, one's eye, and one's taste, just as *intimacies* between schoolmates can distort [fausser] sentiment. In general, the bad bent thus given to one's sensibility does come to fade, but never completely; there remains a taste for anomaly. (Tarde's emphasis)[88]

Deviations in artistic and sexual taste are presented side by side and go hand in hand,[89] one serving as a metaphor for the other, through a shared quality of falsity, repeatedly invoked. Much of the anxiety over *le romanesque* that traversed reactions to the Chambige affair was informed by this often unspoken but ever-present parallel. These same concerns and intimations are already present in *Le Rouge et le Noir*. Madame de Rênal, as we have seen, initially imagines that Julien might be a "young girl in disguise"; Julien's first impression of his later conquest, the aristocratic Mathilde de la Mole, in turn focuses on her "stiff, haughty and almost masculine countenance."[90] Stendhal describes Mathilde's penchant for the novelistic and the illicit through multiple references to her fascination with the sixteenth century and the turbulent reigns of Catherine de' Medici's three sons, in particular, that of Henri III, whose alleged preference for male favourites – still a topic of dispute among historians – is frequently alluded to in nineteenth-century paintings and novels.[91] Julien falls for Mathilde because, as he watches the way she manoeuvres in order to surreptitiously borrow her father's forbidden books, he begins to see in her "the duplicity of a Machiavel."[92] This reference to cunning, using a male literary archetype to describe a female character, overlaid on a scene of deceit about the procurement of books, suggests that Julien's attraction to Mathilde has to do with his recognizing her as a double, a fellow adroit hypocrite and lover of books. Such oblique but repeated allusions to gender ambiguity (Julien as a novelistic girl in disguise, Mathilde as masculine and Machiavellian) connote the developing relationships between Stendhal's protagonist and each of his two conquests – and, by anticipation, between Henri Chambige and Magdeleine Grille – as transgressive and improper, grounded not in "nature" or in the established social order, but in imaginative misrecognitions and unwholesome identifications with a decadent past circulated by books.

The correlation between literary decadence and the possibility of same-sex liaisons – agilely embodied in Tarde's phrase, "the taste for anomaly" – was discreetly but pointedly alluded to in Trarieux's closing argument:

> living closely [dans l'intimité] with a few young men who shared his tastes, he [Chambige] practised with them, getting drunk, at times, on his own dreams of glory, picturing himself as a great writer. Nothing could be nobler, to be sure, than such veneration of literature, when it is not accompanied by unruly impatience, but the members of this young circle overplayed the deplorable tendencies of a certain school that seeks success in the strangeness of its innovations.[93]

The "school" implicated here is no longer the boarding school, but rather a contemporary literary movement that relishes descriptions of the strange or the unusual – a "literature of diseased brains," according to Trarieux.[94] These two schools are not without relation to each other. Albert Bataille, for instance, deplored how some circles of Parisian students made a heroic figure out of Chambige, as if the death of his alleged victim mattered no more than a fictional death – "There has been, among students, a movement of enthusiasm for this *romanesque* young man, who acted out, as if they were natural, tragedies found in books."[95] Bataille's condemnation points to a multiplicity of threats: Chambige played out in reality a plot that belonged in a novel, and conversely, his fellow students read his unnatural actions as an admirably devised narrative, paying no heed to their very real toll. A group of male students, sharing a proclivity for the strange and the novelistic, stood with an accused killer instead of rallying to the defence of a murdered wife and mother. "A taste for anomaly" united corrupt young men against a threatened familial and social order. When Léopold Martin-Laya was called to testify in Constantine, the prosecution quoted from a compromising letter he wrote to Chambige after his arrest: "I hug you, I hold your heart against mine. Here I place a kiss that you will kindly pick up. Please send some in return."[96] Phrases like *je t'embrasse* have much linguistic ambiguity and should not be over-read; *un baiser* can be a kiss on the cheek or the hand. Still, a sense of the impropriety of these statements can be gleaned from the fact that, while they were reproduced integrally in the more specialized *Gazette des tribunaux*, the otherwise thorough account of the trial in *Le Figaro* limited the citation to "I hold your heart against mine."[97]

Denunciations of the boarding school as a space of potential perversion appeared with some regularity in pedagogical reports and medico-legal discourse in the 1880s and 1890s.[98] The literary schools of Naturalism and the psychological novel – which were very much at odds in the late 1880s,[99] despite Trarieux's conflation of them – each made use of the topic in their portrayals of decadent and morally or sexually ambiguous male characters. Zola, as early as *La Curée* (1872), had alluded to the *collège* as an "environment of depravation."[100] In his 1886 novel *Un crime d'amour*, Bourget broached the subject in a less elliptical manner, which did not go unnoticed.[101] As is typical for Bourget in this period, the novel is a story of adultery. The protagonist, Armand de Querne, described as a dilettante and a nihilist, seduces his best friend Alfred's wife. The adult Armand recalls his years at a boys' school, where he met Alfred:

> Within the walls of the great school ... there was talk of nothing but depraved affairs between older and younger boys. Some of these loves against nature were blatantly sensual, taking place in deserted corners of the building. And among all the young Frenchmen living in similar boarding schools, how many took part in this debauchery, while the others sullied their imagination in refusing it! Other attachments between schoolboys were exalted and chaste. Reading some eclogues by Virgil, a dialogue by Plato, certain sonnets by Shakespeare[102] had gone to the head of those with a literary temperament.[103]

The passage is notable for its direct linkage of certain readings to the possibility of sexual deviation, as well as for its insistence that no student, in the end, escapes the wide reach of this threat: even those who do not indulge are affected in their "imagination." Confirming this, Armand goes on to reflect that while "he and Alfred had been among the small number of boys spared by this contagion," the "great advantage of the disgust" he had felt in being surrounded by unnatural love was "that he had been pushed, at a very young age, toward [female] prostitutes."[104] The boys' school thus produces deviants of all kinds – not only those whose tastes go "against nature," but cynical heterosexual bachelors like Armand.

The tropes of literary seduction and sexual perversion at the boarding school converge scandalously in Octave Mirbeau's *Sébastien Roch*. Undertaken in the last months of 1888, the novel appeared as a serial from mid-January to early April 1890, and was published as a volume on 26 April. Its eponymous protagonist, a sweetly naïve young adolescent from a small town in Normandy, is sent off to a prestigious Jesuit boarding school by his ambitious, petit-bourgeois father, who wants Sébastien to rub shoulders with the sons of aristocrats and go on to a brilliant military or political career. Instead, the unsophisticated Sébastien is met with contempt by his well-bred classmates. He eventually bonds with another lonely student, Bolorec, but they are chastised by one of the Jesuits for spending too much time together. The innocent Sébastien does not understand, and Bolorec has to explain that this is "because ... last year ... they found two boys ... doing dirty things in the music rooms."[105] As the years pass, Sébastien develops an enthusiasm for literature, particularly forbidden poets like Victor Hugo whose works circulate clandestinely among students. Noticing this, another Jesuit, Father de Kern, takes him under his wing, and offers him private lessons:

> [Father de Kern] revealed to him the beauties of literature. Schoolbooks had left him with imperfect glimpses and truncated images, and above all with a burning desire to know ... he introduced him to Sophocles, Dante, and Shakespeare, and made him love them. With bright, exquisite, passionate charm, he told him the stories of their immortal works, and explained them. He recited the poetry of Victor Hugo, Lamartine, Alfred de Vigny, Théophile Gautier, read out pages from Chateaubriand. In his mouth this poetry and prose had a numbing music of their own, unimagined harmonies, unnatural penetrations ... he could not resist the corruption of his little soul, skilfully saturated in poetry, chloroformed by ideas, overcome by the dissolving, emasculating [dévirilisante] morphine of ungraspable desires. For this secret, continuous, invasive work, Father de Kern enlisted the aid of the sun, the mist, the sea ... the whole of nature, yielding like an old matron to the monstrous concupiscence of one man. Together, the two of them [Father de Kern and nature] instilled in him, drop by drop, the mortal poison. The moment was well chosen for the rape of a delicate, passionate soul ... attacked at the very roots of his intellectual life.[106]

This scene of seduction interlaces several recognizable topoi of the fin-de-siècle novel of formation: the list of readings, which emphasizes Romantic poets; the gradual abasement of nature by an onslaught of deceptive mimesis; the metaphor of poison.[107] It culminates in a dramatic literalization of the metaphorical "rape of a soul" that was Sébastien's literary miseducation, as Father de Kern rapes his pupil. When he threatens to denounce his aggressor, Sébastien is instead expelled under the false accusation of having been caught in the act with Bolorec. The traumatic incident leaves him indelibly marked: when he returns to his native Normandy, he finds himself unable to pursue what used to be a carefree childhood friendship with a neighbour's daughter. By the end of the novel, he is drafted into a regiment, and dies in battle against the invading Prussians, a victim of the boarding school by way of the book.

Mirbeau's biographer affirms that the novel, upon publication, met with "a veritable conspiracy of silence" from reviewers of all affiliations. It sold less than two thousand copies in its first year.[108] Sébastien's rape by a Jesuit priest – represented only elliptically, through a line of dots across the page interrupting the narration – was too much of a provocation for Mirbeau's literary colleagues, accustomed though they were to allusions to same-sex acts at boarding school from the likes of Zola and Bourget. In addition to its aggressive anticlericalism, the scene's impropriety lay in its making violently literal the threat of devirilization (to use Mirbeau's term) recurrently alluded to in contemporary debates about young men's seduction at the hands of literature. The scandal was not simply that Mirbeau's novel depicted male rape as the consequence of literary education, but rather, that it made overly explicit a threat of which the discussion, as Tarde's aside to his readers showed, required circumlocution and insistent distanciation. In this regard, Bourget's *Le Disciple*, published only months prior, proved much more palatable.

Seductions and Disavowals: *Le Disciple*

The publication of *Le Disciple* triggered an irreparable falling out between Mirbeau and Bourget, who had been friends for much of the 1880s. In a letter from 6 March 1889 (to Paul Hervieu), Mirbeau furiously declared that he would have to rewrite a scene for his novel-in-progress after he read a similar scene in Bourget's novel, which had begun to appear as a serial. Mirbeau complained that Bourget stole his ideas concerning two details about Sébastien's First Communion, after he "imprudently" discussed them with him.[109] In his anger, he wrote that he found *Le Disciple* "extra-bad, and irritatingly pretentious."[110] There are in fact important thematic similarities between the two works: both tell the story of a young man from the provinces who falls prey to the nefarious teachings of a captivating mentor. Still fuming, Mirbeau penned a scathing article in *Le Figaro* on 11 May 1889, deriding an unnamed writer for giving self-aggrandizing interviews to fawning journalists in his bibelot-filled study, and catering to "the emotions and vices that women love" by making adultery his signature topic.[111] Readers easily recognized Bourget. About their quarrel, Edmond de Goncourt notes in his *Journal* for 15 June 1889 that Mirbeau, during a visit, showed him a letter from Bourget: "I can show you the letter, since you know I love women, but I would not dare show it to others: they could think, given the tenderness of his reproaches, that there had been pederastic relations between us."[112] The editor of Mirbeau's correspondence notes that the letter from Bourget, dated 16 May, is nowhere as incriminating as this reported conversation makes it out to be.[113] Instead, the description of the letter by Mirbeau (or Edmond de Goncourt) employs classic mechanisms of distanciation ("others ... could think") and denial ("I love women") to denounce Bourget as a pederast, complementing his public disparagement in *Le Figaro* with a private condemnation for a restricted audience.[114]

While it cost him Mirbeau's friendship, *Le Disciple* was a resounding critical and popular success for Bourget. The novel sold more than twenty-two thousand copies in six weeks, and revived a broad debate on the question raised by the Chambige affair: were writers morally accountable for the aberrant actions of some of their readers? It marked a turning point in Bourget's literary standing, erasing his earlier image as a delicate novelist of bourgeois adultery. The ambiguity of Bourget's position in the literary field during the first half of 1889 is illustrated by the novel's publication history: while it was printed as a serial in *La Nouvelle Revue* from February to May, *La Vie parisienne* was still publishing the extramarital vignettes of *Physiologie de l'amour moderne* in monthly instalments, and would do so until September 1889.[115] When it appeared in book form on 17 June, augmented by an author's preface, *Le Disciple* was hailed as a triumph. A work of "courage and independence," a "most remarkable," "fine and manly" novel, declared the reviewer for *Polybiblion*.[116] Ferdinand Brunetière, in the *Revue des Deux Mondes*, affirmed that Bourget had demonstrated his undeniable superiority over Zola and Daudet, and that his female fans would find no enjoyment in this latest novel, "the strongest" of his oeuvre, the work of a true "master." (He also, in passing, noted the affinities of the protagonist with Julien Sorel).[117] *Le Disciple* was indeed the masterstroke of Bourget's career. It transformed his literary persona, within the space of six months, from a fashionable women's novelist loosely compromised in a notorious affair, to that affair's most eminent and celebrated commentator, a model of rigorous and trenchant analysis.[118] How had he managed such a turnabout?

Much of the answer lies in the novel's complex network of displacements, denegations, and disavowals. The preface,[119] addressed to "my young countryman [who is] looking, in volumes written by us, your elders, for answers to questions that torment you," formally denies that the narrative contains "allusions to recent events"[120] – which stopped no one from reading the novel through the lens of the Chambige affair. The tone, in a sense, is given right at that moment. This is a novel that will strain to disown what it is about, a novel of denial.[121] The titular disciple is a philosophy student named Robert Greslou, who stands accused of having murdered – poisoned, to be exact – a young woman of noble descent. The reader learns of her death through Robert's mentor, the philosopher Adrien Sixte, whose orderly and ascetic existence is perturbed by a summons to testify in front of a judge enquiring on the case. The alleged murder is eventually revealed to be a suicide pact gone wrong: the young woman killed herself, and Robert was to follow, but did not. The events at Sidi-Mabrouk are thus transposed in several ways. The death and trial are moved from Algeria to the French province of Auvergne; the moral blame for the accused's actions is shifted from literature to philosophy; and his victim is no longer an older, married mother but a young noblewoman. In effect, Bourget rewrites *Le Rouge et le Noir*, simply replacing Madame de Rênal (and Madame Grille) with Mathilde in the role of the victim. His descriptions of Adrien Sixte's philosophy owe much to the works of Hippolyte Taine, a historian and philosopher who was an important early influence; in the 1883 *Essais*, Bourget had described how Taine aroused "an enthusiasm of disciples" among Parisian students, including himself.[122] *Le Disciple* was therefore a public repudiation of his former master, who responded with a pained letter.[123] Meanwhile, the novel's putative concern with philosophy and science is belied by a constant parade of literary references, as well as a series of insistent and increasingly less potent denegations regarding the influence of the novelistic on the character's actions and the narrative as a whole.

Bourget's preface, which addresses the reader as a "friend," ends not only with the affirmation of the novelist's wish to be "beneficial" to him, but with the added and somewhat puzzling avowal of a "passionate wish to be loved" by him.[124] The passionate reading pact between Bourget and his reader anticipates and frames the reading pact around which the novel revolves – one where issues of pedagogy and responsibility find themselves intertwined with desire. After Sixte returns from meeting the judge (who gravely tells him that the case likely involves his "moral responsibility"),[125] Robert Greslou's mother brings him a long letter where his former student attempts to explain the broken suicide pact by detailing his intellectual history. Rather than being printed in *Le Figaro*, as Chambige's had been, the accused's confession becomes a confidential letter to his former master, albeit one to which readers of the novel have unfettered access, as it takes up more than half of its three hundred pages.

The defining moment of Robert's intellectual autobiography is his discovery of Sixte's works, an experience he describes using a literary parallel: "it was, in the domain of pure ideas, the same instant attraction [coup de foudre] as earlier, with the works of Musset, in the domain of imagined sensations."[126] Following this revelation, he sought out Sixte in Paris to become his student, a prospect he envisioned with delight.

> I saw you as something of a modern-day Spinoza, fully identical to your books ... I dreamed up for myself a whole novel of happiness at the thought that I would know the hour of your walks ... to my eyes, you were Certainty incarnate, a Master, what Faust is to Wagner in Goethe's psychological symphony.[127]

Robert's anticipation is expressed in a multitude of analogies to reading and literature. Sixte would be like Spinoza in that he would be identical to his books; master and student would be like Faust and his assistant; the happy pupil's life would be like a novel of uninterrupted bliss. This tendency to picture an idealized future through the deforming prism of literature is an important trope in many of Bourget's earlier works – a narrative device possibly borrowed from Flaubert. Inevitably, it leads to disappointment with reality. Looking back on his youth, Armand, in *Un crime d'amour*, lucidly observes that

> my overactive imagination ... destroyed my capacity to feel, because it always erected a ready-made idea between myself and reality. I expected to feel a certain way – and reality never matched up ... Life at boarding school, and modern literature, had sullied my thoughts before I had a chance to live.[128]

In *Le Disciple*, Robert himself states that "the way [his] imagination anticipates emotion" is one of the fundamental traits of his character, and he goes on to recount a pivotal moment of his childhood, the chilling disappointment he felt when, after much imaginary build-up, he failed to experience ecstasy at the moment of his First Communion (this is the scene that Mirbeau found too similar to one he had written for *Sébastien Roch*).[129] That anticlimax, according to Robert's confession, marked the beginning of the erosion of his faith, a process that was to be finalized, at age fourteen, by his discovery of contemporary literature.

Before she hands over his letter, Robert's mother, believing her son must be innocent, makes an impassioned plea to the philosopher. "'Men don't just become murderers or poisoners from one day to the next. A criminal's childhood foretells his crimes,'" she protests. "'But my son, Monsieur, even as a little boy, with his poor father, was always in his books ... I always had to say: Come on, Robert, go outside; you should go outdoors, get some air, enjoy yourself ...'"[130] Her son's confession sheds an ironic light on this statement: indeed, a murderer's path is traced from childhood, and it is precisely because of, not despite, his lifelong passion for books, that he is led to infamy. Robert describes himself as "a passionate reader" from a young age. "By chance, there fell into my hands," he writes, echoing Stendhal's ironic characterization of Madame de Rênal, "some volumes that were very different from the prize books we received in school": Shakespeare, Walter Scott, Dickens, George Sand, all of which "fed my imagination,"[131] until his concerned mother discovered and removed the dangerous books to a locked bookcase. From the beginning, Robert's practice of reading is thus characterized as both illicit and fateful. Outside of school, he befriends a sickly neighbour named Émile (a name with a marked Rousseauian affiliation), an equally voracious reader who has the added privilege of not being monitored by a watchful parent. Together, free from supervision, the boys indulge in their passion secretly. One day, they manage to procure a volume by Musset from an unscrupulous bookseller:

> I was trembling, as if about to commit a great wrong, and we let ourselves be taken over by this poetry as if by wine, slowly, softly, passionately. From that time on, employing ruses like those of a threatened lover, I held in my hands, in Émile's bedroom as well as my own, a great number of illicit volumes, which I have loved dearly.[132]

In this vaguely homoerotic formative scene, reading about romance is inverted into a romance of reading. Robert imagines himself as a tragic or heroic lover, the object of whose wiles are not women but texts themselves. The bedroom becomes the hidden space of clandestine contact, not with a body, but with a book, amorously held in the hand. Musset's poetry fills the heart and the mind, it takes over like a wine or a drug; it is, as Bourget had written about the novels of Stendhal, an intoxication.[133]

Years later, as a serious philosophy student, Robert will claim to have weaned himself from the intoxicating power of poetry and novels. On his way from Paris to a small town in Auvergne, where the Marquis de Jussat has hired him as a preceptor for his younger son, he reflects how little he resembles the ambitious heroes who have, in famous novels by Stendhal or Balzac, made similar journeys across class and geographical lines. Yet his proud and repeated assertion of being nothing like the protagonists of *Le Rouge et le Noir* and *Illusions perdues* does not constitute a complete escape from literary paradigms: to define oneself negatively is still to rely on a model. In fact, his very insistence invites a reading of his statement as denegation:

> I am recounting this childish reflection to prove to you ... how little I resembled, as the carriage sped down the road to Aydat, the poor and ambitious young man depicted in so many novels ... I remember having noticed that difference even back then, and not without a sense of pride. I recalled Julien Sorel in *Le Rouge et le Noir*, arriving at Monsieur de Rênal's; Rubempré's

> temptations, in Balzac, in front of the house of the Bargetons; some pages from Vallès's novels as well. I analysed the sentiment that lies hidden behind these heroes' envy or their revolt ... I found no trace of them in myself.[134]

One is reminded of the example provided by Freud in a short essay entitled "Verneinung" ("Denegation") from 1925: when a patient states preemptively, "'You ask who this person in the dream can be. It's *not* my mother,'" the analyst can usually conclude, "'it *is* the mother.'"[135] At this point in Bourget's novel, the protagonist's story in fact resembles Julien Sorel's in several ways. Halfway through *Le Rouge et le Noir*, Julien also makes a long carriage journey before entering the employ of a marquis, whose daughter Mathilde soon catches his eye. Robert, though he claims it is not for love or for social advancement, but as a purely psychological experiment, will likewise undertake a campaign to seduce his own marquis's daughter, who bears the very Goethean name of Charlotte – while her younger brother, Lucien, happens to share a first name with the protagonist of Balzac's *Illusions perdues*. Before narrating his arrival at the castle, Robert repeats his denegation using a most Stendhalian term: "I am not writing in order to depict myself in a *romanesque* light."[136]

Having resolved to seduce Charlotte, Robert begins to study her character for flaws. He observes that she herself has "a taste for the *romanesque*," perhaps more akin to the pent-up Madame de Rênal than the well-read Mathilde: "not because she had read a lot of novels, but because she had ... an overly intense sensitivity ... that faculty shared by great poets and great lovers, the ability to forget and disperse oneself, to lose oneself completely."[137] In a first attempt at breaching her heart, he confides in her, when she remarks on his melancholy air, the invented story of a tragically broken engagement. The scene, as Robert recounts it in his confession, is saturated with references to reading and literature. It takes place in his personal library, to which Charlotte has gone up to borrow a book – another echo of Stendhal's Mathilde. Robert's made-up story is a "novel" prepared in advance, to which he adds lyrical details in an effort to better "poetize," and in which Charlotte "is unable to read his lies"; it is a "scene from a comedy" that plays out while she lays her hands listlessly against a thick book. Robert is pleased with his own performance: "hypocrisy," he observes in yet another reminiscence of *Le Rouge et le Noir*, "grows bolder as it passes our lips."[138] When she takes leave of him, seemingly unmoved by his tale, he observes that she resembles an engraving he once admired in a religious tome. His sustained use of a military analogy as he reflects on this apparent failure – "these numerous manoeuvres had not earned me the slightest advance in that heart I wanted to conquer"[139] – brings to mind both *Le Rouge et le Noir* and another urtext of literary seduction,

Les Liaisons dangereuses (1782), throughout which Valmont describes his seduction of Madame de Tourvel as a warlike campaign.

Valmont and the Marquise de Merteuil, Laclos's cynical libertines, famously make use of literary sources on which they model their discourse to better dupe their victims. For instance, in an early letter to the Marquise, Valmont mischievously displays his new-found mastery of the religious idiom he has been using around the devout Madame de Tourvel.[140] Yet while he fancies himself a master of language, Valmont eventually becomes ensnared in his own discursive web, and finds himself unable to put an end to his affair. In *Un crime d'amour*, the cynical seducer Armand, in whose personal library Laclos's novel features prominently as one of the few books he still enjoys, ponders this irony when he asks, "between the Valmont of the *Liaisons* – my dear Valmont – and Madame de Tourvel, who was really the dupe?"[141] In *Le Disciple*, when Robert eventually professes his (supposedly false) love to Charlotte during a promenade, she runs off, leaving him to the terrifying discovery that he, like Valmont, is "caught in [his] own trap,"[142] and in fact enamoured of her. Parallels to *Les Liaisons* abound in this episode: Charlotte, precisely like Madame de Tourvel, goes to live with her aunt, and Robert, just like Valmont, writes her numerous letters, which, although they remain unanswered, he later learns she has read and cherished feverishly: "She read and reread these letters, and their poison was surely taking hold."[143]

Before confessing his love to Charlotte, Robert had prepared his campaign by feeding her a steady diet of sentimental literature – everything from *La Princesse de Clèves* to *Le Lys dans la vallée* and the poems of Musset and Vigny. "There are no bad books," he muses. "There are merely bad moments in which to read even the best books."[144] Citing his mentor Sixte's observations, he summarizes what he calls "the general law of literary intoxication ... you once compared the wound created by reading in certain imaginations, to the well-known phenomenon that occurs in bodies poisoned by diabetes, where even a harmless needle prick becomes infected with gangrene."[145] Soon after Charlotte returns to her father's castle, the metaphor of fatal intoxication, which has traversed the entire narrative, comes to be literalized in a promise of double suicide, as the pair make a pact to drink poison after what is to be their first and only night together. Having formed this thoroughly literary project (Shakespeare, Vigny, and the suicidal victims of *Wertherfieber* come to mind), Robert even consults a book about suicide by the physician Brierre de Boismont in preparation for the fateful night.[146] After they consummate their love, however, he has a sudden change of heart – not unlike the protagonist of Martin-Laya's *Yvon d'Or* – which he explains with the Latin saying, *Omne animal post coitum triste*.[147] Robert leaves, Charlotte drinks the poison, and he is soon accused of her murder.

Following this broken suicide pact and the end of Robert's written confession, the remainder of the narrative derives suspense from two related reading pacts. Before the poison took effect, Charlotte wrote to her older brother, explaining the circumstances of her death, and this brother finds himself honour-bound to clear Robert of the charge of murder, despise him though he may. Meanwhile Robert has written to Sixte, and the scholar, his belief in the supremacy of abstract thought deeply shaken, decides to intervene in his student's trial, at the risk of having to accept some of the moral blame for the all too real consequences of his conceptual philosophy. As the trial closes, Robert is spared the guillotine only to be shot in the face by Charlotte's brother – exchanging, in a way, Julien Sorel's fate for Werther's. At the very end of the novel, the troubled Sixte wonders whether a Heavenly Father might not exist after all, yet even this instant of repentance is expressed through the passage from one set of textual references to another. Sixte, in his moment of doubt, disavows Kantian idealism, and ponders a quote by Pascal.

Bourget had placed an annotated clipping of Barrès's article on the Chambige affair in the manuscript of *Le Disciple*, indicating that he had not only read the article but intended to make use of it in the process of writing.[148] Some of Barrès's comments – "The Chambige I imagine would not have allowed love to dominate him ... The best analysts do not let themselves get carried away. They keep a firm grasp on themselves" – read like an anticipative critique of Bourget's completed narrative. The story itself provides little in the way of "crucial guidelines" for impressionable young readers;[149] instead, at every turn, Bourget seems to get carried away with his own love for the literary, rather than coolly analysing it. It may be that, like Robert, the novelist ended up "caught in his own trap," or that, like Charlotte, he succumbed to his own "taste for the novelistic." The penultimate chapter describes how, four weeks after having read Robert's confession, Sixte was still prey to a disconcerted uncertainty, a great "trouble caused by this reading."[150] Readers of the serial version published in *La Nouvelle Revue* from February to May 1889 may have been left with similar feelings of irresolution. In the end, was Sixte truly morally responsible for Robert's actions, which appear much more inflected by literary tropes than by any philosophy? The very reproach addressed to Barrès's *Sous l'œil des Barbares* by Bourget, in his preface to *Le Disciple* – that it lacked a clear conclusion – could be said to apply to his narrative. Yet that same preface, dated 5 June 1889, does away with much of this ambiguity. It vigorously argues for the novel as a demonstration of the "responsibilities" of writers, providing the conclusion lacking in the story.[151] The preface is Bourget's act of atonement, the confession of his moral guilt in the Chambige affair, displaced onto a disavowal of his former masters, Taine included. "Every one of us has been, at some point in the past, this type of young man ... spellbound by the paradoxes of an overly eloquent master," he writes, pleading his blamelessness as a disciple just as he accepts his responsibility as a master.[152] Fittingly, his preface was published – like Bataille's reports on the trial, and Chambige's novelistic confession – in *Le Figaro*, on 17 June 1889.

"A Homosexual in Denial"

The only detailed biography of Bourget, a doctoral thesis published in 1960, signals in a footnote and in hushed tones ("the time has come to mention ...") his friendship with Oscar Wilde during the 1880s.[153] Like Wilde's rumoured acquaintance with the young Marcel Proust, a topic of much speculation,[154] this friendship is attested only through second-hand accounts, as letters written by or addressed to Wilde were likely destroyed in the wake of his 1895 trials. A more recent biography of Henry James likewise offers intriguing anecdotes – on trips to Dover and Venice, James spent much time with the "handsome ... interesting and sympathetic Bourget" – but allows little in the way of conclusions.[155] The authors of a biography of the gender-transgressive aristocrat Mathilde de Morny (1863–1944) twice claim that Bourget was "overtly homosexual" in the first decade of his career, but they do not cite their sources.[156] Their claim is made dubious by their assertion that the Wilde trials of 1895 were what prompted Bourget to "renounce his homosexuality ... and court the salon hostesses who would open the gates of the Académie française for him,"[157] since Bourget was elected to the Académie in 1894. His return to Catholicism (publicly announced in 1901) and his embrace of political conservatism were a long, gradual process that began at least as early as 1889. Still, one documented source exists: Bourget's passionate 1869–70 letters to Maurice Bouchor,[158] then a fourteen-year-old student at the Collège Sainte-Barbe, a Parisian establishment near the Panthéon, not unlike the fictional boarding school that Armand recalls having attended in *Un crime d'amour*. We read in one such letter, written when Bourget was seventeen: "I need to see you again, to gaze into your pretty green eyes ... I love you and hold your hand, while begging you to grant me more. You know what that means, and you will not get upset."[159] While the cerebral and cynical Armand was no exemplar of reproductive virility, the novelist projected onto his character an unblemished heterosexuality – he was one of "the small number of boys spared by [the] contagion" of same-sex liaisons at boarding school – that he, like Gabriel Tarde,[160] appears not to have shared.

André Gide's *Journal* for 26 November 1915 recounts an anecdote involving Bourget.[161] Gide is travelling with Edith Wharton, and they pay a visit to the older writer in the south of France. When Wharton leaves the room, Bourget turns to Gide and asks him a question about a book he had published thirteen years earlier:

> "Now that we are alone, can you tell me, Monsieur Gide, whether or not your *Immoralist* is a pederast?"
>
> As I remained somewhat taken aback, he insisted: "I mean, a practising pederast?"
>
> "He is more likely a homosexual in denial instead," I answered, as if I had little knowledge of the matter; and I added: "I believe there are many of them."[162]

It would be hard to improve on Gide's mordantly sly, insinuative reply, but one might wish he had turned the question back on Bourget: was his *Disciple* a practising pederast, or, perhaps more likely, a self-repressed homosexual? The text features some remarkable ambiguities in its depictions of relations between men.

The master-disciple relationship that structures the novel both outside and within the narration – "my young country countryman ... by whom I passionately wish to be loved," writes Bourget in the preface; "it was [an] instant attraction," writes Robert about his first encounter with Sixte's works – is repeatedly characterized as fervent, shot through with questions of desire and guilt. No less strangely passionate is Robert's relationship with his eventual murderer, Charlotte's brother André, whose name, as we have seen in other fin-de-siècle novels, connotes an idealized masculine double.[163] Recounting his first meeting with the Marquis de Jussat and his family, Robert introduces each character in turn, including the Marquise, their younger son Lucien, and their daughter Charlotte, whose description takes all of four lines. By contrast, Robert spends the next ten pages describing their older son André's robust physicality in the smallest detail ("nimble as an athlete, with broad shoulders and a small waist ... a face like a soldier ... a square forehead ... clenched and firm lips"), their covertly hostile first conversation, and his troubled reaction to both.[164] While Charlotte sits down to a game of cards with her father, Robert chats with the Marquise, but can't seem to take his eyes off André: "While stealing glances toward Comte André playing billiards ... I followed, my mouth agape, the young man's every move."[165] Robert attempts to analyse his strange reaction for Sixte's benefit:

> Neither that evening, nor in the days that followed, did I envy Comte André's name, nor his fortune ... Nor did I feel that strange hatred of one male for another, so finely observed in your pages on love ... I am telling you this

> not out of vanity, but instead to prove to you that vanity never played the slightest part in the kind of sudden rivalry that made me, from those very first moments, Comte André's adversary, almost his enemy ... Let me repeat, in that rivalry there was as much admiration as antipathy. Upon reflection, I have discovered in the sentiment I am trying to define for you the trace of some unconscious atavism.[166]

Robert's frenzy of negation (neither, nor, not, never ...) invites us to ponder what might be entailed by the unconscious atavism – the resurgence of a previously latent genetic trait, or, metaphorically, of a dormant formative influence – which he claims to have discovered through his tortuous self-analysis. The double invocation of his master and of "love," meanwhile, only contributes to the queerness of his non-confession. The menace implicitly described by Tarde and Trarieux in their reflections on the Chambige affair, and made scandalously literal in Mirbeau's *Sébastien Roch* – a network of relations between male students and their decadent masters that threatens innocent women and families, and therefore the entire social edifice – traverses *Le Disciple*. By the close of the novel, the fascinated and fascinating opposition between the bookish student and his virile double ("action in the shape of a man")[167] ends in the death of one at the hands of the other, a symbolic murder that amalgamates the forces of denial, projection, and renunciation driving the narrative. Bourget kills his *Disciple* – enacting the death sentence that Chambige had been spared – and upholds in his place a paragon of familial honour and idealized masculinity. Robert's murder by André is the novel's true crime of passion.

In Eve Kosofsky Sedgwick's definition, male homosocial relationships, which are characterized by a "slippery relation ... between desire and identification," can take the form of "a desire to consolidate partnership with authoritative males in and through the bodies of females."[168] One reading of *Le Disciple* bears out this proposition: since Robert cannot admit he desires to be like (or perhaps plainly desires) André, he settles instead for seducing his sister. Yet I have resisted describing the network of male-to-male relations around Robert – between Robert and Sixte, Chambige and Bourget, Bourget and Stendhal, and other readers and writers around them – as "homosocial," precisely because contemporary commentators of the Chambige affair saw little social function in them. As depicted by Trarieux, Maillet, Bataille, and others, these relationships are in fact unsettlingly antisocial. They are seldom mediated "through the bodies of females," and those women who do get tangled in their network, Madame Grille and Charlotte, end up dead. Instead, the body through which readers like Robert and his boyhood friend Émile play out their slippery relations of desire and identification is the corpus of literature.

The Chambige trial was underlain by the threat that this network of queer literary relations posed to the social, familial, and national order – but unlike in the Wilde trials in London a few years later, prosecutors and commentators did not make the queerness of this threat openly legible, relying instead on circumlocutions and intimations. "Is it not time," Trarieux asked, "that we stop this tide of aberrations? Where would we be headed, dear God, and what would become of our poor nation, which already suffers from so many moral afflictions," if Chambige were to be exonerated?[169] In addition to putting Chambige to death through the fictional mirror of Robert, the success of Bourget's novel lay in its paradoxical claim to redirect this very network of antisocial literary forces, through a passionate but emphatically moral pact between young male reader and older novelist, in the service of the social order – towards what his preface calls "our great duty, the restoration of the fatherland."[170]

The Picture of Dorian Gray, first published in *Lippincott's Magazine* in July 1890, can be read as an alternate version of *Le Disciple*.[171] Dorian, young and beautiful – like Robert, who in Bourget's novel describes himself as "a pretty boy"[172] – falls under the amoral influence of an older mentor, Lord Henry Wotton, who fills his head with "subtle poisonous theories." He causes the death of a young actress, not by murdering her, but by coldly abandoning her, after which she kills herself using poison. His life is further transformed by Lord Henry's gift of a "book bound in yellow paper,"[173] to which Wilde had given a French title in his typescript,[174] but that published versions, in *Lippincott's* and later as a volume, leave unnamed. His emulation of "the hero of the dangerous novel that had so influenced his life" is such that the narrator observes, "Dorian Gray had been poisoned by a book."[175] Like Robert, Dorian dies in the end, but his death is not an unambiguous moral retribution. A queer reading of the final scene – where Dorian stabs the painting that has aged and borne the physical traces of his depraved actions – suggests that what dies, what Dorian kills, is the real Dorian, murdered by a Dorian who has long ceased being real, subject to the principles of reality (ageing, moral consequences), and has instead become a character in a novel, a Julien Sorel, ever charming, ever lucky, ever young. The *romanesque* Dorian slashes the painting because it is too ugly, too real; and in its place, the beautiful young Dorian reappears in the frame, untouched. That Dorian, the Dorian that has crossed over into representation, into fiction, is the one that survives. For the 1891 book version, Wilde added a short preface[176] that reads, in its provocative aphorisms, like an inverted image of Bourget's: instead of announcing a "study" of "the seriousness of [the novelist's] art" for "the moral life" of the nation, Wilde states that "No artist desires to prove anything."[177] He places under his own signature a statement that, in Bourget's novel, had been ascribed to the wayward Robert, and disavowed by both the outcome of the narrative and Bourget's preface – "There is no such thing as a moral or immoral book."[178]

In writing *Le Disciple* and its preface, Bourget claimed to end his own infatuation with the *romanesque*, a queer attachment intertwined with fervent same-sex readerly and writerly relations of identification and desire, rivalry and mentorship, to his schoolmate Maurice, to Stendhal, to Julien Sorel, perhaps to Octave Mirbeau, perhaps to Henri Chambige himself. While Bourget was working on his novel in January 1889, Wilde published "The Decay of Lying," a philosophical dialogue where his textual double defiantly expounds, as Wilde himself would fatefully do on the stand a few years later, a posture that embraces art as more beautiful and more important than truth, and the novelistic as greater than reality – an anti-ethos whose queer slant is captured in the pronouncement, "One of the greatest tragedies of my life is the death of Lucien de Rubempré."[179] The twin front-page headlines of *Le Gaulois* on 13 June 1895 sum up the contrast between the fate of the author of *Le Disciple* and that of the Irish writer. That day, as Bourget was formally inducted to the Académie française, Wilde was doing hard labour at Pentonville Prison.[180]

5 Barrès and the Ghosts of Balzacian Ambition

In an article from 1886, Paul Bourget heralds the upcoming publication of *Répertoire de la Comédie humaine de H. de Balzac*, a directory of the thousands of characters that populate Balzac's fiction. Bourget's reflections on Balzac's enduring appeal for young male readers are consistent with his recently completed *Essais de psychologie contemporaine* (1883–5), where he examines writers from earlier decades as "influences that continue to weigh on today's youth."[1] The following year, the first edition of the *Répertoire* was greeted by an article from the young Maurice Barrès, a Bourget protégé who, aged twenty-four, had yet to publish his first novel. That article, "La Contagion des Rastignacs," follows Bourget in describing how young Frenchmen are still enthralled by the "fever-inducing novelist," but also notes that this decades-old fascination might at last be on the wane. Barrès claims to be weary of ambitious young provincials who flock to Paris, and of those who write novels about them, both under Balzac's spell; he has had enough, in reality as in fiction, of "all these false Rastignacs, as ridiculous as they are odious."[2] He suggests that the time has come for something else: a new paradigm for young men, led by a new writer – perhaps Barrès himself. Would he succeed?

Critics have often noted Barrès's deliberate "refusal" of Balzacian models in his first trilogy of novels, *Le Culte du Moi* (The cult of the self, 1888–91), as well as his "clear return" to Balzac in *Les Déracinés* (*The Uprooted*), published in 1897,[3] which inaugurated a second trilogy, *Le Roman de l'énergie nationale* (The novel of national energy, 1897–1902).[4] Whereas this trajectory is usually described as a two-step process of departure and return, I propose that Balzacian schemas of ambition and ascent exert a tenacious and deeply paradoxical hold on Barrès, particularly in *Les Déracinés*, where they are held up as both possibility and impossibility, subject to simultaneous citation and denegation.[5] Barrès, through a series of pronouncements about Balzac in his early career, attempts to define himself by renouncing this powerful model; yet Balzac and his iconic characters, the socially triumphant Eugène de Rastignac first among them, have an effaced but lingering presence in Barrès's 1897 novel that might be best described as a haunting. Rastignac (the eventually successful hero of *Le Père Goriot* [*Father Goriot*, 1834–5]) and Lucien Chardon/de Rubempré (the ultimately tragic protagonist of its sequel *Illusions perdues* [*Lost Illusions*, 1837–43]), along with a cavalcade of nineteenth-century figures of conquering virility from Napoleon to the seafaring adventurer Edward Trelawny (1792–1881), are paraded in Barrès's novel as models for young male characters to emulate. But these invocations of famous men both fictional and real are systematically signalled as evocations of something gone – as if these figures were the spectres of a ghostly masculinity that can no longer be embodied at the fin de siècle.

Bourget opens his 1886 article by imagining how, with the news of the impending publication of the *Répertoire*, "up on the hill where he was laid to rest – that same hill atop which his Rastignac launched his challenge to Paris – the bones of the great novelist must have ... shivered with joy."[6] The reference to Père-Lachaise Cemetery is striking in its juxtaposition of the site of Rastignac's famous challenge to Paris at the end of *Le Père Goriot* and that of Balzac's tomb: in a single place, the loudly proclaimed potential of youthful ambition and the still slumber of death are made to coexist in a non-verbal, cadaverous tremor. Conflating the geographies of fictional life and real entombment, Bourget describes a site where Rastignac lives on, in a way, even as Balzac the novelist lies dead.

For his preface to the second edition of the *Répertoire* in 1887 (reworked from his 1886 article), Bourget employs similar terms to describe the experience of reading *La Comédie humaine* as an uncanny blurring of fiction and reality: "for some readers, the world of Balzac [has] been more alive than ours: afterwards, it [has] shaped their actions in its likeness."[7] To some of Balzac's young male readers, then – "Let us not talk about women," Bourget specifies in his 1886 article[8] – the world of fiction can appear more vivid than life. In an inversion of the expected relationship between fiction and what is usually called real life, Balzac seems truer, more alive than life: enthralled, his living readers become akin to a horde of the living dead, modelling their actions after those of characters who never lived, imagined by a long-dead novelist. Rastignac's enduring challenge, made atop a hill that is also a cemetery, resonates and shapes the lives of these imagined readers more than fifty years after the publication of *Le Père Goriot*. In Barrès's *Déracinés*, this challenge persists, as Bourget suggests, in something of a ghostly state: a compulsively repeated utterance, never forthrightly spoken nor fully silenced, whose effect is to make reality seem dead to actual possibilities, and alive only with literary reminiscences.

Le Père Balzac

Bourget's 1887 preface to the *Répertoire* describes how adolescent readers imagine themselves following the paths traced by Balzac's characters:

> Are you a Balzacian ...? Have you felt, as you read some tome of the *Comédie humaine* clandestinely at school, a sort of exaltation ...? ... at that age where one harvests in advance all the fruits of the tree of life – even as it has yet to flower – did you dream of being Daniel d'Arthez, covering yourself in glory by writing great works ... perhaps, more ambitious and less literary, you dreamed of seeing the gates of high society open in front of your desires, as for a new Rastignac ...?[9]

While Bourget here depicts an exhilarating confusion of fiction and reality, Barrès's article of the same year ("La Contagion des Rastignacs") uses a more negatively connoted medical lexicon, in line with Bourget's earlier *Essais de psychologie contemporaine*, to describe Balzac's deleterious effect on rising generations since the middle of the century. The novelist's ambitious and amoral heroes, Barrès writes, have become dangerous models for young men from the provinces who dream of emulating their social and amorous triumphs, because these impressionable young readers confuse the possibilities afforded by fiction with prospects for their own life:

> [Balzac's] adventurers ..., among whom Rastignac is the prince, have overstimulated the nerves and brains of all those young ambitious types who, since 1847, have appeared one after the other ... How many dashed hopes and misled lives, all due to a concept of existence that had enthused them at the age of twenty![10]

Yet Barrès also adds a qualification, noting that "these days, only the least estimable and the most defective continue to dream of Rastignac's romantic, adventurous, and rakish life."[11] In the mid-1880s, he claims, Balzac's influence has started to decline: while an abased version of the Balzacian fever of earlier decades subsists, it affects readers who are morally flawed or constitutionally vulnerable. No sophisticated or sensible young man can fall completely under the spell of Balzac's fictions in 1887 – only, as we will see, those who have little to lose.

Barrès's statements about Balzac at different stages of his early writing career trace an evolution towards self-definition through claims of exception and renunciation. "I repudiate all of them, except Balzac," the eighteen-year-old Barrès writes in a letter, professing his contempt for "common, vulgar novelists."[12] Nine years later, in *Un homme libre* (A free man, 1889), Balzac remains the exception even as Barrès takes the opposite stance, describing, through his protagonist, the meditative dilettante's ideal library: "Only Balzac was excluded, since that passionate writer highlights the struggles and the bitterness of social life ... we would have found in his works, on certain days, a nostalgia for that which we have renounced."[13] A logic of renunciation governs both positions. That Balzac is the gold standard of the novel is never in question; Barrès's shift from implicit identification to symbolic exclusion illustrates a growing writerly sophistication, an acknowledgment that individuality can only be claimed by venturing out of the master's shadow. For the protagonist of *Sous l'œil des Barbares* (Under the eye of the barbarians, 1888), the contagion of Balzacian types is so widespread that to think and feel like Rastignac has become distastefully commonplace:

> His heart filled with desire and with an intoxicating melancholy – but then he realized he was thinking more or less like young men who sat at brasseries and similar Rastignacs. He felt a flood of bitterness. "From now on," he said, "I will no longer look kindly on requests, smiles and other niceties. All they ever brought me were vulgar impressions."[14]

To write a Balzacian novel in the 1880s, the intimation seems to be, would be just as vulgar: hence Barrès's renunciation of the mise en scène of social ambition, in his first trilogy of short novels, in favour of the exploration of psychological intricacies that define *Le Culte du Moi*. This aesthetic program is laid out, again through a reference to Balzac, in an article from 1885 in his self-published and short-lived literary magazine, *Les Taches d'encre* (The ink blots):

> [Balzac painted] a fixed image of the torment of passions pitted against social codes and mores ... He has not aged. Even today, the best novelists are merely retouching the background of his pictures. He has said almost everything there was to say, it seems to me, about men who act ... only men who feel, have yet to be written about: they alone are of interest to us.[15]

For the Barrès of *Le Culte du Moi*, to represent new social climbers after Balzac would be artistically vulgar, since everything worth saying on the topic has already been said. For the author of "La Contagion des Rastignacs," it would even be perverse, since the ambitious young man is twice over a creation of *La Comédie humaine*: it is a fictional type created by Balzac, as well as a real-life type made epidemically common by the widespread reading of Balzac. A novel about a new Rastignac would be a representation of an imitation of a fictional type – a Platonic aberration, many times removed from ideals or reality. In order to be a new Balzac, one has to renounce the old Balzac, whose influence has spread to too many imitators in literature as in life.

Only some years later, in the mid-1890s, does a return to Balzacian representations of social struggles become palatable for Barrès, since a new object of analysis, untouched by the master because unknown in his time, has by then finally emerged: the anarchist. Desperate and nihilistic rather than ambitious, the anarchist constitutes a new type of young man unforeseen in the encyclopaedic repertoire of the *Comédie humaine*. In an article commenting on the bombing of the Café Terminus in Paris on 12 February 1894, Barrès boldly declares that the incident is remarkable because it shows that Balzac has aged at last ["Enfin, Balzac a vieilli"]:

> The bombing of the "Terminus" will become a date in literary history. It marks the arrival of a way of feeling that had not been foreseen by Balzac ... [U]ntil 1890 ... nothing new appeared in France that had not already been catalogued in *La Comédie humaine* ... Our entire century could be seen through a Balzacian lens: young men from the bourgeoisie came up from the provinces, eager to take their share of power and pleasure ... But today a new species emerges. Because of universal schooling, a third class rises ... [Y]oung people ... who are literate, yet have no real education ... want their share of power and pleasure. But the grave novelty is that they do not want whatever crumbs are within their reach: those are either too little, or not flavourful enough for their rough appetites ... Rastignac did not threaten the noble townhouses of the faubourg Saint-Germain, he dreamed of entering them ... That is no longer the case for a *bachelier* like the one who bombed the Terminus. His dream is not to enter the townhouse, which represents, in his eyes, a higher echelon in the social hierarchy: his dream is to blow it up.[16]

In pointing to universal primary education as the agent responsible for the rise of the anarchist, Barrès takes up the anxious discourse on *déclassement* that had accompanied pedagogical reforms in the 1880s and 1890s,[17] making an implicit nod to Vallès's *Le Bachelier*, and therefore to the trauma of the Commune recounted in Vallès's subsequent novel *L'Insurgé* (1882–6). The bomber of the Café Terminus, Émile Henry – the son of a Communard – had attended a prestigious boarding school thanks to a state scholarship; he himself described the failed promises of the meritocratic educational system as the root of his anarchist convictions when he stood trial.[18] Barrès later reported on his execution in May 1894, expressing a certain fascination, if not sympathy, for what he described as the "tragic beauty of his revolt."[19]

The originality of Barrès's February 1894 article – to some extent its provocation – lies not in placing the blame with republican reforms, but in stating that the very real event at Café Terminus (which left about twenty patrons wounded, one of them fatally)[20] is in fact a literary milestone: the end of the Balzacian era. With mock detachment, he predicts that some cynically ambitious writer will see this as an unmissable opportunity for innovation: "'At last,' some psychology enthusiast will say, 'we'll be able to create new types, – ever since Balzac, that had been impossible!'"[21] The real cynicism here is Barrès's own, since the opportunity he identifies would become the impetus for his best-known novel, *Les Déracinés* of 1897.[22] The anarchist cannot be accused of being a creation of Balzac; the novelist who paints him,[23] it seems to follow, would be free from the bitter sentiment of being a mere imitator among many. Yet Barrès's return to Balzac would not be entirely triumphant or without ambivalence. The "type" of the anarchist, for one, is almost completely absent from *Les Déracinés*. Mouchefrin, one of the novel's seven protagonists, mutters at one point that "I'd happily blow up all of Paris!,"[24] but this statement is never followed through, and he ends up instead a petty thief and murderer.[25] Instead, Barrès opts to represent the Parisian travails of a group of young men from the provinces, including their enduring struggles with the long shadows of Eugène de Rastignac and Lucien de Rubempré, Balzac's ambitious heroes.

Echoes of Rastignac

For Barrès, Rastignac is the Balzacian character that best embodies ruthless ambition: he is "the man of prey, [a] type ... which, through the genius of the novelist, became in our society ... the most fashionable vice."[26] That Rastignac's would-be emulators populate reality and fiction alike was itself, by the 1890s, a contagious notion. It even spread across the Channel; Oscar Wilde, well versed in contemporary French letters, recast the observation as a maxim on the relationship of art to life in his 1889 essay "The Decay of Lying":

> Literature always anticipates life. It does not copy it, but moulds it to its purpose. The nineteenth century, as we know it, is largely an invention of Balzac. Our Luciens de Rubempré, our Rastignacs, and De Marsays made their first appearance in the *Comédie humaine*. We are merely carrying out, with footnotes and unnecessary additions, the whim or fancy of a great novelist.[27]

The idea that Balzac's characters spawn legions of real-life imitators had already been expressed, nearly thirty years earlier, in Jules Vallès's spirited article "Les Victimes du Livre" of 1862.[28] Having described the perils of childhood readings and romantic poetry, Vallès saves his ultimate volley for Balzac, since the author of the *Comédie humaine*, he argues, "sums up the greatness of the book and its dangers":

> Oh! under the footsteps of this colossus, so many souls crushed, so much dirt, so much blood! How he has kept judges busy, and mothers in tears!
>
> How many men were lost, how many have sunk, while waving above the mire where they were about to die, a page ripped from some volume of the *Comédie humaine*.
>
> These men, alongside Rastignac, from the heights of an attic or standing on the Pont des Arts, raised their fist in a challenge to life, and cried out to the world: "It's between you and me now!" ["À nous deux!"] They swore, on *Le Père Goriot* or some other tome next to it, to carve out a place for themselves with a sword – or with a knife ...[29]

Eugène de Rastignac's fictional exploits – a fortuneless son of modest provincial nobility, he rises to the pinnacle of Parisian influence and status, seducing the wife of a rich banker and later marrying her daughter, accruing titles of nobility and prestigious posts in government, all the while amassing considerable wealth – make him the quintessential Balzacian hero, the emblem of successful ambition.[30] In *Le Père Goriot*, which introduces Rastignac, Balzac insistently uses the term "ambition" and its derivatives ("the ambitious young man," "his ambitiously amorous reverie")[31] to describe his character. Vallès states that this model, with its impossible promises of success, sends the many young men who make the *Comédie humaine* their guide to life (waving its pages like a flag, in the image he uses) down a road of misery and crime. He imagines Rastignac's challenge to Paris – "À nous deux maintenant!" ("It's between you and me now!"), shouted from the heights of Père-Lachaise Cemetery, overlooking the capital, at the very end of *Goriot*[32] – derisorily restaged time and again, as readers act out the famous scene from the much lower altitude of a top-floor room, or on the Pont des Arts, a flat, pedestrian bridge built in 1804, near the Louvre. The change in elevation makes for a comical symbol of the insuperable gap between the glittering world of Balzacian fiction ("Paris ... where the lights were beginning to shine," reads the scene in *Goriot*)[33] and the deadly "mire" of young men's real lives in the capital.

Rastignac's iconic challenge is in fact restaged a number of times in novels of formation of the last decades of the century. In Armand Charpentier's *L'Enfance d'un homme* (1890), the protagonist Georges Maltier – whose "proclivity for literature" emerges early on – issues a repeated and earnest challenge to the city after he passes the *baccalauréat* and begins to work on a grand historical drama in verse: "And now, *à nous deux*, old Paris! ... À nous deux, Paris! ... À nous deux!"[34] (It should be noted that Rastignac's exclamation at the end of *Le Père Goriot*, although explicitly addressed to Paris, is actually "À nous deux maintenant!," not "À nous deux, Paris!" The phrase, as we will see, is frequently misquoted.) Yet Georges has already begun to understand that books offer a warped picture of the world: his novelistic fantasies of being swept up by an aristocrat riding in her carriage contrast unfavourably with his sexual initiation in the arms of a lowly prostitute. After much time spent "in the literary underworld," he sees his first novel rejected by publishers: "the work lacks virility," he realizes upon rereading it. Equating his flawed literary output to a deficiency in reproductive potential, Georges comes to see the manuscript as "a skinny little runt, a blackish fetus." He recalls his outburst of Balzacian aspiration with bitterness: "The cry still buzzes in his ear. Ah! No way! Paris doesn't give a damn about him! Paris has crushed his puny little bones!"[35]

In novels by Vallès and Barrès, by contrast, this sequence of apprenticeship – from the naïve emulation of a Balzacian model to the embittered realization of that model's fallaciousness and inadequacy – is collapsed into a single scene that references Rastignac's ambitious declaration as an impossibility. In *Le Bachelier*, Vallès's protagonist, while commenting "I've read my Balzac," rents a dingy furnished room in an evocatively named boarding house, the Hotel Jean-Jacques-Rousseau.[36] As he settles in the room, he notices that the view from his window has little to do with the scintillating panorama of Paris that closes *Le Père Goriot*:

> Balzac likely chose the hotel that seemed best suited to the ambition and temperament of his hero. ... My window faces a wall. I can't look at Paris and raise my fist at it like Rastignac! I can't even see Paris. There's a wall in front of me, with bird crap all over it.[37]

The titular *Bachelier*'s perspective, worlds removed from the elevated viewpoint of Rastignac at the moment of his novelistic apotheosis, is recast as a literal dead end. A scatological detail completes the picture, a crude reminder that only actual birds, not Balzacian "men of prey," will ever soar in this story.

In *Les Déracinés*, Rastignac's famous exclamation is similarly evoked not through an earnest restaging, but as an ironic jab between two of Barrès's young protagonists. In the third chapter ("Their installation in Paris"), the seven ambitious provincials are discussing their first impressions of the capital over late-night drinks in the Latin Quarter. When one of them, Sturel, begins to explain how one Parisian locale has drawn his attention more than any other, he is interrupted by wisecracking guesses. One of his comrades makes an (unspecified) dirty joke, then another makes a mocking reference to Balzac:

> – He went to the Père-Lachaise, interrupted Racadot in a loud voice; he restaged Rastignac's challenge, after old Goriot is buried, when he shouts out: "*À nous deux, Paris!*" Monsieur François's pleasures are quite sophisticated![38]

Sturel has not, it turns out, been shouting out at Paris from the heights of the hillside cemetery: instead he has been busy browsing the wares of booksellers.[39] His response leads another companion to interject:

> – This very day, right under your eyes there was a display that could have taught you more than any book; but you didn't even bother to watch the funeral procession for Gambetta![40]
>
> – It was splendid! added Léontine.
>
> – Anyone can watch a Parisian spectacle, but you have to be able to read it, Renaudin continued, with the haughty tone of a "Parisian" returning to his village.[41]

The conversation shows the members of the group jockeying to claim a discursive position of worldly sophistication, a claim made salient (and ironically undercut) by the narrator's remark that Renaudin, who has only days before arrived from Lorraine, is already affecting a Parisian tone. Renaudin dismisses Léontine's (Racadot's mistress) exclamation as the naïve response of someone who does not know how to interpret real-life events; Sturel, in his judgment, is likewise at fault for spending his time reading largely useless books when he should instead be "reading" and learning from the world around him. Renaudin goes on to explain the political implications of Gambetta's death and the popular fervour it aroused. "The friends of the deceased will keep their grasp on the republic for years to come," he muses pseudo-prophetically.[42] "What circumstances ... what struggles ... will make them allow a new generation to enter?"[43] This is precisely the question at the heart of *Les Déracinés*: what will it take for the seven ambitious young men to make it in the capital? The question is left hanging at the end of the novel; its ultimate answers, the rout of Boulangisme and the Panama scandal, structure the narrative of subsequent tomes in the trilogy, *L'Appel au soldat* (The call to the soldier, 1899–1900) and *Leurs figures* (Their figures, 1901–2).

In *Les Déracinés*, the only answer ventured – circumstances and struggles replicating a Balzacian model of brash ambition and dazzling success – is put forward without seriousness, as a taunt. When Racadot mockingly imagines Sturel re-enacting Rastignac's iconic challenge, he intimates that the members of the group are much too sophisticated to partake in or approve of such a display, and, by extension, to wholeheartedly believe in Balzacian models.[44] The success of Racadot's joke depends on his audience's expected understanding that no savvy reader, including Sturel, would ever show himself as puerile as, say, the hapless protagonist of Charpentier's *L'Enfance d'un homme*. This proclaimed rejection of Balzacian models is repeated in a later scene where Sturel and another member of the group, Roemerspacher, venture up the slopes of Montmartre: when Roemerspacher again brings up Rastignac's challenge, Sturel replies dryly that "I, François Sturel, find Rastignac, with his oath to dominate Paris, shamefully mediocre."[45] Barrès seems to share his protagonist's dislike for Rastignac's overdone, over-quoted exclamation. In the article "La Contagion," he denounces the phrase's degradation, through overuse, to the status of a cliché that cannot be cited "seriously" without incurring ridicule.[46] The phrase can therefore only appear, in *Les Déracinés*, as an ironic or derided citation.

And yet it appears there twice; Rastignac is also mentioned two further times in the novel.[47] The character who first brings him up, Racadot, happens to share Balzac's first name, Honoré. Barrès's drafts even reveal that the character of Sturel had been explicitly conceived as an updated version of Rastignac, a "thinking little beast," whereas Balzac's hero had been a "beast of prey."[48] "I repudiate all [novelists], except Balzac," Barrès had stated in 1880; in writing *Les Déracinés*, conceived as a novel that Balzac could not have penned, Barrès conversely and insistently proclaims his renunciation of the master, but cannot help citing him.

A Shadowy Pact

The novel's central scene, in which the seven young men gather at Napoleon's tomb, make a solemn oath "to become men" ("être des hommes"), and resolve to join efforts in launching their Parisian careers, is unmistakably Balzacian.[49] Barrès's first chapter explicitly sets up the comparison: during the description of the young men's nascent "association," the reader is reminded that "Balzac had invented thirteen men who, around 1828, were said to have sworn to come to each other's aid in any circumstance, and whose occult power successfully challenged the social order."[50] While the scene at Napoleon's tomb makes no direct mention of Balzac's *Histoire des Treize* (*The Thirteen*, 1833–9), a number of echoes (in addition to the oath itself) reveal their filiation.[51] Most significantly, both descriptions are placed under the sign of literary exemplarity. Balzac and Barrès alike describe an aspiration to bring literary examples to life in "reality" – the fictional reality of a novel, in both cases. In the preface to *Ferragus* (1833), which introduces the *Histoire des Treize*, Balzac insistently describes his band of men through references to fiction: while they have led a "secret and curious life, like something out of the darkest novels by Madame Radcliffe," he writes, "these thirteen men have remained unknown, even though each of them gave reality to the most bizarre ideas suggested to the imagination by the fantastic power falsely attributed to a Manfred, a Faust, a Melmoth."[52] Balzac claims, in keeping with generic conventions, that his stories and his characters are real; this claim is complicated, though, by his simultaneous assertion that they in fact make real ("réalisé") the false, imaginary ones made famous by Goethe or Byron. What's more, he ascribes to a literary source the characters' idea for the pact that binds them: "One day, a member of the group, having just reread *Venise sauvée* and admired the sublime union of Pierre and Jaffier, came to reflect on the particular virtues of those men who are thrown outside the social order."[53] For Balzac's narrative voice as for the characters themselves, then, the oath of the Treize is the realization – that is, the making "real," in the space of fiction – of literary fantasies of masculine complicity and power.

The seven young men of *Les Déracinés* similarly give themselves a model in the figure of Napoleon, at whose tomb they gather: he is to be their "professor of energy," in Barrès's famous formulation.[54] The narrative voice and the characters alike conceive of the emperor through the lens of literature: "with the force of their imagination, nourished by books, [they] bring into the ranks of Napoleon's followers the poets who, for the past century, have been the voices of the great man."[55] Sturel, the most literarily inclined member of the group, makes a long speech about Napoleon's life, emphasizing Napoleon's nature as a reader ("At fifteen ... in secret and with passion he discovers himself in Rousseau") and telescoping his status as a figure that anticipates or inspires literary characters into outright identification ("at sixteen, he is René").[56] Barrès's narrative voice, likewise, makes literary comparisons that find in Napoleon both the incarnation of older literary types ("at Saint Helena ... he was king Lear") and the origin of a profusion of nineteenth-century figures ("He was also Byron's corsair, the emperor of Musset and Hugo, the liberator according to Heine, the Messiah for Mickiewicz, the social-climber for Rastignac [*sic*], the individual for Taine").[57] The historical reality of Napoleon's life, nourished and anticipated by texts, itself becomes a text to be read by the young men in the literary productions it inspired: crystallizing this logic, the emperor's dead body is compared to "a most beautiful parchment to decipher."[58]

Barrès's mention of Byron's *Corsair* (1814) provides a further link to Balzac's preface to *Histoire des Treize*, where we read that "The Thirteen were men as sturdy as Trelawny, the friend of Byron who is said to be the original of the *Corsair*."[59] Balzac's comparison invites the reader to read his thirteen characters as equivalent to the real man who inspired a literary figure, denegating the characters' own status as literary creations. In turn, Barrès's invocation of Byron's *Corsair* sets up a more complex nexus of representation and imitation, making Napoleon the model of a fictional character through which the seven *déracinés* are meant to "read" the emperor so that they may model themselves after him – perhaps in the way that Balzac's Treize translate the fictional version of the corsair back into "real" sturdiness of character. The group of young men is thus not only made to indirectly emulate a real-life model, but to emulate a fictional group's imitative relationship to a real figure made famous by fictionalization. These students of masculine energy find themselves at multiple degrees of remove from their potential professors, Napoleon, Trelawny, Byron's *Corsair*, Balzac's Treize, all of whom appear as reflections of each other, in a literary hall of mirrors where historical reality blends into fiction. The young men seem to barely exist in the same realm – reflections of reflections, shadows of shadows. Barrès's seven cannot be straightforwardly like Napoleon the way that Balzac's thirteen are "as sturdy as" the seafaring Trelawny: too many layers of text, of fiction, stand between them and their model. "Between himself and the objects of his desire, he felt a slight veil. He wanted to dominate men and caress women," writes Barrès about Sturel, who has been reading – perhaps like Napoleon? – *Julie ou La Nouvelle Héloïse*.[60] While the future emperor was able to make his ambitions reality, the veil of fiction hangs too heavily between the seven *déracinés* and the possibility of fulfilling their desires and "becoming men." In the shift from Balzac's thirteen to Barrès's seven, the possibility of heroic realization seems to have dissipated, to the point that the young provincials are left to wonder, after they have sworn the pact, what it is exactly that they will set out to do. "There was an anxious silence," writes Barrès. "Each of the young men felt afraid of being inept."[61]

A Republic of Invalids

Barrès fills this silence with a full chapter (under the title "France disunited and decerebrated") where he expounds on the ills affecting the nation – bureaucratization, low birth rates, the invasion of "the German spirit" – from his narrator's pulpit.[62] While he dissertates about their incapacity for action, the seven young men are left to their anxious hesitation at the site of Napoleon's tomb, the fittingly named Les Invalides.[63] Likely not indifferent to this symbolic toponym, Barrès stages not only the scene of the pact but also two other key scenes of the novel near that location, with explicit references. Roemerspacher's encounter with his intellectual mentor Taine ends at the square des Invalides, where their discussion about a plane tree results in the botanical metaphor of the book's title; the Armenian heiress Astiné Aravian's first meeting with Mouchefrin, who along with Racadot will later become her murderer, likewise takes place in the cour des Invalides.[64] When the narration finally returns to the group of anxious and incapable youths, a new chapter title quips that "There is no easy way out of a tomb," suggesting that they are more akin to hesitant revenants than to heroes triumphantly reborn.[65] The seven settle on a double course of action that is neither particularly daring nor grandly ambitious: they will await the rise of a new heroic personage, a "man for the nation" who will bring them, and indeed all of France, out of its moral and political decadence.[66] In the meantime, they are to join forces in running a newspaper, *La Vraie République*, which they envision as a necessary "stepping stone" towards their greater writerly and political ambitions.[67]

A newspaper, Renaudin suggests, will prove a useful forum from which to support France's new leader when he arises, since France, in his view,

> is a nation ready to be enthralled by the novelistic [romanesque] adventures of a likable hero. A little bit of social justice would please them, but not nearly as much as a great novel. They would hold their breath as it unfolds day by day. I speak as a journalist who knows what readers want.[68]

France under the Third Republic, according to this line of reasoning, is above all a republic of readers: the French will enthusiastically rally behind a new heroic figure if they can follow his ascent in their daily paper, as if it were a serial novel. In making this pronouncement, Renaudin is again striking a sophisticated discursive pose, claiming to speak as someone "who knows." Trumpeting his worldly capacity to figuratively read the world in a more penetrating manner than common readers, he proposes that he and the other *déracinés* can make use of their countrymen's readerly disposition to further their own careers. As it had done earlier, however, the narrative voice undercuts Renaudin's claim when it goes on to explain that journalism, far from being a brilliant or original avenue to pursue, is in fact a near inevitability for young men such as him: "everything had been prearranged so that journalism would be the path they follow."[69] Renaudin may claim to know French readers, then, but he fails to recognize himself as one of them. Rather than a means for him and his companions to exert influence on the mass of the nation's readers, their pursuit of ambitions through journalism is in fact the result of their own status as readers. "Journalism is the true calling of bookish beings,"[70] Barrès's narrator had observed earlier.

When Racadot, following Renaudin, suggests that the group take stewardship of the struggling *La Vraie République*, the narrator comments again:

> They had been raised by books alone: the moment had now come where their education produces its logical and complete effect. They will now add more print to the existing mass. All young Frenchmen, in our *lycées*, are trained [dressés] to become Parisian men of letters.[71]

Young Frenchmen at the fin de siècle, in this damning picture, are thoroughly bookish beings, so saturated with the influence of print that they are unable to direct their efforts towards anything but writing, incapable of producing anything but more print. For the members of Renaudin and Racadot's generation (to which Barrès also belongs: he was twenty-two in 1884, the year in which the novel is set),[72] journalism is not a clever strategy or an expression of individuality: it is the sole prospect their highly literary education affords them, one for which they have been trained like docile show animals ("dressés"). The seven young men's resolution to join forces in putting out a newspaper, then, falls well short of their earlier resolution to emulate heroic models, Napoleon and Balzac's band of thirteen. For young men coming of age in the 1880s, to aspire to write is barely an ambition at all; it is instead a near-slavish emulation of all-too-numerous literary models. Far from the wilfully defiant impulse of a Rastignac, the group of seven's plan, in this view, amounts to the unwitting resignation of a generation of bookish invalids to the tyranny of print – and yet it is still, in a different mode, a decidedly Balzacian endeavour.

Lucien, in Balzac's *Illusions perdues* (1836–43), is the son of a provincial pharmacist who is driven to Paris – and to journalism – by his writerly and social ambitions. In his native Charente, he reads the works of poets and novelists (Schiller, Goethe, Walter Scott, Lamartine, Chénier ...) with a devouring passion, and composes his own poems, making him, in the narrator's ironic characterization, the "Byron of Angoulême."[73] Once he arrives in the capital, Lucien soon experiences one disenchantment after another: his collection of poems and his grand historical novel both fail to secure a publisher, and he turns to writing articles, in spite of the dire warnings of his artist friends. During his initial visit to the offices of a newspaper at the Palais-Royal, he comes to see journalism as a cynical and debased marketplace, where opinions, artistic and political, are bought and paid for:

> Lucien ... saw politics and literature converge in this shop. As he watched an eminent poet prostitute his muse to a journalist, humiliating Art, as Woman was humiliated and prostituted under these same ignoble galleries, the great

> man from the provinces absorbed a terrible lesson. Money! was the name of the game.[74]

Barrès may have remembered Balzac's depiction of the lessons learned by Lucien at the ruthless school of journalism when he described, in an article from 1906, the kind of training that aspiring writers acquire by running a literary magazine:

> It is a difficult exercise: finding funds, a publisher, subscribers, readers ... For a young man preparing for a literary career, founding and managing a little magazine is an excellent training ground, where he will learn two essential truths:
> 1. money is everything;
> 2. the literary business is a wretched business [une industrie de gueux].[75]

The lessons enumerated by Barrès are precisely those learned seventy years earlier by the fictional Lucien: literature is not an artistic endeavour but a commercial enterprise beholden to the rule of money; it is a profession populated by the desperate and the destitute, by the male equivalents of prostitutes. The feminine of *gueux*, the somewhat untranslatable term Barrès uses to describe literary men (beggar, lowlife, wretch), is in fact *gueuse*, prostitute. Balzac's analogy between the poet peddling his talents and the woman selling her wares, an ancient comparison that traverses the nineteenth century, finds a new iteration in Barrès's choice of words, as if the (no doubt very real) lessons learned by Barrès as a young writer could only be described through a retelling of Lucien's lost illusions.

Despite some early successes, Lucien's journalistic career does not end well: when, in a bid to curry political favour and earn more money, he changes allegiance from a liberal to a royalist paper, he ends up losing everything and having to retreat back to his native Charente. Barrès's seven *déracinés* fare no better in their common project. *La Vraie République* loses money,[76] driving Racadot, the member of the group most personally embroiled in its finances, to concoct an extortion scheme that ends in the murder of Astiné Aravian. The narrative thus follows a downward arc from lofty ambitions to petty crime, and, concurrently, from a fictional, Balzacian model – the bustling life of scrappy Parisian journalists – to a real-life news story: Astiné's death at the hands of Racadot and Mouchefrin is inspired by the 1878 murder of a milkmaid by two destitute *bacheliers*, which Barrès had read about in the scandal rag *Le Petit Journal illustré*.[77] From the 1894 bombing that provided the impetus for the novel to the 1878 murder that was reworked as its climax, *Les Déracinés* comes full circle, as journalistic accounts of crimes committed by desperate, overeducated young men are mapped onto to each other. Conceived when the anarchist bombing of the Café Terminus made it possible – or so he claimed – to finally write fiction outside the shadow of Balzac, Barrès's spectrally Balzacian novel ends with Racadot's sentencing and decapitation (Mouchefrin is spared). Renaudin covers the trial for the press, as Barrès had that of the real-life bomber Émile Henry. For Racadot, improbable Balzacian aspirations to heroic advancement, brotherly association, and journalistic productivity result in a lowly end. Unlike Lucien, he is not granted a second act.

Lucien's downward trajectory, over the course of *Illusions perdues* and *Splendeurs et misères des courtisanes* (1838–47), features more than a few dazzling novelistic highs, among them the love of aristocratic women and coveted beauties; a sinister, homoerotic pact with a Mephistophelian figure; and a very nearly successful scheme to extort millions from a love-struck banker. The young provincials of Barrès's *Déracinés*, by comparison, lead a rather lacklustre existence, Racadot and Mouchefrin in particular. A conversation between the two reveals the tenacious hold of Balzacian models of social ascent on Racadot's imagination, deny and mock them though he may in the presence of other members of the group:[78]

> – Are you suffering from all this privation? There are many powerful men who were sneered at when they were our age. But ten years later, still young enough to enjoy it all, they had money, mistresses at the theatre, fine suits they could ruin without care, handshakes on every boulevard; they paid at restaurants without even looking at the bill.[79]

Racadot might well be thinking of Rastignac or Lucien at the height of their Parisian triumph when he describes such brilliant rises; the narrative voice, decrying his "typically scholarly misapprehension of the conditions for success,"[80] confirms that the path to wealth and influence he envisions has less to do with reality than with his readings. For the grand schemes detailed in Balzac's fictions have no possibility of application in the Paris of Racadot and Mouchefrin. Barrès declares this explicitly at least twice, first when he depicts the lowly brasserie where the two most destitute *déracinés* spend the better part of their nights, and later when he describes the daily operations of their newspaper:

> Racadot and Mouchefrin are hungry and cold, they debase and torment their own youth ... This much-decried brasserie ... is not the ice-cold boarding room of Balzac's heroes ... Rubempré, Rastignac, at midnight, in their solitude, saw visions of their own future, which always resembled the adventures of the young Bonaparte.[81]
>
> That newsroom, what a strange place! Could anything be more different from those newspapers, which were quite real [d'ailleurs fort réels], of which

> Balzac told us the ebullience, the verve, the disappointments, the frivolities, the great dinners, the pretty women?[82]

"This is not a Balzacian novel," Barrès's narrator seems to insist, even as he strangely clings to the reality of Balzac's descriptions ("d'ailleurs fort réels"). He purports instead to represent a new, harsher reality – a more real reality, stripped bare of novelistic trimmings.[83] "Could anything be more different from ... Balzac?" The answer is rather mixed: in his repeated, simultaneous invocations of, and distanciations from, a Balzacian model, Barrès appears to be constantly exorcising a ghostly presence that lingers over his novel. Racadot understands and acknowledges that Balzacian models of ascent cannot apply to the world he lives in; he loudly proclaims so, in front of his peers, by turning Rastignac's famous exclamation into a joke. In retrospect, though, given that a few scenes later he indulges in what amounts to a Balzacian daydream about his future, his mocking dismissal of these models reads rather like an unwittingly revealing denegation. Barrès, likewise, asserts repeatedly that the events and characters he describes differ and depart from Balzacian models, yet his very insistence betrays the hold that Balzac continues to exert on his narrative. Character and novelist alike seem compelled to renounce, over and again, the Balzacian illusions they claim to have already lost – hinting that this loss is never quite consummated. *Les Déracinés* stages, over the course of its frequent and often simultaneous citations and denegations of Balzacian models, an insistent and, as that very insistence reveals, intractably incomplete renunciation – the unceasing loss of purportedly already lost illusions.

Lingering Illusions

The city of Paris is both the glittering background and the elusive prize in this drama of perpetual renunciation. Balzac's provincial heroes had puerile and, in Lucien's case, literary illusions of their own, which they had to renounce as they learned the ways of the capital and embarked on their social ascent. Barrès's protagonists know this, and so regard their own Balzacian illusions with suspicion, as chimeras to be discarded – perhaps hoping, paradoxically, that if they renounce their illusions, as Balzac's heroes had, they too will achieve Parisian success. The loss of naïveté, for Rastignac and Lucien, is compensated by unforeseen possibilities of advancement. For Barrès's seven *déracinés*, such compensation is slow to come, if it comes at all – for Racadot and Mouchefrin, none is in store, only more disillusion. Newly arrived from the provinces, the seven do not meet a world-savvy aristocrat like Rastignac's Madame de Beauséant, who offers valuable guidance; the newspaper for which they write does not, like Lucien's *Constitutionnel*, trade in theatrical scandals and high-flying political manoeuvres. As they attempt to make their way in a Parisian world that they know cannot conform to their literary knowledge of the capital, they confront the loss of their own illusions, including the paradoxical fallacy that they might somehow follow in the fictional footsteps of Balzacian models by renouncing them.

La Fille aux yeux d'or (*The Girl with the Golden Eyes*, 1834–5), the third instalment of *Histoire des Treize*, famously opens with a dizzying panoramic tour of Paris, as Balzac reels off a chain of metaphors linking the city to gold – the gold of ears of wheat, as the bustling capital becomes "a vast field incessantly rustled by a storm of opposing interests," and the gold of molten metals, as it turns to a hellish forge where "everything glows, everything smoulders, everything blazes."[84] This is the Balzacian city of the Treize, of Rastignac, of Lucien: a tempestuous, dangerous place, but also a space of immense possibilities, where fortunes are made and lost in thrillingly novelistic plot twists. The seven *déracinés* have heard its siren call, ironically echoed by Barrès's narrative voice: "Paris! ... The meeting-point of men, the great crossroads of humanity! ... the chosen place where they will fulfil their destiny." "To Paris!" they exclaim in response, like countless other provincials who lack what Barrès calls "a sense of reality."[85] Their image of Paris is based not on reality but derived from literary references: Barrès writes that Renaudin, "when he first arrived from Nancy, would repeat to himself: 'Here I am in the centre of Paris ... the centre of Paris ...,' with the intonation of a poet."[86]

In Pierre Gauthiez's *L'Âge incertain*, published a year after *Les Déracinés*, the young protagonist, Adrien, similarly abandons the town of his birth, seduced by "the idea of a literary Paris, where some of the Romantic age still lived, and the men of Balzac or Hugo would not have felt out of place." For this naïve provincial, Gauthiez writes, "Paris stood in front of him as a city of books. He was going to be able to embrace all knowledge, every text; he would find masters to guide him, and libraries to nourish his insatiable appetite."[87] In a slight but significant shift, "the city of books" of the young man's imagination, the city described in countless works (including, explicitly, those of Balzac), becomes a city that contains an endless number of further books to be read, an infinite expanse of library shelves. Like *Les Déracinés*'s Sturel, Adrien ends up preferring the booksellers' quarter at l'Odéon to the capital's other pleasurable offerings.[88] The literary city's promise of social, amorous, and financial possibility becomes, for the bookish provincial, the mere possibility of more reading. Even Balzac's Lucien experiences this shift – a temporary one, in his case – during his unsuccessful first weeks in the capital. He writes, in a letter to his sister who has remained in Charente: "I spend half of every day at the Bibliothèque Sainte-Geneviève ... in Paris ... immense libraries are always open, they provide the mind with intellectual nourishment [une pâture] ... in the air and in every smallest detail, there is a spirit that one breathes in, steeped in literary creations."[89] For the disabused young man from the provinces, the dreamed-of capital of opportunities has turned into a city of books; it is no longer a windswept field of gold, but a pasture for literary ruminations. Confounded by the dissimilarity of his Parisian experience to his book-fuelled aspirations, Lucien temporarily turns his back on reality, embracing pure literariness.

Gauthiez's Adrien and Balzac's Lucien acknowledge the loss of their illusions, yet cling to them, fleeing the city's reality for the consoling atmosphere of further readings. In *Les Déracinés*, this comforting spirit of literariness lingers, for Sturel and Roemerspacher, in ghostly form, as a succession of reminiscences of readings past:

> As they strolled through Paris – although the city was overrun with too many footsteps, transformed by new constructions – they evoked, like magicians uncovering unseen treasures beneath the ground, ghosts that kept them company. They had often breathed life into the boar of the Tuileries, where Fontanes and Chateaubriand used to lean.[90]

In this vaguely Baudelairian evocation of a Paris transformed by the passage of time and Haussmann's redesigns, literary ghosts haunt the cityscape. Sturel and Roemerspacher imagine themselves walking alongside the writerly figures of generations past, conjured up from the memory of their vast readings. For them, Paris no longer appears as a city of present and future possibilities, but as a museum of the literary past, an open-air library of phantomatic references. In such company, the two young men begin to seem like ghostly *flâneurs*, oblivious to the present realities of the city they stroll in, engrossed instead in readerly illusions. Barrès's fin-de-siècle protagonists are not merely haunted by models from the earlier half of the century – Rastignac, Trelawny, Napoleon, and in this scene, Chateaubriand – whom they invoke as exemplars of ambitious, active, triumphant masculinity. Rather than wellsprings of "national energy" (the title of the trilogy the book inaugurates), the *déracinés* themselves speak and act like shadows for most of the novel. Pale copies of models that never truly were, since these models are all diffused through literature, the seven young men glide around Paris without making a mark on it, like spectres of an idealized manliness that they have read about in books, and that they cannot hope to embody, precisely because they have been reading books.

And yet, Barrès's novel is not *L'Éducation sentimentale*, Flaubert's melancholic reworking of the novel of ambition as a meditation on the inadequacy of Balzacian models of romantic and social conquest.[91] In his review of *Les Déracinés*, published in February 1898, André Gide astutely points out that Barrès's thesis – that young men from the provinces are drawn to Paris by false hopes, and doomed to trials and miseries they could avoid by staying put – is belied by the novel's concluding events:

> [T]he events you recount, taken on their own, if we remove the way you describe them, seem less eloquent than yourself. They do not persuade as much as you would like them to. After all, Suret-Lefort, Renaudin, Sturel, Roemerspacher all succeed; with more money, one could imagine Racadot would have succeeded as well.[92]

Indeed a majority of the seven *déracinés* do eventually succeed: Suret-Lefort's adroit defence of Racadot in court launches his political career; Renaudin makes a name for himself as a journalist through his articles about the trial; the trilogy's next instalments, already written but unpublished at the time of the review, bear out Gide's prognosis for the remaining three.[93] In the end, the destinies of Barrès's protagonists are less triumphant, perhaps, than that of Balzac's Rastignac, but they are certainly grander than they would have been had the young men remained rooted in Lorraine. Their hesitant challenge to Paris – the challenge they did not dare shout out, ridiculing it as "shamefully mediocre" and lacking in readerly sophistication – turns out to be successful. Barrès's own reservations about writing a Balzacian novel have dissipated by the novel's conclusion. In the subsequent tomes of the trilogy, he appears content to refresh the background of the old master's works with recent events, a practice he had once lamented: *L'Appel au soldat* and *Leurs figures* chronicle a series of high-stakes political and financial manoeuvrings, with a supporting cast of influential aristocratic women and caricatural bankers that would not be out of place in *La Comédie humaine*. The loss of illusions insistently proclaimed, in *Les Déracinés*, by characters and narrator alike makes way for a return to Balzacian models of social ascent. The success of Barrès's own ambitions, all the while, would prove to be anything but illusory: following the publication of the trilogy, he would go on, Rastignac-like, to accumulate wealth, national honours, and political influence, even acquiring a storied provincial castle – a feat that Lucien, in *Splendeurs et misères des courtisanes*, attempts but never quite manages.[94]

PART III

Forming the Reader

(Case Study: *L'Écornifleur*, 1892)

In the late 1880s, around seven hundred novels were published each year in France. The figure had been increasing dramatically since the middle of the century, when it hovered near two hundred. This marked growth would come to a halt in the 1890s, as publishers faced a crisis of overproduction. The market reached saturation, books went unsold, and manuscripts were left unpublished.[1] As the critic Jules Case put it with dramatic flair in September 1891, "in the doorways of bookstores and publishers' offices, in editorial rooms and literary circles, there is talk of nothing but the crash of the book, the crisis of the novel, the collapse of literature."[2] Meanwhile, the novel as a genre found itself in a paradoxical position. Having at last attained critical and institutional legitimacy, it faced a problem of stagnation, as novelists failed to significantly renew established narrative forms, and languished instead in the shadow of illustrious predecessors like Balzac and Stendhal. By 1887, Zola's claims to scientificity were losing their lustre of novelty;[3] the fleeting reprieve of Bourget's "novel of analysis" was still two years away. Guy de Maupassant, in a short essay on "Le Roman" written that same year, summed up the situation in self-deprecatingly hyperbolic terms. "One must be either quite mad, quite bold, quite overconfident, or else quite stupid, to still write in our day!"[4] The contemporary writer, for Maupassant, not only exposed himself to the judgment of a public and of critics who had already read it all, he faced a deeper problem of originality due to his own status as a reader of literary greats:

> After so many masters ... what is there left to do that has not been done, what is there left to say that has not been said? Who among us can claim to have written a page or even a sentence that does not already exist somewhere else, in more or less identical form? When we read, we who are so saturated with French writing that our entire body feels like a pulp [pâte] made of words, do we ever come across a single line or a single thought that is not already familiar, of which we have never had, at the very least, some vague inkling?[5]

Reading, in this remarkable account, shapes the male reader to such a profound degree that its mental influence is described in corporeal terms. The reader's body is so thoroughly saturated with print that it becomes a pulp of words ("pâte" is a term used in the paper-making process), an impersonal mass of French language that can only be reshaped into more of the same. The physical devolves into the textual, and possibilities for labour productivity or sexual reproductivity are implied to fade, as the reader becomes a writer who will inevitably imitate rather than create. For Maupassant and his literary contemporaries (his first-person plural pronouns, like Bourget's, address an imagined community of educated male readers and writers), writing is an unwitting process of recycling, where every supposedly new page in fact unfailingly reprises or rearranges old material. Even reading, for such wordy beings, becomes an experience of uncanny familiarity, as a sense of *déjà lu* awaits at every page. To add to the mass of existing novels in such a context, Maupassant writes with a grin – for he is doing just that, since this essay was published as a preface to his own novel *Pierre et Jean*[6] – is an act of great audacity, if not of overconfidence, or simple foolishness.

Many late-century novels of formation, as we have seen, describe their protagonist's aspiration to writing as a direct and obvious consequence of excessive reading. While some narratives depict this desire as a vague impulse barely acted on, others represent the would-be writer's travails in sustained and pathetic detail, from the vagaries of inspiration to the difficulty of finding a publisher.[7] More didactic novels organized around a dichotomy of values situate writing, like reading, on the side of unproductivity or passivity, as a desire to be renounced, or else expiated through death. In André Mellerio's *Jacques Mérane* (1891), for instance, the protagonist, an avid reader who as a student "had started to scribble ... columns for newspapers, short stories for magazines,"[8] eventually comes to a clear-cut dilemma: he can choose either the hopeless pursuit of writing a novel or marriage to his childhood sweetheart. He opts for the latter, and lives.[9] Jules Renard's *L'Écornifleur* [*The Sponger*], published the following year, forgoes such rigid binarism and instead depicts the would-be writer's dilettantism[10] as an intermediate state of continually frustrated attempts, a persistent impotence in matters of productivity and seduction alike. Balzac had described Paris as a city where every action is motivated by the twin pursuits of "gold and pleasure";[11] the fin-de-siècle aspiring writer, in Renard's novel, fails in both regards, to tragicomic effect.

As its title suggests, Renard's novel describes the sponging relationship of its first-person narrator, Henri, a young and penniless would-be writer, to the Vernets, a modestly wealthy couple who regularly invite him to dinner. The Vernets are childless, a significant characteristic in a context of national anxieties over low birthrates; they take an interest in him out of boredom, hoping to be entertained by Henri's poetry and his gossipy stories about literary milieus.[12] The narrative depicts their unspoken arrangement as an exchange of one type of oral fare for another: "I dine well and often; I recite verses until all have had their fill."[13] As such, the relationship between the couple and the writer allegorizes that of the petit-bourgeois classes to literature: men who earn money – and, even more so, their wives – subsidize books as an escapist diversion from what should be a pressing familial and social concern, having and raising children. The question of adultery soon takes centre stage, as Henri wonders, confusing the salacious stories he is required to share for an expected course of action, "am I not obligated, given my literary education and society's demands, to become Madame Vernet's lover?"[14] His attempts at seduction, spurred by literary models, remain systematically ineffectual due to this very origin. At first, he hesitates in taking the lead, since he "can only glean what a declaration might sound like from [his] readings"; later, he relies on "memories of the theatre" as he and Madame Vernet, finding themselves alone, fail to come up with things to say to each other – "It seems to me that a scene is about to play out, and we are silent, as if mentally going over our parts, listening inwardly to the rising tide of things that should be said."[15] Nothing in their interactions is spontaneous or impulsive; instead, their actions and responses in matters of passion are shaped by internalized literary norms. When Madame Vernet at last gives Henri a kiss – on the neck – he awkwardly tries to embrace her, but he does not quite know how to do it, and again falls back on a literary cliché, set off from the text by ironic quotation marks: "I have no idea. I want to hold 'my mistress against me,' but she breaks free."[16] Refusing him, she proposes, as a consolation, that he write a novel about her, or, failing that, that he suggest novels for her to read. He agrees to the latter, fittingly beginning with *Madame Bovary*, the century's most notorious novel of adultery. This compromise is less a sublimation than an acknowledgment of the bookish nature of their relationship. For Henri, adultery is a literary convention, rather more seductive than Madame Vernet herself, and he finds himself unable, or unwilling, to perform the role of seducer in his own existence.[17] His relation to writing is much the same. Henri, having read voraciously, imagines that writing must be a desirable pursuit, or perhaps simply that it must be his pursuit, yet he rarely actually writes, and never very successfully. Instead he finds himself – as Maupassant's essay had earlier warned – simply rewriting things he has read.

The scene of Henri's first meeting with Monsieur Vernet is neatly symbolic in this regard. They trade calling cards: Monsieur Vernet's states his full name, address, and occupation, but the sponger's is blank except for a corner bearing his highly common given name, "Henri" (the cards are reproduced to scale in the novel's pages). The implications are clear. The bourgeois Monsieur Vernet has a solidly anchored identity, including a full name, a residence, a professional rank, and a place of employment, whereas Henri's identity is undefined, down to the absence of a family name. He presents himself as a social cipher, an entity with no traceable origin, only pure potential: as he explains to his interlocutor, he likes to have nearly blank cards on hand since "above my name, I can write a few lines, it's handy."[18] The empty card emblematizes the writer's imagined social mobility, his purported freedom to define himself through what he writes. As a creator, this image suggests, the writer gets to invent himself. Yet the narration quickly shows that what Henri writes and says – the material he uses to fill the blank of his social identity – is not an original signature, but rather a mere copy of texts he has read, and an abased one at that. When he dines at the Vernets' table, images of oral exchange are again summoned as he repays his meal by offering up half-digested literary morsels for his hosts' enjoyment:

> as my teeth enjoy the Château Palmer wine, my mouth fills with words and pours them out. The notes I go over every two or three days come in handy at such moments. They distil everything a young man should know in order to appear superior: an excerpt from Taine's *On Intelligence*, simplified to suit the worldly; an irony by Renan, enlarged and brought into focus for an average eyesight; a verse by Baudelaire that startles, to which we listen inwardly for a long time, like the echo of a sound in a cellar.[19]

The sponger reveals himself to be a vulgarizer in a basely literal sense. What he regurgitates, while drinking his hosts' wine, is *Intelligence* dumbed down, subtle irony magnified to the point of mediocrity, poetry reduced to noise echoing in the hollow space of his interlocutors' minds, like sound in cellar – a comparison that circles back to the Vernets' role as providers of wine. In life as in love or in dining-table conversation, the would-be writer appears incapable of having a thought or impression of his own, and relies instead on what he has read.

When the Vernets invite Henri to accompany them on vacation (at their expense) at a seaside resort, he brings along several books about the sea and the country, so that he may experience these new settings properly.[20] As he settles into his room, he looks out to the ocean, awaiting inspiration:

> I stare fixedly at the sea. I seem to be saying: "It's between you and me now!" ["À nous deux!"] But the sea holds out longer than I do ... The Deep Blue

> leads me to despair, because I cannot offer it an image of my own. I would be better off reading a page by Pierre Loti ... I am exasperated by the triviality of what the sea arouses in me ... Jules Verne's Nautilus brought me more wonder. I push these commonplaces away, but they bounce back to me like a ball on a string. My memory is overlain with the junk of comparisons: seaweed is the hair of the drowned, the lobster is the cardinal of the seas![21]

In this new iteration of Rastignac's challenge,[22] the sea replaces the city as a space for the ambitious young man to conquer. The contest is short-lived, though, as this particular young man soon abdicates, unable to come up with an original pronouncement. As Henri fishes around for something to write, he discovers that his mind is rather like a polluted shore, where all that wash up are fragmented and discoloured literary reminiscences, the flotsam of lifeless clichés. When, towards the end of the novel, he goes out to sea by himself to reflect on the events of his stay, he again finds himself unable to think an authentic thought: "A little dizzy from the rocking, I recite poetry to myself; having nothing of worth to say to myself, I call upon my favourite poets to think and speak for me."[23] The blank slate of Henri's identity as a writer, symbolized by his calling card, turns out to be less a space of potential than a perpetual vacuum, a permanent state of writer's block. In a final indignity, even the novel's very last sentence turns out to be a citation, as he reflects, "There is nothing left to do but to stick a label on my back, taken from the Goncourt brothers' *Journal*: 'Free to good home, a second-hand parasite.'"[24] The quotation is meant as a summation of his relationship to the Vernets, now come to an end, but it applies equally well to his relation to literature. In artistic as well as economic terms, Henri is not a producer but a parasite, who lives on his readings just as he feeds on the largesse of a bored bourgeois couple. As a would-be writer, he is not merely a sponger but a sponge. The very essence of his being – his lifeblood, in a sense – is a thin broth of diluted literary texts, without much colour or substance. Given a squeeze, whether by his hosts' dinner-table expectations or by his own aspirations to literary productivity, he can only render what he has previously absorbed from outside sources. Henri fulfils Maupassant's glum imagining of the state of the writer at the fin de siècle: he is a flavourless pulp of readings, made up of the barely digested words of others, incapable of writing or even thinking anything truly new. His story offers no resolution to any of the three common plots of the novel of formation (education, seduction or ambition), whether in a negative and dramatic, or positive and edifying end. He remains in a state of impotent suspension, and it is implied he will simply move on to leech off another household, as he came from one at the beginning of the narrative.

In a fin-de-siècle literary climate of which Renard's parasitic protagonist and Maupassant's bleak statements are emblematic, how could a reader succeed in becoming a writer over the course of a novel of formation? One answer requires that the question be split along levels of fictional and authorial success – that is, that we differentiate between the success or failure of the protagonist's writerly aspirations, as represented within a narrative (usually quite clearly, as in the case of *L'Écornifleur*), and the author's own degree of success (a rather more subjective measure) in depicting these travails and their outcome, in a manner that has literary value. In the last decades of the nineteenth century, few depictions of successful writerly ambitions are to be found, a tendency that can be accounted for by several factors: recurrent discourses about the dangers of reading and literary inclinations, the real-life context of a crisis of overproduction in the publishing industry, received ideas and literary conventions about the higher dramatic potential of failure, and the possibility that a failed artistic attempt is easier to represent convincingly than a successful one. Many authors chose to represent failure, yet their own potential success was complicated by a further problem, as the aspiring writer's failure to emancipate himself from literary models had become a well-worn topos.[25] In other words, to write about the difficulty of writing something new was itself not terribly original – perhaps at any point in literary history, but especially at a time of pronouncements like Maupassant's. To write successfully about failure, then, required a strategic approach. Facing this challenge, some young writers, Renard among them (born in 1864, he was twenty-six when he wrote *L'Écornifleur*), turned to modes of irony that allowed them to distance themselves from their narrative, and succeed, to some degree, at the expense of their protagonist's failure.

~

The three chapters that follow highlight strategies devised by turn-of-the-century novelists to overcome the paradox discussed in earlier chapters: writing a novel of formation in response to the supposed dangers of reading. Chapter 6 traces the progression of one such writer, Jean de Tinan (1874–98), from failed candour to fervent irony, as well as the successful appropriation of this lesson by Roger Martin du Gard (1881–1958). Tinan's increasing irony resulted in a novel in pieces, *Penses-tu réussir!* (So you think you'll succeed!, 1897), a patchwork of citations and gaps that paradoxically manages to convey sincere feeling; Martin du Gard, adopting these tactics in *Devenir!* (Becoming!, 1909), later turned to a strategy of distanciation as he revisited the fin-de-siècle novel of formation in subsequent decades.

In chapter 7, I show how, from the 1890s to the 1920s, André Gide drew on both fragmentation and distanciation to take the potential of irony ever further. Reversing dominant discourses about reading and its perils, Gide asserted instead that the alleged antisocial dangers of reading could be valuable for some select readers, usually envisioned as younger and male. In proposing a pedagogy of distance, he sought to initiate these privileged readers into a mode of reading at once leery and playful.

Finally, in chapter 8, I consider how Marcel Proust tackled late nineteenth-century representations of reading, particularly in his unfinished work *Jean Santeuil* (c. 1895–9). With close attention to his manuscripts and correspondence, I show how Proust came to develop his conception of the possibilities afforded by reading through an unlikely intermediary: his own reading of Ralph Waldo Emerson's essays on friendship and love. I propose that Emersonian fantasies of queer recognition and empathy, more explicitly present in the earlier *Jean Santeuil*, underlie the purportedly asexual relationship between narrator and reader in *À la recherche du temps perdu* (*In Search of Lost Time*, 1913–27), one of the most celebrated novels of the twentieth century.

6 Martin du Gard, Tinan, and the Uses of Irony

How often we hide – like cowards! – our emotion behind irony!

Tinan, Letter to André Gide, 15 January 1885[1]

In *Le Cahier gris* (The grey notebook, 1922), the first volume of Roger Martin du Gard's long novel cycle *Les Thibault*, two adolescent boys run away from their bourgeois Parisian homes with the mad project of crossing over to Africa. Having reached Marseille, they come, like the protagonist of Renard's *L'Écornifleur*, to a first encounter with the sea:

> The closeness of the sea filled them with glee. They ran out of the path toward it, shouting: "*Thalassa! Thalassa!*," lifting their hands forward to dip them in the blue waters ... But the sea did not let itself be touched. At the place where they came near it, the shore did not gently descend toward the water in a slope of fine sand, as their desire had imagined. Instead they overlooked a precipitous gorge [...] where waves shattered on sharp rocks. Beneath them, a breakwater of fallen boulders seemed to lurch forward, like some ancient jetty laid by the Cyclops.[2]

The boys' cry of "Thalassa! Thalassa!" is a citation, a re-enactment even, of a famous scene from a classical text, Xenophon's *Anabasis*, where an army of Greek soldiers shout with joy as they reach the Black Sea after a perilously long journey. *Anabasis* is traditionally one of the first texts read by students of classical Greek. The soldiers' cry, on the strength of this pedagogical diffusion, is cited or alluded to in a number of nineteenth-century adventure novels, including those of Jules Verne, which a later dialogue shows the boys, Jacques and Daniel, have read.[3] The scene thus reveals how they conceive of their own escapade through the lens of adventures they have read about, in school textbooks or in novels. Neither the boys' encounter with the sea nor their project of adventure end up corresponding to the picture conjured up by their readerly imagination: a precipitous, impassable drop separates them from the waves, and the police are soon notified of their whereabouts by a suspicious innkeeper. The physical gap between the boys and the sea is emblematic of the mental gap between their experience of reality and the imaginary objects of their overly enthusiastic impulses and desires; as if to confirm the literary nature of this rift, the narrative compares the rocky obstacle that separates them from the object of their longing to the work of the mythical Cyclops. Reduced to the distant and idle contemplation of this object in place of its possession ("the sea did not let itself be touched"), one of the boys expresses a new desire: "'Oh! to be able to describe all this!' sighed Jacques as he fingered the notebook in his pocket."[4] His impulse to write is presented as a continuation of his frustrated desire to live out what he has read about in books. Finding himself blocked from direct action or experience, Jacques hopes to at least sublimate his desire through representation. Yet his youthful attempts at literary creation are no more successful than his project of fleeing home: in trying to write about his frustrations, he comes up against a similar gap – the chasm between what he imagines he urgently needs to express and the stultified, disappointing results. The boys face a continuum of frustrated desires; as a distraught Daniel puts it, "Oh! how awful, these hopeless aspirations!"[5] To simply throw oneself earnestly towards the mirages of one's imagination, as Jacques and Daniel imagined throwing themselves in the Mediterranean, proves either impossible or disappointing. Bridging the gap, like defeating the Cyclops, requires a ruse.

Distance, or Objective Irony

In the first tomes of *Les Thibault* (1922–40), Roger Martin du Gard revisits not only the years before the First World War but a literary genre that proliferated during that period, the novel of formation. The narrative relies on a number of tropes that would have been largely familiar to readers who, like the author, came of age in the era of *Le Disciple*, *Les Déracinés*, and similar examples of the genre from the turn of the century.[6] The plot of *Le Cahier gris*, for instance, revolves around the discovery and gravely apprehensive discussion, by various figures of pedagogical and parental authority, of a notebook in which Jacques and Daniel detail their illicit readings and exchange feverish declarations of ambition and passionate friendship. Under the influence of forbidden materials (Rousseau, Musset, Zola ...), the boys have been aping the language of romantic passion in the notebook they use to correspond. Relying on the reader's familiarity with the assumption of a corollary between bad readings and so-called corruptive friendships among adolescent boys (concerned authorities speak elliptically of the "influence of a dangerous schoolmate" or "such contagions"),[7] the narrative builds hermeneutic tension – are they or aren't they?[8] – eventually relieved by the revelation that Jacques and Daniel have not gone beyond a "chaste love."[9] The alarmist discourse linking forbidden readings and close adolescent friendships with same-sex practices[10] is revealed to have been the object of an ironic citation.

Jacques's father and, most conspicuously, the overzealously interpretive priest for whom the content of the notebook leaves "simply no doubt as to the nature of this friendship"[11] find their discursive authority undercut by a narrative perspective that turns out to have known better all along. This practice of authorial irony, in which various discourses are cited by characters without immediate commentary from the narrative voice yet understood by or eventually revealed to the reader as being comically wrong, is particularly felt in descriptions of the young protagonists' literary aspirations. Jacques and Daniel's notebook is replete with amusingly puerile statements: "OUR LOVE," "you!!," "my ART!!!,"[12] Jacques writes in one entry, decidedly unafraid of overemphasis. Though the notebook is presented without comment, narrator and reader alike are understood to be well above such pronouncements. The distance that separates them from the charmingly juvenile Jacques and Daniel unites reader and narrator in a humorous complicity. Friedrich Schlegel, one of the most original theorists of irony, observed that in *Wilhelm Meister*, Goethe "seems to take the characters and incidents so lightly and playfully, never mentioning his hero except with some irony and seeming to smile down from the heights of his intellect upon his work"; Schlegel named this stance "objective irony."[13] Martin du Gard, then, could be said to place himself in the filiation of the Goethean *Bildungsroman* by inviting his reader to look onto his naïve protagonists with a mixture of amused distance and somewhat more tender sympathy. In doing so, he adopts irony as a strategy through which to surmount the pitfalls of overeager desire and sincerity that plague aspiring writers like the ones he depicts.

Martin du Gard's account of his own youth, in the short memoir *Souvenirs autobiographiques et littéraires* (1955),[14] reads rather like the typical narrative of a turn-of-the-century adolescence shaped by books. In a section on secondary school, a few lines about life at the *lycée* quickly give way to a detailed account of his illicit reading practices, through which he developed a taste for the likes of Zola, Mirbeau, and Jean Lorrain.[15] When the young Roger is sent to live with a professor and his wife, he is given unfettered access to their extensive library, which the memoirist remembers "overflowed with modern works": Bourget, Barrès, Vallès, Abel Hermant, Paul Adam, Henry Bordeaux, "all of Huysmans," "all of

Daudet," "all of Flaubert," and many others. "In that atmosphere thick with literature, and especially 'novelistic' [romanesque] literature," he writes, "I breathed with delight; it was all new to me, and intoxicating. I naïvely thought I had found my true environment."[16] These reminiscences, although fond, are tinged with ironic distance, manifested most strongly in the close juxtaposition of the adjective "true," in a thought attributed to the young Roger, and the adverb "naïvely," a commentary from the older Martin du Gard. Only a naïve youth, the juxtaposition suggests, would believe he found his true place in life among shelves stocked with fictions. Looking back, the writer indicates that he now knows better; he acknowledges how much his youthful experience of unabashed readerly enthusiasm (soon to be followed by grand writerly ambitions) is typical of a certain type of adolescent narrative, how well it corresponds to a script that has attained the status of cliché. Yet Martin du Gard did not wait until he reached memoir-writing age, or even until the mature enterprise of the sweeping novel *Les Thibault* to develop this kind of pointed, if also tender irony. According to the narrative he traces in *Souvenirs autobiographiques et littéraires*, he might very well not have had a literary career had he not honed this skill in what was to become his first published novel.

Irony as Exorcism

If Martin du Gard's use of overenthusiastic punctuation, as demonstrated in Jacques and Daniel's notebook, can be read as a sign of ironic citation, the very title of his novel *Devenir!* (Becoming!, 1909),[17] with exclamation mark, is an invitation to read the concept of becoming, of formation, and indeed the very genre of the novel of formation with critical detachment. Punctuation in the titles of the novel's three sections – "Wanting!," "Achieving?," "Living ..."[18] – likewise underscores, almost to the point of parody, the familiar arc of the protagonist's evolution from exclamatory ambition to pensive disillusion.[19] Indeed the novel was conceived, according to Martin du Gard's *Souvenirs*, as an exercise in distanciation. A life-changing encounter with Tolstoy's *War and Peace* at the age of seventeen, he writes in his memoir, had sparked the imitative desire to write a monumental novel – an enterprise that would later come to occupy two decades of his career. Still under the spell of Tolstoy at twenty-five, the aspiring author, after a series of aborted attempts, set out to write a vast three-part cycle, *Une Vie de saint* (A saint's life), detailing the life of a small-town priest, from cradle to grave, surrounded by a wide cast of characters. Between 1906 and 1908, Martin du Gard worked tirelessly on this project, but he eventually had to acknowledge it was going nowhere. In a moment of lucidity, he saw himself as the very thing he yearned not to be: a weak imitator who, in his desire to emulate Tolstoy, actually betrayed the master novelist, whose naturalness and lack of mannerism he admired above all.[20] After a few months of literary inactivity, he again took up the pen and, in a sudden burst of inspiration, completed the draft of *Devenir!*. "I have always considered *Devenir*," Martin du Gard writes some forty-five years later, "as a kind of exorcism meant to break [conjurer] the spell I had lived under since the failure of *Une Vie de saint*." If he managed to successfully depict the failure of a would-be writer, the reasoning went, he would prove himself not to be one:

> I suddenly felt an impulse to write the life of a young, presumptuous writer ... full of "illusions about his talent," and whose existence would be a succession of sterile hopes and failures. (I had convinced myself that if I succeeded in this portrayal of "failure," I would somehow prove that I was not destined to share the deplorable fate of my protagonist.)[21]

There is something mathematical to this calculation: the negativity of failure, negatively portrayed in an ironic mode, is expected to amount to positive "proof" of the author's potential. There is also, tellingly, something rather esoteric, close to the realm of wishful thinking – "exorcism," "breaking a spell" – through what amounts to a writer's sleight of hand. At the level of biography, *Devenir!* was successful in that it did allow its author to go on to a celebrated career. As a literary endeavour, the result is more ambiguous. The novel succeeds in its ironic citation of fin-de-siècle tropes about bookish young men's ambitions (a strategy made visible in Martin du Gard's frequent use of quotation marks as he retrospectively describes the project in his memoirs)[22] yet remains unable to surmount the more paradoxical aspects of its conceit. It reveals itself, most conspicuously in the last of its three parts, to not always be in control of its ironies.

The shadow of Tolstoy, who had inspired the failed project of *Une Vie de saint*, still looms over *Devenir!*. The Russian master, for Martin du Gard, represents a writerly ideal: the pure representation of reality, unencumbered by literariness. After reading Stefan Zweig's biography of Tolstoy in 1930 ("with a personal and passionate interest," he specifies), Martin du Gard notes some of Zweig's characterizations in his diary: "Tolstoy's eyes *can only see life as it is* ... without dreams, fancies or illusions"; "[his] art ... is as clear as water." He confides that "my dearest, most secret and timid wish is to deserve, some day, that through some more or less distant analogy, someone might quote a few of these pages about my own work."[23] The protagonist of *Devenir!*, André Mazerelles, is introduced as the opposite of this ideal of directness and transparency. The son of a notary, he was born with "an enviable intelligence" but, fatefully, "from a very young age, had used it to systematically contradict everything he saw and heard around him."[24] André, in other words, is unable to hear or see reality as it is; his intelligence instead leads him to denature it, to view the world in a warped, unreal way. Predictably, he is drawn to the distorting lens of literature: "As soon as he was old enough to read, he gravitated towards books: such a vice was in his nature."[25]

By the age of twenty-two, André's twisted nature has become visible in his physicality, from his "narrow, feminine gestures," to "the softness of his voice and the mannered grace of his movements," to the point that older men "called him ambiguous names – without really believing it."[26] André is the very picture of the decadent, denatured fin-de-siècle young man,[27] so much so that even his androgynous demeanour is not taken as a reliable indication of particular sexual proclivities; men may call him names, but they do not believe them to be necessarily true, seeing him instead as a symptom of the times. André, in short, embodies the unreliability and unreality of the gendered sign, and the literary sign, at the turn of the century. Here, as in *Le Cahier gris*, Martin du Gard cites and plays with certain queer conventions of the novel of formation. André's gender ambiguity, like the possibility of a sexual relationship between Jacques and Daniel, is both suggested and disavowed by the narrator. André's poses are borrowed from an earlier literary era: he puts on, as if it were a garment, "an 1830s '*mal du siècle*' attitude that suited him."[28] The quotation marks underscore the citational nature of André's stance, as well as the narrator's ironic distance from this borrowing. Distancing quotation marks again recur in a long description of André's choice of literature as a vocation:

> He had no intention of deviating from his "vocation," which clearly was "literary." He had carefully shaped for himself a literary intelligence, a literary sensitivity, a whole literary temperament, which could now be nothing else ... His tastes, his ways of thinking, his ways of acting, the slightest of his tendencies were literary: he had a literary way of viewing painting, of listening to music, of dreaming about women; he even had a literary way of thinking about literature, since he deliberately wanted to devote his life to it.[29]

Clearly, André is the very opposite of Martin du Gard's Tolstoian ideal of the writer's direct, untainted experience and representation of reality – a little too clearly, perhaps, for this characterization to be taken entirely seriously, given the narrator's comically redundant use of the term "literary." André emerges as a near caricature of Bourget's diagnosis of fin-de-siècle readers, who according to him suffer from "the illness of having known the image of reality before encountering reality itself."[30]

Having introduced this protagonist, Martin du Gard goes on to stage a conflict between his bookish disposition and reality, in the form of a stint of military service – "ten months of purely animal existence," according to André. Yet proclivities die hard, and the first thing André does upon returning home is reread his favourite authors, foremost among them, as it happens, the author of *Le Disciple*: "Some Bourget, some Régnier, some France ... Ibsen ... Barrès ... I reread *La Débâcle*, *Le Rouge et le Noir*, *Madame Bovary* ..."[31] In conversation with a friend, André describes his flustered disappointment at discovering that his favourite books have little to do with what he has just experienced as the reality of life:

> After living [...] a simple life for ten months, when you stick your nose in those yellow books[32] again, you no longer see yourself in them ... You find yourself asking: 'What? what is this? This is supposed to be observation? life? ideas? Oh, my! ...' Once you've breathed in life, the real one, [...] you naïvely believe you'll find some of it reproduced in books ... Pfft! Not at all, my friend. Not at all![33]

One of the ironies at play here is that André's favoured readings include a number of narratives of disillusion with literature; he may have read Bourget, Barrès, Stendhal, and Flaubert many times over, but he has not read them particularly well. Or perhaps he has read them too well and is now reciting their lesson too literally: Zola's *La Débâcle*, for instance, pits the virile grandeurs of military self-sacrifice against the pitfalls of over-intellectual decadence.[34] For André to momentarily adopt a new pose as a proponent of the invigorating benefits of martial life – especially if this pose comes from reading Zola – is rather amusing. Obstinately blind to such paradoxes, he dismisses the works of his predecessors and instead imagines himself as the innovator who will rescue literature from the miasma of excessive literariness: "I dream of a new art form ... I want to create a book that would contain 'life' and nothing else."[35] Martin du Gard thus places, in his protagonist's mouth, the very ambition he derived from his reading of Tolstoy. In introducing his own aspirations through those of the comically oblivious André, he deploys a strategy of simultaneous affirmation and disavowal. Irony saturates the statement, masking it but also, for the sharp-eyed reader, marking it as a roundabout confession: what we are reading is not only the laughably grandiose project of a naïve would-be writer, but also, presented indirectly, almost surreptitiously, the author's own discreetly avowed ambition.

The predictable failure of André's grand literary project, in the novel's central section, is depicted no less ironically. The would-be writer flees the hustle of Paris in order to work on a play in the small town of

Fontainebleau, at a hotel deserted for the winter. The location itself is intertextually significant, Fontainebleau being the setting of a famous episode in Flaubert's *L'Éducation sentimentale* during which the protagonist likewise seeks to escape from a series of disappointments in Paris. At this hotel, André encounters a mysterious woman, whom he first lays eyes on as she cuts the pages of a new book. A few days later, they have their first conversation when she asks him about a volume of poetry he brings to every meal; they go on to discuss contemporary books and authors. When André starts to wonder about her identity, he attempts to "solve her mystery using various novelistic formulas." He recalls a certain word she said that suggests the possibility of an "*intrigue*" (in French, a conspiracy or liaison, but also a plot).[36] Eventually he learns that her name is Ketty Varine, and that she is a globetrotting Russian orphan who first came to Paris as a maid-in-waiting to a Slavic princess. A romance develops between them; she helps him write his play, but soon his fear of failure leads him to abandon both the woman and the project, and precipitously return to Paris, where we are told he indulges in memories of her "with literary fondness."[37] Critics have noted that the name Ketty Varine is a reminiscence of *Anna Karenina*, where the character Kitty Levina (Levine, in the French translation) crosses paths with a Russian orphan girl named Varenka (in French, Varinka).[38] The allusion is made even more transparent when André, shortly after his return from Fontainebleau, is invited to see a stage version of *Anna Karenina*, and decides to reread the novel.

If Ketty's confidence and worldliness have little to do with Tolstoy's charitable, selfless Varenka, they can be ascribed to another easily identifiable model: Astiné Aravian, the alluring Armenian adventuress of Barrès's *Les Déracinés*.[39] Many layers of literariness are in play in this episode: in a literarily significant setting, a man with a literary project meets a woman through the pretext of a book; they discuss literature. Wondering who she is, he imagines her story through "novelistic formulas," until her real identity is revealed: it turns out to be a composite of literary models. Eventually, he renounces her companionship, preferring instead to remember her with "literary fondness." Everything that happens between André and Ketty is mediated by literature, from physical books to intertextual references. The episode stages an erasure, at every level, of the authentic or the real behind the literary; as such, it carries out, at the level of plot, what we are told early on about the protagonist's thoroughly "literary temperament." It is the narrative equivalent of the hyperbolic repetition of the term "literary" in the earlier description of André's vocation. Irony is born of this insistent redundancy, as well as of the juxtaposition of André's project – "to create a book that would contain 'life' and nothing else" – with such an antithetical set of circumstances.

Living-dead Attachments

Astiné Aravian embodied, in *Les Déracinés*, the seduction of exotic adventure narratives; the inclusion of her alluring tales of the Caucasus, followed by her brutal murder, allowed Barrès's novel to both take pleasure in and stage a dramatic renunciation of the poetry of the foreign. Considering that *Devenir!* not only features its own version of Astiné, but recounts the Parisian travails of a group of eight ambitious young men – *les Huit*, the next number up from Barrès's seven – we may wonder whether Martin du Gard's references to Barrès betray a similar stance of ambiguously coupled partaking and denegation. *Les Huit* are the object of the some of the narrator's most successfully biting irony. Everything they do, every pose they strike reveals or results in the very thing they try to hide or combat:

> Their greatest fear was to seem immature, which itself showed their extreme lack of maturity ... They looked down on snobs and on those who put on airs, to the point that this revulsion became their own snobbishness, the air they naïvely put on. They had such a great fear of forming a "clique" that, preemptively, they made every effort to mock each other: in doing so they formed a clique of self-admiring mockery, more "cliquish" than any other. They were, in the end, everything they desperately tried not to be.[40]

Attitudes of detachment and sophistication, in this picture, end up revealing what they were meant to hide. It is tempting to apply this interpretation to Martin du Gard's own adopted stance of ironic citation of Tolstoy or Barrès: the result would be the unwitting avowal of an enduring attachment and identification with models that, on the surface, are derided. The presence in *Devenir!* of an ersatz Astiné (Ketty) and group of seven (here, eight) allows the author to live out his infatuation with the stories and characters of Barrès, all the while disavowing this fascination through distance. This is a fundamental characteristic of romantic irony. Schlegel defines irony as a stance that allows a writer to both endorse something and reject it, to simultaneously hold up an ideal and tear it down, to have it both ways. The true artist, he claims, not only writes about what he loves but "rises above his affection and is able to destroy what he adores."[41]

Another theorist of irony, the psychoanalyst Theodor Reik, similarly proposes that irony is the mark of a lost ideal, at once reawakened and "contradicted and rejected by better insights":

> The contradiction and contrast between an old and a new attitude and the accompanying emotions form the soil from which irony springs ... The

> corpse of old emotions is awakened to a mock-life which demonstrates how dead it really is ... In the ironic expression not only are the old illusion and the old disenchantment reawakened from the past, but also the indignation and the bitterness, which are the more deeply felt, the more genuinely and sincerely the old faith was once embraced.[42]

According to Reik, the lost or renounced ideal is brought up only to be beaten into submission with the bludgeon of irony. We see this pattern at work in *Devenir!*, where the aspiration to become a writer or be part of a group of up-and-coming talents is staged, only to be mocked by the narrator. Yet Reik's description does not suggest an ideal that "really is" dead as much as one that subsists in a state of living death, as a phantom that isn't as easily cast out – through exorcism, the breaking of a spell (*conjurer l'envoûtement*, in Martin du Gard's words) – as the ironist might like to believe. "Conjuration" has opposite meanings in French, where it means to cast out a danger or an evil spirit, and in English, where it means to summon one. The ironic citation of buried ideals reflects this double meaning and produces a contradiction: the cited model is both renounced and held on to.

Schlegel's and Reik's definitions can help us characterize the complex relationship of *Devenir!* to its other main intertext, *Penses-tu réussir!* (So you think you'll succeed!, 1897) by Jean de Tinan. A bright young thing of French letters, Tinan died at age twenty-four in 1898, making him a cult figure in Parisian student circles. Dedicated to Tinan, Martin du Gard's novel both mocks and partakes in its precursor's world-weary cynicism. When André, who, we are told, has read too much Tinan, attempts to replicate a scene from *Penses-tu réussir!* and starts to philosophize in a brothel, we are simultaneously invited to share in his detachment and deride it as a pose.[43] Likewise, when his friend Bernard reads Tinan out loud, the narrator cynically notes that *les Huit* listen rapturously, not because the text is a revelation but because they already know it by heart; in doing so, he acknowledges both the text's appeal and its status as a cliché.[44] A slight syntactic ambiguity invites us to ask if, rather than Bernard having a solid command of the text ["il le possédait à fond"], it might not be the other way around – Bernard possessed by the text – which in turn allows us to wonder if the passages he recites are indeed appropriately illustrative of "the day's mood" or whether the passages might not actually have dictated the mood in the first place. The scene shows *les Huit* under the spell of Tinan, inviting the reader to stand with the narrator in a position of ironic detachment and (to use Reik's term) disenchantment; yet the spell, by virtue of this very conjuration, shows itself not to be entirely banished. The influence of Tinan haunts Martin du Gard's novel, even as the text repeatedly calls up this spectre in an effort to show how dead it really is; the bitterness of its reproof of *les Huit* and André's fascination for a dead author reveals the depth of its own lingering attachment to this purportedly rejected model.

When André confesses his writerly ambitions to Bernard and bemoans the absence of reality in the works of his favourite authors, they have the following exchange:

> – ... They left everything in the margins. You have to wonder what they made their books with!
>
> – With those that came before.[45]

The remainder of the narrative shows the would-be writer doomed to repeat the faults he ascribes to his predecessors, as prophesied in Bernard's mordant reply. In spite of André's efforts, his literary temperament spoils every one of his attempts at capturing life. When, having abandoned his legal studies, he spends his days wandering the streets of Paris in search of inspiration, he turns out to be blind to anything that does not evoke a literary reminiscence.[46] Later, as he diligently trudges through what he considers difficult but required readings like Goethe or Shakespeare, he is struck by flashes of inspiration that turn out to be nothing more than a compulsion for pastiche.[47] By the last third of the novel, André comes to forsake his ambition, although his essentially imitative nature continues to dictate his choices. When he sees one of his friends give up his life as a Parisian bachelor and settle instead on a country estate that he plans to transform with modern farming techniques imported from America, he decides to do exactly the same. Not that a flight to the country represents a complete escape from literary models; it might well be that André now fancies himself a benevolent pastoral reformer along the lines of Balzac's *Le Médecin de champagne* (*The Country Doctor*, 1833), although the result is more akin to the agronomic disaster described with relish in Flaubert's *Bouvard et Pécuchet* (1881, posth.). One might even read this final rural debacle as a send-up of Barrès's injunction to take root in the provinces. The novel ends with the double death of André's new wife and her stillborn child, in what one critic described as a slovenly amalgam of similar scenes from *Anna Karenina*, *War and Peace*, Gide's *L'Immoraliste* (1902), and Zola's *Pot-Bouille* (1882–3).[48] *Devenir!*, by this point, has run out of breath, and the amusing detachment that characterized its first two-thirds has waned. It is no longer André but the author himself who is attempting to make a new book out of old ones. In a final and unintended irony, the young Martin du Gard falls prey to the phantom of excessive literariness he had conjured in order to exorcize.

A Formula for Sincerity

The aspiration to represent reality free from the encumbrance of literariness – "'life' and nothing else" – is often accompanied by a corollary desire for sincerity in expression that would be equally free of literary clichés. Like the impulse towards transparent description, we find this desire manifested by the young Jacques in *Le Cahier gris*:

> Oh! imagine not doing anything artificial, following your nature, and feeling that since you were born to create, your mission is the gravest and most beautiful of all, a great duty to accomplish. Yes! Being sincere! Being sincere in all things, at all times! Oh! How cruelly this thought haunts me! A thousand times, I've caught a glimpse in myself of the falsity of false artists, of false geniuses, that Maupassant describes in *Sur l'eau*. My heart heaved with disgust.[49]

The mature Martin du Gard's mastery of irony is on full display here: Jacques's very ideal of the true artist's natural sincerity is based on a negative example culled from a literary work, a paradox to which he appears blind. A thousand times over, Jacques has sensed the contrived falsity of his own expression, yet he refuses to abandon his claim to achieving sincerity. As he anxiously analyses himself and his own revulsion at falsity – in writing, since this confession is taken from the notebook he shares with Daniel – he comes to resemble nothing so much as Maupassant's description of the woeful "man of letters," a being split into "a reflection of himself ... condemned to observe himself feel, act, love, think, suffer."[50] The proliferation of exclamation marks in close proximity, as well as the lyrically overwrought "Oh!," twice repeated, underscores the naïveté of Jacques's posturing; and yet, at the same time, his very failure to achieve sophistication manages to convey something akin to youthful sincerity. As readers, we are invited to stand above Jacques – we, along with the narrator, know better than to line up so many exclamations – but also, as Schlegel put it, "smile down" on him, since his failed attempt betrays a juvenility that is more real, by virtue of being involuntarily displayed, than any of his literary affectations. In *Devenir!*, Bernard ponders the question of writerly sincerity when he tells André, "the most difficult, you see, is [...] the formula of one's sincerity ... Barely anyone gets it right."[51] What if, as Jacques unwittingly suggests, the failure to properly formulate things could itself turn out to be a formula for sincerity?

As he began work on what would become *Penses-tu-réussir!*,[52] Jean de Tinan expressed an aspiration similar to that which Martin du Gard would later attribute to Jacques – to write a book where every idea and sensation is represented in a perfectly heartfelt and original manner, without recourse to literary commonplaces:

> So I'm gathering notes, I've made an outline of my chapters and I *think* them through often. But that's too simple, you see: I want there not to be a single sentence that isn't right, not one idea, not one sensation that's "ready-made," I want *everything* to pulsate, and the psychology to be thorough. It's heavy stuff, and my back is not that solid.[53]

The addressee of this confession is André Gide, whose first book, *Les Cahiers d'André Walter* (1891), had made such an impression on Tinan that when he finished his own first work, *Un document sur l'impuissance d'aimer* (A document on the incapacity to love, 1894), he brought it to the same small publisher, La Librairie de l'Art Indépendant.[54] *Un document*, like Gide's *Cahiers*, is a slim volume that combines transparently fictionalized diary entries, poems, and letters, all presented, also like Gide's *Cahiers*, as a text collected by a friend of a young man writing in the first person.[55] It is a decidedly fin-de-siècle affair, managing to namecheck, in under seventy pages, Schopenhauer, Nietzsche, Maeterlinck, Wagner, Tolstoy, and Flaubert, along with citations in German, Greek, and Latin. Marcel, the young man who writes in the first person, confesses his impotent desire to love ("My God, how *I would love to love*!");[56] his daily occupations are recorded in entries such as "I lock myself in my room all day to write – dream – read in a cool semi-darkness."[57] He appears to have read Bourget, or at least be familiar with the diagnosis put forth in *Essais de psychologie contemporaine*: "love has been ruined for me up until now, because I always saw, between reality and myself, some ready-made idea."[58] Tinan's first effort is thus largely an exercise in imitation, overflowing with literary and cultural references: the story, and the work, of a young man who has read too much, including works such as Bourget's about young men who read to much.

Yet *Un document* includes a few flashes of what would become Tinan's signature self-irony, such as this "note" found at the bottom of an attempt to classify (using Greek letters) intense attachments into three types:

> Note. – All of this is too complicated, and I truly envy those who are able to love simply.
>
> And yet – no, I don't envy them – in fact, I remember reading somewhere: "We've read too many books that cost 7,50F to love as everyone else does."[59]

The note shows the protagonist Marcel oscillating between contrary positions: immediately after proposing a complex typology of affections, he dismisses this proposition and expresses envy for those who can "love simply." This new statement is in turn immediately rejected in favour of a citation that would seem to reinstate the initial proposition: people like Marcel are too sophisticated to love simply; their attachments instead follow the kinds of complex models they have read about, and of which Marcel was cataloguing examples a few lines above. Yet this last reversal of position is introduced flippantly ("I remember reading somewhere"), and with the ironic distance afforded by quotation marks. The citation itself is rather self-mockingly ironic, its claim to sophistication laced with a good measure of self-derision. The price mentioned is about double the standard cost of a book in turn-of-the-century Paris.[60] A "book that costs 7,50F" is likely a small print run, a more rarefied cultural product unlike those consumed by "everyone else" – but the very mention of a price reduces such a book to the status of fashionable commodity. The final position adopted by Marcel (the "note" comes at the very end of his diary entry for that day) is thus at once characterized by pronounced self-consciousness – the acknowledgment of being a consumer of expensive books – and the careful remove of ironic citation. The note effects a systematic crossing out of his pronouncements, until we are left with a blur. Borrowing another term from Schlegel, we could say that Marcel "hovers" between the acknowledgment of literary influences on his conception of love, and the desire to love simply; between the pompous claim to loving differently from the masses, and the recognition of that claim as an affectation.[61]

A later scene of shared reading features a similar effect of crossing out, as Marcel once more dismisses a proposition he has just made:

> We were reading, and I said:
>
> "I enjoy reading next to you – it feels like our gazes cross paths over certain words, it's a very subtle caress which I find charming."
>
> It wasn't very clever, you'll admit, nor was it very new, and yet.[62]

The successive affirmation and rejection of the statement – again concerning the intertwinement of reading and desire – leaves it in a state of limbo, crossed out but not erased. The suggestion that reading together could be like a caress is both put forward and brushed off by Marcel's narrative voice; he is left hovering between the two positions, neither fully embracing the statement – since it is, by his own admission, too poorly put, too much of a cliché – nor fully rejecting it, since the rejection is tempered by an incomplete clause. This "and yet" ("mais enfin") is both truncated and loaded with meaning. An addendum that dares not speak itself fully, it nevertheless makes itself heard: we as readers are led to understand what Marcel cannot bring himself to say, that his initial affirmation, though admittedly stated in a manner at once awkward and affected, was in some way heartfelt.

In addition to Schlegel's dictum that the artist should simultaneously set up and tear down his creation, Tinan's technique of figuratively crossing out statements immediately after they are made brings to mind what Roland Barthes called "stammering" (bredouillement) – a characteristic of spoken language, where mistakes or unsatisfactory attempts cannot be, as in writing, completely excised and erased, but must instead be crossed out after the fact, with a "cancellation through addition."[63] "Stammering," for Barthes, reveals "the dysfunctions of language,"[64] the occasional failure of speech to present a seamless surface. In devising a written work that "stammers" in precisely this manner, self-consciously dismissing its own affirmations, Tinan not only evokes the greater intimacy and immediacy associated with spoken language, he also invites the reader to catch a glimpse, through the avowed failures and dysfunctions of his style – too mannered, too cliché, too self-conscious even – of the sincerity of his effort, as if through the cracks of a thickly but imperfectly applied veneer of literariness. This is the saving grace of *Un document*, which Tinan's preface, with precisely this kind of stuttering hesitation, introduces as a "document whose value, *I think*, resides in its being *more or less* sincere" (my emphasis).[65] It would become the guiding principle of his next major endeavour, the novel *Penses-tu réussir!*.

Self-fragmentation, or Subjective Irony

Penses-tu-réussir! (1897) is full of narratorial asides with multiple levels of parentheses, where emotions and the ways they are expressed are simultaneously dismissed and embraced, as here: "(Verbose and inadequate monotony of these trite little memories – I love you, poor ways of being of our erased and fluttering sensibilities ... (and here it's on purpose that I pile up so many inaccurate adjectives) ...)"[66] Such interruptions correspond to what Schlegel termed "subjective irony," the disruption of a scene by an intrusive comment from the narrator. This ironic doubling, between a protagonist and a narrator who both frequently interrupt and comment on the story, is inscribed in the very structure of the novel. Like *Un document*, *Penses-tu réussir!* is introduced as the work of a friend of the protagonist. Whereas in the former the friend disappears between the introduction and a brief postscript, here two narrative voices coexist. The nameless friend writes a preface and narrates five of the nine chapters, describing the protagonist, Raoul de Vallonges, in the third person; in the remaining chapters, Raoul recounts his amorous experiences in the first person. The result is a commingling of distance and proximity that replicates, at the level of narrative structure, the characteristic duality of irony, as Raoul pours fourth his emotions yet constantly remains subject to both self-derision and outside scrutiny. Except for the grammatical person they each use, the two voices are not markedly different; the preface even invites us to conflate them when it specifies, "The man who wrote this book is as young as the man who is its 'hero.'"[67] Here, as throughout the novel, quotation marks are systematically used to denote the ironic use of a term or phrase – a device that would be taken up again by Martin du Gard.

The first chapter opens in Raoul's tiny apartment, filled with bookshelves and writing tables piled high with papers. Raoul has come across a letter from a former mistress – "a fine holograph,"[68] he calls it, comparing the letter to a bibliophile's collectible – and he and the narrator begin discussing past loves. Like *Un document*'s Marcel, Raoul and his friend's experiences with love have come short of an ideal they recognize as false and unattainable, which they name "the blue Dream" ("with a capital D," they specify).[69] Raoul expounds on this phenomenon:

> "My apologies for returning to it – I'm well aware that this makes for a 'long-winded' passage – but the little scene above, repeated six thousand times, that is our sentimental life ... I've known the blue Dream thoroughly, it has caused me much suffering, and its faded petals are now drying between the first few pages of the book of my life – 'a supreme book,' as Mr. A. de Lamartine called it." ...
>
> Vallonges opened a drawer, scattered some pages covered in handwriting, and picked one; he read it with exaggeration:
>
> "Here, this is a sample of its dear literature."[70]

Like the Ketty Varine sequence in Martin du Gard's *Devenir!*, this scene is saturated with references to reading and writing. In an apartment lined with bookshelves, Raoul discusses his penchant for excessive sentimentality and his yearning for an inaccessible ideal; he compares his life to a "supreme" book, citing Lamartine; he reaches into a drawer and starts reading some of what he derisively calls the "dear literature" that his unattainable dream once inspired him to write. The crucial difference between Martin du Gard's and Tinan's use of irony is that the protagonist Armand, in *Devenir!*, unwittingly bears the brunt of the narrator's various ironies, whereas Raoul, in *Penses-tu réussir!*, makes his own self-consciously ironic declarations. Martin du Gard's irony is consistently one-directional: at all times, the narrator knows better than Armand. Tinan's Raoul, by contrast, does not need the narrator – he himself knows better, and judges himself unrelentingly. "Yes, I used to write this kind of thing at that time," he tells his friend after reading his old work. "It was some very bad literature, and some shamefully facile philosophizing – and yet it meant a lot to me ..."[71] In many ways Raoul *is* the narrator: the preface indirectly tells us as much, and what's more, he comments on his own discourse as if it were a printed literary work, referring to what he has previously said as "the little scene above" and self-deprecatingly condemning its redundancies as "'long-winded'" (the later in quotation marks, as if to acknowledge the predictable nature of such a critique). His nameless friend is a placeholder, more of a narrative device than a narrator proper. The friend/narrator holds Raoul at arm's length, allowing Tinan to avoid the excessive self-absorption that marred *Un document*. By dialoguing with this double, Raoul (and through him, Tinan) is able to look at himself both closely and at a remove, subjectively and critically.

In *Devenir!*, the authorial self is neatly split between a failed protagonist who holds on to juvenile literary ideals, and a narrator who stages or proclaims the renunciation – the "exorcism" – of these ideals through irony. Through Armand, Martin du Gard composes an unflattering image of his younger self, to be held at a distance, and, through this distance, overcome. Armand, though certainly self-conscious in the sense that he fears and bemoans his eventual failure, is never made to look at himself with ironic remove. Only the narrator is given the privilege of distance, as if the novel were a one-way mirror, where Armand sees only his close reflection, and does not see himself being observed. Tinan, by contrast, constructs a veritable hall of mirrors, where Raoul and the narrator are both, at different times and possibly simultaneously, character and author, spoken and written, self-pitying in their confessions and self-conscious of their affectations. Raoul and the narrator are both constantly quoting their own beliefs, past and present, "with exaggeration," and then dismissing them with a smirk or a snide comment. The result is a proliferation of quotation marks, dashes, italics, and multiple levels of parentheses that at times make it difficult to know who is speaking, and consistently make it impossible to distinguish what is sincerely said. Tinan's irony does not have a master and a dupe, but rather makes a conscious dupe of all involved, including the author. It is not a tool but a condition. Although nothing in his novel is said with complete sincerity, without literal or figurative quotation marks, the recognition of this condition – the infiltration of the literary into all aspects of the writer's and the characters' existence – is in many ways an act of greater sincerity than its disavowal through projection and one-directional irony.

Penses-tu réussir! is ponderously heavy with literary references. The novel opens with epigraphs from Stendhal and Racine; it is dedicated to Tinan's friend, the poet and novelist Pierre Louÿs; each of the nine chapters bears an additional dedication to one of the author's literary contemporaries (among them Jean Lorrain, Willy, and André Lebey.)[72] The preface – titled, with Tinan's characteristic self-conscious hesitation, "To serve as a preface" – is dedicated to Barrès and quotes the original 1888 preface to *Sous l'œil des Barbares*: "This is a short realist monograph."[73] Barrès is named seven times in the novel, more than any other writer. These references are to the author of *Le Culte du Moi*, since *Penses-tu réussir!* was written in 1896, a year before *Les Déracinés* appeared. Tinan's narrator and protagonist worship *Le Culte du Moi* in what amounts to a cult of Barrès, highlighting the trilogy's problematic status as a work that could end up propagating the symptoms it depicted, despite Barrès's later claims that it aimed to denounce these ills.[74] Raoul encapsulates this paradox when he cites *Sous l'œil des Barbares* to describe the effect Barrès has had on him:

> Here is a sentence by Mr. Maurice Barrès which I find too perfect not to gloss: "*He had gorged on the most audacious paradoxes of human thought; it is likely he would hardly have been able to develop their structure, but he turned them into a sentimental substance* ..." There was a time when Mr. Barrès's own books were all the dearer to me, because I myself could not *develop their structure* – they filled me with an intense fever ... [...] it is to them that I owe the care I have had, since that time, to introduce some order into the readings I had previously done haphazardly ... they made me want to be "*intelligent*" ... I do not exaggerate their importance.
>
> (The young men on whom Mr. Barrès had an influence have not yet spoken about him. He was more than the man of letters, the ideologue, the writer who was much talked about six or so years ago – he was our *teacher*. [...] He knew how to be our *master* without taking any of our initiative away ... [...])[75]

Far from guiding the young Raoul away from excessive reading and intellectualism, Barrès's early novels had the perverse effect of leading him to desire additional (if better-ordered) readings, to want to be more "intelligent." In a biting irony, Barrès's already cynical observation about young readers – that they make sentimental mush out of complex systems of thought because they fail to properly comprehend and integrate the philosophical framework that supports these systems – is turned against Barrès's own works. Raoul admits that he could not fully understand or process Barrès's novels, and that they instead filled him with a "fever." The lesson Barrès retrospectively attributed to his early works ("these monographs are *a form of teaching* [*un enseignement*]")[76] is not the lesson that Raoul and, according to him, his contemporaries took away from these novels. Young Frenchmen may have made Barrès their intellectual "master," but the influence he exerted escaped his own control. Raoul's generation (which is Tinan's generation) has yet to be schooled in matters of life and reading. Barrès, at least before *Les Déracinés*, is not the master who can cure their literary fever; instead, he contributes to it. Conversing with the narrator, Raoul asks, exasperated, "'What masters will teach young men to detest the Dream!'"[77]

Reaching the Reader

Throughout *Penses-tu-réussir!*, the protagonist and the narrator self-consciously (and yet also, as is characteristic of Tinan's ironic stance, sincerely) pose as negative examples for the novel's young readers. In one of his long parenthetical asides, Raoul addresses the reader directly:

> (Young man who will perhaps read these words – I lay out before you my former ridicule, my weakness, my stupidity ... [...] I show myself to you as I was, without any effects of style – I put my finger on the grotesque disproportion between my bloated dream, empty and false – and reality, where I despair that I will never be able to make it fit ... Reality is not what is wrong – my Dream, my recklessness are – as for you, do not be reckless ... [...] do not do as I did. [...] Here is the reason I leave this bleak and boring chapter in my book: if a single youth, a brother to the youth I once was, can be spared through these few lines from the disease that nearly killed my heart, I will not have been useless.)[78]

The address functions both straightforwardly and as a send-up of similar addresses to the young male reader in novels of formation of the period.[79] The message appears to be largely the same (do not do as I did), as are the rhetorical manoeuvres, for instance the claim that the edifying story is purposefully free of literary flourish in order to preserve its status as an example culled from lived experience. Yet there are more than a few hints of irony in Raoul's excessive self-deprecation of his purported lack of style – the passage that precedes it may be somewhat telegraphic, but the address itself, with its emphatic repetitions and liberal use of punctuation, is certainly not "without any effects of style." The drawn-out parenthetical aside concludes by abruptly proposing a concrete solution to the "disproportion" between young men's book-fed yearning for an idealized love and the realities of life: "*Go see some whores*" ("*Va voir des filles*").[80] This surprisingly pragmatic bit of advice, definitely unlike anything found in Barrès or Bourget, does not escape the novel's rampant irony; it is both exaggeratedly emphasized – repeated three times, always with italics – and self-consciously deprecated as soon as it is offered: "None of this is very poetic! I can't help it – I know of no other cure."[81]

In the face of an eminently literary problem, discussed and analysed to no end in a profusion of contemporary novels and essays about melancholic, bookish young men, Tinan's protagonist ends up citing – wryly, as he does everything – the rather prosaic remedy implicitly endorsed by the socio-medical discourse of his time.[82]

On the question of reading, Raoul ultimately reaches a more complex conclusion. Again dissertating about the discrepancy between love as it is imagined and love as it is experienced, as well as about his own propensity for excessive and ultimately circuitous analyses of this discrepancy, he offers a throwaway comment – "Some say that our readings are to blame for all this"[83] – to which he returns some pages later, by citing (with irony, it goes without saying) an essay he wrote some time before:

> "And, because we dreamed before we even lived, because we carry within ourselves the atavism of a race that, going back centuries, has been dreaming, our ideal is now very distant ...
>
> All of you, my unknown ancestors, over the course of centuries, you have thought as I have about happiness, and you have bequeathed me the crushing weight of all your weary love. Oh! You have dreamed too much! Books are not to blame: books and the time we live in may well be causing us much grief, but we also owe them mockery, which sustains our spirit like alcohol sustains our bodies."[84]

According to this fragment, the intellectual heritage of earlier generations, symbolized by books, is indeed the cause of contemporary young men's bitter disappointments in matters of life and love; in making this pronouncement, Raoul essentially repeats the diagnostic proposed in Bourget's *Essais* of the 1880s. He goes on to assert, though, that books also provide a remedy for the ills they cause: "la raillerie," that is, mockery, flippancy, irony. The cure for fin-de-siècle literary maladies, then, would not be to read less, or to limit oneself to less noxious texts, but to read more, and to learn, through the bitter disillusions of prior generations, to look mockingly at one's own disappointments. The proposition is itself – fittingly – ironically presented: "mockery" is compared not to a restorative cure but to alcohol.

Before he even cites this fragment of his own work, Raoul dismisses it as "the sighs of a fifteen-year old" and "a gongorism";[85] after the citation, he reiterates his dismissal, yet also, at the same time, makes a claim for the fragment's sincerity:

> I know this can seem pretentious, disjointed, bombastic, even useless, but what can I do? My nascent "positivism" was struggling – as it does throughout

> this volume – against so many old things. (Even still, you are quite aware that the word "positivism" is worthless.)
>
> It at least had all the sincerity of the sherry that was missing from the empty decanter. One loves – what can I say – as one can, and this is itself somehow quite touching. It is not impossible that some might understand the true emotions to which such exaltations correspond.[86]

As is typical of Tinan's affirmations, the word "positivism" is twice disavowed, first through the use of ironic quotation marks, then through an aside that dismisses it as a worthless signifier. What remains, after this repeated crossing out, is the notion of a struggle ("luttait"), an effort that extends "throughout this volume" – a struggle against "so many old things," against inherited ideals and inevitable disappointments, against literary ways of feeling and their rote expression. If nothing else in the volume is, that struggle is sincere. It might even – as Raoul dares to suggest through a litote ("not impossible"), the mask of irony slipping for a moment – be "somehow quite touching," the imperfect and roundabout intimation of truly felt emotions.

Tinan's narrator, in a postscript to the novel, reflects on the use of constant self-irony as a paradoxical formula for achieving a touching sincerity:

> I believe that the books I will not fail to publish subsequently, and to which this one is largely meant to serve as a preface, will not touch me as directly as this handful of badly arranged lyricisms, so brutal, and so thoroughly contradictory [...] – seeing as my "eighteen-to-twenty" self somehow made itself heard in these pages ...[87]

Although he would write two other novels,[88] Tinan's death in 1898, at the age of twenty-four, left unrealized the works for which *Penses-tu réussir!* could have served as a mere preface. It would be up to others to find a way out of his struggle with the paradoxes of fin-de-siècle literariness.

7 Gide and the Novel as Formation

André Gide's *Les Faux-Monnayeurs* (*The Counterfeiters*), published in November 1925, bears a doubly significant dedication: "To Roger Martin du Gard, I dedicate my first novel, as a token of my deepest friendship."[1] Like Martin du Gard's novel cycle *Les Thibault*, which had begun publication three years earlier – and like the bulk of *À la recherche du temps perdu*, the penultimate volume of which appeared posthumously that same November – *Les Faux-Monnayeurs* revisits the pre-war period. Several indicators, among them the prominent role played by gold coins (which were taken out of circulation in France after 1914) and a brief appearance by the playwright Alfred Jarry (1873–1907) appear to situate the narrative before the war, although closer consideration reveals a deliberate flaunting of historical verisimilitude, in line with Gide's tactic of a simultaneous embrace and transgression of the codes of the realist novel.[2] Indeed Gide's "first novel" is often described as a "roman du roman,"[3] a novel that tells the story of a novel – also called "Les Faux-Monnayeurs" – being written (or rather, planned, discussed, and only very partially written and left unfinished by the end of the narrative), a meta-novel that functions as a reflection on the novel as a genre. Yet while it presents a novel *in* formation, *Les Faux-Monnayeurs* is also very much a novel *of* formation: the narrative revolves around three adolescent boys, Bernard, Olivier, and Armand, and, in large part, their relationship to literature. The novel opens in the conventional gathering place of Parisian students, the Jardin du Luxembourg,[4] where Bernard, Oliver, and a few "schoolmates ... had made it a habit to meet, every Wednesday between four and six ... They discussed art, philosophy, sports, politics and literature."[5] On that particular day one of their schoolmates describes his latest literary project. Later scenes take place in settings that are just as resonantly formational: outside the Lycée Condorcet, or in the courtyard of the Sorbonne, where Olivier and Bernard discuss the written component of the *baccalauréat*, a commentary on La Fontaine. Also like *Les Thibault*, *Les Faux-Monnayeurs* plays with a number of tropes of the fin-de-siècle novel of formation: in an early scene, for instance, Bernard's father proudly asserts his confidence (soon to be proven wrong) that his sons have been raised to steer clear of "dangerous friendships and dangerous readings."[6]

Among the cast of adolescent characters, Bernard is the most typically bookish. As the narrator pauses to judge his characters, in one of the novel's metaleptical moments, he reflects that Bernard "has already read too much, memorized too much, and learned much more from books than from life,"[7] a comment that could easily describe the protagonists of a number of works by Martin du Gard, Tinan, Barrès, Bourget, and other turn-of-the-century novelists. Bernard indeed displays a tendency to view life through literature: when he discovers his status as an illegitimate son, he manages, over a mere few lines of inner monologue, to compare himself to three literary exemplars of the young man with an absent father, Fénelon's *Télémaque*,[8] the mythological Theseus, and Hamlet, before going on to cite a verse by Bossuet.[9] A later episode where he professes his love to Armand's sister Laura – as she happens to be reading a book – introduces two familiar problems: the bookish would-be lover's disappointment that the experience of love does not live up to his literary imaginings ("I had envisioned something volcanic ... and Byronesque"),[10] and his difficulty in achieving sincerity as he attempts to express personal sentiments ("Oh! if you only knew how maddening it is to have heaps of quotes by great writers in your head, and feel them come uncontrollably to your lips when you try to express something with sincerity").[11]

Questions of authenticity and imagination, of the conflict between reality and representation, occupy a central place in the novel. Olivier's uncle Édouard, the writer planning a book called "Les Faux-Monnayeurs," states that this work will deal with "the struggle [lutte] between the facts put forward by reality, and ideal reality"; later he notes in his journal that "the 'core subject' of my book ... will be ... the rivalry between the real world and the representation we make of it."[12] Yet the narration undermines Édouard's project, not only by showing him struggling to get it off the ground ("this whole chapter needs to be rewritten," he muses after going over the one section of his work we are given to read), but by commenting, even as he describes his goals, that his chosen subject is intractably difficult, even antinomic ("the illogical nature of his statements was flagrant, it jumped out at him in a painful way").[13] Gide's novel does not seek to reconcile reality and representation, as was Martin du Gard's disavowed yet overarching ambition,[14] but rather to highlight their struggle through a series of self-conscious and self-reflexive allegories.[15] In one of the final scenes, for instance, Bernard (upon entering, as at the beginning of the novel, the Jardin du Luxembourg) is made to wrestle with an angel that is both figurative and literal. This strange commixture of reality and allegory – the sudden intrusion, in a realist narrative, of a mythical figure that also happens to be the literalization of figurative expression[16] – is left unresolved, as two competing levels of reading (the scene is real; the scene is an allegory) are concurrently solicited and challenged, without one being declared the winner. The reappearance of the term *lutte* links Bernard's struggle with the literal and the allegorical to Édouard's own struggle with reality and representation; the narrator specifies that the scene ends "without a clear winner."[17] The scene exemplifies Gide's fascination with and repeated claims to positions of irreconcilable oppositionality,[18] as well as his invitation, indeed his stipulation, that readers should read his novel, and in fact all literature, on a multiplicity of levels, as something to be both partaken in and viewed with suspicion, enjoyed and critiqued, taken literally and lightly – never one without the other, always both at once. Gide's "roman du roman," in addition to its being a novel of the novel of formation, is a novel of formation *of the reader* – of the multiplicity of (mostly male) readers that populate the narrative, but also of Gide's own readers.

The Novel in Formation: *Les Cahiers d'André Walter*

Gide's struggles with the novel were long-standing. Rather than an affectation, his labelling *Les Faux-Monnayeurs* (published when he was fifty-six) as "my first novel" is the culmination of a decades-long trajectory of flirtation with, distanciation from, and suspicion of the novel as a genre. Early on, Gide identified the novel as the province of his authorial ambitions: "Mallarmé for poetry, Maeterlinck for drama – and although next to them I feel rather puny, I add Myself for the novel," the twenty-one-year-old wrote to Paul Valéry in January 1891, in a letter announcing his allegiance to the then-ascendant school of Symbolism.[19] Yet his first published work, which appeared that same winter, was not labelled "roman," nor was it signed with Gide's name. The cover page simply gave the title, *Les Cahiers d'André Walter* (*The Notebooks of André Walter*), with the indication, "posthumously published."[20] The very first edition bears a "note" signed P.C. (Pierre Chrysis, a pseudonym of Gide's friend Pierre Louÿs), stating: "André Walter wrote these notebooks, which we now publish, and a novel, which shall never be published."[21] *Les Cahiers*, some thirty-five years before *Les Faux-Monnayeurs*, is thus already a novel of the novel, albeit in the negative mode: it is the (non-)novel of the impossibility of writing or completing a novel.

In his preparatory notebook, Gide describes *Les Cahiers* as a "book" (never as a "novel") that would be about an "impossible novel," which would provide "the scaffolding for the book."[22] The narrative – made up of André Walter's diary entries, along with a number of poems, reading notes, and literary or biblical quotations – follows the young Walter as he reminisces about his lost love, Emmanuèle,[23] and labours on the composition of a novel, "Allain." Walter dies of "brain fever" before completing his work; he leaves explicit directions that his notebooks should be published, but not the novel.[24] About "Allain" we are told very little; the title suggests that is was to be the novel of a young man, perhaps in the mould of "mal du siècle" classics like Benjamin Constant's *Adolphe* (1816) or Eugène Fromentin's *Dominique* (1863). What we do know about André Walter is that he is a tremendously voracious and disorderly reader – to the point of insatiability, madness, and ultimately, death.

In the same notebook, Gide defines Walter as an avid reader who seeks to expand and intensify his mental life through identification with a variety of texts:

> Intellectual life is increased tenfold by reading, and he makes a theory out of this ... since the whole purpose of life is to intensify it in every manner possible, he will identify his life with every one of his readings (take care not to veer into banality here). Rather exaltation than identification. That is better: life through imagination, that is the way to burn it at both ends.[25]

Significantly, the young author voices concern that his topic might veer into the banal; the aside makes visible, in nascent form, Gide's characteristic suspicion towards the commonplace and the formulaic.[26] The question of young male readers' overheated imagination is certainly in the air between the spring of 1889 and the fall of 1890, when Gide works on the *Cahiers*: Barrès's *Un homme libre* (April 1889) and Bourget's *Le Disciple* (June 1889) have just appeared, and will soon inspire a number of emulators. Gide had read *Le Disciple* and followed the Chambige affair with what he later described as great emotion; his preparatory notebook even includes a parenthetical reference to the affair – "(Some research is needed on Chambige)" – as a model for Walter and his shared readings with Emmanuèle.[27] He expresses confidence that the topic of readerly excess is a timely one, so timely in fact, that he fears that a similar book might come along and steal his thunder before his is completed.[28]

Looking back at this first literary endeavour in his memoir *Si le grain ne meurt* (*If It Die*, 1924–6), Gide remembers that he conceived of the readerly crisis he felt compelled to depict, not as an individual predicament, but as a pervasive problem with broad implications: "It seemed to me that this book was among the most important books in the world, and that the crisis I described was of the most general, the most urgent interest."[29] Upon publication, *Les Cahiers* was indeed received as such – not, as the ambitious author had hoped, by a large public, but by a number of established or rising literary figures, including Barrès, with whom he shared a publisher; Bourget, who sent him a letter admiring his talent but admonishing his style;[30] and Marcel Schwob (1867–1905), who read the work as the depiction of a "crisis" among young Frenchmen: "you have described, with remarkable acuity, that terrible disease of the will that afflicts young men from the second half of the century, a disease that is the result of the magnificent education of their intellect ... coupled with their weak will ... You make a magnificent description of this crisis."[31] Schwob's reading, with its diagnosis of a widespread "disease of the will," bears the clear imprint of the *Essais de psychologie contemporaine*[32] and reveals how André Walter, in the eyes of contemporary readers, embodied the ills analysed by Bourget. Walter's personal crisis, brought on by the excesses of his intellectual education, was thus both conceived by Gide and understood by his readers as mirroring a larger crisis afflicting contemporary youth.

Walter's readerly education is an autodidactic enterprise: he is the disciple of no intellectual master, and instead reads broadly, even chaotically, across genres, historical periods, and languages. The narrative begins with Walter's evocation, following the death of his mother, of happier times, when he and Emmanuèle read together:

> First, the Greeks, who have since remained our favorites: the *Iliad*, *Prometheus*, *Agamemnon*, *Hippolytus* ... The violent harshness of Shakespeare ... the eloquence of Lamennais ... Then we reread some tomes from childhood ... Pascal, Bossuet, Massillon ... And so many more still – and all the others. Later, once our ambitions had been spurred, came Vigny, Baudelaire, – Flaubert, the friend we had so wished for! – The rhetorical subtleties of the Goncourt brothers ... Stendhal ... the *Oriental Travels* by Du Camp and Flaubert ... the *Temptation of Saint Anthony*, once again.[33]

Over the course of the book, the list grows and grows, soon incorporating other European literatures (in one particular bout, Hoffmann, Schiller, Heine, Turgenev), the Bible, and a rather eclectic list of philosophers (in a mere few pages, Spinoza, Schopenhauer, Kant, and John Stuart Mill).[34] In addition to these enumerations of authors and texts, *Les Cahiers* is woven through with literary citations, often without attribution or explicit demarcation: no less than three hundred, according to Gide's biographer Claude Martin, an "overabundance"[35] that weakens the text's legibility as a narrative, and threatens to reduce it, in the words of another critic, to the status of a mere "anthology."[36]

Walter's relationship with Emmanuèle consists of a series of shared readings; even when they are not reading, they recite texts they have learned by heart, or else reminisce about readings past:

> We loved to lose ourselves together in the most distant memories ... a single word sufficed and could elicit endless daydreams. For it was never the word alone; to us, each word had a legend, which we shared; it evoked an abundance of past emotions, of readings, and the times we had uttered it, and the times we had read it: – it was never the word alone, it was a reminiscence of days gone by.[37]

Every word, in this relationship, carries the weight of intertextuality. It is "never the word alone," and it is never Walter and Emmanuèle alone either; everything that happens between them is not only mediated by reading but superseded by it. A reference to Paolo and Francesca, literature's most iconic pair of amorous readers, provides a literary model but also a significant contrast. Whereas Dante's young lovers, spurred on by the tale of Lancelot and Guinevere, eventually lift their eyes from the book and give in to their adulterous passion ("that day we read no farther"), Walter and Emmanuèle never stop reading.[38] Scenes and settings that, in other coming-of-age narratives, would be expected to lead to amorous explorations, here lead only to more reading: "In the mornings you busied yourself with housework; I would see your pale apron drift by in the long hallways: I would wait for you on the stairs ... we would go up to the linen room, so vast – and sometimes, as you were folding the linens, I would chase you around while continuing to read aloud."[39]

Walter's literary ambition, to write the novel "Allain," likewise leads less to the act of writing than to a perpetual deferment through yet more readings, envisioned as a necessary intellectual preparation for the composition of his masterpiece. His reading program, constantly renewed, grows to encompass almost comically disparate elements, as in these two diary entries:

> I would like an empty cell ... with an enormous oak table, and laid out on it, a profusion of open books. A tall lectern so I can work standing up; on it, an open book. Above the bed, rows of books. I would read the Bible, the Vedas,[40] Dante, Spinoza, Rabelais, the Stoics; I would learn Greek, Hebrew, Italian – and my mind would feel itself come alive with pride.[41]
>
> After I finish Schopenhauer, I will take on *The Origin of Species*. I have finished Berlioz's *Memoirs* and the second volume of *The History of France* by Michelet ... Such delights! – I live in a state of perpetual overexcitement.[42]

The juxtaposition of Rabelais and the Stoics appears just as incongruous as the envisioning of a strict, ascetic existence as a space of "perpetual overexcitement." And yet, lest we read too much irony into these enumerations, it should be noted that Gide's own preparatory notebook features similar reading lists: the very first entry reads, "Read *Paul and Virginie*, *Adolphe*, the Thérèse episode in Michelet. *Last Day of a Condemned Man*."[43] *Les Cahiers* incorporate, often with little modification, passages from the diaries Gide started keeping at the age of seventeen. It may be that the *Cahiers* ended up performing the kind of "exorcism" of literary influences later envisioned by Martin du Gard, though less through a strategy of sustained irony than through projection and distanciation. If there is irony in the *Cahiers*, it is not easily visible: no narrator, as in Martin du Gard, systematically knows better than Walter; no quotation marks or narrative asides, as in Tinan, indicate that things are said or done tongue in cheek. Walter's story, instead, unfolds with seamless (if occasionally overblown) lyricism, following its principle of all-engulfing readerly enthusiasm to the point of death. Gide describes it as such, thirty-five years later: "That book stood before me and blocked my sight, to the point that I did not envision I could ever move beyond it. I was not able to consider it as the first book of my career; instead I viewed it as a unique book, beyond which I could not imagine anything ... after it, there was only death, or madness."[44] If we believe this reflection, André Gide the author saved himself from the fatality of the book only by making André Walter its victim instead.

Walter envisions "Allain" as the supreme novel, nothing less than the summation and meeting point, in the mathematical sense, of the evolutionary trajectories of literary history, art, and philosophy. The second of the two *Cahiers* includes a series of "notes" for the composition of the novel, set off from the text of the diary by an editorial remark from Walter's friend P.C. These compositional notes cite a number of eclectic references – the book of Genesis, Dante, Taine, Flaubert – and spell out Walter's aspirations, laying bare untenable contradictions. On the one hand, the novel "Allain" is to be a rigidly structured demonstration: "The order of Spinoza for the *Ethics*, transposed into the Novel; geometric lines. A novel is a theorem."[45] On the other, it is to exceed this rigid structure, along with the very strictures of narrative, logic, and even spelling, in order to attain a "form so lyrical, so pulsating, that poetry pours forth from it, despite its rigid lines ... Spelling! At first I thought I would have to observe it, but ... In French? No. I would like to write it in music."[46] The genre of the novel, to which Walter stakes a repeated claim ("the Novel," capitalized), is thus envisioned as the site of an improbable synthesis of philosophy and poetry, of structure and music, that would somehow transcend the rules of language. The very bases of Walter's literary project reveal its impossibility.

Here again, we might be tempted to read outright irony, even parody, in the seemingly absurd contradictions and outsize ambition of Walter's statements. Yet the text gives no clear indication that Walter is to be read as a caricature, since he himself gives no sign of auto-irony, and no narrative voice exists that could judge him at a distance; even P.C., in his introductory notice, mostly relies on Walter's own statements, describing him as the author of a "strange work, at once 'passionate and scientific,' he used to say."[47] Walter is thus framed less as an object of derision than as a doomed experimenter, a philosophical-literary alchemist in the mould of Balzac's *Louis Lambert* (1832), that "immense brain, which likely cracked in multiple places, like an overly vast empire" and ultimately gave in to "the desire to hurl himself into infinity."[48] The radical renovation of the novel as a genre was a seriously debated proposition in some quarters of the Parisian literary world in the early 1890s,[49] and Walter's project has much in common with Stéphane Mallarmé's dreamed-of "Livre,"[50] a parallel made all the more tempting by Gide's 1891 statement that he aimed to attain, in the novel, Mallarmé's achievement in poetry. *Les Cahiers d'André Walter* follows one of Mallarmé's key dictums in that it suggests this pursuit obliquely rather than attempt its direct representation or realization.[51] It is the book of an impossible Book, the tale of an all-encompassing Novel dreamt up by an all-devouring reader. Walter's death from "brain fever" literalizes, by pushing it to the point of fatal consequence, the literary fever diagnosed by his contemporaries.[52] It represents an end point, an impasse that, if we believe Gide's recollection, the author himself did not envision he could overcome. Seeing as he did survive, the question became, where to go from there? Gide's answer would stem from the strategy that spared him the fate of his doomed double: the ability to write – and read – at a remove.

Learning to Read

After 1892, Gide did not allow *Les Cahiers* to be reprinted for thirty years. In 1930, a "definitive edition" appeared bearing an author's preface that expressed his misgivings: "It is not very readily that I allow my first book to be reprinted ... at that age, I did not know how to write."[53] In the years since his first effort, the preface intimates, Gide has mastered his craft as a writer. He goes on to explain his ambivalence at seeing *Les Cahiers* re-edited as a fear that the book might veer some impressionable readers off the path to becoming better writers or better thinkers: "[M]ay no suggestible reader look to these pages as a model, whether for ways of writing, ways of feeling, or ways of thinking. I believe André Walter to be a terrible example ... I write in order to warn, to exalt, or to instruct; to me, a book that leaves its reader unchanged is a failed book."[54] This admonition to a reader imagined as young or, at the very least, susceptible to influence ("tendre") reveals a pedagogical impulse, which Gide had expressed before.[55] The very purpose of writing, according to this preface, is to leave an imprint on the reader, who is systematically figured as male (a grammatical feature of French, where the masculine serves as a neutral form, but also a central feature of Gide's pedagogical drive): to instruct him, elevate him, and, most importantly, to "warn" him, make him more aware.[56] Just as he taught himself how to write, Gide aims to teach his reader to tread carefully in matters of literature, so that he may become, if not as well-honed a writer, at least a reader on par with him – a *lecteur averti*, that is, a sophisticated reader, or, translated literally, a "warned" reader.

Les Cahiers suggests, in embryonic form – perhaps visible only to a reader *averti* by way of Gide's later works – two related potential ways out of the impasse of all-encroaching literariness. First, Walter compiles, especially in the last *Cahier*, citations about the inadequacy of literature, indeed of words themselves, to describe pure or authentic feeling, for instance three untranslated verses from Goethe's first *Faust*: "*Gefühl ist alles / Name ist Schall und Rauch / Umnebelnd Himmelsgluth.*"[57] This leads him to a paradoxical (and, it turns out, rather partial and short-lived) renunciation of reading:

> his readings embolden him ... but to what effect? When the mind reads, the heart slumbers – and its fervour cools under the dust of erudition.
>
> Therefore, no more readings, except a lot of the Bible, – and perhaps a quiet rereading of some tame classic.[58]

There would appear to exist something – "fervour" (ferveur), soon to be a key term in *Les Nourritures terrestres* (*The Fruits of the Earth*, 1897) – underneath the accumulated dust of erudition. This is the first apparent way out: rejecting books, embracing *Gefühl*, "the heart," fervour. Yet not only does this epiphany strangely lead Walter to more reading (rereadings, even), it was brought on by reading Goethe. The promise of a state of existence untouched by literariness is undercut by the indication that this promise is itself a literary conceit. A second potential way out, to which Walter remains blind, begins to emerge: that the impossibility of escaping all-encroaching literariness could itself be yet another literary conceit. In other words, the anxiety that true fervour is smothered by reading might itself be the product of reading; the all-invasive reach of books may be inescapable, but it is also, strangely, dismissible as a literary cliché, and as such, open to being put in question. These two potential ways out of Walter's impasse – the idea that something exists outside of books, and the acknowledgment that both the desire to escape books and the realization of the impossibility of this desire are literary commonplaces that should be viewed with suspicion – are separately imperfect, yet taken together, they amount to one of Gide's most important lessons in reading.

The impulse to escape books and the undercutting of this impulse frame Gide's next narrative text, *Le Voyage d'Urien* (1893), the symbolist imagining of a sailing ship's journey to an icy land. In the first chapter, one of the adventurers declares: "We have left behind our books because they bored us, because some unavowed memory of the sea and the real sky made us lose faith in our studies; something else existed."[59] The nautical journey is thus introduced as a return to the real, a flight from books and erudition in the pursuit of "something else." The end of the narrative, however, is followed by an *envoi*, a short concluding stanza in verse that sends up everything that preceded:

> Forgive me! I lied.
> This journey is but my dream,
> We have never left
> The room of our thoughts, –
> And we have passed by life
> Without seeing it. We were reading.[60]

The moral of this strange tale seems to be a double warning to the reader, not to take everything he reads at face value (since it may very well be a lie), and not to seek an escape from books through yet another book.

These same two lessons would become the pedagogical axes of Gide's next two major works, *Paludes* (*Morasses*, 1895), an ironic send-up of rarefied writerly experiments and Parisian literary milieus, and *Les Nourritures terrestres* (1897), an invitation to what amounts to literary detoxification ("désinstruction")[61] through travel and a rediscovery of nature. It is tempting to read *Les Nourritures* as the anti-*Cahiers* or the anti-*Paludes*, an earnest exhortation to the reader that he leave behind the Parisian hothouse of books and ideas, and rediscover instead what lies beneath the dust of his erudition – "Nathanaël, I will teach you fervour"[62] intones the narrator, in an echo of Walter's short-lived renunciation of reading. Gide himself describes the book as such in a preface to its 1927 reprint,[63] and his narrator orders the reader "to burn every book inside you."[64] Yet the book also systematically undercuts its own claims, starting with its potential status as an anti-Book. "Toss away this book," reads the preface; "toss my book. Free yourself from it," repeats the *envoi*.[65] The narrator warns, from the outset, that the book's premises may well be false: neither his own teacher, Ménalque, nor the reader he imagines and addresses, Nathanaël, are real ("Ménalque has never existed, no more than you have"); the travels he describes may likewise be imaginary ("sometimes I describe countries I have never seen, scents I have never inhaled").[66] Indeed his impulse to "remake a new vision for my eyes, to wash them of the grime of books"[67] by travelling through Italy and North Africa, as well as his descriptions of these travels, turn out to be informed by literary reminiscences from the Bible, Theocritus, Virgil, Terence, and Goethe – starting with the names Nathanaël and Ménalque, respectively culled from the Gospel of Saint John and the *Idylls*. Even the book's pedagogical drive is put in question by the time of the final *envoi*: "I am weary of prentending to educate someone ... Educate! Who could I claim to educate, other than myself?"[68] *Les Nourritures* thus not only invites the reader to free himself, through what it describes as a mental auto-da-fé, from the books he has internalized, it repeatedly exhorts the reader to include this particular book among them. It insistently refuses its potential status as an antidote to other books, and instead instructs the reader to question everything it tells him, including the very notion that it has something to teach him. The lesson of *Les Nourritures* repeats and magnifies the moral of *Le Voyage d'Urien*: everything one reads about in books, including aspirations or entreaties to escape books, is to be questioned.

Gide described some of his works, for instance *L'Immoraliste* (1902) and *La Porte étroite* (*Strait is the Gate*, 1909), as diptychs, opposing and complementary entities that did not, taken individually, constitute his final word on any given topic.[69] Instead, he preferred to characterize his literary output as a trajectory, over the course of which it would be a mistake to attempt to pin him down at any one point: "Every one of my books turns its back on the fans of the previous one. This is in order to teach them to applaud me for the right reason only, and not to take any one of my books for something other than what it is: a work of art."[70] Setting aside the question of "art," to which we will return shortly, the statement is remarkable for its emphasis on pedagogy ("to teach them"). From one work to the next – from, for instance, the claustration of *Les Cahiers* to the imagined escape of *Le Voyage*, or from the suffocating literary atmosphere of *Paludes* to its antithesis in *Les Nourritures* – as well as, increasingly over the course of his trajectory, within individual works (as we have seen in *Les Nourritures* and, even more so, in *Les Faux-Monnayeurs*), Gide moves between opposites, demanding that his reader follow him in renouncing the complacency of fixed positions and settled questions, preferring the ambivalence of a roving middle.

Examples of this privileging of an unsettled middle position abound in Gide's oeuvre: the narrator of *Les Nourritures*, as the intermediary between Ménalque and Nathanaël, is at once student and teacher, and expresses ambivalence about both roles; Bernard and Olivier, in *Les Faux-Monnayeurs*, are the middle children in families of three sons, neither fully identified with their father like their older brother nor completely given over to rebellion like their younger one; Gide even gave the name "la Mivoie" (The halfway) to a property he purchased in 1948, a few years before his death. By giving him to read, from one work to the next but also within a single work, everything and its opposite, Gide teaches his reader to read oppositionally, to shun passive identification or acceptance of what he reads, and instead actively question it. In this light, the character Lafcadio, in *Les Caves du Vatican* (*The Vatican Cellars*, 1914) – like Bernard an illegitimate son – emerges as an emblematic figure of the delegitimizing reader when he proudly proclaims:

> I know how to read handwriting or print, fluently, in reverse or against the light, on the other side of the page, in mirrors or on blotters; three months of study and two years of training [apprentissage]; all for the love of the art.[71]

Reading is thus a matter of training, of "apprentissage," of formation, a skill to be learned and honed. To appreciate a work of art is not, as Gide's 1925 statement might have seemed to suggest, a matter of passively applauding the author, but rather of being able to take on the work aggressively, or at least playfully. Lafcadio's boast multiplies images of reading as an act of going against the grain of the text: reading upside down, reading through, reading in reverse, reading in mirrors. A true "love of the art" of literature demands this kind of dexterous, almost acrobatic reading, an engagement with the text not unlike Bernard's wrestling with the angel – an athletic struggle from which no definite winner emerges, but that leaves the reader "more mature."[72] In thoroughly Gidean fashion, of course, Lafcadio turns out to be less efficacious as a reader than he had bragged, since he eventually fails to decipher and link together (that is, to read) various signs that his former mentor Protos is toying with him[73] – a new reminder to readers not to take everything they read at face value, including affirmations of reading prowess. Even the best readers, through Lafcadio's example, are advised to keep up their "training."

One of the earliest memories recounted in *Si le grain ne meurt* is a reading lesson of sorts from Gide's father to his six-year-old son. Before he gets to the readings themselves, Gide the memoirist depicts a peculiar scene:

> I entered [his study] as if it were a temple; in the darkness, the bookshelves stood like a tabernacle ... There was a lectern near one of the two windows; in the middle of the room, an enormous table was covered with books and papers. My father would reach for a large tome, the *Customary Laws of*

> *Brittany* or *Normandy*, a heavy folio which he would lay open on the armrest of a seat, and he would scrutinize along with me, from sheet to sheet, how far the work of some burrowing insect went. The lawyer, while leafing through an old text, had admired these clandestine passageways, and had told himself: "Look at that! it will amuse my son." And it did amuse me, because of the amusement he himself seemed to find in it.[74]

The setting, the father's study, is initially evoked as a space heavy with religious severity; it appears significant that the description of the furnishings finds an uncanny echo in the much earlier *Cahiers*, in the entry where Walter entertains the fantasy of a strictly ascetic retreat ("an enormous oak table, and laid out on it, a profusion of open books. A tall lectern so I can work standing up; on it, an open book. Above the bed, rows of books").[75] Yet instead of the dour reverence suggested by the church-like furnishings and law books, the father's attitude turns out to be quite playful. In this pedagogical primal scene, the father presents a book as an object of delight and amusement, worlds removed from the austere seriousness and feverishness of reading in *Les Cahiers*. His is a lesson in irreverence: the most delightful aspect of the book is the "clandestine," unexpected web of galleries that the insect has managed to burrow through its pages, by virtue of its perseverance and work.[76] This diligent insect, like the reader Lafcadio, has patiently worked its way against, literally *through* the text, digging deep into it, creating new paths that go in admirably unexpected directions.

The scene of a father-son initiation is restaged across Gide's oeuvre, for instance in *Les Caves du Vatican* when Lafcadio, as a young man, dreams about a night from his childhood, when an "uncle" (one of his mother's lovers) woke him from his sleep – although perhaps that was another dream, the boy Lafcadio wondered the next morning. In this queer dream within a dream, the "uncle" leads the boy around their darkened abode, room by room, "clandestinely" – a word that recurs in the scene in the father's study from *Si le grain ne meurt* – as if they were on some secret mission, or faced with a grave danger. Boy and "uncle" delight in exploring the ordinary, domestic world of daytime (the world of the mother, who the boy momentarily imagines may be "dead, or sick") under a different, much darker light, and the boy starts to understand that "this is but a game"[77] – an intensely homoerotic game, where things are not what they had earlier seemed, where events that appear to be happening may in fact not be happening at all, and where the reverse, hidden side of life is explored, or imagined. The game is both gravely serious (the pair take great pains not to make the slightest noise or leave the smallest trace of their nocturnal escapade) and highly playful (there is no actual need for them to be so careful: no one is standing guard, there is no real danger).

Like the insect's burrowing through the thick tome of ancient laws – a telling choice – the nocturnal game is an allegory for initiated, trained, *averti* reading. Indeed, Lafacadio dreams about this earlier "dream" immediately after he makes his boast of being a highly accomplished reader.

Over the course of his career, Gide claims the place of this benevolent father-uncle, positioning himself as a wise teacher who initiates his younger reader into a mode of reading where books are the object of both wonderment and irreverence. Gide the pedagogue invites his reader to be like the perseverant insect that does not slavishly follow the letter of the text but instead struggles with it, digging ever deeper, uncovering new possibilities. In his trajectory as a writer, the impossible novel "Allain," a novel *in* formation that could never fully take shape, gives way to a series of works that repurpose the novel *as* formation, as a veritable training manual for the reader, awakening him to reading's multifarious possibilities. From *Les Cahiers d'André Walter* to *Si le grain ne meurt*, Gide plays with and reverses dominant discourses about reading and its perils, turning the likes of Bourget and Barrès on their heads, exposing and openly playing with the paradox that they left unresolved – the paradox of books about the danger of books. In their prefaces, essays, and novels of the 1880s and 1890s, Bourget and Barrès told young male readers: I have much to teach you; do not do as I did, or as others like you have done; as I have come to recognize my errors and renounce them, so should you, for your own good and that of the nation. A generation later, Gide instead tells them: I have much to teach you, including why you should doubt and discard my teaching; do as I do, and then do the opposite; come play. His queer pedagogy of play and distance proposes to teach select readers – always implicitly male – to become keener, more astute, and more artful analysts of texts. The good of the nation never enters the frame. In Lafcadio's words, Gide teaches his readers that reading is an ever-perfectible training, an endless formation ("apprentissage"), whose sole true goal is "the love of the art."

8 Proust and the Fantasy of Readerly Recognition

If someone else resembles me, I must in fact be someone.

Proust, *Jean Santeuil*[1]

On at least one infamous occasion, Gide proved to be, like Lafcadio, a fallible reader: in November 1912, he and the other directors of the young Nouvelle Revue française turned down a typescript of what was to become *Du côté de chez Swann* (*Swann's Way*, 1913).[2] After the novel was published by Grasset (at the author's expense) a year later, Gide sent Marcel Proust a pained letter describing this refusal as "one of the most bitter regrets of my life."[3] A history of the NRF suggests that the typescript had been read hastily, if at all:[4] in his letter of atonement, Gide suggests as much, and blames himself for having been put off by his image of Proust as a "high-society amateur."[5] That image was in part a holdover of the lukewarm reception of what was by 1912 Proust's only published book of fiction, the collection of short stories and poems *Les Plaisirs et les Jours* (1896).[6] Since then, Proust had published two translations of Ruskin, as well as occasional articles; much of his time, though, had been occupied by the creation of a work that, after much permutation, eventually became *À la recherche du temps perdu*. A first version of this project was largely set aside after 1899: that unfinished manuscript would be published only posthumously, in 1952, under the title *Jean Santeuil*.[7]

"Should I Call This Book a Novel?"

In addition to being shelved by their authors as a works of juvenilia, *Jean Santeuil* and *Les Cahiers d'André Walter* have much in common: both are, to some degree, the story of an avid reader who struggles towards becoming a writer. Both works come up against the apparent impossibility of writing a novel that would not only describe but solve this struggle: the fictional Walter dies before completing "Allain," and the real Proust abandons *Jean Santeuil*. Gide artfully denied *Les Cahiers* the status of "novel"; similarly, in referring to the work, Proust often appeared to prefer terms like "my work" or "my book."[8] In fact *Jean Santeuil*, as structured by its posthumous editors, opens with the question, "Should I call this book a novel?" "It is something less, perhaps," comes the ambivalent response, "and yet much more, the very essence of my life, with nothing extraneous added."[9] The question of whether literature amounts to less or more than life occupies a central place in *Jean Santeuil*, as it will in *À la recherche du temps perdu*; the notion of an "essence" hints at the possibility of an answer, suggested or developed in different places throughout the work, without reaching the climactic pronouncements of *Le Temps retrouvé* (*Time Regained*, 1927, posth.). The unfinished state of the manuscript is not a matter of length but of structure and resolution. Proust wrote fragments and scenes without a discernable overall narrative frame, and left unanswered the question of how or even whether Jean manages to become a writer – quite possibly because he had yet to find his own answer.

In terms of genre, *Jean Santeuil* adheres to a number of conventions of the fin-de-siècle novel of formation: it recounts scenes from the protagonist's childhood and familial life, his time in school, his first experiences with love, and his first contacts with Parisian high society. Two examples highlight the work's proximity to contemporaneous iterations of the genre such as *Crise de jeunesse* (1897): like Fabien Després, the protagonist of Albert Sueur's forgotten novel,[10] Jean's professed desire to become a writer faces parental opposition; like him, he daydreams about Stendhal, rather than pursuing women. As do the young hero's parents in the *Recherche*,[11] Jean Santeuil's family voices apprehension, even outright condemnation, about his literary aspirations. Jean's maternal grandfather expresses this hostility most forcibly, denouncing the choice of a literary career as shameful, "dishonourable," a dissipation of respectable bourgeois patrimony, the equivalent of a suicide.[12] In the stark contrast between Jean and his father, an influential personage of the republican regime,[13] we find a familiar opposition between a father described as an established and potent social figure, and an adolescent son who, under what is presented as the devirilizing influence of the mother, prefers to occupy himself with literature.[14] Indeed Jean's mother, while she describes in front of guests her and her husband's determination "that he should grow up to be a manly little fellow," appears to undermine this goal by initially encouraging his inclination towards letters – "I think Jean will have a feeling for poetry," she confides to the father when they are alone, with an ambivalent mix of enthusiasm and apprehension.[15] When Jean fails to do well in school ("he wants to write extravagant nonsense, to think about nothing at all, to read novels and poetry," she tells her husband), she ascribes his worrisome tendencies to a potentially fatal lack of willpower: "this lack of willpower ... is a terrible rock indeed."[16] The novel thus paints Jean, through the anxious discourses cited by his family, as yet another victim of the late nineteenth-century "diseases of the will" that are alternately described as the cause and the result of young's men susceptibility to debilitating literary influences.[17]

The parental anxiety that the book-loving Jean will not become a productive and respectable man is predictably twinned with intimations that he may not quite become reproductive either. In a scene that would not be out of place in a novel by Bourget or his *Essais de psychologie contemporaine* of the 1880s, the narrator describes the adolescent Jean's reveries about a slightly older woman – or rather, about the reminiscences of readings that she enables him to indulge in:

> It was precisely to Stendhal ... that Jean found his thoughts returning as he sat dreaming of the flawless profile ... which for the last few weeks had given a new charm to his existence. He would not have gone so far as to say that he was very much in love with Madame S., and perhaps it was for this very reason that he reveled in the pleasure of feeling he was in love ... It was happiness for him to feel himself invaded, all the time he was with her, all the time he was being driven away from her, all the time he sat at home thinking of her, by that pleasure which detaches us from other pleasures and gives us new ones, the intensity of which he had realized through the predicament of Julien Sorel and Fabrice del Dongo, and in the pages of *De l'amour*, without ever having felt it since. It had not taken him long to realize that he could not sleep with this young widow, who was reckless (she received him every night from ten o'clock until two in the morning; his desire for her was quite faint) yet decent; he could not even so much as give her a kiss.[18]

We hear echoes of the trial of Henri Chambige, the young man who inspired Bourget's *Disciple*, in the narrator's affirmation that Jean Santeuil does not love the woman in question, but rather the impression of love that their frequentation allows him to feel. The woman's presence does not matter: Jean is filled with the same "pleasure" whether he is with her or away from her. Returning home after seeing her late at night, his thoughts do not drift to her but to Stendhal and his young male protagonists, Julien and Fabrice. These characters have shown him a type of intense pleasure, he reflects, that he has not not experienced "since" reading about it (significantly, not "until now," when he is seeing "Madame S."). The woman's abbreviated name, a convention of eighteenth-century libertine novels and nineteenth-century narratives of adultery, is here symptomatic: her actual name, her subjectivity, her potential sexual availability do not matter. To Jean she is a not person but a novelistic situation that allows him to feel an intense pleasure connected to what he truly loves – novels. She is Madame S[tendhal].

Proust was certainly aware of Bourget's works and the controversy surrounding *Le Disciple* of 1889. In a letter to his mother from September 1899, he references the Chambige affair of 1888 (as well as the bombing of Café Terminus by an anarchist in 1894, which inspired Barrès)[19] while describing a friend, Jean Lazard, about whom little is known today:[20]

> I have received ... these two letters from Jean Lazard, and forward them to you ... They allow many conclusions regarding the danger that a strong intellectual culture represents for men who do not choose an intellectual career: because they apply the finesse of their mind to life, which contains no such finesse, they end up ranting and raving, as he does here. Though he (Jean Lazard) is a more innocuous product of this state of mind (applying a literary intelligence to life), it seems to me he is as much a product of it as Émile Henry or Chambige.[21]

Lazard's letters to Proust have not been found. Why does Proust forward them to his mother? Possibly as a warning: the question of his settling on a proper career is still very much on Proust and his parents' mind in the late 1890s. That Proust felt the need to specify "he (Jean Lazard)," as though there could be confusion as to who he was talking about, hints at the possibility of identification, as if Proust – and his mother – could see potential images of himself in Lazard, in Émile Henry, and in Henri Chambige, those worrisome products of a common fin-de-siècle danger, the conflict between the expectations of a "literary intelligence" and the disappointing experiences of a non-literary life. Could Jean Lazard have inspired the name of Proust's protagonist? Lazard at the very least played at a small role in the composition of *Jean Santeuil*: Proust's only known letter to him, from mid-October 1896, suggests that it was likely Lazard who recommended the Hôtel de France et d'Angleterre at Fontainebleau as a quiet place to write.[22] Proust spent a week at that hotel later than month, working on his manuscript. It was there he wrote a key scene about the shock of hearing his mother's disembodied and bereaved voice on the telephone, which he later transposed into the *Recherche*.[23]

While resonances of genre-defining characters like Bourget's *Disciple* and related fin-de-siècle discourses about "diseases of the will" traverse the unfinished narrative of *Jean Santeuil*, other features distinguish it from the mass of late nineteenth-French century novels of formation and announce the developments to come in the *Recherche*. Foremost among these innovations are the manuscript's reflections on reading.

Readerly Expectations

Many elements of the character Jean's life amount to thinly disguised autobiography, from the familial dynamics of the Santeuils (who largely correspond to what we know of the Prousts) to a series of excursuses into political and artistic events of the late 1890s (including Zola's 1898 trial following the publication of "J'accuse ...!"), which Proust followed with a chronicler's interest.[24] To place himself at a remove, if only as a matter of convention, Proust framed Jean's story, as Gide had *Les Cahiers*, as a found work – a novel within a novel – by means of a sequence he labelled "1st chapter" on a revised section of the manuscript, and referred to as "preface" elsewhere.[25] In these framing scenes, a first-person narrator recounts how he and an unnamed friend once made the acquaintance of a writer whose works they greatly admired (identified by the initial C. or B.) while vacationing on the coast of Brittany. Every evening, the writer read to them from the novel he was writing about a young man named Jean; some years later, when the writer dies unexpectedly, the narrator of the preface decides to publish the novel. The pretext is paper-thin and somewhat maladroitly set up (a scene where the writer summons the two friends to his deathbed was left unfinished), yet the sequence introduces a number of key questions about the potential purposes of reading as well as the structure and content of novels as a genre.

An initial scene of reading out loud begins with a description of the fictional writer's reservations as well as the narrator-auditor's expectations:

> After he had read to us one afternoon the beginning of the novel he was writing, ... every evening, once he had finished his dinner, he would take the papers that were next to him, secured under a plate, and he would start reading them to us, but only after many oratory precautions, and interspersing his reading with constant critiques about his own work ... Often his narrative was interrupted by passages of comment in which the author expressed his opinion on this and that, in the manner of some English novelists[26] of whom at one time he had been very fond. These reflective asides, which some readers find tiresome, because they break the current of narrative and destroy the illusion of life, were what we most liked to hear, so eager we were to know his personal thoughts.[27]

In addition to setting the stage for "the beginning of the novel" (this is, after all, the "1st chapter") the scene uncannily mirrors our own experience of reading *Jean Santeuil*, a work in progress, a collection of the author's loosely held together "papers" that is prefaced, as is C.'s reading of his novel, by a series of writerly precautions and reservations, including the scene we are reading. It also functions as a reader's manual of sorts: the narrator and his friend, in differentiating themselves from ordinary readers whose sole interest lies in "the illusion of life" generated by the flow of plot, inflect our own reading and direct our attention towards the writer's digressive reflections, in which they profess to find greater enjoyment. Their posture, as they listen to him reading, is one of receptive avidity: they await the writer's opinion on matters great and small, as if he were an oracular voice proffering wisdom from a plane of deeper awareness.[28] Two possible pitfalls of reading are thus outlined in this brief description: reading for "the illusion of life," and reading for the writer's opinions, with, in each case, the expectation or the desire that what is culled from the book will supersede the reader's own experience or ideas. Other reading scenes in *Jean Santeuil* will offer further examples of these two pitfalls, but also begin to suggest a third possibility for reading, one that will provide a key to the character Jean's evolution towards the status of writer – an evolution left unrealized in *Jean Santeuil*, but for which the *Recherche* gestures towards fulfilment in its final volume.

In a related, unfinished scene from the frame story, the narrator and his friend come down from their room intent on asking the writer for his opinion on works by Balzac and Stendhal.[29] This literary conversation is deferred, though, by a discussion of the sunset:

> We had played the traitor by bringing down with us, my friend, Balzac's *Le Curé de village* and I, Stendhal's *La Chartreuse de Parme*, since being halfway through these two works which we were reading with all the concentrated enthusiasm that any new and splendid book excites, especially when one has not finished it, we had minds for nothing else and were burning to know C.'s opinion of them ... But we wanted first to ask him whether he had seen the sunset, which had transported us to the point that we forgot for a moment *Le Curé de village* in my friend's case, *La Chartreuse de Parme* in mine, and were filled with a hope that he might sum up his impression in a few words that would shed light on [éclaircirait] our own, and make us more certain of what we had been feeling.[30]

The passage again shows the readerly pair avidly expecting revelation from the writer, whose opinion and impression on disparate matters they imagine having superior value. The juxtaposition of literary masterpieces to the sunset as objects of discussion suggests a rivalry between reading and the natural world – a frequent trope in fin-de-siècle scenes of reading[31] – where the intense experience of one can make the reader-observer forget about the other. In the readers' eyes, however, both the books named and the sun itself are eclipsed by the capacity for illumination attributed to the writer. On their own, Stendhal and Balzac generate "passion," yet this passion is exceeded by the burning desire to hear B.'s opinion of them (a matter apparently more pressing than finishing the books); the transporting experience of the sunset, likewise, produces the strange desire to have the writer shed his own light on it ("éclaircirait"), as if the sun itself were not enough. This elevation of the writer to the status of ultimate authority, like similar great expectations to come in the *Recherche*, sets the stage for great disappointment, and indeed B.'s response – a simple indication of the best nearby locale from which to observe the sunset – leaves the two friends feeling a "disappointment ... of the kind a patient with a neurotic illness feels" when he hopes to receive some profound answer from a doctor, and receives only mundane advice instead.[32] A related danger is alluded to when the narrator describes how, when he tried to ask B. about that evening's sunset, he began to feel himself imitating the writer's style – "I felt that, in spite of myself, I was beginning to sound like him."[33] The writer's pronouncements, when elevated to oracular status, can thus come to supersede both the reader's experience (be it of nature or of reading itself) and his self-expression (as well as his will or self-mastery, since the parroting occurs "in spite of" himself). Yet this avidly desired substitution of the writer's words for the reader's fails to fulfil expectations; some process other than supersession will have to be brought into play for the reader to attain a greater understanding of his experience, and gain self-assurance in his own voice.

The character Jean Santeuil, in the narrative framed as the creation of the writer met by the two friends in the preface, is equally susceptible to the invasive influence of what he reads. A scene set during his childhood shows him getting so engrossed in the classical or religious histories he reads that he takes himself to be the personage they describe:

> Jean ... seeing only something very vague and shadowy when he thought about himself ... had no clear conviction about his moral worth, and accordingly, if a book he happened to be reading condemned his faults or glorified his good qualities, he would think of himself as Nero or as Saint Vincent de Paul.[34]

So malleable and impressionable is Jean as a young reader that his own self is merely "something very vague," prone to self-identification with the most unlikely models. Even in this early example, however, we begin to see how the self-identification of the reader (who exists outside the text) to what he reads about (inside the text) is a function of self-recognition: it is because Jean sees what he understands to be *his own* faults or qualities magnified in descriptions of Nero or Saint Vincent that he momentarily comes to believe he *is* one or the other. The process of readerly identification thus carries, or perhaps is even founded on, the possibility or risk of misrecognition, of believing oneself to *be* the text when one is merely *like* the text, with important differences of scale, not to mention place or time. The mistake is apparently childish, yet it persists, in a subtler but no less treacherous form, into Jean's early adolescence, when his mother introduces him to the poetry of Hugo and Lamartine:

> By this time Jean could manage to read "La Tristesse d'Olympio," and other poems as well. The poets ... now stood beside him while he read with a seemingly greater understanding ... helping him, as it were, to find words for something that had long been weighing on his heart, giving him the right words, understanding his vague, uncertain thoughts better than he did himself, and reflecting them back to him filled with light and power and with a depth of sadness and sweetness that, until then, he had found it impossible to express.[35]

As in the preface, the reader's cognizance of his own thoughts or experience are characterized as deficient ("vague, uncertain"), in contrast to the writer's authoritative and illuminating statements on similar matters. Jean again falls victim to misrecognition when the role of the poets he imagines sitting beside him slips from "helping him" express his emotion to replacing his expression with theirs ("giving him the right words"). Instead of recognizing a measure of resemblance between what he has experienced and what he reads, Jean sees only similitude. He forgets everything that differentiates him from the text and reads himself into it.[36]

The question of readers' expectations and misrecognitions is taken up again in the first few lines of the frame story, as the unnamed narrator of the preface (or "1st chapter") reflects on the experience of reading historically and geographically distant texts and finding within them striking similarities to contemporary concerns:

> The language of our own day striking at us [reconnu] from a canto of the *Iliad*, some crisis in the history of Egypt revealing a similarity with contemporary events – such things serve to show how the basic substance of humanity, often invisible and as though intermitted, nevertheless does not die and can be found again [se retrouve], identical to itself, where we least expect it.[37]

The notion of finding again – *reconnaître*, *retrouver* – is the keystone of the edifice of the *Recherche*, inscribed in its very title (*temps perdu/temps retrouvé*, time lost and regained), and to find it again at the beginning of this once-lost text can itself be a stirring reading experience. What the passage tells us about the process of reading happens to be confirmed by our experience of reading it. Someone who has not read the *Recherche* could very well read this same passage and not feel the shiver of recognition; the difference lies not in the text but in what the reader brings to it. The common fount or "substance" of humanity imagined by the narrator is "invisible," "intermitted"; it does not float freely at the surface of the text, available for any reader to passively receive it (as the narrator and his friend, later in the preface, expect to receive wisdom from the writer). Rather it needs the reader to find it, to piece it together and make it visible. It is up to readers to decipher it or dig for it (images suggested by the passage's reference to a classical text and to Egyptology), and *recognize* it by making connections to what they have already read, be it elsewhere in the same text or in a vastly different text like the day's paper reporting on "contemporary events." Reading is thus envisioned as an active endeavour rather than the passive reception of wisdom, an activity that requires work – the capacity and willingness to read broadly and attentively enough to make fruitful connections.

The novel's "1st chapter" closes with a related reflection on reading and writing as complementary, even symmetrical, endeavours. The narrator wonders to what extent the character Jean Santeuil corresponds to the lived experiences of the writer C.:

> But to what extent did he appear in what he wrote? ... especially in the character Jean, who has many of C.'s faults, but even more of his good qualities, his sensitiveness in particular and his warmth of heart, though unlike C. he is cursed with delicate health, has known much unhappiness, and is without talent for any of the arts. We dared not question him on these points ... but they interested us more than anything else. We thought that a lifetime devoted to solving them would be well employed, because we should be led to ... learn what are the secret relations, the necessary metamorphoses, which exist between a writer's life and his work, between reality and art, or, rather ... between appearances and reality – a reality which underlay all things and can be uncovered only by art.[38]

Proust's biography makes it tempting to answer the initial question by simply dismissing the writer C. as a screen, and a fairly transparent one at that: Jean the character may or may not have much to do with C., but he has almost everything in common with the Marcel Proust of the years 1895–9, from a fragile constitution to the profession of doubts about his aptitude for a literary career. Yet the passage avoids making this question a matter of direct coincidence (is Jean C.?) and insists instead on a more complex relation of correspondence ("secret relations") based on measured similitude but also difference, the result of a labour of transformation ("necessary metamorphoses") on the part of the writer. The reader's work in asking questions, uncovering secrets, making connections – a pursuit worthwhile and exacting enough, according to the narrator, that it could itself fruitfully occupy a whole lifetime – thus mirrors and complements the writer's endeavour, which would be to set up these questions, bury these secrets, lay the groundwork for these connections. The higher reality to which the narrator aspires can be "uncovered" only through the corresponding efforts of reader and writer. Before the reader can get to work, though, the writer needs to have done his.

Learning to Write

Perhaps more so than in the lessons it suggests about reading, the value of *Jean Santeuil* lies in showing us the writer in formation – the character Jean, but also, through him and all around him, the writer Proust. More directly and somewhat more nakedly than the *Recherche*, where the narrator's formation as a writer-to-be takes the shape of a general aesthetic education through models in painting and music,[39] *Jean Santeuil* features two important lessons in writing. These lessons are present in the *Recherche* in that they have been realized in the style and structure of the novel, integrating them but also to some extent masking them. During its depictions of Jean at the *collège* – scenes that are absent from the *Recherche*, which does not include recollections of school – the narrative introduces its first lesson through a character seldom found in other novels of formation of the period: a stern but benevolent (and beneficial) literary mentor.

Jean's initial lesson in writing comes at the hands of his philosophy teacher, Beulier.[40] The sections depicting Jean's adolescent experiences with reading and writing introduce Beulier as a foil to Jean's previous intellectual mentor, "the poet Rustinlor, Director of Studies at the Lycée Henri IV." Rustinlor favours contemporary poetry over the classics – he has nothing but disparaging remarks for Ovid or Horace – and although Jean emulates him, he continues reading older texts:

> Like his master [Rustinlor], Jean held the view that Verlaine and Leconte de Lisle were the greatest among all the poets and, again like him, felt deadly bored when he read the classical authors. But ... he kept on forcing himself to reread *Phèdre*, *Cinna*, and the *Fables* of La Fontaine ... It was only later that he came to appreciate the value for the mind of [such] exercises.[41]

Already, the narrative contrasts Rustinlor's facile enthusiasm for poetic novelties with a notion of reading as a form of training or "exercise" that involves effort and can yield intellectual benefits. This notion is found to also apply to writing when Beulier critiques one of Jean's school assignments, whereas Jean had imagined the composition would reveal him to teacher and classmates alike as a precocious talent:

> It is full ... of all those current clichés, those literary bad manners, which you have picked up from newspapers and magazines. It is not your fault: you are not responsible ... You must learn to prune your style of all those metaphors, of all those images ... it is a mistake ... to raise your voice in order to utter banalities.[42]

To write well, for Beulier, requires a sustained effort of self-discipline, an unlearning of commonplace tricks acquired by reading too much mediocre contemporary poetry. This defamiliarization with language is the equivalent, in the practice of writing, of Jean's self-imposed habit of reading Racine and Corneille. Such exercises have the potential, according to the narrator, "by forcing us to strip a thought of all conventional formulae, of the beauties of style we may have been taught to find in it, of all the academic aura with which, unconsciously, we have come to see it surrounded," to bring the reader or writer closer to "grasping its very reality."[43] The sustained effort of divesting oneself of one's linguistic habits[44] emerges as one of the keys to becoming a probing reader and writer. This is confirmed in a later episode where Jean runs into Rustinlor, who announces he has given up poetry because of its lack of "reality":

> Monsieur Rustinlor replied that poetry with him was a thing of the past, that the matters which were now occupying his attention were a great deal more real ... being "politics, immorality and cycling." According to him those were what really mattered, and not literature, which merely sought to imitate the true emotions which they provided ... All the while Jean was listening to him, he was vaguely conscious that what gives literature its reality is the result of the work of the spirit ... the value of literature is never in the material worked on by the writer, but in the nature of the work his mind performs upon it.[45]

With his statement, the mediocre poet joins the ranks of pedestrian readers who, like those alluded to in the preface, find in the text only "the illusion of life," a superficial and ultimately disappointing pleasure. The passage's repeated emphasis on literature as "work" shows how Jean, albeit "vaguely," has assimilated his first lesson – that the value of a literary work lies not in the imitation of real material but in the transformation of that material through the writer's spiritual effort of discovery. (The episode also highlights one of the structural weaknesses of *Jean Santeuil*, as the narrator finds himself detailing theories that Jean does not yet quite grasp – a discrepancy solved in the *Recherche* by the use of the first person and the general deferral of aesthetic revelations until the last volume.) The precise nature of these discoveries is the object of the novel's second lesson.

Jean meets Madame Gaspard de Réveillon, "a nineteen-year-old poetess,"[46] through his friend Henri, and her extended portrait is the occasion of a new lesson on the relationship of literature to a deeper reality. According to the narrator (and again it is unclear to what extent the reflections occasioned by his description are shared by Jean), the poetess is an artist for whom the "the true essence of things ... was all that really mattered"; her works "expressed something that went so deep in her, that she could not even think, still less speak, of it."[47] The assertion that her work touches something essential and deep, more important than reality and beyond the reach of ordinary thought, anticipates similar pronouncements in the *Recherche* and its preparatory manuscripts, and in fact leads to one of *Jean Santeuil*'s developments on the phenomenon of involuntary memory, characterized as the simultaneous experience of something from the past and something in the present. The narrator describes how this capacity to make connections extends to the poetess's aptitude for conversation:

> She was for ever making people laugh by some amusing comparison [des rapprochements comiques], by her witty manner of recounting the least little incident ... because a sensitive person with the faculty of sympathy, which means being able to place oneself in another person's shoes, and not always being locked up in one's own concerns, can see an element of the comic everywhere.[48]

The conversation of the writer has more to do with salon wit (*l'esprit*) than with the solitary spiritual work ("travail spirituel") described earlier, yet the close juxtaposition of this description to that of the poetess's works reveals that they share the fundamental characteristic of making parallels, of bringing separate realities together ("rapprochement"). The writer has the ability to go beyond the immediate concerns of her mind – the present, the self – and makes connections to more distant, less easily accessible realms – the past, the other – that reveal what these disparate pairs actually have in common. In other words, for a writer to be *spirituel* (in either sense of the word, witty or spiritual) requires that she exercise a "capacity for sympathy," that she be able to move away from the close and the familiar (commonplace language, egotistical concerns) in order to make unexpected connections to the distant. The writer's task, in that sense, very much mirrors the reader's.

This new lesson leads to a further elaboration by the narrator in a related scene where Jean, still a guest at the château de Réveillon, is kept awake at night by the sound of the howling wind: "Poetry and inspiration, these it was that the wind seemed to wake in Jean for the more he listened to it with a growing pleasure, the more he thought he would discover new ideas, which in their turn would give birth to others."[49] The thoughts stirred in Jean by the wind are described, in a long development, as fundamentally different from another kind of thought defined as childish and hollow, and linked, in a significant comparison, to certain types of mimetic literature:

> not those mad ideas that turn inwards on ourselves, such as imaginative children have (and in this respect, there are many who remain children all their lives) ... ideas of this kind are insubstantial things, and call up others no more substantial than themselves. For they imitate reality, and substitute themselves for it ... All this is useless, like what we find in Impressionist and Naturalist novels. We feel the need of new ones each time that new things happen. Such ideas are in mere competition [concurrence], and vain at that, with an inexhaustible and unsatisfying reality.[50]

This first, negatively characterized type of thought is imitative and substitutive: such thoughts, in what amounts to a childish drive for wish fulfilment, seek to replace reality with a representation, a process described as leading inevitably to more disappointment. Their description echoes the lessons in reading proffered elsewhere in the manuscript: to read for "the illusion of life" or for ideas and experiences that would simply supersede one's own is a juvenile and ultimately disappointing mental activity – though many, the narrator points out, fail to outgrow it. With the association of such mental processes with certain types of novels, reinforced by the use of the term "competition" [concurrence] – possibly a reference to Balzac's much-cited statement that the novel as a genre aims to "compete with the civil registry" [faire concurrence à l'état civil][51] – the discussion of Jean's "thoughts" inches towards the elaboration of a literary philosophy. (Here, yet again, the split in *Jean Santeuil* between narrative voice and protagonist causes a strange disconnect, as Jean, although he experiences a poetic epiphany, is not made privy to the more theoretical revelations made by the narrator.) Literature that is merely mimetic is condemned as "useless," shallow, a Danaidean endeavour that fails to transcend the perpetually unsatisfactory experience of reality.

This reflection on the nature of thoughts *not* had by Jean is a prelude to the description of a second, positively characterized type of thought:

> But the ideas that came to Jean as he listened to the wind were of another kind. They seemed not empty, but packed full, not only of the past ... but of the present, too; ideas that went deeper, and, linking the present and the past, were more real, for they showed the value of the moment past and of

> the moment present ... For that reality is something of which we are not conscious in the passing moment, connecting it as we do with some self-regarding project. It is something that in the sharp return of disinterested memory sets us floating between the present and the past, in the essence common to both ... a reality that we spread about us as we sit writing pages which are the synthesis of different moments of life.[52]

The poetic thoughts Jean *is* having are fuller, deeper, more real, more valuable. Linking this scene back to the description of Madame Gaspard de Réveillon's poetic talents, these thoughts are said to create links between the past and the present, revealing that they share an "essence." Such an essence cannot be experienced in the present alone since the mind is habitually closed in on itself, preoccupied with selfish concerns. The sudden rush of memory is able to offer us a glimpse of this essence because it is "disinterested," because it momentarily jolts the mind out of its exclusive focus on the present and the self. The passage again moves to consider literature and suggests that the writer can aim for a similar, and less fleeting, effect by crafting pages that are a "synthesis" of moments past and present. Key to the writer's art, then, is an ability similar to the "capacity for sympathy" ascribed to the poetess: a power of disinterestedness, a willed distanciation from the self and its immediate concerns. The literary works produced by such writers are not mimetic but synthetic, encompassing the present and the past, the self and the other, the familiar and the distant. The two lessons in writing proposed in *Jean Santeuil* thus complement one another: in matters of style as in matters of content, the writer should strive for a defamiliarization that allows the literary work to go beyond the habitual, the immediate, the superficial, and suggest connections that reach deeper into the shared "essence" of things, moments, and people. Jean Santeuil, the character, does not go on to implement these lessons – but Marcel Proust would.

Du côté de chez Swann makes mention of a book the adult narrator once began to write but abandoned, a reference often interpreted as a nod to *Jean Santeuil*: "in later years, when I began to write a book of my own, and the quality of some of my sentences seemed so inadequate that I could not go on with the undertaking, I would find the equivalent in Bergotte."[53] There are indeed important differences in style and sentence construction between the earlier work and the *Recherche*, but it is notable that the narrator of the mature novel links the lack of quality of his early literary attempt to the servile imitation of an admired model. In doing so, he hints – but does not explicitly state – that he eventually came to learn the first lesson introduced in *Jean Santeuil*: the need for the writer to break free of the influence of contemporary models, of which Bergotte is the embodiment in the *Recherche*.[54] The young hero, in his unabashed enthusiasm for Bergotte, shows himself to be rather similar to the overly avid readers described in the preface to *Jean Santeuil*, down to observations that "I was disappointed when he resumed the thread of his narrative" or that " I longed to have some opinion, some metaphor of his, upon everything in the world."[55] Whereas in *Jean Santeuil* the roles are divided between a naïvely avid reader (the anonymous narrator of the preface), an adolescent protagonist who learns a few lessons about writing but does not get to put them into practice (the character Jean), and a fictional writer who elaborates a theory of the "secret relations" that can be revealed through literature (the writer B./C., who becomes the narrative voice telling the story of Jean in the body of the novel), the *Recherche* solves the structural problem of the earlier abandoned novel by combining these roles into a single entity, the hero/narrator, and making the progressive transformation of one into the other the plot of the novel.

In terms of style (addressing the qualm expressed by the narrator about his past attempt at at writing "a book of my own"), the *Recherche* also corrects the inconsistency of the earlier work by integrating and demonstrating its lessons rather than simply stating them. Many of the lessons in reading and writing found in the *Recherche* not only teach, but also put into practice the twin principles of defamiliarization and analogy proposed in *Jean Santeuil*. The painter Elstir, for instance (who has more than a little in common with the solitary writer B./C. encountered on the coast of Brittany in the preface to *Jean Santeuil*), offers the narrator a lesson in the practice of aesthetic "metamorphosis ... analogous to what in poetry we name metaphor," through a series of paintings that represent the seashore as a mountainous landscape. "It was by taking away their names or giving them other names that Elstir created [things] anew," writes the narrator; his technique "surprises us, takes us out of our cocoon of habit, and at the same time brings us back to ourselves by recalling to us an earlier impression."[56] In the few pages between these statements, the lesson is virtuosically illustrated through a long ekphrasis of the paintings. Elstir's lesson in painting is twice over a lesson in writing: not only is it *about* the twin movements of defamiliarization and analogy, it is presented, integrating this lesson, *through* an analogy between two arts, taking a detour by way of the visual to talk about the written in a new, unfamiliar way. Indeed, although everything is in place to suggest a link between the passage's lesson in painting and a potential lesson in literature, this is never explicitly presented as such: it is up to the hero, and the reader along with him, to make the connection. Instead of mimetically representing them, Proust the writer (like Elstir the painter) has subjected his experiences and ideas to "necessary metamorphoses," creating "secret relations" that the reader (like the adolescent hero viewing the paintings) is invited to uncover.

Shared Readings

Jean Santeuil fleetingly but auspiciously alludes to the possibility of a reading experience that could lead to something other than supersession (the replacement of the reader's experiences or opinions by what is found in a text) or egotistic misrecognition (the misreading of a text as a mirror of how the reader already sees himself). What if, instead of diving headfirst into full (and therefore erroneous) identification, the reader was able to experience a measured, analogical self-recognition that preserved the coexistence of similarity and difference between himself and the text – and in doing so, was able to gain greater insight into both? What if there existed some text, some mode of reading, that could provide a respite from the opposition between self and other? Proust's unfinished novel stages a fantasy of reading as recognition (imagined to be different from egotistic identification), in scenes where shared reading is presented as a kind of silent but resonant communion.

One such reading scene, where Jean, now a young adult, reads outdoors with his friend Henri de Réveillon, hints at such a potential, suggested through a coexistence of reading with the sensorial experience of the natural world:

> Jean had not yet started to read ... They could hear, although they could feel nothing but a gentle breeze, a continuous murmuring, as though of the sea. Whenever Jean raised his eyes he could see a great spread of sky like a shoreless ocean, blue and calm to the horizon ... Filmy white clouds were floating across the sky with a scarcely perceptible motion, like homing sails ... Jean resumed his reading and then when he felt tired, laid aside his book, letting the sun beat upon him and illuminate the thoughts that his reading had set afloat within his mind, one by one, while the wind, with the faint stir it gave [imprimait] to everything, quickened their movement ... He would have liked to talk to Henri, and felt disappointed to find that he was absorbed in his reading.[57]

In this precursor to the extended scenes of solitary outdoor reading in "Sur la lecture"[58] and "Combray," elements of nature (sky, sun, wind) commingle with reading instead of competing with it for the reader's attention. The relationship of exclusion suggested in the preface, where sunset makes the narrator forget about literary questions, is replaced with one of felicitous coexistence. Rather than reading supplanting nature or vice versa, nature complements and deepens the experience of reading. In another reversal from the preface, where the narrator hopes the writer will "shed light" on his experience of the sun, the sun is imagined to shed further light on the reader's thoughts, in a description that blurs the figurative and the literal meanings of illumination. The verb *imprimait*, here used in a slightly archaic definition to describe how the wind transmits movement, suggests a further analogy between the world of nature and that of print: the reader's thoughts, stirred by way of an *imprimé* (a printed document, a book), rustle like pages in the breeze. These thoughts are said to be launched onto the water inside the reader ("set afloat within his mind"), a richly significant image, for there is no actual water in the physical setting of the scene – the pair are at Réveillon,[59] not on the Breton coast – only the continual murmur of the breeze that makes the immense blue sky seem like the sea. A conjunction of physical stimuli (the sound of the wind, the blue of the sky) generate an image in Jean's mind (the wispy white clouds are like sails on the water) that is then reconfigured as a metaphor for the mental process set in motion by reading (his thoughts are like sailboats). The blue of the sky above has become an inner sea where Jean's thoughts are blown along by the real wind. The scene thus presents reading as an experience rich with the potential of a concurrence of opposites, a fruitful[60] porosity between outside and inside, literal and figurative, presence and absence, reader and text. This feeling of exhilaration appears to come up against the obstacle of incommunicability: Jean finds himself unable to verbally convey his experience to Henri, who is sitting close to him but remains absorbed in his own reading. But Henri's presence, reading at Jean's side as he was reading, enabled the experience.

As critics have often noted, Henri de Réveillon bears the reverse initials of Reynaldo Hahn (1874–1947), the composer with whom Proust shared a passionate amorous relationship during the years 1894 to 1896, and who later remained his closest, most intimate friend. As Philip Kolb decisively showed, based on an examination of the types of paper used by Proust in certain sections of the manuscript, it was during the fall of 1895, when the pair took a trip to the coast of Brittany by themselves, far from their parents and other interferers, that Proust began to write *Jean Santeuil*.[61] Jean and Henri (who bears different names in other sections of the manuscript, and who also incorporates traits from other real-life and fictional sources, like all Proust's characters) have much in common with Proust and Hahn, as do the two unnamed friends vacationing in Brittany, in the frame story of the preface. What if, in the well-known scenes of solitary reading in "Combray" analysed by Paul de Man, Antoine Compagnon and, more recently, Adam Watt,[62] there might be an invisible trace of earlier scenes from the manuscript of *Jean Santeuil*, such as the scene at Révellion cited above, where reading is not experienced in isolation but instead connects two bookish young men? In that regard *Jean Santeuil* is not entirely unique: other, vastly forgotten novels like Paul Flat's *L'Illusion sentimentale* (1905) stage similar queer meetings through reading.[63] What makes the question interesting in *Jean Santeuil* is the possibility that this dormant fantasy might underlie, in the later, more mature *Recherche*, the dynamics of recognition between reader and book, described by the narrator of *Le Temps retrouvé* with a much-cited and thoroughly desexualized optical metaphor ("in reality, every reader is, while he is reading, the reader of his own self. The writer's work is merely a kind of optical instrument").[64]

Queer recognition through shared reading, in Proust's early novel but also in his correspondence from the same period, is placed under the sign of one of his own formative readings: the essays of Ralph Waldo Emerson.[65] Emerson's name appears twice in *Jean Santeuil*; by comparison it occurs four times in the earlier *Les Plaisirs et les Jours* (1896), but only once in the whole of the *Recherche*.[66] In both of its appearances in *Jean Santeuil* the name is linked to a pleasurable experience of discovery, recognition, and similitude. In the first of these scenes, the protagonist Jean Santeuil goes to meet his friend Henri de Réveillon at a garrison town. He is greeted by a low-ranking officer, a member of a different social class in whom he nevertheless recognizes a kind of intellectual kin (in this and a few later examples I cite the manuscript in semi-diplomatic transcription, as Proust's additions and cross-outs are often revealing):[67]

> He was the son of a peasant
> from the area. ["]Hello Monsieur Santeuil he said joyously is it Monsieur
> de Réveillon who brings you here, Are you bringing M. de Réveillon or is it
> ~~c~~Chance that brings you both?" At that moment St Gervin entered and
> asked
> Jean and Henri to follow him, but ~~charmed by that~~ phrase ~~which might~~
> ~~have been one of the~~ prettiest ~~image~~ <~~most graceful allegory~~> ~~of Chance~~
> ~~that had b these words alone had been~~
> ~~enough to show Jean that the~~ <poor> ~~soldier was a young lad whose cul~~
> ~~is~~ Jean promised himself he would come back to see this soldier ~~whose in~~
> ~~whose mouth~~
> <from> whom he had been stupefied to hear ~~that phrase~~ <~~so~~> that
> charming phrase uttered
> so naturally. If you were to find ~~on the shelves of your~~ in the bedroom
> of your innkeeper in a faraway ~~bedroom~~ <province> ~~most~~ the poems of
> Alfred de

> Vigny, Emerson's Essays and le Rouge et le Noir, would <you> not feel as if in the presence of a friend, full of yourself, with whom you would want to converse.[68]

Here Emerson is imagined to signal, along with Vigny and Stendhal, not just a common sensibility, but a shared readerly identity with an otherwise unknown other.[69]

The contents of the bookshelf allow the hypothetical innkeeper to be recognized as a kindred spirit – of the narrator, but also of his reader, implicated here through the impersonal "you" used by Proust in a number of similar digressions throughout *Jean Santeuil.* The great social and geographic distance between the "innkeeper" from a "faraway province" and the reader, presumed to be Parisian, bourgeois, and male, is abolished by a feeling of "presence" (a key word to which we will return shortly). The interchangeability between the two male friends ("is it Monsieur de Réveillon who brings you here, are you bringing M. de Réveillon?") is reflected in the fantasized sameness of readers of certain works ("a friend, full of yourself"). Reading is not imagined as a conversation with an illustrious author – a fallacy Proust will denounce in the 1905 preface to his translation of Ruskin's *Sesame and Lilies*[70] – but rather as a prelude to a conversation with *another reader* who, by virtue of this shared reading, is not entirely an other but rather a brother of sorts. It is worth noting that the corporal who charmingly recognizes the bond between Jean and Henri is described, in a marginal addition, as a "sickly" [maladif],[71] a term akin to "malade," which Proust often uses to describe himself in his correspondence. Proust crossed out, about the corporal's "charming phrase," the words "in whose mouth" [dans la bouche de], possibly because they are too suggestive of something like cruising – another, more explicitly erotic mode of recognition, one that also collapses social distances, and is perhaps not entirely absent from the dynamics of this scene. Like many female heroines in Proust's early works, whose socially transgressive or same-sex desires systematically lead to their deaths or the deaths of those they love,[72] the charming corporal commits suicide soon after his encounter with Jean and Henri, on the reverse of this same manuscript folio.[73] The continuum of recognizability between males who share a similar sensibility across class and geographic lines evidently carries a dangerous potential, here displaced onto a very minor character.

The second occurrence of Emerson's name in *Jean Santeuil* is found in an extended scene where Jean and Henri read together on the beach, during a trip to the Brittany coast that mirrors Proust and Hahn's shared sojourn of 1895. In a long digression, the narrator muses on Jean's attachment to certain readings from childhood, a development that again prefigures similar reflections in "Sur la lecture," and later, "Combray": "When we were young there was always one special book that we carried under our arm to the park, and read with a passion that no other book could ever quite supplant."[74] The book in childhood is an object of love, manifested in physical contact ("under our arm"), and its company is best enjoyed out of doors: as such it occupies a somewhat parallel, perhaps even analogous position to Henri, Jean's reading companion. A major evolution between childhood and adult reading, according to the narrator, is that the child sees no difference between the book's material aspect and the text it contains. The adult reader, it is implied, has renounced this attachment to materiality, and this is where Emerson is invoked: "Today, we should be enchanted to find in some manuscript, in some newspaper instalment, a few new pages from George Eliot or from Emerson. But in our younger days the book and what it contained made for us a single unity."[75] Here as in the earlier sentence, Proust uses an ambiguous, impersonal plural pronoun, as he will throughout "Sur la lecture" a decade later: "today" (as opposed to earlier, when we were young), "we" (the narrator and his implied adult readers) would be delighted to discover a hitherto unpublished text by Eliot or Emerson in a medium that is not a book (a newspaper, a manuscript), whereas as children we would not have been able to recognize that it belonged to the same oeuvre since it was not enclosed in the same binding.

Paradoxically, and perhaps perversely, this renunciation of the child's material attachment to a favourite book, serves as a pretext for the narrator to indulge a lush description of childhood reading as a sensual, corporeal experience:

> Its [the book's] physical enchantment [charme de corps] was one with the story that we loved, with the pleasure it gave us when on a warm afternoon, in the shady arbours of the park, hidden from sight so as not to be interrupted ... we sat holding it in our hands and looking at its pages. We never, in our mind, separated its contents from the softness of its thin pages, from its lovely smell, from the fine, stiff binding with the gilded corners, which contained it.[76]

It is impossible to read this passage without recognizing its links to comparable moments in "Combray," but the similarity between these scenes should not blind us to a significant difference: unlike the solitary young hero reading out of doors in the first section of the *Recherche*, the reader in *Jean Santeuil* is not alone. At such moments of shared reading in the manuscript of the early work, Proust's handwriting tends to get busy or agitated; it bristles with corrections, additions, crossings out, and rewrites, which get cleaned up in published versions:

> [...] Jean and Henri went to lie down
> with some books on the little sand dunes that ~~rise~~ begin west
> of the beach. They would lie down and sometimes did not read for a long
> time. ~~What~~ In order to read
> and not disturb one another, they placed themselves at some distance from
> one another
> and thanks to the undulations of the dune sometimes ~~one was~~ while being
> only a few steps apart
> from one another they could not see each other[,] hidden by a fold in the
> dune, and each
> could think he was ~~thousands of yards~~ <cut off> from any human, seeing
> only[,] above
> the sand[,] the sky and the sea and the seagulls that flew endlessly.
> ~~Jean lying with his feet up let himself be filled with It T Cut off~~
> ~~from nature and exhausted as we are Such a life is sweet It is because they~~
> ~~make us think about such a life~~ [*ill.*] ~~wholly blindly given over to~~
> ~~the beneficial forces of physical nature that we think fondly~~
> ~~of animals, of the boa for who it retires to digest for~~
> ~~three days and remains all the while in a kind of~~ When one was
> done reading before the other he stepped further away and walked silently
> so as
> not to disturb the other, although truth be told the desire of someone who
> has completed his
> work or his reading is a desire to be done with it and to discuss which
> excludes any
> respect of the other's reading.[77]

There would be a lot to unpack in these crossings out – including the phallic and rather unexpected comparison of the well-fed friends to a boa – but it is the concomitance of presence and absence, coexistence and separation, awareness and invisibility that appears most remarkable. As fellow readers, Jean and Henri are similar to the point of interchangeability: grammatically they become "one" and "the other." The scene unfolds as an allegory for a sense of shared reading. Although each reader is by himself, there is another reader out there just like him, not directly seen, but nevertheless keenly felt, as in the provincial innkeeper's bedroom with its resonant selection of books.

Proust's Emerson

Why does Emerson's name recur in these scenes of shared reading? Of what might "Emerson" be a sign? A letter from Proust to Reynaldo Hahn from mid-January 1895 (the winter before the trip to Brittany in September) provides a clue:

> My beloved child
> This morning I'll go to the Bois if I
> get out of bed early enough, for I'm still lying down,
> reading Emerson with exhilaration. Come see me [...]
> [Mademoiselle Lemaire] wrote me that my verses <(to you)> were good.
> I replied that inspiration comes easily
> when we talk about what we love.
> In truth, we should talk about that alone
> and nothing else. Those verses are the only ones <of mine> that
> you would please me by showing and reciting
> as often as possible. Know that in catho-
> lic liturgy real presence precisely means ideal
> presence. _ . But no I'm a little off.
> I am your pony
> Marcel[78]

Emerson's name, glimpsed on a provincial bookshelf, was interpreted as a sign of the "presence of a friend," an unknown and idealized other who was so "like" the reader as to be brimming with sameness – "full of yourself," the imagined reader of *Jean Santeuil* being drawn into the analogy. Here the friend is Reynaldo Hahn, and the letter evokes the same principle of reversibility, since it is ambiguous whose presence is conjured by the poem mentioned (perhaps the verses about Hahn that Proust added to a manuscript copy of the "Van Dyck" poem from his *Portraits de peintres* which Hahn had set to music; these additional verses were not included in the published version of the poem in *Les Plaisirs et les Jours*).[79] It could be Hahn who is imagined to be "present" in Proust's verses dedicated to him, or Proust who is imagined to be present when Hahn recites the poem. "Real presence" is a significant theological concept for Proust – according to Thomas Aquinas, it is the presence of the body of Christ in the Eucharist, "not ... as in a place" (i.e., materially), "but after the manner of substance" (i.e., essentially)[80] – that will inform the narrator's reflections on the link between artistic practice and involuntary memory in *Le Temps retrouvé.* This is therefore a key letter for Proust's personal and novelistic aesthetics, and not simply because he writes it from bed.

Reading Emerson in January 1895 – in bed, between wakefulness and sleep, like the adult hero reading, in the very first page of the *Recherche* – is a sign of the potent blurring of Emersonian definitions of friendship and love, deployed around a male same-sex object. For Proust in this period (he will begin to write *Jean Santeuil* later that year), "Emerson" becomes a name for this kind of attachment. In reading some of the texts by Emerson that were available to him in French translation, Proust may have recognized what he felt for Reynaldo Hahn; conversely, he may also have invested Hahn with the idealized relationship he read about in Emerson. In *Jean Santeuil* and texts of that era, "Emerson" comes to name both that type of relationship *and* its fundamental mediation through shared reading.

According to Philip Kolb, Proust had access to two single-volume editions of selected *Essays* by Emerson in French: a translation from 1851 that included the essays "Love" and "Friendship" from the *First Series* (1841), and an 1894 translation (1894 being the year he met Reynaldo Hahn) with a preface by Maurice Maeterlinck that included the essay "Character" from the *Second Series* (1844).[81] What did Proust read about friendship and love in these volumes? Three important points stand out (as a complement to Emerson's text, I cite and retranslate in brackets some of the words used in the translations read by Proust, as these often depart from the original in significant ways):

1) Close friendship between men surpasses the love of women; it is the very highest form of relationship, of which heterosexual relations can only be a secondary image.

> What is so excellent as strict [*close*] relations of amity, when they spring from this deep root? ... I know nothing which life has to offer so satisfying as the profound good understanding, which can subsist ... between two virtuous men, each of whom is sure of himself, and sure of his friend ... Of such friendship, love in [*between*] the sexes is the first symbol ... Those relations to the best men, which, at one time, we reckoned the romances of youth [*novels of childhood*], become, in the progress of the character, the most solid enjoyment.[82]

Significantly, here, true friendship between men is described as a "roman de jeunesse" in the translation read by Proust: a novel read in childhood, something one read and dreamt about, but later deemed too good to be possible, until one encountered it.

2) True friendship is a meeting of equals that are concurrently similar and different.

> Friendship requires that rare mean betwixt likeness and unlikeness, that piques each with the presence of ... the other party [*of his companion*] ... [*For*

> *their union to be complete,*][83] There must be very two, [*apart*], before there can be very one. Let it [*their friendship*] be an alliance of two large, formidable natures ... before yet they recognize the deep identity [*unity*] which beneath these disparities unites them.[84]

In *Jean Santeuil*, it is precisely this concomitance between resemblance and dissemblance that signals the "presence" of a friend.

3) Friendship makes a god of the friend.

> The essence of friendship is entireness, a total magnanimity and trust. It must not surmise or provide for infirmity. It treats its object as a god, that it may deify both [*so that the two human beings who have established the relation of friendship between them may be, so to speak, deified, one by the other*].[85]

This is taken up again in the essay "Character," where Emerson reflects that, as gods to each other, friends are destined to find and recognize one another:

> If we are related [*akin in whatever way*], we shall meet. It was a tradition of the ancient world, that no metamorphosis could hide a god from a god; and there is a Greek verse which runs,
>
> "The Gods are to each other [*one to another*] not unknown."
>
> Friends also follow the laws of divine necessity; they gravitate to each other [*one toward the other*], and cannot otherwise ...[86]

The grammatical device of "one" and "the other" ("l'un" / "l'autre," "un" / "un autre") recurs throughout the French translations; these same reversible terms are used to designate the two interchangeable friends Jean and Henri in many episodes from *Jean Santeuil*.

Emerson's reference to the myth of Apollo guarding the flocks of Admetus in disguise is used as an epigraph by Proust for the short story "La Mort de Baldassare Sylvandre" in his first book, *Les Plaisirs et les Jours* (1896). Proust had published that short story in *La Revue hebdomadaire* on 29 October 1895, with a dedication to Reynaldo Hahn.[87] The dedication was removed from *Les Plaisirs et les Jours*, but the Emersonian epigraph that replaces it acts as a hidden sign, a "disguise" through which Hahn can recognize himself. The same reference appears in a letter from Proust to Hahn from March 1896, about Hahn's place in the "novel" he is writing – the novel we now know as *Jean Santeuil*:

> [...] How good you are Reynaldo.
> Maman was touched by
> your kindness and I //

thank you and embrace you
with all my heart. I had
brought you little things
by me and the beginning of
the novel which Yeatman[88] himself
next to whom I was writing
found very pony. You will
help me correct what might
be too much so. I want you to be in it
at all times, but like
a god in disguise that no
mortal can recognize. Otherwise,
you'd have to write
["]to be torn up" on the whole novel. [...][89]

This letter is often cited as a key to Hahn's presence in *Jean Santeuil*,[90] but it takes the Emersonian intertext to give it its full affective charge. Critics have tended to downplay the queer significance of the term "poney" in the context of this particular letter, proposing that, while it is understood to be an affectionate pet name given to Proust by Hahn,[91] it must somehow when applied to *Jean Santeuil* have a broader definition of "overly sentimental or mawkish, too delicate."[92] Yet the sentences that immediately surround the oft-quoted passage about the Emersonian "god in disguise" belie this: "you [vous] will help me correct what might be too much so" (i.e., too "poney"), "otherwise, you'd [tu] have to write [']to be torn up' on the whole novel." The slippage from the more conventional "vous" used everywhere else in the letter to a more intimate "tu" at this very moment (whereas Proust and Hahn use "tu" in relatively few letters, even at the height of their love, and very largely revert to "vous" after 1896) appears significant, as is the phrase "to be torn up," a command one might find as a postscriptum to a compromising letter.[93] The "beginning of the novel" – that is, the frame story, the preface or "first chapter" of *Jean Santeuil* – is not particularly mawkish: it is, however, possibly compromising, with its description of two young male friends travelling together to a remote village on the Breton coast. That section of the manuscript appears to have been written in March 1896,[94] five months after Proust and Hahn's trip to Brittany, but also less than a year after the Wilde trials in London.

Emerson's essays "Friendship" (completed in 1839) and "Love" (from 1840) both derive from a lecture entitled "The Heart," delivered in Boston on 3 January 1838. In that lecture, Emerson states that the heart of each person should aspire to find its harbour in another person either of the opposite sex or of the same, "in the natural Society of Marriage or in the (celestial) Society of Friendship."[95] As Caleb Crain observes, much in the lecture suggests that "Emerson follows Plato in preferring same-sex relationships."[96] Indeed while "The Heart" extols the model male-male friendship of Montaigne and La Boétie,[97] it has little to say on the topic of opposite-sex marriage. The lecture exalts the moment of recognition between two hearts – belonging to two "men" – meant for each other:

> The Heart ... really does bind all men into a consciousness of one brotherhood. Of this the look between man and man is the expression.
>
> One of the most wonderful things in nature, where all is wonderful, is, the glance, or meeting of the eyes; this speedy and perfect communication which transcends speech and action also and is in the greatest part not subject to the control of the will.[98]

The fantasy of such meetings, mediated by reading, is described in both Proust and Emerson's long-unpublished manuscripts.

Meetings in Manuscripts

Proust could not have known Emerson's complete *Journals*, which remained unpublished, not unlike *Jean Santeuil*, until well after the author's death.[99] An entry written around 9 August 1820 (when Emerson, age seventeen, was a junior at Harvard College) reads as follows (see figures 3a and 3b):

> There is a strange face in the Freshman class
> whom I should like to know very much. He
> has a great deal of character in his features & should //
> [be] a fast friend or a bitter ~~enemy~~. His name ~~is Gay.~~
> I shall endeavor to be<come> acquainted with him
> & wish if possible that I might be able to
> recall at a future period the singular
> sensations which his presenc[e] produced at
> this.[100]

The editors of the *Journals* note that "when Emerson set down his feelings about Gay, he usually went back later and carefully deleted or disguised them."[101] Emerson never did become much acquainted with Martin Gay at all,[102] but that encounter, with its fantasized recognition of an idealized friend, was to be crucial to his later writings in "Friendship," "Love" and "Character" – readings through which Proust experienced his own fantasy recognition of Reynaldo Hahn. Fittingly, Emerson's essay "Friendship," which Proust read in translation, opens with a description of the moment of recognition (reworked from the earlier lecture "The Heart" extolling same-sex

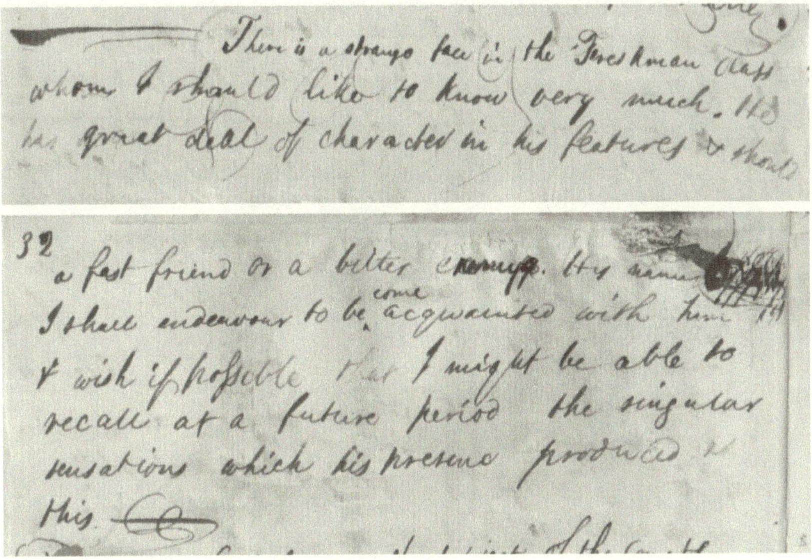

Figures 3a and 3b. Excerpts from Ralph Waldo Emerson journals and notebooks, 1820–1880, "Wide World" [1820], MS Am 1280h (2), p. 31 (detail) and p. 32 (detail). Ralph Waldo Emerson Memorial Association deposit, Houghton Library, Harvard University.

friendship and "the meeting of the eyes") that uses reading as a metaphor: "Read the language of these wandering eye-beams. The heart knoweth."[103]

Later, in a notebook used by Emerson between 1820 and 1822, a number of poems dedicated to Gay are veiled by name changes and other literary disguises (see figure 4):

From Frodmer's Drama "The Friends"
[...]
~~Malcolm, I love thee more than women love~~
Your ~~And pure and warm and equal is the feeling~~
Your ~~Which binds us and our destinies forever~~
Your ~~But there are seasons in the change~~ of times
Yours When strong excitement kindles up the light
Of ancient memories [...][104]

As the editors of the *Journals* note succinctly: "There is no dramatist named Frodmer. The title is apparently Emerson's – to describe his own theme. The thought parallels others he wrote to or about Gay. 'Malcolm' may well be a substitute for 'Martin.'"[105] Another poem in the same notebook ends with a declaration of renunciation, described through ancient myth:

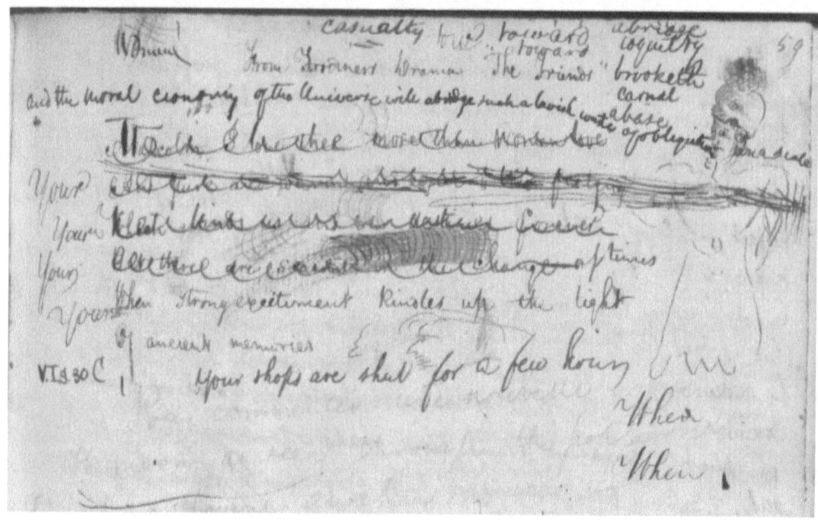

Figure 4. Excerpts from Ralph Waldo Emerson journals and notebooks, 1820–1880, "No. XVIII," MS Am 1280h (4), p. 59 (detail). Ralph Waldo Emerson Memorial Association deposit, Houghton Library, Harvard University.

By the unacknowledged tie
Which binds us to each other
By the pride of feeling high
Which friendship's name can smother

By the cold encountering eyes
Whose language deeply thrilling
Rebelled against the prompt surmise
~~Confessed~~ <Which told> the heart was willing

By all which you have felt and feel
My eager gaze returning
I offer you this silent zeal
On youthful altars burning,

All the classic hours which ~~come~~ <fill>
This little urn of honour;
Minerva guide & pay the pen
Your hand conferred upon her.[106]

The poem describes a textbook case of sublimation: since the "thrilling" meeting of eager gazes did not lead to anything, the burning energy of the encounter will be channelled into the pursuit of wisdom, of which Minerva is the virginal, female symbol.

In what amounts, across manuscripts, at an ocean and many decades' remove, to one of those peculiar meeting of strangers, Minerva also appears in a scene from *Jean Santeuil*, in a passage suffused with Emersonian themes of recognition through reading, fantasized sameness, and the sublimity of male friendship.[107] In that scene, as the young Jean sits in detention at school translating a passage from the *Odyssey*, the narrator describes his ardent desire to become friends with a fellow student, the young nobleman Charles de Réveillon, an alternate name – a mask, like "Malcolm" for Martin Gay – for the character whose name elsewhere in the manuscript, Henri de Réveillon, as we have seen, bears Reynaldo Hahn's initials in reverse. Tellingly, in making Réveillon an aristocrat, Proust followed Emerson's dictum about the true friend, from the translation of his essay "Friendship": "give him the rank of a prince" ("donne-lui le rang d'un prince")[108] (see figures 5 and 6):

> [we see] at the moment ~~when Ulysses longs to see her, Minerva~~
> when Ulysses laments that he is so far from Minerva
> the goddess appear ~~in~~ to the hero in the <disguised> aspect
> of an old man. Jean ~~held~~ knew that
> such apparitions are impossible and that ~~if the~~
> ~~things we desir~~ children alone believe that
> their desire is the law of the world. [...]
> [...] And yet
> he loved, ~~at in the evening during those uncertain hours~~
> ~~spent~~ in his bed ~~before~~ <at the time> he went to sleep ~~and that~~
> combine [...]
> [...] and the daytime at those certain hours that
> look like it, to imagine Réveillon ~~who was then~~
> ~~far from him~~, the distance of whose dwelling was not
> alone in keeping them apart, coming to knock at
> his bedroom door, holding out his hand, explaining
> why he had until then had to hide his sympathy.
> ~~If his reason~~ The experience of his reason protested
> ~~such~~ the absurdity of such a fairytale [*roman*]. But imagination has no experience, [...] //[109]
>
> As a ~~sick man en~~ fool enjoys ~~listening~~ ~~<list>~~ <meeting> ~~a~~
> a kindly friend who listens without contradicting him,
> so Jean sought the innocent complicity
> of the poet. [...]
> [...] He had reached

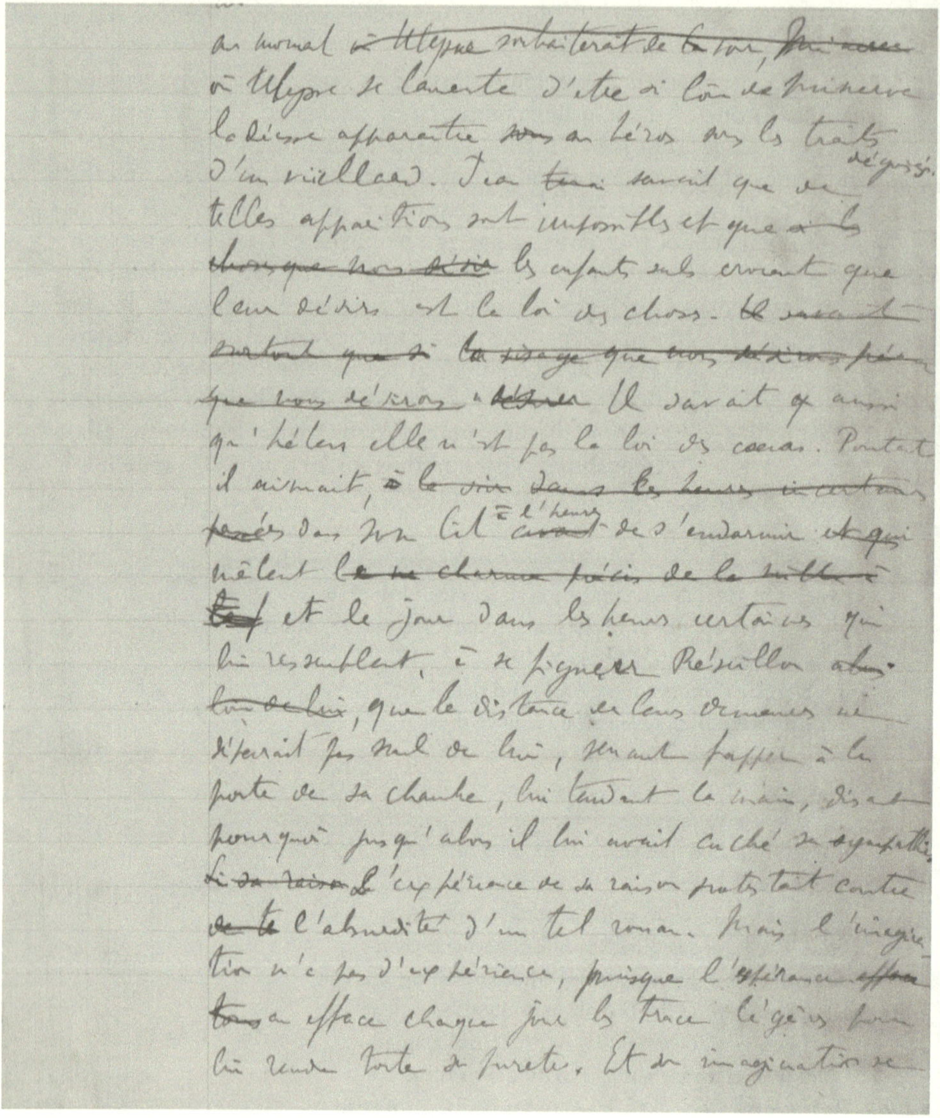

Figure 5. Marcel Proust, "Charles [Henri] de Réveillon," [*Jean Santeuil*], Philip Kolb Collection of Marcel Proust Papers, Box 3, Item 100g, f° 3, recto (detail). Image Courtesy of the Rare Book & Manuscript Library, University of Illinois at Urbana-Champaign.

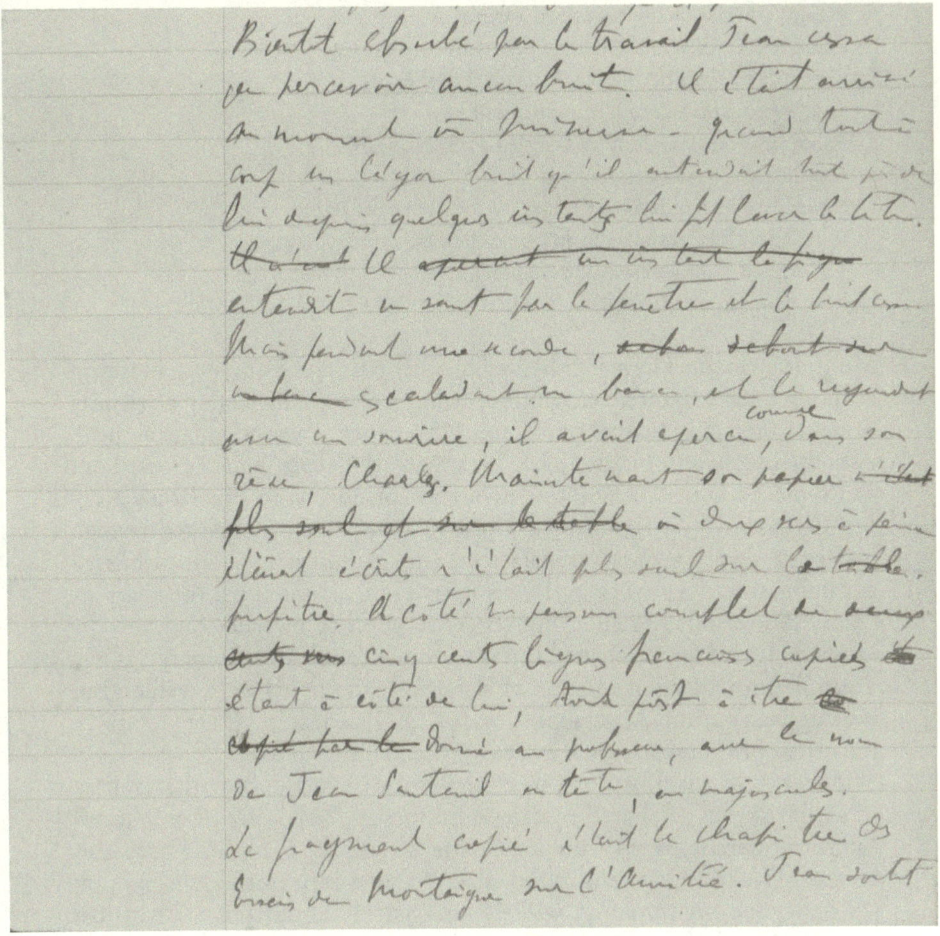

Figure 6. Marcel Proust, "Charles [Henri] de Réveillon," [*Jean Santeuil*], Philip Kolb Collection of Marcel Proust Papers, Box 3, Item 100g, f° 3, verso (detail). Image Courtesy of the Rare Book & Manuscript Library, University of Illinois at Urbana-Champaign.

the moment where Minerva – when all of a
sudden a light noise he had been hearing very close to
him for a few moments made him raise his head.
~~He didn't~~ He ~~saw for a few instants the face~~
heard a jump from the window and the noise ceased.
But for a second, ~~standi standing on~~
~~a bench~~ climbing a bench, and looking at him
with a smile, he had seen, <as he had> in his

> dream, Charles. Now his paper ~~was no~~
> ~~longer alone and on the table~~ where only two verses
> were written was no longer alone on the ~~table~~
> desk. Next to it a complete pensum of ~~two~~
> ~~hundred verses~~ five hundred copied French lines ~~wa~~
> was next to it, ready to be ~~co~~
> ~~copied by the~~ handed over to the teacher, with the name
> Jean Santeuil atop the page, in capital letters.
> The copied fragment was the chapter
> from Montaigne's Essays on Friendship.[110]

Multiple elements I have highlighted in other passages from the manuscript coalesce here: disguise, recognition, being isolated but feeling a friendly presence through a textual connection ("his paper ... was no longer alone"), even the overly autobiographical "sick man" ("malade"), here crossed out and replaced with "fool" ("fou"). In this episode, as in Emerson's essay on "Character," idealized friendship/love – the bringing-together through instant recognition of two separate yet highly similar men – is dismissed as "impossible," a *roman* in the pejorative sense, something the heart ardently desires but the mind knows is too good to be true. And yet, the idealized friend appears, like Minerva appears to Ulysses, literally "as in a dream," through the mediation of a shared text, copied by Réveillon but bearing Jean's name, Montaigne's essay "On Friendship" ("De l'amitié"), the urtext of Emerson's own essays on friendship and love.[111]

If scenes of reading alone in nature in "Combray" bear the imprint of earlier scenes of shared reading outdoors in *Jean Santeuil*, might not the very opening page of the *Recherche*, where the adult hero oscillates between wakefulness and sleep after having just put down a book ("I had gone on thinking, while I was asleep, about what I had just been reading")[112] likewise carry an echo of that 1895 letter to Reynaldo Hahn ("I'm still lying down, reading Emerson with exhilaration")? A hidden lineage connecting the two runs through the manuscript of *Jean Santeuil*, and particularly this folio about Jean's daydream in detention, with its agitated passages about quivering desire and the imperviousness of other hearts, about night and day, proximity and distance, and the "uncertain hours spent in ... bed" when the lines between all of these become blurred.

Behind the somnolent adult reader of the very first page of "Combray," who reads about churches and quartets, we learn, in *Le Temps retrouvé*, that there is another, fantasized reader, distinct yet profoundly akin to the hero (and perhaps to the narrator, or even the author), encountered and recognized through reading. The narrator of *Le Temps retrouvé* expresses a deep care, a form of love for this potential reader, who he imagines as replacing, in his affections, the friends he will no longer have time to see once he sets down to the task of writing:

> Was it not, surely, in order to care for them that I would live apart from these people who would complain that they did not get to see me, to concern myself with them more deeply than would have been possible in their presence, to seek to reveal them to themselves, to realize their potentialities?[113]

In an earlier passage from *La Prisonnière* [*The Captive*, 1923, posth.], the narrator uses an amalgam of themes that, for Proust, are associated with Emerson – invisibility, recognition, reading, desire – to describe the hero's experience of suddenly recognizing, in the mysterious newness of Vinteuil's posthumous septet, the sonata he is familiar with:

> What artist's work was I immersed in? I longed to know, and, seeing nobody near me whom I could ask, I should have liked to be a character in those *Arabian Nights*, which I never tired of reading and in which, in moments of uncertainty, there appears a genie, or an adolescent girl of ravishing beauty, invisible to everyone else but not to the perplexed hero to whom she reveals exactly what he desires to know ... so, all of a sudden, I found myself, in the midst of this music that was new to me, right in Vinteuil's sonata.[114]

In that scene, the mature work of art (Vinteuil's septet, the ultimate model for what the narrator will imagine his book to be) takes the place of the dreamed-of friend in *Jean Santeuil*, that desired double who is "betwixt likeness and unlikeness," in Emerson's terms, and who brings companionship, consolation, and knowledge. The work of art, the future book that the narrator will set down to write, "reveals precisely" to the reader "what he desires to know": it is the true friend that no real-world friend could be, encountered and recognized at last.

The best reading, Proust's *Recherche* insists, does not usurp or supersede the natural, the real, the true. It allows instead for the concurrent experience, indeed the synthesis, of the familiar and the other, the present and the past, the self and the outside world, and yields the potential, for the reader, of a deeper understanding of each. This pedagogical function, presented in desexualized, optical terms by the narrator in *Le Temps retrouvé*, is suffused with an earlier queer fantasy of recognition, derived from a selective reading of Emerson when Proust was in his twenties. Like Gide, Proust reworked anxious discourses that circulated at the fin de siècle, according to which an excess of reading could lead to deviations from normative sexual and gender roles. Unlike Gide's decidedly male-focused scheme of apprenticeship, however, Proust's pedagogical model is not exclusionary: the *Recherche* opens the positively queer possibilities of reading and recognition to readers of all kinds.

Epilogue: The Afterlives of Bad Masters

During the First World War and the interwar period, young people's reading practices continued to preoccupy French cultural commentators and literary critics. In 1922, the conservative writer Léon Daudet (son of Alphonse) published *Le Stupide XIXe siècle* (The stupid nineteenth century); under the subtitle "Exposé on the murderous insanities that have befallen France for the past 130 years," this three-hundred-page screed laid out its case, in chapters such as "The Romantic aberration and its consequences."[1] That same year, Jean Carrère launched a polemic with a book, *Les Mauvais Maîtres* (The bad masters), that blamed writers from Rousseau to Zola for "the state of intellectual trouble, moral lassitude and public uneasiness"[2] the author claimed to have observed among contemporary youth. While *Les Mauvais Maîtres* generated fresh debate, drawing responses from eminent critics like Albert Thibaudet, Paul Souday, and (as we have seen) André Beaunier,[3] the arguments it laid out were anything but new. It appears significant that Carrère's book, with its chapters on Balzac, Stendhal, Flaubert and the like, is entirely composed of articles he had published much earlier, between 1902 and 1904. Two decades into the new century, fin-de-siècle anxieties lived on under the pen of reactionary critics, particularly following the recent Great War.

A further two decades later, in the wake of France's 1940 surrender to Germany, Carrère's essay would be evoked again through what became known as the "quarrel of the bad masters,"[4] as one faction of intellectuals accused modern writers of having demoralized recent generations, leading to France's defeat, while others defended literature's freedom from social responsibility. So familiar were the arguments being rehashed in 1940 that the title of a 1922 book, made up of essays written around 1903, could be applied to a contemporary debate. In July 1940, an unsigned article in *Le Temps* titled "La Jeunesse de France" (The youth of France) singled out the "nefarious" influence of André Gide.[5] Later that month, a longer article by

Guy de Pourtalès in *Le Journal de Genève* made use of a time-worn image, the library as a graveyard of the will, a dying-place of truth, tinged with queer menace: "Simply glance at your bookshelves: pessimists, defeatists, immoralists and *corydons* (many of them indubitably talented) ... writers have abused a false truth ... reason has been silenced, and we have been made instead to listen to the voices of enchanters."[6] Save for its reference to twentieth-century works, such a sentence would not be out of place in any number of fin-de-siècle novels of formation; well past the turn of the century, discourses about the dangers of literature for young Frenchmen had not entirely faded away.

Yet by the 1940s, books and writers were no longer the sole culprits identified by pundits and would-be censors. In an oft-repeated and unattributed anecdote, a nameless Vichy bureaucrat is said to have exclaimed: "we lost the war because of Jean-Paul Sartre and *Le Quai des brumes*"[7] (in another version, the blame is cast on "paid holidays, André Gide, and the *Quai des brumes*").[8] Shortly before the Second World War, the writer Lucien Rebatet (soon to be a leading collaborationist and author of virulent anti-Semitic pamphlets) had repeatedly lambasted the films of Marcel Carné, including *Le Quai des brumes* (*Port of Shadows*, 1938), for their depictions of unmanly, tormented male protagonists, which he compared to "larvae": "nothing could be less virile," he wrote about Carné's *Hôtel du Nord* (also released in 1938).[9] Beginning in 1928, a French government commission oversaw the granting of licences for projecting films; criteria introduced in 1937 included a provision for denying licences to works that "might have a pernicious influence on young people."[10] Under the Occupation, more than one hundred films (including *Le Quai des brumes*) were banned under a directive that forbad "depressing, morbid, immoral films, and those detrimental to youth."[11]

Similar arguments about morality and the behaviour of youth were deployed in the United States to gather support for the regulation and censorship of movies, through what became known as the Hays Code.[12] These arguments are neatly synthesized in the title of a 1935 tract, based on studies commissioned and funded by supporters of the code: *Our Movie Made Children*.[13] On both sides of the Atlantic,[14] antimimetic discourses gradually shifted from reading towards the viewing of films. The ill effects of cinema, as decried by twentieth-century proponents of censorship, were quite similar to nineteenth-century descriptions of the dangers of books: people who consumed them, particularly when young, were given precocious exposure to sexuality, confusing or corrupting examples of immoral behaviour, and false expectations about reality or the possibilities open to them in their own life. Soon these same discourses would be transferred to a newer medium, television. A long discursive lineage can be traced from ancient condemnations of theatre to current-day concerns about young people's (and increasingly, adults') consumption of electronic media. In fin-de-siècle France, these anxieties were, for a time, given a peculiar new shape, through the vicissitudes of history and the evolution of the literary field, as a crisis about young men.

In our twenty-first century, by contrast, articles in French newspapers ask, in concerned headlines, "Are Teens Flunking Reading?"[15] Academic volumes take stock of profound "mutations" in young people's reading habits, noting that "statistics about reading show a clear move away from fiction and from sustained reading more generally."[16] Sociological studies, citing extensive data about engagement with digital media, challenge long-standing cultural paradigms, including the way "reading," as a practice, is usually understood to mean "reading books, and particulalrly reading novels."[17] In the United Kingdom, a 2011 study commissioned by the National Literacy Trust highlights a significant "gender gap" among pre-teens: 43.3 per cent of boys reported enjoying reading, compared to 58.3 per cent of girls. The report describes this as "a very worrying trend ... not simply for literacy but for boys' wider educational attainment and ultimately their life prospects."[18] An uncanny continuity is visible across centuries and cultures, even as practices change and the observed or imagined relation of books to gender shifts: reading remains described as a problem, a cause for concern, a practice to be monitored, guided, corrected – and written about.

Notes

Introduction

1 "Jean recueillit dans des lectures de poètes et dans des promenades rêveuses son âme endolorie. Sa tête s'emplit de visions. Ce fut bientôt un désordre sublime." France, *Les Désirs de Jean Servien* [1882], in *Œuvres*, 1:195. Anatole France (1844–1924) wrote this novel in 1875 or 1876, but it was not published until 1882, to fulfil a contractual obligation after the success of *Le Crime de Sylvestre Bonnard* (1881).

2 "Romans. Pervertissent les masses." Flaubert, *Le Dictionnaire des idées reçues*, in *Œuvres complètes*, ed. A. Thibaudet and R. Dumesnil, 2:1021.

3 "D'où venait donc cette insuffisance de la vie ...?" Flaubert, *Madame Bovary* [1856–7], in *Œuvres complètes*, gen. ed. Claudine Gothot-Mersch, 3:400.

4 A phrase coined by José Ortega y Gasset in *Meditations on Quixote* (1914), 162. Flaubert's correspondence reveals that he indeed reread and reflected on *Don Quixote* during the composition of *Madame Bovary*. Letter to Louise Colet, 19 June 1852, in *Correspondance*, 2:111.

5 The first part of Cervantes's novel was translated as early as 1614. See Bardon, *Don Quichotte en France*.

6 Genette adopts the label "antinovel" (despite its being "too narrow and too vague") to describe works in which "an intellectually weak hero, unable to see the difference between fiction and reality, mistakes as real (and present) the world of fiction, takes himself for one of its characters, and 'interprets' the world around him according to these mistakes." *Palimpsestes*, 164–75. See also Hodgson, "Du *Francion* de Sorel au *Pharsamon* de Marivaux," 29–38.

7 "eût pris Astrée pour modèle et imitât toutes ses actions et ses discours," "un poison." Furetière, *Le Roman bourgeois* [1666], 1005–6. See also Sabry, "Les lectures des héros de romans," 189.

8 Gleize, *Le Double Miroir*, 55.

9 See Weil, *L'Interdiction du roman et la librairie, 1728–1750*.

10 "dont le cerveau est fort tendre." Condillac, *Essai sur l'origine des connaissances humaines* [1749], 90.
11 See Ferrand, *Livre et lecture dans les romans français du XVIIIe siècle*, 23–5. On representations of reading in works by eighteenth-century women, see Mainil, *Don Quichotte en jupons*.
12 See Ferrand, "Élève séduite," in *Livre et lecture*, 69–93, as well as Brown, "The Constraints of Liberty at the Scene of Instruction."
13 Rousseau, *Julie ou la Nouvelle Héloïse* [1761], in *Œuvres complètes*, 2:61.
14 "La mère en prescrira la lecture à sa fille." Sade, *La Philosophie dans le boudoir* [1795], in *Justine et autres romans*, 641.
15 On these transformations, see Allen, *In the Public Eye*.
16 On the relationship between familial and social models of education, see Surkis, *Sexing the Citizen*, 21–9.
17 Lyons, *Readers and Society in Nineteenth-Century France*. For Lyons, "The problem was defined not only in terms of *what* the new readers read, but also in terms of *how* they read. They would read unwisely, it was feared, unable to distinguish reason from falsehood, truth from fantasy." 11.
18 Sainte-Beuve, "La Littérature industrielle."
19 Lise Dumasy observes that "the typical reader of serialized novels, as depicted by its critics, is usually female and young or childlike (cf. the *topos* of the people-as-child) ... she is characterized by passivity; the absence of political, aesthetic and often even moral judgment; and an attraction to immediate pleasure." *La Querelle du roman-feuilleton*, 19.
20 "le désordre littéraire"; "cette ivresse intellectuelle, plus dangereuse cent fois que l'ivresse physique." Nettement, *Études critiques sur le feuilleton-roman*, 1:71.
21 See Matlock, *Scenes of Seduction*, 199–280, esp. 203–19, as well as Dumasy, *La Querelle du roman-feuilleton*, 5–21, and Lyon-Caen, *La Lecture et la vie*, 25–88.
22 Lyons writes, "The anxious dreams of the nineteenth-century bourgeois were peopled by all those who threatened his sense of order, restraint and paternal control." For the patriarchal bourgeois order, "the existence of a mass of lower-class readers was a new and troubling social phenomenon" that raised the question, "How could the new reading public be controlled?" *Readers and Society*, 11–12. For Dumasy, similarly, "in contradistinction" to the (female or childlike) figure of the reader of serial novels "we find the figure of the political subject: male, adult, educated, belonging to the dominant classes, a bearer of authority and reason, guarantor of morals and actor in the public sphere." *La Querelle du roman-feuilleton*, 19.
23 Anne-Marie Thiesse shows how denunciations of the consumption of popular literature by the working classes extend to the first decades of the twentieth century in *Le Roman du quotidien*, 47–58. A treatise from 1883 featuring a number of dramatic case studies, Eugène de Budé's *Du danger des mauvais livres et des moyens d'y remédier* (On the dangers of bad books

and the means to cure them) highlights the persistence of alarmist discourses about women and working-class readers in the last decades of the nineteenth century, as does, for the early twentieth (and in the context of Catholic ideology), the Abbé Bethléem's bibliographic guide *Romans à lire et romans à proscrire* (Novels to be read and novels to be proscribed), first published in 1904 and reprinted and updated until the 1940s. On the latter, see Chartier and Hébrard, *Discours sur la lecture*, 53–73.

24 On educational reforms and the institution of mandatory primary instruction under the Third Republic, see chapter 3, pages 95–6.

25 On the "crisis of the novel," see part III, pages 169–70.

26 Neubauer, *The Fin-de-Siècle Culture of Adolescence*, 6.

27 For a detailed bibliography on this question, see Surkis, *Sexing the Citizen*, 10n20.

28 Buisson, "Le Devoir présent de la jeunesse," 231–54. Buisson's title references an 1892 treatise by Paul Desjardins, *Le Devoir présent*.

29 Agathon, *Les Jeunes Gens d'aujourd'hui*. On these texts to and about adolescents, see Pernot, *La Jeunesse en discours (1880–1925)*. Pernot proposes that "fears about young men at the turn of the century ... created by an unstable institutional situation and fed by the memory of the fires of the Commune ... gave rise to an intense pedagogical agitation ... Expressing concern about the future of youth, many were drawn to observe and counsel it" (243).

30 "parler de la jeunesse ou plutôt parler à la jeunesse." Buisson, "Le Devoir présent," 231.

31 On interpellation as a social mechanism of production of subjectivity, see Althusser, "Idéologie et appareils idéologiques d'État" [1970], 67–125.

32 I discuss an example of each archetype in chapters 3, 4, and 5, respectively.

33 Pernot, *La Jeunesse en discours*, 243.

34 An example of the latter would be Vallès's Jacques Vingtras (see chapter 3), and of the former, Proust's Jean Santeuil (see chapter 8).

35 On the *baccalauréat* and the question of *déclassement*, see chapter 3, pages 93–7.

36 "Racine, les tragiques grecs, Shakespeare, les vers de Voltaire"; "sa paresse, sa stérilité, ses scrupules et ses délicatesses l'arrêtaient dès les premières lignes"; "Pourquoi n'avez-vous pas fait de lui un relieur?" France, *Œuvres*, 1:107, 196, 80.

37 Boes, *Formative Fictions*, 21.

38 See for instance Rogers, *Career Stories*; Monicat, *Devoirs d'écriture*; Waelti-Walters, *Feminist Novels of the Belle Époque*; and Clark, *Schooling the Daughters of Marianne*.

39 Dean, *The Frail Social Body*, 5.

40 "les enfants ... nous n'en avons point dans notre littérature," Taine, "Charles Dickens" [1856], in *Essais de critique et d'histoire* (1858), cited in Bornecque, "*Le Petit Chose* devant l'histoire littéraire," 85.

41 "les poètes et les romanciers n'ont pas assez connu ce sujet d'observation, cette source de poésie qu'offre ce moment rapide et unique dans la vie d'un homme ... l'adolescent." George Sand, *Histoire de ma vie* [1854–5], cited in O'Brien, *The Novel of Adolescence in France*, 3.

42 Denis Pernot asserts: "the young man becomes the major character of the novel in the years 1890–1910." *Le Roman de socialisation*, 7. See also Neubauer, *The Fin-de-Siècle Culture of Adolescence*, 75–82; O'Brien, *The Novel of Adolescence*, 1–14, as well as Dupuy, *Un personnage nouveau du roman français*, and Tison, *Une mosaïque d'enfants*.

43 "excès d'adolescents ... dans le roman," Edmond Jaloux, *Les Nouvelles littéraires*, 4 January 1930; "le très jeune homme ... occupe dans cette période une place centrale," Albert Thibaudet, "Les Lettres au collège," *La Nouvelle Revue française*, March 1927. Both cited in O'Brien, *The Novel of Adolescence*, 9.

44 Notable examples include Anatole France, *Le Livre de mon ami* (1885), and Pierre Loti, *Le Roman d'un enfant* (1890).

45 Angenot, *1889: Un état du discours social*, 832–3.

46 Lefebvre, *André Lebey, intellectuel et franc-maçon sous la IIIe République*, back cover.

47 Valéry and Lebey, *Au miroir de l'histoire*.

48 Lebey's name appears on an alphabetical list of names of acquiantances written in Proust's own hand between 1903 and 1905 (*Marcel Proust: Collection Marie-Claude Mante*, lot 148). No letters from Proust to Lebey have yet been found.

49 André Mellerio dedicates *La Vie stérile* "TO YOUNG MEN, To my contemporaries in age, To those who already follow us" ("AUX JEUNES, À mes contemporains d'âge, À ceux qui déjà nous suivent"). Mellerio's emphasis. Poinsot and Normandy's *La Faillite du rêve* is likewise dedicated "To young men of our generation" ("Aux jeunes hommes de notre génération"). I discuss further examples in chapter 1, pages 37–9.

50 See Boes, *Formative Fictions*, 1–6. Morgenstern was a professor at the Universität Dorpat (now Tartu, Estonia). The term remained little used until it was reintroduced by Wilhelm Dilthey in 1870 and 1906. See also Boes, introduction to "On the Nature of the *Bildungsroman*," 647–9, as well as Martini, "Bildungsroman, Term and Theory," 1–25.

51 "On the Nature of the *Bildungsroman*," 654–5. Michael Minden points out that Morgenstern himself was already "uneasy about the lack of moral rigour and masculine character displayed by the heroes of the novels for which he had just found a name." *The German Bildungsroman*, 2.

52 Moretti, *The Way of the World*, 16–17.

53 Marianne Hirsch, "The Novel of Formation as Genre," 294. Dennis Mahoney discusses the history of *Bildung* as a concept in more detail in "The Apprenticeship of the Reader," 109–12. Like Hirsch, he observes that "in

contrast to the concept of education ... *Bildung* was supposed not just to come from outside mentors but to also represent a process of self-development ... affecting the entire human being – mind, body and spirit," 109.

54 *Authoritarian Fictions*, 66. Suleiman uses *Bildungsroman* in her discussion of Lukács, acknowledging the term *Erziehungsroman* but stating that the distinction is "not ... essential," 266n3; Pernot, meanwhile, points out that Lukács never uses the term *Bildungsroman* (*Le Roman de socialisation*, 2).

55 Neubauer, *The Fin-de-Siècle Culture of Adolescence*, 77–80.

56 Denis Pernot, "Du *Bildungsroman* au roman d'éducation," 115–17; *Le Roman de socialisation*, 5–9.

57 See for instance Grusec and Hastings, *Handbook of Socialization*, and Henslin, *Essentials of Sociology*, 57–77.

58 Hirsch, "The Novel of Formation as Genre," 295. Many of the themes that characterize French novels of formation of the period 1880–1914 were indeed present in other European contexts. For instance, Neubauer notes that the 1890s saw "a wave of novels and plays depicting how German secondary education led to adolescent miseries and even suicides" (*The Fin-de-siècle Culture of Adolescence*, 2). On this topic, see Houtteville, *Le Thème de l'aliénation par l'éducation dans la littérature allemande autour de 1900*.

59 *Le Roman de socialisation*, 9.

60 Boes points out Lukács's *Theory of the Novel* (itself an important source for Moretti's propositions) "borrows many of its central concepts from Hegel's aesthetic lectures." *Formative Fictions*, 14–15 and 21–2.

61 Lukács, *The Theory of the Novel*, 97–123.

62 Lukács, *Studies in European Realism*, 124–43.

63 "Le jeune homme, à vrai dire, commençait à éprouver le besoin d'un autre amour, qui ne donnât plus satisfaction aux seules exigences physiques, mais qui eût quelque résonnance en la partie sentimentale de son être. ... Dès les premiers temps de sa formation littéraire, il avait fait ce rêve ambitieux d'une communion à la faveur de l'intelligence. Son imagination avait travaillé sur les œuvres qu'il aimait. À cet âge, et quand les dures leçons de l'expérience n'ont pas encore apporté leur désenchantement, il n'est qu'un pas, à la lettre, du rêve aux réalités que celui-ci convoite." Flat, *L'Illusion sentimentale*, 79–80.

64 See in particular "Special Issue: The Way We Read Now," ed. Sharon Marcus and Stephen Best, *Representations* 108 (Fall 2009).

65 Cohen, "Narratology in the Archive of Literature," 51.

66 The practice was named (as "lecture symptômale") by Louis Althusser in 1965 ("From *Capital* to Marx's Philosophy," 28), and further theorized by Fredric Jameson in *The Political Unconscious: Narrative as a Socially Symbolic Act*.

67 Best and Marcus, "Surface Reading," 7.

68 The term is proposed by Franco Moretti in "Conjectures on World Literature," 56–7.

69 Definitions are offered by Stephen Best and Sharon Marcus in "Surface Reading," 9–13. Marcus defines "just reading" in *Between Women*, 75. A critique of their definitions of surface reading as well as of Moretti's project of distant reading is made by Nancy Armstrong and Warren Montag in "'The Figure in the Carpet.'"

70 Cohen, "Narratology in the Archive of Literature," 62.

71 O'Brien, *The Novel of Adolescence*, and Pernot, *Le Roman de socialisation*. I am indebted to these two works for the composition of my corpus.

72 Cohen, "Narratology in the Archive of Literature," 51, 57.

73 Ibid., 59–61. Cohen credits Marcus with the phrase "reading for patterns." She also notes that reading a representative example "could be confused with close reading, since it focuses on a single text. But the text takes on its importance as the abstraction of a class rather than in its unique specificity" (61).

74 Love, "Close but not Deep: Literary Ethics and the Descriptive Turn," 383.

75 See Eve Kosofsky Sedgwick's critique of the spread of symptomatic reading (characterized as "paranoid reading") to the status of "common currency of cultural and historicist studies" in "Paranoid Reading and Reparative Reading," 21.

76 In this book I use "denegation" in its psychoanalytic acceptation, to differentiate it from broader terms like "negation," "denial" (expressing disbelief, or asserting that something is false), or "disavowal" (renouncing an earlier statement or a previously embraced position). Denegation, for Freud (*Verneinung*), refers to the strangely insistent denial of a desire or sentiment by a patient, which can be read as a symptom of its repression. See Laplanche and Pontalis, *Vocabulaire de la psychanalyse* [1967], 112–14. The *Standard Edition* of Freud's works in English uses "negation" to render *Veneinung*.

77 Roger Bellet, "Notice" to *L'Enfant*, in Vallès, *Œuvres*, 2:1499–1500.

78 Contributors to the 2014 volume *Lire de près, de loin* (ed. Cabral et al.) suggest similar metaphors of complementarity between close and distant reading: "bifocals" (77), "zooming" (105), "back and forth" (168).

Part I: Youth in Crisis

1 *Lettre à la jeunesse* (Letter to youth) and *Lettre à la France* of 6 January 1898 were published as pamphlets, after Zola's first three articles in support of Dreyfus, in *Le Figaro* of 25 November, 1 and 5 December 1897, were met with inflamed responses from readers threatening to cancel their subscriptions. Alain Pagès, introduction to Zola, *La Vérité en marche* [1901], in *Œuvres complètes*, 18:411.

2 See Forth, *The Dreyfus Affair and the Crisis of French Manhood*. Many of the novelists I examine took position during the Affair: Maurice Barrès was a notorious anti-Semite ("Dreyfus's race is proof enough that he is capable

of betrayal" ["Que Dreyfus est capable de trahir, je le conclus de sa race"]), he writes in *Scènes et doctrines du nationalisme,* 1:161. Paul Bourget was also aligned with anti-Dreyfusards. Octave Mirbeau was one of the first writers to answer Zola's call in support of the Dreyfusard cause. Marcel Proust later claimed to have secured the signature of Anatole France, one of the most eminent French writers at the time, for a pro-Dreyfus petition published on 14 January 1898. See Tadié, *Marcel Proust*, 367–8.

3 Denis Pernot proposes a survey of this topic in *La Jeunesse en discours (1880–1925).*

4 "Ô jeunesse, jeunesse! ... songe à la grande besogne qui t'attend. Tu es l'ouvrière future ... Et nous ne te demandons que ... de nous dépasser par ton amour de la vie *normalement* vécue, par ton effort mis tout entier dans le travail." *Lettre à la jeunesse* [1897], in *Œuvres complètes*, 18:430. My emphasis.

5 "le quartier Latin ... la jeunesse des Écoles." Ibid., 18:427.

6 The fire occurred on 4 May 1897. See Winock, "Un avant-goût d'apocalypse: L'incendie du Bazar de la Charité," in *Décadence fin de siècle*, 233–52.

7 *Les Déracinés* appeared as a serial in *Revue de Paris* from 15 May to 15 August 1897, before being published as a volume in late August.

8 "une régression des sentiments domestiques." Durkheim, "Suicide et natalité: Étude de statistique morale," 462.

9 Durkheim, *Le Suicide*, 226. See Judith Surkis's discussion of *anomie* in *Sexing the Citizen*, 149–55.

10 "The orientation of youth is the topic of the day" ("L'orientation de la jeunesse est un sujet à la mode"), writes Henry Bérenger in his review of Charles Wagner's *Jeunesse* (1891), in *Revue pédagogique* 1 (1892): 205. Cited in Pernot, *Le Roman de socialisation*, 19.

11 Also published in 1897: Henri Lavedan, *Les Jeunes, ou l'espoir de la France* (Young men, or the hope of France); Alfred Fouillée, "Les Jeunes Criminels, l'école et la presse" (Young criminals, schools and the press) in *La Revue des Deux Mondes*, and its responses, Félix Pécaut, *L'Éducation publique et la vie nationale* (Public education and national life), Gabriel Tarde, "La Jeunesse criminelle" (Criminal youth) in *Archives d'anthropologie criminelle, de criminologie et de psychologie normale et pathologique*, and Ferdinand Buisson, "La Jeunesse criminelle et l'éducation" (Criminal youth and education) in *La Revue pédagogique* – all discussed in chapter 1; André Lebey, *Les Premières Luttes* (The first struggles), also discussed in chapter 1; Jean Morgan, *En genèse* (In genesis), and Henry Bérenger, "Portrait d'un jeune homme" (Portrait of a young man), both discussed in chapter 2.

12 Suleiman, *Authoritarian Fictions*, 67.

13 Ibid.

14 "Fabien Després cessa de lire; il leva les yeux vers la clarté joyeuse de la fenêtre, où s'annonçait la grâce de la matinée printanière, et son visage exprima l'obsession d'une pensée inquiète.

Le livre ouvert sur la table était *L'Amour* de Stendhal. Avec une curiosité aiguë, il avait lu cette analyse si précise et si pénétrante de tous les sentiments de l'amour ... Et dans la vague souffrance d'un désir, il s'abandonnait au charme dolent des images suscitées par sa pensée.

Sa rêverie, obéissant aux suggestions de la lecture, dans la poésie de l'éloignement évoquait les ciels d'Espagne et d'Italie ... Cette ivresse imaginaire peu à peu se dissipa; et le désir obscur qu'elle enveloppait se dégageant, l'image de Jeanne Viliers surgit dans la pensée du jeune homme. L'attrait qu'exerçait sur lui cette jeune fille douce et innocente lui parût faible en comparaison de ces félicités enivrantes, de ces émotions sublimes, de ces craintes et de ces transports. Le sentiment tendre auquel il se sentait enclin pour elle lui semblait comme diminué par les médiocrités d'un milieu banal ... De ses rêves, de ses désirs, de ses lectures, il s'était formé un idéal de l'amour et de la femme ... et dans sa douleur obscure, il sentait une disproportion entre son désir et son objet." Sueur, *Crise de jeunesse*, 1–4.

15 For Sueur as for Zola, "la jeunesse" is a synecdoche where a subgroup of male, bourgeois or upwardly mobile, usually Parisian young men are taken to represent the rising generation of future French citizens.

16 Jean Paul, *Selina* [1827, posth.].

17 Gaultier, *Le Bovarysme*.

18 Stendhal, *De l'amour*, 30–51.

19 "fièvre d'imagination qui pare de toutes les seductions l'objet désiré." Sueur, *Nouveau précis de philosophie*, 61.

20 "Henri Beyle ... se trouve ressembler ... à beaucoup de nos jeunes contemporains, qui reconnaissent dans l'auteur ... comme une épreuve avant la lettre de la sensibilité la plus moderne." Bourget, "Stendhal," in *Essais de psychologie contemporaine* [1883–5], 176. See also chapter 4.

21 "livre extraordinaire, et que j'ai vu produire sur certains cerveaux de jeunes gens l'effet d'une intoxication inguérissable ... il ensorcelle. C'est une possession." *Essais de psychologie contemporaine*, 201.

22 "d'une manière générale ... les sentiments ... qui composent l'âme de Fabrice del Dongo et de Julien Sorel lui-même, faisaient encore la loi de tous les cœurs en France. Ses héros étaient nos frères." Barrès, preface to *La Correspondance de Stendhal*, 1:vii.

23 Stendhal, *Vie de Henry Brulard* [1890, posth.], in *Œuvres intimes*, 2:536.

24 "To the happy few" is the dedication printed, in English, in the original edition of *Le Rouge et le Noir* [1830]. In *Œuvres romanesques complètes*, 1:805.

25 "beaux rêves d'amitié chevaleresque et sublime." Stendhal, *La Chartreuse de Parme* [1839], in *Œuvres romanesques complètes*, 3:186.

26 "à la place qu'il aurait dû occuper"; "cette manie de lecture ... odieuse." Stendhal, *Le Rouge et le Noir* [1830], in *Œuvres romanesques complètes*, 1:363.
27 "son roman"; "mon roman est fini," *Le Rouge et le Noir*, 1:414, 749.
28 See Peter Brooks, "The Novel and the Guillotine, or Fathers and Sons in *Le Rouge et le Noir*," in *Reading for the Plot*, 62–89.
29 Stendhal, *Le Rouge et le Noir*, 1:656.
30 "l'amour passionné était encore plutôt un modèle qu'on imitait qu'une réalité." Ibid., 1:657.
31 "mutilé glorieux," *Crise de jeunesse*, 88.
32 "il lut Balzac, Flaubert ... il tâcha de sortir de soi, de son absorbante personnalité." Ibid., 144.
33 "il eut la sensation d'une scène déjà vue; et des lectures de Balzac et de Flaubert lui revinrent à l'esprit confusément ..." Ibid., 113.
34 "Cette comparaison l'écrasa." Ibid., 168.
35 "It's sadly impossible to earn a living through the book these days ... Even more so when you're starting out! If you don't pay to have your work printed, it's incredibly difficult! And if you do pay, it's terribly awkward! It's impossible to get out of that vicious circle," a friend exclaims in conversation with Fabien. ("Malheureusement, aujourd'hui, il est impossible de vivre du livre ... Et quand on débute! Pour se faire imprimer, si l'on ne paye pas, quelle incroyable difficulté! Et si l'on paye, quelle maladresse! Va donc sortir de ce cercle vicieux ...") Ibid., 189.
36 "This predisposition to illness, already latent in his delicate and nervous temperament, that of a man at the end of his race, had been developed through his readings, his withdrawal into himself, his taste for speculation and analysis. He had read, as early as the *collège*, with great passion ..." ("Cette disposition maladive, en germe dans son tempérament délicat et nerveux d'homme de fin de race, avait été développée par les lectures, le reploiement sur lui-même, le goût des spéculations et de l'analyse. Avec passion, dès le collège, il avait lu ...") Ibid., 11. On late nineteenth-century discourses of degeneration, see chapter 2.
37 "he accomplished all his actions mechanically, incapable of any effort. He was drifting along the course of life like a lost ship, rudderless and without aim, carried by the current [à vau-l'eau]." ("tous ses actes, il les accomplissait machinalement, incapable d'aucun effort. Il s'en allait dans la vie, pareil à un navire désemparé, sans direction, sans but, à vau-l'eau.") Ibid., 202.

Compare to Huysmans, *À vau-l'eau*: "he let himself drift with the current [à vau-l'eau], incapable of fighting off the melancholy that was crushing him. Mechanically, ... he went to his office, left it ... only to start again, the next day, an identical existence; little by little, he was gliding towards an absolute petrification of the spirit." ("il se laissait aller à vau-l'eau, incapable de réagir contre ce spleen qui l'écrasait. Mécaniquement ... il se rendait à son bureau, le quittait ... pour recommencer, le jour suivant, une vie pareille; peu à peu, il glissait à un alourdissement absolu d'esprit.") *Romans*, 1:499.

38 "moi aussi j'ai quelque chose là." *Crise de jeunesse*, 55.

39 "Pourtant, j'avais quelque chose là!" *Œuvres posthumes d'André Chénier*, xix.

40 "contre l'intellectualisme [d'] affirmer philosophiquement [la] valeur de l'idée religieuse." Albert Sueur, *Intellectualisme et catholicisme*, 6–7.

41 "L'imagination: ... Elle est l'embellissement de la vie, la condition du progrès, la faculté maîtresse du génie inventif; et elle est aussi, quand elle est livrée sans frein à elle-même, la faculté capricieuse qui engendre les chimères, attise les passions, pervertit le cœur, désorganise toute la vie mentale. ... Mais ses bienfaits ne l'emportent-ils pas sur ses séductions dangereuses?" Sueur, *Nouveau précis de philosophie*, 106–7.

1. Contagions and Cures

1 "LES VICTIMES DU LIVRE, quel livre à faire!" Jules Vallès, "Lettre de Junius (Casaque blanche)," *Le Figaro*, 7 November 1861, in *Œuvres*, 1:133. Subsequent citations of Vallès's articles and novels refer to this edition.

2 See Roger Bellet, "Notice" and "Notes," in Vallès, *Œuvres*, 1:1238–44. *Jacques Vingtras*, a first version of *L'Enfant*, had appeared as a serial *Le Siècle* in 1878, under the pseudonym La Chaussade.

3 "raconter comment on devient un pamphlétaire." "Lettre de Junius (Casaque blanche)," 1:131–3.

4 Vallès, "Les Victimes du Livre," *Le Figaro*, 9 October 1862. The article was revised again in *Le Progrès de Lyon* on 3 January 1865, and in the volume *Les Réfractaires*, published in November 1865.

5 "Combien j'en sais dont tel passage lu un matin a dominé, défait ou refait, perdu ou sauvé l'existence! Une *pensée* traduite du chinois ou du grec, prise à Sénèque ou à Saint Grégoire, a décidé d'un avenir, pesé sur un caractère, entraîné une destinée.

Souvent, presque toujours, la victime a vu de travers, choisi à faux, et le Livre la traîne après lui, vous faisant d'un poltron un crâneur, d'un bon jeune homme un mauvais garçon ... l'influence est là! Tous la subissent, jusqu'à nous, les corrompus." Vallès, "Les Victimes du Livre," in *Œuvres*, 1:230.

6 Ibid., 1:246. Vallès mentions Madame Lafarge, whose case and its relation to denunciations of the serial novel are examined in Matlock, *Scenes of Seduction*, 249–80.

7 "que de mensonges [le livre] fait faire à soi-même!" Ibid., 1:231.

8 Ibid., 1:230. My emphasis.

9 "dans la diminution de plus en plus évidente des influences traditionnelles et locales, le livre devient le grand initiateur. Il n'est aucun de nous qui,

descendu au fond de sa conscience, ne reconnaisse qu'il n'aurait pas été tout à fait le même s'il n'avait pas lu tel ou tel ouvrage: poème ou roman, morceau d'histoire ou de philosophie. À cette minute précise, et tandis que j'écris ces lignes, un adolescent, que je *vois*, est accoudé sur son pupitre d'étudiant, ... penché sur son livre." Bourget, *Essais de psychologie contemporaine*, 435. Page references in subsequent notes are to this edition.

10 "historien de la vie morale"; "le plus important [élément] peut-être." Ibid.

11 Fouillée, "Les jeunes criminels, l'école et la presse," 417–49.

12 "le principal résultat de l'instruction publique a été l'universelle diffusion des journaux et des romans"; "à l'obligation de savoir lire, on a joint la facilité de tout lire et la presque nécessité de lire ce qu'il y a de pis." Ibid., 426, 417, 435.

13 "c'est au logis paternel que les élèves de nos écoles ont sucé le lait empoisonné du scepticisme religieux, de l'irrespectueuse et ambitieuse vanité, de la cupidité précoce, du vice ... quand ce n'est pas au foyer, c'est à l'atelier, c'est au café, c'est par les suggestions de la Presse." Tarde, "La jeunesse criminelle: Lettre à M. Buisson," 459.

14 "Mais je me demande avec inquiétude pour qui et pour quoi nous travaillons, pour qui et pour quoi nous exerçons ces enfants du peuple à lire, à comprendre ... Est-ce pour livrer ces âmes à peine débrouillées à de nouveaux et étranges éducateurs, à ces livraisons de romans bon marché, à ces feuilles corruptrices à un sou, parées des plus perfides attraits de l'image illustrée ...?" Pécaut, "Notes d'inspection," 307.

15 "Le Français est assurément capable d'étudier en classe, mais il étudie encore plus hors de la classe ... Il a une tendance invincible à étudier ce qui n'est pas inscrit sur le programme des cours. Autant est-il prompt à fuir la mainmise des pédagogues, autant il se laisse prendre, docilement, par les journaux, par le théâtre, par les livres, par la sollicitation des choses et l'exemple des gens." Deschamps, *Le Malaise de la démocratie*, 198–9.

16 "Are you certain that this moral crisis is indeed graver and deeper today than it was before? I can certainly see there is a crisis, and we all observe it with the same anguish. I am less certain, however, that this same crisis ... has not always existed in other eras." ("Tenez-vous pour certain qu'au fond la crise morale soit plus grave, plus profonde aujourd'hui qu'hier? Je vois bien qu'il y en a une, et que nous la ressentons tous avec angoisse. Ce dont je suis moins sûr, c'est que la même crise ... n'ait pas existé à toutes les autres époques.") Buisson, "La jeunesse criminelle et l'éducation: Réponse à M. G. Tarde," 302.

17 "Il y a crise morale parce que les actions pernicieuses qui, jadis, s'exerçaient sur la cour, sur la noblesse, sur la haute bourgeoisie, s'exercent désormais sur les millions d'hommes qui sont la France d'aujourd'hui, et sur les millions d'enfants qui seront celle de demain." Ibid., 303.

18 In *L'Enfer de la IIIe République: Censeurs et pornographes, 1881–1914*, Annie Stora-Lamarre cites another example of this "cascade theory of vice," according to which the "literary immorality" of the pre-revolutionary court trickled down to the working classes through mass publishing over the course of the nineteenth century (60).

19 Pécaut describes literature and pedagogy as opposite forces in a larger contest of uneven influences: "While schooling plays a large role in the education of our nation, I do not forget that there are other influences, some of which are vastly more powerful than ours, more active, and with a greater reach, among the educators of our country: the Church ... the theatre ... literature and its novels, the poor quality of which needs no discussion, and lastly, the daily press." ("Si grande que j'estime la part de l'école dans l'éducation du pays, je n'oublie pas que d'autres influences dont quelques-unes autrement plus puissantes que la nôtre, autrement actives, et d'une portée incroyablement plus étendue, figurent parmi les éducatrices du pays: l'Église ... le théâtre ... la littérature et ses romans, dont je n'ai pas besoin de qualifier le caractère ordinaire; enfin, et surtout, la presse quotidienne.") "Notes d'inspection," 308.

20 Pernot, *Le Roman de socialisation*, 15.

21 As I argue in chapters 3 through 5, Vallès, Bourget, and Barrès all complicate this opposition by showing how state-sanctioned classroom readings (whether in classics, philosophy or literature) can also be detrimental to impressionable young minds.

22 Deschamps, *Le Malaise de la démocratie*, 111. Deschamps's definition of pornography may appear broad by another century's standards; the most thoroughly detailed example he cites is a recent trend of bedroom scenes and actresses in nightgowns appearing on various Parisian stages (114–18). Denunciations of the works of Zola and the Naturalists as "pornography" are frequent in critical discourse of the 1880s; see Angenot, *Le Cru et le Faisandé*, 53–4. "La littérature industrielle" is the title of a famous 1839 article by Sainte-Beuve on the rise of the serial novel.

23 Deschamps, *Le Malaise de la démocratie*, 125–8, 202.

24 "vous flânez devant la boutique de Flammarion. Une lumière crue fait flamber les couvertures bleues, jaunes, rouges, violettes, vertes ou zinzolines de bouquins nouveaux. En grosses lettres, les titres s'étalent, prometteurs. Les plus récentes ignominies s'enorgueillissent du chiffre formidable de leurs éditions. [... D]e tout ce tas de livres semble sortir une cacophonie de supplications câlines et impertinentes: 'Prends-moi, monsieur, achète-moi ... moi ... moi ...'" Ibid., 112. Unbracketed ellipses are original. "Zinzolin" is defined as a reddish purple in the 1873–7 *Littré*.

25 The analogy linking pornography to prostitution is an eighteenth and nineteenth-century commonplace and, as has often been noted, is inscribed in the etymology of the former term; see for instance Carolyn J. Dean, *The Frail Social Body*, 35–41.

26 "non point par le ministère du Commerce, mais par celui de l'Instruction publique ... les gens de pornographie ... sont en effet, eux aussi, des éducateurs." Deschamps, *Le Malaise de la démocratie*, 202.
27 Dean, *The Frail Social Body*, 39.
28 Dean describes this as a "tautology": "pornography was the eerie symptom of a society in the process of dissolution, a process of which pornography was also supposed to be the primary cause." Ibid., 42.
29 For the *Société française de prophylaxie sanitaire et morale*, writes Judith Surkis, "prostitution was ... contiguous with disease itself ... a carrier of contagion, which required regulation." *Sexing the Citizen*, 193.
30 "plus que jamais l'écho de nos paroles, le reflet de nos spectacles, le contre-coup de nos lectures, la contagion de nos plaisirs, atteignent la jeunesse." *Le Malaise de la démocratie*, 199.
31 As with Bourget, Deschamps's "nous" implicitly excludes adult women and the working classes.
32 *Sexing the Citizen*, 197.
33 "l'ennemi"; "exciter prématurément des appétits qui n'ont rien de noble." Buisson, "La Lecture en classe, à l'étude, et dans la famille," 22.
34 The proposition is particularly applicable to nineteenth-century narrative forms such as the serial novel, which are often concerned with nominally unsavoury topics such as adultery, crime and prostitution. See for instance Roddey Reid on *Les Mystères de Paris* in *Families in Jeopardy*, 149–51.
35 *Sexing the Citizen*, 211.
36 Ibid., 198–204.
37 Ibid.
38 See for instance Sohn, *Du premier baiser à l'alcôve*, 215–16, and Angenot, *Le Cru et le Faisandé*, 190. A letter from a sixteen-year-old Marcel Proust to his maternal grandfather from 17 May 1888 recounts how "I had such a pressing need to see a woman in order to stop my bad masturbation habits that Papa gave me 10 francs to go to the brothel" ("j'avais si besoin de voir une femme pour cesser mes mauvaises habitudes de masturbation que papa m'a donné 10 francs pour aller au bordel"). *Correspondance*, 21:550–1.
39 See Jill Harsin, *Policing Prostitution in Nineteenth-Century Paris*, as well as Surkis, *Sexing the Citizen*, 190, and Matlock, *Scenes of Seduction*, 8, 30.
40 Surkis, ibid., 192.
41 "C'est à cet empoisonnement public par une littérature systématiquement démoralisante qu'il faut tâcher d'opposer des lectures aussi faciles et aussi rapides, aussi attrayantes, aussi peu coûteuses, aussi multiples, aussi accessibles à tous ... *Similia similibus curantur*, disait le vieil adage médical; il faut combattre les semblables par les semblables, la presse par la presse, l'image par l'image, la feuille malsaine par la feuille honnête." Buisson, "La lecture en classe, à l'étude et dans la famille," 22–3.
42 Ibid., 13.

43 "[la] lecture libre de l'élève hors de la classe"; "encouragée, guidée, contrôlée autant que la chose est possible"; "faire prendre l'habitude des lectures utiles"; "former ainsi le goût de bonne heure, avant qu'il ait été dépravé ou abaissé"; "inspirer peu à peu le goût des livres, faire aimer les bonnes et belles lectures." Ibid., 9, 13, 23.
44 See Surkis, *Sexing the Citizen*, especially 161–83.
45 "Nous voulons ... créer à notre jeunesse une atmosphère littéraire, l'introduire progressivement ... dans les grands salons de conversation du monde civilisé." Buisson, "La Lecture," 23.
46 Buisson, in "La Lecture," expresses limited interest in contemporary literature, focusing instead on the need to make French and foreign classics available to students in affordable editions or through periodicals to be used in the nation's schools (15–22). While he and other educationalists did not directly respond to some contemporary novelists' newfound concern with representing and intervening in the formation of youths, established critics and commentators welcomed these novelists' effort with "unanimous acclaim," according to Angenot (*Le Cru et le Faisandé*, 56).
47 "À quelques collégiens de Paris et de la province j'offre ce livre"; "J'écris pour les enfants et les tout jeunes gens." Barrès, *Un homme libre* [1889], in *Romans et voyages*, 1:97. Subsequent citations of Barrès's novels and prefaces refer to this edition.
48 Ibid., 1:115, 121–30, 175.
49 "J'ai relevé avec piété, depuis six à sept ans, les noms des enfants qui se sont suicidés. C'est une longue liste que je n'ose pas publier ... S'ils m'avaient lu, je crois qu'ils n'auraient pas pris une résolution aussi extrême. Ces âmes délicates et paresseuses étaient évidemment mal renseignées." Ibid., 1:97.
50 "j'ai tenté la monographie des cinq ou six années d'apprentissage d'un jeune Français intellectuel ... Ces monographies ... sont un *renseignement* sur un type de jeune homme déjà fréquent et qui, je le pressens, va devenir plus nombreux encore parmi ceux qui sont aujourd'hui au lycée. Ces livres ... seront consultés dans la suite comme documents." Ibid., 1:16–17.
51 Ibid., 1:17.
52 I discuss Barrès's evolution in more detail in chapter 5. For further examples of novels of formation structured around an opposition between dilettantism and action, see chapter 2, pages 61–9.
53 "Oui, l'*Homme libre* racontait une recherche sans donner de résultat, mais, cette conclusion suspendue, *Les Déracinés* la fournissent ... Si je ne m'abuse, l'*Homme libre*, complété par *Les Déracinés*, est utile aux jeunes Français, en ce qu'il accorde avec le bien général des dispositions certaines qui les eussent aisément jetés dans un nihilisme funèbre." *Romans et voyages* 1:94.
54 "non pas des contradictions, mais un développement"; "mes erreurs ... demeurent, toujours fécondes, à la racine de toutes mes vérités." "Réponse

à M. René Doumic," *Le Journal*, 8 February 1900, in *Romans et voyages*, 1:179. The article was reprinted in *Scènes et doctrines du nationalisme* (1902) and later included as an afterword in the 1905 edition of *Un homme libre*. See Rambaud, "Notes" to *Romans et voyages*, 1:1260n243.

55 The paratextual characterization of the narrative as a recounting of youthful errors meant to educate the reader is a key topos in the novel of formation of the period. In the preface to Marcel Prévost's *La Confession d'un amant* (Confession of a lover, 1891), for example, we read: "I want, at the threshold of my years of redemption, to spend a few hours in solitude and draw an inventory of my wasted years ... Someone reading these pages will find no rare or novelistic events. But I hope they can teach him a better way than the winding and dangerous path I have travelled, so that he may find a purpose in life." ("Je veux, sur le seuil des années de rédemption, consacrer quelques heures de retraite à l'inventaire des mauvaises années ... Si quelqu'un les recueille, il n'y trouvera point d'événements rares ou romanesques. Mais j'espère qu'elles lui feront connaître, pour mieux atteindre au but de la vie, une voie meilleure que le chemin oblique ou dangereux où j'ai marché.") *La Confession d'un amant*, 15.

56 On the paradoxical status of *Un homme libre* as "an antitextbook," see Beaujour, "Exemplary Pornography: Barrès, Loyola, and the Novel," 334–9.

57 In 1911, two decades after its first publication, Joseph Hudault evokes *Le Disciple* in the preface to his own *La Formation de Jean Turoit*: "It is still to you that I write, my young countryman, to whom one of our most illustrious writers offered, twenty years ago, the dangerous example of his *Disciple*." ("C'est encore à toi que je m'adresse, jeune homme de mon pays, à qui l'un de nos plus illustres écrivains offrait, il y a vingt ans, le dangereux exemple de son Disciple.") *La Formation de Jean Turoit*, v.

58 "C'est à toi que je veux dédier ce livre, jeune homme de mon pays, à toi que je connais si bien quoique je ne sache de toi ... rien sinon que tu as plus de dix-huit ans et moins de vingt-cinq, et que tu vas, cherchant dans nos volumes, à nous tes aînés, des réponses aux questions qui te tourmentent. Et des réponses ainsi rencontrées dans ces volumes dépend un peu de ta vie morale, un peu de ton âme; et ta vie morale, c'est la vie morale de la France même ... Pensant à cela, il n'est pas d'honnête homme de lettres, si chétif soit-il, qui ne doive trembler de responsabilité ... tu trouveras dans *Le Disciple* l'étude de ces responsabilités-là. Puisses-tu y acquérir une preuve que l'ami qui t'écrit ces lignes ... pense à toi, anxieusement ... depuis bien longtemps, depuis les jours où tu commençais d'apprendre à lire, alors que nous autres, qui marchons aujourd'hui vers notre quarantième année, nous griffonnions nos premiers vers et notre première page de prose au bruit du canon qui grondait sur Paris." Bourget, *Le Disciple* [1889], 45–6. Page references in subsequent notes are to this edition.

59 "L'Esthétique de l'observation: *Sous l'œil des Barbares*," *Journal des débats*, 3 April 1888, rpt. in *Essais de pyschologie contemporaine*, 376–84. Bourget states the Barrès's first novel "shines an unforgiving light on a moral malady that is quite common in our age of extreme civilization ... a dangerous excess of literature" ("jette le jour le plus vif sur une maladie morale assez habituelle dans notre âge d'extrême civilisation ... [le] dangereux abus de littérature"), 381.

60 *Le Disciple*, 46.

61 *Authoritarian Fictions*, 84–99.

62 For Suleiman, "the presence of two separate and opposing ideological fields ... is crucial to the demonstration of the *roman à these* [ideological novel]." Ibid., 69. While the "positive" ideological field can be implied rather than illustrated, its near-absence in *Le Disciple* highlights that novel's unresolved ambiguity towards questions of literary influence. See chapter 4.

63 Although he is often grouped with *Les Déracinés*'s ambitious schoolmaster Bouteiller as an example of bad influence ("mauvais maître"), *Le Disciple*'s Adrien Sixte is sympathetically depicted as modest, unselfish and perfectly well intentioned; see chapter 4, page 138.

64 "L'auteur de ce roman est un jeune homme et il dédie son roman aux jeunes gens." André Lebey, *Les Premières Luttes*, iii.

65 "Mais si ... tu es celui que je devine, si toi aussi à ta façon tu es un peu Jacques Dalvèze, feuillette ces pages ... et, de loin ... donnons-nous la main. Tu es mon frère; tu n'as pas vingt ans; tu es venu dans la vie avec un sourire tranquille; au ciel bleu de l'éternel rêve tes illusions déployaient leurs ailes; tu as lu beaucoup de livres; tu as un peu vécu; tu as tenté de nombreux essais et tu hésites." Ibid., iv.

66 "Seul depuis le jour où il commença à regarder avec un peu d'attention ce qui l'entourait, il a souffert de la solitude et a désiré un livre qui l'aidât au milieu de ses hésitations. N'ayant pas trouvé ce livre, il a eu l'ambition de le faire afin d'épargner aux autres, autant qu'il le pourrait, la souffrance qu'il avait intensément vécue." Ibid., iii.

67 "Toute sa famille ... le trouva bizarre pour la première fois. Moins bruyant, il se mit à aimer les promenades solitaires. À Troyes, pendant les vacances, sa tante l'aperçut un jour monté sur une chaise en train de prendre des livres dans la vieille bibliothèque à laquelle personne ne touchait jamais ... à la longue, elle en avait conçu une certaine inquiétude: il lisait trop; et elle lui enleva les volumes de sa chambre: c'étaient *Les Mille et une nuits*." Ibid., 23.

68 "Il les passa [les vacances] penché sur ses livres sans avoir une notion du temps, assistant à peine à la vie extérieure, vivant de la vie d'autrui sans y prendre part, si méditatif et taciturne que sa famille commença vite à s'inquiéter ...

– Je n'ai jamais vu d'enfant pareil ... il reste des heures devant un volume ou un morceau de papier au lieu de se mêler aux autres jeunes gens; il est devenu réservé; il ne parle pas.

– ... il est évident qu'il a quelque chose de bizarre dans la cervelle. Personne n'est comme lui." Ibid., 62–4.

69 "il revécut des désillusions successives une à une et s'indigna à nouveau de la tristesse de la vie. Il se persuada qu'il n'y avait rien que le rêve, que le rêve était en réalité la vraie vie." Ibid., 142.

70 "il regardait maintenant la littérature avec un sourire de scepticisme détaché; tout à la vie et emporté par elle il se trouvait incapable de la vivre s'il ne la vivait pas en action." Ibid., 267.

71 "Homme libre de tous côtés, aussi bien vis-à-vis des autres que vis-à-vis de lui-même, double vainqueur." Ibid., 372.

72 For Suleiman, "the story told by the roman à these is essentially teleological – it is determined by a specific end, which exists 'before' and 'above' the story." *Authoritarian Fictions*, 54.

73 Suleiman observes that "the persuasive effect of a story of apprenticeship results from the virtual identification of the reader with the protagonist." Ibid., 73. The identification of the reader with the author can be imagined to strengthen this effect.

74 "soucieux uniquement de rendre service aux collégiens que j'aime, je m'en tiens à la forme la plus enfantine qu'on puisse imaginer: un journal." *Romans et voyages*, 1:98.

75 "C'est d'abord le livre d'enfance." Vallès, "Les Victimes du Livre," in *Œuvres*, 1:232.

76 Vallès, *L'Enfant* [1878–9], in *Œuvres*, 2:160. Page references in subsequent notes are to this edition.

77 Alimentary metaphors for the reception of texts have a long history, of which "the Bible is the principal source"; see Curtius, *European Literature and the Latin Middle Ages*, 134–6.

78 "À ceux qui, nourris de grec et de latin, sont morts de faim." Vallès, *Le Bachelier* [1879–81], in *Œuvres*, 2:445. Page references in subsequent notes are to this edition.

79 "Ai-je été nourri par ma mère? Est-ce une paysanne qui m'a donné son lait? Je n'en sais rien"; "Quel que soit le sein que j'ai mordu, je ne me rappelle pas une caresse du temps où j'étais petit; je n'ai pas été dorloté, tapoté, baisoté; j'ai été beaucoup fouetté." Ibid., 2:141.

80 "On me fait apprendre à lire dans un livre où il y a écrit en grosses lettres, qu'il faut obéir à ses père et mère: ma mère a bien fait de me battre." Ibid., 2:143.

81 *L'Enfant* and Vallès's thoughts on education are indeed heavily indebted to Rousseau: see chapter 3, pages 111–13.

82 *Œuvres*, 2:157.

83 "Il avait su ... traîner ce grand filet le long d'une page et faire passer cette rivière dans un coin de chapitre." Ibid., 2:160.

84 "dévoré par la curiosité, collé aux flancs de Robinson." Ibid., 2:211.

85 "Je me rejette dans le livre que j'avais caché entre ma chemise et ma peau, et je le dévore – avec un peu de thon, et des larmes de cognac – devant la flamme de la cheminée. Il me semble que je suis dans une cabine ou une cabane." Ibid., 2:212.

86 "J'en verrai des dures sur le navire. Il faut que je me *rompe* d'avance, ou plutôt qu'on me *rompe* au métier; et me voilà pendant des semaines disant que j'ai cassé des écuelles, perdu des bouteilles d'encre, mangé tout le papier! – Il faut dire que je mange toujours du papier et que je bois toujours de l'encre, je ne peux pas m'en empêcher. Mon père ne se doute de rien ...!" Ibid., 2:247.

87 An earlier version of this scene in the "Lettre de Junius" is less ambiguous, though it can still be read metaphorically: "In class, I was happy! I ate paper; I drank ink." ("En classe, j'étais heureux! Je mangeais du papier; je buvais de l'encre.") *Le Figaro*, 7 November 1861; *Œuvres*, 1:132.

88 "hypocrite que je suis!" *Œuvres*, 2:247.

89 "depuis un siècle le classique de l'enfance." France, *Le Livre de mon ami* [1885], in *Œuvres*, 1:557. On rewritings of *Robinson Crusoe* in nineteenth-century children's literature for girls in France, see Monicat, *Devoirs d'écriture*, 31–48.

90 Alphonse Daudet, *Le Petit Chose*, in *Œuvres*, 1:6–10; Zola, *La Joie de vivre*, in *Œuvres complètes*, 12:42; Bourget, *André Cornélis*, 171. *Robinson Crusoe* is famously extolled by Rousseau as the only book worthy of being given to children; see *Émile ou De l'éducation*, 291–3. Élisabeth Parinet notes that most French versions of Defoe's novel made available over the course of the nineteenth century are geared towards children and are "always bowdlerized and largely rewritten rather than truly translated." *La Librairie Flammarion: 1875–1914*, 93.

91 *Robinson* by Alfred Capus is written as a letter from a twenty-six-year-old provincial to his former teacher, recounting his failed attempt to make it in Paris. "I was about to wash up, after the wreck, in a place wholly unknown to me [Paris], a place where I would be alone, and where I would have to display, in order to live, the same creativity, the same power of endurance, the same energetic fatalism as Crusoe on his island" ("j'allais aborder après un naufrage dans un endroit inconnu de moi [Paris], un endroit où je serais seul, et où il me faudrait pout vivre déployer la même ingéniosité, la même force de résistance, le même fatalisme énergique que Robinson dans son île") 11–12.

92 "Je suis effrayé comme un Robinson débarqué sur un rivage abandonné, mais dans un pays sans arbres verts et sans fruits rouges." *Œuvres*, 2:451.

93 "Furieusement Racadot et Mouchefrin se débattent ... Perdus au désert parisien, comme Robinson dans son île, ils ne comptent que sur leur industrie." Ibid., 1:562.

94 A few further examples: "*gorged on* the most audacious paradoxes of human thought" ("*gorgé* des plus audacieux paradoxes de la pensée humaine"), Barrès, *Sous l'œil des Barbares*, 1:33; "certainly it would have been better for me not to *feed* my imagination with such disparate elements" ("il est certain qu'il eût mieux valu pour moi ne pas *nourrir* mon imagination d'éléments aussi disparates"), Bourget, *Le Disciple*, 143; "Voltaire, whom he *fed on* more and more" ("Voltaire, dont il se *nourrit* de plus en plus"), Charpentier, *L'Enfance d'un homme*, 85; "he *devoured* tomes about adventures and travels" ("il avait *dévoré* des volumes d'aventures et de voyages"), Mellerio, *Jacques Mérane*, 43; "books *digested* to various degree" ("des bouquins *digérés* tant bien que mal"), Mellerio, *La Vie stérile*, 31; "through the power of their imagination, *nourished* by books" ("par la force de leur imagination *nourrie* de livres"), Barrès, *Les Déracinés*, 1:610; "the young man's *devouring* pen had consumed tales of chivalry" ("les romans de chevalerie avaient passé sous la plume *dévorante* du jeune garçon"), Gauthiez, *L'Âge incertain*, 26; "all this intellectual *sustenance* turned to sentimentaliy inside her" ("toute cette *nourriture* intellectuelle se convertissait en elle en sentimentalisme"), Hudault, *Le Pavillon aux livres*, 111. My emphasis.

95 The image of schoolchildren as livestock is linguistically fixed in the expression "bêtes à concours" (prize specimens) which survives today. See for instance Hermant, *Confession d'un enfant d'hier*, 73.

96 "remâchaient des rudiments quelconques." *Romans et voyages*, 1:493.

97 "nourriture peu assimilable"; "épidémies morales"; "fièvres d'imagination"; "dose trop forte." Ibid., 1:502, 493, 499, 500.

98 "mélancolique"; "profondément, continûment pessimiste"; "Toute une partie de la jeunesse contemporaine traverse une crise ... elle offre les symptômes ... d'une maladie de la vie morale arrivée à sa période la plus aiguë." *Essais de psychologie contemporaine*, 438.

99 "Les œuvres de littérature et d'art sont le plus puissant moyen de transmission de cet héritage psychologique." Ibid., 437.

100 "la contagion de ce mal"; "le germe de mélancolie." Ibid., 439–40.

101 "la loi générale de l'intoxication littéraire." *Le Disciple*, 222.

102 "ma rêverie s'est repue des poisons les plus dangereux de la vie." Ibid., 159.

103 "ces lointains parfums orientaux de la mort, filtrés par le réseau des penseurs allemands"; "exaltation quand, à dix-sept ans, l'étoile de poésie avait surgi des livres ... tous ces éléments et bien d'autres flottaient dans ce jeune homme." *Romans et voyages*, 1:500, 553.

104 "vapeurs mélancoliques"; "condensation générale." Ibid., 1:553.

105 "invasion énervante de l'Asie"; "poussières toxiques"; "coupe de poison"; "précipité de mort." Ibid., 1:553–4.

106 "Astiné, c'est un livre admirable qu'il feuillette; il s'empoisonne avec avidité de toutes ses paroles." Ibid., 1:555.

107 Vallès, *Le Bachelier*, in *Œuvres*, 2:445.
108 *The Republic* (III.401b–c), in *The Dialogues of Plato*, 3:87.
109 See Léoni, *Le Poison et le Remède*, 1–28, 121–76.
110 "un empoisonneur public." Cited in May, *Le Dilemme du roman au XVIIIe siècle*, 24.
111 "ces sirènes dont parle Isaïe"; "le poison qu'elles répandent par leur chant." Bossuet conflates the Homeric episode of the sirens and the Book of Isaiah, where, in the Latin Vulgate, the word "siren" is used to translate the Hebrew *tenim* [jackal] (13:22). Cited in Léoni, *Le Poison et le Remède*, 151.
112 *The Republic* (III.395c–d), in *The Dialogues of Plato*, 3:80.
113 See Derrida's famous essay, "La Pharmacie de Platon," in *La Dissémination*, 79–213.
114 *Le Poison et le Remède*, 3–4.
115 It should be noted that Fouillée, a professor of philosophy, was the author of a two-volume study of Plato, *La Philosophie de Platon*.
116 "un médecin qui vante son remède"; "vous redeviendrez un homme." Hudault, *La Formation de Jean Turoit*, vii.
117 "pour te montrer"; "bienfaisant." *Le Disciple*, 53, 56.
118 "définir quelques-uns des exemplaires de sentiments que certains écrivains de notre époque proposent à l'imitation des tout jeunes gens." *Essais de psychologie contemporaine*, 436.
119 "Apportez-vous un remède au mal que vous décrivez si complaisamment?"; "j'avoue humblement que, de conclusion possible, je n'en saurais donner aucune à ces études." Ibid., 440.
120 "[des] maladies morales de la France actuelle ... le christianisme est à l'heure présente la condition unique et nécessaire de guérison." Ibid., 442.
121 On the question of Bourget's sexuality, see chapter 4.
122 "La Maladie de la volonté: Une guérison"; "je le donne aujourd'hui au terme de ces *Essais*, auxquels il peut servir de conclusion." *Essais de psychologie contemporaine*, 417.
123 "il lisait en cachette ... les plus récents volumes des poètes contemporains "; "il s'imprégnait, il se saturait de cet Idéal complexe et dangereux que fut celui du romantisme." Ibid., 419. I discuss the trope of the reading list in further detail in chapter 2, pages 80–3.
124 "victime d'un même déséquilibre ... [de] toutes les antithèses ... des pires angoisses de son âge." Ibid., 420.
125 "un mélancolique"; "un tourmenté"; "romantisme d'éducation"; "ils ne rêvent que littérature." Ibid., 418, 422.
126 "guérison"; "rares de nos jours"; "elles sont possibles." Ibid., 417–22.
127 "je pouvais lire infatigablement." Ibid., 425.
128 "L'âge me touchait. Je ne lui fis pas un accueil aimable. *Mais je me soumis*. Je commandai un binocle." Ibid.

129 "Remarquez, Messieurs, ce mot, *je me soumis*, et de quel accent il est prononcé. Il va vous éclairer sur la suite de cette très simple mais très significative anecdote. Ce n'est pas à l'âge seulement que l'écrivain l'adresse, comprenez-le bien. C'est à la vie toute entière, c'est à la réalité, c'est à la communauté sociale dont il voudra désormais être un membre utile, un ouvrier bienfaisant." Ibid.

130 "relique de la chère vieille France." Ibid.

131 "L'enfant du siècle, fatigué de passions vaines, d'inutiles mélancolies, d'aventures romantiques, se transforme en un vigoureux, en un vaillant ouvrier de la plume qui n'aura devant lui désormais qu'une seule œuvre, mais large, mâle, civique." Ibid., 424. "Enfant du siècle" is of course a reference to Musset's *Confession d'un enfant du siècle* (1836).

132 "romanesques." Ibid., 426. By 1894, Bourget had published seven novels, in addition to three collections of poetry, three books of short stories, four collections of critical essays, and a travelogue. As "romans psychologiques" or "romans d'analyse," his novels arguably strive to avoid "le romanesque," but this tension remains very much unresolved. I argue in chapter 4 that the "romanesque" constantly resurfaces in *Le Disciple* despite the intentions stated in the preface and by Bourget's narrator.

133 "je saisis quelque chose de résistant sur quoi je pouvais m'appuyer." Ibid.

134 "Ne se servir de la parole que pour la pensée, et de la pensée que pour la vérité." Ibid., 427. The citation is from Fénelon, *Dialogues sur l'éloquence* (1718, posth.).

135 "Eût-il essayé d'animer en décors et en personnages romanesques la vaste enquête où il s'engageait ... il eût de nouveau avivé en lui-même les puissances d'imagination et de sensibilité qu'il fallait endormir. Il n'eût pas pratiqué cette absolue soumission à l'objet, qui le guérit." Ibid., 426. This passage can be read as a thinly veiled attack on Zola, who famously conducted extensive documentary and on-site research in order to write many of the volumes of his *Rougon-Macquart* cycle. Zola was repeatedly denied admission to the Académie française in the 1890s and Bourget's election in his place amounted to a sharp rebuke from its members. The re-edition of the *Discours* as a complement to the *Essais* in 1899 occurs at the height of the Dreyfus Affair, a year after "J'accuse ...!"

136 "*J'ai été discipliné par la vérité*." Ibid., 427.

137 On male renunciation as a "new norm" and a "rearticulation of male subjectivity" at the turn of the century, particularly in the German context, see Stewart, *Sublime Surrender*, 13.

138 Theodor W. Adorno and Max Horkheimer, *Dialectic of Enlightenment*, 25, 35, 43–4.

139 Ibid., 26–7.

140 *Essais de psychologie contemporaine*, 427.

141 *Dialectic of Enlightenment*, 26, 44.
142 I discuss literary representations of these developments in chapter 3.
143 Buisson, "La Lecture," 23.
144 "Esprit de famille, esprit de corps, esprit de traditions et de religion commune: voilà des attaches sérieuses ... Jean sent que s'il va souvent à la dérive, et porte son énergie dans les sens les plus contradictoires, c'est qu'il n'a pas tiré parti de ces attaches-là." *La Formation de Jean Turoit*, 119.
145 "chimère impossible! ... à la façon *Ruy Blas*. J'ai surtout aimé Simone avec mon cerveau." Ibid., 153. *Ruy Blas* is an 1838 play by Victor Hugo.
146 "le centre de ce paysage." Ibid., 183.
147 "La plaine de Beauce s'étend autour de lui, immense ... Et pendant qu'il travaille, ayant oublié sa complication, il est heureux. Il est fatigué. Il songe au repos prochain, à la joie d'aimer et d'être aimé. Tout le reste, il l'oublie. Il ne souffre plus pour des choses insignifiantes et imaginaires." Ibid., 244–5.
148 Hudault, *Le Pavillon aux livres*, 57.
149 "Les yeux perdus au foyer, il regardait se dissiper les fictions qui l'avaient autrefois attiré. Il lui semblait que sur l'aile des flammes, elles s'en allaient semer ailleurs, dans les cœurs innocents et avides, leurs ferments d'incroyance et de désenchantement ... Il les voyait défiler, les sorciers et les magiciens qui avaient abusé de leur art: les romantiques avec leur orgueil et leur maladive passion pour eux-mêmes, les naturalistes qui avaient oublié de donner une âme à leurs héros, les sceptiques autrefois préférés, destructeurs d'idéal, professeurs d'impuissance et d'incertitude." Ibid., 246.
150 Foreword to the 1883 *Essais*, in *Essais de psychologie contemporaine*, 435.
151 Association des écrivains combattants, *Anthologie des écrivains morts à la Guerre 1914–1918*, 1:361–7. The entry on Hudault cites Barrès's praise of his novels: "they find their rightful place ... like *Le Disciple* ... in the lineage of novelistic books that aim to cure us from the novelistic" ("ils se placent tout naturellement ... comme *Le Disciple* ... dans la série des livres romanesques désireux de nous guérir du romanesque").

2. Representing the Fin-de-Siècle Reader

1 "Vous savez comment on appelle ceux de ma génération: les enfants de la conquête. Il est admis que les faits de la guerre, dont nous fûmes les témoins à peine conscients, nous ont marqué d'une empreinte indélébile, qu'ils ont humilié notre énergie, appauvri notre tempérament ... Ils nous ont fait secs, égoïstes, pessimistes." *Confession d'un enfant d'hier*, 71.
2 See Swart, *The Sense of Decadence in Nineteenth-Century France*, 123–38.
3 Daniel Pick, *Faces of Degeneration*, 97.
4 As Christopher E. Forth notes, "observations about the illness of the national body had been widespread since France's defeat at the hands of

Prussia in 1870 and were a recurring theme in political and social discourses as the newly formed Third Republic limped from crisis to crisis." *The Dreyfus Affair and the Crisis of French Manhood*, 2. See also Nye, *Crime, Madness & Politics in Modern France*; Taithe, *Defeated Flesh*; and Dean, *The Frail Social Body*.

5 Pseudonym of Gabriel Lagros de Langeron (1861–1928).

6 "Depuis quelques années les expressions: fin de siècle, fin de race, décadence, corruption, symbolisme, naturalisme, morale de l'intérêt, règne de l'argent, constituaient des expressions-facettes, sur lesquelles brillaient un instant une étincelle de vérité. C'étaient les manifestations étiquetées d'un mal général dont le pronostic n'avait pas encore été établi ... Il fallait, pour l'estampiller, le mot type qu'un docteur allemand nous a soufflé: dégénérescence!" Provins, *Dégénérés!*, 3–4.

7 Dean, *The Frail Social Body*, 69.

8 Nordau, *Degeneration*, 42.

9 Pick, *Faces of Degeneration*, 25, 101.

10 Nye, *Crime, Madness & Politics*, 143.

11 See Forth, *The Dreyfus Affair and the Crisis of French Manhood.*

12 Dean, *The Frail Social Body*, 71.

13 Ibid., 69.

14 Michelle Perrot, "The New Eve and the Old Adam," 58–9.

15 Judith Surkis provides a wide survey of critical positions on this question in *Sexing the Citizen*, 11–12n23.

16 "for these authors, loss of virility is a sign and cause of the social degeneracy and decadence thought to be prevalent during the period. The political left and right joined in denouncing this decadence." Perrot, "The New Eve and the Old Adam," 59. Significantly, Perrot also notes that "the crisis of masculinity marked an awakening consciousness of what it means to be a man ... Hence the intense tone of adolescence in this period, expressed in 'novels of apprenticeship.'" Ibid., 57–8.

17 Nordau, *Degeneration*, viii.

18 Pick notes that some critics ironically decried Nordau's "hysterical" style; one British reviewer even characterized his enterprise as a "display of graphomania," turning Nordau's recurring accusation against him. *Faces of Degeneration*, 26.

19 "Beaucoup de ceux qui se sont usés à la vie fébrile et factice des grands centres sont, à des degrés différents, des dégénérés ... depuis les dégénérés supérieurs dont la fêlure est surtout un excès d'intellectualité, jusqu'aux simples mattoïdes, en passant par les graphomanes." Michel Provins, *Dégénérés!*, 4–5.

20 On the significance of "fêlure" in Zola, see Deleuze, *Logique du sens*, 373–86, and Beizer, *Ventriloquized Bodies*, 169–204.

21 Bourget proposed a "theory of decadence" in his 1881 essay on Baudelaire; he had used the word "decadence" in his criticism as early as 1876. See Călinescu, "The Idea of Decadence," in *Five Faces of Modernity*, 169–70.

22 "L'usure physiologique ... se manifeste par les déformations du type humain qui se rencontrent à chaque pas dans les grandes villes. L'homme moderne, tel que nous le voyons aller et venir sur les boulevards de Paris, porte dans ses membres plus grêles, dans la physionomie trop expressive de son visage, dans le regard trop aigu de ses yeux, la trace évidente d'un sang appauvri, d'une énergie musculaire diminuée, d'un nervosisme exagéré ...

L'usure du sentiment par la pensée s'accomplit, elle aussi, de façons diverses. Tantôt c'est la conception d'un idéal raffiné qui crée la passion [et] précipite l'homme à d'étranges et dangereux excès ... Tantôt c'est l'habitude acharnée de l'analyse ...

L'usure de la volonté achève l'œuvre destructive, et ici les maladies encore non classées pullulent redoutablement. L'abondance des points de vue, cette richesse de l'intelligence, est la ruine de la volonté, car elle produit le dilettantisme et l'impuissance énervée des êtres trop compréhensifs." Bourget, *Essais de psychologie contemporaine*, 99–100.

23 *La Curée*, in *Œuvres complètes*, 5:87; *Le Docteur Pascal*, in ibid., 15:496.

24 "l'hypercivilisation ... a aussi pour effet d'affiner les systèmes nerveux, de les rendre délicats à l'extrême." *Le Suicide: Étude de sociologie* (1897), 365.

25 See Nye, *Crime, Madness & Politics*, 148, and Forth, *The Dreyfus Affair*, 74.

26 Léon Bouveret, *La Neurasthénie* (Paris: Baillière, 1891); Fernand Levillain, *La Neurasthénie* (Paris: Maloine, 1891). Cited in Nye, *Crime, Madness, & Politics*, 149.

27 Proust and Ballet, *L'Hygiène du neurasthénique*, 1–2, 7–8, 10, 14–24.

28 Nye, *Crime, Madness & Politics*, 149.

29 Proust and Ballet, *L'Hygiène du neurasthénique*, 11, 45, 75, 80.

30 Ibid., 11–12.

31 Forth cites Tissot, *De la santé des gens de lettres* (1768), and Réveillé-Parise, *Physiologie et hygiène des hommes livrés aux travaux de l'esprit* (1834). *The Dreyfus Affair*, 73. See also Vila, *Enlightenment and Pathology*, 95–7.

32 *The Dreyfus Affair*, 13, 221.

33 Nye affirms that "the series of 'nervous' and physical symptoms associated with neurasthenia were regarded as signs of the onset of degeneracy." *Crime, Madness, & Politics*, 148.

34 Elder, *Une crise*, 5, 202.

35 "il descendait presque directement aux quais, dont les bouquinistes le connaissaient bien. C'était un garçon de petite taille, aux membres grêles, au front bombé sous des cheveux châtains, plats, peu abondants, à la bouche mince et serrée, à peine ombrée par un léger duvet roussâtre. Sa myopie, qui l'avait fait dispenser du service militaire, l'obligeait à porter un pince-nez

dont les verres grossissaient ses yeux gris. Il avait des mains pâles, maigres, toujours chaudes, d'une extrême maladresse. Sa figure plutôt terne, très mobile ... reflétait un orage intérieur où se mêlaient des sentiments complexes ... qu'aiguisaient une imagination trop active." Rod, *L'Indocile*, 1–2.

36 "Il n'avait pas fait de la réalité une expérience graduelle, proportionnée à un grandissement normal d'esprit. Tout de suite, il avait été très haut par les livres, se perdant et s'absorbant en eux, sans vivre la vie. Ses conceptions avaient eu l'éclat étrange, la croissance hâtive, maladivement exubérante des plantes poussées en l'atmosphère chaude et factice des serres. Et son physique était l'image de cela ... le front trop développé, sa taille maigre, ses grands membres grêles ... Il y avait là une contradiction, une défectuosité de l'être, un manque d'équilibre et de saine corrélation, comme au moral." Mellerio, *La Vie stérile*, 199.

37 Zola, *La Curée* [1872], in *Œuvres complètes*, 5:149–51.

38 "un bourgeonnement précoce pourrissant fatalement sur la tige trop faible, – la décomposition, l'anéantissement avant la maturité. C'était cela qui avait tué Philippe!" *La Vie stérile*, 236.

39 "des promenades solitaires, de longues songeries." Ibid., 177.

40 "À le voir, on devinait une vie d'honneur, de discipline, de désintéressement; et son infirmité le grandissait, évoquait la charge glorieuse, là-bas, d'où si peu étaient revenus.

Quand il parlait de Fabien, il disait parfois: 'Il tient de sa mère.'" *Crise de jeunesse*, 66.

41 "– Il y a beau temps que j'ai reconnu l'absurdité du métier militaire! ... je veux être écrivain ...

– Alors, tu crois que je vais te garder ici, à ne rien faire? ... A-t-on jamais vu pareille chose? Qui donc lui a mis ces idées dans la tête? ...

Son fils! C'était son fils! Et dans l'affolement des idées, il se souvint de la religion qu'il lui avait donnée, de la patrie qu'il lui avait apprise quand il était enfant ... Son fils! C'était son fils, cet anarchiste!

Une larme jaillit de ses yeux, roula sur sa barbe blanche pour tomber sur sa pauvre jambe mutilée." Ferri-Pisani, *Les Pervertis*, 270–5.

42 The passing on of a traumatically acquired trait echoes neo-Lamarckian concepts of heredity famously espoused by Zola. For a discussion of the enduring influence of Lamarck on late-nineteenth century theories of degeneration, see Nye, *Crime, Madness, & Politics*, 119–31.

43 "C'est très normalement, à travers deux générations, sans secousse ni heurt, qu'il est devenu un *cérébral*, c'est-à-dire un de ces êtres bizarres pour qui le jeu des facultés intellectuelles passe en volupté toutes autres formes d'activité. Le grand-père était un rural; le père un homme d'affaires: nulle brusquerie dans ces étapes qui, tout naturellement, ont abouti à un intellectuel." *L'Illusion sentimentale*, 33.

44 "une vigueur intacte et la plus robuste charpente que nulle tare n'est encore venue altérer"; "mince de corps, très élégant, très affiné, avec une charpente frêle et peu de robustesse ... chez lui, tout est cérébralité." Ibid., 30, 33.

45 Ibid., 21–4, 173, 198. The name "Lucien" and the title *L'Illusion sentimentale* are clear allusions to Lucien Chardon/de Rubempré, the protagonist of Balzac's *Illusions perdues* and *Splendeurs et misères des courtisanes.* On Lucien and "male same-sex sexuality," see Lucey, "Queer Capital: Lucien and Vautrin," in *The Misfit of the Family*, 171–223. The adjective "sentimentale" likewise evokes Flaubert's *L'Éducation sentimentale*, and Charles is the name of *Madame Bovary*'s husband. Flat's novel can be read as a same-sex rewrite of these classics, one in which the handsome Lucien and a male Emma Bovary elope to Italy.

46 "rien ne servait mieux les aspirations du jeune rêveur que l'état d'esprit du père, un modèle de probité, d'affabilité et d'exactitude, dans cette étude d'avoué où, depuis plus de vingt ans qu'il travaillait, il avait, par le doyennat, conquis le droit au respect ... ce père enfant de braves paysans au milieu desquels il avait reçu une éducation bien primaire ... ce père, en définitive, se demandait, parfois, soucieux, si cette belle éducation qu'il donnait à son fils, au prix d'immenses sacrifices produirait un jour quelques fruits.

Ce qui le disposait à ces sacrifices, c'est qu'il avait, dans le cœur de Claudius, reconnu les mêmes qualités, les mêmes défauts que les siens; semblables aspirations à l'étude, à la lecture saine des livres qui complètent l'éducation intellectuelle mieux que les meilleurs professeurs. Aussi, se disait-il, si je donne, dès la vingtième année à mon fils le bagage que j'ai mis, moi, un demi-siècle à entasser, il est impossible qu'il ne se crée pas, un jour ou l'autre, une situation." Alcanter de Brahm, *L'Arriviste*, 44–5.

47 "humeur évaporée." Ibid., 46–8.

48 Henry Bérenger, *L'Effort*, 2–3.

49 "Mme Lauzerte était avant tout une intellectuelle ... Les aspirations que Lamartine et George Sand firent naître en elle furent brisées de bonne heure ... À vingt ans, elle avait lu tous les livres et jugé la plupart des hommes ... Elle n'avait point le don de l'amour: elle ne s'intéressait qu'aux idées. Dans ce monde-là, elle était extraordinaire; ses lectures étaient immenses. Les œuvres, nouvelles alors, de Taine, Flaubert, de Stuart Mill, de Spencer, la ravissaient. Mais surtout elle prenait goût aux labeurs curieux et précis d'un Max Muller ou d'un Huxley, et plus encore aux analyses cruelles d'un Baudelaire ou souriantes d'un Renan." Ibid., 14–16.

50 "ils se ressemblaient ... mais la forte ossature du père s'était atténuée dans le fils. Chaque trait du visage, devenu plus subtil, s'était comme spiritualisé." Ibid., 21.

51 "était-il donc bien vraiment son fils, ce grand garçon pâle et trop distingué ... N'avait-il donc tant essayé de le pétrir et de le pousser dans le monde que pour en faire une sorte d'Hamlet intellectuel?" Ibid., 33–4.

52 "le type parfait de l'intellectuel ... de notre génération." Ibid., xv, xxiv. On the use of this term prior to the Dreyfus Affair, see Idt, "L''intellectuel' avant l'affaire Dreyfus."

53 "Le contraste était grand entre les deux gens: Georges plus frêle ... son visage un peu mince ... Jean plus vigoureux, plus mâle avec sa haute taille." Ibid., 11.

54 "atteint comme lui, de dix-sept à vingt ans, par les mêmes maladies intellectuelles, [il] les avait courageusement vaincues et réalisait maintenant un assez beau type d'harmonie morale." Ibid., 81.

55 Zola's *La Débacle*, serialized in February 1892 (*La Vie stérile* also appeared in 1892, and *L'Effort* in 1893), used this device to contrast between two male protagonists respectively representing decadent and rural France, as noted by critics like Pick (*Faces of Degeneration*, 83). In that novel, Maurice, an overintellectual army officer described as having "a woman's nervous temperament, shaken by the disease of the era" ("d'une nervosité de femme, ébranlé par la maladie de l'époque"), goes insane and dies fighting on the side of the Communards, while Jean, a physically strong and morally upright soldier from the countryside, survives and looks towards "the renewal promised to all who hope and work" ("le renouveau promis à qui espère et travaille"). *La Débâcle* [1892], in *Œuvres complètes*, 15:124, 362. Significantly, Maurice is an avid reader of newspapers (15:48), while Jean is never depicted reading.

56 "Je n'aurais pas songé à décrire l'invasion de l'intellectualisme dans une âme destinée au suicide, si je n'avais conçu une façon d'échapper au mal, et si à un Georges Lauzerte je n'avais pu opposer un Jean Darnay ... Au passif, si immense fût-il, j'avais la conviction d'opposer un actif." *L'Effort*, xxvii.

57 The differentiation of males between "actives" and "passives" carries a connotation of homosexuality. Alexandre Lacassagne's entry for "Pédérastie" in the *Dictionnaire encyclopédique des sciences médicales* uses these terms to describe roles in sexual acts, citing an earlier usage by Ambroise Tardieu (22:255).

58 As described in chapter 1, pages 40–1.

59 The device is prominent in *L'Effort*, *La Vie stérile*, *Une crise*, *Le Vertige de l'inconnu* (1892) and Alphonse Daudet's *Soutien de famille* (1898); it is also present in *Le Disciple* and *Les Déracinés*. On contrasting "active" and "passive" characters in *Soutien de famille*, see chapter 3, pages 97–8.

60 *Authoritarian Fictions*, 147–97. Suleiman writes that characters in ideological novels can be "doubly damned" through "the technique of the amalgam": "a character is constructed in such a way that his or her culturally negative qualities are redundant with qualities whose pertinence is specifically ideological" (190). The reverse applies to characters constituted from an amalgam of ideologically positive qualities.

61 "de vagues notes sans style ni ordre, prises au hasard des impressions fugitives, presque immédiatement oubliées." *La Vie stérile*, 177.

62 "Souvenez-vous d'il y a cinq ans. Étais-je assez la proie de mauvaises chimères? ... Je ne me trouvais pas à ma place. Paris et les livres m'avaient tourné la tête. J'avais trop lu Balzac et Baudelaire. J'aurais voulu être tout de suite un grand homme ou un homme très riche ... J'étais tout simplement détraqué." *L'Effort*, 119–20. "Par deux remèdes infaillibles [:] J'ai agi et aimé. Quand, après le romantisme et le pessimisme, j'ai senti le dilettantisme m'envahir, je me suis jeté à corps perdu dans l'action." Ibid., 185.
63 "Cet ami enterré le matin si misérablement, n'établissait-il pas une ligne de démarcation dans l'existence d'André? C'était toute sa jeunesse gaie, inexpérimentée, inconsciente, qui était terminée là." Ibid., 235.
64 "toujours plongé dans les livres, dans l'étude des lettres"; "dès le premier regard ... séduisait les amateurs de la vigueur physique, de la beauté masculine"; "étudiant Fernand à fond d'âme, lisant en lui ainsi qu'un livre ouvert ... Il lui avait suffi de le regarder une fois, pour deviner sa nature positive, toute matérielle, pour pressentir ses appétits, ses besoins. Celui-là devait être son antithèse en tout, au moral aussi bien qu'au physique, et il en ressentit immédiatement, non pas positivement une répulsion, mais une méfiance instinctive comme en présence d'un danger caché." Toudouze, *Le Vertige de l'inconnu*, 110, 115, 120–4.
65 "en même temps, il se reprochait avec une redoublante amertume ce trouble bizarre qui le travaillait. Était-ce simplement l'aveugle et fanatique passion du foyer qui lui faisait immédiatement considérer comme un ennemi du bonheur des siens, de son propre bonheur, ce nouveau venu ... Était-ce quelque autre sentiment plus redoutable, plus dangereux à analyser? ... Un peu de honte monta du fond de lui-même, poussant le sang à sa face." Ibid., 128–9.
66 In Bourget's *Le Disciple*, the bookish protagonist's dislike and fascination for his female pupil's virile brother is similarly fraught with sexual ambiguity. See chapter 4, pages 145–6.
67 See chapter 1, page 27.
68 "À cette minute précise, et tandis que j'écris cette ligne, un adolescent, que je *vois*, s'est accoudé sur son pupitre d'étudiant par ce beau soir d'un jour de juin. Les fleurs s'ouvrent sous la fenêtre, amoureusement. L'or tendre du soleil couché s'étend sur la ligne de l'horizon avec une délicatesse adorable. Des jeunes filles causent dans le jardin voisin. L'adolescent est penché sur son livre, peut-être un de ceux dont il est parlé dans ces *Essais*. C'est *Les Fleurs du Mal* de Baudelaire, c'est la *Vie de Jésus* de Renan, c'est la *Salammbô* de Flaubert, c'est le *Thomas Graindorge* de Taine, c'est *Le Rouge et le Noir* de Beyle ... Qu'il ferait mieux de vivre! disent les sages ... Hélas! C'est qu'il vit à cette minute, et d'une vie plus intense que s'il cueillait les fleurs parfumées, que s'il regardait le mélancolique Occident, que s'il serrait les fragiles doigts d'une des jeunes filles. Il passe tout entier dans les phrases de son auteur préféré. Il converse avec lui de cœur à cœur, d'homme

à homme. Il l'écoute prononcer sur la manière de goûter l'amour et de pratiquer la débauche [...] des paroles qui sont des révélations. Ces paroles l'introduisent dans un univers de sentiments jusqu'alors aperçus à peine. De cette première révélation à imiter ces sentiments, la distance est faible, et l'adolescent ne tarde guère à la franchir. Un grand observateur a dit que beaucoup d'hommes n'auraient jamais été amoureux s'ils n'avaient entendu parler de l'amour. À coup sûr, ils auraient aimé d'une autre façon." Bourget, *Essais de psychologie contemporaine*, 435–6. Bourget's emphasis; unbracketed ellipses are original.

69 Jean Rousset analysed the importance of the window as the privileged place of reading and daydreaming in *Madame Bovary* in *Forme et Signification*, 123–31.

70 See part I, page 19.

71 "continuent à peser sur la jeunesse"; "ce que l'on appelait, en 1830, le mal du siècle." Bourget, 1885 preface to the *Essais*, in *Essais de psychologie contemporaine*, 438, 440.

72 For a classic definition of male homosocial relationality, see Sedgwick, *Between Men*, 1–5.

73 Maxim 136 of the 1678 edition reads: "Some people would never have fallen in love if they had not first heard of love." La Rochefoucauld, *Maximes et réflexions diverses*, 56.

74 For a survey of historical studies on the policing of male homosexuality in late nineteenth-century France, see Surkis, *Sexing the Citizen*, 10–11; on homosexuality and the boarding school, see 47–8, 82–4 and passim.

75 "savante et dominatrice," *L'Effort*, 83, 94. Since *L'Effort* is from 1893, the reference is likely to the trilogy *Le Culte du Moi.*

76 "elle avait lu des livres d'une illicence extrême, elle interrogeait Philippe ... sur des vices putrides, des passions inavouables." *La Vie stérile*, 126–7.

77 In *Monsieur Vénus* (1884), Rachilde similarly links the masculinity of the protagonist Raoule de Vénérande to her extensive literary education (25–7). Jean Borie describes "the effeminate male and the emancipated woman" as a recurring twin figures in "the abundant semiological paraphanelia of degeneration." Preface to Zola, *La Curée*, 19.

78 "entraînée par sa passion pour la littérature, avait mis entre les mains de son neveu bien des livres, couramment interdits avant la naissance des moustaches." Jourdain, *L'Atelier Chantorel*, 37, 109.

79 "Et puis les poètes la lui avaient gâtée à plaisir, cette nature dont le sens intime lui échappait. Pas une branche, pas un brin d'herbe, pas une fleur, pas un ruisseau, pas un caillou derrière lesquels ne fut embusqué un hémistiche, auprès desquels ne se faufilât une épithète. Avec ... ses points d'exclamation charlatanesques, ses vibrations en simili-bronze ... ses ébats idyllesques de momie, le lyrisme universitaire avait défloré ses premiers épanchements. Il ressentait un haut-le-cœur au moment de porter à ses lèvres le verre dans

lequel la cuistrerie du monde entier se gargarisait depuis des siècles. Gaston se rappelait les flots d'encre versés pour glorifier le chant des oiseaux, les rames de papier recouvertes de lithographies et de gravures représentant les joies célestes procurées par le gazouillement du rossignol. Or, de bonne foi, le plus mélodieux pépiement d'oiseau valait-il une sonate de Beethoven ou une mélodie de Schumann?" Ibid., 237–8.

80 The notion that Baudelaire privileges the artificial over the natural is an oversimplification; nevertheless, it has currency as a received idea about his poetics. In poems like "Obsession," Baudelaire describes how the natural world – the forest, the ocean, the night sky – inexorably brings him back to human concerns and thoughts of mortality and loss. In this sense, Gaston's failure to see nature as itself is reminiscent of certain aspects of *Les Fleurs du Mal*, although the poetic tropes he cites (lyrical epithets celebrating birdsong and the like) are decidedly un-Baudelairian. His trailing of a *promeneuse* likewise recalls the well-known "À une passante." *Les Fleurs du Mal* [1857–61], in *Œuvres complètes*, 1:75, 92.

81 "affaibli, énervé, moralement désemparé"; "Il s'essayait à écrire des paroles rythmées, dépourvues de sens, mais dont le rythme l'enchantait. La mémoire meublée de milliers de vers français et latins, mais ignorant les règles les plus élémentaires de la prosodie, il ébauchait des poèmes boiteux"; "Parfois aussi, d'autres bruits, plus proches, auxquels il ne se trompait plus, et qui faisaient perler la sueur à ses flancs, – chuchotements assourdis, fuites de pieds nus, murmures de baisers." Rouquès, *Le Jeune Rouvre*, 162, 199, 200.

82 "Alberti ferma le roman et se prit à rêver d'amour ...

Peu à peu ses nerfs s'engourdirent pour ne plus transmettre à son cerveau les impressions extérieures: le lycéen ne perçut plus les chuchotements de ses voisins ni le bruit des pupitres qu'on ouvre ... La lumière crue du gaz, tamisée par ses paupières baissées, venait emplir ses yeux d'une lueur légèrement rose et tiède ... [...] Alors, sa pensée, tout à elle-même, chercha des souvenirs: des silhouettes entrevues, l'une après l'autre, passèrent en sa mémoire ... [...]

Être irréel, forme impalpable, mais qu'Alberti croyait pouvoir saisir, s'il l'eût voulu ... Autour d'Elle, le décor ondoyait avec une vitesse étourdissante [...]

Voilà que soudain il se trouvait seul dans une chambre avec Elle ... Comment était-il venu là?

Une chose était réelle: Il la voyait en face de lui; il se mettait à ses genoux, il pressait sa taille, mais ne sentait point sous ses doigts la résistance du corset ni des chairs; [...]

Alberti avait une envie folle de toucher cette cheville, puis doucement de caresser, avec la main, plus haut, mais il ne touchait que du vide ... [...]

Lentement, les nerfs sensitifs se réveillaient sous l'action du bruit extérieur ... De très loin, semblant sortir d'un gouffre, une voix, celle de la femme peut-être, criait:

– On m'a chipé un roman de Lorrain! L'as-tu trouvé?" Ferri-Pisani, *Les Pervertis* (1905), 149–54. Unbracketed ellipses are original.

83 Dante, *The Divine Comedy I: Inferno*, 5:127–38.

84 Paul Bonnetain's *Charlot s'amuse* (Bruxelles: Kistmaeckers, 1883) famously describes the tragic life of a chronic masturbator, in a decidedly dark, Naturalist manner.

85 "Tous les souvenirs affluaient à son cerveau bouillant, les poèmes de luxure et les poèmes d'amour chantaient à ses oreilles et de la chair vive et belle s'offrait. – Puis, se rappeler les ivresses ardentes! Oh! étreindre un corps! l'enlacer dans une crispation féroce! – Il s'accrochait aux draps. – [...] oh! viens! Je t'en prie, je t'aime! ... – Il parlait tout haut dans le silence. Puis c'était un apaisement et il connaissait les 'plaisirs solitaires.'" Marc Elder, *Une crise*, 211. Unbracketed ellipsis is original.

86 "le pouvoir que nous avons de réveiller nos perceptions en l'absence des objets nous donne celui de réunir et de lier ensemble les idées les plus étrangères." Condillac, *Essai sur l'origine des connaissances humaines* [1749], 87, 90.

87 Goldstein, *The Post-Revolutionary Self*, 53. See also Laqueur, *Solitary Sex*, and Bennett and Rosario, *Solitary Pleasures*.

88 "Quelle conquête, ardue ou périlleuse, de femme en chair et en os valait à mes yeux celle que je possédais sans effort, librement, comme un magicien créant les plus suaves et les plus beaux fantômes?" Margueritte, *Les Jours s'allongent*, 157.

89 This is, of course, a central point in Derrida's seminal analysis of Rousseau's *Confessions* in *De la grammatologie* (141–64).

90 "Quand le potache se retrouva seul dans la rue, un immense dégoût l'étreignit. C'était donc là tout cet amour qui hantait ses rêves d'enfant!" Ferri-Pisani, *Les Pervertis*, 165.

91 "La réverbération du soleil sur l'asphalte obligea le Corse à fermer les yeux: et voilà qu'il eût des visions inconnues ... Ce ne furent d'abord que des nudités vagues, puis, peu à peu, les lignes se précisèrent pour former des femmes dont les seins se fondaient en des torses d'enfants ... Celui qui avait aimé Marguerite et rêvé à Camille, s'était cru fort; mais la loi était inexorable et la semence des instincts insexuels [*sic*], puisée dans le lycée, allait enfin germer sous le souffle des désillusions féminines pour croître, impérieuse, dans son âme." Ibid., 305–6.

92 "Les peaufins, – peaux fines, – ce sont les imberbes, les jolis adolescents. Ils sont sûrs de trouver des protecteurs ... pour eux des mâles se 'pocheront.' Nul ne s'étonnera de l'aspect féminin, yeux en coulisse, taille ondulante que prendra, naturellement, tel blondin à la grâce molle, tel brunet provocant. Ils ont des surnoms de femme: la belle Anglaise, Bébé ... On se confie, à voix basse, ce qui se passe au dortoir des plus grands: une prostitution sans

femmes, avec femmes pourtant. C'est fatal: l'instinct naturel, insatisfait, dévie." Margueritte, *Les Jours s'allongent*, 131.

93 "une émotion inconnue ... coupée de langueur attiédie, de sursauts fiévreux." Ibid., 57.

94 "La conception exclusivement livresque où s'enlisaient ma casuistique (?) et mon expérience (!) de l'amour, l'envahissement aussi complet d'une âme par le rêve, ne tendaient à rien moins qu'à la paralyser, cette âme ... à fausser en elle la conscience du possible et le goût du vrai. Le dégoût de l'action, la peur d'oser étaient la rançon de ces délicieuses ivresses d'un dormeur éveillé. ...

Je ne pense pas que cette étrange maladie ait été personnelle à moi seul: elle me devait durer des années. ... Elle n'influa pas seulement sur mon cœur et sur mes sens, mais elle dévia le fonctionnement même de mon esprit, la manière dont j'envisageais de plus en plus de choses. Rapportant mes actes à un critérium uniquement sentimental, jugeant la vie d'après les livres, – et quels? les romans romanesques, les moins faits pour me l'apprendre, – j'appartins à l'illusion. J'en fus le jouet." Ibid., 156–7; original parentheses.

95 Bourget, *Essais de psychologie contemporaine* [1883], 99.

96 "Il préférait lire, c'était là sa grande occupation, dès qu'il était libre des leçons et des devoirs. Alors il avait dévoré des volumes d'aventures et de voyages. Tout un monde s'évoquait pour lui. Sa poitrine se dilatait, ses tempes battaient, son esprit s'enfiévrait. Et des courses lointaines l'entraînaient par delà des mers immenses, en d'étranges pays." Mellerio, *Jacques Mérane*, 43.

97 "lassitude de tout"; "elle ne lisait pas de romans, elle n'analysait point. Et c'était justement pour cela qu'elle restait sincère et profonde"; "par elle il recommençait une autre famille qui croîtrait." Ibid., 96, 196–7, 214.

98 Other examples include *La Vie stérile*, where Philippe experiences reading as a depleting fever: "he liked to read in the evenings, during long hours that gradually made him feverish ... he lived a deep and exquisite life through multiple characters, far from time and reality. Then he emerged exhausted, drained of nervous energy – as after exhausting bouts of love ... he sat inert and heavy." ("il aimait à lire le soir, pendant de longues heures qui l'enfiévraient graduellement ... il vivait une vie exquise et profonde à multiples personnages, en dehors du temps et des réalités. Puis il sortait de là harassé, dépouillé de force nerveuse – comme après d'épuisants efforts d'amour ... il végétait alourdi.") *La Vie stérile*, 87. A reading scene from Paul Flat's *Pastel vivant* (1904) uses many of the same terms: "Sébran recalls this or that gripping reading ... begun some morning of the most melancholy autumn, continued all day with hasty meals as the only interlude, and finished late into the night, his temples burning, in such a fever of emotion that he could hardly contain the beating of his heart." ("Sébran se rappelle ainsi telle passionnante lecture ... commencée par un matin du plus mélancolique automne, continuée toute une journée avec le seul intervalle

des repas pris à la hâte, et finie très avant dans la nuit les tempes brûlantes, dans une telle fièvre d'émotion qu'il avait eu peine à contenir les battements de son cœur.") *Pastel vivant*, 51.

99 "C'est, d'ailleurs, l'époque des grandes découvertes littéraires: Stéphane, pour ses étrennes, a reçu les œuvres complètes de Musset, Varenne les poésies de Hugo; Margelin, en explorant la bibliothèque héritée de son grand-père, a fait la trouvaille d'une édition originale de Lamartine ... C'est une fièvre de lectures passionnées, sans répit, sans choix. Pas une pièce qui ne les émeuve jusqu'au fond de leur âme et qui ne leur révèle un peu de leur âme à eux-mêmes. C'est leur peine, leur désir, leur espoir qui s'expriment dans Le Lac, Olympia, Souvenir. C'est au propre, après la révélation de la vie et de l'amour, la révélation de la beauté poétique qui commence.

Bientôt, elle ne leur suffit pas.

Hugo, Musset, Lamartine, Chénier, Vigny, lus et relus, au hasard, Baudelaire admiré un peu de confiance, ils en appellent aux prosateurs. Balzac, les stupéfie. Zola, pour eux, a surtout l'attrait du fruit particulièrement défendu. Les Goncourt, enfin, et Daudet les plongent dans un trouble étrange par leur modernisme, par ces analyses d'impressions et de sentiments qu'ils imaginent si proches des leurs mêmes." Rouquès, *Le Jeune Rouvre*, 240–1.

100 Ibid., 243, 260.

101 A typical example of this trope appears in Jourdain's *L'Atelier Chantorel*: "The boy had hastily devoured, in a jumble: Dickens, Walter Scott, Chateaubriand, Gustave Aymard, Nodier, Cooper, Alfred de Vigny, two or three novels by Balzac and Alexandre Dumas, a few pages by George Sand, poems by Hugo, Lamartine, Mme Desbordes-Valmore, Chénier, and a few passages by Musset. He would have been incapable of ordering or judging his readings with any reason, and anyway he had digested them poorly." ("L'enfant avait dévoré à l'aventure, pêle-mêle: Dickens, Walter Scott, Chateaubriand, Gustave Aymard, Nodier, Cooper, Alfred de Vigny, deux ou trois romans de Balzac et d'Alexandre Dumas, quelques pages de George Sand, les poésies d'Hugo, de Lamartine, de Mme Desbordes-Valmore, de Chénier, et certains passages de Musset. Il eût été incapable de classer et d'évaluer d'une façon raisonnée ses lectures, mal digérées du reste.") *L'Atelier Chantorel*, 37.

102 Rouquès, *Le Jeune Rouvre* (1909), n.p.

103 On Lanson's career and the rise of literary history as a university discipline, see Compagnon, *La Troisième République des lettres*, 21–220, especially 55–8 on Lanson's positions against subjective criticism.

104 "la recherche de l'usage et des applications actuelles de l'œuvre étudiée"; "les jeunes gens seront toujours avertis des grands problèmes qui se posent à toute conscience et à toute société." *Méthodes de l'histoire littéraire* (1925), 49; "Les Véritables Humanités modernes" (1901), 512; both cited in Compagnon, *La Troisième République des lettres*, 83.

105 In the preface to *Histoire de la literature française*, Lanson defends the "broad place I have made ... for the nineteenth century" (x). See also Compagnon, *La Troisième République des lettres*, 95–102.
106 "La Neutralité scolaire" (1912); cited in Compagnon, *La Troisième République des lettres*, 83.
107 "Né délicat, mais sans résistance morale, il avait été successivement victime de toutes les maladies psychologiques qui ont si curieusement travaillé l'Europe au XIXe siècle et qui pourraient bien, si elles se prolongeaient, indiquer l'usure d'une race. Romantique à dix-sept ans, baudelairien à dix-huit, pessimiste à dix-neuf, il s'était retrouvé en fin de compte renanien et barrésiste de vingt à vingt-trois ans." Bérenger, *L'Effort*, 80.
108 Rouquès, *Le Jeune Rouvre*, 240–1.
109 "Mais, cette fois, ils ne jouissent déjà plus en aveugles, avidement: leur trouble se nuance d'une curiosité nouvelle; le métier les attache autant que la fable et leur parenté obscure avec les héros; ils ont sous les yeux des modèles à imiter, des maîtres, d'une génération seulement leurs aînés, dont ils veulent surprendre les secrets." Ibid., 241.
110 That the students' vocational "revelation" is described ironically does not imply straightforward mockery. On irony as the ambiguous mark of a personal disillusion, see Pierre Schoentjes, *Poétique de l'ironie*, 87–90. Rouquès (1873–1935) eventually became an inspector general for primary schools. In his twenties, he published three collections of poetry (1897, 1900, 1903) and a one-act play (1901). *Le Jeune Rouvre* is his only novel.
111 "ce fut la révélation, l'illumination suprême [...] qui décide des vocations [...] Écrire! ... Soudainement ils ne doutaient plus, la clarté les éblouissait; c'était leur destinée: ils écriraient!" Rouquès, *Le Jeune Rouvre*, 248. Unbracketed ellipsis is original.
112 "on leur a caché la vie"; "le mal de notre âge." Ibid., 296, 268.
113 " il ne put dégager une impression générale de cette formidable lecture qui entremêlait *Charles Demailly*, *La Curée*, *Manette Salomon*, *Le Ventre de Paris*, *Fromont jeune*, *Salammbô*, *L'Éducation sentimentale*, etc., etc., etc. ..." Margueritte, *Tous Quatre*, 179. Original ellipsis.
114 Flaubert, *Madame Bovary* [1856], in *Œuvres*, 1:200.
115 See Matlock, *Scenes of Seduction*, 199–280, as well as Dumasy, *La querelle du roman-feuilleton*, 5–21.
116 "un chapitre du Sopha, une Lettre d'Héloïse et deux Contes de La Fontaine." Laclos, *Les Liaisons dangereuses* [1782], 70.
117 In Letter LXXXI, the Marquise describes her literary self-education: "I fortified my observations through reading: but do not think that it was of the kind you imagine. I studied our manners in novels; our opinions in philosophers; I even consulted the strictest Moralists to find out what they demanded of us." ("Je les fortifiai [mes observations] par le secours

de la lecture: mais ne croyez pas qu'elle fût du genre que vous la supposez. J'étudiai nos mœurs dans les Romans; nos opinions dans les Philosophes; je cherchai même dans les Moralistes les plus sévères ce qu'ils exigeaient de nous.") Ibid., 250–1. Her claim that she remains "unstirred by passion" ("emportée par aucune passion," ibid.) is a stark contrast to descriptions of fin-de-siècle adolescents' "fevers of passionate reading" ("fièvre de lectures passionnées," Rouquès, *Le Jeune Rouvre*, 240).

118 In Boyer d'Argen's *Thérèse philosophe* (1748), for instance, Thérèse accepts a wager from the libertine Comte de ***: he will loan her his personal library for a year if she can resist pleasuring herself after perusing it. She loses. *Romans libertins du XVIIIe siècle*, 557–658. For a detailed study of the trope of the library in the eighteenth-century novel, see Ferrand, *Livres et lectures dans les romans français du XVIIIe siècle*, 237–338, especially 311–16 on the library as an "erotic space."

119 "Serrés les uns contre les autres, les livres ne paraissent former qu'un seul volume; ils se soudent en une sorte d'armée pacifique, quoique souvent destructive, invincible et hautaine ... Un néant condensé s'évapore de tout cela. Malgré le merveilleux qu'il contient et la vie dont il s'anime, ce bloc plat qui colle au mur n'est que du papier; chaque dos de livre vacille, s'effile, ondule, se gonfle, précise tantôt une urne, tantôt une bière, et la bibliothèque apparaît une nécropole sublime." Lebey, *L'Âge où l'on s'ennuie*, 2.

120 "Charner se retourna, rôda le long des murs, jeta un regard de dégoût sur cette table de travail qui n'était plus qu'une table de torture, et vint se planter en face de sa bibliothèque. Là s'entassaient ses confidents les plus chers, et aussi ses ennemis les plus redoutés, les chefs d'œuvre. Tantôt ils l'exaltaient jusqu'à l'héroïsme, tantôt ils le déprimaient jusqu'au suicide. Selon qu'il aspirait à les égaler, ou qu'il en désespérait, ils étaient pour lui de précieuses chasses ou d'ignobles tombeaux. Ils contenaient toute l'essence de la beauté, tout son néant aussi. Et le dégoût d'ajouter quelques cadavres à ces cadavres l'écœurait plus souvent qu'il n'était enivré par l'enthousiasme d'ajouter une immortalité à leurs immortalités." Bérenger, "Portrait d'un jeune homme" (1897), 664. "Portrait" appeared as a "Study of interior life to serve in a future novel" in the November 1897 issue of the periodical *L'Art et la Vie*, but the projected novel was never published.

121 "tout mourait, dans ses livres." Margueritte, *Tous Quatre*, 333. I examine depictions of the reader-protagonist as an aspiring writer in more detail in chapters 5 and 6.

122 "regardant autour de lui, dans la chambre où les livres meublaient seuls"; "Oh, les livres ... les meilleurs amis, les pires ennemis!" Jean Morgan, *En genèse*, 147.

123 "Vous souffrez du mal inhérent à la génération actuelle ... nous avons des dilettantes, des hommes merveilleusement corrompus ... mais nous n'avons pas d'hommes de volonté; c'est un élément qui tend à disparaître parmi les

intellectuels. Des sensitifs, des analystes, des penseurs subtils ... c'est une brillante dégénérescence, mais c'est tout de même une dégénérescence ... Pour vous, mon enfant, ce qui vous fait défaut, c'est l'énergie." Ibid., 24–8.

124 *Essais de psychologie contemporaine* [1883], 99–100.

125 "couverte de livres et de papiers en désordre." Bérenger, *L'Effort*, 248.

Part II: The Three Dangers of Literature

1 André Beaunier (1869–1925) would go on to become the literary critic for the *Revue des Deux Mondes* and write many more novels and works of criticism. The novel's publisher, Fasquelle, was a leading literary editor at the turn of the century, also publishing works by Zola, Barrès, and Mirbeau.

2 "je ne suis pas bachelier, moi ... Coppée non plus!" *Les Trois Legrand*, 70. François Coppée (1842–1908), a successful poet initially associated with the Parnasse movement, was elected to the Académie française in 1884.

3 "[Ange] en est là aujourd'hui, déchu de ses ambitions magnifiques, à bout d'orgueil, réduit à cette extrémité de donner à boire à des gars de barrière. Rêves prodigieux, art et littérature, la gloire filiale trop vite escomptée, la fortune, le luxe et leurs mirages décevants! ... L'homme de lettres [Pierre] est en ballade, on ne sait où. De tout le jour, on ne l'a vu. Au toquet familial et sur les talus, à la barrière, il fait des relations. Et il n'écrira pas 'Fortifs'; mais ce roman de naguère, il le vivra." Ibid., 344–8.

4 Linda Hutcheon's useful definitions distinguish parody from satire according to the notion of "target." While the target of satire is "extramural," with satire taking aim at political, social, or moral questions, the target of parody is "intramural": literary parodies, for instance, target literary texts, topoi, or genres. See *A Theory of Parody*, 42–4.

5 "la rencontre des idées et des âmes ... est l'objet de tous mes livres." Beaunier, *L'Homme qui a perdu son moi*, i. Beaunier's dedication echoes Bourget's project in *Le Disciple*: "I have attempted to show the contact between pure ideas and the minds that receive them, that make them into rules for their own lives, and yet, in spite of this, cannot help altering them." ("j'ai tâché de mettre ici en contact les idées pures et les âmes qui les reçoivent, qui font d'elles la règle de leur vie et, pour cela, ne manquent pas de les altérer.") Ibid.

6 André Beaunier, "Sur les dangers de la littérature," in *Au service de la déesse*, 7–21. Jean Carrère, *Les Mauvais Maîtres*. On Carrère, see epilogue, p. 244.

7 I describe characters' ambitions as *writerly* (their ambition is often to become a writer – not always a novelist, but sometimes instead a journalist, as we will see in chapter 5) in order to avoid confusion with *authorial* ambitions, i.e., the literary ambitions or aspirations of the author.

8 *Les Trois Legrand*, 1.

9 Abel Faure, *La Clé des carrières* (1904).

10 "un prolétariat de bacheliers." Barrès, *Les Déracinés*, in *Romans et Voyages*, 1:557. On this topic, see Judith Surkis, *Sexing the Citizen*, 73–103.

11 On these reforms, see chapter 3, pages 95–6.

12 "Il lui prêta des livres ... Elle demanda des romans, avec perversité, car elle avait été élevée à regarder ces ouvrages comme frivoles et dangereux ... George Sand lui causa le plus vif étonnement et d'abord l'indigna, puis la séduisit. Elle n'avait jamais pensé aux droits irréductibles de l'amour." *Les Trois Legrand*, 94.

13 See Ferrand, *Livre et lecture dans les romans français du XVIIIe siècle*, 69–93, and Baudry, *Lectrices romanesques*, 129–50.

14 Ruth Harris writes that "While women were generally considered to be suggestible, *Le Disciple* implied that the most susceptible to deleterious influences were young men with effeminate casts of mind. In this way, the cultural association between femininity and susceptibility was maintained, only to be perverted further by young men whose excessive intellectualism was a source of extreme cultural debilitation." *Murders and Madness*, 320. In chapter 4, I complicate Harris's offhand characterization of Bourget's protagonist as "effeminate" (a term that nowhere appears in the novel), and instead propose to situate him in a more intricate network of social and sexual threats revolving around the notion of "le romanesque."

15 "chaque fois que Rostand fait un drame, ça lui rapporte à peu près un million." *Les Trois Legrand*, 36.

16 "c'est un fait assez connu que les grands poètes ont forcément une assez mauvaise conduite." Ibid., 77.

17 "Un Corps de femme, Chair en folie, l'Amour qui tue, les Passionnés, les Courtisanes des salons, les Démoniques." Ibid., 137.

18 "– Je crois que la poésie est en baisse, hasarda M. Legrand [...]
– Assurément, les vers! ... Si on n'avait pas la pornographie pour se rattraper, la librairie ne serait plus possible [...] On écrit de plus en plus et on lit de moins en moins. C'est ça la crise du livre! Quiconque, jadis, aurait lu, maintenant écrit ..." Ibid., 137–40. Unbracketed ellipses are original.

19 "Dante écrirait 'Chair en folie.' Homère aussi, Virgile aussi. Ou bien ils seraient des ratés." Ibid., 154.

20 Beaunier splits financial ambition and literary aspirations, two defining traits of Balzac's Lucien Chardon/de Rubempré, between father and son. In *Illusions perdues*, Lucien eventually betrays his literary and aesthetic ideals (represented by the group of artists and thinkers of the "Cénacle") in order to achieve social and financial advancement through for-hire political journalism. Balzac, *Illusions perdues*, in *La Comédie humaine*, 5:529–39.

21 "Oui, c'est à l'auteur de la *Comédie humaine* que nous devons l'assaut toujours plus croissant des ambitions les plus grossières ... C'est lui qui ... va, dans toutes les provinces, sonner à l'oreille trop complaisante des plébéiens encore mal débarbouillés de leur terre natale la diane d'appel pour la conquête de

Paris! C'est lui enfin qui ... par l'éclat des exemples ... a fait surgir du fond troublé de la race ce type innombrable et malfaisant, dont le bourdonnement est la plaie de notre pays ... l'arriviste!" Carrère, *Les Mauvais Maîtres*, 77.

22 Barrès, "La Contagion des Rastignacs," *Le Voltaire*, 28 June 1887, 1. I discuss this article in chapter 5, pages 149–54.

23 Bourget's *Le Disciple* and Barrès's *Les Déracinés* are customarily studied together, for instance as literary responses to the Ferry educational reforms of the 1880s: see Chaitin, *The Enemy Within*, 45–138.

24 The title "prince de la jeunesse" was given to Bourget in an article by Jules Lemaitre, "M. Paul Bourget" (*Revue Bleue*, 12 February 1887); the article was reprinted in Lemaitre, *Les Contemporains*, 364. Two years later, Barrès was given a medal inscribed "Princeps Juventutis" (the prince of youth) by Paul Adam: see Éric Roussel, "Préface," in Barrès, *Romans et voyages*, 1:xxxix.

25 Bourget was elected to the Académie française in 1894, Barrès in 1906.

26 See Suleiman, *Authoritarian Fictions*, 74–100 (on *L'Étape*) and 118–32 (on *Le Roman de l'énergie nationale*). For a more recent example of a similar reading, see Béatrice Laville, "Un roman à thèse de Paul Bourget, *L'Étape*," in Fougère and Sangsue, ed., *Avez-vous lu Paul Bourget?*, 21–30.

27 See chapter 1, pages 36–7 and 46.

28 Bompaire-Evesque, "Paul Bourget collaborateur de Maurice Barrès." *Sous l'œil des Barbares* is written as a series of impressionistic scenes or meditations that provide little in the way of plot or information on the characters' backgrounds; each scene is preceded by a "concordance" that fills in some of these details. Bompaire-Evesque provides manuscript evidence that many of the revisions to these concordances for the 1892 edition were made on Bourget's advice.

29 "Sorel, Rubempré, ... la Madame Bovary de Flaubert, le Jacques Vingtras de Jules Vallès ... sont des sensibilités en transfert de classe"; "le danger que représente [ce] que Barrès a très heureusement appelé le déracinement." Bourget, preface to *Pages de critique et de doctrine*, 1:v–vi. Bourget's 1882 essay on Stendhal (integrated in the 1883 *Essais de psychologie contemporaine*) also draws an important parallel between Stendhal's Julien Sorel and Vallès's Jacques Vingtras. *Essais de psychologie contemporaine*, 205–6.

30 "une forte atmosphère familiale, professionnelle et locale." *Pages de critique et de doctrine*, 1:vii.

3. Vallès, the *Déclassé*, and the Pitfalls of Education

1 A *bachelier* is someone who has passed the *baccalauréat* examination, established by Napoleon and originally required for admission to university faculties (law, medicine, theology). As Theodore Zeldin explains, "under the Restoration, it became necessary for admission to the civil service and the liberal professions; in 1830 the written examination was introduced." *France, 1848–1945*, 269.

2 "l'énorme machine à formatter universitaire qui, à l'arrivée, sort un produit ... trop souvent inadapté aux besoins du marché." François Moureau, *Le Nouveau Prolétariat intellectuel*, back cover.
3 Bérenger, "Les Prolétaires intellectuels en France," 1–51. I discuss Bérenger's 1893 novel *L'Effort* in chapter 2, pages 65–8.
4 I discuss alimentary metaphors for reading in chapter 1, pages 41–6.
5 See Cham, *Piled Higher and Deeper* 608 and 759.
6 Patton, "The Ph.D. Now Comes with Food Stamps."
7 "les merveilles de notre civilisation." Brulat, *Le Nouveau Candide*, 10. Brulat (1866–1940) was a journalist and the author of over a dozen novels as well as short biographies of Zola and Jules Ferry. In 1892, he published *L'Âme errante*, a novel inspired, like Bourget's *Le Disciple*, by the Chambige affair of 1888 (see chapter 4).
8 "deux licences et un doctorat, plus qu'il n'en faut pour crever de faim, au temps où nous vivons. Loin de m'aider à gagner ma vie, tant d'érudition m'abrutit. J'ai usé à l'acquérir toute la vigueur et toute l'énergie de ma jeunesse, et me voici maintenant désarmé dans l'âpre conflit vital. Sans doute, aurais-je réussi à quelque chose, si mon père, un brave homme de paysan, ne s'était saigné à toutes les veines pour faire de moi quelqu'un [...] Mes professeurs m'avaient promis un brillant avenir, car j'étais bon élève. [...] J'avais appris par cœur le *De viris illustribus*, livre néfaste, s'il en fut, et qui, dès la cinquième, fit de moi un candidat à la gloire et, plus tard, un hurluberlu, un enflammé, un déclassé, un pauvre bougre enfin dénué de sens pratique, rêveur et gobeur, inapte aux affaires jusqu'à ignorer, bien que licencié en droit, la nature d'une lettre de change et d'un billet à ordre ... Auriez-vous cent sous à me prêter?" Brulat, *Le Nouveau Candide*, 78–9. Unbracketed ellipsis is original.
9 Many works exist under this title, including collections by Jerome and Petrarch. The first known example, by Cornelius Nepos (c. 100–24 BC) is lost but is referenced by Aulus Gellius (c.125–c.180 AD).
10 Historians note that the *baccalauréat classique* continued to enjoy important symbolic privilege over the programs that did not include Latin or Greek well after 1902. See Hanna, *The Mobilization of Intellect*, 173.
11 The Commission, chaired by Alexandre Ribot, began its work in 1899. See Ringer, *Fields of Knowledge*, 122–6, as well as Surkis, *Sexing the Citizen*, 105n3, and Guiney, *Teaching the Cult of Literature in the French Third Republic*, 175. Ringer points out that the 1902 decree was "largely written by Ribot himself." Ibid., 125.
12 Michel Bréal, for instance, introduces an 1872 essay with a reference to the recent defeat: "If we want to correct the flaws of our education system, now is the time to set ourselves to work. History has shown that in the aftermath of great wars ... especially those that ended badly, the public's attention turns to education. We can use our adversaries as a model." ("Si nous voulons

remédier aux défauts de notre enseignement, c'est maintenant qu'il faut nous mettre à l'œuvre. L'histoire nous montre qu'après les grandes guerres ... malheureuses surtout, l'attention publique se tourne vers l'éducation. Nous pouvons prendre modèle sur nos adversaires.") *Quelques mots sur l'instruction publique en France*, 2. Bréal, a distinguished philologist, held a chair in comparative grammar at the Collège de France.

13 See Ozouf, *L'École, l'Église et la République, 1871–1914*, 22–5, as well as Prost, *Histoire de l'enseignement en France 1800–1967*, 184. Jules Simon, in 1874, cites these arguments to justify the greater importance of geography and modern languages in his new curriculum. *La Réforme de l'enseignement secondaire*, 306.

14 "notre enseignement supérieur ne tend à rien autre chose qu'à former un peuple de dilettantes et de beaux-esprits, d'avocats diserts, de penseurs de salon et d'écrivains agréables ... De là viennent cette légèreté et cette imprudence pratique qui nous ont précipités dans de si terribles désastres." Paul Leroy-Beaulieu, *Le Journal des débats*, 16 November 1871. Cited in Ozouf, *L'École, l'Église et la République*, 25.

15 These reforms have been the focus of much scholarly work; a selected bibliography is provided by Judith Surkis in *Sexing the Citizen*, 75–6n7.

16 For a contemporaneous account of this surprising stability, see Bréal, *Quelques mots sur l'instruction publique en France* (1872), 152–7. The historian André Chervel describes this continuity in terms of disciplinarity: "As had been the case in the *collèges* of the Ancien Régime, secondary education until 1880 is limited to a single discipline in the strong sense of the term: the reading and imitation of classical authors, especially Latin." *Les Auteurs français, latins et grecs au programme de l'enseignement secondaire, de 1800 à nos jours*, 3.

17 See Cibois, "La Question du latin," 7–28, especially 11–15.

18 By contrast, the figure of the governess in Victorian literature – typically "born and bred in comfort and gentility," but forced to seek employment due to familial misfortune – is an example of status incongruence due to downward mobility. See Peterson, "The Victorian Governess."

19 Brulat, *Le Nouveau Candide*, 78–9. Fritz Ringer describes this as the "widespread French conservative view" of *déclassés* as "misguided students ... who tried to rise too fast, by means of a general and literary education, when they should have been content with a more modestly 'practical' training." *Fields of Knowledge*, 135.

20 Jules Ferry makes this promise explicit in an address to teachers at the *Congrès pédagogique* of 1880: "you have earned the right to bourgeois status in our great University of France" ("vous est reconnu le droit de bourgeoisie dans cette grande Université de France"). Cited in Ozouf, *L'École, l'Église et la République*, 133.

21 On representations of the schoolteacher, François Jacquet-Francillon writes: "A narrative schema of misery traverses the whole [nineteenth] century, and anchors itself ... in the novel between 1880 and 1914." *Instituteurs avant la République*, 18. See also Tison, "Figures de maîtres," in *Le Roman de l'école au XIXe siècle*, 11–62.

22 "La Comédie pastorale"; "Les Aventures d'un papillon bleu." Alphonse Daudet, *Le Petit Chose* [1868], in *Œuvres*, 1:150.

23 "le vrai soutien de famille"; "Après tant d'avatars, d'efforts stériles en littérature, en médecine, en politique ... j'ai pensé qu'au moins je serais bon à quelque chose." Alphonse Daudet, *Soutien de famille*, 436, 441.

24 "mes garçons sauront le latin." The father's determination, as he pleads with the director of the *lycée*, is presented as borne of unmistakable class envy: "Ah! Monsieur, when I was a boy, I used to stand by the gates of Charlemagne with envy, as I looked at those sons of rich families who entered there to study. How I suffered from my ignorance! But I consoled myself by saying: my sons will learn what I did not." ("Ah! Monsieur, moi qui, tout gamin, m'arrêtais devant la grille de Charlemagne avec envie, à regarder ces enfants de riches qui entraient là pour apprendre, moi qui ai tant souffert de mon ignorance et dont c'était la gloire de me dire: mes garçons seront savants.") Ibid., 6.

25 "je vous en prie, que mon enfant ne sache pas le latin, qu'il ne fasse pas d'études classiques. En demandant le contraire pour son fils, mon père m'a porté malheur." Ibid., 445.

26 Ringer states that "even a summary review of the literature on the 'intellectual proletariat' in France around the turn of the century must ... include a brief reference to Bourget's *Le Disciple*, along with somewhat fuller discussions of Barrès' *Les Déracinés* and of [Henry] Bérenger's tracts." *Fields of Knowledge*, 128.

27 *Sexing the Citizen*, 104–14. On Bérenger, who was invited to deliver testimony as an expert on the "intellectual proletariat" by the Ribot commission, see Ringer, *Fields of Knowledge*, 137–40, as well as Surkis, *Sexing the Citizen*, 106–7.

28 Ringer, *Fields of Knowledge*, 90; Surkis, *Sexing the Citizen*, 75.

29 The phrase was made famous by Raoul Frary's polemical essay *La Question du latin* (1885).

30 Bourget, preface to *Pages de critique et de doctrine* (1912), 1:v; Barrès, "La Leçon d'un insurgé," *Le Voltaire*, 11 June 1886.

31 Regarding these portrayals, Jean-François Massol observes that "*L'Insurgé* can be interpreted as a warning" that Ferry and Simon "are nothing but bourgeois politicians." *De l'institution scolaire de la littérature française: 1870–1925*, 172–3. Roger Bellet suggests that Vallès's profound antipathy for the likes of Ferry and Simon, whom he viewed as bourgeois political

opportunists rather that true republicans, may have driven him to embrace the revolt of the Commune. "L'image de l'école chez Jules Vallès," 52.

32 "Contemporary readers were quick to understand that Vallès's critique was aimed as much at the ideology of the new republican education reforms as at the pedagogy of former regimes," writes Gilbert D. Chaitin. "The Thesis Novel as a Weapon in the Education Wars of the Third Republic," 32–3. See also Massol, *De l'institution scolaire de la littérature française*, 162.

33 See Ozouf, *L'École, l'Église et la République*, 55–102.

34 Séverine (pseud. of Caroline Rémy, 1855–1929), a journalist and feminist polemicist, was Vallès's collaborator from 1879 to his death.

35 See for instance Alexandre Vessiot's response, *La Question du latin de M. Frary et les professions libérales* (1886). According to Judith Surkis, "A veritable tidal wave of works in the late 1880s and 1890s by figures inside and outside the academy debated the past and future of French secondary education." *Sexing the Citizen*, 75.

36 "Nous venons de la campagne. Mon père est un fils de paysan qui a eu de l'orgueil et a voulu que son fils étudiât pour être prêtre. On a mis ce fils chez un oncle curé pour apprendre le latin, puis on l'a envoyé au séminaire. Mon père ... n'y est pas resté, a voulu être bachelier, arriver aux honneurs ... il rentre, le soir, pour faire la cour à une paysanne qui sera ma mère ... Je suis le premier enfant de cette union bénie. Je viens au monde dans un vieux lit de bois qui a des punaises de village et des puces de séminaire." Vallès, *L'Enfant* [1878–9], in *Œuvres*, 2:144–5. Page references in subsequent notes are to this edition.

37 "J'aime mieux faire des paquets de foin que lire ma grammaire [latine]." Ibid., 2:178.

38 As discussed in chapter 1, Vallès's "Lettre de Junius" from 7 November 1861 describes his uncle (a clear stand-in for his father) as "a cold man, thin-lipped, whose hard gaze made me shiver. He was a victim of the book ... He wanted to be the *paterfamilias* of Antiquity ... to be feared, to appear severe." ("un homme froid, aux lèvres minces, à l'œil dur, dont le regard me faisait frémir. C'était une victime du livre ... Il voulait être le *pater familias* antique ... Il désirait être craint, paraître austère.") *Œuvres*, 1:133.

39 "C'est plus fort que moi! Ce professorat a fait de moi une vieille bête qui a besoin d'avoir l'air méchant, et qui le devient, à force de faire le croquemitaine ... *On veut avoir l'air romain*, on est cruel." Ibid., 2:387. The passage in italics appears in the 1878 serial but was removed by Vallès for the book edition of 1879 (see *Œuvres* 2:1600, note 387). On the excision of references to classical antiquity in *L'Enfant* and *Le Bachelier*, see pages 108–9.

40 "voilà le petit Chose qu'on fouette." Ibid., 1:141.

41 "A hundred years ago, Mercier published the book that would become a companion, as a work of action, to the *Encyclopédie* ... today ... the

Tableau de Paris needs to be redone!" ("Il y a juste un siècle que Mercier publia le livre qui fit pendant, comme œuvre d'action, à l'Encyclopédie ... aujourd'hui ... Le *Tableau de Paris* est à refaire!") Vallès, "Le Tableau de Paris" (*Gil Blas*, 26 January 1882), in *Œuvres*, 2:762–3.

42 "Aujourd'hui le petit bourgeois (qui ne sait pas lire) veut faire absolument de son fils un latiniste. Il dit ... à tous ses voisins auxquels il communique son sot projet: Oh! le latin conduit à tout; mon fils saura le latin. C'est un très-grand mal. L'enfant va au collège, où il n'apprend rien: sorti du collège, c'est un fainéant qui dédaigne tout travail manuel ... et méprise l'état de son père ... Cependant il faut qu'il vive; quel état va-t-on lui faire prendre? À quoi est-il propre? Son père n'a point de fortune: on le lance dans l'étude poudreuse d'un procureur ou d'un notaire, & puis voilà mon jeune homme qui postule une place de clerc, de commis, d'homme d'affaires: le plus souvent il ne l'obtient pas. Oh! le latin conduit à tout. N'est-il pas ridicule et déplorable de voir des boutiquiers, des artisans, des domestiques même, vouloir élever leurs enfants ainsi que font les premiers citoyens, se repaître d'une profession imaginaire pour leurs descendants, et répéter imbécilement d'après le régent de sixième: Oh! le latin conduit à tout." Mercier, "Latiniste," in *Tableau de Paris* [1781–8], 1:1146–8.

43 "L'imprimeur m'a répondu: 'Il fallait venir à douze ans. – Mais à douze ans, j'étais au bagne du collège! Je tournais la roue du latin. – Encore une raison pour que je ne vous prenne pas! Par ces temps de révolution, nous n'aimons pas les déclassés qui sautent du collège dans l'atelier. Ils gâtent les autres.'" Vallès, *Le Bachelier* [1879–81], in *Œuvres*, 2:470. Page references in subsequent notes are to this edition.

44 See introduction, pages 7–8.

45 For instance, after the success of *L'Onanisme* in 1760, Tissot published a treatise on *De la santé des gens de lettres* in 1767, translated as *An Essay on Diseases Incident to Literary and Sedentary Persons* in 1769.

46 "marchand de langues mortes." *Œuvres*, 2:448.

47 A typical statement, which would not be out of place in *Le Bachelier*, is found in Paul Margueritte's *Les Jours s'allongent* ("The days grow longer," 1908): "Nothing – given my oldfangled education, my incomplete instruction, my burden of Greek and Latin humanities, my distance from the hard sciences – prepared me to enter a society where, without money, it is a struggle to even live, and where merit is only rewarded at the cost of great determination and effort, when it is rewarded at all." ("Rien dans mon éducation convenue, mon instruction incomplète, dans cette surcharge d'humanités grecques et latines, dans mon éloignement des sciences exactes, ne me préparait à entrer dans une société où, faute d'argent, on doit lutter pour vivre, et où le mérite ne s'impose, quand il s'impose, qu'à force de volonté et de labeur.") *Les Jours s'allongent*, 158.

48 “la clé qui ouvre toutes les portes!” Faure’s narrator deploys many of the arguments commonly made against the institutions of secondary education: “Torn in childhood from his natural environment, the family, he had endured the distorting cerebral influence of the *lycée*. Isn’t the boarding school, as it exists in France, the great producer of men gone astray, of *déclassés*, in a word of the intellectual proletariat?” (“Arraché, depuis son enfance, à son milieu normal, la famille, il avait subi l’influence cérébrale déformante du lycée d’internes. L’internat n’est-il pas, tel qu’il se pratique en France, la grande cause productrice, de dévoyés, de déclassés, en un mot de prolétaires intellectuels?”) Faure, *La Clé des carrières*, 52.

49 “et l’allemand? – Non, Monsieur. – L’espagnol? – Pas davantage! Vous savez, au lycée ... – Oui, le grec et le latin. Malheureusement, nous n’entretenons aucunes relations avec Thémistocle et Brutus.” Jourdain, *L’Atelier Chantorel*, 49. Original ellipsis. In one of the last scenes of this novel, the protagonist recognizes himself when he reads Vallès’s *L’Enfant*: “its bitter sarcasm and laughter full of pain expressed, with such power! his own grievances against society” (“l’amer sarcasme et le rire douloureux exprimaient, et avec quelle puissance! ses propres rancunes contre la Société”). Ibid., 320.

50 “‘Que savez-vous faire?’ [...]

‘Je suis bachelier.’

M. Bonardel répète sa question plus haut; il croit sans doute que je suis sourd.

‘Que-sa-vez-vous-fai-re?’

Je tortille mon chapeau, je cherche ... M. Bonardel attend un moment, me donne deux minutes. Les deux minutes passées, il étend la main vers un cordon de sonnette et tire.

‘Reconduisez monsieur.’ [...]

CE-QUE-JE-SAIS-FAIRE????

J’ai encore cherché toute la nuit, je n’ai rien trouvé.” *Œuvres*, 2:675. Unbracketed ellipsis is original.

51 The scene finds a current-day echo in Jorge Cham’s *PhD Comics*, for instance in two strips where Mike Slackenerny visits the campus career centre, only to be told that as a PhD holder he has no “skills that could be useful in a ‘real’ job” save for typewriting. *Piled Higher and Deeper* 910 and 911.

52 “Les collèges ... indiscrètement ouverts à tout le monde, ne font que verser sur le pavé de Paris une multitude d’inutiles sujets qui, avec une éducation ébauchée, vont corrompre tous les états où ils se glissent. Ce fléau s’étend et se propage, et menace la société d’un déluge de fainéants et d’oisifs. ... il serait temps de fermer ces collèges, si le gouvernement ne veut pas que la prochaine génération des Parisiens ne soit composée que de parleurs, de libertins, de demi-docteurs, et de toute cette race qui va achever de ruiner la fortune paternelle en vaquant toute l’année dans les spectacles, dans les cafés

et dans les mauvais lieux. ... Il faudrait qu'il fût enjoint au petit bourgeois de donner un métier à ses enfants, au lieu de les envoyer sur les bancs de ces classes ... La gangrène augmente dans la petite bourgeoisie; le mal presse, et il est temps que l'on y porte remède sérieusement." *Tableau de Paris*, 1148–9.

53 On this commission and debates about the "intellectual proletariat" in fin-de-siècle France, see Ringer, *Fields of Knowledge*, 127–40, as well as Surkis, *Sexing the Citizen*, 85–90 and 96–103.

54 "l'invasion de plus en plus menaçante de ces bacheliers"; "L'enseignement classique ne prépare les jeunes Français à aucune profession productive ... il les déclasse ... en les lançant dans le monde avec un diplôme dans la poche, du latin dans la tête et rien de plus pour vivre. Le Gouvernement ... fait tort à la société en poussant aux carrières improductives une foule toujours plus nombreuse de Français qui auraient pu se rendre utiles ... si on leur avait donné une éducation moins littéraire." Frary, *La Question du latin*, 73–6.

55 Roger Bellet analyses a similar contrast in Vallès's early journalism: to his loathed Latin schoolbooks, Vallès opposes "blue books" (seafaring adventure novels), "black books" (novels by the likes of Walter Scott or Balzac) and "red books" (militant histories of the Revolution). *Jules Vallès, journaliste*, 171–208.

56 On the importance of *Robinson Crusoe* in *L'Enfant*, see chapter 1, pages 43–5.

57 "Ce n'était plus du latin, cette fois. Ils disaient: nous avons faim! Nous voulons être libres! ... j'ai sauté d'un monde mort dans un monde vivant. – Cette histoire que je dévore, ce n'est pas l'histoire des dieux, des rois, des saints ... c'est l'histoire de Pierre et de Jean, de Mathurine et de Florimond, l'histoire de mon pays, l'histoire de mon village ... J'ai entendu parler du peuple et des citoyens, on disait *Liberté* et non pas *Libertas*." *Œuvres*, 2:363–7.

58 As Roger Bellet notes about the 1862 article "Les Victimes du Livre": "to counteract the Book, [Vallès] does not hold up facts, pure ideas, or nature, but more books, different books." *Jules Vallès, journaliste*, 175.

59 "I will always cover my innermost emotions with the mask of insouciance and the wig of irony" ("Je couvrirai éternellement mes émotions intimes du masque de l'insouciance et de la perruque de l'ironie"), Vallès writes elsewhere in *Le Bachelier. Œuvres*, 2:449.

60 "93, CE POINT CULMINANT DE L'HISTOIRE; LA CONVENTION, CETTE ILIADE; NOS PÈRES, CES GÉANTS." Ibid., 2:481. Vallès's emphasis.

61 "Les Tombes révolutionnaires." Ibid., 2:510.

62 "Je répétais toujours la même chose, et toujours en appelant les morts ... Et j'avais mis du latin ... Sparte, Rome, Athènes ... J'en plaisantais au collège et je trouvais que c'était inutile, bête, les républiques anciennes, grecques, romaines! ... Je vois à quoi cela sert maintenant. On ne peut écrire pour les journaux républicains sans connaître à fond son Plutarque." Ibid., 2:511.

63 "Est-ce qu'il y a une seule page ... de nos écrivains jacobins, où il ne soit pas question d'Annibal, de Fabricius, d'Aristogiton ... On ne peut pas s'en passer. Ce serait une impolitesse à faire aux hommes de 93 que de ne pas leur dire qu'ils ressemblent aux grands hommes de nos livres de classe." Ibid.

64 "Il est sûr qu'on rapporte de l'étude de la langue latine un certain goût pour les républiques, et qu'on voudrait pouvoir ressusciter celle dont on lit la grande et vaste histoire ... en entendant parler du sénat, de la liberté, de la majesté du peuple romain, de ses victoires, de la juste mort de César ... C'est cependant dans une monarchie que l'on entretient perpétuellement les jeunes gens de ces idées étrangères." Mercier, "Collèges, etc.," in *Tableau de Paris*, 207–8.

65 "Notre révolution a été produite en partie par des gens de lettres qui, plus habitants de Rome et d'Athènes que de leur propre pays, ont cherché à ramener dans l'Europe les mœurs antiques." Chateaubriand, *Essai historique, politique et moral sur les révolutions anciennes et modernes considérées dans leurs rapports avec la Révolution française* [1797]. Cited in Hartog, "La Révolution française et l'Antiquité," 30.

66 "les doctrines subversives auxquelles on a donné le nom de socialisme ou communisme sont le fruit de l'enseignement classique, qu'il soit distribué par le Clergé ou l'Université ... est-il permis de douter que cet enseignement n'y ait mêlé [à l'opinion publique] une foule d'idées fausses, de sentiments brutaux, d'utopies subversives, d'expérimentations fatales?" Frédéric Bastiat, *Baccalauréat et socialisme*, 12, 48.

67 More recent scholarship tends to agree with this position: citing Claude Mossé (*L'Antiquité dans la Révolution française*, 1989), Philippe Cibois states that "the use of the [classical] tradition during the Revolution ... is above all a matter of rhetoric" ("La Question du latin," 10).

68 "Ce sont ces livres classiques si vantés, ces poètes, ces orateurs, ces historiens, qui, mis sans discernement aux mains de la jeunesse ... qui, leur offrant pour modèles certains hommes, certaines actions, l'ont enflammée du désir si naturel de l'imitation ... qui, étant également au-dessus de sa conception, n'ont servi qu'à l'affecter du sentiment aveugle appelé enthousiasme." Volney, *Leçons d'histoire* [1795], cited in Hartog, "La Révolution française et l'Antiquité," 32.

69 Victor de Laprade writes in 1869: "The young man does not attend the *collège* to acquire concrete knowledge, but in order to learn how to study ... Study, in a word, must at a young age be a sort of gymnastics, practised to develop strength and health, whatever application these capacities will later be directed toward." ("L'enfant est au collège moins pour acquérir des connaissances positives que pour apprendre à étudier ... L'étude, en un mot, doit être au premier âge comme une sorte de gymnastique destinée à accroître les forces et la santé, quelque soit l'application que ces forces doivent recevoir ensuite.")

Le Baccalauréat et les études classiques, 63–4. Laprade had advocated for physical education in *L'Éducation homicide: Plaidoyer pour l'enfance* (1868).

70 "Does physical gymnastics cause an aversion for athletic exercise?," asks Frary, explicitly targeting Laprade. ("Est-ce que la gymnastique du corps nous donne le dégoût des exercices athlétiques?") *La Question du latin* (1885), 116.

71 Frary asks, "Is it true that keeping company with Greeks and Romans is particularly suitable to shaping men and citizens?" and goes on to answer in the negative, citing revolutionaries' imperfect knowledge of ancient texts as well as classical authors' numerous moral flaws. ("Est-ce vrai que la fréquentation des Grecs et des Romains soit particulièrement propre à former des hommes et des citoyens?") *La Question du latin*, 131–46.

72 "Des jeunes gens âgés de seize ans s'habituent à regarder le sujet comme une chose accessoire et à faire passer le mérite littéraire avant le fond des idées ... [Q]uand la jeunesse de tout un pays est élevée dans la préoccupation exclusive de la forme, il y a danger pour l'esprit et pour le sens moral de la nation." Bréal, *Quelques mots sur l'instruction publique en France* (1872), 275.

73 As Corinne Saminadayar-Perrin notes about a speech given by Jacques during *Le Bachelier*'s description of the turbulent events of 1851: "with biting irony, Vallès shows how a few crumbs of Antiquity and 1793 stir up immediate enthusiasm, even though they are assembled in an incoherent and nearly surrealist manner." *Modernités à l'antique*, 244.

74 "belle et triste victime de l'Antiquité ... mon éloge la rapproche plus d'Emma Bovary ... un dur Spartiate ou un vieux Romain." Vallès, "Les Livres nouveaux" [*Le Progrès de Lyon*, 29 August and 6 September 1864], in *Œuvres* 1:371–85.

75 "le XVIIIe siècle républicain vise seulement à imiter l'Antiquité, et sacrifia à sa manie les idées et les hommes! Orateurs et proconsuls de cette époque tourmentée et sombre s'inspiraient de Plutarque et citaient Tacite, sans savoir que ce qui était pour Tacite et Plutarque la liberté n'était que l'égoïsme féroce de la patrie." Ibid., 1:380.

76 "Vous la croyez spontanée et libre cette femme, quand elle écrit ses confessions. Non, elle n'est qu'un élève faisant du zèle et c'est pour singer Rousseau qu'elle a ces audaces puériles. ... Cette préoccupation reparaît en maint endroit et se trahit d'une façon décisive et sûre ... Voilà l'écrivain jugé, *o imitatores, servus pecus*! Elle imite, voilà tout. Vous allez voir qu'il en sera de même en politique." Ibid., 1:374.

77 Book I, Epistle XIX, verse 19.

78 "vase non sacré.." These classical citations and tropes are signalled by Roger Bellet, editor of the Pléiade edition, in *Œuvres*, 1:373n1–2 and 374n1.

79 Many elements in *L'Enfant* recall Rousseau, including the mention of *Robinson Crusoe*, prescribed to the titular pupil in *Émile* (291).

80 "Quand elle oublie l'histoire et qu'elle redevient elle-même, c'est-à-dire naturelle et simple, alors on se sent pris d'attachement et presque d'admiration." Vallès, "Les Livres nouveaux" [1864], in *Œuvres*, 1:382.

81 "J'ai dit cela hier, je le dis aujourd'hui. Je le dirai demain. *Delenda Carthago*. La Carthage d'aujourd'hui, c'est cette cité de cuistres qui a pour forteresse la Sorbonne." Vallès, "Au travail!" [*Le Réveil*, 7 August 1882], in *Œuvres*, 2:818. The famous phrase "Carthage must fall" is attributed to Cato the Elder.

82 "Lui, dont le génie est fait de la meilleure Antiquité, s'est réjoui à la bafouer comme aucun." Barrès, "La Leçon d'un insurgé."

83 "J'ai de l'éducation. 'Vous voilà armé pour la lutte – a fait mon professeur en me disant adieu. Qui triomphe au collège entre en vainqueur dans la carrière.' Quelle carrière? ... Entrer dans la carrière veut dire: s'avancer dans le chemin de la vie; se mettre, comme Hercule, dans le carrefour. *Comme Hercule dans le carrefour*. Je n'ai pas oublié ma mythologie. Allons! c'est déjà quelque chose." *Œuvres*, 2:447. Vallès's emphasis.

84 "the contradictory attitude of a writer who makes spontaneous use, with great effectiveness, of the arsenal of classical rhetoric, even as he proclaims his rejection of the rules of 'writing well,' with its stifling commonplaces and its empty tropes." *Modernités à l'antique*, 18.

85 Ibid., 300–1.

86 Ibid., 301.

87 *Rejet* a metric term for the displacement of a key word to the following verse – a form of enjambment. Like the English "reject," it also evokes detritus. Roger Bellet points out the many learned references and wilful inaccuracies that Vallès plays with in his description of Jacques's schoolwork. *Œuvres*, 1:1570–1.

88 "Je vole à droite, à gauche, je ramasse des *rejets* au coin des livres. Je suis même malhonnête quelquefois. J'ai besoin d'une épithète; peu m'importe de sacrifier la vérité! Je prends dans le dictionnaire le mot qui fait l'affaire, quand bien même il dirait le contraire de ce que je voulais dire." *Œuvres*, 2:320. Vallès's emphasis.

89 See chapter 1, pages 41–5.

90 "vous n'êtes au collège que pour ça, mâcher et remâcher ce qui a été mâché par les autres!" *Œuvres*, 2:321.

91 On this discovery, Gilbert D. Chaitin writes: "The implication is that the authority of the father and the state is not grounded in some transcendent extra-textual principle ... but in a series of textual copies whose never-ending play of imitations it stops arbitrarily." "The Thesis Novel as a Weapon," 36.

92 Michel Bréal, for instance, writes that "Instead of saying that versification helps us to better understand poets, we would be closer to the truth, if we admitted that we read poets to help us with versification ... this reversal has more serious consequences than one might imagine. It prevents us from

reading poets the way they are meant to be read ... when they read Virgil or Lucan, [students] do little more than mentally compose a poetic dictionary for their personal use." ("Au lieu de dire que la versification nous sert à mieux comprendre les poètes, on serait plus près de la vérité, si l'on disait que la lecture des poètes sert à la versification ... ce renversement a plus de conséquences qu'on ne paraît le croire. Il empêche de lire les poètes dans l'esprit où ils doivent être lus ... en lisant Virgile ou Lucain, [les élèves] font-ils autre chose que de se composer mentalement un dictionnaire poétique pour leur usage personnel?") *Quelques mots sur l'instruction publique en France* (1872), 223.

93 "Est-ce bien l'imagination qu'on développe, en demandant aux jeunes gens des vers latins? N'est-ce pas plutôt la mémoire? Leurs vers sont-ils autre chose que des centons? Ce qu'ils appellent trouver une idée, n'est-ce pas plutôt trouver un hémistiche, et même le trouver tout à fait dans le *Gradus*? Et quelle est cette imagination, qui n'a rien de commun ni avec le goût, ni avec le bon sens, et qui consiste à faire de sang-froid le plus de vers possible sur un sujet donné, sans y mettre une idée ni un sentiment?" Simon, *La Réforme de l'enseignement secondaire* (1874), 319. A *centon* is a literary or musical piece composed of excerpts of other works.

94 "j'ai renfoncé en moi-même ma douleur, j'ai essayé de la noyer dans l'idée d'un livre ... Je me suis heurté contre les stupidités de la *bachellerie* qui m'a laissé la tête gonflée de grec ... Avant d'écrire un livre comme on charge une pièce, il faut avoir jeté au vent le bagage qui gène ... Mon livre est dans mon cœur et point sur le papier. À quoi bon! Je ne connais pas de champ de roseaux auxquels je puisse crier mes fureurs!" *Œuvres*, 2:1713n618a. Vallès's emphasis.

95 "Il faut être soi, jeter au loin les livres." Vallès, "Les Livres nouveaux" [1864], in *Œuvres*, 1:385.

96 *Metamorphoses*, Book XI. The reference is signalled by Roger Bellet in *Œuvres* 2:1713n618 (2).

97 Raymond Trousson explains: "Between 1878 and 1912, a movement for the recuperation of Rousseau as a great national writer gained pace ... Rousseau was slowly integrated into the institutional discourse of the Third Republic, and appropriated by the dominant ideology." *Défenseurs et adversaires de J.-J. Rousseau, d'Isabelle de Charrière à Charles Maurras*, 301. See also Goulemot and Walter, "Les Centenaires de Voltaire et de Rousseau," 1:381–420.

98 "à l'auteur d'*Émile* et du *Contrat social.*" John Grand-Carteret, "La Statue de Rousseau à Paris," in *J.-J. Rousseau jugé par les Français d'aujourd'hui*, 522–3.

99 "Tous nos programmes d'enseignement, d'éducation, se trouvent énoncés dans l'*Émile.*" Ibid., vii.

100 Rousseau writes, anticipating Mercier's critique of the social-climbing aspirations of the working and petit-bourgeois classes through education: "The poor man has no need for education ... it is less reasonable to raise a poor

man to be rich than to raise a rich man as if he were going to be poor, since ruined men are more numerous than successful upstarts." ("Le pauvre n'a pas besoin d'éducation ... il est moins raisonnable d'élever un pauvre pour être riche qu'un riche pour être pauvre; car à proportion du nombre des états il y a plus de ruinés que de parvenus.") *Émile ou De l'éducation* [1762], 103. Page references in subsequent notes are to this edition.

101 On this topic, see Thiéry, *Rousseau, l'Émile et la Révolution*, and Py, *Rousseau et les éducateurs*.

102 Michel Bréal writes, in 1872: "it is in Germany that, in the late eighteenth century, Rousseau's ideas on education, those 'winged seeds' as Jean Paul described them, found the terrain where they took root and bore fruit ... Twenty years after Rousseau laid down in his *Émile* the principle that the child should be made to discover everything by himself (a principle that, as we have seen, become the soul of German education), the University of Paris ... had made itself the imitator of the clergymen it had succeeded. Later, we, the University of France, in turn adopted, spread widely, and imposed those same methods on young people." ("c'est en Allemagne qu'à la fin du dix-huitième siècle, les idées de Rousseau sur l'éducation, ces 'semences ailées' dont parle Jean Paul, ont trouvé le terrain où elles ont germé et porté leurs fruits ... Vingt ans après que Rousseau eut posé ce principe dans son Émile qu'il fallait obliger l'enfant à trouver tout par lui-même [principe qui, nous l'avons vu, est devenu l'âme de l'éducation allemande], l'Université de Paris ... s'était faite l'imitatrice des Pères dont elle avait recueilli la succession. Et nous, Université de France, à notre tour, nous avons adopté, répandu à profusion, imposé à la jeunesse les mêmes méthodes.") *Quelques mots sur l'instruction publique en France*, 9, 172.

103 Jean-François Massol, for instance, observes that "mistrust and the obsession of the past always win out: Vallès only seems able to propose a critical view of any educational system." *De l'institution scolaire de la littérature française*, 178.

104 "Avec un système d'éducation rajeunie et toute pleine de modernité, on apprendrait sans effort, au fur et à mesure de la marche dans la vie, les sciences ... Il n'y aurait qu'à lâcher dans la campagne, les jardins, dans les forges, ou les hôpitaux tous ces enfants qu'on enferme en tête-à-tête avec des livres qui ne parlent que de morts, sous le toit de maisons tristes et malsaines." Vallès, "Au travail!" [*Le Réveil*, 7 August 1882], in *Œuvres*, 2:817–18.

105 "la lecture est le fléau de l'enfance"; "J'ai donc refermé tous les livres. Il en est un seul ouvert à mes yeux, c'est celui de la nature." Rousseau, *Émile ou De l'éducation*, 193, 460, 306, 312. The question of the narrative voice in *Émile* is notoriously complex: the treatise is written in the first person by a voice that shifts between the roles of essayist, narrator, and preceptor to Émile within the narrative (the latter named "Jean-Jacques"). For the sake of efficiency, I refer to Rousseau as the author of the work.

106 "L'usage familier de ces langues étant perdu depuis longtemps, on se contente d'imiter ce qu'on trouve écrit dans les livres, et l'on appelle cela les parler. Si tel est le Grec et le Latin des maîtres, qu'on juge celui des enfants! À peine ont-ils appris par cœur leur rudiment, auquel ils n'entendent absolument rien, qu'on leur apprend ... à coudre en prose des phrases de Cicéron et en vers des centons de Virgile." Ibid., 183.

107 "One must learn Latin to know French," Rousseau writes, leaving unexamined a commonplace of seventeenth and eighteenth-century defences of Latin. ("Il faut apprendre le latin pour savoir le français.") Ibid., 511–12.

108 For an insightful analysis of the role of Fénelon's novel in *Émile*, see Brown, "The Constraints of Liberty at the Scene of Instruction," 288–313, in particular 297–304.

109 "je me suis égaré moi-même." *Émile*, 599.

110 "Il ne rit jamais, ce Rousseau, il est pincé, pleurard; il fait des phrases qui n'ont pas l'air de venir de son cœur; il s'adresse aux Romains, comme au collège nous nous adressions à eux dans nos devoirs ... Il sent le collège à plein nez." *Œuvres*, 2:482. Vallès's ellipsis.

111 Frédéric Bastiat writes, "Read the speeches made at the Legislative Assembly and the National Convention. It is the language of Rousseau and [the Abbé] Mably. Nothing but prosopopoeiae, invocations, apostrophes to Fabricius, Cato or the two Brutus's." ("Qu'on lise les discours prononcés à l'Assemblée législative et à la Convention. C'est la langue de Rousseau et de Mably. Ce ne sont que prosopopées, invocations, apostrophes à Fabricius, à Caton, aux deux Brutus.") *Baccalauréat et socialisme* (1850), 48.

112 "J'entendis le brave serviteur dire à grand-père: – S'il savait lire, cela l'occuperait, le distrairait, l'intéresserait ...

Il n'eut pas le temps d'achever, grand-père le foudroya d'un regard impérieux: – Tais-toi, dit-il d'une voix sévère, tais-toi, m'entends-tu? Lire? ... Je ne veux pas qu'il sache lire ... Cela le rendrait malheureux, comme moi, comme les autres hommes ... [...] je demandai naïvement à mon grand-père si lire était un jeu. – Non, mon enfant, dit tristement grand-père. Ce sont les hommes qui ont inventé cela, et c'est surtout parce qu'ils savent lire qu'ils sont vicieux et méchants. – Alors, dis-je, je ne veux pas savoir lire." L. Achille, *Âme neuve*, 13–14. Unbracketed ellipses are original.

113 "Yves? Le plus beau type d'adolescent qu'une femme puisse rêver! Cet air martial, cette taille, ces muscles." Ibid., 26.

114 In *Émile et Sophie ou les Solitaires* (1781, posth.), Rousseau's unfinished sequel to *Émile*, things take a similar turn for the worse when the tutor leaves the newly married couple, after they have been raised on Rousseauian principles, to face the world on their own. See Brown, "The Constraints of Liberty," 304–9.

115 "le bagage qui gène." Manuscript of *Le Bachelier*, in *Œuvres*, 2:1713n618a.

4. Bourget, the Chambige Affair, and the Queer Seductions of the Novel

1 "Vous croyiez entendre un soupir, c'est une citation, – serrer une femme sur votre cœur, c'est un volume." Bourget, *Physiologie de l'amour moderne*, 140.

2 Albert Bataille, "Une cause célèbre: L'affaire Chambige." *Le Figaro*, 2, 3, and 4 November 1888. These articles, as well as Bataille's reports from the trial which took place from 8 to 11 November, are reprinted with slight modifications in Bataille, *Causes criminelles et mondaines de 1888*. For a summary of accounts of the Chambige affair across the French and European press, see Angenot, "On est toujours le disciple de quelqu'un."

3 "la littérature dite décadente." France, "Un crime littéraire: l'affaire Chambige."

4 For an overview of the debate and the novels inspired by the affair, see Ginn, "'Il a vu les choses de trop haut': Henri Chambige and His Literary Destiny."

5 A reappraisal of Bourget's work is proposed in Fougère and Daniel, *Avez-vous lu Paul Bourget?* Out of print in France between the 1960s and the mid-1990s, *Le Disciple* was re-edited in the widely available *Livre de poche* series in 2010, with a preface and notes by Antoine Compagnon.

6 Bataille, "Une cause célèbre," 2 November 1888, 3.

7 Charles F. Gill, "Plea of justification filed by the defendant in Regina (Wilde) v. Queensberry" [1895], reproduced in Holland, *Irish Peacock and Scarlet Marquess*, 290.

8 Sherard, *The Life of Oscar Wilde*, 242. Cited in Ellmann, *Oscar Wilde*, 228, and Mansuy, *Un moderne: Paul Bourget de l'enfance au Disciple*, 280n73 and 382. Ian D. MacFarlane provides a few additional details (based on interviews with Bourget's brother-in-law, Albert Feuillerat) in *Paul Bourget et l'Angleterre*, 73–4.

9 "Il se fit des hommes et de la société des idées romanesques et fausses dont tant d'expériences funestes n'ont jamais pu le guérir"; "Les femmes aiment la peine, pourvu qu'elle soit bien romanesque." www.littre.org.

10 In *Le Figaro* of 12–13 May 1891 (a few years after the Chambige affair), Marcel Prévost published an article stating that *antiromanesque* literary schools were now dominant. This lead *Le Gaulois* to invite thirty-seven contemporary writers, including Zola, Daudet, and Huysmans, to share their thoughts on the question in a series that ran from 14 to 25 May 1891. See Seillan, "Ce qu'on appelait romanesque en 1891," in *Enquête sur le roman romanesque: Le Gaulois, 1891*, 139–78.

11 "le premier caractère du roman naturaliste, dont *Madame Bovary* est le type, est la reproduction exacte de la vie, l'absence de tout romanesque." Zola, "Gustave Flaubert et ses œuvres," in Zola, *Les Romanciers naturalistes*, 126.

12 On the "masculinization of the novel" in the mid-nineteenth century, see Cohen, *The Sentimental Education of the Novel*, notably 112–18.

13 See chapter 1, pages 49–51.

14 On Bourget's life leading up to 1889, see Mansuy, *Un moderne: Paul Bourget de l'enfance au Disciple*, including 440–1 on his friendship with Geneviève Straus. A number of objections and corrections to Mansuy's work are made by Raymond Pouillart in "Littérature et documents confidentiels."

15 Stendhal, *Le Rouge et le Noir* [1830] (Paris, Lemerre, 1886).

16 Chambige made his literary debut in 1887 with the article "Les Goncourt: Le modernisme," in *La Revue générale, littéraire, politique et artistique*. After his prison sentence, he published a memoir of the Greco-Turkish war of 1897 under the pseudonym Marcel Lami in 1899. Following his death in 1909, a few travel narratives and a novel were posthumously published under the same pen name.

17 "la plus pure, la plus naïve, la plus honnête des femmes ... elle était anti-romanesque et ignorait le mal. C'était une mère de famille et une épouse modèle"; "romanesque, d'un caractère sombre." [Anonymous], "Affaire Chambige – Assassinat – Tentative de suicide," 1097.

18 "mince ... il est pâle et paraît profondément triste." *Gazette des tribunaux*, 9 November 1888, 1084. "grand, fort ... la figure intelligente et sérieuse." Lèbre, "L'Affaire Chambige," 26.

19 "Nous avions les mêmes idées, les mêmes goûts pour les exercices du corps." *Gazette des tribunaux*, 12–13 November 1888, 1097. "la vie de braves gens, travaillant en commun, s'aimant et aimant leurs enfants ... Il m'avait intéressé vivement; c'était un faible et un maladif." *Revue des grands procès contemporains* 7 (1889), 27.

20 "En face de Grille, un hercule, elle m'a aimé, parce que j'étais *un faible très doux*." Albert Bataille, "Une cause célèbre: L'affaire Chambige," 3 November 1888, 3. Original emphasis.

21 "communauté de la douleur." Ibid., 2.

22 "cette manie inoffensive des hommes de science qui consiste à railler les poètes." Ibid., 2.

23 "le Julien Sorel de la brasserie." Henry Fouquier, "Femmes et criminels," 1. On Parisian *brasseries* (female-staffed beer halls) as frequently denounced spaces of moral and sexual corruption for young men in the late nineteenth century, see Tanner, "Turning Tricks, Turning the Tables."

24 In May 1826, Stendhal recommended the *Gazette des tribunaux* to readers of a British journal as "extremely entertaining" and offering "the most accurate pictures of French society." *The New Monthly Magazine and Literary Journal* 16 (1826): 510. The *Gazette des tribunaux* was founded in 1825. According to Sylvie Châles-Courtine, it played a "central role" in "staging and broadcasting criminal affairs" for a broad reading public in the nineteenth century. See "La place du corps dans la médiatisation des affaires criminelles," 179. It should be noted that Albert Bataille's articles in *Le Figaro* appear under a rubric similarly titled "La Gazette des tribunaux."

25 "mince et d'une complexion délicate ... une frêle constitution peu propice aux fatigues du corps, une intelligence supérieure à sa position, un goût manifesté de bonne heure pour les études élevées." [Anonymous], "Accusation d'assassinat, commis par un séminariste dans une église," 226.
26 "réputation intacte"; "âme perverse." *Gazette des tribunaux*, 28 December 1827, 226, and 31 December 1827, 238.
27 On the importance of term in Stendhal, see François Vanoosthuyse, "Romanesque et ironie chez Stendhal," in Seillan, *Enquête sur le roman romanesque*, 93–120.
28 "Le teint de ce petit paysan était si blanc, ses yeux si doux, que l'esprit un peu romanesque de madame de Rênal eut d'abord l'idée que ce pouvait être une jeune fille déguisée." Stendhal, *Le Rouge et le Noir* [1830], in *Œuvres romanesques complètes*, 1:372. Page references in subsequent notes are to this edition.
29 "l'extrême beauté de Julien"; "la forme féminine de ses traits"; "l'air mâle que l'on trouve communément nécessaire à la beauté d'un homme lui eût fait peur." Ibid., 1:375.
30 On my use of "denegation" for Freud's *Verneinung*, see introduction, note 76.
31 "elle regardait comme une exception, et même tout à fait contre nature, l'amour tel qu'elle l'avait trouvé dans le très petit nombre de romans que le hasard avait mis sous ses yeux. Grâce à cette ignorance, madame de Rênal, parfaitement heureuse, occupée sans cesse de Julien, était loin de se faire le plus petit reproche." *Le Rouge et le Noir*, 1:388.
32 "À Paris, la position de Julien envers madame de Rênal aurait vite été simplifiée; mais à Paris, l'amour est fils des romans. Le jeune précepteur et sa timide maîtresse auraient retrouvé dans trois ou quatre romans ... l'éclaircissement de leur position. Les romans leur auraient tracé le rôle à jouer, montré le modèle à imiter ... Dans une petite ville ... un jeune homme pauvre ... voit tous les jours une femme de trente ans sincèrement sage, occupée de ses enfants, et qui ne prend nullement dans les romans des exemples de conduite. Tout va lentement, tout se fait peu à peu dans les provinces, il y a plus de naturel." Ibid., 1:383.
33 For instance, Louvet de Couvray's *Les Amours du chevalier de Faublas* recounts the numerous seductive exploits of an often cross-dressed hero. *Faublas* and its sequels (1787–90) were an enduring publishing success, well into the nineteenth century. See Michel Delon, "Notice" to *Les Amours du chevalier de Faublas*, 1114. The novel is cited in the epigraph to chapter 5 of book 2 of *Le Rouge et le Noir*, in *Œuvres romanesques complètes* 1:586.
34 "son cœur palpitait"; "les livres les plus infâmes"; "Il faudrait spécifier que le domestique ne pourra prendre aucun roman. Une fois dans la maison, ces livres dangereux pourraient corrompre les filles de madame, et le domestique lui-même." Ibid., 1:385–6.

35 "il n'osait les ouvrir que de nuit. Souvent il eût été bien aise de n'être pas interrompu par une visite." Ibid., 1:433.

36 In the most recent Pléiade edition of Stendhal's works, Yves Ansel chides critics who, as early as the 1850s, presented *Le Rouge et le Noir* as a novelization of a famous affair, when in fact "*L'affaire Berthet* ... does not exist – in the *Gazette des tribunaux*, it is only one trial, one case among many others." What was a mere trial in 1827 became an "affair" only decades later, as readers revisited Berthet's story through the prism of *Le Rouge et le Noir. Œuvres romanesques complètes*, 1:1141.

37 "C'est Werther, c'est Antony, c'est Julien Sorel, c'est ... Raskolnikoff." Trarieux, "Affaire Chambige: Cour d'assises de Constantine," in *Cinq plaidoiries*, 170–1. *Antony* is an 1831 play by Alexandre Dumas; in the final act, a married woman begs her lover to kill her after they consummate their adulterous passion. The first French translation of Dostoyevsky's *Crime and Punishment* appeared in 1884.

38 "inventions romanesques et mensonges purs." *Cinq plaidoiries*, 148.

39 "un romancier pervers [qui] imagine toute une histoire calomnieuse sur les mobiles qui l'ont fait agir." Ibid., 82.

40 "dans tous nos sentiments, même dans celui de l'amour, ce sont des chimères que notre imagination poursuit." Ibid., 169.

41 "un comédien redoutable"; "hypocrite." Ibid., 93, 130.

42 "quant aux artifices de faux, ce n'est pas ce qui peut nous surprendre de la part d'un homme passé maître dans l'art de composer des romans"; "suggestion magnétique." Ibid., 139, 158. On the affair as a case of hypnotic suggestion, see Harris, *Murders and Madness*, 236–7 and 314–15.

43 "sinistre héros de roman"; "imagination dévoyée." *Cinq plaidoiries*, 93, 97.

44 "M. Martin Laya, intime de Chambige." Ibid., 99.

45 "Regardez ... au milieu du groupe d'artistes se dresse, dans une pose affectée et prétentieuse ... le personnage mis en scène sous le nom d'Yvon d'Or. Ce sont les traits, c'est la figure de Chambige." Ibid., 101.

46 On Ernest Biéler's work as an illustrator in this period, see Ruedin, "Ernest Biéler illustrateur des Goncourt dans la 'Collection Edouard Guillaume' à Paris (1880–1892)." In the lead-up to the 1888 trial, Biéler was interviewed after one of his drawings was found among Chambige's belongings. Biéler, *Ernest Biéler: sa vie, son œuvre*, 40.

47 "un scepticisme supérieur"; "j'ai le cœur vide, mon amie, je ne puis pas aimer"; "j'irai à l'échafaud, n'est-ce pas?" *Cinq plaidoiries*, 101, 104, 106.

48 "C'est Chambige lui-même." Ibid., 101.

49 "Il n'y a, dans tout ce hideux roman, qu'une monstrueuse aberration." Ibid., 130.

50 "Voilà son roman à lui, le roman où sa vanité s'est complue, où son égoïsme féroce a cherché son heure de joie. Malheureusement le roman est devenu de

l'histoire, et il en sort couvert d'un sang que toutes les larmes de son corps ne parviendraient pas à effacer." Ibid., 171.

51 "notre Yvon." Ibid., 102.

52 "cet Yvon, leur Yvon ... qui leur appartient à tous les deux." Ibid.

53 "idées romanesques," *Le Rouge et le Noir*, 1:492.

54 "son roman"; "mon roman est fini." Ibid., 1:414, 749.

55 "cette confession générale de sa vie." Bataille, "Une cause célèbre: l'Affaire Chambige," *Le Figaro*, 2 November 1888, 3. The term has strong literary associations, with Rousseau's *Confessions* (1782) but also Musset's *La Confession d'un enfant du siècle* (1836). In *Le Disciple*, the protagonist's long autobiographical letter is given the title "Confession of a contemporary young man" ("Confession d'un jeune homme d'aujourd'hui"). Bourget, *Le Disciple*, 121.

56 Jacqueline Carroy and Marc Renneville provide details about the composition of this narrative by Chambige and his lawyer's role in leaking it to the press in "Le crime de Chambige: entre psychologie et littérature," 197–8.

57 "je me précipitais dans les récits merveilleux avec une fougue véhémente"; "je passais des nuits à lire Hugo ... Je lus prodigieusement, les poètes surtout." Henri Chambige, cited in Albert Bataille, *Causes criminelles et mondaines de 1888*, 7.

58 "j'étais un être manqué, impuissant, une fin de famille! ... un pathologique, un cérébral." Ibid., 8–10.

59 "Ma pensée prenait un galop effréné. Je retrouvais dans les livres toutes les questions que, seul, j'avais agitées ... dans mon cerveau fumant et désordonné." Ibid., 10.

60 Eugénie de Guérin (1805–48) and her brother Maurice (1810–39) were minor Romantic poets. Maurice's death famously left Eugénie inconsolable.

61 *Causes criminelles et mondaines de 1888*, 11, 13, 17, 21.

62 "Chambige n'est pas une victime du livre ... Il n'est que sa propre victime ... C'est à tort qu'on attribue cette grande névrose aux études psychologiques admirables des descendants du grand Balzac. La grande névrose, c'est la névrose des ratés comme Henri Chambige; de ceux qui ont la fièvre de vivre et qui s'absorbent et s'aigrissent dans leur impuissance. S'il faut s'en prendre à certains livres de l'état d'esprit de l'accusé, il faut sortir de cette France où la jeunesse acclame encore la devise de Montaigne et de Molière: 'Haut et clair!'. Il faut porter les yeux vers les brouillards d'outre-Rhin." Cited in Bataille, *Causes criminelles et mondaines de 1888*, 68–9. Schopenhauer and Kant – respectively caricatured as perilously pessimistic and relativistic – are favourite targets of French critics in the 1880s. See Digeon, *La Crise allemande de la pensée française, 1870–1914*.

63 "devrait donner à réfléchir aux chefs d'une certaine école." *Cinq plaidoiries*, 95.

64 On the influence of Spencer's theory of "social Darwinism" in late nineteenth-century French novels including *Le Disciple*, see Lyle, "Le *Struggleforlife*."

65 "esprit nourri d'Herbert Spencer et des jeunes maîtres du roman contemporain." Bataille, *Causes criminelles et mondaines de 1888*, 5.

66 "descen[d] de Julien Sorel sur qui l'on se pâme, entre adeptes de l'amour moderne et de la cristallisation." Caliban (pseud. of Émile Bergerat), "La Rime en bige," 1. Stendhal famously developed a theory of "crystallization" in his essay *De l'amour* (1822).

67 "problème psychologique." Caliban, "La Rime en bige," 1.

68 "M. Paul Bourget publie *Physiologie de l'assassinat moderne*, avec lettre-préface de M. Henri Chambige." *L'Illustration*, 1 December 1888. Cited in Carroy and Renneville, "Une cause passionnelle passionnante."

69 See Mansuy, *Un moderne*, 482–3, and Feuillerat, *Paul Bourget*, 141.

70 "je suis comme stupéfié." Chambige, letter to Paul Bourget. Marc Angenot proposes that Bourget himself was likely behind this publication in a Brussels newspaper ("On est toujours le disciple de quelqu'un," 53). Publishing in Belgium is a time-honoured means of circumventing the French justice system while still reaching a readership in France.

71 "Bourget (huh!) will testify for you." ["Bourget (hein!) témoignera pour toi."] Letter from Léopold Martin-Laya to Henri Chambige, cited in *Gazette des tribunaux*, 15 November 1888, 1105. What the interjection implies is open to interpretation; it may simply mean "can you believe it?"

72 "Je le vois encore, ce jeune homme aux yeux brillants, à la physionomie si mobile, si intelligente, tel qu'il entrait dans mon cabinet de travail, il y a moins de deux ans. Il m'apportait des essais de critique, des fragments de nouvelles où se devinait l'espérance d'un beau talent." Bourget, preface to Bataille, *Causes criminelles et mondaines de 1888*, viii.

73 "Il est facile de rendre la littérature responsable de la maladie morale élaborée dans cette âme ... Ceux qui ont déclamé contre les écrivains particulièrement aimés du condamné de Constantine, auraient dû plutôt se demander si, depuis cinquante ans, il a été fait quoi que ce fût en France pour recréer à la jeunesse une vie morale, une atmosphère de volonté saine. Il est plus aisé de flétrir ceux qui précisément ont voué leur vie à montrer les plaies intellectuelles et sentimentales de la jeunesse contemporaine, en cherchant de leur mieux le remède." Ibid., ix–x.

74 Ibid., x. In *Le Rouge et le Noir*, the passage appears in a long parenthetical aside where the narrator playfully defends himself against those who would condemn his portrayal of the amorous Mathilde (1:670–1). The ironic tone of Stendhal's narrator is unmistakable: while ostensibly defending real-life aristocratic young women against the possibility of any comparison to Mathilde's passionate and compromising actions, he is in fact accusing them, through hyperbolic antiphrasis and double-edged compliments, of being materialistic, self-serving, and passionless. That Bourget would read and cite Stendhal at face value is symptomatic of a significant shift, from the

relationship of complicity with a sophisticated reader imagined by Stendhal – "to the happy few," reads the novel's famous dedication (1:805) – to the more pedagogical, if not pedantic, relationship between author and reader devised by Bourget – "To a young man," he titles the preface to *Le Disciple*.

75 "la littérature dite décadente"; "Tout est sujet de trouble aux insensés"; "une irrémédiable névrose"; "un attentat odieux à la majesté des lettres." France, "Un crime littéraire: L'Affaire Chambige," 2. France would comment further on the affair in the summer of 1889 when, following the publication of *Le Disciple*, he traded volleys with Ferdinand Brunetière, the conservative critic for the *Revue des Deux Mondes*. On their debate, see Foucaud, *L'Œuvre d'Anatole France*, section I.1.3.b.

76 "les Muses qu'il a trahies et compromises." France, "Un crime littéraire: L'Affaire Chambige," 2.

77 "parmi ses livres"; "à dix-huit ans, il était gorgé des plus audacieux paradoxes de la pensée humaine." Barrès, *Sous l'œil des Barbares* [1888], in *Romans et voyages*, 1:33.

78 "les traits principaux de l'âme contemporaine"; "a décrit et même créé quelques-unes des façons de sentir qu'on trouve en Chambige"; "la haute littérature de ce temps"; "force"; "Le Chambige que j'imagine n'eût pas permis à l'amour de le dominer. Cela est essentiel. Les meilleurs analystes ne s'autorisent pas à s'emballer. Ils se tiennent vigoureusement en main." Barrès, "La Sensibilité d'Henri Chambige," 1.

79 "Des indications essentielles." Ibid. On Barrès in the 1890s, see chapter 5; on *Le Culte du Moi* and self-control, see also chapter 1, pages 34–7.

80 Fesdis, "Le cas de Chambige." Jean Fesdis was a pseudonym of Paul Margueritte, the author of *Tous quatre* (1885) and *Les Jours s'allongent* (1908), which I discuss in chapter 1. In his memoir *Le Printemps tourmenté*, Margueritte describes how, years after the trial, Chambige and the prosecutor Jules Maillet both attended a gathering at his residence, and did not recognize each other (196–7).

81 "Plus encore que les femmes, j'aimais le mensonge." France, "Un crime littéraire: L'Affaire Chambige," 2. The sentence is syntactically ambiguous: while likely best translated as "I loved deceit, even more than women do," it allows a parallel reading as "I loved deceit more than I loved women."

82 "Celle que j'aime n'est pas si belle que je la vois. En croyant aimer une femme, je n'aime que l'erreur de mon propre esprit." Barrès, "La Sensibilité d'Henri Chambige," 1.

83 This article was commissioned by Alexandre Lacassagne, the director of the journal and one of the founding figures of French criminal anthropology. An early specialist of sexual "inversion," Lacassagne was the author of the entry on "Pédérastie" in the 1886 edition of the seminal *Dictionnaire encyclopédique des sciences médicales* (t.22, 239–59). See chapter 2, page 67n57.

84 Here Tarde inserts a footnote, where he cites Chambige's own written confession as reported by Bataille: "Is this not what he alludes to in his narrative, when he states that the 'melancholy crisis of puberty (in 1883–84), was in his case disproportionate and *almost* exclusively intellectual'?" ("N'est-ce pas à cela qu'il fait allusion dans ses notes, quand il dit que la 'crise mélancolique de la puberté [en 1883–84], fut pour lui hors de toute proportion et *presque* exclusivement intellectuelle'?") Tarde's emphasis. "L'Affaire Chambige," 96. The article is dated "décembre 1888."

85 "Voici un autre [événement] qui, dans l'histoire de son cœur, a pu avoir une importance aussi grande, si je suis bien renseigné. Mais j'ai besoin de quelques circonlocutions pour être bien exactement compris. On nous dit qu'à l'époque où il faisait sa seconde, c'est-à-dire, à l'âge des précoces pubertés, 'une de ces *liaisons* qui se font au collège entre camarades' parut modifier profondément son caractère. 'Il devenait rêveur, il correspondait journellement avec son ami, souvent en vers. Il paraissait prendre la chose très au sérieux et conserva cette intimité tant qu'il resta au collège.'" Ibid., 96. Tarde's emphasis.

86 "répugnants"; "aberrations"; "corruptions"; "dégénérescences monstrueuses." Ibid., 96–7.

87 "Je me souviens avoir vu, avec stupeur, de pareils attachements ... J'accuse ici l'internat qui rend à un certain point ces confusions du cœur presque inévitables"; "une des victimes les plus lamentables de l'internat." Ibid., 97.

88 "Rien de plus excusable, soit, mais rien de plus fâcheux que de débuter ainsi. Apprendre la musique sur un piano faux, avoir pour premier modèle de dessin des lithographies pleines de fautes d'anatomie, s'initier à la poésie par des vers boiteux et contrefaits, cela n'est pas plus propre à fausser l'oreille, l'œil et le goût que les *intimités* de pensionnaires à fausser le sentiment. En général, le mauvais pli donné de la sorte à la sensibilité s'efface, il est vrai; mais jamais tout à fait; il en reste le goût de l'anomalie." Ibid. Tarde's emphasis.

89 I discuss examples of this trope in the fin-de-siècle novel of formation in chapter 2, pages 72–9.

90 "air dur, hautain et presque masculin." *Le Rouge et le Noir*, in *Œuvres romanesques complètes*, 1:572.

91 Henri III (1551–1574–1589) is named on pages 566, 622, and 628 of the Pléiade edition. In Huysmans's *À rebours* (1884) for instance, the decadent and sexually ambiguous Des Esseintes is introduced as a descendant of "one of the closest intimates of the Duc d'Épernon and the Marquis d'O" ("un des plus intimes familiers du duc d'Épernon et du marquis d'O"), an erudite reference to two prominent members of Henri III's court; later the novel again alludes to his "heredity dating back to the reign of Henri III" ("hérédité datant du règne d'Henri III"). Huysmans, *À rebours*, 77, 214. On Henri III, see Katherine B. Crawford, "Love, Sodomy, and Scandal."

92 "la duplicité de Machiavel." *Le Rouge et le Noir*, in *Œuvres romanesques complètes*, 1:636.

93 "vivant dans l'intimité de quelques jeunes gens qui partageaient ses goûts, il [Chambige] s'essayait avec eux, se grisait, par moments, en se voyant déjà grand écrivain, de rêves de gloire. Rien de plus noble et de plus respectable assurément que ce culte des lettres quand il n'est pas accompagné d'impatiences déréglées, mais ce jeune cénacle renchérissait sur les déplorables tendances d'une école qui cherche le succès dans l'étrangeté de ses innovations." Trarieux, *Cinq plaidoiries*, 98–9.

94 "littérature des cerveaux malades." Ibid., 112.

95 "il s'est fait dans la jeunesse des écoles une sorte de mouvement d'enthousiasme autour de ce romanesque, qui a joué au naturel les drames racontés dans les livres." Bataille, *Causes criminelles et mondaines de 1888*, 24.

96 "Je t'embrasse, je te serre le cœur. Ici je mets un baiser que tu auras la bonté de reprendre. Prière d'en renvoyer." *Gazette des tribunaux*, 15 November 1888, 1105.

97 Bataille, "Une cause célèbre: l'affaire Chambige," *Le Figaro*, 11 November 1888, 2.

98 See Surkis, *Sexing the Citizen*, 44–8 and 82–4.

99 See Charle, *La Crise littéraire à l'époque du naturalisme*, as well as Angenot, "Champ littéraire," in *1889: Un état du discours social*, 781–845.

100 "milieu de souillure." Zola, *La Curée* [1872], in *Œuvres complètes*, 5:90.

101 Bourget, *Un crime d'amour*. On reactions to the publication of this passage in Bourget's circle and in the press, see Mansuy, *Un moderne*, 425. Mansuy himself notes that "there are whispers here and there that if Bourget describes youthful debauchery with such precision, it must be that he himself ..." Ibid., 425n18 (original ellipsis).

102 During cross-examination in 1895, Oscar Wilde quipped in response to a question about "a certain tendency" that "the whole idea was borrowed from Shakespeare's ... sonnets." Ellmann, *Oscar Wilde*, 449.

103 "entre les murs du grand lycée ... il n'était question que d'amours infâmes entre ces grands et ces petits. Parmi ces amours contre nature, les unes étaient franchement sensuelles et avaient pour théâtre les coins déserts de la maison. Et parmi les jeunes Français internés dans des collèges semblables, combien participaient à cette luxure, et les autres se salissaient l'imagination en la repoussant! Il y avait aussi entre ces collégiens des liaisons exaltées et chastes. La lecture d'une certaine églogue de Virgile, d'un dialogue de Platon, de quelques sonnets de Shakespeare montait la tête aux plus littéraires." Bourget, *Un crime d'amour*, 38.

104 "Alfred et lui avaient été du petit nombre de ceux que la contagion n'avait pas atteints ... le plus grand avantage de ce dégoût avait été ... de le conduire tout jeune à la poursuite des filles." Ibid., 39.

105 Mirbeau, *Sébastien Roch*, trans. Nicoletta Simborowski, 101. ("Parce que ... L'année dernière ... on en a surpris deux ... qui faisaient des saletés dans les salles de musique.") *Sébastien Roch*, in *Œuvre romanesque*, 1:621.

106 Mirbeau, *Sébastien Roch*, trans. Nicoletta Simborowski, 126–38. Translation modified. "Il lui révéla les beautés de la littérature dont ses cahiers ne lui avaient laissé que des aperçus imparfaits, des images tronquées, et surtout le désir ardent de savoir ... il lui fit connaître et aimer Sophocle, Dante, Shakespeare. Avec un charme clair, exquis, passionné, il racontait leurs immortelles œuvres, et les expliquait. Il récita des vers de Victor Hugo, de Lamartine, d'Alfred de Vigny, de Théophile Gautier, lut des pages de Chateaubriand. Et ces vers et ces proses avaient, dans sa bouche, des musiques engourdissantes, des harmonies encore inentendues, de surnaturelles pénétrations ... il ne put pas résister à la démoralisation de sa petite âme, habilement saturée de poésies, chloroformée d'idéal, vaincue par la dissolvante, par la dévirilisante morphine des tendresses inétreignables. Et ce travail sourd, continu, envahisseur, le Père de Kern en rendit complices le soleil, les brumes ... toute la nature soumise, comme une vieille matrone, aux concupiscences monstrueuses d'un homme. Tous les deux, elle et lui ... ils insinuèrent, goutte à goutte, le mortel poison. Le moment était bien choisi pour le viol d'une âme délicate et passionnée ... attaquée dans les racines mêmes de la vie intellectuelle." *Sébastien Roch*, in *Œuvre romanesque* 1:643–52.

107 I discuss the topos of poison in chapter 1 and the other tropes in chapter 2.

108 Pierre Michel, "Introduction" to *Sébastien Roch* in Mirbeau, *Œuvre romanesque*, 1:528.

109 "je suis furieux, car il y a là une première communion, dont deux sensations m'appartiennent, que j'ai mises dans *Sébastien Roch*, et que j'avais eu l'imprudence de confier à Bourget ... Non, j'aurai l'air de l'avoir copié, et il faudra que je raye cela, quoi qu'il m'en coûte." Letter to Paul Hervieu, 6 March 1889. Mirbeau, *Correspondance générale*, 2:48.

110 "extra-mauvais, et d'une prétention irritante." Ibid.

111 "les sentiments, les vices qu'elles [les femmes] aiment." Mirbeau, "Le Manuel du savoir écrire," 1.

112 "Cette lettre, à vous je la montrerai, parce que vous savez que j'aime les femmes; mais à d'autres, je n'oserais pas la montrer: on pourrait croire, à la tendresse des reproches, qu'il y a eu des rapports de pédérastie entre nous." Edmond and Jules de Goncourt, *Journal: Mémoires de la vie littéraire*, 3:282.

113 Pierre Michel, in Mirbeau, *Correspondance générale*, 2:108n6.

114 An expunged version of the *Journal* was published between 1887 and 1896 (with the volume about the years 1889–91 appearing in 1895), but the full *Journal*, including suppressed passages like the one about Bourget, was not published until the 1950s.

115 *Physiologie de l'amour moderne* is a collection of tableaux of adultery, interspersed with reflections in the style of Stendhal's *De l'amour*, which features a strange mix of real Parisian personalities and characters from Bourget's other works. It would not be published as a volume until two years later, in 1891.

116 "Il a fait preuve d'un courage et d'une indépendance dont il convient de le louer ... le roman le plus remarquable que M. Paul Bourget ait écrit ... il n'a rien produit encore de plus viril et de plus beau." Firmin Boissin, "Romans, contes et nouvelles," 293.

117 "le *Disciple* n'est peut-être pas le 'plus amusant' de ses romans, les femmes préféreront toujours *Mensonges* ou *Crime d'amour* – mais il en est le 'plus fort' ... il y est maître." Ferdinand Brunetière, "À propos du *Disciple*," 217. Brunetière's enmity towards Zola was long-standing, as demonstrated in his essay *Le Roman naturaliste* (1883). He would accede to the Académie française in 1893, a year before Bourget. On the triumphant reception of *Le Disciple* as a reaction to Zola, see Angenot, *1889: Un état du discours social*, 838–9.

118 Bourget's oft-repeated claim to performing psychological analysis "with a scalpel" is derided by Mirbeau in his article from 11 May 1889. The masculinizing analogy comparing the novelist's pen to a surgeon's scalpel was first proposed by Sainte-Beuve in an 1857 article on *Madame Bovary*. See Ladenson, *Dirt for Art's Sake*, 33–4.

119 I discuss the preface in more detail in chapter 1, pages 37–8. On the preface as a key moment in Bourget's trajectory from a member of Parisian literary youth to one of its masters, see Denis Pernot, "Paul Bourget, observateur de la jeunesse (1880–1889)," in *Avez-vous lu Paul Bourget?*, 97–108.

120 "jeune homme de mon pays ... tu vas, cherchant dans nos volumes, à nous tes aînés, des réponses aux questions qui te tourmentent"; "des allusions à de récents événements." Bourget, *Le Disciple*, 45, 55. Page references in subsequent notes are to this edition.

121 A note in Bourget's diary on 1 November 1888 indicates: "avoid it being the Chambige affair" ("éviter que ce soit l'affaire Chambige"). Institut catholique de Paris, Bibliothèque de Fels, Manuscrits français, Fonds P. Bourget, 663/4. Cited by Antoine Compagnon, preface to Bourget, *Le Disciple*, 24.

122 "un enthousiasme de disciples." Bourget, "Taine," in *Essais de psychologie contemporaine*, 126. On *Le Disciple* as Bourget's rupture with Taine, see Thomas Loué, "Les fils de Taine entre science et morale."

123 The letter, dated 29 September 1889, is reproduced in the Livre de poche edition of *Le Disciple*, 361–6.

124 The preface's final words are "my young countryman, to whom I would like to have been beneficial at least once, by whom I passionately wish to be loved – and to be worthy of it" ("jeune homme de mon pays, à qui je voudrais avoir été une fois bienfaisant, par qui je souhaite si passionnément d'être aimé – et de le mériter"). *Le Disciple*, 56.

125 "votre responsabilité morale." Ibid., 89.

126 "Ce fut, dans le domaine des idées pures, le même coup de foudre que jadis, avec les œuvres de Musset, dans le domaine des sensations rêvées." Ibid., 164.

127 "Vous m'étiez apparu comme une sorte de Spinoza moderne, si complètement identique à vos livres ... Je me forgeais d'avance un roman de félicité à l'idée que je saurais les heures de vos promenades ... vous étiez pour moi la Certitude vivante, le Maître, ce que Faust est pour Wagner dans la symphonie psychologique de Goethe." Ibid., 169.

128 "mon imagination excessive ... a détruit ma sensibilité en faisant toujours se dresser entre moi et la réalité une idée façonnée d'avance. Je m'attendais à sentir d'une certaine manière, – et puis ce n'était jamais cela ... La vie de collège et la littérature moderne m'ont souillé la pensée avant que je n'eusse vécu." Bourget, *Un crime d'amour*, 56.

129 "cette imagination anticipée de l'émotion." *Le Disciple,* 152.

130 "'On ne devient pas un assassin, un empoisonneur d'un jour à l'autre. La jeunesse des criminels annonce leur crime ... [...] Mais lui, monsieur, depuis qu'il était tout enfant, avec son pauvre père, toujours dans les livres ... C'était moi qui lui disais: Allons, Robert, sors; il faut sortir, prendre l'air, te distraire ...'" Ibid., 113. Unbracketed ellipses are original.

131 "J'étais, à cette époque déjà, passionné de lecture, et le hasard m'avait mis entre les mains des volumes très différents de ceux qui se donnaient en prix dans les distributions"; "nourrir mon imagination." Ibid., 141, 143.

132 "J'en tremblais, comme d'une grosse faute, et nous nous laissions envahir par cette poésie comme par un vin, longuement, doucement, passionnément. J'ai eu, depuis, entre les mains, dans cette même chambre d'Émile et dans la mienne propre, grâce à des ruses d'amant en danger, bien des volumes clandestins et que j'ai bien aimés." Ibid., 157.

133 As we have seen, Bourget described *Le Rouge et le Noir* in his 1883 *Essais* as a "an extraordinary book, which I have seen produce on the brains of certain young people the effects of an incurable intoxication ... it casts a spell. It is a possession" ("un livre extraordinaire, et que j'ai vu produire sur certains cerveaux de jeunes gens l'effet d'une intoxication inguérissable ... il ensorcelle. C'est une possession"). *Essais de psychologie contemporaine*, 201.

134 "Je vous raconte cet enfantillage pour vous prouver ... combien je ressemblais peu, tandis que le landau roulait sur la route d'Aydat, au jeune homme ambitieux et pauvre que tant de romans ont dépeint ... je me souviens d'avoir, dès cette heure-là, constaté, non sans orgueil, cette différence. Je me rappelais le Julien Sorel de *Rouge et Noir* [*sic*], arrivant chez M. de Rênal, les tentations de Rubempré, dans Balzac, devant la maison des Bargeton, quelques pages aussi du *Vingtras* de Vallès. J'analysais la sensation qui se dissimule derrière les convoitises ou les révoltes de ces divers héros ... je ne trouvais pas une trace en moi." *Le Disciple*, 174.

135 "Negation" ("Die Verneinung," 1925). Freud's emphasis. *The Standard Edition of the Complete Psychological Works of Sigmund Freud*, 19:235. Translation modified.
136 "je ne vous écris pas pour me peindre sous un jour romanesque." *Le Disciple*, 176.
137 "le goût du romanesque; non qu'elle eût lu beaucoup de romans, mais elle avait ... une sensibilité trop vive ... cette faculté qui fait les grands poètes et les grandes amoureuses, de s'oublier, de se disperser, de s'abîmer tout entière." Ibid., 195–6.
138 "roman"; "poétiser"; "n'avait pas su lire le mensonge dans mon récit"; "scène d'une comédie"; "l'hypocrisie ... se redouble d'elle-même en s'exprimant." Ibid., 207, 209–11.
139 "autant de ridicules manœuvres qui ne m'avaient pas avancé d'une ligne dans ce cœur que je voulais conquérir." Ibid., 211.
140 *Les Liaisons dangereuses*, 52.
141 "entre le Valmont des *Liaisons* – mon cher Valmont – et la présidente, qui a été dupe?" *Un crime d'amour*, 50.
142 "pris à mon propre piège." *Le Disciple*, 250.
143 "Elle lisait et relisait ces pages, dont le poison agissait sûrement." Ibid., 248.
144 "Il n'y a pas de mauvais livres. Il y a de mauvais moments pour lire les meilleurs livres." Ibid., 223.
145 "la loi générale de l'intoxication littéraire"; "dans votre chapitre sur l'âme littéraire quand vous assimilez la plaie ouverte sur certaines imaginations par certaines lectures au phénomène bien connu qui se produit sur les corps empoisonnés de diabète. La plus inoffensive piqûre s'y envenime de gangrène." Ibid., 222–3.
146 Ibid., 270. Bourget references a real treatise by Alexandre Brierre de Boismont (1798–1881), *Du suicide et de la folie suicide, considérés dans leurs rapports avec la statistique, la médecine et la philosophie*.
147 "All animals are sad after intercourse." Ibid., 278.
148 See Michel Mansuy, *Un moderne*, 485 and 530.
149 Barrès, "La Sensibilité d'Henri Chambige," 1. See note 78 above.
150 "trouble infligé par cette lecture." *Le Disciple*, 291.
151 "ces responsabilités-là." Ibid., 45. Denis Pernot proposes that "the preface to *Le Disciple* corrects a misunderstanding in the reception" of Bourget's earlier œuvre. "Paul Bourget, observateur de la jeunesse," in *Avez-vous lu Paul Bourget?*, 107.
152 "ce jeune homme-là ... nous que les paradoxes d'un maître trop éloquent ont trop charmés; nous l'avons tous été un jour, une heure." *Le Disciple*, 53.
153 "le moment est venu de signaler." Mansuy, *Un moderne*, 280n73. See also Ellmann, *Oscar Wilde*, 252.
154 For a well-documented survey of this question, see Eells, "Proust et Wilde."

155 Novick, *Henry James: The Mature Master*, 71 and 93.

156 Francis and Gontier, *Mathilde de Morny: La scandaleuse marquise et son temps*, 182.

157 "reniera son homosexualité"; "En 1895 ... Paul Bourget se dépense à faire oublier sa jeunesse ouvertement homosexuelle en courtisant les hôtesses qui lui ouvriront les portes de l'Académie française." Ibid., 126 and 182.

158 Maurice Bouchor (1855–1929) later published poetry as well as plays for marionette theatre.

159 "J'ai besoin de te revoir, de regarder tes beaux yeux verts ... Je t'aime et te serre la main, en te suppliant de me permettre plus. Tu sais ce que cela veut dire et tu ne t'en fâcheras pas." Paul Bourget, letter to Maurice Bouchor, 29 March 1870 (manuscript copy by Georges Hérelle). Ms 3141, fonds Georges Hérelle, Médiathèque Grand Troyes. The text of this letter was displayed in the exhibition *Fières archives, documents autobiographiques d'homosexuels fin de siècle*, curated by Philippe Artières and Clive Thomson, Mairie du IVe arrondissement, Paris, 1 June to 31 August 2017. On Bourget's letters to Bouchor, see Daniel Carl Ridge, "Maurice Bouchor – Paul Bourget – Georges Hérelle – Adrien Juvigny (1869–1874), Correspondances croisées inédites."

160 Jacqueline Carroy and Marc Renneville point out that Tarde's first published work, a collection of literary juvenilia (*Contes et poèmes* [Paris, Calmann Lévy, 1879]), features several masked allusions to queerness. They write, "the stupefied recollection and condemnation of 1888 [in the article about Chambige] directly confront a topic that had remained encrypted or shrouded in poetry in the early literary work." "Une cause passionnelle passionnante: Tarde et l'affaire Chambige (1889)."

161 The anecdote is analysed for its many implications concerning Gide by Michael Lucey in *Never Say I*, 31–46.

162 "'Maintenant que nous voici seuls, apprenez-moi, monsieur Gide, si votre Immoraliste est ou n'est pas un pédéraste?' Et, comme je reste un peu interloqué, il insiste: 'Je veux dire: un pédéraste pratiquant?' – 'C'est sans doute plutôt un homosexuel qui s'ignore,' répondis-je, comme si je n'en savais guère trop rien moi-même; et j'ajoutai: 'je crois qu'ils sont nombreux.'" Gide, *Journal*, 1:907.

163 See chapter 2, page 63.

164 "découplé comme un athlète, des épaules larges et une tournure mince ... avec cela le visage le plus martial ... un front carré ... des lèvres serrées et fermes." *Le Disciple*, 158.

165 "tout en regardant à la dérobée le comte André jouer au billard ... je suivais bouche bée les moindres gestes de ce jeune homme." Ibid., 180. Citing this scene, Jean Borie asks whether Robert might not be more enamored with André than with his sister. "Esquisse d'une étude littéraire et idéologique du *Disciple* de Paul Bourget," in *Avez-vous lu Paul Bourget?*, 18.

166 "Ni ce soir-là, ni durant les jours qui suivirent, je n'ai jalousé le nom du comte André, ni sa fortune ... Je n'ai pas ressenti non plus cette étrange haine de mâle à mâle, très finement notée par vous dans vos pages sur l'amour. ... Je vous dis cela non par vanité, mais pour vous prouver au contraire que la vanité n'entra pas pour un atome dans la sorte de rivalité subite qui fit de moi, dès ces premières heures, un adversaire, presque un ennemi du comte André ... Je le répète, dans cette rivalité il entrait autant d'admiration que d'antipathie. À la réflexion, j'ai trouvé dans le sentiment que j'essaie de vous définir la trace d'un atavisme inconscient." *Le Disciple*, 181.

167 "l'action faite homme." Ibid., 179.

168 Sedgwick, *Between Men*, 24 and 38.

169 "N'est-il pas temps ... d'arrêter ce débordement d'aberrations? Où irions-nous, grand Dieu, et que deviendrait notre pauvre nation, déjà atteinte de tant de misères morales." Trarieux, *Cinq plaidoiries*, 172.

170 "le grand devoir du relèvement de la patrie." *Le Disciple*, 46.

171 Wilde had read Bourget's novel, or at least knew of it: in a revised version of his dialogue "The Decay of Lying," published in his collection *Intentions* in 1891, he adds a mention of *Le Disciple* to a list of books favoured by Cyril, the character who acts as a foil to Wilde's mouthpiece, Vivian. "The Decay of Lying" [1891], ed. Josephine M. Guy, in *The Complete Works of Oscar Wilde*, 4:80.

172 "joli garcon." *Le Disciple*, 181.

173 Late nineteenth-century French paperbacks, such as the first edition of Huysmans's *À rebours* (Paris: Charpentier, 1884), were frequently wrapped in yellow paper covers.

174 "*Le Secret de Raoul*, par Catulle Sarrazin." The title amalgamates code words of decadence and gender-bending: the novel *Monsieur Vénus* by Rachilde (1884), whose protagonist is named Raoule; Catulle Mendès (1841–1909), author of numerous tales and novels depicting lesbianism; and possibly the novella *Sarrasine* (1830) by Balzac. See Michael Patrick Gillespie, note to Wilde, *The Picture of Dorian Gray*, 258.

175 Wilde, *The Picture of Dorian Gray* [1890 version], 234, 259, 273, 275.

176 Wilde's preface was published in *The Forthnightly Review* in March 1891, ahead of publication of the volume in April.

177 Wilde, *The Picture of Dorian Gray* [1891 version], 3.

178 Ibid., 4. In *Le Disciple*, Robert writes to Sixte that "There are no bad books" ("Il n'y a pas de mauvais livres"), 223.

179 Wilde, "The Decay of Lying: A Dialogue," 41. On Balzac's Lucien de Rubempré as a queer figure, see chapter 2, note 45.

180 Larroumet, "Paul Bourget à l'Académie française"; A.G., "Oscar Wilde à la prison de Pentonville." *Le Gaulois*, 13 June 1895, 1. The same day, and later again in July, Octave Mirbeau published articles expressing outrage at the

harsh punishment inflicted on Wilde ("À propos du 'Hard Labour,'" 1; "Sur un livre," 1). Other French writers including Henry Bauer, Paul Adam, and Hugues Rebell penned similar articles. Bourget did no such thing. Though his name was mentioned in a list of potential signatories for a petition, the plan was never carried out, after writers including Barrès, Daudet, and Zola refused to sign. No trace exists of Bourget's response to the request. See Brunet, "L'échec de la pétition," and Ellmann, *Oscar Wilde*, 482 and 493.

5. Barrès and the Ghosts of Balzacian Ambition

1 "des influences qui continuent de peser sur la jeunesse actuelle." Bourget, 1885 preface, in *Essais de psychologie contemporaine*, 440.

2 "enfiévrant romancier"; "tant de faux Rastignacs, ridicules et odieux." Barrès, "La Contagion des Rastignacs," 1.

3 *Les Déracinés* appeared as a serial in *Revue de Paris* from 15 May to 15 August 1897; it was published as a volume by Fasquelle at the end of that summer.

4 Rambaud, "Barrès et Balzac," 397 and 400–1; see also Borie, preface to *Les Déracinés*, 28; Frandon, *Barrès tel qu'en lui-même*, 98; and Marie-Odile Germain, "Un Déraciné à la pension Vauquer," 78.

5 On my use of "denegation" for Freud's *Verneinung*, see introduction, note 76.

6 "sur la colline où il repose, – cette colline du haut de laquelle son Rastignac défiait Paris, – les os du grand romancier ont dû ... frémir de joie." Bourget, "Un nouveau dictionnaire," 3.

7 "pour certains lecteurs, ce monde de Balzac [a] été plus vivant que l'autre, et, par la suite, [a] modelé leur activité à sa ressemblance." Bourget, preface to *Répertoire de la Comédie humaine de H. de Balzac*, by Cerfberr and Christophe, xii.

8 "Je ne parle pas des femmes." Bourget, "Un nouveau dictionnaire," 3.

9 "Êtes-vous balzacien ...? Avez-vous éprouvé, en lisant au collège et clandestinement quelque tome dépareillé de la *Comédie humaine*, une sorte d'exaltation ...? ... à cet âge où l'on vendange à l'avance tous les fruits de l'arbre de la vie – encore à fleurir, – oui, avez-vous rêvé d'être Daniel d'Arthez et de vous couvrir de gloire à force d'œuvres ... ou bien, plus ambitieux et moins littéraire, avez-vous souhaité de voir, nouveau Rastignac, les portes de la haute vie ouvertes devant vos convoitises ...?" Bourget, preface to *Répertoire* (1887), i–ii. The fictional novelist Daniel d'Arthez appears in a dozen texts of the *Comédie humaine*.

10 "Ces aventuriers ... dont Rastignac est le prince, ont surexcité les nerfs et le cerveau de tous les jeunes ambitieux qui, depuis 1847, se succèdent ... Combien d'espoirs déçus et de vies fourvoyées à cause d'une conception de

l'existence, pour laquelle on s'échauffe à vingt ans!" Barrès, "La Contagion des Rastignacs," 1.

11 "aujourd'hui seuls les moins estimables et les plus débiles s'obstinent à rêver la vie romantique, aventurière et canaille de Rastignac." Ibid.

12 "Je les renie tous, sauf Balzac"; "le commun vulgaire des romanciers." Barrès, letter to Léon Sorg, 10 October 1880, cited in Rambaud, "Barrès et Balzac," 395.

13 "Seul Balzac en fut exclu, car ce passionné met en valeur les luttes et l'amertume de la vie sociale ... nous trouverions dans son œuvre, à certains jours, la nostalgie de ce que nous avons renoncé." Barrès, *Un homme libre* [1889], in *Romans et voyages*, 1:108.

14 "Son cœur se gonflait d'envie et d'une enivrante mélancolie, mais soudain il songea qu'il pensait à peu près comme les jeunes gens de brasserie et autres Rastignacs. Et un flot d'âcreté le pénétra. 'Désormais, dit-il, je ne prendrai plus en grâce les prières, les sourires et autres lieux communs. Je n'y trouvai jamais que des visions vulgaires.'" Barrès, *Sous l'œil des Barbares* [1888], in *Romans et voyages*, 1:68.

15 "[Balzac] a fixé la tourmente des passions à travers les codes et les bienséances ... Il n'a guère vieilli. Les meilleurs romanciers de cette minute ne font que rafraîchir les cadres de ses tableaux. Il a presque tout dit, ce me semble, des hommes qui agissent ... reste encore à parler de ceux qui sentent, les seuls qui nous intéressent." Barrès, "Le Sentiment en littérature," *Les Taches d'encre*, January 1885. Cited in Rambaud, "Barrès et Balzac," 398.

16 "La bombe du 'Terminus' est, en outre, une date littéraire. Elle marque l'avènement d'une façon de sentir que n'avait pas prévue Balzac. ... jusqu'en 1890 ... rien de caractéristique n'est apparu en France qui ne fût déjà catalogué dans *La Comédie humaine*. ... Tout ce siècle a vécu de la sensibilité balzacienne: des jeunes gens de la bourgeoisie, accourant pour l'ordinaire de la province, et avides de prendre leur part de pouvoir et de jouissance ... Mais voici surgir une nouvelle espèce. Par l'instruction universelle, une troisième classe se présente, ... des jeunes gens ..., instruits, mais sans éducation ... veulent eux aussi une part du pouvoir et de ses jouissances. Et la grave nouveauté, c'est que les parcelles qui sont à leur portée ne les tentent point, soit qu'elles soient trop petites, soient qu'elles n'aient pas de saveur pour leurs rudes appétits ... Rastignac ne menaçait guère les nobles maisons du faubourg Saint-Germain, où son rêve était de pénétrer ... Il n'en sera pas de même avec des bacheliers comme celui du Terminus. La maison, qui représente, pour lui, un degré supérieur de la hiérarchie sociale, il ne rêve point d'y pénétrer, mais de la faire sauter." Barrès, "Enfin Balzac a vieilli," 1.

17 See Ringer, *Fields of Knowledge*, 127–40, as well as chapter 3.

18 Henry's statement to the court describes his lost illusions on questions of education and class: "the educators of today's rising generation too often

forget one thing: that life ... will readily ... make the scales fall from the eyes of the ignorant ... I had been told that this life would be easy, that it was wide open to the bright and those who were full of energy; but experience showed me that only cynics and those who are willing to crawl can earn themselves a seat at the banquet ... I had been told that social institutions were based on justice and equality, but around me I saw only lies and deceit. With each day I lost another illusion." ("les éducateurs de la génération actuelle oublient trop fréquemment une chose, c'est que la vie ... se charge bien ... de dessiller les yeux des ignorants ... On m'avait dit que cette vie était facile et largement ouverte aux intelligents et aux énergiques, et l'expérience me montra que seuls les cyniques et rampants peuvent se faire bonne place au banquet. ... On m'avait dit que les institutions sociales étaient basées sur la justice et l'égalité, et je ne constatais autour de moi que mensonges et fourberies. Chaque jour m'enlevait une illusion.") Émile Henry, "Déclaration," reprinted in Henry, *Coup pour coup*, 162. On Henry's life, see Langlais, "Biographie," in *Coup pour coup*, 15–45; for a thorough account of the bombing, the trial, and their aftermath, see John Merriman, *The Dynamite Club*.

19 "beauté tragique de sa révolte." Barrès, "Un témoin de la guillotine."

20 Merriman, *The Dynamite Club*, 157.

21 "Enfin, dira quelque maniaque de psychologie, on va pouvoir créer des types, – ce qui, depuis Balzac, était impossible!" Barrès, "Enfin Balzac a vieilli," 1.

22 As Marie-Odile Germain puts it, "Writing a novel had once again become possible, since the figure of the ambitious young man had been supplanted by that of the man in revolt." See "Genèse d'un roman: *Les Déracinés*," 33. Germain first proposes this observation in "Un Déraciné à la pension Vauquer" (1980), 73–83, especially 78; it is also developed by Vital Rambaud in "Barrès et Balzac" (1991), 397 and 400–1.

23 A thinly fictionalized version of Émile Henry appears (as "Victor Mathis") in Zola's *Paris*, which began publication as a serial a few months after *Les Déracinés*. See *Œuvres complètes*, 17:318–19.

24 "Je ferais sauter avec joie tout Paris!" *Les Déracinés*, in *Romans et voyages*, 1:588.

25 Barrès's 1892 novel *L'Ennemi des lois* is purportedly about an anarchist, but critics noted that its plot, about a man who loves two women at the same time, describes "a sort of aristocratic anarchism destined for rich and cultivated individuals." Jules Lemaitre in *Le Figaro*, 22 November 1892, cited in Rambaud, "Introduction" to *L'Ennemi des lois*, in *Romans et voyages*, 1:263.

26 "l'homme de proie, [le] type ... qui, par le génie du romancier, devint dans notre société ... le vice à la mode." Barrès, "La Contagion des Rastignacs" (1887), 1.

27 Oscar Wilde, "The Decay of Lying: A Dialogue," 48. Wilde may have been familiar with Bourget's preface to the *Répertoire de la Coméde humaine*, which states that "Balzacian men, in literature as in life, have appeared

mostly after the death of the novelist. Rather than having observed the society of his era, Balzac seems to have contributed to shaping one." ("On a remarqué que les hommes de Balzac, tant dans la littérature que dans la vie, sont apparus, surtout après la mort du romancier. Balzac semble avoir moins observé la société de son époque qu'il n'a contribué à en former une.") Bourget, preface to *Répertoire* (1887), vi. On Wilde and Bourget's acquaintance in the 1880s, see chapter 4, pages 116 and 144.

28 Though "La Contagion des Rastignacs" makes no mention of Vallès, Vital Rambaud notes the similarity of its tone to Vallès's journalism of the 1860s in "Barrès et Balzac," 399. Hélène Millot points out that, on the critique of educational institutions and the question of formative reading, "there are numberous ... points of convergence between Vallès's trilogy and Barrès's trilogy." See "Vallès contre Barrès, ou du bon usage des racines," 46.

29 "résume la grandeur du livre et ses dangers [...] Ah! sous les pas de ce géant, que de consciences écrasées, que de boue, que de sang! Comme il a fait travailler les juges et pleurer les mères! Combien se sont perdus, ont coulé, qui agitaient au-dessus du bourbier où ils allaient mourir une page arrachée à quelque volume de la *Comédie humaine*. Ceux-ci, avec Rastignac, du haut d'une mansarde ou debout sur le pont des Arts, ont montré le poing à la vie et crié au monde: À nous deux! jurant, sur *Le Père Goriot* ou le volume à côté, de faire leur trou à coups d'épée – ou de couteau ..." Unbracketed ellipsis is original. "Les Victimes du Livre" (*Le Figaro*, 9 October 1862), in *Œuvres*, 1:244–5. I discuss this essay in more detail in chapter 1, pages 26–7.

30 According to Cerfbeer and Christophe's *Répertoire* of 1886, Rastignac appears in thirteen installments of *La Comédie humaine*, and is mentioned in at least three others (427–9).

31 "son ambition," "le jeune ambitieux," "sa méditation ambitieusement amoureuse." Balzac, *Le Père Goriot*, in *La Comédie humaine*, 3:74, 75, 79 and passim.

32 Ibid., 3:290.

33 "Paris ... où commençaient à briller les lumières." Ibid.

34 "tendances vers la littérature"; "Maintenant, à nous deux, mon vieux Paris! ... À nous deux, Paris! ... À nous deux!" Charpentier, *L'Enfance d'un homme*, 86, 128–9.

35 "dans les bas-fonds littéraires"; "l'œuvre manque de virilité"; "avorton malingre, fœtus noirâtre"; "Ce cri vibre encore à son oreille. Ah! Je t'en fiche! Ce que Paris se fout de lui! Ce que Paris a broyé son pusillanime squelette!" Ibid., 106, 140, 228, 282.

36 "J'ai lu mon Balzac." The narrator-protagonist goes on to explain: "I recall that Lucien de Rubempré lived on rue des Cordiers, at the hotel Jean-Jacques-Rousseau" ("je me rappelle que Lucien de Rubempré demeurait rue des Cordiers, hôtel Jean-Jacques Rousseau"). Vallès, *Le Bachelier*, in *Œuvres*,

2:552. While there is no mention of such an address in either of the novels that feature Lucien, *Illusions perdues* and *Splendeurs et misères des courtisanes*, a scene in the former does compare Lucien's very modest living quarters to Rousseau's. Balzac, *Illusions perdues*, in *La Comédie humaine*, V, 306.

37 "Balzac, sans doute, a choisi l'hôtel qui lui paraissait répondre le mieux à l'ambition et au caractère de son héros ... Ma fenêtre donne sur un mur. Je ne puis pas regarder Paris et le menacer du poing comme Rastignac! Je ne vois pas Paris. Il y a ce mur en face, avec des crottes d'oiseau dessus." Vallès, *Le Bachelier*, in *Œuvres*, 2:552–3.

38 "Il est allé au Père-Lachaise, intervint de sa forte voix Racadot; il a refait le serment de Rastignac, après l'enterrement du père Goriot, quand il s'écrie: 'À nous deux, Paris!' C'est un jouisseur délicat que M. François!" Barrès, *Les Déracinés*, in *Romans et voyages*, 1:537. Page references in subsequent notes are to this edition.

39 "he explained that ... it was the galleries at the Odéon he enjoyed most of all." ("il expliqua que ... dans tout Paris, c'étaient les galeries de l'Odéon qui lui plaisaient le plus.") Ibid., 1:537. In the late nineteenth century, booksellers' stands at the Odéon were popular with students and bibliophiles. See for instance France, "Les galeries de l'Odéon," in *La Vie littéraire*, 3:255–65.

40 Léon Gambetta, one of the architects of the Third Republic, held a number of important government positions between 1877 and 1882. Barrès specifies that Sturel arrives in Paris on the day of his death, 31 December 1882; his funeral took place on 6 January 1883. *Les Déracinés*, 1:524–6.

41 "– Aujourd'hui même, tu avais sous les yeux un spectacle plus instructif que tous les bouquins; tu n'as pas daigné regarder l'enterrement de Gambetta!

– C'était splendide! jeta la Léontine.

– Tout le monde peut regarder un spectacle parisien, mais encore faut-il savoir le lire, continua Renaudin, du ton dédaigneux d'un 'Parisien' qui rentre dans son village." Ibid., 1:537.

42 Prominent republicans of Gambetta's generation, whose careers were launched at the fall of the Second Empire in 1870, would indeed continue to dominate French politics well into the 1890s, when Barrès writes the novel.

43 "Les amis du mort tiendront la république pendant des années ... Quelles circonstances faudra-t-il ... quelles luttes ... pour qu'ils autorisent une nouvelle génération à entrer ...?" *Les Déracinés*, 1:537.

44 Underscoring the complexity of Racadot's exclamation, Vital Rambaud points out that "this allusion ... shows how, in spite of his irony, Racadot belongs, or more precisely wants to belong, to the race of Rastignacs." Note to Barrès, *Les Déracinés*, in *Romans et voyages*, 1:1360n121. One can indeed read Racadot's statement as a pose not unlike Renaudin's, a denegation, in front of his literarily sophisticated group of friends, of a not entirely renounced belief. A later scene supports this reading: see page 164.

45 "moi, François Sturel, je trouve Rastignac, avec son serment de dominer Paris, honteusement médiocre." *Les Déracinés*, 1:603.

46 Barrès writes: "And I recall, as one of the most amusing moments in the history of the defunct Naturalist movement, that Paul Alexis once wrote quite seriously, in a chronicle from the month of October: 'Here comes winter! I am back in the city. *À nous deux Paris*!'" ("Et je me rappelle, comme une des choses les plus cocasses du défunt naturalisme, que jadis Paul Alexis écrivait très sérieusement, dans une chronique d'octobre: 'Voici l'hiver! je rentre dans la ville. À nous deux Paris!'") "La Contagion des Rastignacs," 1.

47 *Les Déracinés*, 1:568, 607.

48 "petite bête pensante"; "bête de proie." Marie-Odile Germain cites four explicit comparisons of Sturel to Rastignac in various stages of Barrès's manuscript. "Un déraciné à la pension Vauquer," 74–6.

49 The resonance is signalled by Borie, "Préface," 28–9, as well as Frandon, *Barrès tel qu'en lui-même: Modernité et déracinement*, 98–9.

50 "Balzac a inventé treize hommes qui, vers 1828, auraient juré de se soutenir dans toute occasion et dont la puissance occulte bravait avec succès l'ordre social." *Les Déracinés*, 1:511. The date given by Barrès is erroneous, since the three novellas of Balzac's *Histoire des Treize* are set under the Empire (1804–15), or around 1820. The preface to *Histoire des Treize* specifies that the secret society was dissolved at the death of Napoleon in 1821.

51 The analogy between the emperor and the novelist is fairly common: Bourget, for instance, ends his 1887 preface with the words "Balzac, notre Napoléon littéraire." Cerfberr and Christophe, *Répertoire*, xii.

52 "vie secrète, curieuse, autant que peut l'être le plus noir des romans de madame Radcliffe, ... ces treize hommes sont restés inconnus, quoique tous aient réalisé les plus bizarres idées que suggère à l'imagination la fantastique puissance faussement attribuée aux Manfred, aux Faust, aux Melmoth." Balzac, Preface to *Histoire des Treize*" [1833], in *La Comédie humaine*, 5:787–8. References are to Ann Radcliffe (1764–1823); the dramatic poem *Manfred* (1817), by Byron; Goethe's *Faust*; and the gothic novel *Melmoth the Wanderer* (1820), by Charles Robert Maturin.

53 "Un jour, l'un d'eux, après avoir relu *Venise sauvée*, après avoir admiré l'union sublime de Pierre et de Jaffier, vint à songer aux vertus particulières des gens jetés en dehors de l'ordre social." Ibid., 371. The reference is to *Venice Preserv'd* (1682), a Restoration tragedy by Thomas Otway. This play is also mentioned in *Le Père Goriot* by Vautrin, as he seductively offers to pay Rastignac's debts (*La Comédie humaine*, 3:186).

54 "professeur d'énergie." *Les Déracinés*, 1:608.

55 "par la force de leur imagination nourrie de livres [ils] mêlent aux Napoléonides les poètes, qui depuis un siècle sont les voix du grand homme." Ibid., 1:610.

56 "À quinze ans ... en secret et avec passion il se découvre dans Rousseau ... à seize ans, c'est René." Ibid., 1:611. Chateaubriand's *René* was published in 1802, when Napoleon was thirty-three.

57 "À Sainte Hélène ... il était le roi Lear ... Il fut également le corsaire de Byron, l'empereur des Musset, des Hugo, ... le parvenu de Rastignac, l'individu de Taine." Ibid., 1:607.

58 "un des plus beaux parchemins à déchiffrer." Ibid., I, 607.

59 "Les Treize étaient tous des hommes trempés comme le fut Trelawney, l'ami de lord Byron et, dit-on, l'original du *Corsaire*." Balzac, preface to *Histoire des Treize*, in *La Comédie humaine*, 5:791. The reference is to Edward John Trelawny (1792–1881), an English adventurer who went on to write his memoirs; Balzac may have known his *Adventures of a Younger Son* (1831), translated into French in 1833, the same year the preface to *Histoire des Treize* first appeared in the *Revue de Paris* (Trelawney, *Mémoires d'un cadet de famille*).

60 "Entre lui-même et les objets de son désir il sentait un voile léger. Il voulait dominer les hommes et caresser les femmes." *Les Déracinés*, 1:540. Napoleon's enthusiasm for Rousseau is well documented; it is referenced by the *déracinés* in the scene at his tomb.

61 "Il y eut un silence anxieux ... Tous ces jeunes gens craignaient d'être des incapables." Ibid., 1:616.

62 "La France dissociée et décérébrée"; "l'esprit allemand." Ibid., 1:616, 619.

63 The complex was built under Louis XIV as an *hôpital des invalides* for military veterans. Napoleon's remains were transferred there in 1840, on the order of Louis-Philippe.

64 *Les Déracinés*, 1:596, 625, 640.

65 "On sort du tombeau comme on peut." Ibid., 1:620.

66 "homme national." Ibid., 1:622. Barrès is here laying the groundwork for Sturel's embrace of General Boulanger in the trilogy's second volume, *L'Appel au soldat*.

67 "marchepied." Ibid., 1:623.

68 "C'est un pays passionné pour les aventures romanesques d'un héros sympathique. Un peu de justice sociale leur ferait plaisir, mais moins qu'un beau roman qui, au jour le jour les tiendrait en haleine. Je parle en journaliste qui connaît les lecteurs." Ibid., 1:622.

69 "Tout était préordonné de façon que le journalisme devait être leur voie tracée." Ibid., 1:623.

70 "Le journalisme, voilà le vrai moyen des êtres livresques." Ibid., 1:584.

71 "On ne les a élevés qu'avec des livres: les voici arrivés au moment où leur éducation produit son effet normal et complet; ils vont ajouter à la masse des imprimés. Tous les jeunes Français, dans les lycées, sont dressés pour faire des hommes de lettres parisiens." Ibid., 1:647.

72 Barrès started his own literary career as a journalist. At twenty-two, he launched a monthly review, *Les Taches d'encre*, which would publish only four issues. A decade later, in 1894 and 1895, he was the director of *La Cocarde*, a newspaper with a large team of writers. By his death in 1923 he had published over two thousand articles in more than one hundred newspapers. See Germain, "Barrès journaliste et l'écriture au quotidien," and Broche and Roussel, preface to Barrès, *Journal de ma vie extérieure*, 7.

73 Balzac, *Illusions perdues*, in *La Comédie humaine*, 5:147, 193.

74 "Lucien ... voyait la politique et la littérature convergeant dans cette boutique. À l'aspect d'un poète éminent y prostituant la muse à un journaliste, y humiliant l'Art, comme la Femme était humiliée, prostituée sous ces galeries ignobles, le grand homme de province recevait des enseignements terribles. L'argent! était le mot de toute énigme." Ibid., 5:365.

75 "C'est un rude exercice que de découvrir des fonds, un éditeur, des abonnés, des lecteurs ... La fondation et la direction d'une petite revue, c'est pour un jeune homme qui s'entraîne dans la carrière littéraire un excellent apprentissage où il reconnaîtra ces deux vérités essentielles, à savoir: 1. que l'argent est tout-puissant; 2. que l'industrie littéraire est une industrie de gueux." Barrès, "Victor Hugo ou la méthode pour organiser sa renommée."

76 Jean Borie notes that "part of Racadot's experience, the newspaper sliding toward bankruptcy, the father who cuts off funds and wants his son to become a lawyer, corresponds to Barrès's own experiences in his early career"; he later observes that "Racadot, about to sink, changing the political orientation of his paper ... resembles Rubempré." Preface to Barrès, *Les Déracinés* (1988), 27n10 and 28.

77 The link is convincingly established by Ida-Marie Frandon in "Fait divers et littérature." Barrès mentions the murder in article on Dostoyevsky, "La Mode russe," in *La Revue illustrée* on 1 February 1886.

78 In this regard, when contrasted with other members of the group, Racadot fulfils Barrès's 1887 statement that "only the least worthy and the most wretched cling to their dream of Rastignac's romantic, adventurous and raffish life." See note 11 above.

79 "Tu souffres de ton dénûment? Il y a beaucoup de puissants qui à nos âges étaient méprisés et qui, dix années plus tard, assez jeunes encore pour jouir, avaient de l'argent, des maîtresses au théâtre, des habits à détruire, des poignées de main sur tous les boulevards, et qui payaient au restaurant sans même vérifier la note." *Les Déracinés*, 1:588–9.

80 "méconnaissance tout universitaire des conditions d'une réussite." Ibid., 1:590.

81 "Racadot et Mouchefrin souffrent la faim, le froid, avilissent et martyrisent leur jeunesse ... Cette brasserie décriée ... n'est point la chambre glacée des héros de Balzac ... Rubempré, Rastignac, à minuit, dans leur solitude, se disaient la bonne aventure, qui ressemblait toujours aux aventures du jeune Bonaparte." Ibid., 1:568.

82 "cette salle de rédaction, quel étrange endroit! Rien peut-il différer davantage de ces journaux, d'ailleurs fort réels, dont Balzac nous a dit le tourbillon, la verve, les amertumes, les frivolités, les soupers, les jolies femmes?" Ibid., 1:665.

83 Vital Rambaud describes the relationship between Balzacian fictions and the narrative of *Les Déracinés* as one of degradation: "characters in *Les Déracinés*, far from re-living the occasionally dazzling adventures of Balzac's heroes, experience a degraded version." "Barrès et Balzac," 404.

84 "un vaste champ incessamment remué par une tempête d'intérêts ... tout brille, tout bouillonne, tout flambe." Balzac, *La Fille aux yeux d'or*, in *La Comédie humaine*, 5:1039–40.

85 "Paris! ... Le rendez-vous des hommes, le rond-point de l'humanité! ... le lieu marqué pour qu'ils accomplissent leur destinée ... 'À Paris!'"; "le sens des réalités." *Les Déracinés*, 1:513.

86 "aux premiers temps de son arrivée de Nancy, répétait: 'Me voilà au centre de Paris ... le centre de Paris ...,' c'était l'accent d'un poète." Ibid., 1:574. Barrès's ellipses. With "Me voilà au centre de Paris," Renaudin (or Barrès) may be parroting Julien Sorel's similar exclamation ("Me voici donc dans le centre de l'intrigue ...!") at the start of his own Parisian sojourn. Stendhal, *Le Rouge et le Noir,* in *Œuvres romanesques complètes*, 1:560.

87 "l'idée d'un Paris littéraire encore un peu romantique, où les hommes de Balzac et d'Hugo n'auraient pas été dépaysés. ... Paris se montrait devant lui comme la cité des livres: il allait pouvoir étreindre toute la science, tous les textes: il trouverait les maîtres pour le diriger, les bibliothèques pour nourrir son appétit insatiable." Gauthiez, *L'Âge incertain*, 37–8.

88 "He would walk all the way to the Odéon to feel the intoxicating contact of the newest books; he discovered intimate pleasures." ("Il poussait jusqu'à l'Odéon pour se griser au contact des livres neufs, il découvrait des plaisirs intimes.") Ibid., 279.

89 "je passe la moitié de la journée à la bibliothèque Sainte-Geneviève ... dans Paris ... d'immenses bibliothèques sans cesse ouvertes offrent à l'esprit des renseignements et une pâture ... il y a dans l'air et dans les moindres détails un esprit qui se respire et s'empreint dans les créations littéraires." Balzac, *Illusions perdues*, in *La Comédie humaine*, 5:293.

90 "Comme les magiciens qui retrouvent sous le sol des trésors invisibles, ils évoquaient, à se promener dans Paris, trop piétiné pourtant, bâti, bouleversé, des fantômes, dont ils faisaient leur compagnie. Ils avaient souvent animé le sanglier des Tuileries où s'accoudèrent Fontanes et Chateaubriand." *Les Déracinés*, 1:602. According to his biography by Sainte-Beuve, Chateaubriand and his friend Louis de Fontanes used to promenade in the garden of the Tuileries, where there stood a statue of Meleager and the Calydonian boar. Sainte-Beuve, *Chateaubriand et son groupe littéraire sous l'Empire* (Paris: Garnier, 1848), 2:122. Cited by Rambaud in Barrès, *Romans et voyages*, 1:1377–8n273.

91 On the relationship of Flaubert's novel to Balzacian models, see Peter Brooks, "Retrospective Lust, or Flaubert's Perversities," in *Reading for the Plot*, 171–215.

92 "les événements que vous dites, après que vous en avez parlé, semblent, pris hors du livre, moins éloquents que vous-mêmes, ou ne pas persuader toujours comme vous voudriez qu'ils persuadent. Car enfin Suret-Lefort, Renaudin, Sturel, Roemerspacher réussissent; s'il avait plus d'argent, on peut croire que Racadot réussirait." Gide, "À propos des *Déracinés*," *L'Ermitage*, February 1898, reprinted in *Prétextes*, 45–52. Gide's review famously took a swipe at Barrès's theory of uprootedness [déracinement]; he would develop his critique of this theory in an article from 1903, "La Querelle du peuplier" (*L'Ermitage*, November 1903), also reprinted in *Prétextes*, 53–60.

93 In *L'Appel au soldat* and *Leurs figures*, Sturel becomes a key member of the Boulangist movement; Roemerspacher becomes a successful historian, and Saint-Phlin, the aristocrat of the group, returns to Lorraine to manage his family's lands.

94 In *Les Comédiens sans le savoir* (1845), Balzac's readers learn that Rastignac "has three hundred thousand *livres* of private income, he sits in the Chamber of Peers, the king has made him a Count ... and he is one of the two or three great statesmen whose careers were launched by the July Revolution" ("a trois cent mille livres de rentes, il est pair de France, le roi l'a fait comte ... et c'est un des deux ou trois hommes d'État enfantés par la Révolution de juillet"). See Cerfberr and Christophe, *Répertoire de la Comédie humaine* (1887), 429. Barrès was elected to the Académie française in 1906 and became a member of the Assemblée nationale that same year, representing a district of Paris until his death in 1923. Jean Borie notes that he, like Balzac, "married for money." Preface to *Les Déracinés* (1988), 16. Barrès purchased the château de Mirabeau, which had belonged to the eighteenth-century writer and revolutionary, from the writer Gyp in 1907. In *Splendeurs et misères des courtisanes*, Lucien purchases the Rubempré estate and castle with funds he extorted from the love-struck Nucingen, but he is driven to suicide shortly afterwards when the scheme is revealed.

Part III: Forming the Reader

1 See Charle, *La Crise littéraire à l'époque du naturalisme*, 30–2 and 51; as well as Angenot, *1889: Un état du discours social*, 827–8. It should be noted that, although literacy rates rose, the French population increased only slightly from 1840 to 1890, from c. 35 to c. 40 million.

2 "Sur le seuil des libraires et dans les boutiques d'éditeurs, dans les salles de rédaction et les cénacles, on ne parle plus que de krach du livre, de la crise du roman, de l'effondrement littéraire." Case, "La débâcle du réalisme."

3 In August 1887, as the serialization of Zola's *La Terre* drew to a close in *Gil Blas*, five young writers published a pamphlet, later known as the "Manifeste des Cinq," that vehemently criticized his "profound medical and scientific ignorance" ("ignorance, médicale et scientifique, profonde"). Paul Bonnetain et al., "*La Terre*, À Émile Zola."

4 "Il faut être, en effet, bien fou, bien audacieux, bien outrecuidant ou bien sot, pour écrire encore aujourd'hui!" Maupassant, "Le Roman" [1887], in *Romans*, 711.

5 "Après tant de maîtres ... que reste-t-il à faire qui n'ait été fait, que reste-t-il à dire qui n'ait été dit? Qui peut se vanter, parmi nous, d'avoir écrit une page, une phrase qui ne se trouve déjà, à peu près pareille, quelque part. Quand nous lisons, nous, si saturés d'écriture française que notre corps entier nous donne l'impression d'être une pâte faite avec des mots, trouvons-nous jamais une ligne, une pensée qui ne nous soit familière, dont nous n'ayons eu, au moins, le confus pressentiment?" Ibid., 711–12.

6 *Pierre et Jean* appeared as a serial in *Le Journal* from December 1887 to January 1888 and was published by Ollendorff in January 1888; the preface is dated September 1887.

7 See for instance my earlier discussions of *Crise de jeunesse* in part I and *Les Trois Legrand* in part II. Many influential nineteenth-century works describe the Parisian travails of aspiring writers, among them Balzac's *Illusions perdues* (1837–43) and the Goncourt brothers' *Charles Demailly* (1860).

8 "avait commencé d'écrivailler ... des chroniques pour les journaux, des nouvelles dans des revues." Mellerio, *Jacques Mérane* (1891), 10.

9 Ibid., 180.

10 For a study of this topic in the late nineteenth century, see Hugot, *Le Dilettantisme dans la littérature française d'Ernest Renan à Ernest Psichari*. Hugot examines Paul Bourget and Henry Bérenger's slightly differing definitions of the term "dilettante" (40–50 and 535–51); he does not discuss Renard.

11 "l'or et le plaisir." Balzac, *La Fille aux yeux d'or*, in *La Comédie humaine*, 5:1040.

12 "They have no children; they are bored." ("Ils n'ont pas d'enfants et s'ennuient.") Renard, *L'Écornifleur* [1892], in *Œuvres*, 1:316. Page references in subsequent notes are to this edition.

13 "Je dîne bien et souvent. Je dis des vers à la satiété de tous." Ibid., 1:330.

14 "Mais ne dois-je pas à mon éducation littéraire et aux exigences du monde d'être l'amant de Mme Vernet?" Ibid.

15 "ne devine ce que peut être une déclaration que par mes lectures"; "Des souvenirs de théâtre me reviennent. Il me paraît qu'une scène se prépare, et comme si nous repassions nos rôles, nous nous taisons, et nous écoutons en nous la montée lente des choses à dire." Ibid., 1:332, 357.

16 "Je ne sais pas. Je veux serrer 'ma maîtresse contre moi,' mais elle se dégage." Ibid., 1:384.

17 "I have to admit it: I had not seriously believed that Madame Vernet's adultery would actually become a reality. I thought of it, I caressed its image complacently: but its only seduction was its literary beauty." ("Il faut l'avouer, je n'avais jamais cru que l'adultère de Mme Vernet se réaliserait. J'y pensais, j'en caressais complaisamment les images: mais il n'offrait que la séduction d'une beauté littéraire.") Ibid., 1:382.

18 "Au-dessus je puis écrire quelques lignes, c'est commode." Ibid., 1:311.

19 "tandis que mes dents s'amusent d'un Palmer, ma bouche s'emplit et se vide de mots. Les notes que je repasse tous les deux ou trois jours me sont alors bien utiles. Elles condensent ce qu'un jeune homme doit savoir pour paraître supérieur. C'est un extrait de l'*Intelligence* de Taine vulgarisé à l'usage des gens du monde. C'est une ironie de Renan grossie, mise au point des vues moyennes. C'est un vers de Baudelaire qui étonne et qu'on écoute longtemps en soi-même comme l'écho d'un bruit dans un caveau." Ibid., 1:333. Château Palmer is a famed vineyard of the Bordeaux region, acquired by the Englishman Charles Palmer in 1814. Hippolyte Taine's *De l'intelligence* was published in 1870.

20 "We were going to admire the sea. I packed some authorities: *La Mer* by Michelet and *La Mer* by Richepin ... I also brought along Balzac's *Les Paysans*, in case I found myself having to make some excursion in the countryside." ("Nous allions voir la mer. Je pris avec moi mes autorités: *La Mer* de Michelet, *La Mer* de Richepin ... J'ajoutai à ces deux livres *Les Paysans* de Balzac, pour le cas où je serais obligé de faire quelque excursion en pleine campagne." Ibid., 1:336.

21 "Je regarde la mer avec fixité. J'ai l'air de dire: 'À nous deux!' Mais elle tient plus longtemps que moi ... La Grande Bleue me désespère, car je ne peux lui offrir une image de mon cru. Mieux vaudrait lire une page de Pierre Loti ... la trivialité de ce que la mer me fait éprouver m'exaspère ... Le Nautilus de Jules Verne m'a causé plus d'étonnement. Je repousse ces communes associations d'idées: elles rebondissent sur moi comme des boules de bilboquet. La camelote des comparaisons surcharge ma mémoire: le varech est une chevelure de noyé, le homard est le cardinal des mers!" Ibid., 1:341–2. Nautilus is the name of the submarine in Verne's *Vingt mille lieues sous les mers* (*20,000 Leagues under the Sea*, 1869).

22 On the frequent reference to Rastignac's iconic challenge in late-century novels of formation, see chapter 5, pages 155–7.

23 "Un peu étourdi par le balancement, je me récite des vers et, comme je n'ai rien de bon à me dire, je demande à mes poètes préférés de penser et de parler pour moi." Ibid., 1:432.

24 "Il ne me reste plus qu'à me coller au dos cette étiquette trouvée dans le *Journal* des Goncourt: 'À céder, un parasite qui a déjà servi.'" Ibid., 1:435.

25 Multiple novels of formation describe aspiring writers who unwittingly rely on literary reminiscences. In the aforementioned *Jacques Mérane* (1891), for instance, we read that the protagonist "had thrown himself, like so many young men, into literature, a vague word for an even vaguer thing ... he had published, with a small press, a tiny volume of verse – a feeble effort that mirrored his adolescent readings, a hodgepodge of imitations of ideas and styles." ("[il] s'était jeté, comme beaucoup de jeunes gens, à la littérature, mot vague, chose qui l'est plus encore ... il avait déjà publié, chez un petit éditeur, un infime volume de vers, de faibles élucubrations reflétant ses lectures d'adolescent, ramassis de réminiscences d'idées et de style.") Mellerio, *Jacques Mérane* (1891), 92. See also my discussion of *Crise de jeunesse* in part I, as well as *Tous Quatre* in chapter 2, pages 82–3.

6. Martin du Gard, Tinan, and the Uses of Irony

1 "Nous cachons si souvent – lâchement! – notre émotion derrière l'ironie!" Letter transcribed in Sicard, "Jean de Tinan et André Gide: Une amitié à sens unique," 213.

2 "La proximité de la mer les enivra. Ils quittèrent le chemin pour courir vers elle, criant: '*Thalassa! Thalassa!*,' levant déjà les mains pour les tremper dans l'eau bleue ... Mais la mer ne se laissa pas saisir. Au point où ils l'abordèrent, le rivage ne s'inclinait pas vers l'eau par cette pente de sable fin que leur convoitise avait imaginée. Ils surplombaient une sorte de goulet profond [...] où la mer s'engouffrait entre des rocs à pic. Au-dessous d'eux, un éboulis de quartiers rocheux s'avançait en brise-lames, comme une jetée édifiée par des Cyclopes." Unbracketed ellipsis is original. Roger Martin du Gard, *Les Thibault* [1922–40], in *Œuvres complètes* 1:645. Page references in subsequent notes are to this edition.

3 On the enduring presence of the citation in modern literary texts, see Tim Rood, '*The Sea! The Sea!': The Shout of the Ten Thousand in the Modern Imagination*. Rood points out that the narrator's single exclamation of "La mer!" in Jules Verne's *Voyage au centre de la Terre* (1864) was understood as a citation of Xenophon by the novel's English translator, who rendered it as "The sea! The sea!" (29). In *Le Cahier gris*, Jacques complains that, unlike Daniel, who has free access to his mother's library, he is only ever given books "of the Jules Verne type, imbecilities" ("genre Jules Verne, des imbecilités.") *Les Thibault*, 1:649.

4 "la mer ne se laissa pas saisir"; "'Ah! pouvoir décrire tout ça!' murmura Jacques en palpant son carnet de poche." Ibid., 1:645–6.

5 "Ah! c'est affreux, ces aspirations sans issue!" Ibid., 1:623.

6 Another example is found in a following volume, *La Belle Saison* (1923), where Jacques describes the rapid succession of his youthful artistic and

literary enthusiasms as a series of maladies: "I read like a madman ... I contracted every disease of adolescence: an acute *vincitis*, a hopeless *baudelairitis*! But none of my afflictions were long term! I would wake up one morning a Classic, and that same night go to bed a Romantic." ("Je lisais comme un forcené. ... J'ai eu toutes les maladies de l'adolescence: une *vincite* aiguë, une *baudelairite* exaspérée! Mais jamais d'affection chronique! Un matin, j'étais classique; le soir, romantique.") Ibid., 1:960–1. Through this description, Martin du Gard lightly parodies the discourse characterizing adolescent readings as feverish and disorderly. See chapter 2, pages 79–83.

7 "influence d'un camarade dangereux"; "de semblables contagions." Ibid., 1:583, 597.

8 It may be useful to recall Roland Barthes's definition of the hermeneutic code: "all the units whose function it is to articulate, in various ways, a question, its answers, and the various accidents that can bring about the answer or delay it. In other words, to formulate an enigma and bring about its decipherment." *S/Z* [1970], 21.

9 "amour chaste." *Les Thibault*, 1:631.

10 See chapter 4, pages 131–6.

11 "aucun doute sur la nature de cette amitié." Ibid., 1:584.

12 "NOTRE AMOUR!," "toi!!," "mon ART!!!" Ibid., 1:622. Original emphasis.

13 F. Schlegel, "On Goethe's *Meister*" [1798], 275.

14 Martin du Gard, "Souvenirs autobiographiques et littéraires," in *Œuvres complètes*, 1:xli–cxlii. The memoir was written for publication in that volume, a few years before Martin du Gard's death.

15 "I spent most of my time surreptitiously reading some lowbrow serials, novels and magazines I stole from my parents, or that a schoolmate lent me." ("Le plus clair de mon temps se passait à lire en cachette des feuilletons à bon marché, des romans et des revues que je chipais à mes parents, ou que me procurait quelque condisciple.") Ibid., 1:xliii.

16 "abondait surtout en œuvres modernes"; "Dans cet air saturé de littérature, et de littérature 'romanesque,' ... je respirais avec délices; c'était nouveau pour moi, et grisant. Il me semblait naïvement avoir trouvé mon vrai climat." Ibid., xlvi. Martin du Gard goes on to deploy a dietary metaphor: "What didn't I devour during that semester!" ("Que n'ai-je pas ingurgité durant ce semestre!" Ibid.) On the recurrence of this metaphor in discourses about reading, see chapter 1, pages 41–6.

17 Claude Sicard points out that the novel, written in 1908, was not published until June 1909, contrary to the chronology published in the Pléiade *Œuvres complètes*. See *Roger Martin Du Gard: Les années d'apprentissage littéraire (1881–1910)*, 565.

18 "Vouloir! "; "Réaliser? "; "Vivre ..." Original ellipsis.

19 Sicard notes that Martin du Gard's manuscripts include an indication that the section titles are punctuated "in a deliberate manner." *Les Années d'apprentissage littéraire*, 444. These punctuation marks were neglectfully changed or omitted in the 1955 *Œuvres complètes*, but they appear in the original 1909 edition of the novel as well as its 1930 re-edition at Gallimard.

20 "Tolstoy is the master of masters ... There is no risk, in frequenting him, of becoming afflicted with a 'mannerism.' [His hallmarks are] the natural, an extreme simplicity." ("Tolstoï est le maître des maîtres ... Aucun risque, auprès de lui, de contracter une 'manière'"; "Le naturel, l'extrême simplicité.") Martin du Gard, *Souvenirs autobiographiques et littéraires* [1955], in *Œuvres complètes*, 1:xlviii–xlix.

21 "J'ai toujours considéré *Devenir* ... comme une sorte d'exorcisme, destiné à conjurer l'envoûtement que je subissais depuis la faillite d'*Une Vie de saint* ... le désir m'a pris d'écrire l'histoire d'un jeune écrivain présomptueux ... plein d''illusions sur ses capacités,' et dont l'existence ne serait qu'une suite de velléités stériles et déconvenues. (Je m'étais mis en tête que si je réussissais ce portrait d'un 'raté,' la preuve serait faite que je n'étais pas menacé d'avoir la destinée lamentable de mon héros.") Ibid., 1:liii.

22 Quotation marks, like overemphatic punctuation, can serve as a sign of irony. See Schoentjes, *Poétique de l'ironie*, 164–7, and Hutcheon, *Irony's Edge*, 141–59.

23 "avec un intérêt personnel et passionné"; "Les yeux de Tolstoï, *ne peuvent apercevoir la vie que telle qu'elle est* ... sans rêves, sans chimères, sans illusions"; "[son] art ... transparent comme l'eau."; "Mon plus cher, secret et timide vœu, c'est de mériter qu'un jour, à propos de moi, par une analogie plus ou moins lointaine, on cite quelques-unes de ces pages." Martin du Gard, "10 Septembre 1930," in *Journal*, 2:869. Martin du Gard's emphasis. The reference is to Stefan Zweig, *Tolstoï*, trans. Alzir Hella and Olivier Bournac (Paris: Victor Attinger, 1928).

24 "une part estimable d'intelligence"; "dès le plus jeune âge, l'avait appliquée à contredire obstinément ce qu'il entendait et voyait autour de lui." Martin du Gard, *Devenir!* [1909], 13. Page references in subsequent notes are to this edition.

25 "Dès qu'il fut en âge de lire, le livre l'attira: c'était un vice de nature." Ibid.

26 "gestes étroits, féminins"; "la douceur de sa voix et la grâce maniérée de ses mouvements"; "lui appliquaient des substantifs équivoques – sans d'ailleurs y croire." Ibid., 16–17.

27 The novel is set around the turn of the century, but without mention of dates or specific political events, for instance the Dreyfus Affair. See Denis Boak, *Roger Martin du Gard*, 16–17.

28 "une attitude 1830, 'mal du siècle,' qui lui seyait." *Devenir!*, 16.

29 "Il entendait ne pas se laisser détourner de sa 'vocation,' qui, définitivement, était 'littéraire.' Il s'était insensiblement façonné une intelligence littéraire, une sensibilité littéraire, tout un tempérament littéraire, et qui ne pouvait plus être que cela ... Ses goûts, ses modes de penser, ses habitudes d'agir, ses moindres tendances, étaient littéraires: il avait une manière littéraire de goûter la peinture, d'écouter la musique, de songer aux femmes; il avait même une manière littéraire de concevoir la littérature, puisqu'il voulait délibérément lui consacrer sa vie. " Ibid., 15–16.

30 "le mal d'avoir connu l'image de la réalité avant la réalité." Bourget, "Flaubert," in *Essais de psychologie contemporaine*, 98.

31 "dix mois de vie purement animale"; "Du Bourget, du Régnier, du France ... Ibsen ... Barrès ... J'ai repris *La Débâcle*, *Le Rouge et le Noir*, *Madame Bovary* ..." *Devenir!*, 37. Original ellipses.

32 While in *The Picture of Dorian Gray* the colour of the "book bound in yellow paper" is part of a cluster of signifers of Frenchness and literary decadence, in a French context, the colour simply connotes paperback editions. See chapter 4, page 147.

33 "Quand on a vécu [...] la vie simple, pendant dix mois, et qu'on remet le nez dans ces bouquins jaunes, on n'y est plus ... On se dit: 'Quoi? qu'est-ce que c'est? de l'observation, ça? de la vie? des idées? Oh là là! ...' On a respiré la vie, la vraie, [...] On croit naïvement, qu'on va retrouver un peu de tout ça dans les livres ... Pfuit! Rien, mon cher. Rien!" *Devenir!*, 38. Unbracketed ellipses are original.

34 On *La Débâcle*, see chapter 2, note 55.

35 "Moi, je rêve d'un art neuf ... Je voudrais faire un livre qui serait 'de la vie,' et rien que ça." *Devenir!*, 39. Original ellipsis.

36 "à son mystère diverses formules de romans"; "intrigue." Ibid., 155.

37 "avec une tendresse littéraire." Ibid., 182.

38 The link is established most clearly by Sonia Spurdle in "Some sources of Roger Martin du Gard's inspiration in *Devenir!*."

39 See chapter 1, page 47.

40 "Ils ne craignaient rien tant que de paraître jeunes, ce qui l'était excessivement ... Ils redoutaient le snobisme et le cabotinage, au point de faire de cette répulsion un snobisme à eux, un cabotinage ingénu. Ils avaient si grand'peur de former 'chapelle,' que, préventivement, ils s'appliquaient à se railler, et composaient ainsi une chapelle de blague admirative, plus 'chapelle' qu'aucune autre. Ils étaient, en fin de compte, tout ce qu'ils s'efforçaient de ne pas être." *Devenir!*, 44.

41 Schlegel, "On Goethe's *Meister*," 273. Translation modified.

42 Reik, "Saint Irony," in *The Secret Self*, 166.

43 "– Say ... says André, – who, having read Tinan with too much passion, has developed an affectation of spouting psychology in places of pleasure ..."

("– Dites donc ... commence André, – qui, pour avoir lu trop passionnément Tinan, affecte de psychologuer dans les lieux dits 'de plaisir' ...") *Devenir!*, 70. Original ellipses.

44 "[he] reached on the shelves for a well-worn book and looked for passages that suited the day's mood. It was often Tinan. Bernard read it expertly because he mastered it well, and they listened to him equally well because they knew it by heart. It touched them, without fail." ("[il] atteignait sur ses rayons un livre débroché, et cherchait des passages appropriés à la mentalité du jour. C'était souvent du Tinan. Bernard le lisait bien parce qu'il le possédait à fond, et ils l'écoutaient de même parce qu'ils le savaient par cœur. Ils s'émouvaient, sans se lasser.") Ibid., 83.

45 "Ils ont tout laissé dans la marge. C'est à se demander avec quoi ils les ont faits, leurs bouquins! – Avec ceux d'avant." Ibid., 38.

46 "In the evening, he made an effort to write down on notecards his observations, his thoughts, all the acquisitions of the day. He believed he was accumulating 'material': but in reality, he only wrote down things that, in his book-stuffed brain, had evoked a 'literary reminiscence'; he foolishly neglected everything else." ("Le soir, il s'astreignait à consigner sur fiches les observations, les pensées, toutes les acquisitions de la journée. Il pensait s'approvisionner de 'matériaux': en réalité, il notait tout ce qui, en son cerveau farci de lettres, avait pu éveiller une 'réminiscence littéraire'; et il négligeait ingénument le reste.") Ibid., 123.

47 "A drive to create, which was in fact a mere need for pastiche, took hold of him so completely that, at times, his imagination, guided by reading, suddenly glanced the outline of a great new work. And yet, as soon as he attempted to make it 'real,' the mirage of the topic to cover, of which he had merely caught a glimpse, dissipated in the disconcerting whiteness of the paper, and, once again, he butted into his own impotence." ("Une soif de créer, qui n'était qu'un besoin de pastiche, le possédait si impérieusement, que, parfois, son imagination, guidée par la lecture, découvrait d'un coup le plan d'une œuvre nouvelle. Mais, dès qu'il tentait de 'réaliser,' le mirage du sujet, sommairement entr'aperçu, s'évanouissait sur la blancheur déconcertante du papier, et, une fois de plus, il butait contre son impuissance.") Ibid., 128.

48 Sonia Spurdle, "Some sources of Roger Martin du Gard's inspiration," 264–8. Other critics agree that the novel's last section is less successful than the first two. See for instance Robert Roza, *Roger Martin du Gard et la banalité retrouvée*, 25.

49 "Ah! vois-tu, ne rien faire d'artificiel, suivre sa nature, et quand on se sent né pour créer, se considérer comme ayant en ce monde la plus grave et la plus belle des missions, un grand devoir à accomplir. Oui! Être sincère! Être sincère en tout, et toujours! Ah! comme cette pensée me poursuit cruellement! Mille fois j'ai cru apercevoir en moi cette fausseté des faux artistes, des faux

génies, dont parle Maupassant dans *Sur l'eau*. Mon cœur se soulevait de dégoût." *Les Thibault*, 1:626.

50 "He seems to have two souls, one that notes, explains, comments every sensation of its twin, the natural soul, common to all mankind; and he is condemned to always be, at every moment, a reflection of himself and a reflection of others; condemned to observe himself feel, act, love, think, suffer, and to never suffer, think, love, feel like everyone else, directly, frankly, simply, without analysing himself after each moment of joy or of sorrow." ("Il semble avoir deux âmes, l'une qui note, explique, commente chaque sensation de sa voisine, l'âme naturelle, commune à tous les hommes; et il vit condamné à être toujours, en toute occasion, un reflet de lui-même et un reflet des autres, condamné à se regarder sentir, agir, aimer, penser, souffrir, et à ne jamais souffrir, penser, aimer, sentir comme tout le monde, bonnement, franchement, simplement, sans s'analyser soi-même après chaque joie et après chaque sanglot.") Maupassant, *Sur l'eau* [1888], in *Œuvres complètes*, 14:310–11.

51 "le difficile, vois-tu, c'est [...] la formule de sa sincérité ... Presque tous la ratent." *Devenir!*, 39. Unbracketed ellipsis is original.

52 *Penses-tu réussir!* was completed in 1896, and published by Mercure de France in April 1897.

53 "Enfin je réunis des notes, j'ai fait les plans de mes chapitres et je les *pense* souvent. Mais c'est trop simple, voyez-vous, il faudrait qu'il n'y ait pas une phrase manquée, pas une idée, pas une sensation 'toute faite,' il faudrait que *tout* soit vibré, et qu'il n'y ait pas une lacune de psychologie: c'est lourd et je n'ai pas les reins bien solides." Tinan, letter to André Gide, 9 March 1895. Cited in Sicard, "Jean de Tinan et André Gide," 216–17. Tinan's emphasis.

54 On Tinan's relationship to Gide, see Claude Sicard, ibid.

55 On Gide's *Cahiers*, see chapter 7, pages 199–205.

56 "Mon Dieu, comme *j'aimerais à aimer*!" Tinan, *Un document sur l'impuissance d'aimer* [1894], in *Œuvres complètes*, 1:310. Tinan's emphasis.

57 "Je m'enferme toute la journée dans ma chambre pour écrire – rêver – lire dans une demi-obscurité fraîche." Ibid., 340.

58 "ce qui m'a gâté l'amour jusqu'à présent, c'est que toujours entre moi et la réalité je vois se dresser une idée faite d'avance." Ibid. See above, note 30.

59 "Note. – Tout cela est trop compliqué et j'envie vraiment les gens qui aiment tout simplement.

Et puis – non je ne les envie pas – d'ailleurs, j'ai vu quelque part: 'Nous avons lu trop de volumes à 7,50F pour aimer comme tout le monde.'" Ibid., 318.

60 Around 1900, the usual price for a book (including many of the novels discussed in chapter 2) was 3,50F. A satirical scene performed in March 1897 mocked the high price of Proust's *Les Plaisirs et les Jours* (1896), 13,50F. That volume was published in a large format, with illustrations by

Madeleine Lemaire and musical scores by Reynaldo Hahn. See Dreyfus, *Souvenirs sur Marcel Proust*, 123.

61 Ann K. Mellor writes that "In Schlegel's terms, the ironic artist must constantly balance or 'hover' between self-creation (*Selbstschöpfung*) and self-destruction (*Selbstvernichtung*)." *English Romantic Irony*, 14.

62 "Nous lisions, j'ai dit: 'J'aime lire auprès de vous – il me semble que nos regards se mêlent sur les mots, c'est une caresse très subtile qui me charme.' Ce n'était pas très fort si vous voulez, ni très neuf, mais enfin." Tinan, *Un document sur l'impuissance d'aimer* [1894], in *Œuvres complètes*, 1:338–9.

63 Barthes, "Le Bruissement de la langue" [1975], 99.

64 Ibid.

65 "document dont l'intérêt, je pense, est d'être à peu près sincère." Tinan, *Un document sur l'impuissance d'aimer* [1894], in *Œuvres complètes*, 1:304.

66 "(Monotonie prolixe et étriquée de ces petites idées pieuses de souvenirs – je vous aime, pauvres façons d'être de nos sensibilités effacées et battantes ... (et c'est exprès que je réunis ici tant d'adjectifs inexacts) ..." *Œuvres complètes* 1: 47. Original ellipses.

67 "Celui qui a écrit ces pages est aussi jeune que celui qui en est le 'héros.'" Tinan, *Penses-tu réussir!* [1897], in *Œuvres complètes*, 1:27. Pages references in subsequent notes are to this edition.

68 "un bel autographe." Ibid., 1:31.

69 "avec un R majuscule." Ibid., 1:40. The expression "conte bleu" (blue tale) refers to "a fantasy, a fairytale; or else a baseless story, a lie" (*Dictionnaire de l'Académie francaise*, 6th edition, 1835.) "Bleu" also designates excessive, juvenile or outdated sentimentality; that usage derives from "fleur bleue," an expression that finds its origin in the motif of the blue flower [die blaue Blume] in Novalis's unfinished novel *Heinrich von Ofterdingen* (1802).

70 "'Excuse-moi d'y revenir – je sais bien que ça fait "longueur" – mais la petite scène ci-dessus six mille fois répétée, c'est ça la vie sentimentale ... J'ai connu tout le Rêve bleu, et j'en ai souffert, et ses pétales déteints sèchent entre tous les premiers feuillets du livre de ma vie – "un livre suprême," nous a dit M. A. de Lamartine ...' Vallonges ouvrit un tiroir, éparpilla des feuillets d'écriture, en choisit un; il lut avec exagération: 'Tiens, v'là un échantillon de sa chère littérature.'" Ibid., 1:44–5.

71 "Oui, J'écrivais cela vers ce temps-là"; "C'était de la bien mauvaise littérature, et c'était d'une philosophie bien facile et honteuse – et j'y tenais ..." Ibid., 1:45. Original ellipsis.

72 I discuss Lebey's *Les Premières Luttes*, which appeared the same year as *Penses-tu réussir!*, in chapter 1, pages 38–41.

73 "Pour servir de préface"; "'Ceci est une petite monographie réaliste.'" Ibid., 1:27.

74 See chapter 1, pages 34–7.

75 "Voici une phrase de M. Maurice Barrès que je trouve trop parfaite pour ne pas m'en expliquer: '*Il était gorgé des plus audacieux paradoxes de la pensée humaine, il en eût mal développé l'armature, c'est possible, mais il s'en faisait de la substance sentimentale* ...' Les livres mêmes de M. Barrès me furent alors d'autant plus chers que j'en eu mal *développé l'armature* – ils m'imprégnèrent d'une fièvre intense ... [...] c'est à eux que je dois le souci que j'eus dès lors de régler un peu l'ordre des lectures que je faisais jusqu'alors au hasard ... ils me firent souhaiter d'être '*intelligent*' ... Je n'exagère pas leur importance. (Les jeunes gens sur lesquels M. Barrès a agi n'ont pas parlé de lui encore. Il a été mieux que le lettré, l'idéologue, l'écrivain que l'on a discuté il y a une demi-douzaine d'années – il a été notre *éducateur*. [...] Il a su être notre *maître* sans rien nous prendre de notre initiative ... [...])" Ibid., 1:62. Italics and unbracketed ellipses are original. The quotation is from the first concordance of Barrès's *Sous l'œil des Barbares* [1888]: see *Romans et voyages*, 1:33.

76 Barrès, "Examen des trois romans idéologiques" [1891], in *Romans et voyages*, 1:17. Barrès's emphasis.

77 "'Quels maîtres enseigneront aux jeunes gens à haïr le Rêve!'" Tinan, *Penses-tu réussir!*, in *Œuvres complètes*, 1:44.

78 "(Jeune homme qui me liras peut-être – j'étale devant toi mon ridicule d'alors, ma faiblesse, ma sottise ... [...] Je me montre à toi comme j'étais, sans style – je touche du doigt la disproportion grotesque entre mon rêve gonflé, mon rêve vide, mon rêve faux – et la réalité où je me désespère de ne pas pouvoir le faire entrer ... Ce n'est pas la réalité qui a tort – c'est mon Rêve, c'est mon imprudence – toi ne soit pas imprudent ... [...] ne fais pas comme moi. [...] C'est pour cela que je laisse dans mon livre ce chapitre ennuyeux et terne: si un seul enfant, frère de celui que je fus, peut être préservé par ces lignes de la maladie qui a failli me tuer le cœur, je n'aurai pas été inutile.)" Ibid., 1:86–7. Unbracketed ellipses are original.

79 The passage for instance brings to mind Bourget's famous apostrophe, in the preface to *Le Disciple* (1889): "my young countryman" ("jeune homme de mon pays"). See chapter 1, pages 37–8.

80 Ibid., 1:87. Original emphasis.

81 "Tout ceci n'est pas poétique! Je n'y peux rien – je ne connais pas d'autre remède." Ibid.

82 See chapter 1, pages 31–4.

83 "Il paraît que nos lectures sont la cause de cela." Ibid., 1:232.

84 "'Et, parce que nous avons rêvé avant de vivre, parce que nous portons en nous-mêmes l'atavisme d'une race qui, depuis des siècles, rêve, notre idéal est maintenant très loin. ... Vous tous, mes aïeux inconnus, le long des siècles vous avez comme moi pensé au bonheur, et vous m'avez légué le poids trop lourd de tout votre amour lassé. Ah! vous avez trop rêvé! il ne faut

pas accuser les livres; aux livres et au siècle nous devons sans doute bien des amertumes, mais nous leur devons aussi la raillerie qui soutient notre âme comme l'alcool soutient notre corps.'" Ibid., 1:238–9.

85 "des soupirs de quinze ans"; "un gongorisme." Ibid., 1:238. This rare adjective, from the name of the poet Luis de Gongóra y Argote (1561–1627), describes "an affected type of diction and style" (OED).

86 "Je sais bien, cela peut sembler prétentieux, décousu, boursouflé et inutile encore, mais qu'y faire? Mon 'positivisme' tout frais luttait – comme dans tout ce volume – contre tant de vieilles choses. (Et même, vous sentez bien que le mot 'positivisme' ne vaut rien.)

C'était au moins sincère de tout le sherry qui manquait dans la carafe vide. On aime – que voulez-vous – comme on peut, et c'est déjà très touchant tout de même. Il n'est pas impossible de comprendre à quelles vraies émotions de semblables exaltations correspondent." Ibid., 1:239.

87 "Je crois bien que les livres que je ne saurais manquer de publier à la suite, et auxquels celui-ci doit surtout servir de préface, ne me toucheront pas aussi directement que cette poignée de lyrismes mal apprêtés, si brutaux, et si bien contradictoires [...] – parce que mes 'dix-huit-à-vingt-ans' y ont un peu crié tout de même ..." Ibid., 1:295–6. Unbracketed ellipsis is original.

88 *L'Exemple de Ninon de Lenclos amoureuse* (Paris: Mercure de France, 1898); *Aimienne ou le détournement de mineure* (Paris: Mercure de France, 1899, posth.).

7. Gide and the Novel as Formation

1 "À Roger Martin du Gard je dédie mon premier roman en témoignage d'amitié profonde." Gide, *Les Faux-Monnayeurs* [1925], in *Romans et récits*, 2:173. Page references in subsequent notes are to this edition.

2 On the conflicting historical indicators in the novel, which span the years 1896 (the premiere of Jarry's play *Ubu Roi*, alluded to as recent) to 1920 (a mention of Marcel Duchamp's *Joconde à moustaches* [Mona Lisa with moustache], also known as *L.H.O.O.Q.*), see Goulet, *André Gide, Les Faux-Monnayeurs: Mode d'emploi*, 78–83.

3 The designation is used by a number of critics, for instance Alain Goulet in his "Notice" to *Les Faux-Monnayeurs*. Gide, *Romans et récits*, 2:1201.

4 Gide specified he chose the Jardin du Luxembourg as a "mythical" setting. Cited in Goulet, *Mode d'emploi*, 210.

5 "[ses] camarades ... avaient coutume de se retrouver, chaque mercredi entre quatre et six ... On causait art, philosophie, sports, politique et littérature." *Romans et récits*, 2:176.

6 "des mauvaises fréquentations et des mauvaises lectures." Ibid., 2:182. On turn-of-the-century discourses linking the two, see chapter 2, pages

74–9, and chapter 4, pages 131–6. *Les Faux-Monnayeurs* and the first tomes of *Les Thibault* were written concurrently and bear many traces of their authors' close friendship. See Harald Emeis's extensive study, *Reflets littéraires d'une amitié: André Gide dans Les Thibault de Roger Martin du Gard*. Gide's novel alludes to two of the best-known examples of the turn-of-the-century novel of formation by citing Barrès (in a dialogue) and Bourget (as an epigraph noted by Édouard for his novel-in-progress) – both rather derisively (2:194, 257). See also Hecquet, "*Les Déracinés* dans *Les Faux-Monnayeurs*."

7 "a trop lu déjà, trop retenu, et beaucoup plus appris par les livres que par la vie." *Romans et récits*, 2:338–9.

8 On *Les Aventures de Télémaque*, see chapter 3, page 112.

9 "cette verte jeunesse." *Romans et récits*, 2:216. The citation is from Bossuet's "Panégyrique de Saint Bernard." On these references, see Alain Goulet's notes in ibid., 2:1226–7nn4–8.

10 "j'imaginais quelque chose de volcanique ... à la Byron." Ibid., 2:321.

11 "Ah! si vous saviez ce que c'est enrageant d'avoir dans la tête des tas de phrases de grands auteurs, qui viennent irrésistiblement sur vos lèvres quand on veut exprimer un sentiment sincère." Ibid., 2:322.

12 "la lutte entre les faits proposés par la réalité, et la réalité idéale." Ibid., 2:314. "le 'sujet profond' de mon livre ... sera ... la rivalité du monde réel et de la représentation que nous nous en faisons." Ibid., 2:326–7.

13 "tout ce chapitre est à récrire." Ibid., 2:445; "l'illogisme de son propos était flagrant, sautait aux yeux d'une manière pénible." Ibid., 2:314.

14 See chapter 6, pages 179–82. Unlike Martin du Gard who idealized Tolstoy, Gide favoured Dostoyevsky's dialogic approach of the representation of conflicting perspectives. He gave a series of conferences on Dostoyevsky in 1922 (published in 1923). See Masson, "Notule" on *Dostoïevski*, in Gide, *Essais critiques*, 1156–7.

15 The most prominent of these, as indicated in the title, is the novel's use of money (and counterfeit money) as an allegory for representation. See Goux, *Les Monnayeurs du langage*.

16 In French, "lutter avec l'ange" (literally "wrestling with the angel"), a reference to the biblical story of Jacob (Genesis 32), is a figurative expression for internal debate.

17 "sans qu'aucun des deux fût vainqueur." *Romans et récits*, 2:433.

18 Gide made such claims throughout his career, including numerous times in his memoir *Si le grain ne meurt* (which appeared in 1926, a few months after *Les Faux-Monnayeurs*), for instance: "I am a creature of dialogue: everything inside me combats and contradicts itself." ("Je suis un être de dialogue: tout en moi se combat et se contredit.") *Si le grain ne meurt*, in *Souvenirs et voyages*, 267.

19 "Mallarmé pour la poésie, Maeterlinck pour le drame – et quoique auprès d'eux je me sente bien un peu gringalet, j'ajoute Moi pour le roman." Gide, letter to Paul Valéry, 26 January 1891, in Gide and Valéry, *Correspondance (1890–1942)*, 46.

20 "œuvre posthume." *Les Cahiers d'André Walter* [1891], in Gide, *Les Cahiers et les Poésies d'André Walter*, 28. Page references in subsequent notes are to this edition.

21 "André Walter avait écrit ces cahiers que nous publions ici et un roman qui ne le sera jamais." P.C., "Notice," in Gide, *Romans et récits*, 1:138. The notice appears in the very first printing of *Les Cahiers* (Paris: Librairie académique Didier-Perrin, February 1891), but not in subsequent editions (Paris: Librairie de l'Art indépendant, April 1891 and April 1892). See Pierre Masson, "Note sur le texte," in *Romans et récits*, 1:1245.

22 "l'échafaudage du livre." Gide, "Cahier préparatoire" (preparatory manuscript notebook from 1889–1890, unpublished until 1986). *Romans et récits*, 1:140.

23 Emmanuèle is the name Gide used for his cousin Madeleine Rondeaux in all his autobiographical writings; they married in 1895. When *Les Cahiers* appeared in the winter of 1891, Gide had a special copy printed where every occurrence of the name "Emmanuèle" was replaced with "Madelène." Claude Martin, preface to Gide, *Les Cahiers et les Poésies d'André Walter*, 14.

24 "fièvre cérébrale." *Les Cahiers et les Poésies d'André Walter*, 34. "Que Pierre C***, à qui je les donne, publie, si je deviens fou, ces cahiers ... s'il publie mes cahiers – qu'il garde Allain; – l'un ou l'autre." Ibid., 148.

25 "La vie intellectuelle est décuplée par les lectures, il érige cela en théorie ... comme tout le but de la vie est de l'intensifier de toutes les manières, il identifiera sa vie à toutes ses lectures (prendre garde de tomber dans le banal). Plutôt s'exalte que identifie. Cela est meilleur: la vie en imagination, voilà le moyen de la brûler par les deux bouts." "Cahier préparatoire," in *Romans et récits*, 1:140.

26 In *Les Caves du Vatican* (1914), for instance, Gide's narrator systematically refuses to carry out what he deems the commonplaces of the adventure novel.

27 "(Il faudra rechercher Chambige.)" "Cahier préparatoire," in *Romans et récits*, 1:141. Gide mentions the Chambige affair as "a story that moved us deeply at the time" ("une histoire qui nous émut beaucoup à cette époque") in an interview from 1949. Gide and Amrouche, *André Gide: Qui êtes-vous?*, 184–5. See chapter 4.

28 ("Il me semble qu'un tel livre s'impose tellement maintenant que j'ai toujours peur de le voir paraître tout à coup. Si l'on me coupait l'herbe sous le pied!") "Cahier préparatoire," in *Romans et récits*, 1:140.

29 "Ce livre me paraissait un des plus importants du monde, et la crise que j'y peignais, de l'intérêt le plus général, le plus urgent." *Si le grain ne meurt*, in *Souvenirs et voyages*, 243.

30 In a letter to his mother, Gide enthusiastically describes Perrin, where he had the very first edition of *Les Cahiers d'André Walter* printed (at his own expense), as "the publisher of l'*Homme libre*." Cited in Pierre Masson, "Notice" to *Les Cahiers*, in *Romans et récits*, 1:1240. Bourget's letter, from 8 March 1891, is reproduced in ibid., 1:117–18.

31 "je trouve que vous avez noté là, avec une grande acuité, cette terrible maladie de la volonté par laquelle passent les jeunes gens de la seconde moitié du siècle, une maladie qui résulte de la magnifique éducation de l'intelligence ... en présence de faible volonté ... Cette crise, vous l'avez magnifiquement décrite." Letter from Marcel Schwob, undated (1891), in *Romans et récits*, 1:115. Schwob had published his first collection of symbolist tales the same year.

32 See chapter 2, pages 59–60. The psychologist Théodule Ribot published a treatise entitled *Les Maladies de la volonté* (Diseases of the will) in 1883, the same year as the first volume of Bourget's *Essais*.

33 "Ce furent les Grecs d'abord, et depuis, toujours préférés: l'*Iliade*, *Prométhée*, *Agamemnon*, *Hippolyte*, ... L'âpreté violente de Shakespeare ... l'éloquence de Lamennais ... Puis nous reprenions les lectures de l'enfance ... Pascal, Bossuet, Massillon ... Et tant d'autres encore – et tous les autres. Puis, avec les ambitions révélées, ce fut Vigny, Baudelaire, – Flaubert, l'ami toujours souhaité! – Les subtilités rhétoriques des Goncourt ... Stendhal ... le *Voyage en Orient* de du Camp et de Flaubert ... la *Tentation* encore." *Les Cahiers et les Poésies d'André Walter*, 41–3.

34 Ibid., 60, 92–6.

35 Claude Martin, preface to Gide, *Les Cahiers et les Poésies*, 24 and 24–5n48.

36 Walter Geerts, *Le Silence sonore: La poétique du premier Gide, entre intertexte et métatexte*, 234.

37 "Nous aimions à nous perdre ensemble dans les plus lointain souvenirs ... un mot suffisait à lever tant de rêves. Car ce n'était pas le mot seul; pour nous, il avait sa légende et la même; il évoquait bien des émois passés, des lectures, et quand nous l'avions dit, et quand nous l'avions lu: – ce n'était jamais le mot seul, c'était un rappel d'autrefois." *Les Cahiers et les Poésies d'André Walter*, 66–7.

38 Ibid., 108.

39 "Le matin tu vaquais aux soins du ménage; je voyais ton tablier clair circuler dans les longs couloirs: je t'attendais sur l'escalier ... nous montions dans la lingerie si grande – et parfois, tandis que tu rangeais le linge, je t'y poursuivais d'une lecture commencée." Ibid., 48.

40 The Vedas are the most ancient sacred texts of Hinduism.

41 "Je voudrais une cellule nue ... une table de chêne, immense, et dessus, tous ouverts, des livres. Un grand lutrin pour travailler debout; dessus, un livre ouvert. Au-dessus du lit, des livres rangés. Je lirais la Bible, les Védas, Dante, Spinoza, Rabelais, les Stoïques; j'apprendrais le grec, l'hébreu, l'italien – et ma pensée se sentirait orgueilleusement vivre." Ibid., 55–6.

42 "Quand j'aurai lu Schopenhauer, je prendrai *l'Origine des espèces*. J'ai fini les *Mémoires* de Berlioz et le second volume de l'*Histoire de France* de Michelet. ... Que d'ivresses! – je vis dans une surexcitation perpétuelle." Ibid., 100.

43 "Lire *Paul et Virginie*, *Adolphe*, épisode de Thérèse dans Michelet. *Dernier jour d'un condamné*." Gide, "Cahier préparatoire," in *Romans et récits*, 1:138. *Le Dernier Jour d'un condamné* (1829) is a novel by Victor Hugo.

44 "Ce livre se dressait devant moi et fermait ma vue, au point que je ne supposais pas que je pusse jamais passer outre. Je ne parvenais pas à le considérer comme le premier de ma carrière, mais comme un livre unique, et n'imaginais rien au-delà ... après, c'était la mort, la folie." *Si le grain ne meurt*, in *Souvenirs et voyages*, 228.

45 "L'ordonnance de Spinoza pour l'*Éthique*, la transposer dans le Roman; les lignes géométriques. Un roman c'est un théorème." *Les Cahiers et les Poésies d'André Walter*, 92.

46 "Je voudrais la forme si lyrique et frémissante que la poésie en profuse, malgré les lignes si rigides ... L'orthographie! J'ai d'abord cru qu'il fallait s'y plier, mais ... En français? non. Je voudrais écrire en musique." Ibid., 92–3. On the many references to Verlaine in *Les Cahiers*, see Geerts, *Le Silence sonore*, 49–61.

47 "œuvre étrange, 'scientifique et passionnée' disait-il." P.C., "Notice," in Gide, *Romans et récits*, 1:138.

48 "immense cerveau, qui a sans doute craqué de toutes parts comme un empire trop vaste"; "l'envie de se précipiter dans l'infini." Balzac, *Louis Lambert* [1831–5], in *La Comédie humaine*, 11:691–2. On the similarities between the two works, see Geerts, *Le Silence sonore*, 175–6, 182–90.

49 On this topic, see Seillan, *Enquête sur le roman romanesque*.

50 See *Le "Livre" de Mallarmé*.

51 For Mallarmé, "*to name* an object is to suppress three fourths of the pleasure of a poem ... to *suggest* the object, that is the dream" ("*nommer* un objet, c'est supprimer les trois quarts de la jouissance du poème ... le *suggérer*, voilà le rêve"). Mallarmé's emphasis. See Huret, *Enquête sur l'évolution littéraire (1891)*, 103.

52 I discuss the prevalence of "fever" as a trope to describe young men's reading practices at the fin de siècle in chapter 2, pages 79–80.

53 "Ce n'est pas très volontiers que je laisse réimprimer mon premier livre ... à cet âge, je ne savais pas écrire." Gide, "Préface" [1930] to *Cahiers et poésies (édition définitive)* (Paris: Crès, 1930.) Reprinted in *Romans et récits*, 1:3. The first reissue authorized by Gide (and the first edition of the *Cahiers* to bear his name) was printed by the NRF in 1922.

54 "qu'un trop tendre lecteur n'aille pas chercher ici un modèle de façons d'écrire, ou de sentir, ou de penser. Je crois André Walter de très mauvais

exemple ... c'est pour avertir que j'écris, pour exalter ou pour instruire, et j'appelle un livre manqué celui qui laisse intact le lecteur." Ibid., 4.

55 See below, note 70.

56 On the pedagogical drive of Gide's narrative works, particularly *Les Caves du Vatican* and *Les Faux-Monnayeurs*, see Savage-Levrut, "Représentations de lecteurs et pédagogie de la lecture dans les soties et *Les Faux-Monnayeurs*."

57 "Feeling is all /Name is but noise and smoke /Clouding the heavens' glow." *Les Cahiers et les Poésies d'André Walter*, 112.

58 "[L]es lectures l'enorgueillissent ... et de quoi? Quand l'esprit lit, le cœur sommeille, – et sa ferveur tiédit sous les poussières érudites. Donc, ne plus lire, sinon beaucoup la Bible, – et relire doucement quelque sage classique." *Les Cahiers et les Poésies d'André Walter*, 105–6. Original ellipsis.

59 "Nous avons quitté nos livres parce qu'ils nous ennuyaient, parce qu'un souvenir inavoué de la mer et du ciel réel faisait que nous n'avions plus foi dans l'étude; quelque chose d'autre existait." Gide, *Le Voyage d'Urien* [1893], in *Romans et récits*, 1:186.

60 "Pardonnez! J'ai menti.
Ce voyage n'est que mon rêve,
Nous ne sommes jamais sortis
De la chambre de nos pensées, –
Et nous avons passé la vie
Sans la voir. Nous lisions." Ibid., 1:230.

61 Gide, *Les Nourritures terrestres* [1897], in *Romans et récits*, 1:351.

62 "Nathanaël je t'enseignerai la ferveur." Ibid., 1:353, 354.

63 "*Les Nourritures terrestres* is the book, not quite of a sick man, but of a convalescent, of someone cured – someone who had been ill ... I wrote the book at a time when literature reeked of the factitious, of a suffocating atmosphere: it seemed urgent to bring it down to earth again, to let it simply touch the ground with a bare foot." ("*Les Nourritures terrestres* sont le livre, sinon d'un malade, du moins d'un convalescent, d'un guéri – de quelqu'un qui a été malade ... J'écrivais ce livre à un moment où la littérature sentait furieusement le factice et le renfermé; où il me paraissait urgent de la faire à nouveau toucher terre et poser simplement sur le sol un pied nu.") Gide, "Préface de l'édition de 1927," in ibid., 1:443.

64 "que tu brûles en toi tous les livres." Ibid., 1:359.

65 "Jette ce livre"; "jette mon livre. Émancipes-t'en." Ibid., 1:349, 442.

66 "Ménalque, n'a jamais, non plus que toi-même, existé"; "parfois j'y parle de pays que je n'ai point vus, de parfums que je n'ai point sentis." Ibid., 1:349.

67 "refaire à mes yeux une vision neuve, les laver de la salissure des livres." Ibid., 1:358.

68 "Je suis las de feindre d'éduquer quelqu'un ... Éduquer! Qui donc éduquerais-je, que moi-même?" Ibid., 1:442.

69 "This book [*La Porte étroite*] will be the counterpart to my *Immoraliste.*" ("Ce livre formera en quelque sorte le pendant de mon *Immoraliste.*") Letter to Maurice Denis, 7 December 1907, cited in Pierre Masson, "Notice" to *La Porte étroite*, in *Romans et récits*, 1:1433.

70 "Chacun de mes livres se retourne contre les amateurs du précédent. Ceci pour leur apprendre à ne m'applaudir que pour le bon motif, à ne prendre chacun de mes livres que pour ce qu'il est: une œuvre d'art." Gide, "Caractères" [1925], in *Divers*, 33–4.

71 "je sais lire écriture ou imprimé, couramment, à l'envers ou par transparence, au verso, dans les glaces ou sur les buvards; trois mois d'études et deux années d'apprentissage; et cela pour l'amour de l'art." Gide, *Les Caves du Vatican* [1914], in *Romans et récits*, 1:1130.

72 "Bernard était grave. Sa lutte avec l'ange l'avait mûri." *Les Faux-Monnayeurs*, in *Romans et récits*, 1:434.

73 On the proliferation of "possibilities of double readings" in *Les Caves*, in terms of textual but also bodily and queer signs, see Paul J. Young, "Cruising *The Vatican* ...: Reading Gide's Queerest Text."

74 "J'y entrais comme dans un temple; dans la pénombre se dressait le tabernacle de la bibliothèque ... Il y avait un lutrin près d'une des deux fenêtres; au milieu de la pièce, une énorme table couverte de livres et de papiers. Mon père allait chercher un gros livre, quelque *Coutume de Bretagne* ou *de Normandie*, pesant in-folio qu'il ouvrait sur le bras d'un fauteuil pour épier avec moi, de feuille en feuille, jusqu'où persévérait le travail d'un insecte rongeur. Le juriste, en consultant un vieux texte, avait admiré ces galeries clandestines et s'était dit: 'Tiens! cela amusera mon enfant.' Et cela m'amusait beaucoup, à cause de l'amusement qu'il paraissait lui-même y prendre." Gide, *Si le grain ne meurt* [1924–6], in *Souvenirs et voyages*, 85.

75 *Les Cahiers et les Poésies d'André Walter*, 56. See above, note 41. This resemblance is not signalled in the Pléiade edition, which usually goes to great lengths to point out intertextual resonances.

76 It should also be noted that the insect is not characterized as a pest or a parasite; in fact, the early chapters of *Si le grain ne meurt* go on to describe, in great detail, the young Gide's fascination and enthusiasm for entomology.

77 "clandestinement"; "morte, ou malade"; "ce n'est là qu'un jeu." *Les Caves du Vatican*, in *Romans et récits*, 1:1131–2.

8. Proust and the Fantasy of Readerly Recognition

1 "Si un autre me ressemble, c'est donc que j'étais quelqu'un." Proust, *Jean Santeuil*, ed. Clarac and Sandre, 471.

2 In 1912, the novel was still conceived as one of two parts: "Le Temps perdu," to be followed by "Le Temps retrouvé." On Proust's difficulties in finding a publisher, see Tadié, *Marcel Proust*, 674–92.

3 “one of the most bitter regrets, even remorses of my life.” (“un des regrets, des remords, les plus cuisants de ma vie.”) Gide to Proust, [10 or 11 January 1914], in Proust, *Correspondance* XIII:50–1. Abbreviated as *Corr.* in subsequent notes.

4 “the typsescript was not read attentively, it was at most browsed, or leafed through.” Anglès, *André Gide et le premier groupe de la Nouvelle Revue française*, 2:390–3. Jean Schlumberger likewise claims that “none of us, including Gide, Gallimard or Copeau, had actually read the manuscript. At most we had glimpsed, here and there, a few paragraphs written in a style that discouraged us.” Letter to J. Lambert, cited in Tadié, *Marcel Proust*, 686n2.

5 “un mondain amateur.” Gide to Proust, *Corr.*, XIII:50. On Gide’s aversion to “high-society reading” (“la lecture mondaine”), see Cazentre, *Gide lecteur*, 76–109.

6 On the reception of *Les Plaisirs et les Jours*, see Tadié, *Marcel Proust*, 312–15; on the possible impact of this reception on the composition of *Jean Santeuil*, see Kolb, “Historique du premier roman de Proust,” especially 240–4.

7 Proust had not chosen a title for his unfinished novel; Bernard de Fallois, the editor of the 1952 version, gave it the name of its protagonist. A revised edition was published in 1971 (*Jean Santeuil précédé de Les Plaisirs et les jours*, Paris: Gallimard [Pléiade]) by Pierre Clarac and Yves Sandre, who reordered the material thematically and added certain fragments or scenes not included by Fallois. For citations in French, page references in subsequent notes are to the 1971 edition, hereafter cited as *JS*. Citations in English generally refer to the translation of the 1952 version by Gerard Hopkins (New York: Simon & Schuster, 1956), hereafter cited as *JS (Hopkins)*. In some cases, all noted, I have modified this translation; for passages not included in the 1952/1956 version, I provide my own translation.

8 “I say ‘my book,’ as if I were to never write another ... Once I finish the one I am working on now, ...” (“Je dis mon livre comme si je n’en devais jamais écrire d’autre ... Si je puis terminer celui qui est entrepris, ...”) Dedication to Pierre Lavallée on a copy of *Les Plaisirs et les Jours*, [around 12? June 1896], in *Corr.*, II:76. “I have been working for a long time on a very long work, without being able to complete anything.” (“Je travaille depuis très longtemps à un ouvrage de très longue haleine, mais sans rien achever.”) Letter to Marie Nordlinger, [5 December 1899], in *Corr.*, II:377.

9 These are the first sentences of a very brief, unfinished introduction. *JS (Hopkins)*, 1. (“Puis-je appeler ce livre un roman?” “C’est moins peut-être, et bien plus encore, l’essence même de ma vie, recueillie sans rien y mêler.” *JS*, 181.)

10 See part I, pages 19–23.

11 "[M]y father had steadily opposed my devoting myself to literature." Proust, *In Search of Lost Time*, trans. C.K. Scott Moncrieff (except for *Time Regained*, trans. Andreas Mayor and Terence Kilmartin), rev. Terence Kilmartin and D.J. Enright (New York: Modern Library, 2003), 2:13. Hereafter cited as *SLT*. ("[M]on père avait fait une constante opposition à ce que je me destinasse à la carrière des lettres." Proust, *À la recherche du temps perdu*, gen. ed. Jean-Yves Tadié [Paris: Gallimard [Pléiade], 1987–9], 1:431. Hereafter cited as *RTP*.)

12 "[O]ne sees a young man, son of an intelligent and successful father, with money to burn, dissipating a fortune that's been honourably amassed, dragging in the mud a name that's universally repected and ending up starving to death, if not worse, among a scratch lot of good-for-nothing scribblers ... You'd do better to give him a length of rope to hang himself!" *JS (Hopkins)*, 38. ("Et on voit un jeune homme, fils d'un grand homme intelligent, riche et qui pouvait prétendre à tout, dissiper la fortune bien acquise, déshonorer le nom universellement considéré de son père et finir par crever de faim si ce n'est pas pire, dans un ramassis de scélérats d'hommes de lettres ... Autant lui donner la corde pour se pendre." *JS*, 214.)

13 The description of Jean's father is an almost parodic accumulation of functions and powerful relations: "an ex-Senator for the Drôme, a man who had twice sat on the Budget commision, Vice-President of the Commission on Colza, who had been Secretary of the Commission set up to enquire into social conditions in the suburbs, had once been Presiding Officer of the Court of Appeal, an intimate friend of the President of the Republic, a nephew of a former War Minister." *JS (Hopkins)*, 36, translation modified. ("ancien sénateur de la Drôme et deux fois membre de la commission du budget, vice-président de la commission des colzas, secrétaire de la commission des misères suburbaines, ancien président de chambre à la Cour d'appel, ami le plus intime du président de la République et neveu du ministre de la Guerre." *JS*, 212.)

14 See chapter 2, pages 63–6.

15 *JS (Hopkins)*, 25, 35. ("nous voulons, mon mari et moi, l'élever virilement"; "Je crois que Jean aimera la poésie." *JS*, 202, 211.)

16 *JS (Hopkins)*, 68, translation modified. ("il a envie d'écrire des extravagances, de ne penser à rien, de lire des romans ou des vers ... Cette force dont l'absence est un terrible écueil ... c'est la volonté." *JS*, 232.)

17 Théodule Ribot's *Les Maladies de la volonté* (Diseases of the will) was published in 1883; it is cited in an 1897 treatise co-authored by Marcel's father, Adrien Proust, *L'Hygiène du neurasthénique*. See chapter 2, pages 60–1. On Marcel Proust, Adrien Proust and Ribot, see Finn, *Proust, the Body and Literary Form*, 45–56.

18 *JS (Hopkins)*, 580, translation modified. ("C'est justement à Stendhal ... que Jean pensait toujours, en pensant au profil pur ... qui mettait depuis un mois

un charme nouveau dans sa vie. Il ne pouvait pas dire qu'il fût très amoureux de Mme. S., mais justement, peut-être à cause de cela, il jouissait du plaisir qu'il sentait à être amoureux ... il était heureux de se sentir envahi, chez elle, en revenant de chez elle, chez lui en restant à penser à elle, par ce plaisir qui nous détache des autres et nous en fait connaître de nouveaux, dont il avait vu la vivacité chez Julien Sorel, chez Fabrice Del Dongo, dans le livre *De l'amour*, sans l'avoir éprouvé depuis. Il s'était bientôt rendu compte qu'il ne pouvait coucher avec cette jeune veuve imprudente [elle le recevait tous les soirs de dix heures à deux heures du matin; il ne la désirait d'ailleurs que très peu] mais honnête, qu'il ne pourrait même pas l'embrasser." *JS*, 746.)

19 See chapter 5, pages 153–4.

20 Philip Kolb only found one letter from Proust to Jean Lazard (letter addressed to "Mon petit Jean," [around 17 or 18 October 1896], *Corr.*, VI:349–50). Jean Lazard (1871–1950), the son of a wealthy banker, appears to have met Proust in or before 1892. The extent of their friendship and correspondence remains unknown: Lazard is not cited in Tadié's biography. In 1920 Proust includes him in a list of friends that could potentially subscribe to a luxury edition of *À l'ombre des jeunes filles en fleurs* (*Corr.*, XIX:356–7).

21 "J'ai reçu ... les deux lettres ci-jointes de Jean Lazard ... On peut en tirer bien des conclusions sur le danger que présente la culture intellectuelle trop forte chez des gens qui ne prennent pas une carrière intellectuelle de sorte qu'ils appliquent à la vie qui ne les comporte pas la subtilité de leur esprit et les condui[t] à déraisonner ainsi. Pour en être un produit plus innocent il (Jean Lazard) me semble résulter aussi maladivement de cet état d'esprit (appliquer à la vie l'intelligence littéraire) qu'Émile Henry ou Chambige." *Corr.*, II:330.

22 *Corr.*, VI:350n4.

23 See Tadié, *Marcel Proust*, 327–31.

24 See Kolb, "Historique du premier roman de Proust," 245–60. Jean-Yves Tadié notes that this attempt to include a chronicle of contemporary political events (using a combination of real and fictional characters) shows the influence of Barrès's *Déracinés*, which Proust read in 1897. "Préface" to *Jean Santeuil*, 14n22.

25 "1er chapitre." The sequence is named "préface" in other related sections of the manuscript; the latter label was retained for the 1971 edition.

26 The reference to English novelists is principally to George Eliot, who Proust read avidly at the time. There are multiple references to *Middlemarch* and to Eliot in *Jean Santeuil* and in Proust's correspondence of 1896.

27 From "After he had read": my translation. From "Often his narrative": *JS (Hopkins)*, 18. ("après nous avoir lu un après-midi tout le commencement du roman qu'il écrivait alors, chaque soir, ... quand il avait fini de dîner, il prenait les papiers qui étaient à côté de lui, maintenus par une assiette,

et commençait à nous les lire, mais après tant de précautions oratoires et mêlant sa lecture de tant de critiques sur soi-même ... Souvent son récit était interrompu par quelques réflexions où l'auteur exprime son opinion sur certaines choses, à la manière de certains romanciers anglais qu'il avait autrefois beaucoup aimés. Ces réflexions, souvent très ennuyeuses pour le lecteur pour qui elles coupent l'intérêt et ôtent l'illusion de la vie, étaient ce que nous écoutions avec le plus de plaisir, si avides de connaître sa propre pensée." *JS*, 189–90.)

28 In *Du côté de chez Swann*, the narrator remembers having had a similar enthusiasm for the works of Bergotte. See below, pages 224–5.

29 The novel goes on to make significant further references to Balzac and Stendhal, including a long, Barrès-like aside on the psychology of Balzacian types updated for the 1890s. ("le Rubempré moderne," "le Rastignac moderne": *JS*, 427–8.) See chapter 5, pages 151–4.

30 *JS (Hopkins)* 15, translation modified. ("Nous avions traîtreusement descendu avec nous, mon ami *Le Curé de village* de Balzac, moi *La Chartreuse de Parme* de Stendhal, car étant en train de lire ces livres avec la passion qu'excite un ouvrage nouveau et beau, surtout tant qu'on ne l'a pas terminé, nous ne pensions qu'à cela et brûlions d'avoir dessus l'opinion de B. ... Mais nous voulions d'abord lui demander s'il avait vu le coucher de soleil ce soir, qui nous avait transportés jusqu'à nous faire oublier, à mon ami *Le Curé de village*, à moi *La Chartreuse de Parme*, et nous espérions qu'il nous dirait peut-être son impression d'un mot qui éclaircirait peut-être la nôtre et nous rendrait plus certains." *JS*, 197.)

31 See chapter 2, pages 73–4.

32 *JS (Hopkins)*, 15, translation modified. ("la déception d'un névropathe," *JS*, 198.)

33 *JS (Hopkins)*, 15, translation modified. ("je sentais que malgré moi je parlais comme lui," *JS*, 197.)

34 *JS (Hopkins)*, 56, translation modified. ("Jean qui, ne voyant jamais qu'une chose très vague quand il pensait à lui-même, n'avait pas d'idée arrêtée sur sa valeur morale et, selon que tel de ses défauts était flétri dans un livre ... ou que telle de ses qualités y était exaltée, se croyait tour à tour Néron et saint Vincent de Paul." *JS*, 222.) The scene finds an echo in the opening of *Du côté de chez Swann* (1913), where the narrator describes how, after reading and falling alseep, "I felt as though I myself were the subject of the book: a church, a quartet, the rivarly between François Ier and Charles Quint." *SLT*, 1:1. ("il me semblait que j'étais moi-même ce dont parlait l'ouvrage: une église, un quatuor, la rivalité de François Ier et de Charles Quint." *RTP*, 1:3.)

35 *JS (Hopkins)*, 60, translation modified. ("Maintenant Jean pouvait lire *La Tristesse d'Olympio* et bien d'autres poèmes. Les poètes ... se tenaient tout à côté de lui pendant qu'il lisait, comme un homme plus habile, l'aidant pour

ainsi dire à prononcer quelque chose qui lui pesait depuis longtemps sur le cœur, trouvant les mots pour lui, comprenant son obscure et faible pensée mieux que lui-même, et la lui renvoyant pleine de lumière et de force, déroulant en paroles claires ses regrets, d'une tristesse et d'une douceur jusque-là inexprimables." *JS*, 229.)

36 I discuss another example of this trope in descriptions of adolescents (mis) reading poetry in chapter 2, pages 80–2.

37 *JS (Hopkins)* 3–4, translation modified. ("Un langage d'aujourd'hui reconnu dans un chant de l'*Iliade* et la similitude d'une crise de l'histoire d'Égypte avec les événements actuels achèvent de nous montrer que telle substance qui fait le fond de l'humanité, souvent invisible et comme interrompue, ne meurt cependant pas et se retrouve identique là où on s'y attendait le moins." *JS* 183–4.)

38 *JS (Hopkins)* 18, translation modified. ("Mais dans quelle mesure était-il dans ce qu'il avait écrit ... surtout ce Jean qui, avec quelques-uns des défauts de C., plus de qualités peut-être, surtout de sensibilité et même de cœur, mais aussi une santé bien plus chétive, à la différence de C. avait eu tant de malheurs, et de talent pour aucun art? ... Ces problèmes que nous n'osions pas lui poser ... nous intéressaient plus que tout. Nous pensions en consacrant toute notre vie à les résoudre ne pas mal l'employer, puisqu[e] ... nous comprendrions quels sont les rapports secrets, les métamorphoses nécessaires qui existent entre la vie d'un écrivain et son œuvre, entre la réalité et l'art, ou plutôt, ... entre les apparences de la vie et la réalité même qui en faisait le fond durable et que l'art a dégagée." *JS*, 190.)

39 In the *Recherche*, the literary model, Bergotte, is the first model encountered but also the first to be overcome. On the *Recherche* as a series of lessons in reading, including through art and architecture, see Watt, *Reading in Proust's À la recherche*.

40 Beulier is modelled after Proust's philosophy teacher Alphonse Darlu. See Tadié, preface to *Jean Santeuil*, 20, as well Fraisse, *L'Éclectisme philosophique de Marcel Proust*, 111–23.

41 *JS (Hopkins)*, 72–4. ("le poète Rustinlor, maître d'études au lycée Henri-IV"; "Comme son maître Rustinlor, Jean préférait à tous les autres poètes Verlaine et Leconte de Lisle, et comme lui éprouvait à la lecture des classiques un morne ennui. Mais ... il s'efforçait sans cesse de relire *Phèdre*, *Cinna*, les *Fables* de La Fontaine ... Plus tard, Jean eût compris de quel prix pour l'intelligence sont ces exercices." *JS*, 236–8.) *Cinna* (1641) is a play by Corneille.

42 *JS (Hopkins)*, 162. ("il y a ... des banalités courantes, toutes les mauvaises manières d'écrire que vous avez apprises dans les journaux ou les revues. Mais ce n'est pas votre faute. Ce n'est pas à vous. ... Il faudra soigneusement bannir toutes ces métaphores, toutes ces images ... ne grossissez pas la voix pour dire des banalités." *JS*, 262–3.)

43 *JS (Hopkins)* 100, translation modified. ("en l'obligeant à dévêtir une pensée de toutes les formules convenues, de toutes les élégances apprises, de tout le poncif ambiant à travers lesquels nous les [*sic*] apercevons involontairement"; "en saisir la réalité même." *JS*, 238.)

44 The notion of "habit" is of central importance in Proust's theories of memory and aesthetics; see for instance Beckett, *Proust*, 19.

45 *JS (Hopkins)*, 251–2, translation modified. ("Il dit qu'il ne faisait plus de vers, qu'il s'occupait de choses infiniment plus réelles ... 'À savoir la politique, la débauche, et la bicyclette.' D'après lui, c'était cela, et non la littérature, ce qu'il y a de réel, puisqu'elle essaye seulement d'imiter ce que ces choses-là donnent, les vraies émotions de la vie. ... Tout en écoutant, Jean percevait confusément que ce qu'il y a de réel dans la littérature, c'est le résultat d'un travail tout spirituel ... la valeur de la littérature n'est nullement dans la matière déroulée devant l'écrivain, mais dans la nature du travail que son esprit opère sur elle." *JS*, 480–1.)

46 ("une poétesse de dix-neuf ans." *JS*, 520.) The model the character is Anna de Noailles (1876–1933); on her friendship with Proust, see Catherine Perry, "Flagorneur ou ébloui? Proust lecteur d'Anna de Noailles."

47 *JS (Hopkins)*, 463–4. ("cette essence intime des choses ... était en réalité la seule qui fût vraiment importante"; "quelque chose qui en elle était si profond qu'elle n'avait même pas pu y penser, en parler." *JS*, 520–1.)

48 *JS (Hopkins)*, 464–5, translation modified. ("elle faisait rire perpétuellement par des rapprochements comiques, une manière spirituelle de raconter la moindre chose ... car une personne fine, que la faculté de sympathie met à la place de chacun au lieu de rester tout le temps en soi, voit partout du comique." *JS*, 522.)

49 *JS (Hopkins)*, 487. ("La poésie, l'inspiration, ce vent semblait la réveiller en Jean, car au fur et à mesure qu'il prenait plus de plaisir à l'entendre, il pensait de plus en plus à découvrir de nouvelles idées qui en faisaient naître d'autres." *JS*, 535.)

50 *JS (Hopkins)*, 487, translation modified. ("non point ces folles idées qui se rapportent à nous et que les enfants d'imagination [et plusieurs restent toujours enfants pour cela] ont indéfiniment ... de telles idées sont des idées creuses, qui en appellent d'autres, mais creuses aussi. Elles imitent la réalité en s'y substituant, mais sans la dépasser ... tout cela est inutile, c'est comme les romans impressionnistes et naturalistes. Alors, il en faudra de nouveaux, chaque fois qu'il y aura des choses nouvelles. C'est une concurrence inutile à l'inépuisable et insatisfaisante réalité." *JS*, 535–6.)

51 The phrase, from the "Avant-propos à *La Comédie humaine*" (1842), is often cited, for instance in a letter from Bourget to the young Gide following the publication of *Les Cahiers d'André Walter* in 1891: "Remember that the whole art of the novel, whatever the type, can be summarized as what

Balzac called, in his sociologist's lingo, 'to be in competition with the *état civil.*'" ("Rappelez-vous que tout l'art du roman, quel qu'il soit, se réduit à ce que Balzac appelle dans son langage de sociologue: 'faire concurrence à l'état civil.'") Cited in Gide, *Romans et récits*, 1:118. The notion of a need for new novels "each time that new things happen" may be a reminiscence of Barrès's stated project following the emergence of types not described in Balzac. See chapter 5, pages 152–4.

52 *JS (Hopkins)*, 488, translation modified. ("Mais ces idées qui venaient à Jean en écoutant le vent étaient des idées autres qui semblaient non pas creuses mais pleines, à la fois dans le passé ... et le présent, et plus profondes, les reliant, plus réelles, montrant par là le prix de la minute passée et de la minute présente ... Réalité qui est celle que nous ne sentons pas pendant que nous vivons les moments, car nous les rapportons à un but égoïste, mais qui, dans ces brusques retours dans la mémoire désintéressée, nous fait flotter entre le présent et le passé dans leur essence commune ... réalité que nous répandons tandis que nous écrivons des pages qui sont la synthèse de divers moments de la vie." *JS*, 536–7.)

53 *SLT*, 1:132. ("Même plus tard, quand je commençai de composer un livre, certaines phrases dont la qualité ne suffit pas pour me décider à le continuer, j'en retrouvai l'équivalent dans Bergotte." *RTP*, 1:95.)

54 In a parody of fin-de-siècle denunciations of "bad influences" on young male readers, Bergotte's writings are later disparaged by Norpois as "altogether lacking in virility." *SLT*, 2:61. ("mauvaise influence," "bien peu viril," *RTP*, 1:465.)

55 *SLT*, 1:131–2. ("J'étais déçu quand il reprenait le fil de son récit"; "j'aurais voulu posséder une opinion de lui ... sur toutes choses." *RTP*, 1:94.)

56 *SLT*, 2:566, 570. ("celle qu'en poésie on nomme métaphore"; "les choses ... c'est en leur ôtant leur nom, ou en leur donnant un autre qu'Elstir les recréait"; "nous étonne, nous fait sortir de nos habitudes, et tout à la fois rentrer en nous-mêmes en nous rappelant une impression." *RTP*, 2:191, 194.)

57 *JS (Hopkins)*, 268, translation modified. ("Quelquefois Jean ne s'était pas encore mis à lire ... Ils entendaient, sans rien sentir qu'un léger souffle, un murmure continu et auraient pu croire entendre le bruit de la mer. Chaque fois que Jean levait les yeux il voyait le ciel immense devant lui comme une mer sans borne, calmes, bleue et douce au loin ... De légers nuages blancs voguaient insensiblement dans le ciel comme des voiles qui reviennent. ... Jean se remettait à lire, puis quand il était fatigué posait son livre, et le soleil venait frapper et illuminer en lui toutes les pensées que sa lecture avait mises à flot en lui une à une, et le vent par la légère agitation qu'il imprimait à toutes choses, les faisait aller plus vite aussi ... Il aurait voulu parler à Henri et était déçu de le trouver absorbé à lire." *JS*, 491–2.)

58 "On Reading," Proust's essayistic preface to his translation of John Ruskin's *Sesame and Lilies*. This preface and excerpts from the translation

were published in journals in 1905; the book was published in 1906 (Paris, Mercure de France).

59 The location of the fictional Réveillon appears to vary in different sections of the manuscript of *Jean Santeuil*; the real Réveillon (in Seine-et-Marne, ninety kilometres east of Paris) is the château where the artist Madeleine Lemaire hosted Proust and Reynaldo Hahn together a number of times in the mid-1890s, away from their parents.

60 The passage goes on to compare Jean's experience of reading to a "fruitful endeavor" ("travail fécond"), the enthusiasm generated by which proves itself to be equally incommunicable (*JS*, 492).

61 See Philip Kolb, "Historique du premier roman de Proust," 223–35.

62 de Man, "Reading (Proust)," in *Allegories of Reading*, 57–78; Compagnon, "Proust 1, contre la lecture," in *La Troisième République des lettres*, 221–52; Watt, *Reading in Proust's À la recherche*, 27–44.

63 See chapter 2, page 64.

64 *SLT*, 7:322. ("en réalité, chaque lecteur est, quand il lit, le propre lecteur de soi-même. L'ouvrage de l'écrivain n'est qu'une espèce d'instrument d'optique." *RTP*, 4:489–90.)

65 Intriguingly, Emerson's *Essays* appear on a list of titles for an "ideal library" sent to Proust by Paul Desjardins (1859–1940), sometime between 1893 and 1899. *Marcel Proust: Collection Marie-Claude Mante*, lot 138.

66 As signalled by Kate Stanley in "Through Emerson's Eye: The Practice of Perception in Proust," 459n4. Stanley provides a useful overview of exisiting English-language criticism on Proust and Emerson, mostly around questions of perception and memory.

67 These transcriptions of manuscripts and letters by Proust (and later Emerson) observe the writer's lineation and his use of capitals. Cross-outs on the manuscript are rendered in striketrough. Illegible passages are signalled with the abbreviation [*ill.*]. The signs < > indicate interlinear or marginal additions by the writer. The sign // indicates a change of folio or page. The signs [ ] surround editorial interventions, such as the insertion of missing elements (usually punctuation), or cuts in the transcription.

68 [...] C'était le fils d'un cultivateur
des environs. ["]Bonjour Monsieur Santeuil dit-il d'un air joyeux est-ce
Monsieur
de Réveillon qui vous amène, Est-ce vous qui amenez M. de Réveillon
ou est-ce
le ~~h~~Hasard qui vous amène tous les deux?" En ce moment St Gervin entra
et demanda
à Jean et à Henri de le suivre, mais ~~charmé par cette phrase qui avait~~
~~pu être une des plus jolie image~~ <~~gracieuse allégorie~~> ~~du Hasard qui~~
~~n'avait p ces seuls mots avaient~~

~~suffi pour montrer à Jean dans le~~ <pauvre> ~~caporal fourrier un je garçon d’une cul es~~ Jean se promit de revenir voir ce caporal fourrier ~~dont~~ ~~dans la bouche de~~ <par> qui il avait été stupéfait d’entendre ~~cette phrase~~ <~~si~~> naturellement prononcer cette phrase charmante. Si vous trouviez dans la ~~bibliothèque de votre~~ chambre de votre aubergiste dans une ~~chambre~~ <province> éloignée ~~la plu~~ les poésies d’Alfred de Vigny, les Essais d’Emerson et le Rouge et le Noir, ne <vous> sentiriez vous pas comme en présence d’un ami, plein de vous-même, avec qui vous auriez envie de converser.

[*Jean Santeuil*], Bibliothèque nationale de France, ms. BnF, NAF 16615, f° 423r. gallica.bnf.fr/ark:/12148/btv1b53069102f/f710.image.r=NAF%2016615. The passage corresponds to *JS (Hopkins)* 446–7 and *JS* 556–7. My transcription and translation.

69 Proust cites Vigny’s “La Maison du berger” (“The Shepherd’s Cabin,” 1844) with some regularity in his letters to Reynaldo Hahn in this period. Lines from the poem celebrate the meeting of “the shepherd and the stranger” (“le pâtre et l’étranger”) and invite the stranger to “come hide love and your divine sin” (“viens y cacher l’amour et ta divine faute”). In *Sodome et Gomorrhe II*, the hero recites two lines of this poem to Albertine (*SLT*, 4:357; *RTP*, 3:259). On queerness in *Le Rouge et le Noir*, see chapter 4.

70 “Sur la lecture” [1905], in *La Bible d’Amiens, Sésame et les Lys et autres textes*, 420–3.

71 [*Jean Santeuil*], Bibliothèque nationale de France, ms. BnF, NAF 16615, f° 423r.

72 See for instance “Souvenir” [1891], in *Marcel Proust: Le Mensuel retrouvé*, 137–40, and “Avant la nuit” [1893], in *Jean Santeuil précédé de Les Plaisirs et les Jours*, 167–71.

73 [*Jean Santeuil*], Bibliothèque nationale de France, ms. BnF, NAF 16615, f° 423v.

74 *JS (Hopkins)*, 377, translation modified. (“Déjà du reste quand nous étions petits, il y avait un certain livre que nous prenions sous notre bras quand on allait au parc et que nous lisions avec amour, qu’aucun autre n’aurait remplacé.” *JS*, 367–8.)

75 *JS (Hopkins)*, 377, translation modified. (“Aujourd’hui sur un manuscrit, dans le feuilleton d’un journal, nous serions ravis de trouver quelques nouvelles pages de George Eliot ou d’Emerson. Mais quand nous étions plus jeunes, le livre ne se séparait pas pour nous de ce qu’il disait.” *JS*, 368.)

76 *JS (Hopkins)*, 377, translation modified. (“Son charme de corps ne faisait qu’un avec l’histoire que nous aimions et le plaisir qu’il nous donnait, quand

par une chaude après-midi, dans la charmille du parc, nous cachant aux regards pour ne pas être interrompus, ... nous étions assis le tenant à la main, et, regardant ses pages, nous ne le séparions pas de la douceur de ses minces feuillets, de leur fine odeur et de bonne couverture solide qui le fermait de ses coins d'or." *JS*, 368.)

77 [...] Jean et Henri allaient s'étendre
avec des livres sur des petites dunes de sable qui ~~s'élèvent~~ commencent à
l'ouest
de la plage. Ils s'étendaient et quelquefois restaient longtemps sans lire.
~~Quel~~ Pour lire
et pour ne pas se gêner, ils se mettaient à quelque distance l'un de l'autre
et grâce aux replis de la dune quelquefois ~~l'un était~~ n'étant qu'à quelques
pas
l'un de l'autre ils ne s'apercevaient pas caché[s] par un pli de la dune, et
chacun
pouvait se croire ~~à des milliers de lieues~~ <isolé> de tout être humain ne
voyant au dessus
du sable que le ciel et la mer et les mouettes qui ne cessaient de voler.
~~Jean étendu la tête en bas se laissait pénétrer de~~ ~~C'est~~ ~~L'~~ ~~Éloigné que nous sommes de la nature et fatigué~~ ~~Une telle vie est douce~~ ~~C'est parce qu'ils nous font penser à une telle vie~~ [*ill.*] ~~tout entière~~ ~~livrée aveuglément aux forces bienfaisantes de la nature physique que nous pensons avec plaisir aux animaux, au boa~~ ~~pour qui~~ ~~c'est~~ ~~se retire pour digérer~~ ~~pendant trois jours et~~ ~~qui reste pendant~~ ~~ce temps dans~~ ~~une sorte de~~ Quand l'un
avait
fini de lire avant l'autre il s'éloignait et se promenait sans bruit pour ne
pas déranger l'autre, bien qu'à vrai dire le sentiment de quelqu'un qui a
fini son
travail ou sa lecture soit un désir d'en finir et de causer qui exclut le
respect de la lecture de l'autre.

[*Jean Santeuil*], Bibliothèque nationale de France, ms. BnF, NAF 16615, f° 363 r. gallica.bnf.fr/ark:/12148/btv1b53069102f/f606.item.r=NAF%20 16615. The passage corresponds to *JS (Hopkins)* 378 and *JS* 366–7. My transcription and translation.

78 "Mon enfant bien aimé,
Ce matin je vais aller au bois si je me
lève assez tôt car je suis encore couché
lisant Emerson avec ivresse. [...]
[Mademoiselle Lemaire] m'a écrit que mes vers <(à toi)> étaient bien.
Je lui ai répondu qu'on est toujours bien
inspiré quand on parle de ce qu'on aime.

La vérité est qu'on ne devrait jamais parler
que de cela. Ces vers-là sont les seuls <de moi> que
tu me feras plaisir en montrant et récitant
le pl. possible. Sache que d^{s} la liturgie catholique présence réelle veut justement dire présence
idéale. _ . Mais non je me trompe un peu.
Je suis ton poney
Marcel"

Marcel Proust to Reynaldo Hahn, [mid-January 1895]. *Corr.* I:361. Transcription revised on a photocopy of the original letter (Kolb-Proust Archive, University of Illinois). The "bois" is likely the Bois de Boulogne. Mademoiselle Lemaire is Suzette Lemaire (1866–1946), Madeleine Lemaire's daughter. In his letters Proust uses the sign ". _ ." to signal a change of paragraph. "Poney" is Hahn's pet name for Proust during the amorous phase of their relationship.

79 *Portraits de peintres* de Marcel Proust mis en musique par Reynaldo Hahn (Paris, Heugel, 1896). See *Album Proust*, 150–1.

80 Article III.76.5, *La Somme théologique de Saint Thomas*, 7:63.

81 *Corr.*, I:361.

82 Emerson, "Character," from *Essays: Second Series* [1844], in *Collected Works*, 3:64–5. ("Qu'y a-t-il de meilleur que d'étroites relations d'amitié, quand elles ont pour base ces racines profondes? ... Je ne sais ce que la vie peut offrir de plus satisfaisant que cette entente profonde qui subsiste ... entre deux hommes vertueux dont chacun est sûr de lui-même et sûr de son ami. ... D'une telle amitié, l'amour entre les sexes est le premier symbole ... Ces rapports avec les êtres les meilleurs, nous les avons pris autrefois pour des romans de jeunesse, mais avec l'élévation du caractère ils deviennent la plus solide des jouissances." From "Caractère," in *Sept Essais*, 171.)

83 This phrase was added by the translator and has no equivalent in Emerson's text.

84 Emerson, "Friendship," from *Essays* [First Series, 1841], in *Collected Works*, 2:122–3. ("L'amitié exige ce rare juste milieu entre la ressemblance et la dissemblance qui fait sentir à chacun des deux amis la présence ... de son compagnon. ... Pour que l'union s'opère, ils doivent d'abord être deux, séparés, avant de ne faire qu'un. Que leur amitié soit l'alliance de deux formidables natures ... avant d'être la reconnaissance de la profonde unité qui les unit malgré ces contrastes." From "Amitié," in *Essais de philosophie américaine*, 118.)

85 Ibid., in *Collected Works*, 2:127. ("L'amitié ne doit avoir ni soupçons ni défiances, mais elle doit traiter son objet comme un dieu, afin que les deux êtres humains qui ont établi entre eux ces rapports d'amitié puissent être, pour ainsi dire, déifiés l'un par l'autre." From "Amitié." Ibid., 126.)

86 Emerson, "Character," from *Essays: Second Series* [1844], in *Collected Works*, 3:65. ("Si nous sommes apparentés, de quelque façon, nous nous rencontrerons. Dans le monde ancien il était de tradition qu'aucune métamorphose ne pouvait cacher un dieu à un autre dieu, et un vers grec dit: 'Les

dieux ne sont pas inconnus les uns aux autres.' Les amis aussi suivent les lois de la divine nécessité; ils gravitent l'un vers l'autre et ne peuvent faire autrement ..." From "Caractère," in *Sept Essais*, 172.)

87 "To Reynaldo Hahn, singing poet and musician." ("À Reynaldo Hahn, poète chanteur et musicien.") Yves Sandre, note to "La Mort de Baldassare Sylvande," in *Jean Santeuil précédé de Les Plaisirs et les Jours*, 912–13.

88 Proust had met Léon Yeatman (1873–1930) through a mutual friend, Robert Dreyfus (Fernand Gregh, *L'Âge d'airain [souvenirs 1905–1925]*, Paris: Grasset, 1951, 259.) In 1893 Proust dedicated a short prose piece, "Présence réelle," to "L. Yeatmann" [*sic*] (*La Revue blanche* 26, December 1893, 377–80); it was reprinted in *Les Plaisirs et les Jours*, without the dedication (*Jean Santeuil précédé de Les Plaisirs et les Jours*, 134–7). On Proust's use of the theological concept of "real presence," see page 232 above.

89 "[...] Que vous êtes bon Reynaldo.
Maman était émue de
votre gentillesse et je vous //
remercie et vous embrasse
de tout mon cœur. Je vous
avais apporté des petites choses
de moi et le début du
roman que Yeatman lui-
même près de qui j'écrivais
a trouvé très poney. Vous m'
aiderez à corriger ce qui le
serait trop. Je veux que vous y
soyez tout le temps mais comme
un Dieu déguisé qu'aucun
mortel ne reconnaît. Sans cela
c'est sur t[t] le roman que tu serais
obligé de mettre: [«]déchire ». [...]"
Marcel Proust to Reynaldo Hahn [March 1896]. *Corr.*, II: 52.
Transcription revised on a photocopy of the original letter (Kolb-Proust Archive, University of Illinois).

90 For instance in William C. Carter, *Marcel Proust: A Life*, 209.

91 See *Corr.*, I:327.

92 Martin Robitaille, *Proust épistolier*, 219n15.

93 In [September 1894] Proust writes to Hahn: "Do not write anything that would force me to hide your letters" ("Ne m'écrivez pas de choses qui me font cacher vos lettres"). Unpublished letter, Les Autographes (Paris), *Autographes, lettres et manuscrits, documents et souvenirs*, catalogue n° 94 (Noël 2000), lot 232.

94 Kolb, "Historique du premier roman de Proust," 235–6.

95 Emerson, "The Heart" [1838], in *The Early Lectures*, 2:288.

96 Crain, *American Sympathy*, 190.

97 For a historically sensitive queer reading of Montaigne's essay, see Schachter, *Voluntary Servitude and the Erotics of Friendship*, 73–114.

98 "The Heart," in *The Early Lectures*, 2:283.

99 A first version of the *Journals*, published from 1909 to 1914, was heavily censored by Emerson's son; only selected excerpts were translated into French (Paris: Armand Colin, 2 vols., 1914–18). A complete edition was not published until 1960. Proust seems to have been unaware of the *Journals*, in any edition; they are not mentioned in his letters.

100 Emerson, *The Journals and Miscellaneous Notebooks*, 1:22. I simplify the transcription provided in that edition and restitute the original lineation.

101 Ibid., 22n41.

102 On Martin Gay, who died in 1850, see ibid., 22n41, as well as Crain, *American Sympathy*, 153–75.

103 Emerson, "Friendship," from *Essays* [First Series, 1841], in *Collected Works*, 2:113. ("Lisez le langage de ces regards errants; le cœur le connaît." From "Amitié," in *Essais de philosophie américaine*, 103.)

104 Emerson, *Journals and Miscellaneous Notebooks*, 1:292.

105 Ibid., 1:291n54.

106 Ibid., 1:322. (Notebook No. XVIII, p. 100.) I simplify the transcription provided in that edition.

107 In the *Recherche*, Proust again evokes the myth cited by Emerson to describe how "inverts" are able to see through each other's dissimulation: "Ulysses himself did not recognise Athena at first. But the gods are immediately perceptible to one another, like as quickly to like, and so too had M. de Charlus been to Jupien." *SLT*, 4:18. ("Ulysse lui-même ne reconnaissait pas d'abord Athéné. Mais les dieux sont immédiatement perceptibles aux dieux, le semblable aussi vite au semblable, ainsi encore l'avait été M. de Charlus à Jupien." *RTP*, 3:15.)

108 "Amitié," in *Essais de philosophie américaine*, 120. The clause does not appear in Emerson's original essay and seems to be a liberty taken by the translator.

109 [on voit] au moment ~~où Ulysse souhaiterait de la voir, Minerve~~
où Ulysse se lamente d'être si loin de Minerve
la déesse apparaitre ~~sous~~ au héros sous les traits <déguisés>
d'un vieillard. Jean ~~tenai~~ savait que de
telles apparitions sont impossibles et que ~~si les~~
~~choses que nous désir~~ les enfants seuls croient que
leur désirs [*sic*] est la loi des choses. [...]
[...] Pourtant
il aimait, à ~~le soir~~ ~~dans les heures incertaines~~
~~passées~~ dans son lit ~~avant~~ <à l'heure> de s'endormir ~~et qui~~
mêlent [...]
[...] et le jour dans les heures certaines qui
lui ressemblent, à se figurer Réveillon ~~alors~~
~~loin de lui~~, que la distance de leurs demeures ne

séparait pas seul de lui, venant frapper à la
porte de sa chambre, lui tendant la main, disant
pourquoi jusqu'alors il lui avait caché sa sympathie.
~~Si sa raison~~ L'expérience de sa raison protestait contre
~~de te~~ l'absurdité d'un tel roman. Mais l'imagination n'a pas d'expérience, [...] //

"Charles [Henri] de Réveillon," [*Jean Santeuil*], Rare Book & Manuscript Library, University of Illinois, Philip Kolb Collection of Marcel Proust Papers, box 3, item 100g, f° 3, recto. My transcription and translation.

110 Comme un ~~malade ai~~ fou aime à ~~écouter~~ <~~éco~~> <rencontrer> ~~un~~
l'ami docile qui l'écoute sans le contredire,
ainsi Jean recherchait l'innocente complicité
du poète. [...]
[...] Il était arrivé
au moment où Minerve – quand tout à
coup un léger bruit qu'il entendait tout près de
lui depuis quelques instants lui fit lever la tête.
~~Il n'eut~~ Il ~~aperçut un instant la figure~~
entendit un saut par la fenêtre et le bruit cessa.
Mais pendant une seconde, ~~debou debout sur~~
~~un banc~~ escaladant un banc, et le regardant
avec un sourire, il avait aperçu, <comme> dans son
rêve, Charles. Maintenant son papier ~~n'était~~
~~plus seul et sur la table~~ où deux vers à peine
étaient écrits n'était plus seul sur ~~la~~<e> ~~table~~
pupitre. À côté un pensum complet de ~~deux~~
~~cents vers~~ cinq cents lignes françaises copiées ~~ét~~
était à côté de lui, tout prêt à être ~~co~~
~~copié par le~~ donné au professeur, avec le nom
de Jean Santeuil en tête, en majuscules.
Le fragment copié était le chapitre des
Essais de Montaigne sur l'Amitié.

Ibid., f° 3, verso. This and the passage transcribed in the previous note correspond to *JS*, 255–6.

111 The editors of Emerson's *Journals* note that Emerson (or his mother) borrowed Montaigne's *Essays* from the Boston Library in September 1820, about a month after his first encounter with Gay (1:323n84). On reminiscences of Montaigne's "De l'amitié" in Proust, see Smith, *Réécrire la Renaissance, de Marcel Proust à Michel Tournier: Exercices de lecture rapprochée*, 13–25.

112 *SLT*, 1:1. ("je n'avais pas cessé en dormant de faire des réflexions sur ce que je venais de lire," *RTP*, 1:49.)

113 *SLT*, 6:436–7, translation modified. ("Et d'ailleurs, n'était-ce pas pour m'occuper d'eux que je vivrais loin de ceux qui se plaindraient de ne pas me

voir, pour m'occuper d'eux plus à fond que je n'aurais pu le faire avec eux, pour chercher à les révéler à eux-mêmes, à les réaliser?" *RTP*, 4:564.)

114 *SLT*, 5:331–2, translation modified. ("Dans l'œuvre de quel auteur étais-je? J'aurais bien voulu le savoir et, n'ayant près de moi personne à qui le demander, aurais bien voulu être un personnage de ces *Mille et Une Nuits* que je relisais sans cesse et où dans les moments d'incertitude surgit soudain un génie ou une adolescente d'une ravissante beauté, invisible pour les autres, mais non pour le héros embarrassé, à qui elle révèle exactement ce qu'il désire savoir ... ainsi, tout d'un coup je me reconnus au milieu de cette musique nouvelle pour moi, en pleine sonate de Vinteuil." *RTP*, 3:753.)

Epilogue

1 "L'aberration romantique et ses conséquences." Léon Daudet, *Le Stupide XIXe siècle*, 81.

2 Carrère, *Les Mauvais Maîtres*, 7.

3 See part II, page 88.

4 A name coined by André Rousseaux, a literary critic for *Le Figaro*. For a detailed account of the 1922 and 1940 polemics, see Sapiro, *La Guerre des écrivains: 1940–1953*, 123–7 and 161–207.

5 This article and the one referenced in the next note are cited in Sapiro, *La Guerre des écrivains*, 164–5.

6 Pourtalès, "Après le désastre." The sentence is a clear allusion to Gide, whose works include *L'Immoraliste* and *Corydon*. The title of the latter (a book of dialogues about male same-sex attachments, published anonymously in 1911 and 1920, and in a wider edition with the author's name in 1924) is here reduced to a lower-case name to designate homosexuals.

7 Sadoul, *Écrits 1: Chroniques du cinéma français, 1939–1967*, 199. *Le Quai des brumes* (dir. Marcel Carné, 1938), about an army deserter who eventually dies in the seedy underworld of Le Havre, was criticized by the far-right press for its bleak mood and unfavorable depiction of the military. See Carné, *Ma vie à belles dents: Mémoires*, 102.

8 Ehrlich, *Cinema of Paradox: French Filmmaking under the German Occupation*, 215.

9 "misérables larves"; "on ne peut rien imaginer de moins viril." François Vinneuil [pseud. Lucien Rebatet], "Réalisme: 'Hôtel du nord,'" *L'Action française*, 30 December 1938. Cited in Pillard, "Une histoire oubliée: la genèse française du terme 'film noir' dans les années 1930 et ses implications transnationales."

10 Crisp, *The Classic French Cinema, 1930–1960*, 251.

11 Courtade, *Les Malédictions du cinéma français*, 161.

12 See Black, *Hollywood Censored.*

13 Forman, *Our Movie Made Children.*

14 On nineteenth-century American discourses about the dangers of reading, particularly for women, see Millner, *Fever Reading*.

15 Simon, "Ados: Zéro de lecture?"

16 Bessard-Banquy, "Où en est la lecture?" in *Les Mutations de la lecture*, 12.

17 Evans, "Avant-propos: Les mystères de la lecture," in *Lectures et lecteurs à l'heure d'Internet*, 9.

18 The majority of respondents for this study were eleven or twelve years old. Clark and Douglas, *Young People's Reading and Writing*, 8, 115.

Bibliography

Unless otherwise stated, works in French are published in Paris.

Primary Sources

"Accusation d'assassinat, commis par un séminariste dans une église." *Gazette des tribunaux*, 28 to 31 December 1827.

Achille, L. *Âme neuve*. Ollendorff, 1898.

"Affaire Chambige – Assassinat – Tentative de suicide." *Gazette des tribunaux*, 9 to 17 November 1888.

A.G. "Oscar Wilde à la prison de Pentonville." *Le Gaulois*, 13 June 1895.

Agathon (pseud. Henri Massis and Alfred de Tarde). *Les Jeunes Gens d'aujourd'hui: Le goût de l'action, la foi patriotique, une renaissance catholique, le réalisme politique*. Plon-Nourrit, 1913.

Les Autographes. *Autographes, lettres et manuscrits, documents et souvenirs*. N° 94. Noël 2000.

Balzac, Honoré de. *La Comédie humaine*. General editor Pierre-Georges Castex. 12 vols. Bibliothèque de la Pléiade. Gallimard, 1977.

Barrès, Maurice. "La Contagion des Rastignacs." *Le Voltaire*, 28 June 1887.

– "Enfin Balzac a vieilli." *Le Journal*, 16 February 1894.

– *Journal de ma vie extérieure*. Edited by François Broche and Eric Roussel. Julliard, 1994.

– "La Leçon d'un insurgé." *Le Voltaire*, 11 June 1886.

– "La Mode russe." *La Revue illustrée*, 1 February 1886.

– Preface to *La Correspondance de Stendhal*, by Stendhal, I:v–x. Edited by A. Paupe and P.-A. Cheramy. 3 vols. Charles Bosse, 1908.

– *Romans et voyages*. Edited by Vital Rambaud. 2 vols. Robert Laffont (Bouquins), 1994.

– *Scènes et doctrines du nationalisme*. Juven, 1902.

– "La Sensibilité d'Henri Chambige." *Le Figaro*, 11 November 1888.

– "Le Sentiment en littérature." *Les Taches d'encre*, January 1885.
– "Un témoin de la guillotine." *Le Journal*, 22 May 1894.
– "Victor Hugo ou la méthode pour organiser sa renommée." *L'Auto*, 28 May 1906.
Bastiat, Frédéric. *Baccalauréat et socialisme*. Guillaumin, 1850.
Bataille, Albert. "Une cause célèbre: L'affaire Chambige." *Le Figaro*, 2, 3, 4, and 11 November 1888.
– *Causes criminelles et mondaines de 1888*. Preface by Paul Bourget. Dentu, 1889.
Baudelaire, Charles. *Œuvres complètes*. Edited by Claude Pichois. 2 vols. Bibliothèque de la Pléiade. Gallimard, 1975–6.
Bauer, Henry. *Mémoires d'un jeune homme*. Charpentier, 1895.
Beaunier, André. *Au service de la déesse: Essais de critique*. Flammarion, 1923.
– *L'Homme qui a perdu son moi*. Plon, 1911.
– *Les Trois Legrand, ou le danger de la littérature*. Fasquelle, 1903.
Bérenger, Henry. *L'Effort*. Armand Colin, 1893.
– "Portrait d'un jeune homme." *L'Art et la Vie* (November 1897): 661–76.
– "Les Prolétaires intellectuels en France." In *Les Prolétaires intellectuels en France*, edited by H. Bérenger, 1–51. Éditions de la revue, 1901.
Bertrand, Louis. *La Mue*. Annales de la jeunesse laïque, 1903.
Bethléem, Louis (Abbé). *Romans à lire et romans à proscrire: Essai de classification au point de vue moral des principaux romans et romanciers (1500–1932)*. 11th ed. Éditions de la Revue des lectures, 1932.
Boissin, Firmin. "Romans, contes et nouvelles." *Polybiblion, revue bibliographique et universelle* (October 1889): 289–310.
Bonnetain, Paul. *Charlot s'amuse*. Brussels: Kistmaeckers, 1883.
Bonnetain, Paul, et al. "*La Terre*: À Émile Zola." *Le Figaro*, 18 August 1887.
Bourget, Paul. *André Cornélis*. Lemerre, 1887.
– *Un crime d'amour*. Lemerre, 1886.
– *Le Disciple* [1889]. Edited by Antoine Compagnon. Librairie générale française (Livre de poche), 2010.
– *Essais de psychologie contemporaine: Études littéraires (1883–1885)*. Edited by André Guyaux. Gallimard (Tel), 1993.
– "Un nouveau dictionnaire." *Journal des débats politiques et littéraires*, 2 February 1886.
– *Pages de critique et de doctrine*. Plon-Nourrit, 1912.
– *Physiologie de l'amour moderne*. Lemerre, 1891.
– Preface to Stendhal, *Le Rouge et le Noir* [1830]. Lemerre, 1886.
Brahm, Alcanter de. *L'Arriviste*. Jules Souque, 1893.
Bréal, Michel. *Quelques mots sur l'instruction publique en France*. Hachette, 1872.
Brierre de Boismont, Alexandre. *Du suicide et de la folie suicide: considérés dans leurs rapports avec la statistique, la médecine et la philosophie*. Germer-Baillière, 1856.

Brulat, Paul. *Le Nouveau Candide: Roman contemporain*. Villerelle, 1902.
Brunetière, Ferdinand. "À propos du *Disciple*." *Revue des Deux Mondes* (1 July 1889): 214–26.
– *Le Roman naturaliste*. Calmann-Lévy, 1883.
Budé, Eugène de. *Du danger des mauvais livres et des moyens d'y remédier*. Sandoz et Thuillier, 1883.
Buisson, Ferdinand. "Le Devoir présent de la jeunesse." In *Morale sociale*, edited by Émile Boutroux, 231–54. Alcan, 1899.
– "La Jeunesse criminelle et l'éducation: Réponse à M. G. Tarde." *La Revue pédagogique* (April 1897): 295–308.
– "La Lecture en classe, à l'étude, et dans la famille." *La Revue pédagogique* (July 1894): 4–23.
Caliban (pseud. Émile Bergerat). "La Rime en bige." *Le Figaro*, 8 November 1888.
Capus, Alfred. *Robinson*. Fasquelle, 1910.
Carné, Marcel. *Ma vie à belles dents: Mémoires*. L'Archipel, 1996.
Carrère, Jean. *Les Mauvais Maîtres*. Plon, 1922.
Case, Jules. "La Débâcle du réalisme." *L'Événement*, 21 September 1891.
Cerfberr, Anatole, and Jules Christophe. *Répertoire de la Comédie humaine de H. de Balzac*. Preface by Paul Bourget. 2nd ed. Calmann-Lévy, 1887.
Cham, Jorge. *Piled Higher and Deeper* 608 (25 July 2005), 759 (12 September 2006), 910 (7 July 2007), and 911 (10 July 2007). www.phdcomics.com.
Chambige, Henri. "Les Goncourt: Le modernisme." *La Revue générale, littéraire, politique et artistique* 85 (1887): 207–12.
– Letter to Paul Bourget. In "Revue autographe de l'an 1888." Supplement to *L'Indépendance belge*, 1 January 1889.
Charpentier, Armand. *L'Enfance d'un homme*. Lemerre, 1890.
Chénier, André. *Œuvres posthumes*. Edited by D.C. Robert. Guillaume, 1826.
Condillac, Étienne Bonnot de. *Essai sur l'origine des connaissances humaines* [1749]. Alive, 1998.
Dante, Alighieri. *The Divine Comedy I: Inferno*. Translated and edited by Robin Kirkpatrick. London: Penguin, 2006.
d'Argens, Boyer. *Thérèse philosophe* [1748]. In *Romans libertins du XVIIIe siècle*, edited by Raymond Trousson, 557–658. Robert Laffont (Bouquins), 1993.
Daudet, Alphonse. *Œuvres*. Edited by Roger Ripoll. 3 vols. Bibliothèque de la Pléiade. Gallimard, 1986.
– *Soutien de famille: Mœurs contemporaines*. Charpentier, 1898.
Daudet, Léon. *Le Stupide XIXe siècle: Exposé des insanités qui se sont abattues sur la France depuis 130 ans, 1789–1919*. Nouvelle Librairie nationale, 1919.
Deschamps, Gaston. *Le Malaise de la démocratie*. Armand Colin, 1899.
Desjardins, Paul. *Le Devoir présent*. Armand Colin, 1892.
Dreyfus, Robert. *Souvenirs sur Marcel Proust*. Grasset, 1926.

Durkheim, Émile. *Le Suicide: Étude de sociologie*. Alcan, 1897.

– "Suicide et natalité: Étude de statistique morale." *Revue philosophique de la France et de l'étranger* 26, no. 11 (1888): 446–63.

Elder, Marc. *Une crise*. Société française d'imprimerie et de librairie, 1906.

Emerson, Ralph Waldo. *Collected Works*. Edited by Joseph Slater, Alfred R. Ferguson, Jean Ferguson Carr et al. 10 vols. Cambridge, MA: Harvard University Press, 1971–2013.

– *The Early Lectures*. Edited by Stephen E. Whicher, Robert E. Spiller and Wallace E. Williams. 3 vols. Cambridge, MA: Harvard University Press, 1959–72.

– *Essais de philosophie américaine*. Translated by Émile Montégut. Charpentier, 1851.

– *The Journals and Miscellaneous Notebooks*. Edited by William H. Gilman et al. 16 vols. Cambridge, MA: Harvard University Press, 1960–82.

– *Sept Essais*. Translated by I. Will [pseud. Mlle Mali]. Brussels: Paul Lacomblez, 1894.

Faure, Abel. *La Clé des carrières*. Stock, 1904.

Ferri-Pisani, [Camille]. *Les Pervertis: Roman d'un potache*. Librairie universelle, 1905.

Flat, Paul. *L'Illusion sentimentale*. Fontemoing, 1905.

– *Pastel Vivant*. Éditions de la Revue politique & littéraire, 1904.

Flaubert, Gustave. *Correspondance*. General editors J. Bruneau and Yvan Leclerc, 5 vols. Bibliothèque de la Pléiade. Gallimard, 1984–2007.

– *Œuvres complètes*. Edited by A. Thibaudet and R. Dumesnil. 2 vols. Bibliothèque de la Pléiade. Gallimard, 1951–2.

– *Œuvres complètes*. General editor Claudine Gothot-Mersch. 3 vols. Bibliothèque de la Pléiade. Gallimard, 2001–13.

Forman, H.J. *Our Movie Made Children*. New York: MacMillan, 1935.

Fouillée, Alfred. "Les Jeunes Criminels, l'école et la presse." *Revue des Deux Mondes* (15 January 1897): 417–49.

– *La Philosophie de Platon: Exposition, histoire et critique de la théorie des idées*. 2 vols. Ladrange, 1869.

Fouquier, Henry. "Femmes et criminels." *Le Figaro*, 15 November 1888.

France, Anatole. "Un crime littéraire: L'affaire Chambige." *Le Temps*, 11 November 1888.

– *Œuvres*. Edited by Marie-Claire Bancquart. 4 vols. Bibliothèque de la Pléiade. Gallimard, 1984–94.

– *La Vie littéraire*. 5 vols. Calmann-Lévy, 1895–1921.

Frary, Raoul. *La Question du latin*. L. Cerf, 1885.

Furetière, Antoine. *Le Roman bourgeois* [1666]. In *Romanciers du XVIIe Siècle: Sorel, Scarron, Furetière, Madame de La Fayette*, edited by Antoine Adam, 899–1104. Bibliothèque de la Pléiade. Gallimard, 1958.

Gaultier, Jules de. *Le Bovarysme: Essai sur le pouvoir d'imaginer*. Mercure de France, 1902.
Gauthiez, Pierre. *L'Âge incertain*. Ollendorff, 1898.
Gide, André. *Les Cahiers et les Poésies d'André Walter* [1891]. Edited by Claude Martin. Gallimard (Poésie), 1986.
– *Divers*. Gallimard, 1931.
– *Essais critiques*. Edited by Pierre Masson. Bibliothèque de la Pléiade. Gallimard, 1999.
– *Journal*. Edited by Éric Marty. 2 vols. Bibliothèque de la Pléiade. Gallimard, 1996.
– *Prétextes: Réflexions sur quelques points de littérature et de morale*. Mercure de France, 1903.
– *Romans et récits, œuvres lyriques et dramatiques*. General editor Pierre Masson, 2 vols. Bibliothèque de la Pléiade. Gallimard, 2009.
– *Souvenirs et voyages*. General editor Pierre Masson. Bibliothèque de la Pléiade. Gallimard, 2001.
Gide, André, and Jean Amrouche. *André Gide: Qui êtes-vous? Entretiens Jean Amrouche-André Gide*. Edited by Éric Marty. Lyon: La Manufacture, 1987.
Gide, André, and Paul Valéry. *Correspondance 1890–1942*. Edited by Peter Fawcett. Gallimard, 2009.
Goncourt, Edmond de, and Jules de Goncourt. *Journal: Mémoires de la vie littéraire*. Edited by Robert Ricatte. 3 vols. Robert Laffont (Bouquins), 1989.
Henry, Émile. *Coup pour coup*. Edited by Roger Langlais. Plasma, 1977.
Hermant, Abel. *Confession d'un enfant d'hier*. Ollendorff, 1903.
Hudault, Joseph. *La Formation de Jean Turoit*. Perrin, 1911.
– *Le Pavillon aux livres*. Perrin, 1914.
Huysmans, Joris-Karl. *À rebours* [1884]. Edited by Marc Fumaroli. Paris: Gallimard (Folio), 1977.
– *Romans*. General editor Pierre Brunel. Robert Laffont (Bouquins), 2005.
"La Jeunesse de France." *Le Temps*, 9 July 1940.
Jourdain, Frantz. *L'Atelier Chantorel: Mœurs d'artistes*. Charpentier, 1893.
Juhellé, Albert. *La Crise virile*. Mercure de France, 1898.
La Rochefoucauld, François de. *Maximes et réflexions diverses* [1678]. Edited by Jacques Truchet. Flammarion (GF), 1977.
Lacassagne, Alexandre. "Pédérastie." In *Dictionnaire encyclopédique des sciences médicales*, edited by J. Raige-Delorme and A. Dechambre, 22:239–59. Asselin, 1886.
Laclos, Choderlos de. *Les Liaisons dangereuses* [1782]. Edited by Michel Delon. Librairie générale française (Livre de poche), 2002.
Lanson, Gustave. *Histoire de la littérature française* [1894]. 3rd ed. Hachette, 1895.
Laprade, Victor de. *Le Baccalauréat et les études classiques*. Didier, 1869.

– *L'Éducation homicide: Plaidoyer pour l'enfance*. Didier, 1868.
Larroumet, Gustave. "Paul Bourget à l'Académie française." *Le Gaulois*, 13 June 1895.
Lavedan, Henri. *Les Jeunes, ou l'espoir de la France*. Calmann-Lévy, 1897.
Lebey, André. *L'Age où l'on s'ennuie: Chronique contemporaine*. Juven, 1902.
– *Les Premières Luttes*. Fasquelle, 1897.
Lèbre, Gaston, ed. "L'Affaire Chambige." *Revue des grands procès contemporains* 7 (1889): 21–101.
Lemaitre, Jules. *Les Contemporains: Études et portraits, troisième série*. Lecène et Houdin, 1887.
Loti, Pierre. *Le Roman d'un enfant*. Calmann-Lévy, 1890.
Mallarmé, Stéphane. *Le "Livre" de Mallarmé*. Edited by Jacques Schérer. Gallimard, 1978.
Marcel Proust: Collection Marie-Claude Mante. Sotheby's, Paris, 24 May 2018. sothebys.com/fr/auctions/2018/livres-et-manuscrits-pf1803.html.
Margueritte, Paul [as "Jean Fesdis"]. "Le Cas de Chambige." *Le Figaro*, 12 November 1893.
– *Les Jours s'allongent: Souvenirs de jeunesse*. Plon, 1908.
– *Le Printemps tourmenté*. Flammarion, 1925.
– *Tous Quatre*. Giraud, 1885.
Martin du Gard, Roger. *Devenir!* [1909]. Gallimard, 1930.
– *Journal*. Edited by Claude Sicard. 3 vols. Gallimard, 1992.
– *Œuvres complètes*. 2 vols. Bibliothèque de la Pléiade. Gallimard, 1955.
Martin-Laya, Léopold. *Yvon d'Or*. Dentu, 1888.
Maupassant, Guy de. *Pierre et Jean*. Ollendorff, 1888.
– "Le Roman" [1887]. In *Romans*, edited by Louis Forestier, 703–15. Bibliothèque de la Pléiade. Gallimard, 1987.
– *Sur l'eau* [1888]. In *Œuvres complètes*, edited by Gilbert Sigaux, vol. 14, 231–395. Lausanne: Éditions Rencontre, 1962.
Mellerio, André. *Jacques Mérane*. Lemerre, 1891.
– *La Vie stérile*. Lemerre, 1892.
Mercier, Louis-Sébastien. *Tableau de Paris* [1781–8]. Edited by Jean-Claude Bonnet. Mercure de France, 1994.
Mirbeau, Octave. "À propos du 'Hard Labour.'" *Le Journal*, 13 June 1895.
– *Correspondance générale*. Edited by Pierre Michel. 3 vols. Lausanne: L'Âge d'Homme, 2003–9.
– "Le Manuel du savoir écrire." *Le Figaro*, 11 May 1889.
– *Œuvre romanesque*. Edited by Pierre Michel. 3 vols. Buchet-Chastel, 2000–1.
– *Sébastien Roch*. Translated by Nicoletta Simborowski. Edited by Margaret Jull Costa. Sawtry, UK: Dedalus, 2000.
– "Sur un livre." *Le Journal*, 7 July 1895.
Morgan, Jean. *En genèse*. Plon, 1897.

Moureau, François. *Le Nouveau Prolétariat intellectuel*. Bourrin, 2007.

Nettement, Alfred. *Études critiques sur le feuilleton-roman*. Perrodil, 1845.

Nordau, Max. *Degeneration* [1892]. Translator unknown. New York: D. Appleton, 1895.

Pécaut, Félix. *L'Éducation publique et la vie nationale*. Hachette, 1897.

– "Notes d'inspection." *La Revue pédagogique* 25, no. 10 (15 October 1894): 289–319.

Plato. *The Dialogues*. Translated by Benjamin Jowett. Oxford University Press, 1892.

Poinsot, [Maffeo Charles], and [Georges-Charles] Normandy. *La Faillite du rêve: Roman d'un jeune homme d'aujourd'hui*. Fasquelle, 1905.

– *La Mortelle Impuissance: Roman du dilettantisme*. Fasquelle, 1903.

Pourtalès, Guy de. "Après le désastre." *Le Journal de Genève*. 28–9 July 1940.

Prévost, Marcel. *La Confession d'un amant*. Lemerre, 1891.

Proust, Adrien, and Gilbert Ballet. *L'Hygiène du neurasthénique*. Masson (Bibliothèque d'hygiène thérapeutique), 1897.

Proust, Marcel. *À la recherche du temps perdu*. General editor Jean-Yves Tadié. 4 vols. Bibliothèque de la Pléiade. Gallimard, 1987–9.

– *Album Proust*. Edited by Pierre Clarac and André Ferré. Bibliothèque de la Pléiade. Gallimard, 1965.

– *Correspondance*. Edited by Philip Kolb. 21 vols. Plon, 1970–93.

– *Jean Santeuil*. Translated by Gerard Hopkins. New York: Simon & Schuster, 1956.

– *Jean Santeuil précédé de Les Plaisirs et les Jours*. Edited by Pierre Clarac and Yves Sandre. Bibliothèque de la Pléiade. Gallimard, 1971.

– *In Search of Lost Time*. Translated by C.K. Scott Moncrieff (except for *Time Regained*, translated by Andreas Mayor and Terence Kilmartin). Revised by Terence Kilmartin and D.J. Enright. New York: Modern Library, 2003.

– *Marcel Proust: Le Mensuel retrouvé*. Edited by Jérôme Prieur. Éditions des Busclats, 2012.

Proust, Marcel, and John Ruskin. *La Bible d'Amiens, Sésame et les Lys et autres textes*. Edited by Jérôme Bastianelli. Robert Laffont (Bouquins), 2015.

Provins, Michel. *Dégénérés!* Havard, 1897.

Rachilde. *Monsieur Vénus: Roman matérialiste* [1884]. Edited by Melanie Hawthorne and Liz Constable. New York: MLA Texts and Translations, 2004.

Renard, Jules. *Œuvres*. Edited by Léon Guichard. 2 vols. Bibliothèque de la Pléiade. Gallimard, 1970.

Rod, Édouard. *L'Indocile*. Fasquelle, 1905.

Rouquès, Amédée. *Le Jeune Rouvre*. Ollendorff, 1909.

Rousseau, Jean-Jacques. *Émile ou De l'éducation* [1762]. Edited by Charles Wirz and Pierre Burgelin. Gallimard (Folio essais), 1995.

– *Œuvres complètes*. General editors Bernard Gagnebin and Marcel Raymond. 5 vols. Bibliothèque de la Pléiade. Gallimard, 1959–95.

Sade, D.A.F. de. *Justine et autres romans*. Edited by Michel Delon and Jean Deprun. Bibliothèque de la Pléiade. Gallimard, 2014.

Sainte-Beuve, Charles Augustin. "La Littérature industrielle." *Revue des Deux Mondes* (1 September 1839), 675–691.

Schlegel, Friedrich. "On Goethe's *Meister*" [1798]. In *Classic and Romantic German Aesthetics*, edited by J.M. Bernstein, 269–86. Cambridge: Cambridge University Press, 2003.

Simon, Jules. *La Réforme de l'enseignement secondaire*. Hachette, 1874.

Stendhal. *De l'amour* [1822]. Edited by Victor Del Litto. Gallimard (Folio), 1980.

– *Œuvres intimes*. Edited by Victor Del Litto. Bibliothèque de la Pléiade. Gallimard, 1982.

– *Œuvres romanesques complètes*. Edited by Yves Ansel and Philippe Berthier. 3 vols. Bibliothèque de la Pléiade. Gallimard, 2005–14.

– "Sketches of Parisian Society, Politics, & Literature." *The New Monthly Magazine and Literary Journal* 16 (1826): 508–17.

Sueur, Albert. *Crise de jeunesse*. Plon, 1897.

– *Intellectualisme et catholicisme*. Bloud, 1906.

– *Nouveau Précis de philosophie*. É. Croville, 1920.

Taine, Hippolyte. "Charles Dickens" [1856]. In *Essais de critique et d'histoire*, 73–125. Hachette, 1858.

Tarde, Gabriel. "L'Affaire Chambige." *Archives de l'anthropologie criminelle et des sciences pénales* 4 (1889): 92–108.

– "La Jeunesse criminelle: Lettre à M. Buisson." *Archives d'anthropologie criminelle, de criminologie et de psychologie normale et pathologique* 12 (1897): 452–72.

Tinan, Jean de. *Œuvres complètes*. Edited by Hubert Juin. 2 vols. Union générale d'éditions (10–18), 1980.

Tissot, [Samuel-Auguste]. *L'Onanisme; ou Dissertation physique sur les maladies produites par la masturbation*. Lausanne: Antoine Chapuis, 1760.

– *De la santé des gens de lettres*. Lausanne: François Grasset, 1767.

Thomas Aquinas. *La Somme théologique de Saint Thomas*. Translated by abbé Drioux. Eugène Bélin, 1853.

Toudouze, Gustave. *Le Vertige de l'inconnu*. Havard, 1892.

Trarieux, Ludovic. *Cinq plaidoiries: l'Union Générale; l'affaire Chambige; le procès Raynal; le procès de la Ligue des Droits de l'Homme; le procès de Gyp*. Société nouvelle de librairie et d'édition, 1903.

Trelawny, Edward John. *Mémoires d'un cadet de famille*. Translated by Juan Floran. Dumont, 1833.

Valéry, Paul, and André Lebey. *Au miroir de l'histoire (Choix de lettres 1895–1938)*. Edited by Micheline Hontebeyrie. Gallimard, 2004.

Vallès, Jules. *Œuvres*. Edited by Roger Bellet. 2 vols. Bibliothèque de la Pléiade. Gallimard, 1975–90.

Vessiot, Alexandre. *La Question du latin de M. Frary et les professions libérales*. Lecène et Oudin, 1886.

Wilde, Oscar. *The Complete Works of Oscar Wilde*. General editor Ian Small. 10 vols. Oxford: Oxford University Press, 2000–18.

– "The Decay of Lying: A Dialogue." *The Nineteenth Century: A Monthly Review* 25, no. 143 (January 1889): 35–56.

– *The Picture of Dorian Gray*. Edited by Michael Patrick Gillespie. New York: Norton (Critical Edition), 2007.

Zola, Émile. *Œuvres complètes*. General editor Henri Mitterand. 20 vols. Nouveau monde, 2002–9.

– *Les Romanciers naturalistes*. Charpentier, 1881.

Secondary Sources

Adorno, Theodor W., and Max Horkheimer. *Dialectic of Enlightenment: Philosophical Fragments* [1947]. Edited by Gunzelin Schmid Noerr. Translated by Edmund Jephcott. Stanford, CA: Stanford University Press, 2002.

Allen, James Smith. *In the Public Eye: A History of Reading in Modern France, 1800–1940*. Princeton, NJ: Princeton University Press, 1991.

Althusser, Louis. "From *Capital* to Marx's Philosophy" [1965]. In Louis Althusser and Étienne Balibar, *Reading Capital*, 11–69. Translated by Ben Brewster. New York: Pantheon Books, 1970.

– "Idéologie et appareils idéologiques d'État. (Notes pour une recherche)" [1970]. In *Positions (1964–1975)*, 67–125. Éditions sociales, 1976.

Angenot, Marc. *Le Cru et le Faisandé: Sexe, discours social et littérature à la Belle Époque*. Brussels: Labor, 1986.

– *1889: Un état du discours social*. Longueuil, QC: Le Préambule, 1989.

– "On est toujours le disciple de quelqu'un, ou le mystère du pousse-au-crime." *Littérature* 49 (February 1983): 50–62.

Anglès, Auguste. *André Gide et le premier groupe de la Nouvelle Revue française*. 3 vols. Gallimard, 1978–86.

Armstrong, Nancy, and Warren Montag. "'The Figure in the Carpet.'" *PMLA* 132 no. 3 (2017), 613–19.

Association des écrivains combattants. *Anthologie des écrivains morts à la Guerre 1914–1918*. 5 vols. Amiens: Malfère (Bibliothèque du Hérisson), 1924.

Bardon, Maurice. *Don Quichotte en France au XVIIe et au XVIIIe siècle, 1605–1815*. Honoré Champion, 1931.

Barthes, Roland. "Le Bruissement de la langue" [1975]. In *Le Bruissement de la langue: Essais critiques IV*, 99–102. Seuil (Points), 1984.

– *S/Z* [1970]. Seuil (Points), 1976.

Baudry, Marie. *Lectrices romanesques: Représentations et théorie de la lecture aux XIXe et XXe siècles*. Garnier (Classiques), 2014.

Beaujour, Michel. "Exemplary Pornography: Barrès, Loyola, and the Novel." In *The Reader in the Text: Essays on Audience and Interpretation*, edited by Susan Rubin Suleiman and Inge Crosman, 325–49. Princeton, NJ: Princeton University Press, 1980.

Beckett, Samuel. *Proust* [1930]. London: John Calder, 1965.

Beizer, Janet L. *Ventriloquized Bodies: Narratives of Hysteria in Nineteenth-Century France*. Ithaca, NY: Cornell University Press, 1994.

Bellet, Roger. "L'Image de l'école chez Jules Vallès." *Revue des sciences humaines* 174 (June 1979): 37–59.

– *Jules Vallès, journaliste: du Second Empire, de la Commune de Paris et de la IIIe République, 1857–1885*. Les Éditeurs français réunis, 1977.

Bennett, Paula, and Vernon A. Rosario, eds. *Solitary Pleasures: The Historical, Literary, and Artistic Discourses of Autoeroticism*. New York: Routledge, 1995.

Bessard-Banquy, Olivier, ed. *Les Mutations de la lecture*. Pessac: Presses universitaires de Bordeaux, 2012.

Best, Stephen, and Sharon Marcus. "Surface Reading: An Introduction." *Representations* 108 (Fall 2009): 1–21.

Biéler, Madeleine. *Ernest Biéler: sa vie, son œuvre*. Lausanne: Éditions à la Louve, 1953.

Black, Gregory D. *Hollywood Censored: Morality Codes, Catholics, and the Movies*. Cambridge: Cambridge University Press, 1996.

Boak, Denis. *Roger Martin Du Gard*. Oxford: Clarendon Press, 1963.

Boes, Tobias. *Formative Fictions: Nationalism, Cosmopolitanism, and the Bildungsroman*. Ithaca, NY: Cornell University Press, 2012.

– "On the Nature of the *Bildungsroman*." *PMLA* 124, no. 2 (2009): 647–9.

Bompaire-Evesque, Claire. "Paul Bourget collaborateur de Maurice Barrès." *Revue d'histoire littéraire de la France* 92, no. 2 (April 1992): 224–45.

Borie, Jean. "Préface." In *La Curée* [1872], by Émile Zola, 7–35. Gallimard (Folio), 1999.

– "Préface." In *Les Déracinés* [1897], by Maurice Barrès, 7–65. Gallimard (Folio), 1988.

Bornecque, Jacques-Henry. "*Le Petit Chose* devant l'histoire littéraire." In *Le Petit Chose* [1868], by Alphonse Daudet, 85–98. Fasquelle, 1947.

Brooks, Peter. *Reading for the Plot: Design and Intention in Narrative* [1984]. Cambridge, MA: Harvard University Press, 1992.

Brown, Diane Berrett. "The Constraints of Liberty at the Scene of Instruction." In *Rousseau and Freedom*, edited by Christie McDonald and Stanley Hoffmann, 288–313. Cambridge: Cambridge University Press, 2010.

Brunet, Elisabeth. "L'Échec de la pétition." In *Pour Oscar Wilde: Des écrivains français au secours du condamné*, 58–72. Rouen: Association des amis d'Hugues Rebell, 1994.

Cabral, Maria de Jesus, Maria Hermínia A. Laurel, and Franc Schuerewegen, eds. *Lire de près, de loin: Close vs distant reading*. Garnier (Classiques), 2014.

Călinescu, Matei. *Five Faces of Modernity: Modernism, Avant-Garde, Decadence, Kitsch, Postmodernism*. Durham, NC: Duke University Press, 1987.

Carroy, Jacqueline, and Marc Renneville. "Le Crime de Chambige: entre psychologie et littérature." In *Psychologies fin de siècle*, edited by Jean-Louis Cabanès, Jacqueline Carroy, and Nicole Edelman. *Recherches interdisciplinaires sur les textes modernes* 38 (2007): 193–208.

– "Une cause passionnelle passionnante: Tarde et l'affaire Chambige (1889)." *Champ pénal /Penal field, nouvelle revue internationale de criminologie* (15 September 2005). champpenal.revues.org/260.

Carter, William C. *Marcel Proust: A Life*. New Haven, CT: Yale Univesity Press, 2000.

Cazentre, Thomas. *Gide Lecteur: La littérature au miroir de la lecture*. Kimé, 2003.

Chaitin, Gilbert D. *The Enemy Within: Culture Wars and Political Identity in Novels of the French Third Republic*. Columbus: Ohio State University Press, 2009.

– "The Thesis Novel as a Weapon in the Education Wars of the Third Republic." In *Culture Wars and Literature in the French Third Republic*, edited by Gilbert D. Chaitin, 20–43. Newcastle upon Tyne: Cambridge Scholars, 2008.

Châles-Courtine, Sylvie. "La Place du corps dans la médiatisation des affaires criminelles." *Sociétés & Représentations* 18, no. 2 (2004) : 171–90.

Charle, Christophe. *La Crise littéraire à l'époque du naturalisme: Roman, théâtre et politique*. Presses de l'École normale supérieure, 1979.

Chartier, Anne-Marie, and Jean Hébrard. *Discours sur la lecture: 1880–2000*. 2nd ed. BPI Centre Pompidou – Fayard, 2000.

Chervel, André. *Les Auteurs français, latins et grecs au programme de l'enseignement secondaire de 1800 à nos jours*. INRP/Publications de la Sorbonne, 1986.

Cibois, Philippe. "La Question du latin: des critiques du XVIIIe siècle au *revival* du XIXe." *L'Information littéraire* 52, no. 1 (January-March 2000): 7–28.

Clark, Christina, and Jonathan Douglas. *Young People's Reading and Writing: An In-depth Study Focusing on Enjoyment, Behaviour, Attitudes and Attainment*. London: National Literacy Trust, 2011. files.eric.ed.gov/fulltext/ED521656.pdf.

Clark, Linda L. *Schooling the Daughters of Marianne: Textbooks and the Socialization of Girls in Modern French Primary Schools*. Albany, NY: State University of New York Press, 1984.

Cohen, Margaret. "Narratology in the Archive of Literature." *Representations* 108 (Fall 2009): 51–75.

– *The Sentimental Education of the Novel*. Princeton, NJ: Princeton University Press, 1999.

Compagnon, Antoine. *La Troisième République des lettres, de Flaubert à Proust*. Seuil, 1983.

Courtade, Francis. *Les Malédictions du cinéma français*. Alain Moreau, 1978.

Crain, Caleb. *American Sympathy: Men, Friendship, and Literature in the New Nation*. New Haven, CT: Yale University Press, 2001.

Crawford, Katherine B. "Love, Sodomy, and Scandal: Controlling the Sexual Reputation of Henry III." *Journal of the History of Sexuality* 12 (2003): 513–42.

Crisp, Colin. *The Classic French Cinema, 1930–1960*. Bloomington: Indiana University Press, 1993.

Curtius, Ernst. *European Literature and the Latin Middle Ages* [1953]. Princeton, NJ: Princeton University Press, 2003.

Dean, Carolyn J. *The Frail Social Body: Pornography, Homosexuality, and Other Fantasies in Interwar France*. Oakland: University of California Press, 2000.

Deleuze, Gilles. *Logique du sens*. Minuit, 1969.

Delon, Michel. "Notice." In *Les Amours du chevalier de Faublas* [1787–90], by Louvet de Couvray, 1113–21. Gallimard (Folio), 1996.

de Man, Paul. *Allegories of Reading: Figural Language in Rousseau, Nietzsche, Rilke, and Proust*. New Haven, CT: Yale University Press, 1979.

Derrida, Jacques. *De la grammatologie*. Minuit, 1967.

– *La Dissémination*. Seuil (Points), 1972.

Digeon, Claude. *La Crise allemande de la pensée française, 1870–1914*. Presses universitaires de France, 1959.

Dumasy, Lise, ed. *La Querelle du roman-feuilleton: Littérature, presse et politique, un débat précurseur (1836–1848)*. Grenoble: ELLUG-Université Stendhal, 1999.

Dupuy, Aimé. *Un personnage nouveau du roman français: L'enfant*. Hachette, 1931.

Eells, Emily. "Proust et Wilde." In *Le Cercle de Marcel Proust*, edited by Jean-Yves Tadié, 225–36. Honoré Champion, 2013.

Ehrlich, Evelyn. *Cinema of Paradox: French Filmmaking under the German Occupation*. New York: Columbia University Press, 1985.

Ellmann, Richard. *Oscar Wilde*. New York: Vintage, 1988.

Emeis, Harald. *Reflets littéraires d'une amitié: André Gide dans Les Thibault de Roger Martin du Gard*. Harmattan, 2007.

Evans, Christophe, ed. *Lectures et lecteurs à l'heure d'Internet*. Cercle de la librairie, 2011.

Ferrand, Nathalie, *Livre et lecture dans les romans français du XVIIIe siècle*. Presses universitaires de France, 2002.

Feuillerat, Albert. *Paul Bourget: Histoire d'un esprit sous la Troisième République*. Plon, 1937.

Finn, Michael R. *Proust, the Body and Literary Form*. Cambridge: Cambridge University Press, 1999.

Forth, Christopher E. *The Dreyfus Affair and the Crisis of French Manhood*. Baltimore: Johns Hopkins University Press, 2004.

Foucaud, Boris. *L'Œuvre d'Anatole France: À la recherche d'une philosophie du monde par l'écriture du désir*. PhD thesis, Université d'Angers, 2001. tel.archives-ouvertes.fr/tel-01068782/document.

Fougère, Marie-Ange, and Daniel Sangsue, ed. *Avez-vous lu Paul Bourget?* Éditions universitaires de Dijon, 2007.

Fraisse, Luc. *L'Éclectisme philosophique de Marcel Proust*. Presses de l'Université Paris-Sorbonne, 2013.

Francis, Claude, and Fernande Gontier. *Mathilde de Morny: La scandaleuse marquise et son temps*. Perrin, 2000.

Frandon, Ida-Marie. *Barrès tel qu'en lui-même: Modernité et déracinement*. Fontainebleau: La Pirole, 1998.

– "Fait divers et littérature." *Revue d'histoire littéraire de la France* 84 (August 1984): 561–9.

Freud, Sigmund. *The Standard Edition of the Complete Psychological Works of Sigmund Freud*. Edited and translated by James Strachey with Anna Freud, Alix Strachey, and Alan Tyson. London: Hogarth Press, 1956–74.

Geerts, Walter. *Le Silence sonore: La poétique du premier Gide, entre intertexte et métatexte*. Namur, Belgium: Presses universitaires de Namur, 1992.

Genette, Gérard. *Palimpsestes: La littérature au second degré*. Seuil, 1982.

Germain, Marie-Odile. "Barrès journaliste et l'écriture au quotidien." *Cahiers de l'association internationale des études françaises* 48, no.1 (1996): 91–107.

– "Un Déraciné à la pension Vauquer: Note sur quelques réminiscences balzaciennes dans un roman de Barrès." *Littératures* 1 (1980): 73–83.

– "Genèse d'un roman: *Les Déracinés*." In *Barrès: Une tradition dans la modernité*, edited by A. Guyaux, J. Jurt, and R. Kopp, 31–40. Honoré Champion, 1991.

Ginn, L.H. "'Il a vu les choses de trop haut': Henri Chambige and his Literary Destiny," *Nottingham French Studies* 30, no. 1 (1991): 23–32.

Gleize, Joëlle. *Le Double Miroir: Le livre dans les livres de Stendhal à Proust*. Hachette, 1992.

Goldstein, Jan. *The Post-Revolutionary Self: Politics and Psyche in France, 1750–1850*. Cambridge, MA: Harvard University Press, 2005.

Goulemot, Jean-Marie, and Éric Walter. "Les Centenaires de Voltaire et de Rousseau." In *Les Lieux de mémoire*, edited by Pierre Nora, 1:381–420. Gallimard, 1984.

Goulet, Alain. *André Gide, Les Faux-Monnayeurs: Mode d'emploi*. SEDES, 1991.

Goux, Jean-Joseph. *Les Monnayeurs du langage*. Galilée, 1984.

Grand-Carteret, John, ed. *J.-J. Rousseau jugé par les Français d'aujourd'hui*. Perrin, 1890.

Grusec, Joan E., and Paul D. Hastings. *Handbook of Socialization: Theory and Research*. New York: Guilford Press, 2007.

Guiney, Martin. *Teaching the Cult of Literature in the French Third Republic*. New York: Palgrave Macmillan, 2004.

Hanna, Martha. *The Mobilization of Intellect: French Scholars and Writers during the Great War*. Cambridge, MA: Harvard University Press, 1996.

Hardin, James, ed. *Reflection and Action: Essays on the Bildungsroman*. Columbia: University of South Carolina Press, 1991.

Harris, Ruth. *Murders and Madness: Medicine, Law, and Society in the Fin de Siècle*. Oxford: Clarendon Press, 1989.

Harsin, Jill. *Policing Prostitution in Nineteenth-Century Paris*. Princeton, NJ: Princeton University Press, 1985.

Hartog, François. "La Révolution française et l'Antiquité." In *Situations de la démocratie*, edited by Marcel Gauchet, Pierre Manent, and Pierre Rosanvallon, 30–61. Seuil-Gallimard (Hautes Études), 1993.

Hecquet, Michèle. "*Les Déracinés* dans *Les Faux-Monnayeurs*." *Roman 20–50* 11 (1991): 75–81.

Henslin, James M. *Essentials of Sociology*. 4th ed. Boston: Allyn and Bacon, 2002.

Hirsch, Marianne. "The Novel of Formation as Genre: Between Great Expectations and Lost Illusions." *Genre* 12 (Fall 1979): 293–311.

Hodgson, Richard G. "Du *Francion* de Sorel au *Pharsamon* de Marivaux: Histoire de la folie à l'âge de l'anti-roman." In *La Naissance du roman en France: Topique romanesque de L'Astrée à Justine*, edited by Nicole Boursier and David Trott, 29–38. Papers on French Seventeenth Century Literature, 1990.

Huret, Jules. *Enquête sur l'évolution littéraire (1891)*. Edited by Daniel Grojnowski. José Corti, 1999.

Holland, Merlin. *Irish Peacock and Scarlet Marquess: The Real Trial of Oscar Wilde*. London: Fourth Estate, 2003.

Houtteville, Sophie. *Le Thème de l'aliénation par l'éducation dans la littérature allemande autour de 1900*. Bern: Peter Lang, 1998.

Hugot, Jean-François. *Le Dilettantisme dans la littérature française d'Ernest Renan à Ernest Psichari*. Aux Amateurs de livres, 1984.

Hutcheon, Linda. *Irony's Edge: The Theory and Politics of Irony*. London: Routledge, 1994.

– *A Theory of Parody: The Teachings of Twentieth-Century Art Forms*. New York: Methuen, 1985.

Idt, Geneviève. "L''Intellectuel' avant l'affaire Dreyfus." *Cahiers de lexicologie* 15 (April 1968): 35–46.

Jacquet-Francillon, François. *Instituteurs avant la République: La profession d'instituteur et ses représentations, de la monarchie de Juillet au Second Empire*. Presses universitaires du Septentrion, 1999.

Jameson, Fredric. *The Political Unconscious: Narrative as a Socially Symbolic Act.* Ithaca, NY: Cornell University Press, 1981.

Kolb, Philip. "Historique du premier roman de Proust." *Saggi e ricerche di letteratura francese* 4 (1963): 217–77.

Ladenson, Elisabeth. *Dirt for Art's Sake: Books on Trial from Madame Bovary to Lolita.* Ithaca, NY: Cornell University Press, 2007.

Laplanche, Jean, and J.-B. Pontalis. *Vocabulaire de la psychanalyse* [1967]. 5th ed. Presses universitaires de France (Quadrige), 2007.

Laqueur, Thomas. *Solitary Sex: A Cultural History of Masturbation.* New York: Zone Books, 2003.

Lefebvre, Denis. *André Lebey, intellectuel et franc-maçon sous la IIIe République.* Éditions maçonniques de France, 1999.

Léoni, Sylviane. *Le Poison et le remède: Théâtre, morale et rhétorique en France et en Italie, 1694–1758.* Oxford: Voltaire Foundation, 1998.

Loué, Thomas. "Les fils de Taine entre science et morale: À propos du *Disciple* de Paul Bourget." *Cahiers d'histoire* 65 (1996): 45–61.

Love, Heather. "Close but not Deep: Literary Ethics and the Descriptive Turn." *New Literary History* 41, no. 2 (Spring 2010): 371–91.

Lucey, Michael. *The Misfit of the Family: Balzac and the Social Forms of Sexuality.* Durham, NC: Duke University Press, 2003.

– *Never Say I: Sexuality and the First Person in Colette, Gide, and Proust.* Durham, NC: Duke University Press, 2006.

Lukács, György. *Studies in European Realism.* Translated by Edith Bone. New York: Grosset & Dunlap, 1964.

– *The Theory of the Novel: A Historico-Philosophical Essay on the Forms of Great Epic Literature.* Translated by Anna Bostock. Cambridge, MA: MIT Press, 1971.

Lyle, Louise. "Le *Struggleforlife*: Contesting Balzac through Darwin in Zola, Bourget, and Barrès." *Nineteenth-Century French Studies* 36, nos. 3–4 (2008): 305–19.

Lyon-Caen, Judith. *La Lecture et la vie: Les usages du roman au temps de Balzac.* Tallandier, 2006.

Lyons, Martyn. *Readers and Society in Nineteenth-Century France: Workers, Women, Peasants.* Houndmills, UK: Palgrave, 2001.

MacFarlane, Ian D. *Paul Bourget et l'Angleterre.* PhD thesis, Université de Paris, 1950.

Mahoney, Dennis. "The Apprenticeship of the Reader: The *Bildungsroman* of the 'Age of Goethe.'" In *Reflection and Action: Essays on the Bildungsroman*, edited by James Hardin, 97–117.

Mainil, Jean. *Don Quichotte en jupons: Des effets surprenants de la lecture, essai d'interprétation de la lectrice romanesque au dix-huitième siècle.* Kimé, 2008.

Mansuy, Michel. *Un moderne: Paul Bourget de l'enfance au Disciple.* Besançon: Jacques et Demontrond, 1961.

Marcus, Sharon. *Between Women: Friendship, Desire, and Marriage in Victorian England*. Princeton, NJ: Princeton University Press, 2007.

Martini, Fritz. "Bildungsroman, Term and Theory." In *Reflection and Action: Essays on the Bildungsroman*, edited by James Hardin, 1–25.

Massol, Jean-François. *De l'institution scolaire de la littérature française: 1870–1925*. ELLUG, Université Stendhal, 2004.

Matlock, Jann. *Scenes of Seduction: Prostitution, Hysteria, and Reading Difference in Nineteenth-Century France*. New York: Columbia University Press, 1994.

May, Georges. *Le Dilemme du roman au XVIIIe siècle: Étude sur les rapports du roman et de la critique, 1715–1761*. New Haven, CT: Yale University Press, 1963.

Mellor, Anne K. *English Romantic Irony*. Cambridge, MA: Harvard University Press, 1980.

Merriman, John. *The Dynamite Club: How a Bombing in Fin-de-Siècle Paris Ignited the Age of Modern Terror*. Boston: Houghton Mifflin Harcourt, 2009.

Millner, Michael. *Fever Reading: Affect and Reading Badly in the Early American Public Sphere*. Lebanon: University of New Hampshire Press, 2012.

Millot, Hélène. "Vallès contre Barrès, ou du bon usage des racines." *Les Amis de Jules Vallès* 22 (July 1996): 45–57.

Minden, Michael. *The German Bildungsroman: Incest and Inheritance*. Cambridge: Cambridge University Press, 1997.

Monicat, Bénédicte. *Devoirs d'écriture: Modèles d'histoires pour filles et littérature féminine au XIXe siècle*. Lyon: Presses universitaires de Lyon, 2006.

Moretti, Franco. "Conjectures on World Literature." *New Left Review* 1 (February 2000): 54–68.

– *The Way of the World: The Bildungsroman in European Culture* [1987]. Translated by Albert Sbragia. New ed. London: Verso, 2000.

Morgenstern, Karl. "On the Nature of the *Bildungsroman*" (*Über das Wesen des Bildungsromans* [1819]). Translated by Tobias Boes. *PMLA* 124, no. 2 (2009): 650–9.

Neubauer, John. *The Fin-de-Siècle Culture of Adolescence*. New Haven, CT: Yale University Press, 1992.

Novick, Sheldon M. *Henry James: The Mature Master*. New York: Random House, 2007.

Nye, Robert A. *Crime, Madness, & Politics in Modern France: The Medical Concept of National Decline*. Princeton, NJ: Princeton University Press, 1984.

O'Brien, Justin. *The Novel of Adolescence in France: The Study of a Literary Theme*. New York: Columbia University Press, 1937.

Ortega y Gasset, José. *Meditations on Quixote* [1914]. Translated by Evelyn Rugg and Diego Marín. New York: Norton, 1961.

Ozouf, Mona. *L'École, l'Église et la République: 1871–1914* [1963]. Revised edition. Seuil, 1992.

Parinet, Élisabeth. *La Librairie Flammarion: 1875–1914*. IMEC éditions, 1992.

Patton, Stacey. "The Ph.D. Now Comes with Food Stamps." *The Chronicle of Higher Education* (6 May 2012). www.chronicle.com/article/From-Graduate-School-to/131795.

Pernot, Denis. "Du *Bildungsroman* au roman d'éducation: un malentendu créateur?" *Romantisme* 76, no. 2 (1992): 105–19.

– *La Jeunesse en discours (1880–1925): Discours social et création littéraire*. Honoré Champion, 2007.

– *Le Roman de socialisation: 1889–1914*. Presses universitaires de France, 1998.

Perrot, Michelle. "The New Eve and the Old Adam: Changes in French Women's Condition at the Turn of the Century." Translated by Helen Harden-Chenut. In *Behind the Lines: Gender and the Two World Wars*, edited by Margaret Randolph Higonnet et al., 51–60. New Haven, CT: Yale University Press, 1987.

Perry, Catherine. "Flagorneur ou ébloui? Proust lecteur d'Anna de Noailles." *Bulletin Marcel Proust* 49 (1999): 37–53.

Peterson, Jeanne. "The Victorian Governess: Status Incongruence in Family and Society." In *Suffer and Be Still: Women in the Victorian Age*, edited by Martha Vicinus, 3–19. Bloomington: Indiana University Press, 1972.

Pick, Daniel. *Faces of Degeneration: A European Disorder, c.1848–c.1918*. Cambridge: Cambridge University Press, 1989.

Pillard, Thomas. "Une histoire oubliée: La genèse française du terme 'film noir' dans les années 1930 et ses implications transnationales." *Transatlantica, revue d'études américaines* 1 (2012). transatlantica.revues.org/5742.

Pouillart, Raymond. "Littérature et documents confidentiels: À propos d'une thèse récente sur Paul Bourget." *Les Lettres romanes* 17 (1963): 34–48, 147–58.

Prost, Antoine. *Histoire de l'enseignement en France, 1800–1967*. Armand Colin, 1968.

Py, Gilbert. *Rousseau et les éducateurs: Étude sur la fortune des idées pédagogiques de Jean-Jacques Rousseau en France et en Europe au XVIIIe siècle*. Oxford: Voltaire Foundation, 1997.

Rambaud, Vital. "Barrès et Balzac." *L'Année balzacienne* 12 (1991): 395–408.

Reid, Roddey. *Families in Jeopardy: Regulating the Social Body in France, 1750–1910*. Stanford, CA: Stanford University Press, 1993.

Reik, Theodor. *The Secret Self: Psychoanalytic Experiences in Life and Literature*. New York: Farrar, Straus and Young, 1953.

Ridge, Daniel Carl. "Maurice Bouchor – Paul Bourget – Georges Hérelle – Adrien Juvigny (1869–1874), Correspondances croisées inédites." *Histoires Littéraires* 19, no. 73 (January–March 2018): 65–95.

Ringer, Fritz. *Fields of Knowledge: French Academic Culture in Comparative Perspective, 1890–1920*. Cambridge: Cambridge University Press, 1992.

Robitaille, Martin. *Proust épistolier*. Montréal: Presses de l'Université de Montréal, 2003.

Rogers, Juliette M. *Career Stories: Belle Époque Novels of Professional Development*. University Park: Pennsylvania State University Press, 2007.

Rood, Tim. *The Sea! The Sea!: The Shout of the Ten Thousand in the Modern Imagination*. London: Duckworth Overlook, 2004.

Rousset, Jean. *Forme et Signification*. José Corti, 1962.

Roza, Robert. *Roger Martin du Gard et la banalité retrouvée*. Didier, 1970.

Ruedin, Pascal. "Ernest Biéler illustrateur des Goncourt dans la 'Collection Edouard Guillaume' à Paris (1880–1892): Arts industriels ou Beaux-Arts?" *Kunst + Architektur in der Schweiz/Art + architecture en Suisse/Arte + architettura in Svizzera* 47 (1996): 389–403.

Sabry, Randa. "Les Lectures des héros de roman." *Poétique* 94 (1993): 185–204.

Sadoul, Georges. *Écrits 1: Chroniques du cinéma français, 1939–1967*. Union générale (10–18), 1979.

Saminadayar-Perrin, Corinne. *Modernités à l'antique: Parcours vallésiens*. Honoré Champion, 1999.

Sapiro, Gisèle. *La Guerre des écrivains: 1940–1953*. Fayard, 1999.

Savage-Levrut, Sophie. "Représentations de lecteurs et pédagogie de la lecture dans les soties et *Les Faux-Monnayeurs*." *La Revue des lettres modernes* 1452–1457 [André Gide 11] (1999): 81–104.

Schachter, Marc D. *Voluntary Servitude and the Erotics of Friendship: From Classical Antiquity to Early Modern France*. Hampshire, UK: Ashgate, 2008.

Schoentjes, Pierre. *Poétique de l'ironie*. Seuil (Points), 2001.

Sedgwick, Eve Kosofsky. *Between Men: English Literature and Male Homosocial Desire*. New York: Columbia University Press, 1985.

– "Paranoid Reading and Reparative Reading; or, You're So Paranoid, You Probably Think This Introduction Is About You." In *Novel Gazing: Queer Readings in Fiction*, edited by Eve Kosofsky Sedgwick, 1–37. Durham, NC: Duke University Press, 1997.

Seillan, Jean-Marie, ed. *Enquête sur le roman romanesque: Le Gaulois, 1891*. Amiens: Centre d'études du roman et du romanesque de l'université de Picardie, 2005.

Sherard, Robert Harborough. *The Life of Oscar Wilde*. New York: Mitchell Kennerley, 1906.

Sicard, Claude. "Jean de Tinan et André Gide: Une amitié à sens unique." *Littératures* 9–10 (Spring 1984): 209–23.

– *Roger Martin Du Gard: Les années d'apprentissage littéraire (1881–1910)*. Atelier reproduction des thèses, Université Lille III, 1976.

Simon, Catherine. "Ados: Zéro de lecture?" *Le Monde*, 29 November 2012.

Sohn, Anne-Marie. *Du premier baiser à l'alcôve: La sexualité des français au quotidien, 1850–1950*. Aubier, 1996.

Smith, Paul J. *Réécrire la Renaissance, de Marcel Proust à Michel Tournier: Exercices de lecture rapprochée*. Amsterdam: Rodopi (Faux titre), 2009.

Spurdle, Sonia. "Some Sources of Roger Martin du Gard's Inspiration in *Devenir!*" *Neophilologus* 55, no. 3 (July 1971): 261–9.

Stewart, Suzanne R. *Sublime Surrender: Male Masochism at the Fin-de-siècle.* Ithaca, NY: Cornell University Press, 1998.

Stora-Lamarre, Annie. *L'Enfer de la IIIe République: Censeurs et pornographes, 1881–1914.* Imago, 1990.

Suleiman, Susan Rubin. *Authoritarian Fictions: The Ideological Novel as a Literary Genre* [1983]. Princeton, NJ: Princeton University Press, 1993.

Surkis, Judith. *Sexing the Citizen: Morality and Masculinity in France, 1870–1920.* Ithaca, NY: Cornell University Press, 2006.

Swart, Koenraad W. *The Sense of Decadence in Nineteenth-Century France.* The Hague: Martinus Nijhoff, 1964.

Tadié, Jean-Yves. *Marcel Proust.* Gallimard, 1996.

– Preface to *Jean Santeuil*, by Marcel Proust, 7–33. Gallimard (Quarto), 2001.

Taithe, Bertrand. *Defeated Flesh: Welfare, Warfare and the Making of Modern France.* Manchester: Manchester University Press, 1999.

Tanner, Jessica. "Turning Tricks, Turning the Tables: Plotting the *Brasserie à femmes* in Tabarant's *Virus d'amour.*" *Nineteenth-Century French Studies* 41, nos. 3–4 (2013): 255–71.

Thiéry, Robert, ed. *Rousseau, l'Émile et la Révolution: Actes du colloque international de Montmorency, 27 septembre – 4 octobre 1989.* Universitas, 1992.

Thiesse, Anne-Marie. *Le Roman du quotidien: Lecteurs et lectures populaires à la Belle Époque* [1984]. Seuil (Points), 2000.

Tison, Guillemette. *Une mosaïque d'enfants: L'enfant et l'adolescent dans le roman français, 1876–1890.* Arras: Artois Presses Université, 1998.

– *Le Roman de l'école au XIXe siècle.* Belin, 2004.

Trousson, Raymond. *Défenseurs et adversaires de J.-J. Rousseau: d'Isabelle de Charrière à Charles Maurras.* Honoré Champion, 1995.

Vila, Anne C. *Enlightenment and Pathology: Sensibility in the Literature and Medicine of Eighteenth-Century France.* Baltimore: Johns Hopkins University Press, 1998.

Waelti-Walters, Jennifer R. *Feminist Novelists of the Belle Époque: Love as a Lifestyle.* Bloomington: Indiana University Press, 1990.

Watt, Adam. *Reading in Proust's À la recherche: "le délire de la lecture."* Oxford: Clarendon Press, 2009.

Weil, Françoise. *L'Interdiction du roman et la librairie, 1728–1750.* Aux Amateurs de livres, 1986.

Winock, Michel. *Décadence fin de siècle.* Gallimard (L'Esprit de la cité), 2017.

Young, Paul J. "Cruising *The Vatican* ...: Reading Gide's Queerest Text." *Dalhousie French Studies* 78 (Spring 2007): 107–16.

Zeldin, Theodore. *France, 1848–1945: Intellect and Pride.* Oxford: Oxford University Press, 1980.

Index